State and Nature

State and Nature

Studies in Ancient and Medieval Philosophy

Edited by
Peter Adamson and Christof Rapp

DE GRUYTER

ISBN 978-3-11-112197-0
e-ISBN (PDF) 978-3-11-073094-4
e-ISBN (EPUB) 978-3-11-073103-3

Library of Congress Control Number: 2020952257

Bibliographic information published by the Deutsche Nationalbibliothek
The Deutsche Nationalbibliothek lists this publication in the Deutsche Nationalbibliografie;
detailed bibliographic data are available on the Internet at http://dnb.dnb.de.

© 2022 Walter de Gruyter GmbH, Berlin/Boston
This volume is text- and page-identical with the hardback published in 2021.
Cover image: © knape / E+ / Getty Images
Printing and binding: CPI books GmbH, Leck

www.degruyter.com

This volume grew out of a series of workshops held under the aegis of the DFG-funded research group "Natur in politischen Ordungsentwürfen: Antike – Mittelalter – frühe Neuzeit." We are grateful to the DFG for its support and to our colleagues in the group. Our gratitude goes also to Marilù Papandreou, who cheerfully and assidously helped us to prepare the volume for press, and to Fabian Ruge for preparing the index.

Table of Contents

Introduction —— IX

Part I: Plato and Aristotle

Oliver Primavesi
Human Nature and Legal Norms: Antiphon the Sophist as Anonymous Target in Plato's *Republic* IX —— 3

Dominic Scott
Natural Born Philosophers —— 35

Christoph Horn
Normative Naturalism in Aristotle's Political Philosophy? —— 59

Christof Rapp
Whose State? Whose Nature? How Aristotle's *Polis* is 'Natural' —— 81

Fred D. Miller, Jr. and David Keyt
Aristotle on Freedom, Nature, and Law —— 119

Béatrice Lienemann
Aristotle on the Rationality of Women: Consequences for Virtue and Practical Accountability —— 135

Part II: Hellenistic Philosophy

René Brouwer
Cynic Origins of the Stoic Doctrine of Natural Law? —— 159

Tim O'Keefe
The Normativity of Nature in Epicurean Ethics and Politics —— 181

Philipp Brüllmann
Nature and Psychology in Cicero's *Republic* —— 201

Raphael Woolf
Unnatural Law: A Ciceronian Perspective —— 221

Caroline Humfress
Natural Law and Casuistic Reasoning in Roman Jurisprudence —— 247

Part III: **Late Antiquity**

Christopher Isaac Noble
Human Nature and Normativity in Plotinus —— 269

Miira Tuominen
On Justice in Porphyry's *On Abstinence* —— 293

George Karamanolis
Early Christian Philosophers on Society and Political Norms —— 317

Part IV: **Medieval Philosophy**

Peter Adamson
Against Nature: Two Critics of Naturalism in the Islamic World —— 343

Juhana Toivanen
"Like Ants in a Colony We Do Our Share": Political Animals in Medieval Philosophy —— 365

Jenny Pelletier
Ockham on Human Freedom and the Nature and Origin of Lordship —— 393

Index of Names —— 415

Index of Subjects —— 419

Introduction

One of the great differences between ancient and medieval political philosophy on the one hand, and early modern and contemporary political philosophy on the other hand, is (supposedly) that in the earlier period social and political institutions were always thought to be natural. Except, that is, when they went wrong by being *un*-natural. The rule of man over woman, of master over slave, of king over subject, was appropriate and best for all concerned, just as it is appropriate and best that giraffes use their long necks to get at leaves near the tops of trees. From Plato's ideal city, to the long-lived notion of natural law, to the divine right of kings, the "naturalness" of political arrangements was an unquestioned, and self-serving, myth that kept the elite where they reckoned they belonged. This was all undone (again supposedly) by early modern figures such as Hobbes, who drew attention to the artificiality of the state. If the king rules rightly, it is because he *rescues* us from the state of nature, having been installed for precisely this purpose by his subjects, who agree to surrender their natural-born freedom for manufactured security.

No doubt there is some truth in this narrative. But as you'll already have guessed, it is one that we hope to challenge, or at least significantly nuance, in the present volume. In part for the reason historians of philosophy always give when confronted with such sweeping chronological claims: that the change came earlier than usually thought. This comes out best in the final paper of the book, in which Pelletier shows that Ockham, writing hundreds of years before Hobbes, already conceived of "lordship" as being more artificial than "natural." But we can also find problems with the story if we look back to the very beginning.

Classical antiquity was, as it turns out, no stranger to the thought that political norms might be departures from nature. We can see this from the fact that already before Plato, the sophists contrasted *nomos* to *phusis*. As the sophist Antiphon put it, "the greater part of the things that are defined as just by the law (*nomon*) is hostile to nature (*phusis*)." This remark, its context, and the response it elicited from Plato are discussed by Oliver Primavesi in the first paper of this book. This sets the tone for what is to follow. Other schools of thought in antiquity would propose that nature is an alternative to the law, or at least the law as we know it. O'Keefe shows that Epicurus, contrary to what might be assumed, did not simply equate "natural" with "good." Had he done so, Epicurus could hardly have recognized a class of natural but harmful desires, as in *Vatican Saying* 21: "one must not compel nature but persuade her. And we will persuade her

https://doi.org/10.1515/9783110730944-001

by fulfilling the necessary desires, and the [merely] natural ones too if they do not harm [us], but sharply rejecting the harmful ones."

An even wider gulf between political norms and nature was recognized by the early Stoics, followed in this by the Cynics. As Brouwer puts it in his study of this relationship, "the Stoics criticised *all* existing laws and constitutions in no uncertain terms." It's fascinating to see, in the pieces by Brüllmann and Woolf, how Cicero worked to undo the Stoics' anti-conventionalist understanding of natural law. Cicero would have no sympathy for the idea that normativity comes from resisting or departing from nature. Instead, he believed that the traits of human psychology are compatible with, and even lead us towards, subordinating our own private interests to those of the wider political community. Indeed, it turns out that for Cicero the natural law fits very nicely with Roman law, for instance by ratifying the legitimacy of property rights. To be sure, Roman laws were also in part tailored to the specific needs of the Romans: how a given community should govern itself depends in part on natural law, in part on its own special situation. Thus the jurist Gaius, one of numerous Roman legal theorists featured in Humfress' survey of how natural law was invoked in actual legal writings, wrote that "all peoples who are governed by laws and customs use law which is partly theirs alone and partly shared by all mankind."

Of all ancient philosophers, the one whose views on nature as a source of normativity are most controversial is surely Aristotle. Our book thus devotes ample space to his political thought, presenting rival views on how exactly to understand the "naturalness" of the city-state or *polis*. For Horn, this is to be taken in a rather literal sense, namely that the *polis* is a quasi-biological entity. A middle view is adopted by Miller and Keyt, who hold that the *polis* has a "natural order" which it reaches precisely when it facilitates virtue and freedom (in the sense of "freedom" they explore). Rapp, taking a view diametrically opposed to Horn's, argues that the *polis* is "natural" only in the sense that it stems from the nature of the *humans* who build it. In this respect the supposed naturalness of the *polis* does not refer us to non-human or biological nature, but to the nature or essence of human beings. While this might free Aristotle from the criticism of undue naturalism, he would still be open to other objections, given that these very arrangements notoriously include the enslavement of some by others and the subservience of wives to husbands. But Lienemann shows that as far as the role of the wife in the household is concerned, Aristotle's stance is not quite as dismissive as is often supposed. He does recognize women's capacity for practical reasoning and virtue, since they can engage in deliberation.

In the Platonic tradition, the temptation to extract norms from nature grew not out of a "biological" approach to politics, which as Toivanen shows was still at work in medieval Aristotelianism. Rather, it came from the idea that the perfect state of the soul is its natural state. Again, Primavesi's piece is relevant here: it reminds us that it is "natural" for the lower soul to desire things that the human as a whole should not pursue. Similarly, Scott shows that even the philosophers who come to rule in Plato's ideal state are not simply born to it: by nature they have the capacity to achieve virtue and knowledge, but realizing these dispositions takes work and is thus in a sense artificial. The fundamental tension within Platonic psychology – that it is best to be "according to nature" but only if we choose the right nature, namely that of the rational soul – means that for a Platonist, what is truly normative is not human nature as such, but building on the better aspects of human nature and suppressing the worse ones. This conception shows itself also in later Platonism. Thus Plotinus saw nature as normative, but only with reference to the rational soul, which as Noble puts it, was for him "the nature according to which we *ought to* live because it is teleologically prior to the other parts of the organism." This might suggest that in late ancient Platonism, the right ordering within the soul was just a matter of philosophical contemplation, since that was the function of the higher soul. Tuominen, however, shows that Plotinus' student and editor Porphyry expanded the notion of individual "justice" to include humans' relationship with animals.

As we turn from pagan thought to the Abrahamic faith traditions that dominated the medieval period, we need to reckon with a final received opinion about pre-modern political thought. Namely that Christians, and perhaps also Jews and Muslims, simply reasserted ancient naturalism with the new caveat that nature is good because it was created that way by God. Now the political *status quo* could be given an even more powerful justification: not only is it natural for the king to be in charge of you, but God decided it should be that way! But Karamanolis shows that already in late ancient Christianity, things were more complicated. Since the Church Fathers were writing in a majority pagan society, some were ready to critique political institutions and assert an exceptional status for the Christian community. What would matter, for these thinkers, would not be humans' place within nature, but their relation to God. Another reason for Abrahamic thinkers to challenge the normativity of nature was that nature is, in their view, ultimately only provisional. Looking at a Muslim and a Jewish author who both lived in the Islamic world, Adamson shows that at least in the case of these two thinkers there are no universal laws set down in nature, which it would behoove us to observe. Instead nature itself is, to speak in the terms of the sophists, only a matter of custom.

Part I: **Plato and Aristotle**

Oliver Primavesi
Human Nature and Legal Norms: Antiphon the Sophist as Anonymous Target in Plato's *Republic* IX

Abstract: This paper focuses on a passage from Plato's *Republic* book IX, which describes the tripartite soul as a fusion of three animals or 'natures' (*phuseis*), whose growth (*phuesthai*) must be regulated by the legal norms (*nomima*). This is presented as a response to the problem posed earlier in the *Republic* with the example of the Ring of Gyges. In this paper, it is argued that the image is directed at Antiphon's theory of a fundamental antithesis between human *phusis* and *nomima*, so that the fictitious interlocutor of *book* IX, who is introduced as an upholder of the 'Gyges-thesis'—namely that that practicing injustice is beneficial provided that it is committed in complete secrecy—in fact represents the sophist Antiphon.

1 Introduction

From Book II of Plato's *Republic* onwards,[1] Socrates attempts to establish the composition of the human soul according to the model of a much larger and therefore clearer item, the city-state (*polis*). He establishes what he regards as the ideal constitution for the polis, and he does so by acting as imaginary *legislator* (*nomothetês*), with the assistance of his interlocutors Glaucon and Adeimantos.[2] The most important of his laws divides the citizens of the *polis* up into three classes: (i) craftsmen and farmers, (ii) soldiers, (iii) philosopher kings. Socrates aims to legitimize this imaginary class-division as a *natural* one by means of a founding myth that he frankly admits to be an 'indispensable,

---

[1] Plato's *Republic* (= R.) will be cited after Slings 2003 throughout.
[2] From the many references to *nomos* and related terms that underline the legislative character of Socrates' imagination from R. II, 369b5 onwards, we quote only those that precede the key passage III, 414d–415c, to which we will presently return, since for our interpretation of that key passage it will be important that the legislative character of Socrates' imagination is already presupposed: II 380c5 (νόμου); 383c7 (νόμοις); III 398b3 (ἐνομοθετησάμεθα); 403b4 (νομοθετήσεις); 409e5 (νομοθετήσεις).

noble falsehood' (*pseudos en tôi deonti gignomenon* [...] *gennaion*),³ by which ideally even the rulers should be persuaded, and failing that, at least all other citizens. The members of the first generation of the ideal city are apparently meant to believe the following (R. III, 414d–415c): their memories of adolescent education are simply an illusion. In fact they were raised inside the earth and born from the native soil itself only after they had become adults. Especially their future assignment to one of the three classes, or so they are to believe, was already determined at the moment of their emergence from the earth, depending on whether the divine creator, acting within the earth, has equipped them with gold to make them rulers, with silver to make them soldiers, or with iron (or bronze) to make them a farmer or craftsman.

In fact the citizens' assignment to the different classes is, of course, regulated by an assessment, prescribed by Socrates' *laws*, of their character and achievements.⁴ Yet according to the 'noble lie' the civic authorities will pretend to give to each citizen the rank appropriate to his *nature*. The same holds for the citizens of following generations. They too shall be divided into the three classes on the basis of an educational selection prescribed by law, and made to believe that their class membership is based solely on the admixture of metal with which they were born. In some cases, the classification will amount to a social *descent* or *ascent* from the parents' class. A ruler's child who is found to contain iron will, or so it is claimed, be downgraded without hesitation to the status of farmer that is appropriate to his or her *nature* (*phusis*),⁵ while a farmer's child who, in spite of low origin, is found to be equipped with gold or silver due to his or her *natural growth* (*phunai*) will automatically be honoured with promotion into the rulers' or soldiers' class.⁶

The paramount importance of 'nature' (*phusis*) in this context is not only documented by the presence of the noun in 415c2 (*têi phusei*) and of the cognate verb in 415c4 (*phuêi*), but also by the narrative of the 'noble lie' as a whole. For the first inhabitants of the ideal city-state will be told that they were born from

---

3 *R*. III, 414b7–c2: τῶν ψευδῶν τῶν ἐν δέοντι γιγνομένων [...] γενναῖόν τι ἓν ψευδομένους πεῖσαι μάλιστα μὲν καὶ αὐτοὺς τοὺς ἄρχοντας, εἰ δὲ μή, τὴν ἄλλην πόλιν.
4 The selection of the future philosopher rulers from among the guardians is described in greater detail in *R*. III, 412d9–e2; see also *R*. VII, 535a–536d.
5 *R*. III, 415b7–c3: καὶ ἐάν τε σφέτερος ἔκγονος ὑπόχαλκος ἢ ὑποσίδηρος γένηται, μηδενὶ τρόπωι κατελεήσουσιν, ἀλλὰ τὴν τῇ φύσει προσήκουσαν τιμὴν ἀποδόντε ὤσουσιν εἰς δημιουργοὺς ἢ εἰς γεωργούς.
6 *R*. III, 415c3–5: καὶ ἂν αὖ ἐκ τούτων τις ὑπόχρυσος ἢ ὑπάργυρος φύῃ, τιμήσαντες ἀνάξουσι τοὺς μὲν εἰς φυλακήν, τοὺς δὲ εἰς ἐπικουρίαν.

the earth, like *plants*.⁷ Now for native speakers of Ancient Greek there would be an obvious etymological relationship between *phuomai* ('grow', used especially of plants) and its two derivatives *phuton* ('plant') and *phusis* (usually translated as 'nature' but literally meaning 'plant growth'). It is true that the literal meaning of *phusis* was normally generalized to 'natural form of a living being,' but this very generalization indicates that, in Greek, the growth of plants epitomizes the stability and regularity with which *all* genera of organic life reproduce themselves in basically unchanged form – as far as the Greeks could tell.⁸ Thus, when Socrates attempts to legitimize his class-division by tracing it back to a purportedly plant-like growth of human beings, he is just illustrating, for Greek ears, the literal meaning of the claim that the class-division is 'by nature' (*phusei*).

But *why* does the Platonic Socrates go to such lengths to establish that his class-division is *by nature*? He seems to take it for granted that the emphatically anti-democratic character of his legislation stands in need of justification, and that such justification is to be provided by convincing everybody that his laws concerning class-division simply acknowledge and preserve a division produced by *natural growth*. This strategy, however, presupposes an intellectual climate in which human nature (*phusis*) is given preference over the law (*nomos*). Thus, the introduction of the 'noble lie' seems to locate the *Republic* firmly within the debate over the relationship between human nature (*phusis*) and law (*nomos*) that was initiated in the late fifth century AD by the sophists.⁹ This observation leads to the further question as to whether Plato wrote the *Republic* with a particular sophist in mind. Whereas in his early and middle dialogues Plato explicitly engages with almost every prominent sophist,¹⁰ this appears not to apply to the main part of the *Republic*, that is, to Books II–IX which come after the refutation of the sophist Thrasymachus in Book I.

Yet the absence of prominent sophists as interlocutors in the main part of the *Republic* is only an apparent one, as we will see. At the outset of *R*. II, Glaucon tells the story of Gyges and his ring in order to illustrate the thesis (henceforth: 'Gyges-thesis') that practicing injustice is beneficial provided that it is committed in complete secrecy – a thesis adopted by Glaucon just for the sake

---

7 The mythical model of this narrative is the first citizens of Thebes, who sprang out of the earth fully grown and armed for battle from the dragon's teeth sown by Cadmus.
8 On the meaning of the root *phu-* and its derivatives see the useful study by Patzer 1993.
9 Compare the classical study by Heinimann 1945 as well as more recent résumés in Dodds 1959, 263–264; Dihle 1981; Deitz 1989; Kerferd and Flashar 1998, 13–19.
10 All sophists given individual sections by Kerferd and Flashar 1998, 29–86 appear as named interlocutors in Plato: Protagoras (§3), Gorgias (§4), Thrasymachus (§5), Prodicus (§6), Hippias (§7), Kritias (§9) and Callicles (§10) – the conspicuous exception being Antiphon of Athens (§8).

of the argument. In *R.* IX, Socrates comes back to the Gyges-thesis. He introduces a fictitious anonymous exponent of the thesis and refutes him by drawing on his own theory of the tripartite soul as expounded in *R.* IV. This fictitious anonymous interlocutor represents, or so we will argue, Antiphon the sophist.

Our evidence will be an Oxyrhynchus papyrus first published in 1915, which preserves large parts of a treatise (*Aletheia*, 'On Truth') by the late fifth century AD sophist Antiphon of Athens.[11] In this treatise, the sophist defines 'justice', in an entirely legalistic manner, as "obedience to the legal norms (*nomima*) of the state," and he claims that 'justice' is to be recommended if and only if one's actions are observed by others, whereas one should follow one's 'nature' (*phusis*) whenever there are no witnesses around. Now Hermann Diels noted almost immediately, in 1917, that Antiphon's precepts reminded him of the 'Machiavellian' moral suggested by Glaucon's Gyges-story in *R.* II.[12] A few years later, in 1926, Alfred Edward Taylor went in the same direction – independently, as it seems, and more confidently – by making two claims. First, that when Glaucon complains that besides Thrasymachus there are innumerable other upholders of injustice[13] we are meant to think, among others, also of Antiphon.[14] Second, that the moral of the Gyges-story in particular is to be identified with the philosophical position of Antiphon's *Aletheia*.[15] It is true that Diels and Taylor

---

[11] Relations between the Antiphon-papyrus and Plato's dialogues were naturally considered already in the *editio princeps* of the papyrus, cf. Grenfell and Hunt 1915, 94.

[12] Diels 1917, col. 87: "Man ist versucht, bei diesem offenen Bekenntnis der Heuchelei an die Machiavellisten der Platonischen Politeia zu denken, deren höchster Begriff von Ungerechtigkeit darin besteht, durch geschicktes Verstecken ihrer Schurkenstreiche vor dem Volke als die wahrhaft Gerechten zu erscheinen (361 A)."

[13] *R.* II, 358c6–d1: ἀπορῶ μέντοι διατετρυλημένος τὰ ὦτα ἀκούων Θρασυμάχου καὶ μυρίων ἄλλων.

[14] Taylor 1926, 119, n. 1 (quoted after the Second Edition 1927, that "only differs from the first by the correction of misprints, the addition of one or two references and the modification of a few words in two or three of the footnotes"): "Cf. Blake, *Marriage of Heaven and Hell*: 'Those who restrain Desire do so because theirs is weak enough to be restrained; and the restrainer or Reason usurps its place and governs the unwilling. And being restrained, it by degrees becomes passive, till it is only the shadow of Desire.' The recently discovered Oxyrhynchus fragments of Socrates' contemporary, Antiphon 'the sophist,' have revealed to us one of the quarters in which these conceptions found literary expression in the age of the Archidamian war. It is, I believe, of Antiphon among others that Plato is thinking when he makes Glaucon declare that this same theory is widely current in his own circle (*Rep.* II. 358b)."

[15] Taylor 1926, 271: "According to Antiphon, the 'wise man', who means to make a success of life, will practise 'conventional justice' when he believes that his conduct will be observed by others, but will fall back on 'natural justice' whenever he can be sure of not being found out. This is exactly the position Glaucon means to urge in his apologue."

based their remarks on interpretations of the new Antiphon papyrus that were not entirely accurate. According to Diels, Antiphon introduced his legalistic definition of 'justice' just in order to refute it, by demonstrating that it leads to immoral consequences,[16] while according to Taylor, Antiphon used the concept of 'natural justice' as a complement to 'conventional justice'.[17] Both contentions were implicitly refuted by David Furley who, without ever mentioning Diels (1917) or Taylor (1926), demonstrated in 1981 that Antiphon nowhere criticizes or goes beyond a strictly legalistic definition of 'justice'. Or, to put it in Furley's own terms, Antiphon, while annulling the *prescriptive* value of the words 'just' and 'unjust', nowhere proposes a new *descriptive* use of them.[18] Yet Furley's helpful clarification does not undermine the link between the new Antiphon and the Gyges-thesis of *R*. II. On the contrary: the story of Gyges is obviously a perfect example for someone who, as recommended by Antiphon, denies any inherent prescriptive value of 'justice' while fully recognizing the factual power of the legal norms as soon as his actions are observed by witnesses. So it is unfortunate that in subsequent contributions on Antiphon's *Aletheia* and its reception, the important link observed by Diels and Taylor seems to have been overlooked.[19] It was Gerald F. Pendrick, in his useful edition of the fragments of Antiphon (2002), who not only rediscovered, as it were, the link between the Gyges-story and Antiphon, but also restated it in a form compatible with Furley's clarification of Antiphon's position.[20]

---

16 Diels 1917, col. 87: "Allein unser Sophist will durch diese offenbar unmoralische Folgerung aus der vorausgeschickten Definition nur diese selbst als falsch und die Geltung des Nomos als unberechtigt erweisen."
17 Taylor 1926, 271 (already quoted): "According to Antiphon, the 'wise man' [...] will practise 'conventional justice' when he believes that his conduct will be observed by others, but will fall back on 'natural justice' whenever he can be sure of not being found out."
18 See Furley 1981, 81–82.
19 Michael Nill 1985 investigates the relationship between the story of Gyges and Plato's *Protagoras* (40–42), yet when he comes back to *R*. II in his useful treatment of Antiphon (see, in particular, 56–57 and 71–74), he does not mention the story (57): "And third, Antiphon raises the escaping-notice issue. We have already seen that Glaucon and Adeimantus in the *Republic* focus on this issue in raising objections to traditional (Protagorean) defenses of justice." Fernanda Decleva Caizzi 1986 in her paper *Nature and Law in Antiphon and Plato* does not mention the *Republic* at all; instead, she brings to the fore the *Menexenus* and, above all, the *Laws* in connection with her attempt at identifying the sophist Antiphon of Athens with the orator Antiphon of Rhamnus.
20 Pendrick 2002, 64–65: "Glaucon contends that justice is less advantageous than injustice, and is practiced only under compulsion [...]. He illustrates this contention with the famous story of Gyges' ring [...]. The story's cynical presumption that human beings will commit injustice whenever they can get away with it is in perfect agreement with Antiphon's argument that self-

One interesting question, however, seems to have remained unasked so far. Can the link between the Gyges-thesis and Antiphon also enhance our understanding of the *refutation* of the thesis in *R.* IX? In other words, does the refutation of the Gyges-thesis in *R.* IX feature hints at Antiphon's *Aletheia* that go beyond the parallels observed by Diels, Taylor, and Pendrick in the exposition of the thesis in *R.* II? In the following paper we will suggest an affirmative answer to this question. The refutation of the Gyges-thesis in *R.* IX addresses a basic feature of Antiphon's *Aletheia* that does not feature in the exposition of the thesis in *R.* II: the pivotal role of human nature (*phusis*) in Antiphon's argument. According to Antiphon, one should give precedence to one's nature over legal norms (*nomima*) when choosing one's actions. Now in *Republic* IX the theory of the tripartite human soul is illustrated by the bizarre image of a composite organism. This organism consists of three animals or 'natures' (*phuseis*), the growth (*phuesthai*) of which entails the self-destruction of the organism as a whole unless regulated by the legal norms (*nomima*). This image, while officially meant to refute the Gyges-thesis as presented in *R.* II, is clearly directed at Antiphon's theory of a fundamental antithesis between human *phusis* and *nomima*, so that the fictitious interlocutor of *R.* IX, who is introduced as an upholder of the Gyges-thesis, in fact represents Antiphon. We will argue for these points by first expounding the refutation of the Gyges-thesis in *R.* IX and then comparing it with the relevant parts of the *Aletheia*-papyrus.

2 Plato, *Republic* IX, 588b1–589d4

Towards the end of *R.* IX,[21] the just man is compared with the unjust man with regard to their respective happiness. In that context, Plato has Socrates return to the Gyges-thesis raised in his discussion with Glaucon:[22] Glaucon told the story

---

interest is best served by obeying the law in the presence of witnesses, but ignoring it in their absence." Yet Pendrick quotes neither Diels 1917 nor Taylor 1926 here; and he omits Taylor 1926 even in his bibliography (while listing Diels 1917).

21 The direct transmission of the *Republic* rests upon just three independent manuscripts: Par. gr. 1807 (A: latter half of 9th c.), Marc. gr. 185, coll. 576 (D: 12th c.), Vind. suppl. gr. 39 (F: ca. AD 1300). Furthermore, our passage is transmitted by the following quotations: Iamb. *Protr.* 5, 62.17–63.3 des Places (588e6–589b6); Eus. *PE* XII 46.2–6 (588b6–589b7); Stob. III 9.62; 397.20–400.19 Hense (588b1–590a5); *Nag Hammadi Codex* VI.5 (*NHC*: Coptic translation of 588b1–589b3 φύεσθαι).

22 *R.* II, 360e–362c. In *R.* IX, Glaucon again functions as Socrates' interlocutor from 576b onwards.

of Gyges and his ring of invisibility[23] in order to illustrate the claim that the most beneficial conduct of life consists in acting unjustly to one's heart's content as long as one goes unnoticed. Like Mr Hyde in Stevenson's famous novel,[24] Gyges the shepherd is able to enjoy his own outrages – adultery with the queen, assassination of the king, and usurpation of the throne – since like Dr Jekyll he is able to escape the sanctions that society usually imposes upon the unjust.[25] Returning to this Gyges-thesis in *R.* IX, Socrates recapitulates it as follows:[26]

> "All right, then. Since we've reached this point in the argument, let's return to the first things we said, since they are what led us here. I think someone said at some point that injustice profits a completely unjust person who is believed to be just. Isn't that so?" – "It certainly is."

In what follows, Socrates initiates a dialogue with an *imaginary* upholder of the Gyges-thesis, since Glaucon, the original advocate of this thesis, has by now been convinced that justice is beneficial. Socrates intends to bring home to his imaginary opponent the devastating consequences of the Gyges-thesis by confronting him with a bizarre image of the human soul. This image has first to be set forth:[27]

> "Now, since *we* have agreed on the respective powers that injustice and justice have, let's discuss this with *him.*" – "How?" – "Let's fashion an image of the soul in words, so that the person who says this sort of thing will know what he is saying."

---

23 *R.* II, 359c7–360d7. The corrupt introductory sentence 359c7–d2 may be restored as follows: εἴη δ ἂν ἡ ἐξουσία ἣν λέγω τοιάδε μάλιστα, εἰ αὐτοῖς γένοιτο οἵαν ποτέ φασιν δύναμιν τῷ Γύγου τοῦ Λυδοῦ δακτυλίῳ (προγόνῳ codd.) γενέσθαι. That the *dunamis* of the *ring* is at stake is shown by 360a4–6.

24 Stevenson 1886.

25 For the story, retained in its initial form by Plato and reinterpreted by Herodotus, see Reinhardt 1960, 139–143 and 175–183, and Müller 2006, 300–308 (with further references).

26 *R.* IX, 588b1–5 (*Recalling to mind the Gyges-thesis*): Εἶεν δή, εἶπον· ἐπειδὴ ἐνταῦθα λόγου γεγόναμεν, ἀνα-|2|λάβωμεν τὰ πρῶτα λεχθέντα, δι' ἃ δεῦρ' ἥκομεν. ἦν δέ που |3| λεγόμενον λυσιτελεῖν ἀδικεῖν τῷ τελέως μὲν ἀδίκῳ, δοξαζο-|4|μένῳ δὲ δικαίῳ· ἦ οὐχ οὕτως ἐλέχθη; – |5| Οὕτω μὲν οὖν.

27 *R.* IX, 588b6–11 (*Confronting an imaginary proponent of the Gyges-thesis with an allegory of the soul*): Νῦν δή, ἔφην, αὐτῷ διαλεγώμεθα, ἐπειδὴ διωμολογησά-|7| μεθα τό τε ἀδικεῖν καὶ τὸ δίκαια πράττειν ἣν ἑκάτερον ἔχει |8| δύναμιν. – |9| Πῶς; ἔφη. – |10| Εἰκόνα πλάσαντες τῆς ψυχῆς λόγῳ, ἵνα εἰδῇ ὁ ἐκεῖνα |11| λέγων οἷα ἔλεγεν (b6 αὐτῶι ADF Eus. Stob. : not rendered by *NHC* : αὖ οὕτω C. Schmidt || b10 εἰδῆι AD Eus.(I) Stob. : ἴδη F Eus.(ON) : *intellegat NHC*, rendering εἰδῆι rather than ἴδηι || b11 οἷα ADF Stob. : οἵαν Eus.).

The human soul will be portrayed as a quasi-mythical creature in which parts of different animals have grown together (*sumpephukuiai*) into one single organism (*phusis*, literally "result of natural growth").[28] By way of example, Socrates refers to three famous epic monsters: the Chimera[29] who is a lion at the front, a snake at the back, and in the middle a goat; Scylla,[30] who has twelve misshapen feet at the bottom and six long necks at the top, each with a terrible head equipped with three rows of teeth; and Cerberus,[31] Hades' hound with fifty heads who devours raw meat and whose voice is as loud as a brazen trumpet:[32]

> "What sort of image?" – "One like those creatures (*phuseis*) that legends tell us existed in ancient times, such as the Chimera, Scylla, Cerberus, or any of the multitude of others in which many different kinds of things are said to have grown together (*sumpephukuiai*) naturally into one." – "Yes, legends do tell us of such things."

As the *first constituent* of the imaginary organism, Glaucon is to conceive a beast that already by itself possesses a multitude of various heads from both tame and savage animals and that is capable both of changing its heads' character and of bringing forth (*phuein*) new ones:[33]

> "Well, then, fashion a single kind of multi-coloured beast with a ring of many heads that it can grow (*phuein*) and change at will – some from gentle, some from savage animals." – "That's work for a clever artist. However, since a thought is a more malleable object than wax and the like, consider it done."

As the second and third constituents of this imaginary organism, Glaucon is to picture a lion and a human being. He is to ensure that the many-headed beast

---

28 For the function of this image in the larger context of *R.* IX, see Annas 1981, 318–320.
29 *Iliad* 6, 181.
30 *Odyssey* 12, 89–91.
31 Hesiod, *Theogony* 311–312.
32 *R.* IX, 588c1–6 (*The soul pictured as a composite animal*): Ποίαν τινά; ἦ δ' ὅς. – |2| Τῶν τοιούτων τινά, ἦν δ' ἐγώ, οἷαι μυθολογοῦνται παλαιαὶ |3| γενέσθαι φύσεις, ἥ τε Χιμαίρας καὶ ἡ Σκύλλης καὶ Κερβέρου, |4| καὶ ἄλλαι τινὲς συχναὶ λέγονται συμπεφυκυῖαι ἰδέαι πολλαὶ |5| εἰς ἓν γενέσθαι. – |6| Λέγονται γάρ, ἔφη.
33 *R.* IX, 588c7–d1 (*First component: the many-headed monster*): Πλάττε τοίνυν μίαν μὲν ἰδέαν θηρίου ποικίλου καὶ πολυ- |8| κεφάλου, ἡμέρων δὲ θηρίων ἔχοντος κεφαλὰς κύκλῳ καὶ |9| ἀγρίων, καὶ δυνατοῦ μεταβάλλειν καὶ φύειν ἐξ αὑτοῦ πάντα |10| ταῦτα. – |11| Δεινοῦ πλάστου, ἔφη, τὸ ἔργον· ὅμως δέ, ἐπειδὴ εὔπλασ-|d1|τότερον κηροῦ καὶ τῶν τοιούτων λόγων, πεπλάσθω (c7 πλάττε ADF Eus. : πρᾶττε Stob. NHC || c8 δὲ ADF Eus. Stob. : τε Madvig || c9 φύειν AD Eus. Stob. : φύσιν F NHC || c9–10 πάντα ταῦτα ADF Stob. : ταῦτα πάντα Eus. || d1 λόγος ADF Stob. : ὁ λόγος Eus.).

will be the largest, the lion the second in size, and the human the smallest creature:[34]

> "Then fashion one other kind, that of a lion, and another of a human being. But make the first one much the largest and the other one second to it in size". – "That's easier – the sculpting is done."

Thereafter, Glaucon is told to have the three creatures be grown together (*sumpephukenai*) into a single one:[35]

> "Now join the three of them into one, so that they are, in a way, naturally *grown together*." – "They're joined."

Finally, he should envelop this tripartite creature within a human-shaped covering (*elutron*), so that it appears to be a human being when seen from outside:[36]

> "Then, fashion around them the image of one of them, that of a human being so that anyone who sees only the outer covering and not what's inside will think it is a single creature, a human being." – "It's done."

Thus, the image is completed: a natural organism (*phusis*) that appears to be a uniform, purely human *phusis* since its peculiar composition is not visible from outside, whereas in fact it corresponds to an epic *monstrum triforme* in that it encompasses three quite different creatures.

Now Socrates can invite Glaucon to take part in an imaginary discussion based on the image of the tripartite soul. Their interlocutor will be an anonymous advocate of the Gyges-thesis, who holds that disguised injustice pays off whereas consistently doing justice brings no advantage (*ou sumpherei*, 588e5). In the course of this discussion, it will be assumed that injustice corresponds to a specific kind of treatment which the outer man, like an animal keeper, bestows on the three creatures inside himself. The treatment in question consists of (i) nurturing and strengthening both the many-headed beast and the lion, (ii)

---

[34] R. IX, 588d2–4 (*The second and third components: lion and inner man*): Μίαν δὴ τοίνυν ἄλλην ἰδέαν λέοντος, μίαν δὲ ἀνθρώπου· |3| πολὺ δὲ μέγιστον ἔστω τὸ πρῶτον καὶ δεύτερον τὸ δεύτερον. – |4| Ταῦτα, ἔφη, ῥᾷω, καὶ πέπλασται (d2 δὴ AD Stob. : δὲ F Eus.).
[35] R. IX, 588d5–7 (*Fusing the three components*): Σύναπτε τοίνυν αὐτὰ εἰς ἓν τρία ὄντα, ὥστε πῃ συμπεφυ-|6|κέναι ἀλλήλοις. – |7| Συνῆπται, ἔφη (d5 ὄντα ADF Stob. *NHC* : ἔχοντα Eus.).
[36] R. IX, 588d8–e3 (*A human envelope*): Περίπλασον δὴ αὐτοῖς ἔξωθεν ἑνὸς εἰκόνα, τὴν τοῦ |e1| ἀνθρώπου, ὥστε τῷ μὴ δυναμένῳ τὰ ἐντὸς ὁρᾶν, ἀλλὰ τὸ |2| ἔξω μόνον ἔλυτρον ὁρῶντι, ἓν ζῷον φαίνεσθαι, ἄνθρωπον. – |3| Περιπέπλασται, ἔφη (d8 δὴ ADF Eus.(G) Stob. : δὲ Eus.(IN) || e1 τὸ ADF Eus. : τι Stob.).

having the 'inner man'[37] be oppressed by the many-headed beast and lion and thereby starving and weakening him, and (iii) inciting the lion and the many-headed beast to fight against each other to the death. It follows that the advocate of the Gyges-thesis must be prepared to defend the paradoxical claim that this ruinous policy would be beneficial for the outer man:[38]

> "Then if someone maintains that injustice profits this human being and that doing just things brings no advantage, let's tell him that he is simply saying that it is beneficial for him, (i) to feed the multiform beast well and make it strong, and also the lion and all that pertains to him; (ii) to starve and weaken the human being, so that he is dragged along wherever either of the other two (*poteron*)[39] leads; and (iii) to leave the parts to bite and kill one another rather than accustoming them to each other and making them friendly." – "Yes, that's absolutely what someone who praises injustice is saying."

Socrates, however, does not dwell on the formal refutation of this claim, as it is evident that the outer man will not benefit from allowing the three individual creatures inside him to destroy each other. Rather, Socrates temporarily replaces the first imaginary interlocutor with a second one who argues for the opposite thesis, according to which it is justice that is beneficial for the outer man. This second interlocutor will deem it necessary (i) that we strengthen, by means of speech and action, the inner man as much as possible, (ii) that the inner man cultivates the many-headed beast by stimulating the growth of those of its heads that are tame (compare above *R*. IX, 588c7–10), and by suppressing the growth of its savage heads, all with the assistance of the lion; and finally (iii) that he establishes a harmony both between the many-headed beast and the

---

[37] 589a7–b1 ὁ ἐντὸς ἄνθρωπος; cf. Plot. I 1.10 lin. 15 and V 1.10 lin. 10 Henry-Schwyzer, as well as Dorotheus Abbas, *doct*. I 6.3, and, last not least, the New Testament expression ὁ ἔσω ἄνθρωπος 2 *Cor*. 4.16; *Rom*. 7.22.2; *Eph*. 3.16.

[38] *R*. IX, 588e4–589a5 (*The treatment of the composite animal by the proponent of injustice*): Λέγωμεν δὴ τῷ λέγοντι ὡς λυσιτελεῖ τούτῳ ἀδικεῖν τῷ |5| ἀνθρώπῳ, δίκαια δὲ πράττειν οὐ συμφέρει, ὅτι οὐδὲν ἄλλο |6| φησὶν ἢ λυσιτελεῖν αὐτῷ τὸ παντοδαπὸν θηρίον εὐωχοῦντι |7| ποιεῖν ἰσχυρὸν καὶ τὸν λέοντα καὶ τὰ περὶ τὸν λέοντα, τὸν δὲ |a1| ἄνθρωπον λιμοκτονεῖν καὶ ποιεῖν ἀσθενῆ, ὥστε ἕλκεσθαι ὅπῃ |2| ἂν ἐκείνων πότερον ἄγῃ, καὶ μηδὲν ἕτερον ἑτέρῳ συνεθίζειν |3| μηδὲ φίλον ποιεῖν, ἀλλ' ἐᾶν αὐτὰ ἐν αὑτοῖς δάκνεσθαί τε καὶ |4| μαχόμενα ἐσθίειν ἄλληλα. – |5| Παντάπασι γάρ, ἔφη, ταῦτ' ἂν λέγοι ὁ τὸ ἀδικεῖν ἐπαινῶν (e5 ὅτι ADF Stob. : διότι Eus. || e6 φησὶν ADF Eus. : φήσει Stob. : not rendered by *NHC* || 589a1 ὥστε ADF Eus. Stob. : ὡς Iamb. || a2 ἐκείνων A$^{s.l.}$DF Eus. Iamb. *NHC* : ἐκείνω A | πότερον Stob. : ὁπότερον ADF Eus. Iamb. : πρότερον *NHC* || a5 ἂν ADF Eus. : omitted by Stob.).

[39] For the indefinite meaning of πότερον (589a2) see LSJ s.v. πότερος III. Schwyzer II 213, however, distinguishes the interrogative pronoun πότερος and the enclitic indefinite pronoun ποτερος.

lion and between these two creatures and himself. Such a harmony allows for a healthy common upbringing of all three creatures:[40]

> "But, on the other hand, wouldn't someone who maintains that just things are profitable be saying (i) that we should say just those things and do just those things in virtue of which the inner man within the human envelope will gain maximum control; (ii) that he should take care of the many-headed beast like a farmer, feeding and domesticating the gentle ones and preventing the savage ones from growing (*phuesthai*), by making the lion's nature (*phusis*) his ally, and (iii) that he should take care of all parts together, and bring them up in such a way that they will be friends with each other and with himself?" – "Yes, that's exactly what someone who praises justice is saying."

A comparative evaluation leaves no doubt that the thesis of the second imaginary interlocutor must be accepted whereas the Gyges-thesis must be rejected. Measured exclusively by utilitarian calculation, that is, with regard to the acquisition of pleasure, social recognition, and material benefit, just behaviour is consistently beneficial for human beings, whereas acting unjust is harmful, even when it goes completely unnoticed. Through unjust behaviour the soul's tripartite *phusis* destroys itself – irrespective of whether it manages to keep up the appearance of humanity by concealing the inner chaos or not. Consequently, the critique of justice offered by the proponent of the Gyges-thesis must be regarded as altogether unfounded:[41]

> "From every point of view, then, anyone who praises justice speaks truly, and anyone who praises injustice speaks falsely. Whether we look at the matter from the point of view of pleasure, good reputation, or advantage, the one who praises justice tells the truth, while the one who condemns it has nothing sound to say and condemns without knowing what he is condemning." – "In my opinion, at least, he knows nothing about it."

---

40 R. IX, 589a6–b7 (*The treatment of the composite animal by the proponent of justice*): Οὐκοῦν αὖ ὁ τὰ δίκαια λέγων λυσιτελεῖν φαίη ἂν δεῖν |7| ταῦτα πράττειν καὶ ταῦτα λέγειν, ὅθεν τοῦ ἀνθρώπου ὁ ἐντὸς |b1| ἄνθρωπος ἔσται ἐγκρατέστατος, καὶ τοῦ πολυκεφάλου θρέμ-|2|ματος ἐπιμελήσεται, ὥσπερ γεωργὸς τὰ μὲν ἥμερα τρέφων |3| καὶ τιθασεύων, τὰ δὲ ἄγρια ἀποκωλύων φύεσθαι σύμμαχον |4| ποιησάμενος τὴν τοῦ λέοντος φύσιν, καὶ κοινῇ πάντων |5| κηδόμενος φίλα ποιησάμενος ἀλλήλοις τε καὶ αὑτῷ, οὕτω |6| θρέψει; – |7| Κομιδῇ γὰρ αὖ λέγει ταῦτα ὁ τὸ δίκαιον ἐπαινῶν (a7 ἐντὸς ADF Eus. Stob. Dor. : ἔνδον Plot. I 1 : εἴσω Plot. V 1 || b5 οὕτω ADF Eus. : οὕτως αὐτὰ Iamb.).

41 R. IX, 589b8–c5 (*The proponent of justice vindicated, the proponent of injustice refuted*): Κατὰ πάντα τρόπον δὴ ὁ μὲν τὰ δίκαια ἐγκωμιάζων ἀληθῆ |c1| ἂν λέγοι, ὁ δὲ τὰ ἄδικα ψεύδοιτο. πρός τε γὰρ ἡδονὴν καὶ |2| πρὸς εὐδοξίαν καὶ ὠφελίαν σκοπουμένῳ ὁ μὲν ἐπαινέτης τοῦ |3| δικαίου ἀληθεύει, ὁ δὲ ψέκτης οὐδὲν ὑγιὲς οὐδ' εἰδὼς ψέγει ὅτι |4| ψέγει. – |5| Οὔ μοι δοκεῖ, ἦ δ' ὅς, οὐδαμῇ γε (b8 τρόπον δὴ ADF : δὴ τρόπον Stob. || b8–c1 ἀληθῆ ἂν DF Stob. : ἀλήθειαν A || c1 τε ADF : omitted by Stob. || c2 εὐδοξίαν AD Stob. : εὐεξίαν F).

Thus, the comparison of the respective benefits of *justice* and *injustice*, which has all along been the point of discussing the image of the soul,[42] has reached its goal.

Finally, Socrates asks Glaucon to return to the first imaginary interlocutor, the advocate of the Gyges-thesis. He deserves sympathy since he "does not go wrong voluntarily";[43] rather, his mistake rests on ignorance. For his benefit, Socrates applies the gist of what has been established to a re-evaluation of the *nomima*, i.e. established legal norms[44] that determine what is 'fine' and 'shameful'. Socrates concludes that these *nomima* supply the indispensable corrective for the antagonism within the human soul. Only with their help can one prevent the 'shameful' actions that subject the 'fine' aspects of the human character to the control of the beast within:[45]

> "Then let's persuade him gently – for he doesn't go wrong of his own will – by asking him these questions. 'Shouldn't we say that this is the original basis for the legal norms (*nomima*) about both what is fine and what is shameful? Fine things are those that subordinate the beastlike parts of our nature (*phusis*) to the inner man – or better, perhaps, to the divine, shameful ones are those that enslave the gentle to the savage?' Will he agree or not?" – "He will, if he takes my advice."

---

42 Compare *R.* IX, 588b3–4: λυσιτελεῖν ἀδικεῖν τῷ τελέως μὲν ἀδίκῳ, δοξαζομένῳ δὲ δικαίῳ. 588b7–8 τό τε ἀδικεῖν καὶ τὸ δίκαια πράττειν ἣν ἑκάτερον ἔχει δύναμιν. 588e4–5 λυσιτελεῖ τούτῳ ἀδικεῖν τῷ ἀνθρώπῳ, δίκαια δὲ πράττειν οὐ συμφέρει. 589a5: ὁ τὸ ἀδικεῖν ἐπαινῶν. 589a6: ὁ τὰ δίκαια λέγων λυσιτελεῖν. 589b7: ὁ τὸ δίκαιον ἐπαινῶν. 589b8–c1: ὁ μὲν τὰ δίκαια ἐγκωμιάζων ἀληθῆ ἂν λέγοι, ὁ δὲ τὰ ἄδικα ψεύδοιτο. 589c2–4: ὁ μὲν ἐπαινέτης τοῦ δικαίου ἀληθεύει, ὁ δὲ ψέκτης οὐδὲν ὑγιὲς οὐδ' εἰδὼς ψέγει ὅτι ψέγει.
43 *R.* IX, 589c6: οὐ γὰρ ἑκὼν ἁμαρτάνει. This formulation comes as close to the words 'no one errs willingly (οὐδεὶς ἑκὼν ἁμαρτάνει)' frequently, though not entirely accurately, ascribed to Socrates in modern research, as does the *Gorgias*-passage 509e (μηδένα βουλόμενον ἀδικεῖν, ἀλλ' ἄκοντας τοὺς ἀδικοῦντας πάντας ἀδικεῖν) cited by Vlastos 1995, 52 n. 32 as 'approximation' to this; cf. Segvic 2000.
44 Cf. *Cri.* 53c, *Grg.* 488d–e; *R.* VI, 484d2, *Lg.* I, 626a7; *Lg.* VII, 793a10 and d4; *Lg.* IX, 871a3; see further Schöpsdau 2011, 328–329.
45 *R.* IX, 589c6–d4 (*The successful treatment of the composite animal corresponds to the legal norms of good and bad*): Πείθωμεν τοίνυν αὐτὸν πράως – οὐ γὰρ ἑκὼν ἁμαρτάνει – |7| ἐρωτῶντες· Ὦ μακάριε, οὐ καὶ τὰ καλὰ καὶ αἰσχρὰ νόμιμα |8| διὰ τὰ τοιαῦτ' ἂν φαῖμεν γεγονέναι, τὰ μὲν καλὰ τὰ ὑπὸ τῷ |d1| ἀνθρώπῳ – μᾶλλον δὲ ἴσως τὰ ὑπὸ τῷ θείῳ – τὰ θηριώδη |2| ποιοῦντα τῆς φύσεως, αἰσχρὰ δὲ τὰ ὑπὸ τῷ ἀγρίῳ τὸ ἥμερον |3| δουλούμενα; συμφήσει ἢ πῶς; – |4| Ἐάν μοι, ἔφη, πείθηται (c6 πείθωμεν AD Stob. : πείθομεν F || d2 τὰ ADF : omitted by Stob. || d4 μοι [...] πείθηται ADF : ἐμοί [...] πίθηται Stob.).

This final message for the imaginary interlocutor clearly shows that *denying* the inherent value of the *nomima* is considered to be his central contention.

The construction of the image of the soul and the argument of the ensuing discussion itself are closely connected to the famous passage in *R*. IV where Socrates inferred, from the division of the *polis* into three classes, a corresponding tripartition of the soul.[46] He first distinguished the 'rational' (*logistikon*) and the 'appetitive' (*epithumetikon*);[47] afterwards, against Glaucon's initial doubts,[48] he determined a third part as the 'spirited' (*thumoeides*).[49] On that basis, Socrates defined 'justice' (*dikaiosune*) as a constitution of the soul, in which every one of the parts strictly adheres to its proper role according to the soul's nature (*kata phusin*), whereas 'injustice' is a state of the soul in which a single part, the appetitive one, transgresses its rightful competences and subjugates – against the soul's nature (*para phusin*) – the rational and the spirited parts.[50] In the light of *R*. IV, the image of the soul described in *R*. IX has to be decoded as follows. The largest and innately most powerful of the three creatures, the many-headed beast, corresponds to the appetitive part of the soul (*epithumetikon*); the second in size, the lion, represents the spirited part (*thumoeides*); the smallest one, the inner man, embodies the rational part (*logistikon*). The self-destruction arising through the subjugation of the inner man to the many-headed beast and the lion represents the unjust way of life in which the rational part of the soul is prevented from carrying out its natural duty of guiding the whole soul, so that the human being is enslaved by his craving for honour and especially by bodily desires. By contrast, the rule of the inner man over the many-headed beast and the lion corresponds to the just state of the soul in which all its three parts fulfil their proper duties, which is to say that the bodily desires and the craving for honour are regulated by the rational part.

In *R*. IX, then, the Platonic Socrates tries to solve the problem of the benefit of unjust action as raised by the Gyges-story in Book II on the basis of the tripartition of the soul as expounded in *R*. IV. He does so by expressing this tripartition in an image that leaves no doubt as to the harmfulness of any unjust action for the one who performs it. In spite of the close relationship between *R*. IV and *R*. IX, however, a closer comparison between them also reveals a conspicuous *dif-*

---

46 *R*. IV, 434d–435c.
47 *R*. IV, 439d.
48 *R*. IV, 439e.
49 *R*. IV, 440e–441a.
50 *R*. IV, 444d: Οὐκοῦν αὖ, ἔφην, τὸ δικαιοσύνην ἐμποιεῖν (*scil. ἐστι*) τὰ ἐν τῇ ψυχῇ κατὰ φύσιν καθιστάναι κρατεῖν τε καὶ κρατεῖσθαι ὑπ' ἀλλήλων, τὸ δὲ ἀδικίαν παρὰ φύσιν ἄρχειν τε καὶ ἄρχεσθαι ἄλλο ὑπ' ἄλλου, cf. *R*. IV, 442a–b.

ference; this difference, to which we now turn, concerns the nature (*phusis*) of the human soul.

In the exposition of the theory of the tripartite soul in *R*. IV, the term *phusis* is applied to the relation of the three incorporeal parts of the soul to one another and to the soul in its entirety, and in this context it is used in the meaning 'inherent norm' as derived by abstraction from the original meaning 'regular result of (plant) growth.' The normative meaning is evident in the definition of justice as the inner relation of the three parts 'in accordance with their nature (*kata phusin*)' and of injustice as 'against their nature (*para phusin*)'. In this context, *phusis* unequivocally denotes a state of the incorporeal human soul and its parts that conforms to an inherent norm. Even the 'natural' voracity ascribed in *R*. IV to the appetitive part of the soul (*epithumethikon*)[51] conforms to the inherent norm of the soul as a whole in that the appetitive part is said to be destined 'by nature' (*phusei*) for servitude.[52]

In the figurative illustration of the tripartite human soul in *R*. IX, however, where the term *phusis*[53] is associated – in keeping with its word formation – with the process of bodily growth (*phuein, phuesthai*)[54] or its result (*pephukenai*),[55] *phusis* and its cognates completely *lack* the usual normative connotation. At 588c3, the horrifying mythical composite creatures, the Chimera, Skylla, and Cerberus, are called *phuseis* ('grown shapes'), whose individual, often heterogeneous parts are made to 'grow together' (*sumpephukuiai*: 588c4) and to 'become one from many'. There can hardly be any question of a *normative* shape in the case of such unnatural compositions. This is also true of the use of the intransitive perfect verb *sumpephukenai* at 588d5–6, where Glaucon is invited to allow the three individual beings in the image of the soul to grow together in his mind. Here, *sumpephukenai* designates a *misalliance* of three parts that are not only completely heterogeneous, but even mutually antagonistic. At 588c9, the durative active form *phuein* is used to describe the many-headed beast's capacity to grow new heads. Whereas *phuein* is usually applied to processes of natural growth that produce a regular result, such as the teething of a child,[56] in the case of the many-headed beast we have tame heads being transformed into sav-

---

[51] *R*. IV, 442a χρημάτων φύσει ἀπληστότατον (scil. τὸ ἐπιθυμητικόν): "by nature (*phusei*) most insatiable."
[52] *R*. IV, 444b τοιούτου ὄντος φύσει (scil. τοῦ ἐπιθυμητικοῦ) οἵου πρέπειν αὐτῷ δουλεύειν.
[53] *R*. IX, 588c3 φύσεις, 589b4 φύσις, d2 φύσεως.
[54] *R*. IX, 588c9 φύειν, 589b3 φύεσθαι.
[55] *R*. IX, 588c4 συμπεφυκυῖαι, d5–6 συμπεφυκέναι.
[56] Solon Fr. 27, 1–2 West: παῖς μὲν ἄνηβος ἐὼν ἔτι νήπιος ἕρκος ὀδόντων / φύσας ἐκβάλλει πρῶτον ἐν ἕπτ' ἔτεσιν.

age ones and also the ability to grow (*phuein*) new heads, so that any reference to a normative shape is obviously ruled out. The same is true of 589b3, where the middle voice intransitive *phuesthai* is ascribed to the savage heads. This is an anarchic growth that has got out of control, and that the outer man must avoid by acting in conformity with the legal norms (*nomima*). It is true that at 589b4 a *phusis* is also ascribed to the lion, whose form seems to correspond to the zoological norm. Yet it grows together with the many-headed beast and the inner man, forming a surreal whole. The lion is also ambivalent on the level of action, since it can form alliances with either of the other parts. Even more worrying is the 'nature' of the outer man. The *phusis* ascribed to him at 589d2 looks like a human from the outside, but this human shape is really only a covering that conceals the three-bodied creature within. Again, the ambivalence is again reflected on the level of action. The outer man is able to subjugate the beastly components of his nature (*ta thêriōdê tês phuseōs*) to the inner man, the rational part of the soul, by means of noble actions and with the assistance of the lion. Yet he can also allow it to tyrannize the inner man through shameful actions.

All in all, then, the specific use of the term *phusis* in the image of the human soul strongly emphasizes both the correlation of *human nature, unjust action*, and *self-destruction* on the one hand, and the correlation of *suppression of human nature, just action*, and *self-preservation* on the other. For according to 588e6–589a4, unjust treatment strengthens the *natural* superiority of the many-headed beast and the lion, while ultimately eliminating the inner man who is already insignificant by nature. This, in turn, results in the mutual antagonism of the many-headed beast and the lion and thus entails the destruction of the entire three-bodied organism. By contrast, just treatment (589a7–b6) secures supremacy for the inner man – in spite of his *natural* weakness – and enables him to suppress the *natural* anarchic growth of the beast's savage heads in favour of the tame ones. Only this intervention makes possible a 'mutual friendship' between the three beings (*phila poiêsamenos allêlois*, 589b5), which is in turn a necessary condition for the survival of the three-bodied organism as a whole. Furthermore, it is in accordance with the *legal norms* of good and bad that the just treatment corrects the natural distribution of power within the organism and thereby saves it (589c7–d3).

The inconsistency between the use of the term *phusis* in the exposition of the tripartite structure of the human soul in *R.* IV and the extensive use of *phusis* and cognate expressions in the figurative illustration of the same structure in *R.* IX could scarcely be stronger.[57] In *R.* IV, *phusis* designated the 'inherent norm', obedience to which secures the just state of the human soul. In our *R.* IX passage, on the other hand, the *phusis* of the human soul appears as a polymorphous monstrosity whose parts are opposed to each other, and which depends for its mere survival on coercion by the *nomima*. The inconsistency will be resolved, however, in the final section of *R.* IX, which is devoted to spelling out the consequences of the encounter with the imaginary interlocutor. In that context, Socrates introduces a *qualification*. He designates the state of the soul in which the relation between the soul parts has been put in order no longer as its 'nature', but as its '*best possible* nature' (*beltistê phusis*)[58] – as opposed to the soul of, for example, a proletarian in which the best part is *by nature* so weak that it cannot control the other two creatures.[59] Furthermore, in an important passage of *R.* X to which we will return presently, he uses similar qualifications of *nature*: 'truest' (*alêthestatê*, *R.* X, 611b1), and 'primary' (*archaia*: *R.* X, 611c7–d1). So the emphasis on *phusis* and cognate forms in the horrifying portrait of the human soul is clearly not just a poetic device. It amounts, rather, to *a serious criticism of 'nature'* and, as such, it has a lasting consequence: from now on it seems no longer advisable to speak – without qualification – of a '*phusis* of the soul' in the normative sense that Socrates took innocently for granted when using the expressions *kata phusin* and *para phusin* in *R.* IV.

The difference between "nature of the soul" and "*best possible* nature of the soul" (*R.* IX, 591b3–4) foreshadows an important philosophical point that is revealed at *R.* X, 611a4–612a7. In this passage, Socrates emphasizes that "the soul *in its truest nature*" cannot be identified with the tension-ridden composite soul as portrayed in the image of *R.* IX:[60]

"[...] nor must we think that the soul *in its truest nature* is full of multi-coloured variety and unlikeness or that it differs with itself." – "What do you mean?" – "It is not easy for any-

---

57 Mannsperger 1969 failed to note the inconsistency between the use of *phusis* in Book IV and in the image of the soul in Book IX.
58 *R.* IX, 591b3–4: καὶ ὅλη ἡ ψυχὴ εἰς τὴν βελτίστην φύσιν καθισταμένη τιμιωτέραν ἕξιν λαμβάνει.
59 *R.* IX, 590c1–4: βαναυσία δὲ καὶ χειροτεχνία διὰ τί οἴει ὄνειδος φέρει; ἢ δι' ἄλλο τι φήσομεν ἢ ὅταν τις ἀσθενὲς φύσει ἔχῃ τὸ τοῦ βελτίστου εἶδος, ὥστε μὴ ἂν δύνασθαι ἄρχειν τῶν ἐν αὐτῷ θρεμμάτων [...];
60 *R.* X, 611b1–7: [...] μήτε γε αὖ (scil. οἰώμεθα) τῇ ἀληθεστάτῃ φύσει τοιοῦτον εἶναι ψυχήν, ὥστε πολλῆς ποικιλίας καὶ ἀνομοιοτητός τε καὶ διαφορᾶς γέμειν αὐτὸ πρὸς αὐτό. Πῶς λέγεις; ἔφη. Οὐ ῥᾴδιον, ἦν δ' ἐγώ, ἀίδιον εἶναι σύνθετόν τε ἐκ πολλῶν καὶ μὴ τῇ καλλίστῃ κεχρημένον συνθέσει, ὡς νῦν ἡμῖν ἐφάνη ἡ ψυχή.

thing to be *immortal* if it is composed of many parts and composed in a way that is not exactly the finest, yet this is how the soul just [i.e. in the image of R. IX] appeared to us."

So it turns out that in R. IX–X the function of the expressions '*best possible*', '*truest*', or '*primary* nature' – as opposed to 'nature' without qualification – is to designate the nature of the *immortal soul* in its *original state* before its incarnation, still free from all the blemishes that were produced by its connection to a body[61] – a state compared by Socrates to the *archaia phusis* of the sea god Glaucus that is almost beyond the imagination of the fishermen who have successfully called out for the god's help (*exō Glaukē*)[62] and, accordingly, see him in his present state, damaged and disfigured by mussels, seaweed, and stones:[63]

> "Now we have said the truth about it [i.e. the soul] as it appears at present. But we have studied it in a state that is like that of the sea god Glaucus: it seems that for those who manage to see him it is by no means easy to make out his *primary nature* any more, since by now some of his original parts have been broken off, others have been crushed, his whole body has been maimed by the waves, and other things like shells, seaweeds, and stones have attached themselves to him, so that he looks more like a wild animal than like the being *he was by nature*."

It remains puzzling, however, that although 'nature' did not play any role in the exposition of the Gyges-thesis in R. II, the *refutation* of this thesis in R. IX should be so heavily charged with a *criticism* of 'nature'. The Gyges-thesis as presented in R. II could have been refuted simply by pointing out the antagonism between the three parts of the soul as introduced in R. IV, without any emphasis on the 'naturalness' of that antagonism. In what follows, we will argue that the criticism of 'nature' conveyed by the horrifying picture of the soul is in fact directed at the text that according to Taylor 1926 stands already behind the exposition of the Gyges-thesis in Book II: at the treatise *Aletheia* by the sophist Antiphon of Athens.[64]

---

61 R. X, 611b10–c1: [...] λελωβημένον [...] ὑπό τε τῆς τοῦ σώματος κοινωνίας καὶ ἄλλων κακῶν.
62 Phot. ε 1283; II 126 Theodoridis, with parallels.
63 R. X, 611c4–d1: νῦν δὲ εἴπομεν μὲν ἀληθῆ περὶ αὐτοῦ, οἷον ἐν τῷ παρόντι φαίνεται. τεθεάμεθα μέντοι διακείμενον αὐτό, ὥσπερ οἱ τὸν θαλάττιον Γλαῦκον ὁρῶντες οὐκ ἂν ἔτι ῥᾳδίως αὐτοῦ ἴδοιεν τὴν ἀρχαίαν φύσιν, ὑπὸ τοῦ τά τε παλαιὰ τοῦ σώματος μέρη τὰ μὲν ἐκκεκλάσθαι, τὰ δὲ συντετρῖφθαι καὶ πάντως λελωβῆσθαι ὑπὸ τῶν κυμάτων, ἄλλα δὲ προσπεφυκέναι, ὄστρεά τε καὶ φυκία καὶ πέτρας, ὥστε παντὶ μᾶλλον θηρίῳ ἐοικέναι ἢ οἷος ἦν φύσει.
64 Mannsperger 1969 does not take into consideration the term *phusis* as attested by the *Aletheia* papyrus, nor its relation to *Pol.* IX.

3 Antiphon, *Aletheia* (*POxy.* 1364 + 3647)

In 1905, the English papyrus excavations in Egyptian Oxyrhynchus brought to light two extensive textual fragments obviously stemming from the same papyrus scroll, on the relation between human nature (*phusis*) and the legal norms (*nomima*) of the state. Both fragments were published by Bernard Grenfell and Arthur Hunt in 1915 as *POxy.* 1364 Fragments 1–2. This text is rightly regarded as the earliest witness for the thesis that the beneficial or harmful consequences of a person's actions depend primarily on the nature (*phusis*) of the agent, and only secondarily on the legal norms (*nomima*) of his society.[65] Thanks to the assistance of Ulrich von Wilamowitz-Moellendorff, the editors were able to equip their edition[66] with the title *Antiphon Sophistes, Περὶ ἀληθείας* i. He had pointed out to them in correspondence that a citation, by Harpocration, from Antiphon's treatise *Aletheia*[67] is exactly matched by three lines in fr. 1 of the new papyrus text,[68] and accordingly, that *POxy.* 1364 clearly stems from that work by Antiphon.[69] The editorial qualification of the author as a 'sophist' can be supported by the testimony of Xenophon: he reports that a certain 'Antiphon' tried to win over Socrates' students with his hedonist teachings; and he explicitly characterizes this Antiphon as a 'sophist'.[70] In assigning the papyrus text to the *first book* of the *Aletheia*, however, the first editors went beyond the evidence.[71] With re-

---

[65] Cf. Furley 1981, 90: "Antiphon stands, I think, at the very beginning of the tendency to seek for guidance for human behaviour in nature [...]"

[66] Grenfell and Hunt 1915, 92–104, no. 1364; Diels 1916, 932–936; Diels 1922, XXXI–XXXVI; Diels and Kranz 1935, 346–353.

[67] 80 B 44, Diels 1912, 298 (Harp. ed. Dindorf 1853, 4 or ed. Keaney 1991, 2, α7, s.v. ἄγοι): Ἀντιφῶν δ' ἐν τῷ περὶ ἀληθείας φησὶ 'τοὺς νόμους μεγάλους ἄγοι' ἀντὶ τοῦ 'ἡγοῖτο'. τούτου πολλὴ χρῆσις.

[68] The sentence *POxy.* XI, 1364 fr. 1, col. i, lines 18–20 (το[υ]ς νο|μους μεγα[λο]υς | αγοι) in Grenfell and Hunt 1915, 96 corresponds exactly – including the optative ἄγοι – to Harpocration's citation from Antiphon's *Aletheia* as quoted in the preceding note.

[69] See Grenfell and Hunt 1915, 92: "The authorship of the fragment is fortunately established by the coincidence, pointed out to us by Wilamowitz, of ll. 18–20 with a citation in Harpocration from the treatise of Antiphon 'On Truth'." This was the last example of the fruitful "collaboration on several volumes of the Oxyrhynchus papyri" mentioned by v. Wilamowitz-Moellendorff 1929, 257, on which the two Oxford editors could count when preparing parts V (1908) – XI (1915) of the *Oxyrhynchus Papyri*. After the war, the collaboration was not resumed.

[70] X. *Mem.* I 6, 1–15 (= Antipho Soph. T 1 Pendrick): Ἄξιον δ' αὐτοῦ (scil. τοῦ Σωκράτους) καὶ ἃ πρὸς Ἀντιφῶντα τὸν σοφιστὴν διελέχθη μὴ παραλιπεῖν. ὁ γὰρ Ἀντιφῶν ποτε βουλόμενος τοὺς συνουσιαστὰς αὐτοῦ παρελέσθαι προσελθὼν τῶι Σωκράτει ἔλεξε τάδε κτλ.

[71] See Bastianini and Decleva Caizzi 1989, 182 (with a misleading reference to Diels 1916) and Pendrick 2002, 316.

gard to the contents of the new *Aletheia* papyrus, Wilamowitz considered the identification of its author with Xenophon's sophist as certain.[72] The picture that Xenophon draws of 'Antiphon the sophist' seems to indicate that this author should be distinguished from the outstanding orator and politician Antiphon who belonged to the Attic demos of Rhamnus,[73] given that the latter was an ultra-conservative representative of the oligarchy and, as Thucydides reports in his very respectful obituary, strictly opposed to any gathering of the people.[74] We do not need to broach the much-disputed problem as to how to distribute the various prose speeches and fragments transmitted under the name 'Antiphon' between Antiphon the sophist and Antiphon the orator (the *tragedian* Antiphon is yet another person).[75] What Wilamowitz observed is enough for our purposes: the attribution of the papyrus text *P. Oxy.* 1364 to Antiphon's *Aletheia* is entirely plausible, as is the identification of this Antiphon with the hedonist sophist described by Xenophon.[76]

---

[72] The identification of the *Aletheia* author with the sophist was assumed by Diels already before the publication of the papyrus, cf. Diels 1912, 289; see also the report in Diels 1916, 931, v. Wilamowitz-Moellendorff 1920, 84 and especially v. Wilamowitz-Moellendorff, 1932, 217, n. 1: "Xenophon führt ihn als den typischen Sophisten ein, der viel Geld macht und den Sokrates von oben herab behandelt. Er hat also zu der Zeit, da Xenophon mit Sokrates verkehrte, in Athen sein Handwerk betrieben. Gehören muß ihm die Ἀλήθεια, die in zwei Bücher geteilt werden mußte."

[73] As suggested by Stenzel 1924, and more recently by Pendrick 2002, 1–26, who prudently rejects the identification of the two figures with each other as revived for example by Decleva Caizzi 1986. Pendrick's judgement is based on a detailed and well-balanced résumé of the entire debate.

[74] Th. 8, 68; text after Alberti 2000, 264–265: ὁ μέντοι ἅπαν τὸ πρᾶγμα (scil. τὴν δήμου κατάλυσιν) ξυνθεὶς ὅτωι τρόπωι κατέστη καὶ ἐκ πλείστου ἐπιμεληθεὶς Ἀ ν τ ι φ ῶ ν ἦν, ἀνὴρ Ἀθηναίων τῶν καθ' ἑαυτὸν ἀρετῆι τε οὐδενὸς δεύτερος καὶ κράτιστος ἐνθυμηθῆναι γενόμενος καὶ ἃ γνοίη εἰπεῖν, καὶ ἐς μὲν δῆμον οὐ παριὼν οὐδ' ἐς ἄλλον ἀγῶνα ἑκούσιος οὐδένα, ἀλλ' ὑπόπτως τῶι πλήθει διὰ δόξαν δεινότητος διακείμενος, τοὺς μέντοι ἀγωνιζομένους καὶ ἐν δικαστηρίωι καὶ ἐν δήμωι πλεῖστα εἷς ἀνήρ, ὅστις ξυμβουλεύσαιτό τι, δυνάμενος ὠφελεῖν. καὶ αὐτός τε, ἐπειδὴ τὰ τῶν τετρακοσίων ἐν ὑστέρωι μεταπεσόντα ὑπὸ τοῦ δήμου ἐκακοῦτο, ἄριστα φαίνεται τῶν μέχρι ἐμοῦ ὑπὲρ αὐτῶν τούτων αἰτιαθείς, ὡς ξυγκατέστησε, θανάτου δίκην ἀπολογησάμενος.

[75] TrGF I Nr. 55 in Snell and Kannicht 1986, 193–196.

[76] Xenophon's portrait of Antiphon corresponds exactly to the degrading image of the sophists known especially from Plato's early dialogues, so Xenophon's reference to Antiphon as a 'sophist' is likely to be pejorative, *pace* Gomperz 1912, 58. Even stronger evidence is provided by the immoralism found in the *Aletheia* papyrus. Thus, the publication of *P. Oxy.* 1364 (+ 3647) has supported the attribution of the text cited by Harpocration as "Antiphon, *On the Truth*" to Xenophon's sophist, and there is no reason to adopt the sceptical thesis of Bilik 1998 that Harpocration's quotation of the work title *Aletheia* and of the author Antiphon are two independent blunders.

Supplementary to the identification of work and author, Wilamowitz sent suggestions concerning the readings and restoration of the text to the Oxford editors in the summer of 1914, shortly before the outbreak of the World War. Due to the war the letter in question was not delivered, but Herman Diels made known its contents in the *apparatus criticus* of a preliminary edition of the papyrus in 1916.[77] In 1984, Maria Serena Funghi was able to complete fr. 2 of *POxy.* 1364 by means of an important piece overlooked by Grenfell and Hunt, namely, *POxy.* 3647.[78] Thus, she could edit fr. 2 in a substantially enlarged form. Furthermore, she realized that the new text of fr. 2 provides a convincing starting point for the argument of *POxy.* 1364 as a whole. Accordingly, she suggested putting her text of fr. 2 before fr. 1.[79] In our presentation of the text we will follow—unless otherwise stated—Bastianini and Decleva Caizzi 1989,[80] especially in putting Funghi's new text (*POxy.* 1364, fr. 2 + *POxy.* 3674) first and in labelling it Fr. A.[81]

Fr. A offers a readable text from its second column onwards. At the outset of the column, Antiphon generalizes into an ethnological constant the disdain towards foreign peoples that Herodotus had observed among the Persians,[82] and traces it back to the dissimilarity of *nomoi* ('customs, laws'), a dissimilarity that increases with the geographical distance. It never lies in the nature of a

---

[77] Diels 1916, 931: "Hr. von Wilamowitz hatte einige Ergänzungen zu dem Texte noch kurz vor dem Ausbruch des Krieges dem englischen Herausgeber mitteilen wollen. Allein jener Brief ward von der Post nicht mehr befördert. So hat er mich ermächtigt, hier seinen Beitrag zu veröffentlichen."
[78] Funghi 1984, 1–5 recognized in *POxy.* LII 3647 some line endings belonging to lines from *POxy.* 1364 fr. 2, col. ii, as well as the first lines of both following columns.
[79] It is true that a further papyrus has also been plausibly assigned to the *Aletheia* of Antiphon (*POxy.* 1797, completing VS 80 B 44 in Diels 1922, XXXVI–XXXVII and VS 87 B 44 in Diels and Kranz 1935, 353–355, cf. F 44 c Pendrick); it stems from the same excavation and was written by a contemporary, though not identical hand. Yet for our purposes, the evidence provided by *POxy.* 1364 in conjunction with *POxy.* 3674 is entirely sufficient.
[80] Bastianini and Decleva Caizzi 1989 (CPF I*, nr. 17/1, 180–213). For text, translation, and interpretation, we have also consulted Pendrick 2002 throughout.
[81] Pendrick 2002, 316–317, however, leaves the question open and returns, merely for the sake of convenience, to the order of the first editors: he counts *POxy.* 1364 fr. 1 as F 44 (a), and *POxy.* 1364 fr. 2 (+ *POxy.* 3647) as F 44 (b). Laks and Most 2016, 50–59 (D [= Doctrine] 38 a–b) follow Pendrick.
[82] Bastianini and Decleva Caizzi 1989, 188 refer to Hdt. 1, 134, 2 (text after Wilson 2015, 82–83): τιμῶσι δὲ (scil. οἱ Πέρσαι) ἐκ πάντων τοὺς ἄγχιστα ἑωυτῶν οἰκέοντας μετά γε ἑωυτούς, δεύτερα δὲ τοὺς δευτέρους, μετὰ δὲ κατὰ λόγον προβαίνοντες τιμῶσι· ἥκιστα δὲ τοὺς ἑωυτῶν ἑκαστάτω οἰκημένους ἐν τιμῇ ἄγονται, νομίζοντες ἑωυτοὺς εἶναι ἀνθρώπων μακρῷ τὰ πάντα ἀρίστους, τοὺς δὲ ἄλλους κατὰ <τὸν αὐτὸν> λόγον τῆς ἀρετῆς ἀντέχεσθαι. For Herodotus' interest in differing *nomoi* among various peoples, see Dihle 1981, 59–61.

human being to be 'barbarian'; rather, this ascription mirrors the cultural difference between the person perceived as 'barbarian' and the one applying the term to him. The question whether certain human beings are seen as 'Greek', i.e. as civilized, or as barbarians will be answered differently by those close to their culture and those who are further away. Hence, the answer does not depend on their natural equipment:[83]

> [the laws of those nearby] we know and respect, whereas the laws of those who live far off we neither know nor respect. Now in this we have become barbarians *in one another's eyes*; for by our nature (*phusis*), at least, we are all naturally adapted (*pephukamen*) in every respect to be either Greeks or barbarians.

By contrast, the necessities of life and the capacity to attain them are given by human nature and equal for all. With respect to these essential needs and capacities, no one draws a distinction between Greeks and barbarians:[84]

> But the *necessary* ones among the natural things are to be observed in all humans, being provided for all by means of the same faculties; and in these things none of us is set apart as 'Greek' or as 'barbarian'.

First and foremost, these 'necessary things' are physical needs and physiological capacities – breathing by means of the mouth and nose, sense-perception by means of hearing and sight, the use of hands as instruments to work and of feet to walk – but they also include emotional reactions such as laughing and crying:[85]

---

83 Bastianini and Decleva Caizzi 1989, 184–185, Fr. A (= *POxy.* 1364, fr. 2 + 3647 = F44 [b] Pendrick), col. II,1–15 (for the first supplement see Funghi 1984, 4): [τοὺς νόμους τοὺς μὲν τῶν ἐγγυτέρ-]|ii,1|ρων ἐπ[ιστάμε]θά τε κ[αὶ σέβομεν] τοὺς δὲ [τῶν τη]λοῦ οἰκ[ούν]των, |5| οὔτε ἐπι[στ]άμεθα οὔτε σέβομεν. ἐν τ[ο]ύτῳ οὖν πρὸς ἀλλήλους βεβαρβαρώμε-|10|θα, ἐπεὶ φύσει γε πάντες πάντα ὁμοίως πεφύκ[α]μεν καὶ βάρβαροι καὶ Ἕλλην[ες] |15| εἶναι. Cf. Pendrick 2002, 180–181 (text and translation) and 356–360 (commentary).
84 Bastianini and Decleva Caizzi 1989, 185, Fr. A (= *POxy.* 1364, fr. 2 + 3647 = F44 [b] Pendrick), col. II,15–27: σκοπεῖν δ[ὲ] παρέχει τὰ τῶν φύσει [ὄντων] ἀναγκαῖ[α ἐν] πᾶσιν ἀν[θρώ-]|20|ποις, π[οριζόμενά] τε κατὰ τ[ὰς αὐτὰς] δυνά[μεις ἅπασι,] καὶ ἐν [αὐτοῖς τού]τοις οὔτε β[άρβα-]|25|ρος ἀφώρι[σται] ἡμῶν ο[ὐδείς,] οὔτε Ἕλλην. Cf. Pendrick 2002, 180–183 (text and translation) and 360–362 (commentary).
85 Bastianini and Decleva Caizzi 1989, 185–186, Fr. A (= *POxy.* 1364, fr. 2 + 3647 = F44 [b] Pendrick), col. II,27 – III,12: ἀναπνέομέν τε γὰρ εἰς τὸν ἀ-|30|έρ[α] ἅπαντες κατὰ τὸ στόμα[α] [κ]αὶ κατ[ὰ] τὰς ῥῖνας· κ[αὶ γελῶμε]ν χ[αίροντες] |III,1| [καὶ] δακρύομε[ν] λυπούμενοι· καὶ τῇ ἀκοῇ τοὺς φθόγ-|5|γους εἰσδεχόμεθα· καὶ τῇ αὐγῇ μετὰ τῆς ὄψεως ὁρῶμεν· καὶ ταῖς χερσὶν ἐρ-|10|γαζόμεθα· καὶ τοῖς ποσὶν βαδ[ίζο]μεν. Cf. Pendrick 2002, 182–183 (text and translation) and 362–365 (commentary).

For we all breathe into the air by our mouth and nostrils, and we laugh when we are happy, and cry when we are sad, and we take in sounds with our sense of hearing, and thanks to the sunlight we see with our sight, and we work with our hands, and we walk with our feet.

At this point the readable text of Fr. A breaks off. In its completed form, the fragment provides authentic sophistic evidence for an argument that Felix Heinimann once regarded as a starting point for the *nomos/phusis* antithesis.[86] The ethnological observation about how foreign peoples see one another leads to the insight that the *customs* and *laws* of distant peoples differ widely from one another (which is why such peoples regard each other as barbarians), whereas *human nature* is the same everywhere, as our basic needs as well as the functions of the human organism clearly show.

We now turn to Fr. B (= *POxy*. 1364 fr. 1). In this fragment, Antiphon tackles the problem of the *benefit* or *harmfulness* of human actions for the acting person. He concludes that the beneficial or harmful consequences of actions are without exception regulated by the human *phusis* whose universality was established in Fr. A. In certain situations, however, these consequences are also subject to the competing influence of the prevailing *nomoi*. The text of Fr. B is readable from line 6 of the first column onwards. Here, the text immediately offers a definition of justice (*dikaiosune*), in which it is simply equated with obedience to the legal norms of one's *polis*: "Justice, then, is not to transgress the legal norms (*nomima*) of whatever *polis* one lives in."[87]

For a proper understanding of Fr. B as a whole, we must remind ourselves of David Furley's insight (already quoted in our introduction) that Antiphon takes his legalistic definition of justice for granted throughout.[88] Behaviour labelled as 'just' may often be harmful, but this is no reason to question the use of the name. In particular, the name 'just' is never used for the other type of human behaviour, i.e. the one that follows human nature and is, according to Antiphon's judgement, often more beneficial. In a nutshell: Antiphon is going to re-*value* 'justice'– not re-*interpret* it by identifying what 'true justice' might be.

On the other hand, Antiphon insists that the citizen of a *polis* should not aim at a single stance towards justice that is valid in every circumstance. Rather, he ought to make his attitude to justice dependent on the given situation. Before

---

[86] Cf. Heinimann 1945, 78–85. See further Dihle 1981.
[87] Bastianini and Decleva Caizzi 1989, 192, Fr. B (= *POxy*. 1364 fr. 1 = F 44 [a] Pendrick), col. I,6–11: δικα[ιοσ]ύνη [δ' οὖ]ν τὰ τῆς πό[λεω]ς νόμιμα [ἐν ᾗ] ἂν πολι-|10|[τεύ]ηταί τις μὴ [παρ]αβαίνειν. Cf. Pendrick 2002, 158–159 (text and translation) and 321–322 (commentary).
[88] According to Furley 1981, 81–82, Antiphon retains the descriptive force of the word 'just' "while questioning or reversing the prescriptive value (e.g. he might say 'perhaps impartiality *is* just, but I'm against it – down with justice!)"

witnesses, that is, in public, he may do well to uphold the laws; but when he is alone with no one to observe his actions, he will more profitably follow the needs of his own *phusis*:[89]

> Now a man would make use of justice in a way most advantageous to himself if, in the presence of witnesses, he were to regard as great the laws (*nomoi*), but in the absence of witnesses, the needs of human nature (*ta tês phuseōs*).

These lines suggest that violating the laws in order to serve the needs of one's nature is *not always* beneficial, but only under certain circumstances, namely in secrecy. As already suspected by Diels 1917 and clearly seen by Taylor 1926, this recommendation comes remarkably close to the Gyges-thesis expounded by Glaucon in Plato, *R.* II – except that in *R.* II there is no reference to 'human nature' as an authority capable of overruling the laws. The argument offered by Antiphon in support of his claim begins as follows:[90]

> For the norms stated by the laws (*ta tōn nomōn*) are imposed, whereas the needs of human nature (*ta tês phuseōs*) are necessary; and the norms stated by the laws are not naturally grown (*phunta*) but agreed upon, whereas the needs of human nature (*ta tês phuseōs*) are not agreed upon but naturally grown (*phunta*).

This is to say that the legal norms are *external* for human beings in that they are imposed on them on the basis of mere agreements between the citizens. The needs of the human nature (*phusis*), by contrast, are *internal* for human beings in that they are naturally grown (*phunta*) and thereby form part of their own being. It is remarkable that the naturalness of the needs of nature (*phusis*) is underlined by the use of the cognate participle *phunta* ('naturally grown'): a similar stylistic device is put to polemical use by Plato in the description of the three-bodied animal in *R.* IX, where, as we have seen, forms cognate with *phusis* like *phuein*, *phuesthai*, and *pephukenai* bring home to the imaginary interlocutor the 'naturalness' of the pernicious multi-headed beast.

---

[89] Bastianini and Decleva Caizzi 1989, 192–193, Fr. B (= *POxy.* 1364 fr. 1 = F 44 [a] Pendrick), col. I,12–23: χρῷτ' ἂν οὖν ἄνθρωπος μάλιστα ἑαυτῷ |15| ξυμφ[ε]ρόντως δικαιο[σ]ύνῃ, εἰ μετὰ μὲν μαρτύρων τ[ο]ὺς νόμους μεγά[λο]υς |20| ἄγοι, μονούμενος δὲ μαρτύρων τὰ τῆς φύσεως. Cf. Pendrick 2002, 158–161 (text and translation) and 322–324 (commentary).
[90] Bastianini and Decleva Caizzi 1989, 193, Fr. B (= *POxy.* 1364 fr. 1 = F 44 [a] Pendrick), col. I,23 – col. II.1: τὰ μὲν γὰρ τῶν νόμων |25| [ἐπίθ]ετα, τὰ δὲ [τῆς] φύσεως ἀ[ναγ]καῖα· καὶ τὰ [μὲν] τῶν νό[μω]ν ὁμολογη-|30|[θέντ]α οὐ φύν[τα ἐστί]ν, τὰ δὲ [τῆς φύσ]εως φύν[τα οὐχ] ὁμολογη-|II,1|θ[έ]ντα. Cf. Pendrick 2002, 160–161 (text and translation) and 322–325 (commentary).

The external character of the legal norms entails that only those violations of them will be prosecuted that are observed by our fellow citizens:[91]

> When a man transgresses the *legal norms* (*nomima*) he is free from shame and punishment if he escapes the notice of those who agreed on them; but if he does not, he is not.

In contrast, whenever one violates the needs of one's nature beyond endurance, one damages oneself (*blaptetai*) regardless of whether the violation is noticed by third parties or not. The natural needs of a human being are inseparably connected to him, and thus accompany him even into total secrecy. In other words: there is an immediate and objective link (*aletheia* 'truth') between the violation of one's own natural needs and the harm (*kakon*) resulting from such self-violation, a link independent of the opinions of one's fellow citizens:[92]

> If, on the other hand, he violates, beyond endurance, any of the needs grown together with him by nature (*phusei xumphuta*), the harm is no less if in doing so he escapes the notice of all men, and it is no greater if all see him. For in that case he is harmed not on the basis of mere opinion (*doxa*) but on the basis of the truth (*aletheia*).

Here the recommendation given in Fr. B, I,12–23 – to let one's attitude towards justice depend on whether one is observed by others or not – is justified by pointing out that the legal norms are based just on public opinion (*doxa*), whereas the inborn needs of human nature are based on truth (*aletheia*). Now this distinction would be of no practical significance if legal norms were in perfect agreement with natural human needs. But in fact, this is far from being the case. Rather, laws are frequently opposed to the human *phusis*:[93]

---

[91] Bastianini and Decleva Caizzi 1989, 193, Fr. B (= *POxy.* 1364 fr. 1 = F 44 [a] Pendrick), col. II, 3–10: τὰ οὖν νόμιμα παραβαίνων |5| εἰ ἂν λάθη τοὺς ὁμολογήσαντας καὶ αἰσχύνης καὶ ζημίας ἀπήλλακται, μὴ |10| λαθὼν δ' οὔ. Cf. Pendrick 2002, 160–163 (text and translation) and 325–326 (commentary).

[92] Bastianini and Decleva Caizzi 1989, 193–194, Fr. B (= *POxy.* 1364 fr. 1 = F 44 [a] Pendrick), col. II, 10–23: τῶν δὲ τῇ φύσει ξυμφύτων ἐάν τι παρὰ τὸ δυνατὸν βιάζηται, ἐάν |15| τε πάντας ἀνθρώπους λάθῃ, οὐδὲν ἔλαττον τὸ κακόν, ἐάν τε πάντες ἴδωσιν, |20| οὐδὲν μεῖζον· οὐ γὰρ διὰ δόξαν βλάπτεται, ἀλλὰ δι' ἀλήθειαν. Cf. Pendrick 2002, 162–163 (text and translation) and 326–327 (commentary).

[93] Bastianini and Decleva Caizzi 1989, 194, Fr. B (= *POxy.* 1364 fr. 1 = F 44 [a] Pendrick), col. II,23 – col. III,18: ἔστι δὲ τῶνδε ἕνε-|25|κα τούτων ἡ σκέψις, ὅτι τὰ πολλὰ τῶν κατὰ νόμον δικαίων πολεμίως τῇ |30| φύσ[ει] κεῖται· νενο[μο]θ[έ]τηται γὰρ [ἐ]πί τε τοῖς ὀφ[θ]αλμοῖς, ἃ δεῖ |III,1| αὐτο[ὺ]ς ὁρᾶν καὶ ἃ οὐ [δε]ῖ· καὶ ἐπὶ τοῖς ὠσίν, ἃ δεῖ αὐτὰ ἀκούειν καὶ |5| ἃ οὐ δεῖ· καὶ ἐπὶ τῇ γλώττῃ, ἅ τ[ε] δεῖ αὐτὴν λέγειν καὶ ἃ οὐ δεῖ· καὶ ἐπὶ ταῖς χερσίν, |10| ἅ τε δεῖ αὐτὰς δρᾶν καὶ ἃ οὐ δεῖ· καὶ ἐπὶ τοῖς ποσίν, ἐφ' ἅ τε δεῖ αὐτοὺς ἰέναι καὶ ἐφ' ἃ οὐ |15| δεῖ· καὶ ἐπὶ

We conduct the examination of these things for the following reasons (*tônde heneka*):[94] because the greater part of the things that are defined as just by the law (*nomon*) is hostile to nature (*phusis*). For laws have been established (*nenomothetetai*) over the eyes, as to what they must and must not see; and over the ears, as to what they must and must not hear; and over the tongue, as to what it must and must not say; and over the hands, as to what they must and must not do; and over the feet, as to what they must and must not go after; and over the mind, as to what it must and must not desire.

The just behaviour demanded by the laws frequently leads to a disdain for natural human needs which in turn will harm the affected person to some degree, as just ascertained in Fr. B, II, 10–23. It is important to note, however, that Antiphon regularly (though not without exception) designates those natural needs by means of composite expressions, such as 'the *necessary* ones among the natural things',[95] or 'the things belonging to human nature',[96] or 'the things grown together with man by nature'.[97] The point might be that these natural needs are not simply *coextensive* with 'human nature' (*phusis*) itself, since the latter comprises, of course, not only the natural needs, but also the natural if undesirable consequences of violating them. This impression seems to be confirmed by the following remark, according to which unjust (i.e. legally forbidden) actions are as close to human nature as just (i.e. legally permitted) actions:[98] "Now, the things from which the laws try to dissuade people are no more friendly or akin to human nature (*phusis*) than the things to which they encourage them."

On the other hand, it is not immediately clear how this remark can be reconciled with the preceding claim, according to which "the greater part of the things that are defined as just by the law (*nomon*) is hostile to nature (*phusis*)."[99]

τῷ νῷ, ὧν τε δεῖ αὐτὸν ἐπιθυμεῖν καὶ ὧν μή. Cf. Pendrick 2002, 162–165 (text and translation) and 327–331 (commentary).

94 In II,24, the second hand has corrected τῶνδε to πάντων (by adding παν- and deleting -δε); cf. Bastianini and Decleva Caizzi 1989, 206: "La correzione al r. 24 è da attribuire alla stessa mano che ha effettuato gli altri interventi sul testo, verosimilmente il *diorthotes*; non per questo la lezione emendata è da ritenere migliore di quella originaria (cf. POxy 1364 B I r. 19) che anzi, in quanto *difficilior*, sembra preferibile."
95 τὰ τῶν φύσει ὄντων ἀναγκαῖα Fr. A (= POxy. 1364 fr. 2 + POxy. 3647) col. II, lines 16–18.
96 τὰ τῆς φύσεως Fr. B (= POxy. 1364, fr. 1), col. I,22–23, 25–26 and 31–32.
97 τὰ τῇ φύσει ξύμφυτα Fr. B (= POxy. 1364, fr. 1), col. II,10–12.
98 Bastianini and Decleva Caizzi 1989, 194, Fr. B (= POxy. 1364 fr. 1 = F 44 [a] Pendrick), col. III,18–25: [ἔστι]ν οὖν οὐδὲν τ[ῇ] φύσει |20| φιλιώτ[ερ]α οὐδ' οἰκειότε[ρα] ἀφ' ὧν οἱ νόμο[ι ἀ]ποτρέπουσι τ[οὺς] ἀν[θ]ρώπ[ους] ἢ ἐφ' ἃ [ἐπιτρέ]-|25|πουσ[ιν]. Cf. Pendrick 2002, 164–165 (text and translation) and 331–333 (commentary).
99 Bastianini and Decleva Caizzi 1989, 194, Fr. B (= POxy. 1364 fr. 1 = F 44 [a] Pendrick), col. II,25–30: ... ὅτι τὰ πολλὰ τῶν κατὰ νόμον δικαίων πολεμίως τῇ |30| φύσ[ει] κεῖται.

Yet this difficulty, which has led to various suggestions for changing or reinterpreting the text,[100] is not insurmountable. In a sense, the legal norms are often hostile to human nature, since they aim at supressing natural needs which are one aspect of human nature; but in another sense, *fulfilling* these needs does not come closer to human nature than *suppressing* them, since human nature will react to fulfilment as inevitably as to suppression. In other words, the nature of the human species as such can, of course, not be harmed by anyone's obedience to hostile laws any more than by his resistance to such laws, even though the individual human being may easily be destroyed by obeying hostile laws beyond endurance. On this reading of the text there is a satisfactory transition to the next remark, namely that life *as well as* death belong to human *phusis*:[101] "For[102] both living and dying belong to nature; and living comes to men[103] from what is advantageous (*xumpheron*), dying from what is not."

Human nature, then, is the authority that regulates both what is beneficial (*xumpheron*) and what is non-beneficial to the individual's survival. In this sense, a long life attained through an adequate supply of beneficial things is no more natural than an early death, caused by an excess of non-beneficial things.

Finally, it is of course possible that beneficial things are conceded also by the laws; but these concessions are subject to the condition of obedience to other, potentially harmful laws, so that the individual is fettered even by apparently friendly laws, whereas obeying one's nature is an act of freedom:[104] "As to the advantages, those established by the laws are chains on human nature (*phusis*), whereas those established by human nature (*phusis*) are free." Both the laws and human nature offer us their *xumpheronta* when we obey them. But in the

---

100 III,18 [ἐστι]ν Editio princeps : [οὐ μὲ]ν Diels : [ἧττο]ν Bastianini and Decleva Caizzi ‖ III,21–25 ordinem verborum ἀφ' ὧν ἀποτρέπουσι et ἐφ' ἃ προτρέπουσι inversum esse suspicatus est Gernet 1923, 177. See further Pendrick 2002, 331–332.

101 Bastianini and Decleva Caizzi 1989, 194–195, Fr. B (= *POxy*. 1364 fr. 1 = F 44 [a] Pendrick), col. III,25 – col. IV,1: τ[ὸ γὰρ] ζῆν [ἔ]στι τῆς φύσεως κ[αὶ τ]ὸ ἀποθαν[εῖ]ν, καὶ τὸ μὲν [ζ]ῆν αὐτ[οῖς |30| ἐστι[ν ἀ]πὸ τῶν ξυμ[φερό]ντω[ν, τὸ δὲ ἀ[ποθανεῖν] ἀπὸ τ[ῶν μὴ ξυμ-]|IV,1|φερόντω[ν]. Cf. Pendrick 2002, 164–167 (text and translation) and 333–334 (commentary).

102 III,25 τ[ὸ γὰρ] Grenfell / Hunt, Bastianini and Decleva Caizzi : τ[ὸ δ' αὖ] Diels : τ[ὸ δὲ] Pendrick.

103 29 αὐτ[οῖς] edd. : αὐτ[ῇ] Pendrick.

104 Bastianini and Decleva Caizzi 1989, 195, Fr. B (= *POxy*. 1364 fr. 1 = F 44 [a] Pendrick), col. IV, 1–8: τὰ] δὲ ξυμφέρ[οντα,] τὰ μὲν ὑπ[ὸ τῶν] νόμων κε[ί]-|5|μενα δεσμ[οὶ] τῆς φύσεώς ἐ[στι,] τὰ δ' ὑπὸ τῆς φύσεως ἐλεύθερα. Cf. Pendrick 2002, 166–167 (text and translation) and 335–336 (commentary).

case of the laws obedience means the renunciation of one's impulses, whereas the commands of nature coincide, or so Antiphon believes, with what the human being desires of his own accord.

4 Conclusion

Taylor 1926 and Pendrick 2002 identified the Gyges-thesis as expounded in *R.* II with the philosophical position of Antiphon's *Aletheia* and they supported this identification by pointing out, correctly, that there is a sufficiently specific assumption common to both – the assumption that it is advantageous to commit unjust deeds, i.e. to violate the laws, *provided that it can be done in complete secrecy.*[105] We have provided strong additional evidence for this identification by comparing Socrates' *refutation* of the Gyges-thesis in *R.* IX with the Antiphon papyrus. Socrates' refutation proceeds by showing that the *tripartite nature* of the human soul, as first described in *R.* IV, is self-destructive unless supressed by legal norms (*nomima*). He attacks the Gyges-thesis, as upheld by his anonymous interlocutor, for justifying the secret violation of legal norms by an appeal to *human nature* as a self-contained source of ethical orientation. Now it is precisely this appeal to *human nature* that, while being absent from the presentation of the Gyges-thesis in *R.* II, is absolutely central to the argument of Antiphon, as our analysis of Fr. A and Fr. B (I.6–IV.8) of the Antiphon papyrus has shown.

Are there alternative candidates for the role of the sophist hiding behind the anonymous interlocutor of *R.* IX? Only Hippias, Callicles, and Thrasymachus could come into consideration, even though all three appear under their own names in Plato's dialogues. But upon closer examination, all three can be ruled out. The Hippias of the Platonic *Protagoras* does oppose between *nomos* and *phusis* in a rather humorous passage already cited above (337c–338b) and takes the side of *phusis*. However, he simply wants to settle the dispute between Socrates and Protagoras peacefully.[106] Drastic ethical consequences, like a demand to act unjustly, are out of the question.[107] Although the Callicles of Plato's *Gorgias* argues for the priority of *phusis* over *nomos*, he reinterprets the concept of justice as a "law of the stronger."[108] Introducing, quite unlike Antiphon, a new *descriptive* use of 'justice', he can safely be ruled out as a possible representative

---

105 See the quotations from Taylor 1926 and Pendrick 2002 at notes 15 and 20, above.
106 See Kerferd and Flashar 1998, 67–68.
107 This is also true of the long dialogue between Socrates and Hippias on justice, as reported by Xenophon, *Memorabilia* IV, 4, 5–25.
108 *Gorgias*, 482c–484c; see Dodds 1959, 268 (regarding 483e3).

of the Gyges-thesis which insists on the profitability of secret 'injustice' and thereby presupposes Antiphon's legalistic definition of 'justice'. Finally, the Thrasymachus we meet in Book I of Plato's *Republic* cannot be identified with the imaginary interlocutor from *R*. IX either,[109] since he does not refer to *phusis* at all,[110] neither when redefining justice as the "benefit of the stronger" in *R*. I, 338a–339d, nor when extolling the benefits of large-scale injustice in *R*. I, 343a–344c. Moreover, in all three of these sophists we miss the theme of the *secrecy* of injustice, which is of particular importance for the Gyges-thesis and for Antiphon. We conclude that none of Plato's other sophists can compete with Antiphon to fill the role of the nameless sophist who supports the Gyges-thesis with the antithesis between *nomos* and *phusis* in *R*. IX.

Plato's Socrates is not against invoking human nature (*phusis*). Rather, he criticizes Antiphon's totally flawed concept of *phusis*, which has led him to an equally wrongheaded judgement as to the noxious effect of legal norms (*nomima*). In Antiphon's account, the only relevant conflict is between natural disposition and human needs, on the one hand, and legal norms (*nomima*) that restrict and even oppose nature, on the other. He perceives antagonism only between the human *phusis* and the *nomima* of the *polis*, while being blind to the possibility that antagonism could occur *within* the human *phusis*. His theory overlooks basic facts about human nature: the relevant object of investigation is not 'the human being', but rather the human soul; this soul is tripartite by nature[111]; its parts stand in an antagonistic relation to each other; and the strongest part by nature, the *epithumetikon*, destroys the entire soul unless suppressed in accordance with the laws. It is only due to his insufficient understanding of human nature that Antiphon deemed secret injustice to be profitable – in fact it causes great damage to the agent, as does indeed any injustice.

The disagreement between Plato's Socrates and Antiphon does not end there. It is true that, for the sake of an 'immanent critique' of Antiphon, Socrates accepts the restriction of human nature to the person's existence as a corporeal

---

109 An anonymous return of Thrasymachus in Book IX, who was already refuted in Book I, would also be a failure with regard to the literary composition of *R*.

110 Rightly in Furley 1981, 81: "[...] Antiphon in DK 87 B 44 (consisting of the famous papyrus fragments from Oxyrhynchus) criticizes and rejects justice on the ground that to be just is to damage or neglect one's own natural interest. Antiphon's position is thus similar to that of Thrasymachus in Plato, *Republic* I, although Thrasymachus differs in making no explicit appeal to nature."

111 The fact that Antiphon was deceived, as it were, by the human shape of the 'outer human' represents the ignorant and, from a Freudian point of view, 'pre-analytical' character of his glorification of human nature.

being. But the ensuing diagnosis of the soul as riven by internal antagonism, and in need of the state's control, is not Socrates' last word on the subject. According to his own view, we are not supposed to think of ourselves only or mainly as corporeal beings, as Antiphon did, but rather to grasp the nature of our immortal souls. This difference with respect to the concept of nature, which is fundamental for both thinkers, finds expression in the juxtaposition of deficient and normative senses of *phusis* in *R.* IX–X. According to Plato's Socrates, as soon as human nature is identified with the immortal soul, it no longer appears as a source of problems that need to be brought under control through external regulation; rather, it becomes the true source of the norms guiding human behaviour. In this sense, one may describe the opposition between Antiphon's *Aletheia* and Plato's *Republic* as one between a naturalistic defence of the Gyges-thesis and a naturalistic rejection of that same thesis.

One may still ask, of course, why Plato should have introduced Antiphon of Athens *anonymously*, whereas other sophists appear by name in his early and middle dialogues. We venture to suggest a very simple answer to this question: a characteristic feature common to the Gyges-thesis and to Antiphon's account of the tension between *nomima* and *phusis* lies, as we have seen, in the *secrecy* of beneficial injustice. So it makes perfect sense that the upholder of this thesis wears a mask.

Primary literature

Antiphon the Sophist. 1915. "1364. Antiphon Sophistes, Περὶ Ἀληθείας ἰ." In *The Oxyrhynchus Papyri*. Part XI, edited by Bernard P. Grenfell and Arthur S. Hunt. London: Egypt Exploration Fund.

Antiphon the Sophist. 1922. "1797. Antiphon Sophistes, Περὶ Ἀληθείας ἰ?" In *The Oxyrhynchus Papyri*. Part XV, edited by Bernard P. Grenfell and Arthur S. Hunt. London: Egypt Exploration Fund.

Antiphon the Sophist. 1923. *Antiphon: Discours, suivis des Fragments d'Antiphon le sophiste*, texte établi et traduit par Louis Gernet. Paris: Les belles lettres.

Antiphon the Sophist. 1984. "3564. Antiphon, Περὶ ἀληθείας (addendum to 1364)." Edited by Maria S. Funghi. In *The Oxyrhynchus Papyri*. Part LII, edited with translation and notes by Helen M. Cockle, 1–5. London: Egypt Exploration Fund.

Antiphon the Sophist. 1989. Antipho 1–2: De veritate. Edited by Guido Bastianini and Fernanda Decleva Caizzi. In *Corpus dei papiri filosofici greci e latini* (CPF). *Testi e lessico nei papiri di cultura greca e latina*, 176–222. Firenze: L. S. Olschki.

Antiphon the Sophist. 2002. *Antiphon the Sophist: The Fragments, Edited with Introduction, Translation, and Commentary* by Gerard J. Pendrick. Cambridge: University Press.

Harpocration. 1853. *Harpocrationis lexicon in decem oratores Atticos* ex recensione Guilelmi Dindorfii. Tomus I, Oxford: E typographeo academico.

Herodotus. 2015. *Herodoti Historiae.* Recognovit brevique adnotatione critica instruxit, by Nigel G. Wilson. Oxford: University Press.

Plato. 1959. *Plato: Gorgias.* A Revised Text with Introduction and Commentary by Eric R. Dodds. Oxford: Oxford Clarendon Press.

Plato. 2003. *Platonis Rempublicam* recognovit brevique adnotatione critica instruxit, by Simon R. Slings. Oxford: Oxford University Press.

Plato. 2011. *Platon: Nomoi (Gesetze) Buch VIII–XII.* Übersetzung und Kommentar, by Klaus Schöpsdau. Göttingen: Vandenhoek & Ruprecht.

Presocratics. 1912. *Die Fragmente der Vorsokratiker.* Griechisch und Deutsch. Bd. 2, by Hermann Diels. Berlin: Weidmannsche Buchhandlung.[3]

Presocratics. 1922. *Die Fragmente der Vorsokratiker.* Griechisch und Deutsch. Bd. 2, by Hermann Diels. Berlin: Weidmannsche Buchhandlung.[4]

Presocratics. 1935. *Die Fragmente der Vorsokratiker.* Griechisch und Deutsch. Bd. 2, by Hermann Diels and Walther Kranz. Berlin: Weidmannsche Buchhandlung.[5]

Thucydides. 2000. *Thucydidis Historiae.* Volumen III: Libri VI–VIII, by Ioannes Baptista Alberti. Rom: Typis Officinae Polygraphicae.

Tragic poets. 1986. *Tragicorum Graecorum Fragmenta*, Vol. 1, by Bruno Snell and Richard Kannicht. Göttingen: Vandenhoeck & Ruprecht.

Secondary literature

Annas, Julia. 1981. *An Introduction to Plato's Republic.* Oxford: Oxford University Press.

Bilik, Ronald B. 1998. "Stammen POxy. XI 1364 + LII 3647 und XV 1797 aus der Ἀλήθεια des Antiphon?" *Tyche. Beiträge zur Papyrologie und Epigraphik* 13:29–49.

Classen, Carl J. 1976. *Sophistik.* (= Wege der Forschung Bd. CLXXXVII). Darmstadt: Wissenschaftliche Buchgesellschaft.

Decleva Caizzi, Fernanda. 1986. "'Hysteron proteron': la nature et la loi selon Antiphon et Platon." *Revue de Métaphysique et de Morale*, 91/3:291–310.

Deitz, Luc. 1989. "Physis/Nomos, Physis/Thesis." In *Historisches Wörterbuch der Philosophie*, edited by Joachim Ritter, Karlfried Gründer, and Gottfried Gabriel, Band 7, P–Q, 967–971. Basel: Schwabe Verlag.

Diels Hermann. 1916. "Ein neues Fragment aus Antiphons Buch Über die Wahrheit (Oxyrh.-Pap. XI n. 1364)." In *Sitzungsberichte der Königlich Preussischen Akademie der Wissenschaften*, 931–936. Berlin: Georg Reimer.

Diels Hermann. 1917. "Ein antikes System des Naturrechts." In *Internationale Monatsschrift für Wissenschaft, Kunst und Technik,* Band XI:81–102.

Dihle, Albrecht. 1981. "Die Verschiedenheit der Sitten als Argument ethischer Theorie." In *The Sophists and their Legacy. Proceedings of the Fourth International Colloquium on Ancient Philosophy*, edited by George B. Kerferd,54–63. Wiesbaden: F. Steiner.

Furley, David J. 1981. "Antiphon's Case against Justice." In *The Sophists and their Legacy. Proceedings of the Fourth International Colloquium on Ancient Philosophy*, edited by George B. Kerferd 81–91. Wiesbaden: F. Steiner.

Gomperz, Heinrich. *Sophistik und Rhetorik. Das Bildungsideal des εὖ λέγειν in seinem Verhältnis zur Philosophie des V. Jahrhunderts.* Leipzig / Berlin: B. G. Teubner, 1912.

Heinimann, Felix. 1945. *Nomos und Physis. Herkunft und Bedeutung einer Antithese im griechischen Denken des 5. Jahrhunderts*, (= Schweizerische Beiträge zur Altertumswissenschaft 1). Basel: F. Reinhardt.
Keaney, John J. 1991. *Harpocration. Lexeis of the Ten Orators*, Amsterdam: Hakkert.
Kerferd, George. B. 1981. *The Sophists and their Legacy. Proceedings of the Fourth International Colloquium on Ancient Philosophy*, (= Hermes Einzelschriften 44). Wiesbaden: F. Steiner.
Kerferd, George B. and Flashar, Hellmut. 1998. "Erstes Kapitel: Die Sophistik." In *Grundriss der Geschichte der Philosophie. Begründet von Friedrich Ueberweg*, völlig neubearbeitete Ausgabe, Band 2/1: *Sophistik. Sokrates. Sokratik. Mathematik. Medizin*, edited by Hellmut Flashar, 3–137. Basel: Schwabe.
Kühner, Raphael and Gerth, Bernhard. 1898. *Ausführliche Grammatik der Griechischen Sprache von Dr. Raphael Kühner*. Zweiter Teil: Satzlehre. Dritte Auflage in zwei Bänden in neuer Bearbeitung besorgt von Dr. Bernhard Gerth. Erster Band, Hannover and Leipzig: Hahnsche Buchhandlung.
Laks, André and Most, Glenn W. 2016. *Early Greek Philosophy*. Volume IX: *Sophists* Part 2. Cambridge (MA) and London: Harvard University Press.
Mannsperger, Dietrich. 1969. *Physis bei Platon*. Berlin: De Gruyter.
Müller, Carl W. 2006. *Legende – Novelle – Roman: Dreizehn Kapitel zur erzählenden Prosaliteratur der Antike*. Göttingen: Vandenhoek & Ruprecht.
Nill, Michael. 1985. *Morality and Self-Interest in Protagoras Antiphon and Democritus*. Leiden: Brill.
Patzer, Harald. 1993. *Physis. Grundlegung zu einer Geschichte des Wortes*. Stuttgart: F. Steiner.
Reinhardt, Karl. 1960. *Vermächtnis der Antike. Gesammelte Essays zur Philosophie und Geschichtsschreibung*. Göttingen: Vandenhoek & Ruprecht.
Segvic, Heda. 2000. "No One Errs Willingly: The Meaning of Socratic Intellectualism." *Oxford Studies in Ancient Philosophy* XIX:1–45.
Stenzel, Julius. 1924. "15) Antiphon." In *Paulys Realencyclopädie der classischen Altertumswissenschaft*, Neue Bearbeitung, Begonnen von Georg Wissowa, Supplementband IV: Abacus bis Ledon, Stuttgart, 33–43.
Stevenson, Robert L. 1886. *Strange Case of Dr Jekyll and Mr Hyde*. London: Longmans, Green, and Co.
Taylor, Alfred E. *Plato: The Man and His Work*, Second Edition, London: Methuen & Co. Ltd., First Published October 28th 1926, here quoted after the Second Edition 1927.
Vlastos, Gregory. 1995. *Studies in Greek Philosophy*. Volume II: *Socrates, Plato, and their Tradition*, edited by Daniel W. Graham. Princeton: University Press.
Wilamowitz-Moellendorff, Ulrich von. 1920. *Platon*. Erster Band: *Leben und Werke*. Berlin: Weidmannsche Buchhandlung.[2]
Wilamowitz-Moellendorff, Ulrich von. 1929. *Erinnerungen 1848–1914*, zweite ergänzte Auflage. Leipzig: K.F. Kochler.
Wilamowitz-Moellendorff, Ulrich von. 1932. *Der Glaube der Hellenen*. II. Band, Berlin: Weidmannsche Buchhandlung.

Dominic Scott
Natural Born Philosophers

Abstract: In Republic VI, Plato claims that philosophers have as part of their nature a string of qualities including truthfulness, temperance, courage, justice, and mental agility. But is he talking about the qualities of a fully formed philosopher, or about those required earlier on in life if one is to become such a philosopher? This paper argues for a version of the latter view: when he talks about the natural qualities of a philosopher, he is thinking of an unusually talented adolescent, characterized by an intense love of truth and a string of associated moral qualities, which nonetheless fall short of the perfect virtues found in the mature philosopher. The paper also explains how these different qualities are related to one another, and in what sense Plato considers them to be natural.

1 Introduction

In the central books of the *Republic*, Socrates discusses three 'waves of paradox' – three proposals about the guardians of the ideal state that he thinks will prove highly controversial. The one that will provide the focus of this paper is the third, that the rulers of the state should be philosophers. From V 473c9 until VI 502a3, he mounts an elaborate defence of the proposal, first in conversation with Glaucon (473e5–480a13), then with Adeimantus (487b–502a3). Nowadays the best-known part of this defence is probably the very first, the argument conducted with Glaucon, especially the discussion concerning the lovers of sights and sounds (476e4–480a13). This attempts to show that only philosophers have knowledge, knowledge being a necessary qualification for ruling in the ideal state. But there is another strand in Socrates' defence, which comes at the beginning of Book VI as the second part of the conversation with Glaucon (484a1–487a5). Socrates wishes to show that, as well as having the requisite knowledge, philosophers have, as part of their nature, the same qualities we would expect in a political leader. This might sound surprising: his contemporaries (like our own) might assume that the natures of philosophers and leaders are quite different – a point easy enough to convey through caricature and cliché: for us, phrases like "head in the clouds" or "living in an ivory tower" come to mind. Plato was acutely aware of such attitudes, and so at the beginning of Book VI he mounts an argument (less famous than the one that concludes Book V) to show that the natures of the philosopher and the ruler converge.[1]

Unfortunately, the details of the passage are difficult to determine. In outline, Socrates argues that it is in the nature of a philosopher to possess a whole string of qualities, not just the love of truth, but other faculties of mind (quickness at learning, having a good memory) and moral qualities (temperance, liberality, courage and justice). The point of the argument is that these same qualities are needed in a political leader. But there is an ambiguity here. Socrates could be saying that, once someone has become a fully-fledged philosopher, there are certain qualities they will have, qualities that will have become natural to them as philosophers, which are also what we expect in the ideal ruler.[2] Alternatively, he may be saying that in order to become a philosopher one needs, as part of one's nature, certain qualities that are also those required in order to become the best kind of ruler.[3] (Note that on this view, the qualities in question – temperance, courage, justice and the like – are not to be identified with perfect moral qualities; they are approximations to them, immature versions. I shall discuss this in more detail below).

In the next section we shall take a close look at the passage in question (484a1–487a5) and, as we do so, we shall indeed find strong *prima facie* evidence for both views just sketched. However, it is important to note that this passage is not Socrates' last word on the natural qualities of philosophers. At the end of it, Adeimantus interrupts with a famous objection (487d1–5): despite the ingenuity of the preceding argument, he says, most people will balk at the claim that philosophers have all the qualities just listed. On the contrary, people generally think of philosophers as either corrupt, useless or simply bizarre. In reply, Socrates mounts a further defence of his argument, starting at 488a7. This passage offers valuable clues as to how to understand 484a1–487a5, in particular how to resolve the issue I have raised. Later on in this paper, therefore, I

---

[1] It is interesting to note that he had already encountered a parallel problem in his defence of the first wave of paradox (V 452e3–457b5). Critics of his proposal for women rulers claim that it is just not in the nature of women to rule (cf. 452a4–453e5). So it could be said that the crux of the argument here is also about nature.

[2] Those who opt for this view include Kraut 1973, 214–5; Burnyeat 1999a, 283 n. 50, and 1999b, 308; Dahl 1999, 211, 215 and 219.

[3] For this view see Hatzistavrou 2006, 106–9; Lane 2007, 53. Hatzistavrou 2006, 107–8 makes a helpful distinction between two senses of nature in the *Republic*, one corresponding to his reading of the current passage, which he calls "natural abilities and aptitudes", and another corresponding to the "basic traits of a developed personality." (He cites *Resp.* III 395d1–3 for an example of this use of nature).

shall look at the second passage, specifically 491b7–495b7, using it to provide a commentary on aspects of the earlier passage.

2 Analysis of 484a1–487a5

The introduction to this passage comes at the very start of Book VI. At 484a1–485a8, Socrates begins by summarizing the distinction between philosophers and non-philosophers from the end of the previous book (V 476a1–480a13). He then states that rulers need knowledge of being (484b7–d4), but he adds that they also need experience and complete virtue (484d5–485a3). So his task is to examine the nature of the philosopher to see if it allows for these features to be combined:

> Then, as we were saying at the beginning of this discussion,[4] the first thing to understand is their nature;[5] and I think that if we sufficiently agree on this we shall also agree that the combination of qualities that we seek belongs to the same persons, and that we need no others for guardians of states than these. (485a4–8)

The ensuing argument can be analysed into six sections and a conclusion:

> [1] 485a10–b9: Socrates argues that someone with a philosophical nature loves learning about being rather than becoming.
>
> [2] 485b10–d4: next, he attributes a hatred of falsity and love of truth to the philosophical nature.
>
> [3] 485d6–e6: he now introduces the general principle that, the stronger one's desires for one thing, the weaker they are for others. Then he applies the principle to the love of learning, which produces temperance, along with an indifference to bodily pleasures and money.
>
> [4] 486a1–b13: Socrates introduces several more character traits, including magnificence (*megaloprepeia*), courage and justice.
>
> [5] 486c1–d3: he now turns to mental qualities: being quick at learning and having a good memory.

---

4 Cf. V 474b7–c2: once the philosophers are clearly defined, "it will be possible to defend ourselves by showing that to them by their very nature belong the study of philosophy and political leadership." Translations of the *Republic* are from Shorey 1937 with occasional modifications.
5 This is one place where I have modified Shorey. He over-translates τὴν φύσιν αὐτῶν in 485a4–5 as "the nature they have from birth." If this were the literal sense of the Greek, it would of course have serious consequences for our question.

[6] 486d4–12: here he focuses on qualities such as gracefulness, measure and proportion.

[7] 486e1–487a5: by way of a conclusion, he summarizes most of the qualities featured in the passage: philosophers are required to be "by nature of sound memory, good at learning, magnificent, gracious, and with an affinity to truth, justice, courage and temperance".

Let us now go through the text in detail, in order to highlight the problem at issue. To begin with, I shall work with a relatively crude distinction, between the two interpretations sketched above. According to the first, Socrates is talking about the qualities of a mature philosopher, someone who has developed as a philosopher to the fullest extent (which in the ideal state of the *Republic* only happens around the age of fifty). I abbreviate this to 'M'. Alternatively, he may be only talking about someone with the *potential* to reach this level of maturity. I shall call this interpretation 'P'. As we go on, we shall see that this interpretation can be subdivided into more specific versions. But for the purposes of setting up the problem, we can start with the simple binary divide between M and P. In the translations that follow, I have used italics to highlight phrases particularly relevant to the choice between M and P.

[1] 485a10–b7. Someone with a philosophical nature loves knowledge of eternal being:

> "We must accept as agreed this trait of the philosophical nature, that it is ever enamored of the kind of knowledge which reveals to them something of that essence which is eternal, and is not wandering between the two poles of generation and decay." "Let us take that as agreed." "And, further," said I, "that their desire is for the whole of it and that they do not willingly renounce a small or a great, a more precious or a less honored, part of it."

Prima facie, this suggests M: it sounds like the mark of a mature philosopher to have distinguished between being and becoming and to gravitate towards one rather than the other.

[2] 485b10–d4. Hatred of falsity and love of truth:

> "Consider, then, next whether the people *who are going to become such as we have described* (οἳ ἂν μέλλωσιν ἔσεσθαι οἵους ἐλέγομεν) must have this further quality in their nature." "What quality?" "The spirit of truthfulness, reluctance to admit falsehood in any form, the hatred of it and the love of truth." "It is likely," he said. "It is not only likely, my friend, but there is every necessity that he who is by nature enamored of anything should cherish all that is akin and pertaining to the object of his love." "Right," he said. "Could you find anything more akin to wisdom than truth?" "Impossible," he said. "Then can the same nature be a lover of wisdom and of falsehood?" "By no means." "The true lover of learning *then* (ἄρα) must *from youth onwards* (εὐθὺς ἐκ νέου), as far as in him lies, desire all truth?" "By all means."

This section seems to be talking about potentiality: at the beginning, Socrates talks of people who are "going to become such as we have described" (sc. mature philosophers) at 485c1 and refers to their being this way "from youth onwards" in the conclusion (ἄρα) to this section at 485d3–4.

[3] 485d6–e6. Here we encounter what has become known as 'the channel argument': the stronger one's desires for one thing, the weaker they are for others.[6] Socrates connects this to the possession of temperance, along with an indifference to bodily pleasures and money.

> "But, again, we surely are aware that when in a person the desires incline strongly to any one thing, they are weakened for other things. It is as if the stream had been diverted into another channel." "Surely." *"So, when a person's desires have been taught to flow in the channel of learning and all that sort of thing, they will be concerned, I presume, with the pleasures of the soul in itself, and will be indifferent to those of which the body is the instrument, if the person is a true and not a sham philosopher."* "That is quite necessary." "Such a man will be temperate and by no means greedy for wealth; for the things for the sake of which money and great expenditure are eagerly sought others may take seriously, but not he." "That is so."

Although there are no clear signals in favour of either interpretation, intuitively one might favour M: the sense seems to be that the change in the intensity of one's desires takes time, so is something that ought to happen later on in life.

[4] 486a1–b13: Socrates now discusses a string of moral qualities:

> "And there is this further point to be considered in distinguishing the philosophical from the unphilosophical nature." "What point?" "You must not overlook any touch of illiberality. For nothing can more opposed than pettiness[7] to a soul *which is going to long after* (μελλούσῃ [...] ἐπορέξεσθαι) *integrity and wholeness in all things human and divine."* "Most true," he said. *"Do you think that a person to whose mind belongs magnificence and the contemplation of all time and all being can consider human life a thing of great concern?"* "Impossible." *"So, such a person will not consider death to be terrible?"* "Least of all." "Then a cowardly and illiberal spirit, it seems, could have no part in genuine philosophy." "I think not." "What then? Could a man of orderly spirit, not a lover of money (μὴ φιλοχρήματος), not illiberal, nor a braggart nor a coward, ever be unjust, or a driver of hard bargains?" "Impossible." "And when you are considering whether a soul is philosophic or not – *from youth onwards* (εὐθὺς νέου ὄντος), you'll also observe whether it is just and tame or antisocial and savage." "Of course."

---

6 The channel argument is discussed by Kahn 1996, 276–7. He raises the interesting question of whether the desires that become weakened are all of the same type: does Plato really mean to say that the same desire can be turned from one direction to another? Did he not hold that different types of object require radically different types of desire? Interesting though this question is, we do not need to discuss it here.

7 *Symp.* 210d3 also talks of the lack of pettiness (*smikrologia*) in the developing philosopher.

This passage sends out mixed signals. On one hand, some of the language points unequivocally towards the potential for future achievements (cf. 486a5–6: "a soul which is going to long after integrity and wholeness"); also, when he adds that someone who was orderly, and neither mercenary, cowardly or boastful, would not be[8] unjust (486b6–8), he uses an inferential particle (τί οὖν). So he must, as in the lines from which it is inferred, be talking about philosophical potential. As regards the person's indifference to money (486b6), this recalls the second section, where Socrates used the channel argument to show that the philosopher is indifferent to physical pleasures and hence money (485e3–5). At that point we were unsure as to whether he was talking about the potential or mature philosopher. But if he now repeats the reference to money in a passage clearly focusing on potential, we are entitled, retrospectively, to read the channel argument in the same way. Still in Section [4], the next sentence (486b10–12) states that we should check to see if someone is just and gentle (rather than unjust and antisocial) when trying to determine if they have a philosophical nature from youth onwards (εὐθὺς νέου ὄντος, 486b10–11). Again, this clearly supports P.

On the other hand, there is one indication in favour of M, when he talks about the reasons for being courageous: "the spectator of all time and all being" sounds like a mature philosopher (indeed a proto-Stoic, one might say).

[5] 486c1–d3. Mental qualities – being quick at learning and having a good memory:

> "Nor will you overlook this, I think." "What?" "Whether he is quick or slow to learn. Or do you suppose that anyone could properly love a task which he performed painfully and with little result from much toil?" "That could not be." "And if he could not keep what he learned, being steeped in oblivion, could he fail to be empty of knowledge?" "How could he?" "And so, having all his labor for nothing, don't you think *he will have to end up hating himself* (ἀναγκασθήσεται τελευτῶν αὑτόν τε μισεῖν) and this kind of occupation?" "Of course." "The forgetful soul, then, we must not list in the roll of competent lovers of wisdom, but we require a good memory." "By all means."

This is clearly about potentiality. The qualities mentioned here must belong to someone before they become a mature philosopher, because they are instrumental in helping them to become such. (I have highlighted the use of the future tense ἀναγκασθήσεται in 486c10 to drive home the point: someone who lacks

---

8 Admittedly, 'be' could be translated as saying 'become' here (γένοιτο, 486b8) but, given what immediately follows (that the person of a philosophical nature must be just while young), this cannot be taken as a reference to his becoming fully just later in life. So I have translated γένοιτο simply as 'be': cf. *LSJ* sv II.1. (Shorey, whose translation I have modified, had 'prove'). The use of the word γένοιτο in 486b8 is discussed by Lane 2007, 52 n. 14.

these qualities will come to despise themselves and their studies through labouring in vain: 486c10 – 11).

[6] 486d4 – 12. Gracefulness, measure and proportion:

> "But assuredly we should not say that the want of harmony and seemliness in a nature conduces to anything else than the lack of measure and proportion." "Certainly." "And do you think that truth is akin to measure and proportion or to disproportion?" "To proportion." "Then in addition to our other requirements we look for a mind endowed with measure and grace, *which will make its native disposition easily guided* (παρέξει τὸ αὐτοφυὲς εὐάγωγον) to the form of each thing that is." "Assuredly."

Again, this points to the potential to achieve philosophical understanding. Aside from the use of the future tense παρέξει (486d11), the main point is that the quality of gracefulness will guide the soul towards understanding. Hence the quality in question must belong to someone before they reach the philosophical summit.

[7] 486e1 – 487a5. The conclusion:

> "Well then, don't you think all the things we have been listing *follow on from one another* (ἑπόμενα ἀλλήλοις), and are necessary to a soul *that is going to have* a sufficient and perfect grasp of being (τῇ μελλούσῃ τοῦ ὄντος ἱκανῶς τε καὶ τελέως ψυχῇ μεταλήψεσθαι)?" "They are absolutely necessary," he replied. "So (οὖν) is there any fault that you can find with a study which a person could not properly pursue unless he were by nature of good memory, quick apprehension, magnificent, gracious, friendly and akin to truth, justice, bravery and temperance?" "Not even Momus [the god of censure]," he said, "could find fault with such a combination." "Well, then," said I, "*once people of this sort have been perfected by education and maturity of age*, would you not entrust the state solely to them?"

Again, this points towards P. First, Socrates says that all the qualities mentioned are needed if someone is going to achieve full philosophical understanding (486e1 – 3). Then, in a final flourish, he concludes (οὖν, 487a2): no one could find fault with a discipline (sc. philosophy) that requires its students to have by nature all the qualities and virtues listed above. Again, this points to a focus on the potential to become philosophical in the full sense. One final point: in this conclusion, Socrates says that all the qualities listed "follow on from one another" (ἑπόμενα ἀλλήλοις, 487e2). This picks up a crucial feature of the passage as a whole: the way the list of qualities is presented as a string of closely connected inferences.[9] Hence, the fact that at several points he uses future-directed language (and at two points refers to qualities possessed "from

---

[9] This will be picked up by the chorus metaphor of 490c2 – 10, in which the love of truth stands as the chorus leader, and the other qualities as those that follow in its train.

youth onwards") affects how we read the passage as a whole: the clear and unambiguous references to potentiality in some sections must apply to all, if the passage is to succeed as a chain of inferences. (And yet this consideration also cuts the other way: if there are strong indications that he is talking about the mature philosopher, as in the fourth section, then these ought also to 'infect' the whole strong of inferences).

In sum, most of the evidence points to P. But there are still some passages that stubbornly resist such a reading and point to M.[10]

3 Subdividing P: two possibilities

We are trying to identify what stage in a person's life Socrates has in mind when he talks of them as possessing the qualities listed in this passage. According to M, it is at the peak of their philosophical development. But we have just seen that there are very serious obstacles to such a reading, because the text refers to qualities that exist "from youth onwards". If we are thrown back on P, we need to make some refinements. I said above that P would be capable of further subdivision. In itself, P only specifies that the qualities at issue must exist before one becomes a mature philosopher, but it does not say when exactly these exist. Let me set out two different possibilities.

Melissa Lane has proposed that we think of the natural philosopher along the lines of Socrates as characterized in the *Symposium* – that is the Socrates who was wholly immersed in philosophy, while showing enormous courage at the battle of Potidaea and temperance in resisting the allure of the young Alcibiades.[11] Importantly, this is someone who has not gone all the way in terms of understanding the forms. Exceptional though he may be, he is not a perfect phi-

---

[10] Perhaps I am wrong to treat P and M as mutually exclusive. Why can we not adopt both interpretations? Some of the qualities mentioned might belong only to the mature philosopher (e. g. magnificence or courage); others (such as quickness at learning) apply to the emerging philosopher (though they will also, of course, persist in the mature philosopher). In other words, when discussing some of the qualities Socrates is thinking of the mature philosopher, in others the emerging philosopher. A quick response to this proposal is to cite the concluding section, [7] 486e1–487a5: this is clearly talking about the emerging philosopher, and yet it lists almost all the qualities mentioned, including magnificence and courage. So it is not an option for us to claim that some of the qualities (i.e. the more Stoic sounding ones) belong only to the mature philosopher. (In n. 26 below, I shall give a further objection this compromise proposal, based upon the later passage about the corruption of the philosophical nature at 491b7–495b7.)

[11] See Lane 2007, especially 46 and 58. Socrates would have been in his late thirties at the battle of Potidaea (432–30).

losopher. And yet he still has the kind of attitudes mentioned in the passage in the discussion of magnificence, or the channel argument (i.e. the qualities that inclined us towards M). He is someone whose appetitive desires have been weakened by his love of learning, and who takes the kind of perspective that goes with magnificence, generating the sort of courage referred to in the passage. So, taking the *Resp.* VI passage to be referring to Socrates gives us a version of P able to accommodate the texts that seemed to point towards M: the character is not too developed, but still sufficiently developed to fit the Stoic-sounding attitudes described in our passage.

And yet these qualities belong to someone "from youth onwards". So isn't the Socrates of the *Symposium* just too old to be exactly the person Plato has in mind when he talks of the natural philosopher in *Resp.* VI 484a1–487a5? Although this is not a decisive objection, it should give us pause. So another possibility is to go a few stages earlier, and think of a much younger person. As an example, Alcibiades comes to mind. Drawing again from the *Symposium*, one thinks of the way he was literally entranced by Socrates' philosophizing, as he himself admits (215b8–216c3). So we can plausibly assume he had great philosophical potential, and had already made enough progress not just to understand what Socrates was saying, but to be enamoured of it.[12]

Furthermore, citing Alcibiades fits with a crucial feature of the discussion that is central to the second discussion of natural philosophers (489e–497a): here, in response to Adeimantus' objection, Socrates talks of the way the qualities discussed in the earlier passage, those same qualities possessed "from youth on", might later become corrupted. This is presumably what happened in the case of Alcibiades. So if our question is about the stage in life at which might possess the qualities listed in 484a1–487a5, an Alcibiades figure seems like a good fit.[13]

---

[12] This would have been true of Alcibiades even in his late teens. The episode where he attempts to seduce Socrates (*Symp.* 217b–219e), because he himself is so enamoured of his philosophizing, predates the battle of Potidaea, where they both served. Alcibiades, born in 450, cannot have been more than twenty at that stage.

[13] Although Lane 2007 presents the Socrates of the *Symposium* as the prime example of a natural philosopher, she also implies that Alcibiades is one as well (p. 57), although she seems somewhat lukewarm about the idea: "Alcibiades is a natural philosopher in the sense that he is naturally and passionately moved by Socrates' words." I suspect Lane thinks Alcibiades is a natural philosopher only in a restricted sense: he exhibits the basic desire for knowledge of being to an extent, but not all of the other virtues or qualities. In the next paragraph, she implies that he had "vigour, tenacity and high-mindedness." But I am not sure she embraces the idea that Alcibiades might have possessed all the natural virtues of the philosopher, before corruption set in.

This is not to deny that Socrates had the natural virtues of a philosopher. He certainly did, though they would have been far more developed than in the case of Alcibiades, and closer towards the character of the perfect philosopher. However, the suggestion behind my second version of P is two-fold: first, that it is possible for the full list of natural virtues to belong to someone in their late teens; and second that the passage describing these virtues, 484a1–487a5 (with its references to qualities held from "youth onwards"), is focusing primarily on a younger character like Alcibiades.

On the other hand, it might seem quite a stretch to say that a youth like Alcibiades, indeed any youth, could have been so developed in their philosophical outlook that that they possess the qualities of magnificence and fearlessness described in our passage. These are characteristic of the mature philosopher, and probably also applied to Socrates. But did Plato really think they might also have characterized a much younger person, perhaps even an adolescent?

4 Plato's underlying theory

So, although it looks like P is more plausible than M, neither version of P is problem-free.[14] To make progress, let us set our main question on one side for a moment, and try to clarify the underlying theory of this passage. Plato thinks a string of qualities is natural to philosophy. First, I wish to ask how these qualities are related to one another. In the conclusion to the passage, Socrates says that all the qualities listed "follow on from one another" (486e2). This implies that there are certain interconnections between them all. But what are they exactly? Having done that, I shall move back towards our original question and ask exactly what he means by implying that these qualities are natural.

I think we need to start by acknowledging that the qualities mentioned in Section [1] – perhaps also [2] – are the fundamental ones – fundamental, that is, to the philosophical nature.[15] They provide the core definition of what it is to be philosophical: not just desire to learn, but to learn about being or *ousia* (in its entirety). From this basic and apparently simple starting point, which I shall call the 'Ur-desire', Plato thinks he can derive a long list of specific qualities. So how are these other qualities related to the Ur-desire?

---

14 At the end of this paper, I shall briefly consider (and reject) a third version of P, according to which the qualities listed in our passage are manifest from childhood.
15 This is also implied by the chorus metaphor (490c2–10), which could be read as implying that the essence of the philosophical nature is the desire to learn about being; the other attributes are rather like Aristotelian 'necessary accidents'.

Let me start with the qualities of quickness of mind and memory. A close look at the relevant text, Section [5], shows that for Plato we could never fulfil the Ur-desire without these extra qualities. In the text he may be imagining a person who has the philosophical aspiration but lacks quickness of mind and memory (486c9–d2). The result is complete frustration, leading the person to give up on their original aspiration. The lack of these qualities simply blocks any progress towards true philosophy. These qualities stand in an instrumental relation to the fulfilment of the Ur-desire.

How should we understand the relation of the rest of the qualities to the Ur-desire? On the most plausible view, Plato is proposing a rather different account from status of memory and quick-wittedness in Section [5] (486c1–d3). Initially, instead of seeing them as necessary pre-requisites for developing one's philosophical aspiration, they are the consequences of its development. As the Ur-desire starts to be satisfied, it gives rise to temperance. This is the point of the channel argument: the more one satisfies one's intellectual desires, the more one diminishes one's appetitive desires. The result is temperance and a lack of interest in money. Turning to the next section, [4], we might say that love of truth about being, which involves abstracting away from the particular and the human – taking a god's-eye view – gives rise to magnificence, which in turn gives rise to courage. Courage and temperance then give rise to justice, because one has no incentive to cheat others through desire for profit or fear of danger.[16]

So in what sense are all these qualities natural? Let us start with the Ur-desire. Socrates, I suggest, thinks that there is a certain kind of person (a very rare case), who is naturally predisposed to love any kind of inquiry that relates to being as such – indeed they are predisposed to pursue such learning with a passion.

The best way to make sense of this is to appeal to the theory of dispositional innatism that was developed explicitly by Descartes and Leibniz in the slightly different context of the debate over the origin of our ideas.[17] When Descartes argued for the innateness of certain ideas (e.g. of god or cause and effect), he was resisting the empiricist view that the mind comes equipped only with very general powers of concept formation, e.g. abstraction, and that it relies very heavily

---

16 I used the word 'initially' because, once these virtues have resulted from the gradual satisfaction of the Ur-desire, they then act to help its subsequent fulfilment: temperance, courage and the like sustain one along the path to philosophical understanding (cf. 487a2–5). The whole process thus involves a virtuous cycle, or feed-back loop.

17 I have discussed this theory in Scott 1995, 91–5. Descartes espouses dispositional innatism in *Notes Directed against a Certain Programme* (Haldane and Ross 1911, I 442), and Leibniz in *New Essays on Human Understanding*, Preface and I i (Remnant and Bennett 1982, 52 and 80).

on external stimuli to provide the content of its ideas. On the other hand, Descartes did not want to espouse the absurd thesis that babies are born thinking of cause and effect, or of god, not to mention the different geometrical figures. So he steered a middle course, as did Leibniz (in response to Locke's critique of innatism): the mind is born with predispositions to form certain concepts rather than others. External stimuli are needed, but these only prompt the mind to go in a predetermined direction. To illustrate the point Descartes used the analogy of an innate disease, such as gout. Someone might be born with an innate propensity to develop gout later in life. They do not suffer from gout at birth, of course. But when they develop the disease they need not have been exposed to specific gout-inducing stimuli. Thus someone without the innate propensity might have been exposed to identical environmental stimuli without ever developing the disease.[18] To extend Descartes' analogy somewhat, we might say that, by contrast, something like flu depends on specific environmental factors (i.e. the specific virus). The analogue for this would be a concept like that of a pineapple: you would not develop this concept unless you actually encountered objects of this kind (or representations of them); whereas you would develop ideas of cause and effect whatever stimuli you encounter – i.e. in the normal run of experience.

All this can usefully be adapted to explain the sense in which the Ur-desire is natural. Plato is not saying that certain babies or infants are born with an occurrent desire to learn about being. (They might be born with a desire to learn about something, to use their senses, along the lines mentioned by Aristotle at the beginning of the *Metaphysics* – I.1, 980a20–27). But over time, in response to the same stimuli to which others are exposed, they will start to develop an occurrent desire of this kind. One way this would happen would be if they started to study mathematics. Their curiosity would be fired up, in a way that would make them stand out from the other students. As the disposition comes to be realized, the desire for knowledge and truth grows in strength. It is crucial to emphasize the peculiarly Platonic nature of this disposition. Think again of Aristotle's claim that all human beings desire to know. For him, this desire could be satisfied by learning about becoming. He even gives the use of the senses as an example at the opening of *Met.* I.1 980a21–3. Plato has in mind something far more specific, and much rarer – not common to all humans: the desire to know about unchanging reality. So imagine two people studying astronomy when young, one who has the Ur-desire innately, and another who lacks it.

---

[18] An even better example for our purposes would be a genetic disposition to alcoholism, because it has a desiderative aspect.

The latter might become interested in empirical facts about the stars and might even admire the beauty of the night sky. But the former would feel a natural inclination to move beyond the empirical to the underlying mathematical proportions and ratios.

So dispositional innatism is a good way of explaining the origins of the Ur-desire. What about the other qualities? As far as having a good memory or quickness at learning are concerned, we should take these in a straightforward sense: some people are just born with abilities of this kind, which exist alongside the Ur-desire and so enable its fulfilment. But the case of the moral qualities is quite different. As we have seen, these arise as a result of the Ur-desire being gradually fulfilled. So they are not innate in the same basic or primary way; they are only indirectly innate. They owe their existence entirely to the strength of the Ur-desire as it becomes realized. By contrast, the instrumental 'talents' listed in Section [5] do not depend on the Ur-desire for their existence. It depends on them – not for its existence, but for its fulfilment. So they must also be innate in a primary and non-derivative way.

To clarify this point, contrast Aristotle's account of the natural virtues in the *Nicomachean Ethics*. He thought someone might have the natural virtue of courage in the sense that they are from birth predisposed to stand up to dangers. As they grow up, this tendency begins to manifest itself in action.[19] (If all goes well, it will come to be moulded by practical reason, and so become genuine courage.) But Plato is not thinking of the philosopher's moral qualities as natural virtues in this way. The natural philosopher is not born with an innate predisposition for courage. They are born with the innate disposition to form the Ur-desire, and with certain talents necessary for satisfying it. Only when this happens will courage, as well as temperance, magnificence, courage and justice come along. This is quite different form Aristotle's theory of the natural virtues and should not be assimilated to it.[20]

In the light of this, let us summarize what Socrates is saying in our passage. In talking of a person who possesses this long string of inter-connected qualities, he must be thinking of someone who, from birth, had the innate predisposition

---

[19] See *EN* VI.13, 1144b4–6. He also talks of innate tendencies to vice in II.8, 1109a13–16 and IV.1, 1121b14–16. I have discussed Aristotle's natural virtues in terms of dispositional innatism in Scott 1995, 103–4. It is interesting that, when Descartes illustrates the innateness of ideas (Haldane and Ross 1911, I 442), his examples include not just innate diseases (like gout), but also the virtue of generosity. Although he does not elaborate, he probably has something along the lines of an Aristotelian natural virtue in mind: a child is born with an innate predisposition towards the feelings and actions involved in generosity.

[20] See Lane 2007, 45 n. 2.

towards loving truth about being, along with certain natural talents, like quickness at learning; but Socrates must also think that such a person has gone some way towards realizing this basic desire, far enough to have brought into existence a set of moral qualities such as temperance, magnificence, courage and justice (which were not innate in the same way as the Ur-desire).[21]

The question is, therefore, what kind of age could such a person be? How young could they be – only as developed as Socrates in the *Symposium*, or as young as Alcibiades when he associated with Socrates? Let me now turn to the second passage, 489e–497a, to see what light it can throw on this issue. I shall start by showing how it confirms the general theory we have just described, before turning to the choice between our two versions of P.

---

21 As I have stressed, all these qualities are interconnected. This is the point of the chorus metaphor (490c2–10), which suggests that the different qualities of the philosophical nature stand or fall together. However, in a later back-reference to the topic in 503b6–d4, Socrates could be read as suggesting the opposite. He says that it is extremely rare for all the qualities to coalesce, and much more common for them to be found in separation: "Facility in learning, memory, sagacity, quickness of apprehension (εὐμαθεῖς καὶ μνήμονες καὶ ἀγχίνοι καὶ ὀξεῖς) and their accompaniments, and youthful spirit and magnificence (νεανικοί τε καὶ μεγαλοπρεπεῖς) in soul are qualities, you know, that are rarely combined in human nature with a disposition to live orderly, quiet, and stable lives; but such men, by reason of their quickness, are driven about just as chance directs, and all steadfastness is gone out of them. [...] And on the other hand, the steadfast and stable temperaments, whom one could rather trust in use, and who in war are not easily moved and aroused to fear, are apt to act in the same way when confronted with studies. They are not easily aroused, learn with difficulty, as if benumbed, and are filled with sleep and yawning when an intellectual task is set them" (503c1–d4). But note a curious feature of this passage: the vocabulary used differs somewhat from the earlier discussion. The first two terms are the same: facility in learning and memory (εὐμαθεῖς and μνήμονες: cf. 487a4 and 494b1). But the next two – sagacity and quickness of apprehension (ἀγχίνοι and ὀξεῖς) – are new (as is the term νεανικοί, which Shorey translates here as "youthful spirit"). And when in the second half he refers to stability or steadfastness, he does not actually use the term *andreia* (courage) which featured in the earlier discussion. In my view, Socrates does not hold that the very same qualities need exist in the philosophical nature as in the cases discussed here. He probably does allow this for the case of quickness of learning and strictly mental qualities. But steadfastness is like an Aristotelian natural virtue; it should not be assimilated to the courage that is born of the Ur-desire. Nor should "youthful spirit and magnificence" be assimilated to the magnificence (*megaloprepeia*) also born of the Ur-desire, even though the same term *megaloprepeia* is used in both passages. This "youthful spirit" or pride is not equivalent to the Stoic-like attitude of the natural philosopher. (There is a serious textual problem with this passage, but I do not have space to address it here. It will not seriously impact on the issue I have raised. See Adam 1963, II 79–81 for details.)

5 The evidence of VI 489e–497a

Against Socrates' panegyric of the philosophical nature, Adeimantus objects that most people put philosophers into one of three categories: corrupt, bizarre, or useless (487d1–5). To his surprise, Socrates agrees, though he is only speaking of philosophers as they currently are. To explain himself, he goes through each category in turn. (1) The claim that philosophers are corrupt is explained in 491b7–495b7. Some people who have all the qualities or virtues described earlier in 484a1–487a5 may be lured by the prospect of political power into deserting true philosophy and using their natural qualities for bad ends. Indeed, there is a paradox: the very qualities that we have just celebrated as making for a good ruler can, if corrupted, make someone thoroughly dangerous to society. (2) He then describes what happens when philosophy is deserted by those truly suited for it: people who do not possess the natural qualities take it up, and pursue a kind of *faux* philosophy. Instead of pursuing truth about being as their goal, they merely indulge in contentious argument. These 'eristics' are the ones who give philosophy a reputation for being bizarre (495b8–496a9). (3) Finally, Socrates discusses those who are true philosophers but do not allow themselves to be corrupted (or are saved by a lucky fate) and maintain their purity by staying out of power. They give philosophy its reputation for uselessness (496a11–497a7).

Here we can see Socrates going through Adeimantus' three categories quite methodically. Our concern will be with the first, those who have a philosophical nature, but succumb to corruption (491b7–495b7). He starts with the following statement of the paradox (491a8–b10):

> "I think everyone will grant us this point, that a nature such as we just now postulated for becoming the perfect philosopher is a rare growth among men and is found in only a few. Don't you think so?" "Most emphatically." "Observe, then, the number and magnitude of the things that operate to destroy these few." "What are they?" "The most surprising fact of all is that each of the gifts of nature which we praise tends to corrupt the soul of its possessor and divert it from philosophy. I am speaking of courage, temperance, and the entire list."

Note immediately the clear statement of P at 491a8–b1: "a nature such as we just now postulated for becoming the perfect philosopher." If we still had any doubts about excluding M, they can finally be laid to rest.[22]

---

[22] This reading is also implied by the comparison of the philosophical nature to a seed at 491d1–492a5.

He then explains how the corruption works. There seem to be two components involved. The first concerns the role of the *dêmos* (492a5–494a6). Socrates talks of the way in which a youth might come to love the roar of applause in the assembly, if he were ever to put his considerable talents to use by engaging in popular oratory. (Here he must be alluding to the role of spirit, *thumos*, as the source of the desire to shine in front of the crowd.) The specific corruption that follows consists in the young man not just saying what the *dêmos* wants to hear, but over time actually coming to believe it.[23] The second component of the corruption (494a10–e6) emphasizes the role of the person's immediate associates and family. They realize that he has extraordinary qualities, which they seek to use to further their own interests. So they encourage him to go into democratic politics (where he will be corrupted in the first manner described in 492a–493a), and do everything they can to stop him continuing with philosophy. The results of the process are detailed at 494c4–d3. Then, at 494d5–495a3, Socrates imagines someone attempting to set the person back on course, an attempt that ends in failure. Finally, he summarizes the section at 495a4–b6, saying that the finest natures, when corrupted, do the greatest harm.

So how does any of this help with our main question? If we opt for P, should we go with the Socrates or Alcibiades version?

There are three crucial points to note. The first concerns one of the mechanisms by which the corruption takes place. As we have just seen, the person's family (and close citizens) try to use his qualities for their own ends. The implication of this is that the qualities at issue must already be manifest. Now, it is not difficult to imagine someone who is quick to learn and good at remembering being considered an asset by those around him. But Socrates' point is much broader: his family see his temperance, grandness of vision (magnificence), courage, justice and gracefulness, and seek to exploit these.[24] So we are to imagine a young man, who already has such a range of qualities visible to all those around him, about to turn down the wrong track. Note that these cannot be mere potentialities; otherwise his family would not realize the assets they have at their disposal.

The second point is that he must also be recognizably philosophical. That he is actually philosophical is already implied: if the person has the moral qualities of temperance, courage and the like, he must have been caused to exist by some

---

23 In this section, Socrates emphasizes that it is primarily the *dêmos* that does the corrupting, not, as some think, the sophists.

24 In my view, what the family really values are not the qualities of temperance, grandness of vision, courage, justice and gracefulness Platonically conceived, but (respectively) self-discipline, ambition, steadfastness, sociability and charisma.

actual philosophizing.[25] And that he is recognizably philosophical is also implied by the overall context: the whole passage (inspired by Adeimantus' objection) assumes that people widely think that philosophers can be corrupt. So the wider public must already have in mind people who have immersed themselves in philosophy but then turn to politics (with unfortunate results). So when he talks of the natural philosopher, Socrates has in mind someone who has already developed their Ur-desire to the extent that they actually are – and are thought to be – philosophical. This is not someone who has an unrealized philosophical disposition.

The third point to consider is that someone can have all these qualities (occurrently), be recognized as having them, and yet then go on to be corrupted by their families to do great evil. Alternatively, they might, by some happy circumstance, avoid all this and continue on the path towards perfect philosophy. This point seems to me to tilt us in favour of the Alcibiades reading and away from the Socratic one. Although he is not explicitly mentioned, Alcibiades must be in Plato's mind here. Think again of his self-description in the *Symposium*, where he is torn between the love of honour and the love of Socrates' *logoi*. Note that the latter really does count as love: the passage where he describes it, 215b8–216c3, speaks in no uncertain terms of the emotional power of Socrates' *logoi*. Like a lover, Alcibiades is quite mesmerized by the *logoi*, as only someone with the true Ur-desire could be.

My claim is that he has developed this desire to the point where he is recognizably philosophical; and this process has in turn brought about the existence of the other qualities. So when Socrates talks in *Resp.* VI about someone possessing these qualities from youth onwards, I take him to mean the age at which Alcibiades showed such philosophical potential. In other words, if, as most scholars agree, Plato is thinking of Alcibiades as someone who might be corrupted in the way described in 489e–497a, then Alcibiades must have had all the qualities listed before (484a1–487a5), otherwise he would not have been perceived as being useful to his family and so been at risk of this kind of corruption. And if he had these qualities, he must have already started to fulfil his philosophical

---

[25] Socrates clearly implies that the youth is already engaged in philosophy at 494a10–11: "from this point of view do you see any salvation that will allow one who is a philosopher to *remain* in the pursuit and persevere to the end?" A similar implication can be drawn from 495a6–7: "the very qualities that make up the philosophical nature do, in fact, become, when the environment and nurture are bad, in some sort the cause of its *backsliding* [...]" (emphasis added in both cases).

Ur-desire to a significant extent. This in turn explains why he was recognized as a philosopher.[26]

Above I raised an objection: can we really believe that a youth could have the sorts of Stoic-sounding attitudes mentioned in the earlier passage in connection with magnificence and courage? Given the weight of evidence, I think we just have to bite the bullet. Plato believes that such attitudes can manifest themselves well before one has become a 'perfect philosopher'; they *can* occur even in someone like the young Alcibiades. But note that such cases are rare (cf. 491b1– 2), so this may help alleviate any anxieties we may still have.

I have used Alcibiades as my prime example of the natural philosopher. But another figure to consider in this context would be the mathematician Theaetetus.[27] In the dialogue named after him, he is no more than 16 at the time of his conversation with Socrates.[28] He is already a budding mathematician, but in addition to his intellectual qualities, he is also described as courageous and mild (πρᾷον, 144a4; cf. ἥμερος in *Resp.* VI 486b11). More generally, Socrates greatly admired his nature (φύσιν, 142c8). It is therefore tempting to see him as an example of the kind of natural philosopher described in *Resp.* VI. What makes the comparison all the more attractive is that, in the course of describing the young Theaetetus' qualities, the dialogue consciously echoes *Resp.* VI:

> Theodorus: He is quick to learn (εὐμαθῆ), beyond almost anyone else, yet exceptionally gentle (πρᾷον), and moreover brave beyond any other; I should not have supposed such a combination existed, and I do not see it elsewhere. On the contrary, those who, like him, have quick, sharp minds and good memories (οἵ τε ὀξεῖς ὥσπερ οὗτος καὶ ἀγχίνοι καὶ μνήμονες) have usually also quick tempers; they dart off and are swept away, like ships without ballast; they are excitable rather than courageous; those, on the other hand, who are steadier are somewhat sluggish when brought face to face with learning (νωθροί πως ἀπαντῶσι πρὸς τὰς μαθήσεις), and are very forgetful. But he advances toward learning and investigation smoothly and surely and successfully, with perfect gentleness, like a stream of oil that flows without a sound, so that one marvels how he accomplishes all this at his age. (144a3–b6, translation by Fowler 1921 modified)

---

26 This passage also provides another reason to reject the compromise interpretation I mentioned in n. 10 above. This was that some of the qualities at issue might apply only to the mature philosopher, but others also to the emerging philosopher. In the passage we are now considering (491b7–495b7), Socrates attributes the full list of natural qualities to a young man who will go on to be corrupted. Again this shows that he really means to attribute all the qualities to someone who is not a mature philosopher.

27 My thanks to Peter Adamson for pointing me in this direction.

28 See Burnyeat 1990, 3. Although Theaetetus is first and foremost a mathematician, he would still count as someone focused on knowledge of being rather than of becoming. So in this broader sense, he is philosophical.

This is remarkably similar to a passage we discussed in n. 21 above: *Resp.* VI 503b6–d4, where Socrates points out how rare it is for anyone to possess all the virtues he has been discussing. Instead, it is more common for people to have possess some good qualities, but not others. At 503c1–6, he says "Facility in learning, memory, sagacity, quickness of apprehension (εὐμαθεῖς καὶ μνήμονες καὶ ἀγχίνοι καὶ ὀξεῖς)" are seldom combined with the stability of character; instead, such people "are driven about just as chance directs" (just as in Theodorus' simile of the ship without ballast). Then, at 503c8–d4, he says that those of a more stable disposition "learn with difficulty [...] and are filled with sleep and yawning when an intellectual task is set them." (Compare the use of the word 'sluggish', νωθροί, in *Theaet.* 144b1.)[29]

Through the character of Theaetetus, therefore, Plato may well have been consciously giving us an example of someone who had manifested the virtues of the natural philosopher described in *Resp.* VI, even at the age of 16. Of course, this is someone who did not go on to become corrupted, like Alcibiades – far from it, to judge from the eulogy of the dialogue's opening (142b6–c1).

To return to *Resp.* VI: when Socrates talks about someone possessing such qualities from youth on, he means what he says. He thinking about someone quite young, even in late adolescence. The point of the whole passage as it goes on is to ask about what might happen to such qualities. If one resists corruption, the Ur-desire and with it, the moral qualities, will develop and intensify further – reaching the place on the spectrum that Socrates himself occupies (in the *Symposium* and the *Republic*). Eventually, with the right education in place, this process will culminate in the state of the perfect philosophers who rule in the *Republic*.

6 Two objections

Finally, I should mention two texts, both from the second passage (489e–497a), which seem to raise objections to my interpretation. The two objections come from opposite directions, the first suggesting that the natural qualities in question only belong to a more mature stage in life than I have argued; the second that they arise much earlier, even in childhood.

---

[29] The link between these two passages is noted by Ambuel 2015, 20 n. 4, and discussed in some detail by Balansard 2012, 37–8.

[1] Near the beginning of this passage, Socrates makes an obvious back-reference to the natural qualities of the philosopher. But the way he does so might be taken to suggest M rather than P. Here is the passage (490a8–c10):

> It was the nature of the real lover of knowledge to strive emulously for true being and [...] he would not linger over the many particulars that are opined to be real, but would hold on his way, and the edge of his passion would not be blunted nor would his desire fail *till he came into touch with the nature of each thing in itself by that part of his soul to which it belongs to lay hold on that kind of reality – the part akin to it, namely – and through that approaching it, and consorting with reality really, he would beget intelligence and truth, attain to knowledge and truly live and grow, and so find surcease from his travail of soul, but not before.* [...] Well, then, will such a person love falsehood, or, quite the contrary, hate it?" "Hate it," he said. "When truth led the way, no chorus of evils, we, I fancy, would say, could ever follow in its train." "How could it?" "But rather a sound and just character, which is accompanied by temperance." "Right," he said. "What need, then, of repeating from the beginning our proof of the necessary order of the chorus that attends on the philosophical nature? You surely remember that we found pertaining to such a nature courage, grandeur of soul, aptness to learn, memory." (Italics added)

An obvious way to read this is to embrace M. In this text he talks of the way the truth-lover has satisfied their *eros* as far as achieving knowledge. This language is clearly redolent of the *Symposium*, but it takes us well beyond the stage that even Socrates had reached: the *eros* is satisfied, and pregnancy has given birth to actual understanding. Apparently, this is this kind of person to whom Socrates attributes the natural qualities under discussion since the beginning of Book VI.

This reading obviously contradicts the view I have been advocating. But it causes considerable upset for any interpreter. As we have already seen, less than a page later, when Socrates sums up and recalls the list of virtues from before (491a8–b10), he says quite explicitly that these are what one needs in order to develop philosophical knowledge.[30] This unambiguously endorses P.

What are we to do? Something has to give. I do not think we can avoid finding P in 491a8–b10; so can we read 490a8–c10 in such a way that it does not yield M? I think we can.

He starts by talking of the person who has a philosophical nature: someone who is a genuine lover of learning ("it would be the nature of the real lover of knowledge to strive emulously for true being"). This can be read along the lines of P: he is thinking of someone quite young who has already developed an intense desire to understand about being. In the next few lines (which I

---

30 See especially 491a8–10: "a nature such as we just now postulated for becoming the perfect philosopher."

have italicized) he projects into the future to imagine how such a person would develop if they continued to follow this desire along its natural course. Eventually they would attain knowledge. But having done this, Socrates goes back to the developing philosopher at 490b9 (where my italics end): this is the point where he asks, "will such a person love falsehood"; my contention is that he is once again thinking of the young philosopher, not the perfect specimen he has just been envisaging in the previous (italicized) lines. And he continues to have this person in mind in the rest of the text, where he recalls the list of virtues attributed to them before. So the intervening lines, about the progress of this person towards full knowledge, flick forwards to a future stage; but Socrates need not to attributing the natural qualities of temperance and the like to this character (though of course they will have the fully developed versions of those virtues).[31]

I think this is a possible and plausible reading of the text. As it is consistent with what follows in 491a8–b10, I think we should adopt it.

[2] For a very different objection, consider the following text (494b1–10):

> "We agreed that quickness in learning, memory, courage and magnificence were the traits of this nature." "Yes." "Then even among boys such a one will take the lead in all things (οὐκοῦν εὐθὺς ἐν παισὶν ὁ τοιοῦτος πρῶτος ἔσται ἐν ἅπασιν), especially if the nature of his body matches the soul." "How could he fail to do so?" he said. "His kinsmen and fellow-citizens, then, will desire, I presume, to make use of him when he is older for their own affairs." "Of course."

The implication of these lines would be that all the qualities we have been discussing are manifest even in children. This would run counter to my interpretation, where it takes more time for the qualities to develop.

The catch, however, is that this implication is based upon an an emendation of the text from πᾶσιν ('all people') to παισὶν ('boys'). Thus Burnet, followed by most scholars and translators, reads 494b4–5 as saying εὐθὺς ἐν παισὶν ὁ τοιοῦτος πρῶτος ἔσται ἐν ἅπασιν. Literally translated, this means: "such a one will

---

[31] Just to be clear: in n. 10 and n. 26 above, I rejected a compromise interpretation, that some of the qualities at issue might apply only to the mature philosopher, others to the emerging philosopher. Yet according to my interpretation of 490a8–c10, Plato is after all placing the emerging and mature philosophers on the same continuum. However, he is not retracting his claim that the emerging philosopher has *all* the qualities listed; the young man he imagines in this passage (before and after the italicized section) certainly does have those qualities. When Plato then fast-forwards to the mature philosopher, he is not doing so to say that such a person will have natural qualities lacking in the emerging philosopher; he is merely describing what it would be like to have developed the philosophical desire to its ultimate conclusion.

straightaway be first among boys in all things."³² However, the received text reads: εὐθὺς ἐν πᾶσιν ὁ τοιοῦτος πρῶτος ἔσται ἐν ἅπασιν – "such a one will straightaway be first among all people in all things." This is compatible with my reading of *Resp.* VI.

There is no manuscript authority for changing the text. And doing so causes an enormous difficulty with Socrates' account of the qualities natural to the philosopher. As I have shown, earlier in Book VI (484a1–487a5), he clearly makes magnificence and courage consequent on the development of a philosophical perspective. So, unless one is to make highly implausible claims about the philosophical achievements of children, the suggested emendation creates a glaring inconsistency with what has preceded. (In other words, I just don't think children can, in Plato's view, have the proto-Stoic perspective mentioned above. So they cannot have the temperance, magnificence, courage etc. already discussed. They could have some Aristotelian natural virtues – but that is a different matter). So why, one might ask, should we be attracted by the emendation in the first place? It could be said that ἐν πᾶσιν [...] ἐν ἅπασιν sounds clumsy and repetitive; but I do not find this decisive. According to Adam,³³ the emendation makes sense of the contrast that immediately follows: "when they grow older [...]". But, again, this is a weak argument: there can be a contrast between two stages of life, as there has to be, without the earlier one being in childhood. The earlier could be in late adolescence, or around the age of twenty; the second stage could be much later on, even around the age of fifty. So I propose we stick with the manuscript reading.

7 Conclusion

In this paper, I started with the problem of identifying the natural philosopher described at the beginning of *Resp.* VI. Is Socrates talking about the nature of the fully formed philosopher, or is he talking about qualities required earlier on in life if one is to become such a philosopher? Over the course of the paper, I have argued that the figure whom he discusses at the beginning of Book VI is a young person, perhaps even an adolescent, of whom Alcibiades or Theaetetus would have been good examples. Such a character might continue

---

32 Shorey actually magnifies the effect of the emendation by translating "then even as a boy among boys such a one will take the lead in all things."
33 Adam 1963, II 25.

along the path towards philosophical knowledge, or, as is all too likely, they might be corrupted by the influence of society, family and friends.

Our attempt to answer the original question has also led us into an inquiry about what Socrates actually means by calling all these attributes 'natural'. In the event, the term natural (or 'by nature', *phusei*) is somewhat plastic, and means different things depending on the qualities to which it is attributed. [1] To say that the person by nature desires to understand about being is to say that they were born with an innate predisposition towards forming this desire, which they have now gone some way towards fulfilling. [2] They were also born with a facility in learning and remembering, which will aid the successful fulfilment of their desire. [3] But the sense in which the remaining qualities are natural is different: these qualities result from the gradual fulfilment of the innate desire to philosophize. They are thus only derivatively innate.[34]

Primary literature

Descartes, René. 1911. *Descartes' Philosophical Works*. 2 Volumes, edited by Elizabeth Haldane and George Ross. Cambridge: Cambridge University Press.
Leibniz, Gottfried Wilhelm. 1982. *Leibniz: New Essays on Human Understanding*, edited by Peter Remnant and Jonathan Bennett. Cambridge: Cambridge University Press.
Plato. 1921. *Plato: Theaetetus and Sophist*, translated by Harold Fowler. Cambridge, MA: Harvard University Press.
Plato. 1937. *Plato: The Republic*. 2 Volumes, by Paul Shorey. Cambridge, MA: Harvard University Press.
Plato. [1902] 1963. *The Republic of Plato*. 2 Volumes, edited by James Adam. Cambridge: Cambridge University Press.
Plato. 2015. *Turtles All the Way Down: On Plato's Theaetetus. A Commentary and Translation*, by David Ambuel. Sankt Augustin: Academia Verlag.

Secondary literature

Balansard, Anne. 2012. *Enquête Sur La Doxographie Platonicienne Dans La Première Partie Du Théétète*. International Plato Studies, 29. Sankt Augustin: Academia Verlag.

---

[34] Previous versions of this paper were given at the Munich School of Ancient Philosophy (LMU Munich) and Oxford University, where both audiences gave me invaluable feedback. I am also grateful to Melissa Lane for arousing my interest in this topic, and more recently to Peter Adamson for his keen editorial eye and insightful comments. Finally, I would like to thank the Alexander von Humboldt and Carl Friedrich von Siemens Foundations for supporting my research during 2016, when I first started working on this paper.

Burnyeat, Myles. 1990. *The Theaetetus of Plato*. Indianapolis: Hackett Publishing.
Burnyeat, Myles 1999a: "Culture and society in Plato's *Republic*." In *The Tanner Lectures on Human Values*, edited by Grethe Peterson, 20:215–324. Salt Lake City: University of Utah Press.
Burnyeat Myles. 1999b. "Utopia and Fantasy: The Practicability of Plato's Ideally Just City." In *Plato II: Ethics, Politics, Religion and the Soul*, edited by Gail Fine, 297–308. Oxford: Oxford University Press.
Cooper, John. 1977. "The Psychology of Justice in Plato." *American Philosophical Quarterly* 14:151–7.
Dahl, Norman. 1999. "Plato's Defense of Justice." In *Plato II: Ethics, Politics, Religion and the Soul*, edited by Gail Fine, 207–234. Oxford: Oxford University Press.
Hatzistavrou, Antony. 2006. "Happiness and the Nature of the Philosopher-Kings." In *New Essays on Plato: Language and Thought in Fourth-Century Greek Philosophy*, edited by Fritz-Gregor Herrmann, 95–124. Swansea: The Classical Press of Wales.
Kahn, Charles. 1996. *Plato and the Socratic Dialogue: The Philosophical Use of a Literary Form*. Cambridge: Cambridge University Press.
Kraut, Richard. 1973. "Reason and Justice in Plato's *Republic*." In *Exegesis and Argument*, edited by Edward Lee, Alexander Mourelatos, and Richard Rorty, 207–24. *Phronesis* Suppl. I.
Lane, Melissa. 2007. "Virtue as the Love of Knowledge in Plato's *Symposium* and *Republic*." In *Maieusis: Studies in Honour of M. F. Burnyeat*, edited by Dominic Scott, 44–67. Oxford: Oxford University Press.
Sachs, David. 1963. "A Fallacy in Plato's *Republic*." *Philosophical Review* 72:141–58.
Scott, Dominic. 1995. *Recollection and Experience*. Cambridge: Cambridge University Press.
Scott, Dominic. 2015. *Levels of Argument: a Comparative Study of Plato's Republic and Aristotle's Nicomachean Ethics*. Oxford: Oxford University Press.

Christoph Horn
Normative Naturalism in Aristotle's Political Philosophy?

Abstract: This paper defends the view that in his *Politics*, Aristotle embraces 'normative naturalism', the view that nature serves as a criterion of goodness, and provides a standard against which success in the practical sphere can be measured. Accordingly, it is argued that the *polis*' being 'by nature' brings with it teleological implications such as are familiar from Aristotle's biology. It is also argued that at several points in the *Politics*, Aristotle actually presupposes this naturalist theory of norms, for instance in his discussion of constitutions that are 'contrary to nature'.

1 Introduction

In *Politics* I.2, Aristotle famously characterizes the city as something that exists by nature (*pasa polis phusei estin*, 1252b30), and then claims that "man is by nature a political animal" (*ho anthrōpos phusei politikon zōon*, 1253a2–3). Finally, he asserts that the city has a "natural priority to the household and each of us" (*kai proteron de tê phusei polis ê oikia kai hekastos hêmōn estin*, 1253a18–9; cf. a25–6). These three Aristotelian claims regarding the *polis* might be called (i) the natural existence thesis, (ii) the natural anthropology thesis, and (iii) the natural priority thesis. These are surprisingly strong claims; formulated in one of the opening chapters of the *Politics* they are certainly meant to indicate programmatic ideas. Aristotle apparently wants to emphasize his position with force.[1] But what is this position?

One approach is provided by David Keyt (1991) in his classic essay *Three Basic Theorems in Aristotle's Politics*. According to Keyt, Aristotle advances four arguments in favour of claims (i–iii) in *Pol.* I.2: namely (1) the *genetic argument* (1252b27–34), which derives the naturalness of the *polis* from the naturalness of the first impulses and the natural process of transitivity; (2) the *telic argument* (1252b34–1253a7), which claims that man is by nature a political animal since the *polis* is characterized by self-sufficiency (*autarkeia*); (3) the *linguistic argument* (1253a7–18), which concludes from the human natural endowment with

---

[1] This is confirmed by the fact that in this short chapter *Pol.* I.2, the term *phusis* and its cognates appear more than 20 times.

linguistic skills to the correctness of the natural anthropology thesis; and (4) the *organic argument* (1253a18–33), which maintains that, separated from the *polis*, humans are 'human' only homonymously. Keyt ultimately rejects all four arguments as implausible or mistaken, opting finally for the Hobbesian thesis that the state is an artificial entity.

Though Keyt's article is well argued, one can read Aristotle much more favourably. There are several ways to make more positive sense of Aristotle's triple emphasis on naturalness. To begin with a widely shared point: he certainly intends to reject a conventionalist theory, defended e.g. by the Sophist Lykophron, according to which the *polis* and its legal order are simply based on social agreement or a contract. For Aristotle nature, not convention, is the origin of political life. The appeal to naturalness implies that political life is seen by him as 'self-grown', as something immediately given and something that essentially belongs to human identity. It is a direct feature of what it means to live as a human being and is, in this sense, inevitable. But there must be more to it. By describing the city as 'natural' and as 'naturally prior', and human beings as "political animals by nature", Aristotle must also have in mind an evaluative aspect: the natural thing is always the good or appropriate and the normatively preferable option; nature establishes a normative standard of and criteria for success or failure. Aristotle must defend some sort of political perfectionism in which nature serves as criterion of goodness.[2] We should ascribe to him a strong version of normative naturalism.

But does Aristotle really adopt normative naturalism in his political philosophy? What would be its foundation? With regard to the claim of naturalness and the theses (i–iii) in *Pol.* I.2, four main interpretations seem to be available (a-d). (a) According to a *minimalist reading*, the naturalness Aristotle has in mind can be reduced to that aspect of human nature (instead of Nature in general) which renders political community natural; seen from this interpretation, defended by Christof Rapp (2016), Aristotle does not accept any sort of normative naturalism. (b) According to a *eudaimonist reading*, humans fulfil their nature in the *polis* in the sense of reaching *autarkeia* only in this sort of community; his normative naturalism would then be built on a version of eudaimonism (Fred D. Miller Jr. 1995). (c) According to an *internal cause reading*, Aristotle's appeal to nature alludes to the dynamics of *phusis* as an 'inner cause' (Adriel Trott 2014). (d) Finally, according to a *biological reading*, the naturalness under consideration here is part of a biological teleology of nature (Pierre Pellegrin

---

[2] In a number of passages, Aristotle explicitly appeals to *phusis* as the normative standard in ethics: *e.g. EN* I.9, 1099b21–22; IX.9, 1170a13–16; X.7, 1178a5–6.

2015). In this paper, I want to defend (d) and develop the following ideas: I admit that, in *Pol.* I.2, Aristotle's standpoint includes the aspects of origin, *autarkeia*, and internal causality; thus readings (a), (b), and (c) all capture something about his position. But all these aspects should be seen as being formulated against the background of a biological teleology of Nature with a capital N: Aristotle contends that the *polis* is the habitat that is pre-designed by Nature and therefore fully appropriate for human beings. As a consequence, Aristotle's standards of political evaluation are likewise derived from the idea of naturalness. In fact, upon closer inspection, he formulates a number of fundamental points within his political thought from the perspective of normative naturalism.

2 Does Aristotle defend a version of normative naturalism?

The appeal to nature seems a strange and disputable strategy when it comes to the justification of political and moral norms. Human individuals and human society are far from being simply natural; substantive norms of our lives are highly conventional and artificial. As a consequence of this insight (which is fundamental to Hobbes' criticism of Aristotle's naturalism),[3] many of us are in general tempted to reject naturalness as a basic standard in politics and morals. It seems impossible to distinguish satisfactorily between what is natural and what is not. Even if one could do so, we might wonder why the former should be normatively preferable to the latter. And even if some natural things might be preferable due to their naturalness (such as organic food) it would still remain an open question whether *all* (or most, many, some, or rather few) natural things are good. Meanwhile it is far from clear that something that is normatively good, adequate, perfect, desirable, and choiceworthy in politics and morals must in some relevant sense be understood as natural. Thus normative naturalism appears to be highly implausible.

On the other hand, it is a historical fact that naturalness was a crucial normative standard in Greek philosophy, maybe even the most important one. The

---

3 *Leviathan*, Introduction: "Nature (the art whereby God hath made and governs the world) is by the art of man, as in many other things, so in this also imitated, that it can make an artificial animal. […] Art goes yet further, imitating that rational and most excellent work of Nature, man. For by art is created that great LEVIATHAN called a COMMONWEALTH, or STATE (in Latin, CIVITAS), which is but an artificial man, though of greater stature and strength than the natural, for whose protection and defense it was intended."

natural was seen by ancient philosophers not only as the set of given facts from which we must begin, but simultaneously as the norm for the unimpeded development of an entity. Furthermore, the nature of something was considered to consist of its essential attributes and excellent features. Julia Annas is therefore right in her claim that "the life according to nature is the virtuous life, and this alone shows that we do not find what is natural just by looking at children or, indeed, normal adults. As often stressed, nature in ancient ethics is a theoretical term, for we are being given an ethical ideal" (1993, 216).

Nor is normative naturalism absent in our contemporary thought. On the contrary, we are confronted with it in three different forms, forms with quite different degrees of philosophical attractiveness. First, there are positions derived from Neo-Darwinist socio-biology, such as those adopted by Edward O. Wilson, Richard Dawkins, and Matt Ridley; second, Neo-Thomistic accounts of Natural law, like that of John Finnis; and third, a movement which can broadly be characterized as Neo-Aristotelian, which includes the positions adopted by John McDowell, Philippa Foot, Michael Thompson, or Martha Nussbaum.[4] Whereas the first family of theories is naturalistic in a reductionist sense, the other two try to defend the idea of normative naturalism in a non-reductionist way. My goal here will not be to present any of these views, or indeed any contemporary philosophical approach. My intention is simply to give a textual interpretation bringing out Aristotle's own normative naturalism, leaving aside the question whether Aristotle's standpoint is tenable.[5]

On the reading I will defend, Aristotle is in his political and moral thought defending a biological version of normative naturalism. I base this claim on a teleological interpretation of *Pol.* I.2. Aristotle describes the political world in terms of biological teleology. He believes that Nature forms a unified and well-structured totality and that all its parts display such characteristics as purposiveness and goal-directedness, order and regularity, structure and governance, hierarchy and interdependence. Nevertheless, his moral and political normativity is formulated in terms of the flourishing lives of *human individuals*. It is not about the flourishing of *poleis*; political institutions are not seen as quasi-organic entities on their own. So the source of norms in natural teleology does not alter Aristotle's object of normative concern, which remains the *eudaimonia* of individuals.

---

4 For a critical account of what is 'Aristotelian' in these approaches see Rapp 2010.
5 One possible critique of his position is that it implies a sort of normative organicism and social collectivism; for a recent discussion see Weber 2015. We will however see that he is not committed to any such view.

3 The transfer argument and the minimalist reading

At the beginning of *Pol.* I.2 (1252a24–35), Aristotle distinguishes between two original social couplings: the pair of male and female and the pair of master and slave. The community of males and females mentioned here is 'natural' in the sense that they are in a predetermined relationship with one another. They cannot exist only individually, since they need one another to produce offspring – and this is characterized as natural for humans, just as for plants and animals. What is natural, we are informed, is 'not intentionally chosen' (*ouk ek prohaireseōs*). Thereafter the relationship between ruler and subject is likewise characterized as 'natural', in the sense that their mutual preservation (*sōtêrian*) necessitates their social connection. It is then added that master and slave too benefit from this social constellation. From this Aristotle draws the conclusion that in general, the more insightful person who can anticipate the future should rule, while the less intelligent should be ruled. Without further explanation given in this passage, Aristotle amplifies this point by speaking of 'slavery by nature' (*phusei doulos*).

As we can see, the two couplings of persons – and not the singular individuals – are the original social unities from which Aristotle starts when he describes the city as a natural whole; these couplings are the elementary parts that play a causal role in the generation of the city. The first coupling is for the sake of reproduction, the second for preservation. Note that Aristotle's line of argument is not based on human individuals and their conscious interests, but rests from the beginning on (minimal) social communities and their biological conditions. Starting from these considerations, Aristotle discusses the establishment of the household (*oikos*) which is characterized as a "natural community of everyday life" (ἡ μὲν οὖν εἰς πᾶσαν ἡμέραν συνεστηκυῖα κοινωνία κατὰ φύσιν οἶκός ἐστιν, 1252b13–4). He then proceeds to the village which he describes as "the most natural form of community"[6] and as "a foundation from the house, composed of the children and grandchildren, who are said to be suckled 'with the same milk'" (μάλιστα δὲ κατὰ φύσιν ἔοικεν ἡ κώμη ἀποικία οἰκίας εἶναι, οὓς καλοῦσί τινες ὁμογάλακτας, παῖδάς τε καὶ παίδων παῖδας, 1252b16–8).

---

[6] One might ask in which sense the village is 'most natural' (one would expect this to apply to the *polis*). Whatever Aristotle has in mind, we see from his formulation that the more complex social communities – household, village, and city – do not simply receive their naturalness from the first two couplings.

According to the minimalist reading (Rapp 2016), Aristotle merely transfers the naturalness of first human impulses and elementary communities to fully developed cities. One can call this the 'transfer argument'. To some extent this reading is certainly correct. In the process described by Aristotle naturalness is transferred from the first elementary communities, via the household and the village, to the city. Perhaps the strongest support for the minimalist reading is offered by the following sentence (*Pol.* I.2, 1252b27–31):

> [1] When several villages are united into a single complete community, large enough to be nearly or quite self-sufficing, the city comes into existence, originating in the bare needs of life, and continuing in existence for the sake of a good life. And therefore, if the earlier forms of society are natural, so is every city (διὸ πᾶσα πόλις φύσει ἔστιν, εἴπερ καὶ αἱ πρῶται κοινωνίαι).[7]

It is correct to say that in the quoted passage the aspect of naturalness is transferred from the first couplings to the final community, i.e. the city (as the words *eiper kai hai prōtai koinōniai* indicate). Aristotle describes a process of transmitting the naturalness of the first two impulses, i.e. of sexual reproduction and of preservation, to the *polis*. Yet this does not exclude that the process under consideration is ultimately a teleological one. Aristotle often combines, in his explanations of natural processes, efficient or material causes with final ones (as shown in Bolton 1997). Exactly this happens here, as becomes obvious when we look at the wider context of the sentence just quoted (*Pol.* I.2, 1252a24–35):

> [2] If someone might consider things from their beginnings as originating (εἰ δή τις ἐξ ἀρχῆς τὰ πράγματα φυόμενα βλέψειεν), whether a city or anything else, he will obtain the clearest view of them. In the first place there must be a union of those who cannot exist without each other; namely, of female and male in order to procreate offspring – and this is a union which is formed, not of deliberate purpose, but because, in common with other animals and with plants (καὶ τοῦτο οὐκ ἐκ προαιρέσεως, ἀλλ' ὥσπερ καὶ ἐν τοῖς ἄλλοις ζῴοις καὶ φυτοῖς), humans have a natural desire to leave behind them an image of themselves (φυσικὸν τὸ ἐφίεσθαι, οἷον αὐτό, τοιοῦτον καταλιπεῖν ἕτερον) – and of natural ruler and subject, that both may be preserved (ἄρχον δὲ καὶ ἀρχόμενον φύσει, διὰ τὴν σωτηρίαν). For the one who can foresee by the exercise of mind is by nature intended to be lord and master, and the one who can with the body give effect to such foresight is a subject, and by nature a slave; hence master and slave have the same interest.

The passage is not simply about natural impulses in the sense of efficient causes, but implies final causality. This is indicated by the emphasis in [2] on the goals of

---

[7] This quotation and the followings are taken from the revised Oxford translation, with occasional modification.

reproduction and common preservation. Concerning reproduction, it would be mistaken to take the desire to procreate offspring simply in the elementary sense of a sexual desire. To see its full teleological meaning, we should look at a parallel passage from the *De anima*, where Aristotle regards procreation as a strategy of finite living beings to reach some sort of trans-individual continuity (II.4, 415a14–b10):

> [3] The most natural act is the production of another like itself [...] an animal producing an animal, a plant a plant, in order that, as far as they can, they may partake in the eternal and divine (φυσικώτατον γὰρ τῶν ἔργων τοῖς ζῶσιν [...] τὸ ποιῆσαι ἕτερον οἷον αὐτό, ζῷον μὲν ζῷον, φυτὸν δὲ φυτόν, ἵνα τοῦ ἀεὶ καὶ τοῦ θείου μετέχωσιν ᾗ δύνανται). That is the goal towards which all things strive, that for the sake of which they do whatsoever their nature renders possible (πάντα γὰρ ἐκείνου ὀρέγεται, καὶ ἐκείνου ἕνεκα πράττει ὅσα πράττει κατὰ φύσιν). (The phrase 'for the sake of which' is ambiguous; it may mean either the end to achieve which, or the being in whose interest, the act is done). Since, then, no living thing is able to partake in what is eternal and divine by uninterrupted continuance (for nothing perishable can for ever remain one and the same), it tries to achieve that end in the only way possible to it, and success is possible in varying degrees; so it remains not indeed as the selfsame individual but continues its existence in something like itself – not numerically but specifically one.

In Text [3] as in [2], Aristotle declares that human beings have the 'natural', even the 'most natural' (*phusikōtaton*), desire to leave behind them an image of themselves. From quotation [3] it becomes clear that for Aristotle sexual impulses have to be seen within a broader metaphysical framework. He interprets reproduction as the strategy of a perishable individual to achieve some sort of everlastingness, namely through the intergenerational persistence of a species. The individual cannot participate in eternity except by the temporal continuity of its offspring. The continuation of the species is thus an emulation of immaterial, eternal entities. This is what the procreation of progeny is all about, and it is this teleological impulse that is described as 'natural'.

Regarding the naturalness of the relationship between the ruler and the ruled (*archon kai archomenon*) in Text [2], we should take into account a similarly illuminating text, which shows that Aristotle considers governance as part of the general world-order (*Politics* I.5, 1254a28–33):

> [4] For in all things which form a composite whole and which are made up of parts, whether continuous or discrete, a distinction between the ruling and the subject element comes to light (ἐν ἅπασιν ἐμφαίνεται τὸ ἄρχον καὶ τὸ ἀρχόμενον). Such a duality exists in living creatures, but not in them only; it originates in the constitution of the universe; even in things which have no life there is a ruling principle, as in a musical mode.

In [4], Aristotle claims that there exists a universal structure of governance in the universe between ruling entities and ruled ones. According to him, this includes all composite beings, both organic and inorganic; the structure appears even in music. The social couplings of male and female and of master and slave, while very different in their types of governance, fit into this scheme. The Aristotelian world is generally organized in forms of dominance and hierarchy. It is hence plausible to assume that the elementary form of rule introduced in *Pol.* I.2, the master-slave relation, is not only about protection, but additionally corresponds to the structure of Nature.

To return to Text [2], the idea of Nature is introduced in the context of a genealogical method. If one considers things (*ta pragmata*) in their generation (as *phuomena*), then, we are told, one gets the best picture of them. Of course the genealogical method is not meant in a historical sense, as if the underlying claim was the factual emergence of cities in the history of mankind.[8] It would be implausible to assume that at a certain point in history there existed isolated individuals, or couples and master-slave pairings, and only thereafter houses, villages, and finally cities. This is certainly something Aristotle rejects. At least houses or families, if not villages, must always have existed.[9] The genealogical reconstruction is instead based on a causal principle. The controversy concerns what kind of causality is at work – efficient or final – and whether the generation of the city should therefore be characterized as artificial or as natural.

At first glance, both questions, that regarding the alternative of efficient and final causality and that regarding natural or artificial generation, might seem to be easily answered. One is tempted to say that, for Aristotle, it is obviously the founder of the city or its lawgiver who imposes a constitution on a group of people, and that he does so by his competence (*technê*). Seen from this perspective, the process is brought about by efficient causality and in an artificial way. But this simple view is misleading. Even if an effect is brought about by an agent, there is room to acknowledge an impersonal teleological standpoint. It is perfectly possible that the legislator who lays down the constitution intentionally, and the people who accept it willingly, are at the same time guided by the goal-directedness and purposiveness of Nature. Given that a natural generation is, according to Aristotle, a transfer from individual to individual, and given that the master-slave relationship reflects the natural structure of the world, we can infer that Aristotle sees the foundation of a *polis* as both artificial *and* natural. One striking

---

[8] As Schütrumpf 1991, 186–7 points out, the historical development will follow in *Pol.* IV–VI.
[9] But admittedly, cities did not always exist: see *Pol.* I.2, 1252b16–27 on 'pre-political monarchies' and further Pellegrin 2015, 43.

example for this has been admitted by Keyt (1991, 119): the founding of one city by another. Aristotle's genealogical account of the *polis* is, in a sense, not that far away from his genealogical account of bird's nests, beehives, anthills, and the like.

One important piece of evidence for this teleological reading of *Pol.* I.2 is Aristotle's claim that nature is the end of something (τέλος γὰρ αὕτη ἐκείνων, ἡ δὲ φύσις τέλος ἐστίν: 1252b31–2). If we look again at Text [3] from the *De anima*, we find an explanation for this. The nature of an entity actually prefigures its end, and in arriving at its end an entity realizes or perfects its nature. In the context of *Pol.* I.2, the passage reads as follows (1252b31–1253a1):

> [5] For it [sc. the *polis*] is the end of them, and the nature of a thing is its end. For what each thing is when fully developed, we call its nature, whether we are speaking of a man, a horse, or a household [i.e. family]. Besides, the final cause and end of a thing is the best, and to be self-sufficing is the end and the best.

Obviously Text [5] is difficult to reconcile with the minimalist interpretation. Aristotle does not claim that the naturalness of the city is derived from the naturalness of the first impulses in human beings, but contends that the naturalness of the city is based on the naturalness of its end. His idea is that being natural for an *x* is based precisely on *x*'s reaching its essential end. I think that passage [5] even excludes a minimalist reading. The causal process as described in *Pol.* I.2 (starting from singular couplings and ending up with the city) *does not constitute* the naturalness of the *polis*. What Aristotle says is that human beings, and likewise horses or households, are natural *because* they have a tendency, expressed for example in the first social drives that exist in humans, to realize their full natures which are their ends. The naturalness of the *polis* is ultimately based not on efficient, but on final causality. Self-sufficiency (*autarkeia*) is that best state of a human community, its *phusis*, for which the entire process is undertaken. The transfer argument thus amounts to an argument from the goal-directedness of elementary impulses and communities.

To conclude, although the word *phuomena* (1252a24) in our chapter indicates a causal process, the minimalist reading of Rapp, who understands the process as a simple case of efficient causality, is insufficient. For Aristotle efficient causality, which proceeds from basic impulses towards the self-sufficient community, is attracted by its goal and so in a sense moves from the goal to the starting-point. Since Aristotle declares that the city is the *telos* of the other two more elementary communities (*koinōniai*), the household and the village, and since he says that nature is the end of a thing, the entire process should be seen as directed by its final cause, namely the *polis* as the human habitat provided by Nature.

4 *Autarkeia*, *ergon*, and the eudaimonist reading

For Aristotle, human beings are by nature directed towards the end of leading a good and happy life. Such a life cannot be reached outside the *polis*, since only the city enables human beings to live in a perfect and independent way, that is, according to *autarkeia*. This consideration may be seen as favouring a eudaimonist reading of *Pol.* I.2, as suggested by Fred D. Miller Jr. (1995), among others. Miller basically acknowledges the presence of the transfer argument in our text, but reads it from a eudaimonist perspective, roughly as follows. Like all other entities that have a natural *ergon*, human beings too have a specific function, namely the intellectual activity of the highest part of their souls (according to *EN* I.7). Humans cannot, however, achieve this in isolation; they must partake in social communities. On the one hand they have many needs for which only a community of people is sufficient, on the other hand they show a natural inclination to live together even beyond mere necessity (cf. *EN* XI.9, 1169b17–19). The *polis* then appears as a necessary instrument for the realisation of human nature, since only the *polis* guarantees the best circumstances for the fulfilment of the human goal by providing the appropriate preconditions for a life of *autarkeia*. The crucial passage for this is *Pol.* III.9 (1280b39–1281a4):

> [6] Therefore the end of a city is the good life (τέλος μὲν οὖν πόλεως τὸ εὖ ζῆν), and these things are means to that end. And a city is the partnership of clans and villages in a full and independent life (πόλις δὲ ἡ γενῶν καὶ κωμῶν κοινωνία ζωῆς τελείας καὶ αὐτάρκους), which in our view constitutes a happy and noble life (τοῦτο δ' ἐστίν, ὡς φαμέν, τὸ ζῆν εὐδαιμόνως καὶ καλῶς); political fellowship must therefore be deemed to exist for the sake of noble actions, not merely for living in common.

For Miller, the naturalness of the city is hence due to its instrumental role within the process of human self-perfection and *eudaimonia*. Even if he, by contrast with Rapp, broadly accepts that biological teleology is at work in our chapter, he rather emphasizes the eudaimonist element.[10] In my view Miller's interpretation is advantageous compared to the minimalist reading since it can better ac-

---

[10] As Miller 1995, 45 writes: "On Aristotle's view the natural end of human beings can be fully realized only through habituation and education. Hence, this sense of 'nature' as a natural end is closely related to the extended sense in which the *polis* exists 'by nature' in *Politics*, I 2: the *polis* arises out of human nature (in the strict sense) and is also necessary for the fulfilment of human nature (in the sense of an end). Aristotle's failure to distinguish explicitly these different senses of 'nature' is a source of misunderstanding, but [...] his theory that the *polis* exists by nature is internally consistent."

count for Aristotle's remark that the *polis* is the end of human beings (cf. Text [5]). But I think it is still somewhat lacking, because it stresses too much the subjective teleology of the agent striving for a good life. One should go one step further than Miller by accentuating the biological form of final causality at work here. In my view the three Aristotelian theses – the natural existence thesis, the natural anthropology thesis, and the natural priority thesis – are based on the idea of an external goal-directed process that unfolds within biological teleology.

In several of his biological writings, Aristotle spells out the idea that there is a species-appropriate endowment of individuals that helps them to survive. This includes the equipment of living beings with organs, instincts, faculties, and environmental factors[11] – an idea also highly appreciated (although in a modernized sense) by Foot, Nussbaum, and Thompson. 'Having a nature' or 'being by nature' means that something has a *phusis* as an internal principle of goal-directedness (as famously formulated in *Phys*. II.1). It is hence not the case that, first, humans strive for their happiness and only then found cities as a necessary means to that end, but they have in themselves an original drive for founding cities and then realize that, in such a habitat, they can fulfil their endowments. This is valid not only for natural substances, but also for social entities; the three examples Aristotle mentions are human, horse and household (*oikia*, in the sense of a family).

To corroborate this, let us look at Aristotle's transition from the naturalness of the city to his observation that man is by nature a political animal in *Pol*. I.2, 1253a1–7:

> [7] Hence it is evident that the city is a creation of nature, and that man is by nature a political animal. And he who by nature and not by mere accident is without a city, is either a bad man or above humanity; he is like the "tribeless, lawless, heartless one" whom Homer denounces – the natural outcast is forthwith a lover of war; he may be compared to an isolated piece at draughts.

In this passage we find an unambiguous use of the term 'nature' in the sense of a biological teleology. Nature is what is both the goal of an entity and what leads it to strive for that goal. Aristotle wants to point out here the correspondence between the *polis* and the endowment of human beings. Since it is a common tendency of all human beings to live in cities (since otherwise, their lives would be poor and deprived) we have to conclude that the city is the natural habitat for

---

11 One might take as an example the endowment of human beings with hands in *De partibus animalium* IV.10; see Pellegrin 2015, 36.

men. The endowment of human beings is immediately correlated with the natural living conditions for which it is determined. It is hence not enough to read *Pol.* I.2 in a eudaimonist sense without integrating this eudaimonism into the framework of natural teleology.

There is more evidence in support of this point. According to *Pol.* I.2, certain anthropological features confirm that man is destined or determined to live his life in a certain way (1252a35–b9):

> [8] Now nature has distinguished between the female and the slave. For nature is not niggardly, like the smith who fashions the Delphian knife for many uses; she makes each thing for a single use (οὐθὲν γὰρ ἡ φύσις ποιεῖ τοιοῦτον οἷον οἱ χαλκοτύποι τὴν Δελφικὴν μάχαιραν, πενιχρῶς, ἀλλ' ἓν πρὸς ἕν), and every instrument is best made when intended for one and not for many uses. But among barbarians no distinction is made between women and slaves, because there is no natural ruler among them: they are a community of slaves, male and female. Wherefore the poets say, "It is meet that Hellenes should rule over barbarians"; as if they thought that the barbarian and the slave were by nature one.

Following Aristotle, Nature is not parsimonious. What he apparently means is that a natural thing does not resemble a Swiss army knife. Natural arrangements are never multifunctional; they are always definite and unambiguous since they have to be optimally suited for their respective functions. His point seems to be that if nature had produced the female as that which is, at the same time, the slavish, it would have generated something ambiguous, something having a double function. But this is excluded. The principle "Nature does nothing niggardly" (1252b1–3) is clearly a teleological one, hinting in the direction of a perfectionist teleology.

Immediately after this, still in our quotation [8], Aristotle conveys this idea in a slightly different way, claiming that "Nature equips each instrument it produces in the best possible way" (*houtō gar an apoteloito kalliston tōn organōn hekaston*, 1252b3–5). Such a principle is well known from Plato's teleology in the *Phaedo* and the *Timaeus*, although many scholars – such as Leroi (2014) – see fundamental differences between Plato's and Aristotle's accounts of teleology.[12]

---

[12] Leroi 2014, 86–8 regards Plato's teleology as 'unnatural' and based on the idea of a 'natural designer', while he ascribes to Aristotle a 'functional biology'. But I think that this contrast is mistaken. In the *Phaedo*, this approach to natural causality famously appears in Socrates' story of his disappointment with Anaxagoras, whom he expected to expound the thesis that *nous* "ordered everything and is the cause of everything" (*nous estin ho diakosmōn te kai pantōn aitios*, 97b9–10). Aristotle twice gives a very similar criticism of the misleading position of Anaxagoras (*Met.* I.3, 984b8–22 and in I.4, 985a18–22). He fully accepts the Platonic idea, expressed by Socrates, that reason brings everything into an optimal order and locates all things to their

This formula basically amounts to the thesis that natural things must be seen as purposive or goal-directed; they possess endowments which make them optimally suited for the fulfilment of their tasks and ultimately for survival. In this sense, all natural entities can be functionally described, i.e. by a biological teleology.[13]

In our chapter we encounter another indication for such a teleology, namely the principle "Nature does nothing in vain" (οὐθὲν γὰρ [...] μάτην ἡ φύσις ποιεῖ, 1253a9). It appears within the best-known consideration to be found in *Pol.* I.2, namely the argument from the purposiveness of language (1253a7–18):

> [9] Now, that man is more of a political animal than bees or any other gregarious animals is evident. Nature, as we often say, makes nothing in vain, and man is the only animal whom she has endowed with the gift of speech. And whereas mere voice is but an indication of pleasure or pain, and is therefore found in other animals (for their nature attains to the perception of pleasure and pain and the intimation of them to one another, and no further), the power of speech is intended to set forth the expedient and inexpedient, and therefore likewise the just and the unjust. And it is a characteristic of man that he alone has any sense of good and evil, of just and unjust, and the like, and the association of living beings who have this sense makes a family and a state.

Peter Simpson in his commentary (1998, 23) has pointed out, I think correctly, that the linguistic argument cannot be understood if one does not read it as a teleological consideration:

> It may be stated thus: (1) nature makes nothing in vain; (2) only humans possess by nature reasoned speech (*logos*), whereas animals merely possess voice; (3) reasoned speech serves to make plain what is advantageous or harmful, just and unjust, good and bad, or it enables human beings to commune with each other about these things (perception of which they alone have among animals) and community in these things makes a household and a city. From (2) and (3) it follows that (4) only humans have by nature something whose point (or part of whose point) is the community of the city, namely the sharing together about good, bad, just, and unjust. From (4) and (1) it follows that (5) humans must be nat-

---

best (*ton ge noun kosmounta panta kosmein kai hekaston tithenai tautê hopê an beltista echê*: 97c4–5).

[13] Does the *hōs* ('as if', 1252b9) indicate some sort of anti-realism? I don't think so. It may be explained in light of the fact that Aristotle derives his point from the sayings of poets. Apparently the meaning of the passage is that certain things fit together by a sort of pre-established connectedness. They are, on Aristotle's view, parts of a teleological unity. But two further questions arise. The first is whether Aristotle assumes a universal teleology in which the city has a natural place; I will return to this question later. The second problem is whether the "Nature does nothing in vain" formula is to be understood in an anthropocentric sense, as David Sedley (1991; 2000) contended with regard to *Physics* II.8. Is the human the entity in the universe towards which the organisation of everything is directed? I think that Aristotle conceives of the universe as teleologically organized to the best, but not solely to the best of human beings.

urally political and more political than any other animal. For if nature does nothing in vain, she must, in giving humans speech, have made them for what speech is itself for, namely life in the city; and since she gave speech to humans alone, she must have made humans more political than all other animals to which she gave merely voice.

The linguistic argument from passage [9] clearly implies a conclusion from a natural endowment of a species to its appropriate habitat. The habitat, accordingly, precedes its inhabitants in a certain sense; this is what Aristotle means by the natural priority thesis. The *polis* is necessary in order to realize and fulfil a basic endowment of humans, language, and it is therefore the constitutive framework for human life. There exists some sort of pre-established harmony between a species and its habitat. It is in the same vein, I think, that we should also read Aristotle's argument from priority or homonymy (*Pol.* I.2, 1253a18–29):

> [10] Further, the city is by nature clearly prior to the family and to the individual, since the whole is of necessity prior to the part; for example, if the whole body be destroyed, there will be no foot or hand, except in an equivocal sense, as we might speak of a stone hand; for when destroyed the hand will be no better than that. But things are defined by their working and power; and we ought not to say that they are the same when they no longer have their proper quality, but only that they have the same name. The proof that the city is a creation of nature and prior to the individual is that the individual, when isolated, is not self-sufficing; and therefore he is like a part in relation to the whole. But he who is unable to live in society, or who has no need because he is sufficient for himself, must be either a beast or a god: he is no part of a city.

What Text [10] says is, again, that the city as the human habitat in a substantial sense precedes individual beings. According to the natural priority thesis, an isolated human would be a 'human' only in a homonymous sense. To illustrate his point, Aristotle uses the comparison of a hand: the function of a hand depends completely on its being a part of the human body. If we take that comparison literally, it implies that humans receive their full function only in the *polis*. Aristotle thus accepts a pre-established correlation between humans and their habitat in the same sense in which he speaks of an animal's living conditions. Humans have to lead their lives within the teleologically organized context of a city.

Nevertheless, this need not amount to some sort of political organicism. The *polis*, as he been pointed out for example by Wolfgang Kullmann (1991), is not an *ousia*. This context precedes the individual not the way that substance precedes its accidents, but in the sense of a necessary condition for full development. Additionally, while Miller's line of interpretation is basically correct with regard to human happiness, the eudaimonist interpretation somewhat misses the point insofar as it is not the natural endowment of humans that explains the qualities their habitat must have. It is the other way around: the natural endowment of humans depends on the context of the *polis*, the form of cooperation for which it is made. Hence, although Aristotle thinks that the *polis* is not a social organism, but composed of independent individuals (what Miller 1995, 46–7 calls 'priority in separateness'), the living conditions of humans are prior to their natural endowment (in the sense of a 'priority in completeness').[14] The city provides the necessary conditions to such an extent that humans outside the city exist as humans only homonymously. Thus, Aristotle claims that, if a city is lacking, this is seriously detrimental to human beings; an individual outside the city becomes the rudest of all beings on earth (*cheiriston pantōn*, 1253a33). If the lack of an appropriate habitat makes a human the worst creature on earth, its presence allows the human to be the most excellent animal.

As we have already seen, the teleological rationale for the city doesn't rule out its being founded artificially by humans. In *Pol.* I.2 being 'by nature' and being 'by human art' are not mutually exclusive. Cities are founded by people, but essentially pre-established by nature. Aristotle explicitly says that when someone first establishes a city, he is the 'greatest benefactor' (*megistōn agathōn aitios*, 1253a31). The passage runs as follows (*Pol.* I.2, 1253a29–39):

> [11] A social instinct is implanted in all men by nature, and yet he who first founded the city was the greatest of benefactors. For man, when perfected, is the best of animals, but, when separated from law and justice, he is the worst of all; since armed injustice is the more dangerous, and he is equipped at birth with arms, meant to be used by intelligence and virtue, which he may use for the worst ends. Wherefore, if he have not virtue, he is the most unholy and the most savage of animals, and the most full of lust and gluttony. But justice is the bond of men in cities, for the administration of justice, which is the determination of what is just, is the principle of order in political society.

The text emphasizes that the foundation of cities is based on a natural drive present in all humans. Aristotle does not discuss the idea of a natural drive in opposition to reflective decision-making. On the contrary, the natural impulse is precisely what leads a human being to the full moral and intellectual identity of the 'second nature'. This is a point that has also been pointed out by Trott (2014).

5 The internal cause reading

Adriel Trott (2014) develops the idea that, according to Aristotle, nature and reason are not in opposition to one another, as many interpreters have assumed.

---

[14] See also Weber 2015, 118–124.

Nature, Trott contends, should not be understood as the realm of the given, especially not as the materially given. Nor should nature be taken in the sense of that which is constant or invariant. For Trott Aristotelian nature should be understood as the internal source of movement, as *archê kinêseōs*. Conversely, Trott takes *logos* – the characteristic human endowment, following *Pol.* I.2 – not as a faculty to identify the invariant truth, but as practical deliberation within a community.

Trott's line of interpretation might be summarized as follows. Aristotle's thesis that the *polis* exists by nature seems at first glance to be at odds with his remarks about natural entities in *Physics* II.1. There he states that natural beings are animals and their parts, as well as plants and the elemental bodies (earth, fire, air, and water). He contrasts these with artefacts existing by human *technê*; clearly the city seems to belong to the second group. In order to understand why he interprets the city as natural, even though it is deliberatively founded and organized by human beings, one must note that Aristotle leaves room for further entities, to which certain descriptive features of naturalness can be applied. The decisive point for the naturalness of an entity is that it possesses within itself the principle (*archê*) of change and stability. The principle of change in natural entities is a teleological one, the final cause, as can be seen from a crucial passage in the *Physics* (II.1, 193b12–18):

> [12] We also speak of a thing's nature as being exhibited in the process of growth by which its nature is attained (ἔτι δ' ἡ φύσις ἡ λεγομένη ὡς γένεσις ὁδός ἐστιν εἰς φύσιν). The 'nature' in this sense is not like 'doctoring', which leads not to the art of doctoring but to health. Doctoring must start from the art, not lead to it. But it is not in this way that nature (in the one sense) is related to nature (in the other). What grows qua growing grows from something into something. Into what then does it grow? Not into that from which it arose but into that to which it tends. The shape then is nature (ἡ ἄρα μορφὴ φύσις).

According to Trott's interpretation this passage describes nature as a dynamic principle that inspires men to live a life of political activity. The *phusis* of the *polis* is, then, the internal principle that drives the city to realize itself. Trott does not believe that Aristotle defends a natural law-account of normativity (2014, 20). As she says: "Political life is thus not taken to be good just because it is, as if nature is givenness. Political life is good, rather, because it is not imposed on us, but arises in activities whereby we flourish" (2014, 11).

Trott's interpretation may seem to resemble my own reading. I do agree that, in *Pol.* I.2, Nature appears as the end of the developmental process. But contrary to what Trott says, it is the human individual towards which this process is directed. The *phusis* under consideration is the nature of man, not of the *polis*. Some further points against her position are the following:

(1) Trott's claim that the *polis* is natural because it possesses a *phusis* has no sufficient basis in the text. Those entities that are said to have a nature that may be realized are natural substantial beings, namely animals and their parts, plants and the elemental bodies. My own claim is that Nature – not the nature of the *polis* – is the organising principle behind biological teleology.

(2) Aristotle does not say that the *polis has* a nature, only that it exists by nature or naturally (*phusei*). It cannot be said to have a *phusis* since its general end is simply that of the citizens living in it (namely *eudaimonia*), and since its constitutive parts are independent individuals (human beings). Having no *phusis* of its own, the city cannot be said to realize its nature in a developmental process.[15] A *polis* can be *para phusin* as well as *kata phusin*, as we shall see in a moment. But it cannot develop its own *phusis*.

(3) Aristotle's statements regarding the concept of *phusis* do not support the idea of an infinite or open-ended process, like that of political deliberation in a *polis*. The process initiated by nature comes to an end when it is fully actualized in the city. Therefore, it is also incorrect to deny that Aristotelian nature is invariant and eternal. Each entity that possesses a *phusis* has a definite final determination.

Especially the dynamic character of politics, highlighted in Trott's reading, seems to me insufficiently present in the text. As we will see in the next section, Aristotle uses naturalness as a normative criterion for politics precisely in the sense of the later natural law tradition, namely as the transpositive norm which is to be observed in politics.

6 Does naturalness serve as a normative criterion in Aristotle's political philosophy?

One might concede that *Pol.* I.2 contains biological teleology and, nevertheless, have doubts as to whether Aristotle actually uses normative naturalism within his discussions of political and moral reality. Teleology, and the normativity resulting from it, could be seen as merely programmatic ideas or as an irrelevant ornament when it comes to concrete normative questions. But this is wrong. We can show that Aristotle makes a strong use of his normative naturalism. In his discussion of the *phusikon dikaion* and the *nomikon dikaion* in *EN* V.10, he explicitly claims that there is only one political constitution (*politeia*) which is, *by na-*

---

15 These considerations have been already brought forward against an internal cause reading by Miller 1995, 37–40.

ture, everywhere the best: ἀλλὰ μία μόνον πανταχοῦ κατὰ φύσιν ἡ ἀρίστη (1135a5). This statement clearly illustrates that normative naturalism can be applied to political reality, in this case in support of the claim that there is one best constitution.

The importance of normative naturalism for political evaluation becomes evident when we combine two pertinent passages. The first is located in a brief discussion of tyranny (*Pol.* III.17, 1287b37–41):

> [13] For there is by nature both a justice and an advantage appropriate to the rule of a master, another to kingly rule, another to constitutional rule; but there is none naturally appropriate to tyranny, or to any other perverted form of government; for these come into being contrary to nature.

In this passage, Aristotle claims that tyranny is not according to nature (*ouk estin kata phusin*). Like tyranny, he continues, all constitutions which are deviations (*parekbaseis*) are against nature (*para phusin*). The criterion which allows us to distinguish between natural constitutions and unnatural deviations is the orientation of the natural constitution towards common welfare. To this we may add a well-known passage from *Pol.* III.6 (1279a17–21):

> [14] The conclusion is evident: that governments which have a regard to the common interest are constituted in accordance with strict principles of justice, and are therefore true forms; but those that regard only the interest of the rulers are all defective and perverted forms, for they are despotic, whereas a state is a community of freemen.

As we can infer from passages [13] and [14] democracy, oligarchy, and tyranny are, for Aristotle, constitutions contrary to nature. They are against nature by being despotic in their form of governance and by being misdirected in their pursuit of the city's end. One can hardly imagine a more emphatic use of normative naturalism than this application within the debate about constitutions. Additionally, in his criticism of Plato's *kallipolis* Aristotle claims that the *polis* is, by its nature, a plurality; hence, he contends, the idea of unity as advanced in the *Republic* is mistaken (*Pol.* II.2, 1261a18–22; cf. 1261b6–9). In another passage from *Pol.* VII.3 we learn that the principle of rotation – mutual change in leadership – is natural (1325b7–10):

> [15] For equals, the noble and just consists in their taking turns, since this is equal and alike, but for those that are equal to have an unequal share and those that are alike an unlike share is contrary to nature, and nothing contrary to nature is noble (τὸ δὲ μὴ ἴσον τοῖς ἴσοις καὶ τὸ μὴ ὅμοιον τοῖς ὁμοίοις παρὰ φύσιν, οὐδὲν δὲ τῶν παρὰ φύσιν καλόν).

Again, the passage [15] implies an unambiguous appeal to normative naturalism. In *Pol.* VII.3 we are confronted with an interesting passage that throws much light on the natural priority thesis (1326a34–b7):

> [16] Hence that city also must necessarily be the most beautiful with whose magnitude is combined the above-mentioned limiting principle; for certainly beauty is usually found in number and magnitude, but there is a due measure of magnitude for a city as there also is for all other things – animals, plants, tools; each of these, if too small or excessively large, will not possess its own proper efficiency, but in some cases will have entirely lost its true nature and in others will be in a defective condition: for instance, a ship a span long will not be a ship at all, nor will a ship a quarter of a mile long, and even when it reaches a certain size, in some cases smallness and in others excessive largeness will make it sail badly. Similarly a city consisting of too few people will not be self-sufficing (which is an essential quality of a city), and one consisting of too many, though self-sufficing in the mere necessaries, will be so in the way in which a nation is, and not as a city, since it will not be easy for it to possess constitutional government – for who will command its over-swollen multitude in war? Or who will serve as its herald, unless he have the lungs of a Stentor?

Text [16] contends that the right size of a *polis* must be derived from practical considerations: it must be large enough to be self-sufficient, but at the same time small enough to be ruled as a community built on inner connections. As this shows, the *polis* does not possess a nature like an organic substance does. Its nature is derived from the rights and interests of human individuals.

One still might raise a certain objection here. According to what I have called the natural existence thesis, Aristotle claims that each *polis* is by nature (*pasa polis phusei estin*), whereas now he seems to say that the deviations are contrary to nature. I think that the tension can be resolved, though. While every *polis* qua community (*koinōnia*) is by nature, since reproduction and preservation find their ideal habitat in it, it is not the case that each *polis* qua constitution is, since the three deviant constitutions mistake despotic rule for political rule. The *parekbaseis* are hence against nature by their practice of enslavement of a certain group (or all) citizens who are free by nature.

7 Is Aristotle's normative naturalism part of a cosmic order?

My biological understanding of *Pol.* I.2, close to that advanced by Pellegrin (2015), was originally directed against a minimalist reading as proposed by Rapp (2016). The minimalist reading denies that the three Aristotelian theses mentioned above should be traced back to a teleology of nature. Seen from this perspective, Aristotle would not be opposed to Hobbes. The city would not be established by nature, but by humans. According to this interpretation, the existence of the *polis* is simply an expression of elementary human impulses. If we follow the reading of Rapp, Aristotle would transfer the naturalness of these impulses and from elementary communities to the fully developed cities. Although I concede that this 'transfer argument' is in the text and even plays a significant role, I do not believe that *Pol.* I.2 can be sufficiently understood following the minimalist reading. Furthermore, my interpretation is, to some extent, directed against the eudaimonist reading as we find it in, for instance Miller (1995). Again, although it is convincing that the naturalness in *Pol.* I.2 has to do with perfection and *autarkeia*, happiness provides no sufficient ground for Aristotle's position. We have to go one important step further, even if it is a strange step from our contemporary perspective. Finally, nature as internal cause – as we find it in *Physics* II.1 – is present to some extent in our chapter; but the internal cause reading turns out to be overstated, especially in the version advanced by Trott (2014).

Let me now conclude with some brief remarks on the metaphysical context of Aristotle's normative naturalism. What he has to say about human beings leading their lives under the cooperative living conditions of a *polis* is apparently part of a comprehensive, universal sort of teleology. As we already saw, Aristotle formulates a principle of cosmic order in *Pol.* I.5 (Text [4]). Aristotle emphasizes the naturalness and ubiquity of order in the universe. He defends, I think, a *naturalism of order.* What Nature does is to impose regularity and hierarchy onto the changeable entities in the world. The political community is only one form of that ordering activity.

When in the *De Caelo* Aristotle uses the formula "Nature does nothing in vain", he does so by saying: *ho de theos kai hê phusis ouden matên poiousin* (*De Cael.* I.4, 271a33). The reference to the *theos* must clearly mean that an overarching cosmic principle is at work. Aristotle thinks that the order of the world is in its best possible state, as he claims in several passages. A key text is *Met.* XII.10, 1075a11–25:

> [17] We must consider also in which of two ways the nature of the universe contains the good, and the highest good, whether as something separate and by itself, or as the order of the parts. Probably in both ways, as an army does; for its good is found both in its order and in its leader, and more in the latter; for he does not depend on the order but it depends on him. And all things are ordered together somehow, but not all alike, both fishes and fowls and plants; and the world is not such that one thing has nothing to do with another, but they are connected. For all are ordered together to one end, but it is as in a house, where the freemen are least at liberty to act at random, but all things or

most things are already ordained for them, while the slaves and the animals do little for the common good, and for the most part live at random; for this is the sort of principle that constitutes the nature of each. I mean, for instance, that all must at least come to be dissolved into their elements, and there are other functions similarly in which all share for the good of the whole.

The universe, following Text [17], is organized according to the paradigm of an army or a household. This means, as I have argued elsewhere (Horn 2016), that Nature in Aristotle should be seen as the structuring principle that organizes the universe so that the universe can be said to "contain the good and the best" (τὸ ἀγαθὸν καὶ τὸ ἄριστον, 1075a12). For the political sphere this principle implies a strong version of normative naturalism which anticipates the later natural law tradition.

Primary literature

Aristotle. 1957. *Aristotelis Politica*, by William D. Ross. Oxford: Oxford Clarendon Press.
Aristotle. 1990. *Aristoteles' Politik*, edited by Günther Patzig. Göttingen: Vandenhoeck & Ruprecht.
Aristotle. 1991. *Aristoteles, Politik I* (=Aristoteles, Werke in deutscher Übersetzung 9.1), by Eckhart Schütrumpf. Berlin: Akademie.
Aristotle. 1995. *Aristotle, Politics, Books I–II*, by Trevor J. Saunders. Oxford: Oxford Clarendon Press.

Secondary literature

Annas, Julia. 1993. *The Morality of Happiness*. New York and Oxford: Oxford University Press.
Bolton, Robert. 1997. "The Material Cause: Matter and Explanation in Aristotle's Natural Science." In *Aristotelische Biologie. Intentionen, Methoden, Ergebnisse*, edited by Wolfgang Kullmann and Sabine Föllinger, 97–124. Stuttgart: Franz Steiner Verlag.
Fiedler, Wilfried. 1978. *Analogiemodelle bei Aristoteles. Untersuchungen zu den Vergleichen zwischen den einzelnen Wissenschaften und Künsten*. Amsterdam: Grüner.
Horn, Christoph. 2016. "The Unity of the World-Order According to *Metaphysics* Lambda 10." In *Aristotle's Metaphysics Lambda. New Essays*, edited by Christoph Horn, 269–293. Berlin: De Gruyter.
Keyt, David. 1991. "Three Basic Theorems in Aristotle's Politics." In *A Companion to Aristotle's Politics*, edited by David Keyt and Fred D. Miller Jr., 118–141. Oxford and Cambridge: Blackwell.
Kraut, Richard. 2002. *Aristotle. Political Philosophy*. Oxford: Oxford University Press.

Kullmann, Wolfgang. 1991. "Man as a Political Animal in Aristotle." In *A Companion to Aristotle's Politics*, edited by David Keyt and Fred D. Miller Jr., 94–117. Oxford and Cambridge: Blackwell.

Labarrière, Jean-Louis. 2004. *Langage, Vie Politique, et Mouvement des Animaux. Études aristotéliciennes*. Paris: Vrin.

Leroi, Armand Marie. 2014. *The Lagoon. How Aristotle Invented Science*. New York: Penguin.

Miller Jr., Fred D. 1995. *Nature, Justice, and Rights in Aristotle's Politics*. Oxford: Oxford University Press.

Mulgan, Richard G. 1974. "Aristotle's Doctrine that Man is a Political Animal." *Hermes* 102:438–445.

Mulgan, Richard G. 1977. *Aristotle's Political Theory*. Oxford: Oxford Clarendon Press.

Pellegrin, Pierre. 2015. "Is Politics a Natural Science?" In *Aristotle's Politics. A Critical Guide*, edited by Thornton Lockwood and Thanassis Samaras, 27–45. Cambridge: Cambridge University Press.

Rapp, Christof. 2010. "Was heißt 'Aristotelismus' in der neueren Ethik?" *Information Philosophie* 1/10:20–30.

Rapp, Christof. 2016. "'Der Staat existiert von Natur aus' – Über eine befremdliche These im ersten Buch der Aristotelischen *Politik*.' In *Menschennatur und politische Ordnung*, edited by Andreas Höfele and Beate Kellner, 45–77. Paderborn: Wilhelm Fink.

Sedley, David. 1991. "Is Aristotle's Teleology Anthropocentric?" *Phronesis* 36:179–96.

Sedley, David. 2000. "Metaphysics Lambda 10." In *Aristotle's Metaphysics Lambda. Symposium Aristotelicum*, edited by Michael Frede and David Charles, 327–350. Oxford: Oxford University Press.

Simpson, Peter L.P. 1998. *A Philosophical Commentary on the Politics of Aristotle*. Chapel Hill: University of North Carolina Press.

Trott, Adriel. 2014. *Aristotle on the Nature of Community*. Cambridge: Cambridge University Press.

Weber, Simon. 2015. *Herrschaft und Recht bei Aristoteles*. Berlin and New York: De Gruyter.

Christof Rapp
Whose State? Whose Nature? How Aristotle's *Polis* is 'Natural'

Abstract: It is sometimes held that in Aristotle's *Politics*, the *polis* has a nature of its own not unlike an organism, which brings with it a range of teleological norms. Against this, it is here argued that the puzzling claim that 'the state exists by nature' can best be explained by supposing that for Aristotle, the state exists in accordance with *human* nature. This is shown through an analysis of the structure of the opening chapters of the *Politics*, which reveals that not only *poleis* but also more rudimentary social arrangements ('first communities') like families and villages are established by humans in accordance with their natural desires and needs. Thus the *polis* is not legitimized and normalized through arbitrary references to nature, but solely through its relation to human nature.

1 Introduction

Near the beginning of his *Politics*, Aristotle claims that every state (*polis*) exists by nature. He bases this claim mainly on the assumptions (i) that the state emerges from the connection between man and woman, master and slave, from the households that derive from these two earlier connections and from the villages that emerge from several households, (ii) that the first connections (in particular the connection between man and woman aiming at reproduction) are brought together by natural impulses, and (iii) that there is a continuous path leading from the first connections to the foundation of a state. Aristotle's claim raises, above all, two sorts of questions. First, one might wonder in what sense of 'natural' a state can be plausibly called 'natural'. After all, the coming about of a state requires the consent and purposeful intervention of a number of human beings, so that it cannot be natural in the sense that it would come about without human intervention. Second, one might wonder why Aristotle stresses this point so much right at the beginning of the treatise and whether he takes this claim to have important consequences (most notably, normative ones) for the assessment of particular states, their political constitutions and institutions, etc. With regard to the first question I am going to argue that Aristotle's claim should be read as saying – surprising as this may seem – that the state exists *in accordance with human nature*. This suggested reading is not only different from most of the prevailing interpretations, it also limits the range of possible answers to the second question regarding the implications of this claim.[1]

2 A puzzling claim

What does Aristotle mean by saying that the state exists by nature? At first glance this claim is really puzzling, if not outlandish. In everyday life, when we ask whether something is natural or not, we are mostly interested in whether this thing has come about with or without human intervention, e.g. whether it came about through artificial design, whether it was manipulated, whether it contains additives, and so on. In this sense of 'being natural' and 'coming about by nature' a state can never be natural, because it is an assembly consisting of human beings and because it requires some amount of consent, planning and organization, so that it cannot come about without human intervention. In fact, Aristotle himself mentions the merits of the one who first brought about a political community (*Pol.* I.2, 1253a30 – 31). For the same reason, the state is not 'natural' in the sense that it can be found in nature in the absence of humans (e.g. out in the jungle). Some scholars relate the claim to Aristotle's treatment of beehives and ant-colonies, because Aristotle calls animals living in those colonies 'political'; however, non-human animals cannot have a state or *polis* (*Pol.* III.9, 1280a31– 36), so that the attribute 'political' does not relate them to a *polis* in a literal sense, which is in turn why *poleis* cannot be found in non-human nature. Sometimes in the history of ideas and also in the Aristotelian tradition, the notion of nature takes on theological significance, so that, in the end, saying that something is natural amounts to saying that it is 'willed by God'. Adopting such a notion of nature, Aristotle's claim about the state might mean that the existence of states is in accordance with a divine plan. This might work e.g. for Christian Aristotelians; however, the Aristotelian God does not seem to 'will' anything – except thinking all day long.

Other interpreters of Aristotle read the passage in light of Aristotle's theory of nature and natural beings in his *Physics*. There, Aristotle distinguishes natural

---

[1] The first version of this paper I presented at a colloquium of the GANPH (Gesellschaft für Antike Philosophie) in Trier 2015; in 2015 and 2016 more elaborate versions were presented at workshops at the Ludwig-Maximilians-Universität in Munich. An earlier version of parts of the text (especially sections 3 and 4) was published in Rapp 2016. Christoph Horn was so kind as to deliver replies first to the oral presentation and then to the written version of it (see Horn's contribution to the present volume). I am genuinely grateful that he helped me through his criticism to find shortcomings in the previous formulation of my ideas.

from non-natural beings through an "internal principle of motion and rest."[2] These interpreters thus assume that by his puzzling claim in the *Politics*, Aristotle wants to assign such an 'internal principle' to the state. From the beginning, this attempt does not seem very promising (and has often been rejected), since there are significant differences between states on the one hand and the natural beings from Aristotle's *Physics*, and, in particular from natural substances[3] on the other. Nonetheless, variants of this interpretation have appeared again and again. Recently, Adriel M. Trott (2014, 81) wrote: "Since nature is an internal principle by which we move to our end, the *polis* is natural because it moves from within itself to fulfil itself in this activity." In this quote she seems to recognize the challenge that faces every adherent of the 'internal principle'-interpretation, namely the need to identify such a principle within the state: she links this principle with a *polis*' movement to fulfil itself in its specific activity. Elsewhere, she identifies the latter as "the activity that is definitive of it, deliberation about what counts as living well" (Trott 2014, 41). The problem with this sort of reading is that, strictly speaking, states do not deliberate at all, because deliberation is the activity of a soul, and states are not generally understood to have a soul, at least not in the literal sense. In this context, furthermore, we have to insist on the difference between literal and non-literal: the reason Aristotle's claim is so puzzling is that it *literally* says that states exist by nature.

Most scholars who comment on our passage emphasize in one way or another that Aristotle's concept of nature is teleological. What they seem to mean is that we have to look at the end or completion of the development of the state. It is easy to agree on that much. After all this is Aristotle; and he explicitly refers to the end (*telos*) of the development that has started with the initial associations between men and women for the purpose of reproduction. However, the reference to teleology might be misleading for the question of what precisely it means that the state exists by nature. Mostly, interpreters refer to the so-called 'telic argument', by which they mean the passage in which Aristotle points out that "whatever each thing is when its growth is completed, we speak of as being the nature of that thing, for instance of a man, a horse, a house" (*Pol.* I.2, 1252b32–34). The completed development of each thing reveals *its nature*, i.e. its essence, which is indeed an important Aristotelian theorem. However, it does not really pertain to the question whether and how something exists *by nature*, since artefacts – which in an important sense do not exist by nature –

---

[2] Aristotle, *Phys.* II.1, 192b13–15.
[3] It seems that Aristotle ascribes this internal principle to natural substances only: *Phys.* II.1, 192b32–33.

also have an essence or nature, which is also revealed by the completion of the process through which they come into being. It also applies to the nature/essence of a house, as Aristotle himself says in the quoted passage, and to the nature/essence of the tragedy (*Poetics* 4, 1449a15). Neither houses nor tragedies exist *by nature*, at least not in any common sense of existing by nature. For this reason, it is clearly insufficient to refer to the teleological concept of nature or to the 'telic argument' in *Pol.* I.2 to settle the question on what grounds the state can be said to exist by nature.

Finally, a brief remark on the philosophical significance of Aristotle's claim that the state exists by nature. It has often been associated with a position called 'political naturalism'[4] and has even been mentioned in connection with Aristotle's purported theory of natural law and justice (Miller 1991). 'Political naturalism' might be interpreted in various ways, but it seems to imply, at any rate, that the state and its institutions are measured by standards provided by nature. If this is so, it clearly matters whether Aristotle's puzzling claim about the state is part of this political naturalism and what kind of nature is evoked by saying that the state exists by nature. In our review of the basic options for understanding Aristotle's claim that the state exists by nature, we have observed that some scholars tend to align the existence of the state with the existence of natural substances, such as plants or animals. If one grants that this is Aristotle's intention, one might be tempted to evaluate states by the same standards by which we assess other natural beings,[5] such as organisms. Obviously, such an assumption would impose non-trivial constraints on any interpretation of Aristotle's political theory and might even suggest a sort of political organicism. In my view, this is not what we find in the rest of Aristotle's *Politics*: he is not interested in assessing states and their institutions by comparing them to organisms and other natural substances. In any case, the interpretation of Aristotle's claim that the state exists by nature clearly has philosophically salient ramifications for the understanding of his political theory as a whole.

---

[4] Miller 1989; 1991; 1995; 2000; Horn (this volume).
[5] This is how I understand Knoll (2009, 161–62) when he writes (my translation): "Justice, which exists by nature, also dictates, according to Aristotle, who in a *polis* should be the sovereign naturally and legitimately and under what conditions what types of dominion and constitution are natural and just. Just as the inner order of a human being, the inner order of a *polis* has to be guided by the given natural order and its principles of ordering and distribution. In order to make these theses plausible, let us begin by reminding the reader that he (Aristotle) sees both a human being and the *polis* as parts of nature. Aristotle conceives of the *polis* – just like the original communities between man and woman, master and slave, household and village – as an entity that exists by nature."

3 The structure and argument of *Pol.* I.2

Together, Chapters I.1 and I.2 provide a sort of preamble to Aristotle's *Politics*. In the first sentence of the treatise Aristotle claims that the state or *polis* is a sort of community, that each and every community is constituted with a view to some good, and that the political community, i.e. the *polis*, stands out by aiming at the most supreme good that includes all other goods (*Pol.* I.1, 1252a1–7). In a way, this statement provides a template for parts of the discussion that follow in *Pol.* I.2. The connection between the two chapters is slightly obscured though by two brief remarks that follow upon the opening statement in I.1. The first, programmatic, remark (1252a7–16) states – against accounts such as that developed in Plato's *Statesman* – that political leadership is not like ruling a big household but is different in kind from ruling any other type of community. The second, methodological, remark (1252a17–23) points out that, since the *polis* is a composite, one needs to consider its smallest parts. This brings us to the verge of *Pol.* I.2, where Aristotle first briefly announces that in the political subject, as in others, it is recommendable to study the origin of things. Afterwards he immediately enters into a long stretch of argument about the origin and development of the *polis* (1252a26–b30) intended to show that every *polis* exists by nature (*dio pasa polis phusei estin*) (1252b30). This is the first important conclusion reached in this chapter:

C1 The *polis* exists by nature.

3.1 The main argument (leading to C1, C1* and C2)

The argument leading to C1 is commonly called 'the genetic argument'. It is based on a view of the state or *polis* as emerging from the connection between man and woman, master and slave, from the household that resulted when these two unions are combined, and from the villages that are formed through the founding of households. The two main ideas that he first puts forth as evidence seem to be, firstly, that the aforementioned communities originate from a natural impulse, and secondly, that the emergence of the village from the households and the *polis* from the villages constitutes a continuous development. Thus what ultimately emerges, the *polis*, must itself exist by nature, given that the original stimulus for this development was natural and the development itself was continuous, in that it has always been directed toward the gradual attainment of self-sufficiency, a condition unique to the *polis*.

Shortly after stating the conclusion C1 – indeed, only five lines later – Aristotle reiterates this conclusion and expands upon it (1253a1–3), now taking it as proven that the *polis* is among the things that exist by nature and that man is by nature a political animal (ἐκ τούτων οὖν φανερὸν ὅτι τῶν φύσει ἡ πόλις ἐστί, καὶ ὅτι ὁ ἄνθρωπος φύσει πολιτικὸν ζῷον). The argument therefore results in two conclusions (C1* and C2), the first (C1*) just being a variant of C1.

C1* The *polis* is among the things that exist *by nature*.
C2 Man is by nature a political animal.

It is controversial how to describe the argumentative move that took place in the five lines between C1 and C1*. Is it an additional argument for the same conclusion? Or is it more like an explication of how C1 was reached? We will come back to this.

At any rate, after stating C2 Aristotle takes the time to develop the thought that human beings are by nature political animals (1253a3–18). In this section he introduces, among other things, the idea that only human beings are equipped with language and that it is through language that we communicate about what is beneficial/harmful or what is just/unjust, and that the participation in these things are crucial for the *polis*. Apart from minor ambiguities, this is a straightforward and plausible passage.

3.2 The priority argument

The next passage (1253a18–29), by contrast, is perhaps one of the strangest in the *Politics* (and the *Politics* includes plenty of strange passages) and has led to bewildering interpretations. Aristotle argues that the *polis* is prior to the household and to its individual members; hence I will call it the 'priority argument'. Of course, it cannot be prior in a temporal sense, according to the genetic argument. But Aristotle often recognizes alternative senses of being prior, and it seems clear that we should think here of some non-temporal meaning of priority, for example, priority in being, substance, definition, or essence. For example, the boy is temporally prior to the adult man, but, according to Aristotle, the adult man, by constituting the completion of a development, is prior in essence or being. At any rate, Aristotle argues in the present passage of the *Politics* that the *polis* is prior to its parts in the sense that the whole is prior to its parts, and that the parts of the whole taken in isolation are no longer what they used to be (except in a homonymous way), because they are defined by their function and they cannot perform that function when separated from the whole.

This is puzzling, first of all, because it is unclear what Aristotle wants to imply. Does he really want to say that human beings cease to be human beings when they are isolated from the *polis*? Obviously, this is too strong a conclusion and, more than that, it would turn Aristotle's own theory of the priority of particular natural substances upside down. Strictly speaking, the argument only implies that the functional parts of a *polis* taken as functional parts would cease to be in isolation from the *polis*. Isolated from the ship, the captain would cease to be a captain and the rower would cease to be a rower, but they would not automatically cease to exist as natural substances. In the *polis* something like this seems to apply to the citizen or institutional groups, since without the *polis* they could not perform their defining political functions, but neither would they immediately drop dead without the *polis*. In the previous section, Aristotle has said that human beings are 'political animals', which involves that it is natural for them to take over functions within the political communities, i.e. performing the duties and rights of a citizen. In this sense the priority argument could mean – and reasonably so – that in separation from the *polis*, human beings could not live as political beings (possibly implying that this would deprive them of a potential for human development that is crucial for flourishing as a human being).

In a similar vein, Aristotle says in the same passage that, since individuals are not self-sufficient (*autarkes*) in isolation, they are *like* parts of the whole (1253a26–27). First of all, being *like* parts of the whole is weaker than what the homonymy thesis seems to suggest. Second, lacking self-sufficiency does not mean that such people could not exist; it just means (as we know from the genetic argument) that they would have to dedicate most of their time to fulfilling their daily needs, and this, again, would deprive them of the opportunity to fully develop their social and intellectual capacities, and performing these capacities is part of what Aristotle takes to be good life. If we read the priority argument along these lines, it is no longer monstrous and counterintuitive, but seems to be a further elaboration on the thought expressed in C2 that human beings are political animals. This becomes clear when, in the last lines of the passage (1253a28–29), Aristotle concludes that human beings that do not need the *polis* and do not actually live as political animals are a rare exception ("either beasts or gods", as he prefers to put it). On this reading of the priority argument, it is clear that the priority of the *polis* characterizes the relation between the *polis* and people conceived of as social-political beings and *not* as biological beings (since even Aristotle knows and acknowledges that, as a matter of fact, there are human beings in the biological sense that do not live in a *polis*). One could object that Aristotle is not clear enough here in distinguishing the political from the biological understanding of the individual parts of the *polis*; however, given that this argument directly follows upon the introduction of the notion of a 'political animal' and given his emphasis on the fact that people separated from the *polis* do not live *autarkes* (but are still alive!), it seems sufficiently clear that nothing in this passage encourages a biological (or ontological) instead of a political reading.

3.3 The structure of Pol. I.2

There is one remaining passage (1253a29–39), in which he formulates the memorable idea that while human beings may become the best being on earth when they reach their perfection, they may be the worst being when being isolated from justice, laws and human culture.[6] So it is genuinely dangerous to live without human community. Obviously, this is meant to be a concomitant of, and additional support for, the political animal theorem as expressed in C2. How could anyone ever fail to recognize this close connection?

All in all, then, we have the following structure of argument:

1252a24–b30	the 'genetic argument' leading to C1
1252b31–1253a3	transition from C1 to C1* and C2
1253a3–18	the political animal-theorem is further explored
1253a18–29	'priority argument'
1253a29–39	passage on the danger of living without community

3.4 Keyt's reconstruction

In the scholarship of the past decades, the structure of the chapter has turned out to be central to its philosophical interpretation. Originally published in 1987, a well-written paper by David Keyt (cited from Keyt 1991) has had an unparalleled impact on how scholars understood the argument. Keyt's paper is titled "Three Fundamental Theorems in Aristotle's 'Politics'" (1987) or, alternatively, "Three Basic Theorems in Aristotle's 'Politics'" (1991). Accordingly, he highlights three theorems: (I) that the *polis* exists by nature, (II) that man is by nature a political animal and (III) that the *polis* is prior in nature to the individual. Without prioritizing one of these claims over the other, Keyt (1991, 120) suggests that these three ideas together "may fairly be said to characterize Aristotle's standpoint in political philosophy." Next, he distinguishes and discusses four argu-

---

[6] This is more or less what Goethe has his character Mittler say about marriage: "Marriage is the origin and the summit of human culture. It renders the beast-like ones mild, and for the most educated one there is no better opportunity to prove his mildness" (*Wahlverwandtschaften*, Hamburger Ausgabe 6, 306; my translation).

ments that correspond to what he takes to be the four main sections of the chapter:
- The genetic argument (1252b27–34)
- The telic argument (1252b34–1253a7)
- The linguistic argument (1253a7–18)
- The organic argument (1253a18–33)

After a rigorous and thorough (though often unconvincing) discussion, Keyt concludes that the arguments are flawed or invalid, the only exception being the so-called 'linguistic' argument, which however fails to prove what it is supposed to prove. Many interpreters, even interpreters who disagree with his devastating conclusion, possibly driven by some sort of herd instinct, just take over Keyt's division of main theses and arguments, without noticing or acknowledging that this division actually suffers from severe problems. I will briefly address what I take to be the main weaknesses by comparing Keyt's to my own subdivision as presented above.

One problem is that Keyt presents his three key theorems as being on a par. However, it is far from clear that what he takes to be Theorem III is actually as important as the other theorems, both in Chapter I.2 and in the rest of the *Politics* (nor do I think that his Theorem III is a particularly good way to characterize Aristotle's political thinking). Above all, it is unclear which argument is supposed to support which of the three basic theorems. Indeed, he seems to think (and so do many authors who simply accept his division) that all the arguments with the exception of the linguistic argument are somehow meant to support Theorem I, which is that the state exists by nature. I will take issue with this supposed role of the so-called 'telic' argument below in Section 5. With regard to the so-called 'organic' argument (which is spatially separated from the claim that the state exists by nature) Keyt can draw on the fact that the passage includes an *interim* conclusion saying that it is clear that the *polis* exists by nature and that it is prior (1253a25). However, 'nature' is not mentioned in the entire argument, so it seems more likely that Aristotle just wants to take stock of what he takes himself to have established so far, thus repeating a conclusion that he has argued for in a previous section. The so-called 'linguistic' argument is strictly speaking an argument for why human beings are more political, more likely to be political or more appropriately called 'political' than any other animal; so it is strictly speaking not meant as argument for his Theorem II, the claim that human beings are political *animals*. Separating off the so-called 'organic' argument as Keyt does, it gets obscured how the priority argument is embedded and that the chapter concludes with a thought (the danger of living without community) that is independent of the priority argument. Finally, I find it inappropriate to label the passage about the alleged priority of the *polis* 'organic', because Aristotle focuses on the relation of parts and wholes, which need not be an 'organic' one (compare the example of the ship, mentioned above). By speaking of an 'organic' argument Keyt inadvertently gives unwarranted hope to organicist interpreters.

By contrast, the reading I defend can be characterized by the following claims. If we understand the claim that the *polis* exists by nature as saying that it is established by human beings in accordance with their nature (see Section 3 below), it is closely related to the claim that human beings are political animals, so that both conclusions can be inferred from the same premises (set out in the genetic argument and further explicated in the course of the transition from C1 to C1* and C2). From this point on, after the establishment of C2, Aristotle is more interested in elaborating upon the political animal theorem than in defending the naturalness of the *polis*. The reference to linguistic capacities is meant to offer further indications that human beings are suited to live in political communities. The priority argument, and the thought that it is dangerous to live in separation from human society, provide additional evidence that human beings do not randomly choose to live in *poleis*. Rather, they would be deprived of the chance to develop and fully realize their human capacities in isolation from political societies.[7]

4 C1 defused: a schematic disambiguation

The genetic argument concludes with Thesis C1, that the *polis* exists by nature. Aristotle infers (1252b30 – 31) that every *polis* exists by nature, given that the earliest communities also existed by nature (διὸ πᾶσα πόλις φύσει ἔστιν, εἴπερ καὶ αἱ πρῶται κοινωνίαι). The first communities mentioned were those consisting of a man and a woman or a master and a slave. If the *polis* exists by nature in the same way as these, then it would be instructive to ascertain why they, too, exist by nature. The argument is that a man and woman unite to have children, not based on a decision or choice, but rather due to a natural desire to leave behind children. Master and slave unite not for procreation, but for survival; and they do so based on the supposedly natural complementarity between those fit to govern and those in need of governing. The first communities therefore exist *by nature*, because they were established by people (men and women, masters and slaves) in accordance with their nature. In the first case, the community

---

[7] This is why in the remainder of this paper I can focus on how C1 and C2 are established and explicated.

between men and women, nature is speaking, as it were, through the impulse for reproduction, in the second case, the community of masters and slaves, there is the shared, presumably natural, desire to be preserved (*sôtêria:* 1252a31, an almost Stoic element *avant la lettre*), together with the supposedly natural division of labour between the ruling and the ruled.[8]

The first communities can therefore be classed among the things founded or established by humans in accordance with their nature (either as man and woman or governing and governed). In principle, there could be groups or individuals that establish things for no good reason, or contrary to their nature. The first communities, though, are established in accordance with the nature of their founders: male and female individuals on the one hand, and on the other, masters insofar as they govern, and the governed and those in need of governing (whether such a thing actually exists need not concern us at the moment) insofar as they are governed and in need of governing. To put it briefly and pointedly, we could also say that these communities *exist by nature.* Then we would no longer be talking about the individuals who established them in a certain way (namely in accordance with their nature, and not arbitrarily or contrary to their nature), but it would still be clear that what we talk about are communities *of these individuals*, communities that were established by *these individuals.*

The same must also hold for the *polis*, since the *polis* exists by nature *because* the first communities do. From a genetic, or developmental, standpoint it is already relatively far removed from the participants in the first communities. But we should not forget that just like the first communities, the *polis* is supposed to be something that was founded by its participants in a specific way, namely, in accordance with their nature. Granted, the *polis* is no longer characterized as an amalgamation of individuals like the first communities, but as an amalgamation of villages, which arose in turn from an amalgamation of households. Still, each of these amalgamations pursues a single goal, namely the gradual approximation of full self-sufficiency. And strictly speaking, neither households nor villages can pursue a goal; only the people who make them up can do this. To take up the thread again, if *poleis* exist by nature just like the first communities, and the first communities exist by nature in the sense that they are among the things established by people in accordance with their nature, then the *polis*, too, exists by nature in precisely the sense that it is among the things established by people in accordance with their nature. If this reasoning is correct, then instead of C1 or C1* we should rather expect the following conclusion:

---

[8] On this point see the close reading of the section on masters and slaves below in Section 5.2.

> C1***** The *polis* is among the things that are established by people *in accordance with their nature*.

My claim is that C1 should be understood in the sense of C1*****. In my opinion, Aristotle's wording of C1 is deliberately vague and grandiose, entirely in keeping with the style of an introductory section riddled with poetic quotes and appeals to universal human experience. However, the unelaborated generality of C1 does not follow logically from the arguments given.[9] What actually follows from them is C1*****, conceived as an elaboration of C1. As we will see, Aristotle himself appears to be aware of the vagueness of the formulation in C1, and duly attempts to specify it by adding C2. For, it is fairly difficult to see how C1 or C1* (a conclusion regarding the character of the *polis*) could follow directly from the same argumentation as C2 (a conclusion about the nature of mankind), and yet C1 and C2 are deduced in a single step from the selfsame line of argumentation and are even linked via the conjunction 'and'. This peculiarity is dispelled when we understand C1 in the sense of C1*****, since the statement that people combine to form *poleis* in accordance with their nature (and that the *polis* is natural in this sense) obviously stands in the closest possible relation to C2, which states that man is by (his or her) nature a political animal.

The only remaining question, then, is how C***** can be logically understood as an elaboration of C1. This can be shown in the following steps.

Step 1:

C1 The *polis* exists *by nature*.
C1* The *polis* is among the things that exist *by nature*.

C1 is worded almost exactly like the first conclusion in 1252b30–31, which asserts that *every polis* exists by nature; in any case, the universal quantifier is also implied in the generic statement about the *polis*. C1* is the wording of the first half of the second conclusion in 1253a1–3. The step from C1 to C1* is therefore trivial.

---

[9] Basically, this is an old observation; Keyt 1991 already argued that C1 does not follow from any of the previous elements. I will argue that, on a charitable reading, we should understand C1 in the sense of C1*****, because in the latter version it does follow from the previous arguments.

Step 2:

C1*   The *polis* is among the things that exist *by nature*.
C1** The *polis* is among the things that are established *in a natural way*.

While the transition from C1* to C1** is certainly non-trivial, it nevertheless follows necessarily when we make explicit the claim that is asserted implicitly in the scenario regarding the emergence of the *polis*, namely that specific *poleis* neither existed from time immemorial nor fell from heaven, but were formed, established, or created under certain historical and geographical conditions. Nor can this claim be dismissed with the objection that the *polis* has always existed in a generic sense somewhere or other, because Aristotle explicitly argues that *every polis*, i.e. each individual *polis*, exists *by nature* in the manner to be specified. Therefore, every single *polis* belongs to the class of things that are created. But if the *polis* is among the things that are formed or created or that someone established, how can we possibly salvage the claim that it also exists by nature? Answer: in claiming that the *polis* exists by nature, Aristotle does not mean to contrast *poleis* with artefacts and things established by people. His goal is rather to distinguish between various modes of being-established or coming-into-being, namely those that are *natural* in a way that has yet to be specified, and those that are not. This consideration is reflected in the clause 'in a natural way.'

Step 3:

C1**   The *polis* is among the things that are established *in a natural way*.
C1*** The *polis* is among the things that are established in a natural way by someone.

Among things that come into being in a natural way, there are some that come about through reproduction within the same species. *Poleis* are obviously not created in that way, because they do not reproduce themselves. In 1253a30–31, Aristotle refers to the first who established a *polis* as the originator of the greatest goods. We are therefore justified in supplementing the formulation 'things that are established' to initially include at least one anonymous originator of the state, regardless of whether Aristotle means an individual founder or a group of people who combine to form a *polis*. Hence, the *polis* is among the things that are established *by someone*.

Step 4:

C1*** The *polis* is among the things that are established in a natural way by someone.

C1**** The *polis* is among the things that are established in a natural way *by people*.

Regardless of whether we credit the individual founders or a collective with bringing about the creation of *poleis*, it is no coincidence that in both cases we are dealing with *people* who combine to form *poleis* and, in this sense, establish the *polis*. In principle, this has been clear since the introductory statement in the first chapter of the *Politics*, because in this chapter Aristotle emphasizes that if communities are formed with a view to some good, then this implies that *people* unite to form communities with a view to some good: "Every *polis* is as we see a sort of community (*koinônia*), and every community is constituted with a view to some good since all the actions of all mankind are done with a view to what they take to be good."[10]

In order to justify the introductory claim that every community is formed with a view to some good, Aristotle advances the more general proposition that everything that individual or collective agents do is done with a view to some real or apparent good. If the latter proposition is understood to justify the former claim, then this can only mean that when a community is formed, it is once again the people or individuals involved in its formation that do something. From this it follows that the somewhat forced, impersonal manner of speaking about a community's 'being formed' can be translated into a statement about the people who bring this community about. This line of reasoning should be formulated for later use as a general transformation rule:

TR

A community is formed with a view to some good.

⇔

People form a community with a view to a specific good.

Because the introductory sentence quoted above from the *Politics* leaves open the questions what type of community the *polis* is and what type of good people have in view when uniting to form a political community, the intended relationship between this introductory sentence and the argument in Chapter I.2 is probably that the genetic argumentation in I.2 is meant to establish, among other

---

[10] *Pol.* I.1, 1252a1–3, translation based on Rackham's.

things, the type of good that people have in view when establishing a political community.[11] From this premise it also follows that the remarks on the emergence of the *polis* in I.2 are to be understood as a concretization of the introductory claim regarding the formation of communities, meaning that the transformation rule (**TR**) also applies to the statements in I.2. However, **TR** makes it clear that the statements regarding the formation of *poleis* can be translated into statements about the people who united to form such *poleis*. This, in turn, provides adequate justification for the step from C1*** to C1**** (as in Step 4).

Step 5:

C1****   The *polis* is among the things that are established in a natural way *by people*.

C1*****   The *polis* is among the things that are established by people *in accordance with their nature*.

Therefore, the political community is formed or established by people, and this process takes place "in a natural way." What does this mean? The most obvious supposition is that the people who form the *polis* do so neither contrary to their nature nor arbitrarily and without cause, but in accordance with or by virtue of their nature. This supposition is confirmed by the fact that the conclusion of the argument aimed at establishing the naturalness of the *polis* is presented together with C2, a claim about the nature of mankind. Like the *polis*, the first communities, especially between men and women, were declared 'natural' based on the fact that it was in their nature (as living beings) to want to have children. Additional arguments for the claim that the conclusion is geared toward human nature and that the naturalness of the *polis* should be rooted in a desire that accords with human nature will be provided in the following section, where the argument is analysed in detail. Step 5, too, can therefore be taken as established.

4.1 A Closer Look at C1*****

What is achieved by transforming C1 into C1*****? In contrast to the interpretations of C1 that we have considered at the outset, C1***** is neither outlandish nor patently false. C1***** also requires no (far-fetched) appeal to the principles

---

[11] I argue for this connection at some length in Rapp 2020.

of Aristotle's natural philosophy. Furthermore, C1***** avoids several of the ambiguities of C1; in this sense, C1 could clearly be understood as a kind of pithy abridgement of C1*****. The position expressed by C1***** is not vague, but relatively precise. The formation of the *polis* is not arbitrary and certainly not unnatural for mankind. Rather it is a consistent progression in the development of mankind's unique nature. If the *polis* is thus legitimized by an appeal to human nature, then it seems simply mistaken to postulate that the *polis* must be evaluated based on some sort of law relevant to a non-human nature. Furthermore, the arguments that precede C1 or C1***** do not aim to show that the *polis* is a 'natural entity' in the same sense as a dog, cat or mouse, or the sun, moon and stars are natural entities, and is therefore bound like natural entities to obey certain laws of nature. They merely show that the development leading to the founding of *poleis* by human beings is initiated by natural impulses and follows a coherent pattern, and therefore cannot be either arbitrary or contrary to human nature. Finally, the content of C1***** (the thesis that the *polis* was established by people in accordance with their nature) is intimately connected with that of C2 (the thesis that man is a political animal, in other words, a being that by nature exists for life in the *polis*). Conclusion C2 can therefore be reasonably established based on the same premises as C1***** (which seemed out of the question for conclusion C1).

5 A close reading of the genetic argument leading to C1

Having thus far examined the argument of *Politics* I.2 only from a distance, we will now turn our attention in this section to the individual steps of the argument. At the beginning of the chapter, Aristotle suggests that the matter be handled, as in other cases, by examining how things grow from the outset or how they develop naturally (*phuomena*). Accordingly, he distinguishes different communities that develop successively out of each other. This is followed by the already familiar conclusions C1 and C2, which are explained in detail. Put briefly in summary form, the argument consists of the following basic steps:

5.1 Man and woman

> Necessarily then, the first coupling together of persons then is that between those who are unable to exist without one another, such as the union of female and male for the continuance of the species – and this not of deliberate purpose, but with man as with the other animals and with plants there is a natural instinct to desire (*phusikon to ephiesthai*) to leave behind one another being of the same sort as oneself.[12]

Female and male unite for the purpose of sexual reproduction. The point is not only to mate, but also to leave behind something similar to oneself;[13] it is therefore also a question of preserving the species. In doing so, people are acting in accordance with their nature as living beings. And it is in this sense that what they do is natural. A natural impulse drives them to do what is in their nature to do. Even if the union between a man and a woman is based not on a decision or choice (*ouk ek prohaireseôs*), but on this natural drive, we are already dealing here with a community, and a community with a certain purpose, namely reproduction. Nature, as it were, equipped living beings for this end with sexual urge and sexual attraction – and this is why everybody seems happy to accept that this first community comes about in a natural way. Strictly speaking, however, the desire to leave behind a being of the same sort cannot be reduced to sexual drives. In different species it might involve different kinds of efforts (beyond mating, pregnancy and giving birth) to bring up one's offspring. For example, in all higher developed species it requires some amount of parental care. In the case of human beings, it obviously takes multiple efforts to leave behind descendants that are able to live up to the opportunities provided by human nature. So, even if human beings share this desire with all living beings, it is possible (and, indeed, quite likely) that for different kinds of animals this desire is manifested in different kinds of activities (beyond mating).

5.2 Master and slave

> [...] and the union of natural ruler and natural subject for the sake of preservation (*dia tên sôtêrian*), for the one who can foresee with his mind is naturally ruler and naturally master, and the one who can do these things with his body is subject and naturally a slave; so that master and slave have the same interest.[14]

---

12 *Pol.* I.2, 1252a26–30, translation based on Rackham's.
13 On this point see also Schütrumpf 1991, 187–88.
14 *Pol.* I.2, 1252a30–34, Rackham's translation, slightly altered.

This community or cooperation is supposed to exist for the mutual benefit and preservation of two types of people: those whose natural aptitudes make them better suited to plan, govern, give orders, etc. and those whose natural aptitudes cause them to benefit from following the orders of others. Much like the natural instinct for reproduction, which precipitates the community between man and woman, this cooperation could be understood as a natural instinct for preservation. Above all, however, Aristotle dwells here on the thought that it is in accordance with the nature of the party that is capable of reasoning and seeing into the future to rule (and, correspondingly, in accordance with the nature of the party that is not capable to do these things to be ruled), instead of elaborating on the naturalness of the desire to be preserved, which brings masters and slaves together and is the real analogue to the desire for reproduction that brings men and women together.

Anyhow, Aristotle's reflections on the relationship between master and slave seem to include a fair amount of platonically tinged psychology: in the relationship between soul and body, as in the relationship between rational and non-rational parts of the soul, it is *natural* in the sense of the nature of the soul (i.e. in the sense that the several parts of the soul are ordered in accordance with their specific functions) that the soul should rule over the body or for the rational should dominate the non-rational.[15] If the body sought to rule over the soul or the irrational strove to command the rational, then the effectiveness of the structured division of labour within the soul would be threatened, resulting in an unnatural condition in which the parties involved would not perform the functions to which they are suited. Aristotle now applies this logic to cooperation between people. Drawing an analogy to the specific functions of the various parts of the soul, he postulates a sufficient difference in aptitude based on the individual, natural endowments of the people involved. A community formed for the sake of mutual preservation on the basis of this complementary relationship between ruler and ruled is considered *natural* in the same sense as it is natural for the rational part of the soul to lead and command.[16] Whether conditions within the soul can be legitimately carried over to relationships between different people is another question entirely. In any event, it should now be clear in what

---

15 Plato says about the *polis* in which each part performs the function that corresponds to its proper nature, that it is 'natural' (*Resp.* IV, 428e); this has also been observed by Schütrumpf (1991).

16 In accordance with **TR** one might be tempted to say that this community is established by the people involved, i.e. the masters and slaves, but owing to the distinctive nature of this relationship, it would be odd to say that the ruled party enters this community for the sake of preservation.

sense Aristotle understands this relationship to be natural, even though it might be considered a weakness of his argument that he does not further elaborate on the supposedly natural desire for preservation, but, instead, lets himself be distracted by the thought that the supposed complementarity of master and slave (similarly as the complementarity of men and women) provides another respect (though, perhaps not the most pertinent one) in which this community exists 'by nature'.

5.3 The household

> From these two communities then is first composed the household, and Hesiod was right when he wrote "First and foremost a house and a wife and an ox for the ploughing." For the ox serves instead of a servant for the poor. The community therefore that comes about in accordance with [its] nature for everyday purposes is the 'household' [...].[17]

In referring back to man and woman, master and slave, Aristotle is clearly speaking here of 'communities.' This will become important later on, when the question arises what connections Aristotle considers as 'first communities'. The household developed directly out of the first two communities, each of which is natural in its own way (as well as out of the community between parents and children, which is not mentioned here explicitly, but is already implied by the comment about preserving the species). The remark that the household serves everyday purposes or the satisfaction of daily needs refers back to reproduction and preservation on the one hand, and on the other hand forward to the non-routine needs of the village and to the self-sufficiency of the *polis*.

The translation of the final sentence is crucial here. In the Greek it reads: ἡ μὲν οὖν εἰς πᾶσαν ἡμέραν συνεστηκυῖα κοινωνία κατὰ φύσιν οἶκός ἐστιν, which most translators render as something like "The community therefore that comes about in the course of nature for everyday purposes is the house [...]" (Rackham), "The family is the association established by nature for the supply of men's everyday wants [...]" (Everson/Revised Oxford Translation of Aristotle), "Thus the association naturally formed for the supply of everyday wants is a household [...]" (Welldon), etc. This is not entirely impossible from a linguistic perspective and is clearly meant to emphasize that the house, household or family likewise inherits the naturalness of the communities included within it, namely those between man and woman, master and slave. Strictly speaking, however, the claim that the household exists by nature is nowhere to be found. A far more accurate

---

17 *Pol.* I.2, 1252b9–14, Rackham's translation, slightly altered.

interpretation would be that the community characterized as such and such is, *in accordance with nature*, the house or household. 'In accordance with nature' therefore means either the nature of the specified community or the nature of the household. This results in a claim whose ultimate meaning is that the household, in accordance with its nature (its essence), is nothing other than a community formed for daily life, i.e. to meet the needs of everyday life. Consequently, it seems not to have occurred to Aristotle to emphasize that the household, too, *exists by nature*. Instead, he emphasizes that, in accordance with its nature, the household constitutes a community for meeting everyday needs. Far from making an independent claim concerning naturalness, he is rather emphasizing the continuity with the preceding communities, whose goals are reproduction and preservation.

5.4 The village

> On the other hand, the primary community made up of several households for the satisfaction of not mere daily needs is the village. Most plausibly, the village seems to be, according to its nature, a colony from a household (μάλιστα δὲ κατὰ φύσιν ἔοικεν ἡ κώμη ἀποικία οἰκίας εἶνα), formed of those whom some people speak of as 'fellow-sucklings' or "sons and sons' sons."[18]

The village community enables its participants to satisfy needs beyond those required for everyday life; on the one hand, the description refers back to the household community, which meets daily needs, while on the other it refers forward to the *polis*, which makes full self-sufficiency possible. In this respect, Aristotle once again seeks to emphasize the continuity not only with the preceding communities, but also with the remaining community, the *polis*. The characterization as *kata phusin*, *in accordance with nature*, emerges once again, and once again it tempts us to translate that the village exists by nature.[19] But now the

---

[18] *Pol.* I.2, 1252b15–18, based on Rackham's translation.
[19] See Schütrumpf (1991): *Im höchsten Maße scheint aber das Dorf naturgemäß zu sein* [...] More cautiously Everson/Revised Oxford Translation: "And the most natural form of the village appears to be that of a colony from the family, [...]" and Welldon: "It seems that the village in its most natural form is derived from the household, [...]" Horn (in this volume, 63) is still quibbling with the question, in what sense the village is 'most natural', without addressing my argument that this is an unlikely reading of the passage. Aristotle's point here is not that the household and the village exist by nature, but that the household is (by its nature) nothing but the community that takes care of the daily needs and that the village is (by its nature) nothing but a colony of the household, which is to say that the emergence of these communities do

qualification *malista* rears its troublesome head: it can mean "to the highest degree" or 'most likely'. Why should a village be natural to a higher degree (or 'rather') than the communities that exist before or after it? Or why should Aristotle be interested, as some translators presuppose, in distinguishing several forms of the village? As in the passage on the household, the qualification *kata phusin* seems to refer to the nature (essence) of the community in question, in this case the nature of the village; and that nature, we come to learn, consists in being the outgrowth of a household that has grown too large. It is therefore clearly not the case that Aristotle, as if fearful that naturalness might get lost somewhere along the way to the *polis*, is emphasizing the naturalness of the different communities at each station. To the contrary, he is much more interested in showing that the nature or essence of each new form of community stands in an intimate relation to the preceding communities, such that the development follows a kind of internal logic.

5.5 The *polis*

> The community finally composed of several villages is the city-state; it has at last attained the limit of virtually complete self-sufficiency and thus, while it comes into existence for the sake of life, it exists for the good life. **(C1)** Hence every city-state exists by nature, inasmuch as the first communities so exist; for the city-state is the end of the other communities [...][20]

The *polis* or city-state is now introduced in this passage. It is said to consist of several villages and to constitute a 'final' community – clearly in the sense that "it has attained the limit of self-sufficiency" (which in itself already seems to imply that the aforementioned communities, despite aiming for such a condition, did not attain it). Attaining the 'limit of self-sufficiency' is combined with another, even more important change in the goals for which communities are formed, a change that is indicated in the oft-quoted formulation "to come into existence for the sake of life, to exist for the good life." The type of self-sufficiency made possible by life in the *polis* is obviously conceived as a condition enabling the realization of a good life. This doesn't mean that the good life wasn't sought after at the stages preceding self-sufficiency; it simply means that the immediate goal at those stages was to secure what was needed for

---

not have to invoke other motives and causes apart from those invoked for the emergence of the first communities.
20 *Pol.* I.2, 1252b27–31, Rackham's translation, slightly altered.

life, without excluding the possibility that certain steps might be taken toward achieving a *good* life.

But above all, the passage marks the first appearance of the claim in question, namely that the *polis* exists by nature. Although the argumentation resumes after this passage, the sentence presents itself early on as a conclusion, so that one has reason to suppose that the preceding remarks already contain at least the major part of the justification for this thesis. The passage contains two hints indicating how the conclusion might follow from the preceding argumentation: first, the hint that the first communities, too, were natural, and second, the hint that the nature is the goal.

Let us begin with the remark that is directly connected with the statement of the conclusion (C1), namely that the *polis* is natural, because the first communities, too, were natural. The 'first communities' might mean (a) the communities between man and woman, master and slave, (b) the household and village communities or (c) all four of these communities. In his influential reconstruction, David Keyt (1991, 129) assumes without further ado that (b) must be meant. Perhaps he finds it difficult to believe that the formations referred to as (a) could actually be considered real 'communities'; yet Aristotle refers to them explicitly as such, and each is connected with specific forms of leadership, which after all is the actual theme of Book I of the *Politics*. Furthermore, it is precisely in the descriptions of these two communities that the heaviest emphasis is placed on naturalness, whereas our (linguistically preferable) translation of the passages on the household and village communities contain only a remark concerning their nature (in the sense of essence). Finally, the designation '*first* communities' is best suited to these two forms of community; households and villages are by comparison derivative, and hence not exactly 'first' communities. All these considerations make (a) seem the more probable solution and (b) less probable. The argument would therefore be that the *polis* exists by nature because the first communities from which it emerged (presumably those between man and woman, master and slave) were already *natural* communities (in the manner described).

Is this a coherent argument? In his reconstruction, Keyt (1991, 130–31) quite rightly recognized that something like a law of the transitivity of naturalness was assumed here as an unstated premise: if C follows from B and B follows from A, and if A is 'natural,' then B, too, must be natural, as must C by virtue of B. It is not difficult to come up with counterexamples to this law, as Keyt does himself, in order to reject the whole argument as fundamentally flawed. Yet Aristotle is not dealing with just any sequence, but with a very specific process that begins with the reproductive community and leads logically from the establishment of one form of community to the establishment of the next, arriving finally at the *polis*. This process is characterized by two important features. *Firstly*, it is clear how eager Aristotle is to show that the transition from one form of community to the next is accomplished not by means of a leap, but by a continuous development. In other words, the initial goal of the household community in accordance with its nature is nothing other than the satisfaction of everyday needs, which was already the objective of the two more basic communities. Consequently, the village community, in accordance with its nature, is nothing other than the result of the expansion of households that have grown too large, and the *polis* is hence an amalgamation of such villages. *Secondly*, this process involves hierarchically ordered goals as well as striving that is aimed at those goals, with the latter tracing an arc, so to speak, from the natural impulses triggering the first communities all the way up to the foundation of the *polis*. The hierarchical order of the goals is especially clear in the sequence "Satisfaction of everyday needs – satisfaction of more than everyday needs – self-sufficiency," but it can also easily be traced back to the goals of the first communities, namely reproduction and self-preservation.

One can now argue for a kind of 'transferability' of naturalness in this particular case by emphasizing that the striving for each of the goals of the first communities points beyond itself toward the goals of the consecutive communities through to the self-sufficiency of the *polis*, so that the admittedly natural striving/impulses of the first communities set in motion a consecutive process of community formation that finds its consummation in the *polis*. Thus the *polis* ultimately hearkens back to striving/impulses that can be described as natural. To make the argument more plausible, one might point out that the striving of those who unite to form a household, for example, is not limited to meeting everyday needs, but is ultimately directed toward self-sufficiency, even though the latter cannot be achieved without striving to achieve the prior goals. That Aristotle has such an argument in mind becomes clear when he says: "for the *polis* is the end of the other [earlier] communities." In other words, the earlier communities point beyond themselves to a condition that realizes in full what they themselves could only realize in part, namely the kind of self-sufficiency that facilitates a lifestyle oriented toward the good life. The argument would therefore be as follows:

(i) Every community is formed to achieve some good/goal/end (from *Politics* I.1).
(ii) Communities are formed by people to achieve a specific good/goal/end (from **TR**).
(iii) Communities are formed by people because they strive for the good/goal/end inherent in this community (from (ii): in Aristotle's parlance, to seek to achieve a good/goal/end means to strive for it).

(iv) Some communities have a further community as their goal (this follows if, according to 1252b31, certain other communities have the *polis* as their goal).
(v) Certain communities are formed by people because they strive not only for the good/goal/end inherent in the community, but also for a further community, or the goal of that other community (otherwise, communities that were themselves formed with a certain good/goal/end in view could not aim at any other community).
(vi) The 'early' communities (man and woman, master and slave, household, village) are formed by people because they strive not only for the goods/goals/ends inherent in those communities, but also for the good/goal/end inherent in the *polis* or political community, namely self-sufficiency (from 1252b31 and (v)).
(vii) The striving directed toward the inherent goods/goals/ends of the earlier communities is directed toward them as an *interim* goal, and toward another goal as a final goal. Only the final goal fulfils the corresponding striving in full (hypothesis in the style of *Nicomachean Ethics* I.1 to explain how one and the same striving can have different goals).
(viii) If people strive *in a natural way* for an *interim* goal, then they also strive for the corresponding final goal *in a natural way* (nonetheless, in accordance with (vi) and (vii) the striving in question should be the same striving directed toward both the *interim* and the final goal).
(ix) If people strive *in a natural way* for a good/goal/end that is inherent in a community, then the corresponding community can itself be considered *natural*.
(x) If people strive for (at least one of) the goods inherent in the 'earlier' communities as *interim* goals and they do so in a natural way, then they also strive in a natural way for the corresponding final goal, namely the goal inherent in the political community (from (vi) and (viii)).
(xi) If the goal inherent in the *polis* is striven for in a natural way, then the *polis*, too, is natural (from (xi) and (x)).

This looks like a reasonable argument. I therefore claim, against Keyt, that the transitivity of naturalness is tenable – not in general, but insofar as purposeful desiring and subordinated goals, as described above, are involved. Much depends, of course, on the plausibility of (viii) and (ix), as well as on how one interprets the qualification *in a natural way*. Where the plausibility of (ix) is concerned, however, we should bear in mind that the naturalness of the *polis*, according to Section 3 above, can hardly be conceived of as anything but the mode of bringing about used by the people forming the community. For simple and primordial communities such as the reproductive community discussed above, it is not implausible to say that they are *natural* in the sense that their goal is striven for *in a natural way*, namely via a natural impulse. But in the case of goals and communities that are more advanced, could one not object that the 'naturalness' of the initial striving directed toward early *interim* goals becomes increasingly 'diffused'? As if in answer to objections such as these, Aristotle comes to the rescue of the argument underlying his description of the emergence of the *polis* with a completely new strategy, which will be discussed in the following section.

6 C1*, C2 and the political nature of human beings

The sentences that follow directly upon the statement of C1 refer to the *polis* as an end or goal of the previous communities, emphasize that the nature of each thing is revealed once its growth has been completed, and point out that the purpose for the sake of which each thing exists is its chief good. Afterwards Aristotle states C1*, a mere variant of the original conclusion C1, and adds the further conclusion C2. It is crucial to understand the argumentative progress made in these lines. For the purpose of further reference, I subdivide the section into Subsections [i], [ii], and [iii]. The following quotation repeats the statement of C1, just to make the context clear.

> **(C1)** Hence every city-state exists by nature, inasmuch as the first communities so exist; **[i]** for the *polis* is the end of the other communities, and nature is an end, since that which each thing is when its growth is completed we speak of as being the nature of each thing, for instance of a man, a horse, a house (or household). **[ii]** In addition (*eti*), the purpose for the sake of which a thing exists, its end, is its chief good; and self-sufficiency is an end, and a chief good. **[iii]** From these things therefore it is clear **(C1*)** that the city-state (*polis*) is among the things that exist by nature, and **(C2)** that man is by nature a political animal (*phusei politikon zôon*) [...][21]

6.1 The structure of the argument

Keyt quotes Subsection [i] as part of the genetic argument and Subsection [ii] as the beginning of a new argument, which he calls the 'telic' one. Treating [i] as

---

[21] *Pol.* I.2, 1252b30–1253a3, based on Rackham's translation.

still being related to the genetic question seems to be a reasonable step, but I take issue with the idea of treating [ii] as the beginning of a new and independent argument to the effect that the state exists by nature. On the contrary, it seems obvious that the teleological turn, as it were, of the argument, has started already in [i] and is continued in [ii]. While Subsection [i] has established that nature (in the sense of the nature of each thing) is an end, as the nature of each thing becomes obvious when its growth has been completed, Subsection [ii] adds that the purpose, 'that for the sake of which', is also an end, so that self-sufficiency, which the *polis* is supposed to guarantee, is such an end and hence (tacit conclusion) is the purpose, i.e. the end, i.e. the nature of the *polis*, which is revealed when its development is completed. Therefore [i] and [ii] together make up a single argument; they are both similarly 'teleological', so it makes no sense to cut off [ii] and distinguish it as 'telic'.

Most probably, Keyt's subdivision was triggered by the occurrence of 'in addition (*eti*)' at the beginning of Subsection [ii], for usually, this conjunction is used to indicate the transition to a new thought or argument. However, the *eti* need not mean that after the conclusion of the genetic argument an additional argument for the same conclusion will now be presented. It could mean that an addition will now be made to the last thought within the argument, i.e. an argument in addition to the thought included in [i]. And this makes good sense: in [i] the *polis* is considered as the completion of a development of different communities, while [ii] considers, *in addition*, that this end of the development sketched is also an end that was intended, i.e. that for the sake of which people established a *polis*, namely the self-sufficiency that they take to be guaranteed by the *polis*.

The other reason why [ii] could be considered as (the beginning of)[22] an independent argument to the effect that the *polis* exists by nature, consists in the fact that in Subsection [iii] Aristotle more or less repeats conclusion C1, as though he wishes to infer it from the previous lines (= [ii]). Yet we need not think that C1* is meant as the conclusion of an independent argument. I rather take [i] and [ii] as remarks that are meant to explicate how conclusion C1 has come about, in accordance with a phenomenon discussed in the *Topics*, viz. that sometimes one of the dialectical interlocutors is puzzled about how exactly the conclusion came about (VIII.1, 156a15). Along these lines, the current passage does not give a new argument to the same effect, but clarifies for those who are

---

[22] Indeed, the attempt to build an independent argument on [ii] and [iii] is somewhat bold; Keyt has to supply the decisive premise (that which is natural exists for the sake of the best) as a tacit assumption.

not yet convinced by the conclusion of the genetic argument – in the sense that they do not see how naturalness of the first communities can be transmitted to the *polis* – why and how the conclusion C1 actually follows. This is exactly why Aristotle in [iii] repeats C1 with only slight modification as C1*. By doing so, he seeks to round off the entire preceding argument, and clarify and develop it further with the aid of C2. The repetition of C1 in the form of C1* is offered as the closure of the argument, because the first mention of the conclusion that the *polis* exists by nature required additional explication (primarily via [i] and [ii]), resulting in what is effectively a recapitulation of the argument, which in turn calls for a repetition of the conclusion at the end.[23]

6.2 Being 'by nature' and 'being the nature of'

The lines immediately following upon the statement of C1 are particularly puzzling, because Aristotle speaks here of the nature that is the end, where we expect him to comment on why the *polis* is 'by nature'. The nature that is the end is the nature of each thing, i.e. its essence. It is not that nature we usually ask about when inquiring whether something exists by nature. Here (if not elsewhere) one might get the impression that Aristotle is deliberately confusing the concepts 'to-exist-by-nature' and 'to-be-the-nature-of-a-thing', which seem to have little to do with each other. Yet in the Aristotelian terminology there seems to be an extremely close correlation between the two concepts, because the condition into which a thing develops by nature, or in the course of a natural, unhindered growth process, reveals the nature or essence of the thing in question. Admittedly, this correlation is plausible first and foremost in the case of biological development. In processes of this kind, the specific form, as an efficient principle in matter, also functions as a development program that leads through certain stages from a seed to a mature specimen of a certain bio-

---

[23] In this sense, it is not true that my interpretation when using the transitivity of naturalness is based on an efficient cause alone, as Horn (in this volume) objects. It does depend crucially on the intentional or practical teleology of human agents (and where there is teleology, there is final causation), whereas Horn seems to miss in my interpretation what he calls "teleology of nature". Indeed, what I am saying is that the *polis* is brought about by the agency of human beings and not by any (mysterious, direct) agency of nature. I do not deny, though, that human beings do what they do when founding a state in accordance with what is natural for them (i.e. in accordance with their nature/essence) nor that they are 'pushed' by nature to do so, as it were, by (i) their desire for reproduction (see section 4.1 above) and (ii) by their natural drive to live together (*Pol.* I.2, 1253a29 – 30), even without further benefit, which is the basis for their 'social' (not yet political) nature in the narrow sense.

logical species. Because social entities do not have this kind of efficient form, the naturalness of the *polis* cannot be proven by applying this principle. Its applicability seems rather to presuppose the naturalness of the object in question (as argued above in Section 1, even artefacts, such as houses, have a 'nature/essence', which is revealed only when their generation is completed).

In the current context, appealing to the nature of a thing has different function. Its purpose is to emphasize that the previously described emergence of the *polis* is a goal-oriented process, and that processes of this kind are to be determined from their end state – in this case, the attainment of self-sufficiency. Unlike in the biological case, this goal-orientation does not derive from the development program of a natural form, but from the striving of the participants who form the community. The goal toward which the consecutive sequence of community formations tends is the thing for which the participants (the people who form the communities) have striven from the beginning – a beginning that is in some sense *natural*. The corresponding striving can only be fully determined from the perspective of the final goal. The fact that objects of striving are at issue here is initially obscured by the impersonal manner of speaking of "communities that are formed" or "communities that have specific goals." But this fact can unquestionably be derived from **TR**, which Aristotle established in the very first paragraph of the *Politics*.

6.3 Interpretation of [i] and [ii]

Here, in short, is how I understand the function of this section. C1 is clearly meant to be derived from the genetic argument. As discussed above, in Section 4, the thought is that the *polis* exists by nature, if the previous communities existed by nature too. This, we said, is the transitivity of naturalness. Now, Subsection [i] introduces a thought that presents itself as explicating or commenting on the conclusion just drawn, pointing out that the *polis* is the end or goal of the previous communities. On my interpretation, this means that what people were desiring when they desired the subordinate goals of the previous communities, was ultimately a community like the *polis* guaranteeing self-sufficiency. The establishment of the *polis* is, as we saw in Section 4, inextricably connected with self-sufficiency (which again facilitates the good life or living well), and self-sufficiency makes the *polis* a desired end. This connection of finality with self-sufficiency is made explicit in Subsection [ii]. How does this help to shed light on the conclusion C1 just drawn? Aristotle does not suggest that nature (or whatever is natural) is an end, that the *polis* is an end, and that the *polis* is therefore natural. This would be a fallacy: compare "horse is an animal, human is an animal, therefore human is horse". Also, Section [i] does not speak of nature *simpliciter* but of the nature-of-each-thing. What Aristotle wants to say (on a charitable reading that makes the argument sound) is that the earlier stages in the development of a *polis*, i.e. the earlier communities and what people moved to come together in these communities, must be assessed in the light of the end stage of this development. For as shown in section [i], the nature-of-each-thing becomes manifest when its development has been completed. In the case of the genesis of the *polis* this means that even the early communities must be understood as tending towards a life in a community that guarantees self-sufficiency.

Looking from the end stage of the development, even the supposedly brute impulses for reproduction and preservation appear in a new light. Clearly they are natural, and clearly, at least the impulse for reproduction does not require choice or decision (*prohairesis*). But as desires of human beings who ultimately desire a self-sufficient and good life, these impulses are not fully satisfied by mere reproduction of the species, nor by the amount of nourishment that guarantees mere survival, nor by the household and the village that help them with daily needs. Only a community that facilitates the good life will do; and this is, I think, fully in line with what Aristotle says about the non-rational part of the souls of human beings (e.g. in *Nicomachean Ethics* I.13): even non-rational impulses are not just brute and non-rational, but are in touch with the rational part of the soul. Eventually, the natural impulses by which the first communities were brought about turn into something more deliberate, or are complemented by something more deliberate, since acknowledging self-sufficiency and the good life as ultimate goals is no longer the job of our brute instincts.[24] Still, the transitivity of naturalness is given, and the naturalness does not get diluted along the way, if we understand the earlier communities as stages in a development that, from the beginning, was directed at the self-sufficiency guaranteeing *polis*. By emphasizing, in the genetic argument, that the first communities were brought about by natural impulses and that the household and the village by their nature/essence were nothing but consecutive steps in the development ini-

---

24 Within an Aristotelian framework, to be sure, the emergence of reason and reasonable desire in human beings is not less 'natural' than the supposedly 'brute' desires that bring together men and women for the sake of reproduction. Rational desire together with the capacity to make reasoned choices or decisions are capacities that are intimately connected with human nature. Hence, making use of this peculiarly human capacity does not, as some interpreters seem to suspect, interrupt the transitivity of naturalness, as long as this capacity is used for decisions that accord with the content of human nature, i.e. (roughly) as long as they take the good life consisting in the excellent exercise of peculiarly human capacities as the supreme goal and opt for the life in the *polis* for just this end.

tiated by natural impulses, Aristotle portrays the emergence of the *polis* as a process that can be fully explained by natural impulses and by the dynamics of these impulses within human beings. By emphasizing in Subsection [i] that the nature of each thing is revealed by the final stage of a development, he wants to ensure that the naturalness of the first communities is actually indicative of the naturalness of the *polis*, in that they are just phases in a development that leads to the emergence of the *polis*.

Ultimately, the emergence of the *polis* and its alleged naturalness is thus grounded in what human beings desire in accordance with their nature, and it is part of their nature or directly implied by their nature that they are 'political animals'. It is time to move forward to Subsection [iii].

6.4 C2: the political animal

In Subsection [iii] C1* is, as we said, mostly a repetition. The inclusion of C2 though, which states that man is by nature a 'political animal,' is a novelty. Of course, this expression should in no way be associated with 'politics,' 'career politicians,' etc. A living being that is by nature *politikon* is connected by virtue of its own nature to the *polis*, is suited for life in the *polis*, is oriented toward such a life, and strives for it.[25] Living beings that are suited in a similar way to life in another collective that is roughly analogous to the *polis* (packs, herds, colonies, etc.) can also be *politikon*, albeit in a figurative sense that does not connect them with actual *poleis*.

As mentioned above, this passage expresses the conclusion of the entire argumentation up to this point. The main problem with these lines is why Aristotle thinks it possible to derive both parts of this conclusion (C1* and C2) from the self-same premises. After all, C1* is presented here as a claim about *poleis*, while C2 is a claim about people. This problem can be resolved if we understand C1*, too, in precisely the sense that has actually been established in the course of the preceding argument. We have been shown that the *polis* exists *naturally* or *by nature* in precisely the sense that it is formed by people who strive *in a natural way* for the goal inherent in the *polis* (this was Step (x) in our reconstruction of the argument). When we apply this to C1* and C2, we obtain the following:

> [...] that the *polis* is formed by people who strive *in a natural way* for the goal inherent in it, and that man is *by nature* a political animal.

---

25 On the notion of a political animal see Schütrumpf 1991, 207–08.

Finally, we can substitute the passive construction in the first sentence with the corresponding active formulation, resulting in a general conclusion that contains two partial conclusions about people:

> [...] that people who strive *in a natural way* for the goal inherent in the *polis* establish it (*the polis*) and that man is *by nature* a political animal.

Having reached this point, we now see that the two partial conclusions are not much different in meaning, if, as previously stated, *zôiôn politikon* means that a living being is oriented toward life in the *polis* and desires to live in such a community.

Furthermore, few would contest the claim that the second partial conclusion is intended as an expression *about the nature of man*, in other words, that man is a political animal *according to* or *in accordance with his/her nature*. Based on the parallels between the two expressions, we now arrive at the following interpretation of the formula *in a natural way* in the first partial conclusion: when people strive for the goal inherent in the *polis*, they do so *in accordance with their nature* or *by virtue of their nature*. If Aristotle now concludes, on the basis of his actual argumentation, that (C1) the *polis* exists by nature in the sense that (in line with C1*****) it is formed or established by people who strive for the goal inherent in it *by virtue of their nature*, then the second partial conclusion follows as a pithier reformulation of the same thesis, namely that people are by nature *zôia politika*, living beings 'created', as it were, for life in the *polis*.

Thus far, I have argued that conclusion C1 or C1* should be interpreted in such a way that it actually follows from the preceding stretch of argument, and that the argument about the emergence of the *polis* results, as I have shown, in an expression corresponding to C1***** or C1****. If, in line with my strategy, we now apply the conclusions actually established from the line of argumentation, we find them to be in full accordance with C2. This goal could also be achieved as follows: Aristotle initially concludes in a deliberately pointed way (and as a way of polemically differentiating the *polis* from other systems of government) that the *polis* is among the things that exist by nature, but he clearly senses or knows that this thesis is formulated in a vague and ambiguous way and does not really take the course of the argumentation into account. He therefore adds a second conclusion introduced by *kai*, namely C2, to serve as an interpretation or subsequent qualification of the pithier C1*. Translated as 'and,' the Greek conjunction '*kai*' often serves an epexegetic function ('in other words,' 'in the sense of,' 'meaning that'), and in fact C2 could quite easily play this subsequent qualifying or interpretative role: "The *polis* exists by nature, *meaning that* man (who establishes the *polis*) is, in accordance with his nature, a living being who strives for a life in the *polis*."

It is important for the interpretation proposed here that the striving that leads people to establish communities actually be rooted in human nature, because the supposed 'naturalness' of the *polis* by virtue of this striving, a striving that leads to political coexistence, is supposed to be rooted in human nature. On a quite plausible interpretation, Thesis C2 implies exactly this: that in accordance with their nature people strive for a life in the *polis*. Aristotle himself provides the required interpretation of "being a *zôiôn politikon*" in the very next passage.[26] At the end of the chapter Aristotle emphasizes once again that *by nature* there is a drive that underlies every community of this type, i.e. every political community.[27] But even apart from this, there are many references to the nature of human beings. When discussing the connection between man and woman Aristotle refers to a natural impulse that clearly derives from the nature of a living being. And the nature of living being is one aspect of human nature. Furthermore, human nature amounts to more than just these natural, decision-free impulses to form communities. The targeted striving for an independent community that facilitates a happy life is distinctively in accordance with human nature. In *Pol.* I.2 Aristotle does not attempt to show exactly where there occurs a transition from community formation by mere impulse to formation by reason. Nevertheless, he does make it very clear that the communities based on more than just reproduction are formed in continuity with these first communities and with the impulses that prompt them. In a way, both sides of human desire are kept together by the 'political animal' formula. In a passage found in *Pol.* III, Aristotle gives a remarkable retrospective interpretation of this formula:

> It has already been said in our first considerations – those in which the management of household and the despotic rule have been determined – that man is by nature a political animal. This is why, even if they do not need mutual help, they nonetheless desire to live

---

[26] See *Pol.* I.2, 1253a7–19 (Rackham's translation slightly altered): "And why man is called political animal more appropriately (*mallon*) than any bee or any gregarious animal is clear. For nature, as we declare, does nothing without purpose; and man alone of the animals possesses speech (*logos*). The mere voice, it is true, can indicate pain and pleasure, and therefore is possessed by the other animals as well (for their nature has been developed so far as to have sensations of what is painful and pleasant and to indicate those sensations to one another), but speech is designed to indicate the advantageous and the harmful, and therefore also the right and the wrong; for it is the special property (*idion*) of man in distinction from the other animals that he alone has perception of good and bad and right and wrong and the other moral qualities, and it is community in these things that makes a household and a *polis*."
[27] *Pol.* I.2, 1253a29–30.

together. Nevertheless, they are also brought together by common interest (*to koinêi sumpheron*), insofar as each of the citizens achieves a share of living well. For this is, above all, the objective, for all members both collectively and individually.[28]

This is clearly a back-reference to *Pol.* I.2. The passage reveals an important ambiguity in the 'political animal' formula, which is also present in *Pol.* I.2. On the one hand, this formula implies that human beings – in addition to their needful nature and their need for mutual aid – just enjoy the company of other human beings. This could be dubbed their 'social nature'. On the other hand, it can indicate that it is beneficial or advantageous for human beings to live together in a political community, for this is the only way for them – in accordance with their nature – to get a share of the good and happy life.[29] And it is this latter idea that defines the purpose of the *polis*. For this purpose, the for-the-sake-of-which of the *polis* is something that must be consciously and intentionally pursued. It must result from its members' deliberate choice, while the social nature in the narrow sense merely disposes human beings to a sort of instinct. I interpret this as saying that nature endows us human beings with these impulses and instincts in order to push us in the right direction. However, if we live together in a *polis* for the sake of getting a share of the good and happy life, this is no longer the work of brute instincts, but requires choice and decision. If we then choose, or at least reaffirm, life in a *polis*, this is a choice also made in accordance with our nature, given that *eudaimonia* rests on the actualization of our nature, and given that for someone who naturally desires to live in a household or village, it is similarly (or even more) natural to live in a *polis*. After all this is just the form of community into which households and villages will eventually develop when this development is driven by human beings' search for self-sufficiency.

7 Conclusions

In the preceding article I have attempted to explicate a number of initially unspoken assumptions without which Aristotle's thesis that the *polis* exists by nature appears notoriously disconcerting. At the same time, I have attempted to

---

28 *Pol.* III.4, 1278b17–23, my translation.
29 Thus, I wholeheartedly agree with Kullmann (1991, 102): "As we see Aristotle explains the existence of the state as due to the mixed effect of two factors. The biological factor is primary, which is expressed in the innate *orexis* [desire] for living together [...]. The second factor is the conscious, specifically human striving after gain and happiness, which manifests itself in the detailed shaping of the state."

show that certain other interpretations (especially those comparing the existence-by-nature of the *polis* with the naturalness of living beings, elements and heavenly bodies) lead to consequences that are undesirable from both a philosophical and exegetical point of view. In my reconstruction, the *polis* is not legitimized and normalized through arbitrary references to nature, but solely through its relation to human nature. This has enabled me to reduce the confusing number of appeals to nature and claims of naturalness that one seems to encounter in the first book of Aristotle's *Politics* to a single idea about what is natural. Thereby we reduce the philosophically disagreeable heterogeneity of possible normative sources to a single source. If the *polis* is natural in the sense I have indicated, we cannot derive norms for the *polis* and its institutions from references to nature in general, or to non-human nature. What occurs in non-human nature, as in the jungle or in what ants and bees accomplish together – all of this is natural in some sense, but on my reading it has no implications whatsoever for the *polis*. All other references to natural analogies, natural organisms, or other natural systems of classification therefore also remain without (direct) normative consequences.

But the proposition in question certainly does have normative consequences, which show themselves above all in an argument frequently used by Aristotle, namely that certain institutions or constitutions would not correspond to the nature of the *polis* and should therefore be rejected. The nature/essence of the *polis* is revealed when its development has been completed and when it enables self-sufficiency and good life for its citizens. This self-sufficiency and the good life are, at the same time, that for-the-sake-of-which the *polis* was established by human beings. Book III of the *Politics* contains a series of important references back to the argumentation of *Politics* I.2. In III.6, for example, Aristotle refers to the 'initial investigations' into the object for the sake of which the *polis* was established (1278b15–19). He also reminds us that man is a political animal (1278b19) and that the most important goal in the formation of the *polis* is for everyone to share in the good life (1278b21–23). In the course of the same chapter, a distinction crucial to the *Politics* is drawn between true and deviant constitutions, and a reference is made to the purpose of the *polis*, namely that a true *polis* must benefit everyone, that is, allow everyone to share in the good life, for the sake of which the *polis* was formed. When comparing the democratic and oligarchic conceptions of the *polis* in a subsequent chapter (III.9), Aristotle points out in objection to certain claims made by the oligarchs that the citizens joined together in the first place only for the sake of the good life (1280a31–34). He goes on to assert that the *polis* is not merely the sharing of a common location, but rather "[...] a community of families and of clans in living well, and its object is a full and independent life" (1280b33–35). A similar argument is made a few lines later: "The object of a state is the good life, these things are means to that end. And a state is the community of clans and villages in a full and independent life, which in our view constitutes a happy and noble life" (1280b38–1281a2). All of these remarks refer verbatim to *Politics* I.2 and confirm that the rather cursory remarks at the end of the genetic argument, that the *polis* come into being for the sake of self-sufficiency and exists for the sake of good life, were intended as an essential determination of the *polis*. They also show the extent to which this determination of the nature of the *polis* implies substantial normative consequences.

What sort of normativity is at work here? In his analysis of the tyrannical constitution in *Politics* III.17 Aristotle says that it is not natural (*ouk esti kata phusin*), but developed 'unnaturally' (*para phusin*) like the other deviant constitutions (1287b39–41). At first glance this appears to be an example of justifying norms on diffuse naturalistic grounds. What is *natural* is good, and what is *unnatural* is bad. However, the preceding remarks in Book III have clearly shown that we have no grounds for resorting to this kind of indiscriminate naturalism. As in the passages quoted above, 'natural' and 'unnatural' should be understood as referring back to the *nature of the polis*, which consists in the fact that people unite to form the *polis* for the sake of self-sufficiency and the good life. Forms of government that prevent a group of citizens from duly sharing in benefits and the good life are not in accordance with the nature of the *polis*, in that they do not fulfil the aim for which people combined to form *poleis* in the first place. We have thus also answered the question raised in the title of this paper, namely the question of *whose* state und *whose* nature is at stake in the argument of *Politics* I.2. It is the state of all free people who live in a *polis* for the sake of *autarkeia* and living well, and it is by being in accordance with *their* (human) nature that the state exists 'by nature'.

One of the main messages that Aristotle wants to get across in this chapter is that it is not arbitrary or random for human beings to choose or endorse the life in the *polis*; he uses drastic language to convey the idea that the life in isolation is a kind of deprivation. For someone who wants to make use of the potential of human nature (and happens not to be a god) it even seems that there is no alternative to living in a *polis*. This is why my reading is far from equating Aristotle to Hobbes.[30] In this context, it turns out that the term 'artificial' or 'artifact' applied

---

[30] As Horn (in this volume) seems to think. He classifies my interpretation as 'minimalist', which, in general, I take to be a good thing or even a compliment as it seems to imply that he did not find me guilty of drawing hasty or unsubstantiated conclusions (as 'maximalists' would do), presumably the most embarrassing exegetical vice. In some respects, however, my interpretation was not meant to be as minimalist as Horn seems to think when he treats my read-

to the state is misleading: ontologically speaking, the *polis* is dependent on human minds and human desires and is, thus, an artificial entity – even in Aristotle's view. (*Nota bene:* that the *polis* exists by nature is not an ontological thesis and thus not directed against the idea that it is artificial in the ontological sense; it is a thesis that concerns the role of the *polis* in human life.) However it is not, as it were, a 'random artifact' – something that human beings can equally choose or decline. On the contrary, while artificial in the ontological sense, the *polis* is brought about by and ultimately grounded in practical reason and thus by, or in, human nature (which involves, among other things, that human beings are rational, desire happiness, express themselves through language and live together in communities that exist for the sake of the happy life). One might call it a 'non-accidental' or 'essential artifact', for what it's worth, to mark this difference.

Finally, the conception presented here with regard to Aristotle's *Politics* seems particularly compatible with a plausible interpretation of Aristotle's *Ethics*. According to my reading, there is a close analogy between the founding of *poleis* and the development of virtues of character and intellect. In the second book of the *Nicomachean Ethics* Aristotle says that the virtues are neither present by nature (from birth) nor do they emerge contrary to human nature. Rather, it is in accordance with human nature to develop the virtues. It is the same with the *polis*, which neither exists arbitrarily nor emerges contrary to human nature. Rather, it is the nature of mankind to come together to form *poleis*. If, as Aristotle argues, it is human nature to develop virtues, and if the virtues, as Aristotle as-

---

ing as attack on all kinds of normative or political naturalism. On the contrary, I do defend a kind of naturalism, namely the kind of naturalism that is grounded in human nature. For an interpreter of Aristotle this is not even original, for, clearly, Aristotle is almost always interested in the species-specific nature of a thing (and not in Mother Nature or nature simpliciter); and for an interpreter of *Politics* I.2 a species-specific reading is almost unavoidable, if one wants to do justice to the repeated references to the (political) nature of human beings. In my reading of naturalism, it is owing to human nature that people desire a good life and, for this end, endorse a life in the political community; this involves rational desire, practical reason to some extent, and even the possibility to decide against a life in the *polis* (which decision, to be sure, would be *against* human nature). And this is why the coming about of a *polis* is not in the least compatible to nest-building or to the spinning of a spider web. By the same token, the *polis* is not like a preexisting natural habitat to which the life-form of human-beings would be adapted. This would require a quite implausible reading of the priority argument (see section 2.2 above) and would reverse the direction of explanation: the existence of the *polis* is explained by the nature of human beings and not the other way around (since in Aristotle's biology, above all in *Historia Animalium* VIII and IX, the idea of the natural habitat is invoked to explain differences in the life-style, search for food and certain anatomic details of different species – and not the other way around).

sumes, can best be developed through the self-sufficient life made possible by the *polis*, then the union of individuals striving for virtue and for an independent, happy life in a *polis* must be as much a part of human nature as the development of the virtues themselves.

Primary literature

Aristotle. 1879. *Aristoteles' Politik*, by Franz Susemihl. Leipzig: W. Engelmann.
Aristotle. 1923. *The Politics of Aristotle*, translated with an analysis and critical notes by J. E. C. Welldon. London: Macmillan & Co.
Aristotle. 1944. *Aristotle Politics*, English translation by Harris Rackham (= Aristotle in 23 Volumes, Vol. 21). Cambridge (MA): Harvard University Press.
Aristotle. 1957. *Aristotelis Politica*, by William D. Ross. Oxford: Oxford Clarendon Press.
Aristotle. 1991. *Aristoteles, Politik I* (=Aristoteles, Werke in deutscher Übersetzung 9.1), by Eckhart Schütrumpf. Berlin: Akademie.
Aristotle. 1995. *Aristotle, Politics, Books I–II*, by Trevor J. Saunders. Oxford: Oxford Clarendon Press.
Aristotle. 1996. *Aristotle, The Politics and The Constitution of Athens*, by Stephen Everson. Cambridge: Cambridge University Press.

Secondary literature

Horn, Christoph (this volume). "Normative Naturalism in Aristotle's Political Philosophy?"
Keyt, David and Miller Jr., Fred D. (ed.) 1991. *A Companion to Aristotle's Politics*. Oxford and Cambridge: Blackwell.
Keyt, David. 1991. "Three Basic Theorems in Aristotle's Politics." In *A Companion to Aristotle's Politics*, edited by David Keyt and Fred D. Miller Jr., 118–141. Oxford and Cambridge: Blackwell.
Knoll, Manuel. 2009. *Aristokratische oder demokratische Gerechtigkeit*. München: Fink.
Kraut, Richard. 2002. *Aristotle. Political Philosophy*. Oxford: Oxford University Press.
Kullmann, Wolfgang. 1991. "Man as a Political Animal in Aristotle." In *A Companion to Aristotle's Politics*, edited by David Keyt and Fred D. Miller Jr., 94–117. Oxford and Cambridge: Blackwell.
Labarrière, Jean-Louis. 2004. *Language, Vie Politique, et Mouvement des Animaux. Études aristotéliciennes*. Paris: Vrin.
Miller Jr., Fred D. 1995. *Nature, Justice, and Rights in Aristotle's Politics*. Oxford: Oxford University Press.
Miller Jr., Fred D. 1989. "Aristotle's Political Naturalism." *Apeiron* 22:195–218.
Miller Jr., Fred D. 1991. "Aristotle on Natural Law and Justice." In *A Companion to Aristotle's Politics*, edited by David Keyt and Fred D. Miller Jr., 279–306. Oxford and Cambridge: Blackwell.

Miller Jr., Fred D. 2000. "Naturalism." In *The Cambridge History of Greek and Roman Political Thought*, edited by Christopher Rowe and Malcom Schofield, 321–343. Cambridge: Cambridge University Press.

Mulgan, Richard G. 1974. "Aristotle's Doctrine that Man is a Political Animal." *Hermes* 102:438–445.

Rapp, Christof. 2016. "'Der Staat existiert von Natur aus'– Über eine befremdliche These im ersten Buch der Aristotelischen Politik." In *Menschennatur und politische Ordnung*, edited by Andreas Höfele and Beate Kellner, 45–78. Paderborn: Wilhelm Fink.

Rapp, Christof. 2020. "Definitions in Aristotle's Politics: State and Constitutions." *Revue de Philosophie Ancienne* 38/2:361–404.

Schütrumpf, Eckart. 1981. "Kritische Überlegungen zur Ontologie und Terminologie der Aristotelischen Politik." *Allgemeine Zeitschrift für Philosophie* 6 (2):26–47.

Trott, Adriel M. 2014. *Aristotle on the Nature of Community*. Cambridge: Cambridge University Press.

Fred D. Miller, Jr. and David Keyt
Aristotle on Freedom, Nature, and Law

Abstract: Aristotle holds that laws, even if they are conventional, can be evaluated positively or negatively insofar as they accord with nature or are contrary to it. An important application of this idea, which is recognised by Aristotle, is that a law is unjust by nature if it sanctions the enslaving of human beings who are by nature free. Likewise, in the political realm he opposes correct or just constitutions to those which are 'despotic', in which the rulers treat their subjects like slaves. Surprisingly (at least to modern readers) Aristotle includes democratic constitutions among those which are deviant or unjust by nature. His rationale is that democracy is based on a false definition of freedom. Although he does not explicate his own alternative definition, there is evidence for such a conception, which may be called 'aristocratic freedom', consisting in the rule of reason over desire. Hence, on Aristotle's view, the constitution which is "everywhere according to nature the best" will ensure aristocratic freedom for all its citizens.

1 Introduction

That freedom has an important place in Aristotle's political theory is often overlooked, ignored, or even denied (e.g. Barnes 2005; Hansen 1996, 2013). There is some justification for this insofar as Aristotle does not offer an explicit definition of political freedom or even discuss in a very straightforward way the place of freedom in his own political theory. Nonetheless we shall argue in this essay that Aristotle holds that a just constitution will preserve and promote the freedom of its citizens.

First, however, let us explain what we mean by 'freedom' (*eleutheria*) and related words used by Aristotle. We have previously defended a tripartite analysis.[1] For example, if a prisoner has just been released from prison and is free to go, his freedom involves three factors: (i) an agent (the prisoner); (ii) removal of an impediment (the iron bars of his cell); and a goal (to go where he pleases). There are however two different sorts of impediments. For example, if the prison is on an island and no boats are available, the released prisoner faces two sorts

---
[1] Here we follow the analysis of the modern concept of freedom proposed by MacCallum 1967. Our essay builds on, and draws material from, Keyt 2018 and Miller 2018. Extracts from Schmidtz and Pavel 2018 are by permission of Oxford University Press, USA.

of impediments to his further progress: the *presence* of surrounding water and the *absence* of a boat. The *presence* of the water may be called an 'obstructing' impediment, and the *absence* of a boat a 'disabling' impediment.

The triadic analysis fits the ancient Greek term *eleutheros* rather well. We find it in the following passage from Plato's *Lysis:* "in these matters we shall do what we wish, and no one will willingly impede (*empodiei*) us", Socrates says, "but we shall be free (*eleutheroi*) ourselves in these matters" (210b3–4). Note that in the first half of the sentence Socrates mentions all three terms of the triadic relation of freedom – first the agents ('we'), then the goal (to "do what we wish"), and finally the impediments (other people). We shall also assume that freedom can be understood in both a personal and a civic sense. *Personal* freedom is the freedom of a person from impediments to pursue his own goals. *Civic* (or political) freedom is the freedom of a citizen from impediments to his personal freedom resulting from the political system under which he lives.

Having explained what we mean by freedom, we shall now show how it is related to political justice. We shall begin by describing how political justice, according to Aristotle, involves nature as well as convention. We shall then show that within this framework Aristotle takes a favourable view of freedom in some cases while being at the same time highly critical of the democratic definition of freedom. Although he does not explain his own alternative definition of freedom, we shall argue that such a conception – which we call *aristocratic freedom* – can be elicited from passages scattered throughout the *Politics* and ethical works. Moreover, we shall show that the preservation and promotion of aristocratic freedom so understood is a requirement of political justice as Aristotle understands it.

2 Political justice: natural and conventional

Political justice, according to Aristotle in Book V of the *Nicomachean Ethics*, is present "among those who share a way of life with a view to self-sufficiency, who are free (*eleutherōn*) and are equal either proportionately or arithmetically" (*EN* V.6, 1134a26–28).[2] Further, political justice is "according to law, and is present among those for whom law (*nomos*) naturally exists and who have equality in ruling and being ruled" (1134b13–15). Aristotle's discussion proceeds (*EN* V.7, 1134b18–24):

---

[2] The distinction between arithmetical and proportionate equality will be explained in Section 5. All translations are by the authors, unless otherwise indicated.

Of political justice part is natural (*phusikon*), part conventional (*nomikon*) – natural, that which everywhere has the same potential and does not exist by our thinking it [just] or not; conventional, what at first does not make a difference whether it is this way or that, but, whenever it has been laid down, does make a difference, for example, that a prisoner shall be ransomed for a mina, or that a goat and not two sheep shall be sacrificed, and in laws laid down about particular cases, e. g. that there shall be a sacrifice for Brasidas, and in decrees.

It is noteworthy that Aristotle here treats *natural* justice as a part of political justice.[3] He goes on to observe that some have argued that all justice is *merely* conventional, because "that which is by nature is unchangeable and everywhere possesses the same potential (as fire burns both here and in Persia), while they see just things undergo change" (1134b24–27). Aristotle remarks in the *Nicomachean Ethics* along similar lines that "noble and just things, which political science investigates, exhibit much variety and variation, so that they are believed to exist only by convention and not by nature" (I.2, 1094a14–16). Aristotle agrees with the conventionalist about the variability of just things – "with us [as distinct from the Olympian gods] there is something that is [just] by nature, yet all is changeable" (1134b28–30) – but rejects the conclusion that the conventionalist draws from this fact: "nevertheless some [justice] is by nature, some not by nature" (1134b30). Aristotle offers a counterexample in rebuttal: "by nature the right hand is stronger, and yet it is possible for all people to become ambidextrous" (1134b33–35). If all people became ambidextrous, this variation between one state of affairs and another would not show that right-handedness is not a natural quality. Similarly, variation among different systems of justice does not by itself show that no system is just by nature. Thus, the fact that what is just according to the laws of one *polis* is unjust according to the laws of another is not an argument against natural justice (1134b29–35). Aristotle next compares conventional justice to measures: "those things that are just according to agreement and the advantageous are similar to measures; for wine and grain measures are not everywhere equal, but larger where people buy [wholesale], smaller where they sell [retail]. Similarly, also things that are not naturally but humanly just are not the same everywhere, since neither are constitutions, but one alone is everywhere according to nature the best" (1134b35–1135a5).[4]

---

[3] Natural justice looks like a close relative to natural law, although Aristotle does not mention natural law in his ethical or political works, but only in *Rhet.* I.10, 13, and 15 (where it is not clear to what extent he endorses the notion). See Miller 1991, 282–89 for a comparison of these discussions.

[4] On *EN* V.7 see also Keyt 2017; Miller 1991.

This brief discussion has been interpreted in different ways. One way is to understand political justice as comprising two distinct and mutually exclusive sets of just rules: some are merely conventional, based on an arbitrary decision between initially indifferent alternatives, but which are just after enactment, for example, whether or a goat or two sheep should be sacrificed in a particular ritual. Aristotle does not give examples for natural justice, but he may have in mind customary rules which prevail in all societies, for example, that one should do good to benefactors, that one should be ready help friends, and that children should obey their parents (mentioned at *Rhet.* I.13, 1374a23–25 and Ps.-Aristotle, *Rhet. Al.* 1421b35–1422a4). On the first view the same law cannot be both natural and conventional.[5] However, this seems to leave out of account many, if not most, just laws, and it seems hard to square with Aristotle's concluding remark that only one constitution is best according to nature.[6]

Another, arguably better, way to understand Aristotle is to allow that the lawful (*nomimon*) can be just in both the natural and the conventional sense.[7] Although some laws, like "the rule of the road", may be merely conventional, many laws also seem to have a basis in human nature. For example, it is not a matter of indifference whether children are under the authority of adults or the reverse. The subordinate status of children is based on the fact that their rational faculty is 'incompletely developed' as Aristotle points out (*Pol.* I.13, 1260a13–14). However, this fact alone does not tell us how children are to be supervised and cared for, which adults are to have what responsibilities, and what specific rights and duties children and adults are to have toward each other. These are all matters of convention, and societies vary widely in the conventions which they adopt. Yet these different conventions may be viewed as a way in which different societies are able to accommodate the aforementioned fact about the nature of children.

Thomas Aquinas offers an interpretation along similar lines: when Aristotle says that the conventionally just is what at first a matter of indifference, he is

---

[5] See, for example, Peter Trude: "Nicht aber können sich natürliches und nomisches Recht überschneiden, da sie begrifflich verschieden sind" (1955, 154). Other commentators seem to take this for granted, e.g. Broadie and Rowe 2002, 348 who identify the 'legally just' with laws which are "ad hoc or purely conventional."

[6] Some commentators complain that Aristotle is unclear in his use of *nomikon*, shifting from a purely conventional sense to a moralized sense; see Hardie 1980, 205; Wolf 2002, 98.

[7] As Grant 1885, II, n. 126 observes, "*To nomikon* is not to be confused with *to nomimon*, [...] which is justice expressed in the law, and which is nearly equivalent to *to politikon dikaion*, containing therefore both the natural and conventional elements." To avoid confusion, we translate *nomikon* 'conventional' and *nomimon* 'lawful'.

referring to "those enactments which are by way of determination or signification" of naturally just rules. Aquinas explains this with an analogy to the way the crafts give determinate shape to a common form. "Thus, the craftsman needs to determine the common form of a house to the shape of this or that particular house." In an analogous manner the legislator must derive a particular statute from a precept of nature by way of determination: "e.g. the law of nature has it that the evil-doer should be punished, but that he be punished in this or that way is a determination of the law of nature" (*Summa Theologiae* I–II, q. 95 a. 2, English Dominican translation, ed. Pegis). It follows from this, according to Aquinas, that there is a great diversity of positive laws among various peoples, although they fall under common principles of natural law.[8]

The analogy between legislation and the crafts alluded to by Aquinas sheds light on the relationship between nature and convention. Let us first consider how Aristotle distinguishes between nature and craft in the *Physics*: nature is defined as "a principle of being moved or at rest in that to which it belongs primarily, in virtue of itself and not co-incidentally", while craft (*technê*) belongs to a cause external to the thing, namely, a craftsman (*Phys.* II.1, 192a8–32). For example, a seed becomes a tree because it has a nature within it causing it to grow, while bricks and mortar become a house because a carpenter assembles them into the house. A law, as a legal convention, is a product of craft, and thus a creation of human reason rather than of nature. However, because human beings are rational animals, they are able to use the arts and crafts to develop their innate capacities and dispositions which otherwise would remain unfulfilled. When they do so in pursuit of their natural ends, Aristotle describes the art or craft as 'natural', for example, when the head of a household or statesman uses the art of wealth acquisition in pursuit of life and well-being (*Pol.* I.8, 1256b26–39). Likewise, the legislator should lay down laws in order to supplement nature, a point which Aristotle makes early in the *Politics* (*Pol.* I.2, 1253a29–35):

> Though an impulse toward [political] community exists by nature in everyone, whoever first established it [i.e. this community] was the cause of the greatest of goods. For as a human being is the best of the animals when completely developed, so when separated from law

---

[8] Caveat: Aquinas offers this interpretation as only part of his own theory of natural law, which extends well beyond Aristotle's treatment of natural justice. For example, he goes on to state that a particular law may be derived not only by determination (as described in the main text) but also by deduction from the first principles of natural law as a conclusion from first principles, "e.g. that one must not kill may be derived from the principle that one should do harm to no man." This is to view natural-law jurisprudence as a demonstrative science along the lines described in the *Posterior Analytics*. We find no suggestion of this in Aristotle.

and justice he is worst of all. For injustice is harshest when it possesses weapons, and a human being grows up possessing weapons for virtue and practical wisdom to use, weapons which are especially open to being used for opposite purposes.

Aristotle views the legislator as analogous to a craftsman, although the legislator relies primarily on practical wisdom rather than art (*Pol.* VII.4, 1325b40–1326a5, II.12, 1273b32–3; *EN* X.9, 1180a21–2). The function of the laws and the constitution is to create "a sort of order (*taxis*)" in the *polis* (*Pol.* VII.4, 1326a30; cf. III.16, 1287a18; II.5, 1263a23), which is compared to natural order in the *Movement of Animals* (*MA* 10.703a29–36):

> The animal must be conceived as constituted like a *polis* under good laws. For whenever order exists in a city, there is no need of a separate monarch, who must look over each thing that takes place, but each person does his tasks as ordered, and one thing happens after another because of habit. And in animals the same thing happens because of nature and because each part naturally does its own work.

The habit (*ethos*) to which this refers is virtue (*aretê*), which humans are naturally able to receive but which must be fully developed by habituation (*EN* II.1, 1103a24–26). Hence, "legislators make the citizens good by forming habits in them, and this is the wish of every legislator, and those who do not make them good are mistaken, and it is in this that a good constitution differs from a base constitution" (1103b3–6). When individuals are self-controlled the irrational part of their souls obeys their reason, and even more so when they are virtuous (*EN* I.13, 1102b26–27), and Aristotle states at the beginning of the *Politics* that what is natural and beneficial is for the affective (i.e. the desiring) part of the soul to be ruled by the part that has reason (I.5, 1254b6–9). A good political order is one in which individuals are brought into such a natural condition by being habituated to virtue through the laws. In this sense we might say that the natural order of the *polis* is fully developed when it becomes the political order.

Aristotle also maintains that a craft should not merely develop natural capacities, but it must also be delimited by nature. As Aristotle remarks in connection with childhood education: "One should follow upon nature's division; for all art and education wish to fill up what is lacking in nature" (*Pol.* VII.17, 1337a1–3). A craft or the product of craft which does not conform to nature in this way is unnatural, for example, the art of acquisition is unnatural when it is practiced, as by Midas, in the insatiable pursuit of unlimited riches for their own sake (*Pol.* I.9, 1257b14–23). The same holds for the art of legislation, the product of which is a constitution and laws. Even though entire legal systems are created by convention, they can be evaluated in terms of the extent to which they are in accord with nature, as indicated by Aristotle's claim, cited above, that only one constitution is according to nature the best (*EN* V.7, 1135a3–5). The same goes for particular laws since "the laws should all be enacted according to the constitution, and they all are" (*Pol.* IV.1, 1289a13–15).

To sum up, then, although particular laws, as well as entire constitutions, may be just in a conventional sense, they may also be evaluated either favourably or unfavourably from the standpoint of natural justice. In terms of Aristotle's teleology, the laws may be viewed favourably to the extent that they tend to promote the natural ends of human beings, and unfavourably insofar as they tend to impede the realizations of these ends. Let us now consider how this account of political justice applies to various kinds of freedom.

3 Freedom and political justice

We shall consider here three instances in which Aristotle discusses freedom in connection with justice: his distinction between natural and legal slavery, his criticism of the Persian mode of child-rearing, and his critique of democracy. The first two clearly imply that political justice requires freedom, but the third is more problematic in that it seems, if anything, to imply the opposite.

In discussing the issue of slavery Aristotle argues that "by nature some are free (*eleutheroi*), and others slaves (*douloi*), and for the latter slavery is advantageous and just" (*Pol.* I.5, 1255a1–3). Slavery is just provided that the law of slavery conforms to nature, more precisely to the principle that in a natural system the rational part should rule over the non-rational part (see Miller 2013). Here Aristotle clearly has in mind natural justice; for in this sense of 'slave' "one must say that some are slaves everywhere, others nowhere" (6, 1255a31–32). Aristotle considers an opposing view that some persons are slaves according to law, "because the law is a sort of agreement, and they say that what is conquered in war belongs to the conquerors" (6, 1255a6–7). They contend that the victors have a 'just claim' to their human spoils because "the law is a sort of justice" so that the aforementioned law of war implies that slavery is just (1255a7–8, 21–23). Aristotle replies that this argument overlooks his own distinction between natural slaves and legal slaves. His opponent must admit that if the war itself is unjust and if someone happened to be captured in this unjust war and sold, he would be unworthy of being a slave, but nobody would say that someone unworthy of being a slave is a slave [by nature] (1255a24–26). Aristotle concludes, "There is a certain mutual advantage and friendship for a slave (*doulos*) and a master (*despotês*) who are worthy by nature of being related to each other in this way; but for those who are not related in this way but merely due to law and force, the opposite is true" (1255b12–15). Although this argument depends on the highly objectionable premise that some human beings are suited by nature to be slaves, it also presupposes, more defensibly, that a law is not truly just if it is contrary to nature.

Aristotle's distinction between natural and legal slaves provides a helpful backdrop for the second example, his condemnation of the Persian way of rearing children. As previously noted Aristotle regards paternal authority as justified because children are 'incompletely developed'. This presumably means that their rational faculty is incompletely developed, in contrast to natural slaves who never possess a fully developed rational faculty. A father rules over his children according to nature, and he should rule over them like a benevolent king, educating them for their sake, so as to "fill up what is lacking in nature" in them (I.5, 1259a39–b4; III.6, 1278b; VII.17, 1337a1–3). This still allows for considerable variation in modes of child-rearing. The Persian way, however, is beyond the pale, because "they treat their sons as slaves. Tyranny is the rule of a master over slaves; for it is the advantage of the master that is produced in it" (*EN* VIII.10, 1160b27–31). The clear implication is that the Persian mode of paternal rule is unjust because it involves treating sons as if they were slaves, even though they have the potential to grow into free men. Natural paternal rule, we may infer, is just because it enables the child to mature by "filling up what is lacking in nature" (cf. *Pol.* VII.17, 1337a1–3).

The third example, however, Aristotle's critique of democracy, presents difficulties for the thesis that justice and freedom are congenial. In one passage (*Pol.* VI.2, 1317a40–b17) Aristotle says that democrats define freedom by two marks.[9] The first is "ruling and being ruled in turn." This amounts to saying that democratic justice requires that each free citizen have equal political rights. The second is "to live as one wishes." The second mark differentiates a free man from a slave: a slave does not live as he wishes. Aristotle further says that the second mark 'gives rise' to the first, which can be explained as follows. Take the second mark first. Under the triadic analysis the *agents* are all those counted as free adult male natives under the constitution of a given democracy; the *end*, or *goal*, is living as one wishes; and the *impediment* to this goal would seem to be the interference of others. Thus, the second mark yields a definition of *personal freedom*: a man enjoys democratic personal freedom to the extent that he can live as he wishes without interference from others. We would expect a man to enjoy democratic *civic* freedom to the extent that the political institutions under which he lives foster his democratic personal freedom. This is where the

---

[9] Plato describes democracy in similar terms in *Resp.* VIII, 557a–558c.

first mark of freedom comes in, referring as it does to the political institution of ruling and being ruled in turn. For Greek democrats regard the interference of others, particularly that of political officials, as akin to slavery. They would eliminate it altogether if a political community could exist without it. Since this is not possible, they attempt to minimize such interference by distributing it equally among the citizen body. Their idea seems to be that if each citizen is as much a master of other citizens as any other citizen, then no citizen is either a master or a slave of any other.

In another passage Aristotle claims that democrats, in defining freedom as "doing whatever one wishes", define freedom badly (*Pol.* V.9, 1310a25–36). He objects that "one should not think it slavery to live in harmony with the constitution, but safety." What is here called 'freedom' corresponds to the second mark of freedom in the previous passage. Hence, when Aristotle says people define freedom badly, it is the democratic conception of *personal* freedom that he has in mind. His objections to such freedom are both moral and political. The moral objection is given later: "For the license (*exousia*) to do whatever one wants has no power to keep guard over the evil in each man" (VI.4, 1318b39–1319a1). The political objection implied by the passage before us is that the democrats "think it slavery to live in harmony with the constitution." Presumably they think that to live in harmony with a constitution is to obey its laws and to support its political institutions *even if one does not want to*. Their personal freedom, like that of a slave, will be restricted. Aristotle implies that democratic freedom is at heart anarchic.

The foregoing critique of democracy reflects the high value Aristotle places on safety (*sōtêria*) in legal and constitutional matters. He says in one place that "the safety of a *polis* resides in its laws" (*Rhet.* I.4, 1360a20) and in another that "the safety of the community is the function of its citizens, and the community is the constitution" (*Pol.* III.4, 1276b28–29). Since Aristotle opposes *safety*, rather than freedom, to slavery, one might well suppose that he offers no alternative to the democratic conception of freedom. Indeed, Hansen has concluded that, like Plato, "Aristotle seem[s] to have had no problem rejecting democratic freedom as a mistaken ideal without developing an alternative understanding of political freedom" (2013, 96). However, Aristotle's complaint that democrats define (personal) freedom badly implies that he believes there is a good definition, even if he does not say what it is. We shall argue that Aristotle does in fact have his own conception, which we shall call *aristocratic freedom*. But we will first prepare the way by tracing the roots of this idea back to Socrates.

4 Socratic aristocratic freedom

The rudiments of aristocratic freedom can be found in a notable passage in Xenophon's *Memorabilia* IV.5. In a dialogue with Euthydemus Socrates argues as follows. Doing what is best is characteristic of the free person, whereas being incapable of doing the best things is characteristic of the unfree person. A person lacks self-control if he is ruled by the pleasures of the body. Such a person is unfree because he is incapable of doing the best things and is compelled to do the most shameful. But the worst masters are those that prevent the best and compel the worst, and the worst sort of slavery is rule by the worst masters. Therefore, the worst form of slavery is that by which persons are unfree because they lack self-control.

This passage fits the triadic analysis. The agent of personal freedom is the person. His goal is to do the best things. The bodily pleasures, which are said to prevent him from achieving his goal, are the impediment. By this analysis freedom is the ability to do the best things unimpeded by the bodily pleasures. This is the Socratic version of *aristocratic personal freedom* – where 'aristocratic' means "rule by the best."

Such aristocratic freedom also comes into view in connection with Plato's tripartite psychology, as illustrated by some striking images in the *Phaedrus* and *Republic*. In the *Phaedrus* (244a–257b) Plato's Socrates depicts the soul of a lover as a triad in which a charioteer (reason) holds the reins of an undisciplined black horse (sexual desire) and an obedient white horse (presumably spirit or *thumos*). Using this symbolism and the language of freedom and slavery Socrates states that when the lovers' sexual desire for each other is held in check by reason, "they live a life of blessedness and concord here on earth, self-controlled and orderly, having enslaved that [part] by which vice was brought into the soul and having freed that [part] by which virtue was brought in" (256a8–b3). Here, as in Xenophon's *Memorabilia*, self-control is directly associated with aristocratic freedom. If we apply the triadic analysis of freedom, the agent is the soul; the goal is a blessed life; and sexual desire is the impediment. The soul is able to reach its noble goal when reason is able, with the aid of spirit, to restrain its sexual appetites, just as, in the myth, the charioteer is able to guide his chariot to its destination by exerting control over the undisciplined black horse by enlisting the aid of the docile white horse. In applying the triadic analysis, we assume that Plato means to claim that the whole soul is free when its principal part is free, which is implied in the *Republic* where Socrates infers that the soul is enslaved when its better parts are enslaved to its worst part (IX 577d1–8). By implication and parity of reasoning the soul is free when its principal part is free. In the *Republic* (IX 588b) Socrates compares an embodied soul to a creature composed of three parts – a many-headed beast (desire), a lion (spirit), and a man (reason) – wearing a costume (the human body). At 589d2–3 Socrates speaks of the shamefulness of the tame parts of the soul being 'enslaved' to the wild, and at 591b2–3 of the bestial element of the soul being calmed and tamed, and the gentle part being 'set free'. What brings such freedom to the soul are the cardinal virtues, especially temperance, which in the *Republic* is characterized as "a sort of order" consisting in "the self-control over certain sorts of pleasures and appetites" (IV 430e3–7) and defined as the friendship and concord of the three elements of the soul "when the one that rules and the two that are ruled believe in common that the rational element ought to rule and do not engage in faction against it" (*Resp.* IV 442c10–d1). We thus find evidence in Plato's dialogues of a concept of aristocratic freedom – consisting in the rule of reason over desire – which belongs to the soul itself.[10]

We next offer evidence for a similar conception of aristocratic freedom in Aristotle's writings.

5 Aristotelian aristocratic freedom

5.1 Aristocratic personal freedom

We find a basis for an Aristotelian conception of personal freedom by conjoining two passages in the *Politics*. At the very end of the treatise Aristotle distinguishes two sorts of audience at a musical festival, "one free and educated, the other coarse and composed of artisans, laborers, and other such" and goes on to characterize the souls of the latter as "warped from their natural state" (VIII.7, 1342a18–23). At the beginning of the treatise he says that what is natural and beneficial is for the affective (i.e. the desiring) part of the soul to be ruled by the part that has reason (I.5, 1254b6–9). Taking the two passages together we can infer that a free man has a soul in which reason rules desire and that an unfree man has a soul in which it does not. However, Aristotle's conception is not quite the same as that of Plato or of Xenophon's Socrates. It differs from Xenophon's Socrates in that Aristotle distinguishes moral virtue (*aretê*) from mere self-control (*egkrateia*): although desire obeys the rational part in self-controlled men, in virtuous men "it is still more obedient; for in them it speaks, on all mat-

---

[10] Miller 2018 offers evidence from these and other dialogues including the *Laws* that Plato also speaks more widely of freedom as belonging to individual citizens and to the *polis* itself.

ters, with the same voice as reason" (*EN* I.13, 1102b26–28). Aristotle's conception differs from Plato's in that Plato conceives of the soul and its parts as agents which in their relations to each other can be master or slave, free or bound whereas Aristotle treats the soul as a suite of capacities of a human being and attributes actions to the human by means of the soul, which implies that for Aristotle it is the virtuous agent, not the virtuous soul, that is truly free.

Aristotle's conception of personal freedom, moreover, is aristocratic. The free audience mentioned above is educated and listens to more refined music than an audience of artisans, laborers, and others of the same ilk. Since music is provided for the artisans and laborers as well as the free, we may infer that these artisans and laborers are legally free even though they do not qualify as citizens of Aristotle's ideal *polis* (cf. VII.9, 1328b39–40). But in any case, they would not be 'free' in the sense in which the educated audience is free. For the latter possess a freedom that goes beyond and is superior to mere legal and democratic freedom. In a similar vein Aristotle distinguishes tasks that are free from those that are unfree, the unfree being those that "render the body or mind of a free man useless for the practices and activities of virtue" (VIII.2, 1337b5–11). This suggests that craftsmen such as carpenters, stonemasons, and smiths are consigned to a life of toil, drudgery, and unfreedom. In contrast, the person who is free in the aristocratic sense must be educated to perform acts that are 'noble' (*kalon*) and "for the sake of virtue" and not merely "useful or necessary" (VII.1, 1323b12; VII.14, 1333a32–b3; VIII.3, 1338a30–b4; cf. VIII.2, 1337b19–20).

5.2 Aristocratic civic freedom

Although Aristotle is sometimes thought not to have the concept of civic freedom, there are in the *Politics* occurrences of *eleutheros* that seem unmistakably to refer to civic freedom. Aristotle holds, contrary to Plato, that rule over natural slaves is qualitatively different from rule over the naturally free. He calls the former despotic rule (*despotikê archê:* literally rule of a master) and the latter political rule (*politikê archê*) (I.7, 1255b16–18; contrast Plato *Statesman* 258e–261a). Aristotle's conception of political rule accordingly provides the key to understanding his conception of civic freedom.

The opposition of political rule to despotic rule involves the transference of two pairs of opposed concepts from the personal into the political realm: the opposition of free to slave, and opposition of master to slave. The transfer occurs when Aristotle classifies constitutions in *Politics* III.6. Constitutions are divided into six types by two independent differentiae, the number of rulers and the sort of rule. The rulers number one, few, or many; and their rule aims either at the rulers' own advantage exclusively or at the common advantage. Thus, kingship, aristocracy, and polity have respectively one, few, and many rulers and are ruled in the common interest, whereas the 'deviations' of these 'correct' constitutions – tyranny, oligarchy (literally, rule of the few), and democracy – are ruled solely in the interest of the rulers. The reason the three latter constitutions are deviations, Aristotle explains, is that "they are despotic, whereas the *polis* is a community of the free" (III.6, 1279a21).

What he means by this may be understood from another passage where he claims that when a citizen body is divided between those favoured and those disfavoured by fortune, the fortunate never learn how to be ruled, whereas the unfortunate never learn how to rule. The result, Aristotle says, is "a *polis* of masters and slaves, not of free men" (IV.11, 1295b21–22; see also II.9, 1274a17–18). Since the *polis* of masters and slaves and the *polis* with a despotic constitution are each set in opposition to the same thing – a *polis* of free men – we can infer that for Aristotle the two are the same: a despotic constitution divides citizens into masters and slaves. However, since citizens cannot be slaves, these 'slaves' can only be *virtual* slaves, not literal slaves. Aristotle calls them slaves, because their rulers treat them *as if* they were slaves. The expression 'despotic rule' has also shifted its meaning: from being rule of natural slaves it has become rule of virtual slaves.

The citizens enjoy civic freedom where there is political rule. Such rule has three distinguishing features. (1) It is rule that seeks the common advantage (*to koinon sumpheron*) rather than the advantage of the rulers (III.6, 1279a17–19; VII.14, 1333a3–6). (2) It is willingly accepted (III.14, 1285a25–29, b8, b21–22; V.10, 1313a5–6). And (3) it is alternating, rather than continuous, whenever rulers and ruled are equals in the appropriate respect (II.2, 1261a30–b5; VII.3, 1325b7–8; 14, 1332b25–27). We may infer that the citizens enjoy civic freedom when these three conditions are satisfied.[11]

Aristotle's aristocratic conception of civic freedom differs from the democratic in two main respects: whereas the common advantage for the democrats consists in the citizens being able to do whatever they wish, for Aristotle it consists in "the life of virtue sufficiently equipped to partake of virtuous actions" (VII.1, 1323b40–1324a2). And whereas for the democrats all freeborn men should be arithmetically equal (that is, possess equal political rights), for Aristotle the citizens should be proportionately equal (that is, be assigned political rights in proportion to their virtue [cf. III.9, 1281a2–8]).

---

[11] For (1) see Newman 1887, I, 246; Mulgan 1970, 98. For (2) see Long 1995, 795; and for (3) Liddel 207, 325–331; Kraut 2002, 452 n. 35. Civic freedom in fact involves all three features.

6 Aristocratic freedom in the ideal *polis*

Aristotle's "one constitution that is everywhere according to nature the best" will preserve and protect aristocratic freedom as defined in the previous section. Aristocratic personal freedom requires a soul in a natural condition (see *Pol.* VIII.7, 1342a18–23); such a condition, in which reason rules over the non-rational part of the soul (I.5, 1254b6–9), is most fully realized in a virtuous person (*EN* I.13, 1102b27–28); and Aristotle's best constitution aims to make all of the citizens virtuous so that they can act best and live blessedly (VII.13, 1332a32–38; 2, 1324a23–35; 9, 1329a22–24). The constitution will ensure that all the citizens have private property rights. "For happiness necessarily belongs with virtue, and a *polis* must be called happy not by viewing a part of it but by viewing all the citizens" (VII.9, 1329a17–26). It will also ensure that all the citizens have an education appropriate for a free man (VIII.1, 1337a22–23; 2, 1337b4–15). The system of education should be based upon a study of nature, in order to ensure that our birth and education are guided by our natural end which is our reason or intellect (VII.15, 1334b6–17).

Since in Aristotle's ideal *polis* all the mature citizens are fully virtuous, "it is necessary for everyone alike to share in ruling and being ruled by turns. For equality consists in the same thing for those who are similar, and it is hard for the constitution to endure if it has been established contrary to justice" (VII.14, 1332b26–29). A *polis* will be politically free in the aristocratic sense, then, to the extent that its institutions remove the impediments to the life of virtue for each and every citizen and allow for equal political participation by equally virtuous citizens where the impediments that need to be removed are unfavourable political institutions, lack of moral and intellectual education, and insufficient material resources.[12]

A constitution in which the citizens are free in the aristocratic sense perfectly exemplifies ideal political justice because nature and law coincide in every one of its citizens. Because the citizens of the best constitution are virtuous each of them does his tasks as ordered without any need of a monarch (a 'single ruler') over them all (*MA* 10, 703a33–4). And they, like the freemen in a well-regulated household, "have the least opportunity to act haphazardly, but all things or most things have been ordained for them, whereas the slaves and the animals pay little heed to the common interest, and for the most part do act haphazardly" (*Met.* XII.10, 1075a19–22). Because they are virtuous, each citizen has his soul in a natural condition with reason ruling over desires (*Pol.* I.5, 1254b6–9; *EN* I.13,

---

[12] The argument of this paragraph is more fully presented in Keyt 1991; Miller 1995.

1102b27–28). At the same time, because they are virtuous, each citizen of the best constitution is also one who is "refined and possessed of a free character and a law unto himself" (*EN* V.8, 1127b32). Thus, the ideal *polis* is a community of free and autonomous citizens.

7 Conclusion

We have argued that when Aristotle says that political justice is part natural and part conventional, he means that even though laws and constitutions are established by convention they can be evaluated from the standpoint of nature. Hence, there is one constitution that is everywhere according to nature the best. We also argued that this constitution will be committed to freedom. Although Aristotle rejects the democratic idea of personal freedom on the ground of its consistency with psychological bondage, he has an alternative, 'aristocratic', conception of freedom. We found that for Aristotle this conception has two dimensions: personal freedom and civic freedom. Hence, the constitution which exemplifies true political justice – that is, natural as well conventional justice – will ensure aristocratic freedom, personal as well as civic, for all its citizens.

Primary literature

Aristotle. 1887–1905. *The Politics of Aristotle*, 4 Volumes, by William L. Newman. Oxford: Clarendon Press.
Aristotle. 2002. *Aristoteles' Nikomachische Ethik*, by Ursula Wolf. Stuttgart: Wissenschaftliche Buchgesellschaft.
Aristotle. 2002. *Aristotle: Nicomachean Ethics: Translation, Introduction, and Commentary*, by Sarah Broadie and Christopher Rowe. Oxford: Oxford University Press.

Secondary literature

Barnes, Jonathan. 2005. "Aristotle and Political Liberty." In *Aristotle's Politics: Critical Essays*, edited by Richard Kraut and Steven Skultety, 185–202. Lanham: Rowman & Littlefield.
Grant, Alexander. 1885. *The Ethics of Aristotle Illustrated with Essays and Notes*. London: Longmans, Green, and Co.
Hansen, Mogens Herman. 1996. "The Ancient Athenian and the Modern Liberal View of Liberty as a Democratic Ideal." In *Dēmokratia*, edited by Josiah Ober and Charles Hedrick, 91–104. Princeton: Princeton University Press.

Hansen, Mogens Herman. 2013. "Democratic Freedom and the Concept of Freedom in Plato and Aristotle." In *Reflections on Aristotle's* Politics, Museum Tusculanum Press; reprinted from *Greek, Roman, and Byzantine Studies:* 50 (2010):1–27.

Keyt, David. 1991. "Aristotle's Theory of Distributive Justice." In *A Companion to Aristotle's* Politics, edited by David Keyt and Fred D. Miller, 238–278. Oxford: Blackwell.

Keyt, David. 2017. "Nature and Justice." In *Nature and Justice: Studies in the Ethical and Political Philosophy of Plato and Aristotle*, by David Keyt, 1–19. Louvain-La-Neuve: Peeters.

Keyt, David. 2018. "Aristotelian Freedom" In *The Oxford Handbook of Freedom*, edited by David Schmidtz and Carmen E. Pavel, 160–75. Oxford: Clarendon Press.

Keyt, David, and Fred D. Miller. 1991. *A Companion to Aristotle's* Politics. Oxford: Blackwell.

Kraut, Richard. 2002. *Aristotle: Political Philosophy*, Oxford: Oxford University Press.

Liddel, Peter P. 2007. *Civic Obligation and Individual Liberty in Ancient Athens*. Oxford: Oxford University Press.

Long, Roderick T. 1995. "Aristotle's Conception of Freedom." *Review of Metaphysics* 49:775–802.

MacCullum, Gerald. 1967. "Negative and Positive Freedom." *The Philosophical Review* 76:312–334.

Miller, Fred D. 1991. "Aristotle on Natural Law and Justice." In *A Companion to Aristotle's* Politics, edited by David Keyt and Fred D. Miller, 279–306. Oxford: Blackwell.

Miller, Fred D. 1995. *Nature, Justice, and Rights in Aristotle's Politics,* Oxford: Oxford University Press.

Miller, Fred D. 2013. "The Rule of Reason." In *The Cambridge Companion to Aristotle's Politics*, edited by Marguerite Deslauriers and Pierre Destrée, 38–66. Cambridge: Cambridge University Press.

Miller, Fred D. 2018. "Platonic Freedom." In *The Oxford Handbook of Freedom*, edited by David Schmidtz and Carmen E. Pavel, 143–59. Oxford: Clarendon Press.

Mulgan, Richard. 1970. "Aristotle and the Democratic Conception of Freedom." In *Auckland Classical Essays Presented to E. M. Blailock*, edited by Bruce F. Harris, 95–111. Auckland: Auckland University Press.

Schmidtz, David, and Pavel, Carmen E. 2018. *The Oxford Handbook of Freedom*. Oxford: Oxford University Press.

Trude, Peter. 1955. *Der Begriff der Gerechtigkeit in der aristotelischen Rechts- und Staatsphilosophie.* Berlin: Walter De Gruyter and Co.

Béatrice Lienemann
Aristotle on the Rationality of Women: Consequences for Virtue and Practical Accountability

Abstract: In a notorious passage of the *Politics* Aristotle denies women a place in the political sphere on account of the fact that the deliberative part of a woman's soul is *akuron*, here translated as 'without authority'. Drawing on *Nicomachean Ethics* I.13, the paper shows that Aristotle's moral psychology provides the basis for the deficiency in deliberation that he ascribes to women, as well as slaves and children. One result of this is that, although women can have virtues, this is true of them in a rather different sense than is true of mature, non-slavish men. Since women lack the type of practical wisdom needed for political life, they have the virtues characteristic of those who should be ruled, not those who should rule. However they do exercise a restricted sort of practical wisdom, such as is needed for success in the domestic sphere.

1 Introduction

Aristotle's views on women in the *Politics* accord well with the actual situation in Athens in his time. In contrast to Plato's egalitarian tendencies, Aristotle holds a traditional position on women's rights, roles, and social status. He regards women as unsuited to political participation and denies them a place in the political sphere. As he consistently emphasizes, their appropriate domain is the home, and even there they must play a subordinate role.

It seems that Aristotle not only agreed with the traditional Greek view on women, but indeed did so on philosophical grounds. In a crucial passage in the last chapter of Book I of the *Politics*, he seems to use facts about the souls of different kinds of human beings to justify limiting the domain of women to the household and to found his criticism of Plato's egalitarian position. He says that women do have the deliberative part of the soul, the *bouleutikon*, but he describes it as *akuron*, which is best understood, as I will argue below, in the sense of being 'without authority'.

Starting from this often-quoted and widely discussed description of the specific deficiency ascribed to the deliberative abilities of women in *Pol.* I.13, I will explain, in the first part, what Aristotle might have meant when he called the female *bouleutikon* '*akuron*'. As most commentators maintain, this remark is indeterminate and in need of exploration. I will discuss the two leading interpretations of this claim about the female deliberative faculty, both of which face specific difficulties. Comparing the passage from *Pol.* I.13 with Aristotle's description of the human soul in *Nicomachean Ethics* I.13, I will further explore his attribution of specific parts of the soul to women and slaves. In the second part, I will consider the consequences that follow from the specific deliberative deficiency associated with women and their limited role in the household with respect to their share in the moral and intellectual virtues and their accountability for their actions. As I will argue, the claim that women are only partially accountable for their actions can be explained by reference to their limited role in the household – a role that is itself based on women's deliberative deficiencies and the incompleteness of their virtue.

2 A brief summary of the traditional view and Plato's egalitarian vision

On the traditional view, women were considered hereditary free citizens in the same way that men were; a woman could be a citizen if both her parents were citizens.[1] In this respect, women were equal to free men but differed from slaves, who were unfree and excluded from citizenship. With this said, however, women were unequal to free men with respect to their legal, political and social rights. Although women enjoyed various forms of legal protection, they could do nothing to assert those rights themselves: they could not bring charges, defend themselves, or testify, either on their own or on another's behalf. In legal matters, they had to be represented by their husband or another male relative. Moreover, although women brought their fortunes into the household, they did not have the right to dispose of their dowries of their own accord (they enjoyed this right only to a very limited degree).[2] Furthermore, women had no political rights: they could not participate in politics, were not admitted to the assembly, could not sit in the court, and could not serve in office. Finally, they had no social rights: they did not take part in public activities outside the home, with the ex-

---

[1] In developing the following summary, I owe much to Dorothea Frede's paper on Plato's and Aristotle's views on women as citizens, to be published as a chapter in a volume dedicated to the topic of *Equality* edited by Anagnostopoulos and Santas. Cf. Frede (forthcoming).
[2] Foxhall 1989, 32–39. For a very comprehensive description of the economic rights of women in ancient Greece see Schaps 1979.

ception of religious activities, they did not have access to higher education, and they could not exercise in the palaestra.

Against the background of the actual situation of women in Athens, Plato's conception of the equality of women and men in the *Republic* appears revolutionary. In the ideal state of the *Republic*, Plato assumes the equal right of men and women to participate in political activities. Although he allows for differences, these only amount to inequalities of degree that are not specific to the differences between men and women. As far as the guardian class is concerned, Plato believed that holding women and children in common and abolishing private property in favour of collectivism would guarantee justice, stability and the unity of the city. Whereas the family was traditionally considered the foundation of both stable civic life and individual security, Plato viewed the family as a threat to the unity of the state because of the egoistic tendencies inherent in familial structures.

In the *Laws*, Plato does not directly address the question of equality, but his extensive remarks on the legal, political and social rights of women show that he still adheres to an egalitarian view in this late work. Several laws of the nomocracy, which he views as a second-best constitution, offer significant improvements on the actual status of women in Athens. According to Plato's description, under such a constitution, women would have specific rights with regards to managing and disposing of their property, divorce laws would be recognized, and unmarried women over 40 would have further special rights, such as the right to attend the assembly. Moreover, his discussion of public education shows that he advocated the equal participation of girls and boys at the elementary level (reading, writing, sports) and in military training. With this said, Plato never mentions women when he discusses higher education (mathematics, astronomy); nor does he speak of women in connection with higher institutions of the city or the Nocturnal Council. Furthermore, Plato's view seems to vary with the context. In the cosmological context of the *Timaeus*, he reserved for women a position between men and beasts in the cycle of reincarnation: to be born a woman is an unfortunate form of reincarnation, clearly less choice worthy than being reincarnated as a man. Apart from this peculiar deviation in the cosmological context of the *Timaeus*, however, we can conclude that Plato's egalitarian view on the status of women was indeed innovative and differed in important ways from the actual legal and political status of women in his time.

3 The context of *Pol.* I.13

The most revealing passage when it comes to understanding Aristotle's view on women's deliberative deficiencies is the last chapter of Book I of the *Politics*. Let me briefly summarize the context of these remarks on the rationality of women.[3] In most of the previous chapters of Book I, Aristotle considers the household the smallest unit of the *polis*, and he examines whether slavery can be justified – a question which he answers in the affirmative (*Pol.* I.6). Chapter 13 begins with a new question about slaves, namely whether they can possess moral virtues such as temperance, courage, justice and the like (1259b22–26). He construes this question as a dilemma: if slaves possess moral virtues, how are they different from free men? And yet, it would be absurd to deny that slaves have moral virtues, since they are human beings, and human beings participate in reason (*logos*). In the next step, Aristotle includes women and children in the discussion, suggesting that one can ask in the same way whether women and children possess moral virtues (1259b28–32). Abstracting from these cases, he puts the problem in a more general form, connecting it with the relation of ruler and ruled (1259b32–34). A relation of ruler and ruled holds between free men on the one hand and on the other hand women, children, and slaves.

It is important to remember in this regard that Aristotle distinguishes between different types of rule, which he applies to both the political sphere and the family. First, there is the *despotic* rule of the tyrant over his subjects, which in the household is exerted by the master over his slaves. Second, there is the *kingly* rule of the benign king over his subordinates, which in the family is exerted by the father over his children. And third, there is the *political* rule of citizen over citizen, which in the family is exerted by the husband over his wife. Yet, there is an important difference with respect to political rule: in the state, political rule should ideally be such that citizens take turns ruling and being ruled, because in this context the ruler and the ruled tend by nature to be on an equal footing and not to differ (1255b20–24; 1259b4–10; 1277a25–27). By contrast, Aristotle asserts that the political rule of husband over wife should be permanent. In this respect, there is a crucial asymmetry between political rule in the state and in the family. Although women are born free citizens and are in this respect equal to men, Aristotle does not consider women capable of exerting political rule over their husbands. His justification for this significant difference hinges on the difference between the rational capacities

---

[3] In my reconstruction, I follow the main points presented by Scott 2010.

of women and men and on their differing capacities for virtue. I will explore this further in what follows; first, however, I will return to the context of *Pol.* I.13.

Aristotle restates the question of the possible moral virtues of slaves, women and children by asking whether subjects participate in the same virtues as rulers. He presents this question as a second dilemma: if those that are ruled by nature participate in virtue in the same way as those who rule by nature, why are they subjects, unable to rule? Yet if only the rulers participate in virtue, how is it possible for both ruler and ruled to fulfil their respective functions of ruling and being ruled well? Just as the ruler needs the virtues in order to rule well, the ruled needs the virtues in order to be well ruled. Note that the first horns in both dilemmas seem to be equivalent, while the second horn of the second dilemma is different from the first. The new version of the second horn seems to derive from the newly introduced reference to the relation between ruler and ruled, which is in turn connected to the fact that different virtues belong to ruler and ruled. Aristotle then immediately rejects one possible attempt to avoid the second dilemma: the proposal that ruler and ruled participate in the same virtues to different *degrees*. Given that the distinction between ruling and being ruled is not only a matter of degree but a difference in *kind*, he seems to assume that the difference between the virtues of the rulers and the ruled must also be a difference in kind rather than degree.

In the remainder of the chapter, Aristotle develops his solution to these dilemmas by showing that, although both sides of both dilemmas entail some correct and consistent claims, they require further explanation. In sum, the compromise between the two pairs of the apparently inconsistent sides of both dilemmas lies in holding that, while subjects do participate in the virtues, these virtues are different from those exercised by their rulers. Aristotle justifies this solution by referring to moral psychology and to the psychological differences between different kinds of human beings. Thus, he uses facts about the human soul to explain how subjects partake of moral virtue in different ways. The psychological differences also explain why only men are by nature suited to rule, and why women, slaves, and children are unsuited to participation in political activities and to holding a ruling position in the domestic sphere.

4 Moral psychology as a guiding principle

Let us now take a closer look at the passage where Aristotle presents the psychological facts that he uses as evidence for the natural differences between ruler and ruled:[4]

> Consideration of the soul leads immediately to this view [i.e. the view that subjects do participate in the noble-and-good (*kalokagathia*), only differently]. The soul by nature contains a part that rules and a part that is ruled, and we say that each of them has a different virtue, that is to say (*hoion*), one belongs to the part that has reason (*tou logon echontos*) and one to the non-rational part (*tou alogou*). It is clear, then, that the same holds in the other cases as well, so that most instances of ruling and being ruled are natural. For free rules slave, male rules female, and man rules child in different ways, because, while the parts of the soul are present in all these people, they are present in different ways. The deliberative part of the soul (*to bouleutikon*) is entirely missing from a slave; a woman has it but it lacks authority (*akuron*); a child has it but it is incompletely developed (*ateles*) (*Pol.* I.13, 1260a4–14).

In this passage, Aristotle refers to moral psychology to explain why slaves, women, and children are by nature inferior to men and therefore naturally subject to adult males. In addition, he explains why slaves, women, and children are ruled in different ways by their male rulers. To this end, he describes in further detail the psychological differences between different kinds of human beings. The beginning of the passage introduces a distinction between the part of the soul that has reason (*logon echein*), i.e. the rational part, and the non-rational part (*alogon*) of the soul. He then denies slaves any share in the deliberative part of the soul (*bouleutikon*). At first sight, it might seem that he identifies the deliberative part of the soul, the *bouleutikon*, with the rational part of the soul. I will return to this point in the following, arguing that this identification is mistaken and that we must distinguish between the rational part and the *bouleutikon*. Aristotle goes on to assert that women do have the deliberative part, although it lacks authority (*akuron*). Children, finally, also have the deliberative part, although is it immature (*ateles*). The absence or insufficiency of the delib-

---

[4] *Pol.* I.13, 1260a4–14: καὶ τοῦτο εὐθὺς ὑφήγηται ἀτᾶñ περὶ τὴν ψυχήν· ἐν ταύτῃ γάρ ἐστι φύσει τὸ μὲν ἄρχον τὸ δ' ἀρχόμενον, ὧν ἑτέραν φαμὲν εἶναι ἀρετήν, οἷον τοῦ λόγον ἔχοντος καὶ τοῦ ἀλόγου. δῆλον τοίνυν ὅτι τὸν αὐτὸν τρόπον ἔχει καὶ ἐπὶ τῶν ἄλλων, ὥστε φύσει τὰ πλείω ἄρχοντα καὶ ἀρχόμενα. ἄλλον γὰρ τρόπον τὸ ἐλεύθερον τοῦ δούλου ἄρχει καὶ τὸν ἄρρεν τοῦ θήλεος καὶ ἀνὴρ παιδός, καὶ πᾶσιν ἐνυπάρχει μὲν τὰ μόρια τῆς ψυχῆς, ἀλλ' ἐνυπάρχει διαφερόντως. ὁ μὲν γὰρ δοῦλος ὅλως οὐκ ἔχει τὸ βουλευτικόν, τὸ δὲ θῆλυ ἔχει μέν, ἀλλ' ἄκυρον, ὁ δὲ παῖς ἔχει μέν, ἀλλ' ἀτελές. Translations from the *Politics* follow Reeve 1998, sometimes with slight modifications.

erative part of the soul explains why slaves, women, and children are inferior and subject to the rule of men. All members of these classes are psychologically deficient in some respect and therefore naturally ruled by men, who are supposed to possess the rational part of the soul in the fullest sense. Thus, Aristotle invokes these psychological facts to illuminate the different domestic roles and functions of women, slaves, and children. However, while he clearly uses moral psychology as a guiding principle to explain these different domestic roles, his description of these respective deficiencies is brief and requires elucidation. Leaving aside the qualifications concerning slaves and children, I will focus mainly on the case of women.

There are two main interpretations of Aristotle's claim that, while women do partake of the deliberative faculty (*bouleutikon*), it is *akuron*. One interpretation, originally proposed by Fortenbaugh (1977), reads this qualification *intrapersonally*, in terms of women's supposed inability to control their emotions. The other interpretation, offered among others by Deslauriers (2003), construes the qualification *interpersonally*, in terms of women's subordinate status relative to men. I will briefly discuss the two interpretations and explain why both encounter specific difficulties. As we will see, the problems faced by the first are much more serious than those faced by the second.

4.1 The intrapersonal interpretation

According to Fortenbaugh (1977, 138), Aristotle's assertion that women's deliberative faculty is without authority refers not to interpersonal relationships but to an intrapersonal relationship. Fortenbaugh explains that a woman's deliberative capacity lacks authority on Aristotle's view "because it is often overruled by her emotions or alogical side." Women are too often guided by their pleasures and pains, such that they are, as Fortenbaugh (1997, 138) reads Aristotle, "unfitted for leadership and very much in need of temperance."

The intrapersonal interpretation is implausible for various reasons. The first problem is that the interpretation turns all women into natural acratics and renders them unable to become virtuous. Aristotle defines an acratic person as one who acts against her right decision (*prohairesis*) because the deliberative part of her soul is overruled by her non-rational emotions. What speaks against the assumption that Aristotle conceives of women as acratics by nature? He never asserts that women are naturally prone to *akrasia*. On the contrary, at *EN* VII.6, 1148b31–34, Aristotle denies the view that women, by virtue of playing the passive rather than the active role in sexual intercourse, are thereby acratic.[5] This assumption is misleading, he argues, because *akrasia* does not have nature as its cause. Furthermore, he repeatedly insists that women and children must be educated to become good (1260b13–20):

> […] both women and children must be educated with an eye to the constitution, if indeed it makes any difference to the virtue of the city-state that its children be virtuous, and its women too. And it must make a difference, since half the free population are women, and from children come those who participate in the government.

This clearly shows that Aristotle allows that women can become virtuous, although he assumes different standards of virtue with respect to women and men, as we will see below (cf. 1260a14–17).

The second objection is based on linguistic observations. In connection with the first difficulty, it is important to note that *akuron* is not synonymous with *akratês*. In general usage, *akuros* refers not to a psychological inability to control oneself but to a lack of authority in a legal, political, or socio-economic sense. It is most often used with reference to people who lack authority or certain powers, but also to invalid laws, decrees, or decisions in a legal or political context. A woman in Athens may be considered *akuros* to the extent that she has lived her life under the guidance of a male relative – perhaps her father or her husband – who is *kurios* over her in legal and economic matters. Such a woman is powerless in the sense that she is not capable of deciding and acting autonomously in the political arena, which comprises legislative, executive and judicial decision-making. Furthermore, she cannot make independent decisions about the household, or can only do so to a very limited extent. This general use of *akuros*, which accords with Aristotle's occasional use of the word, speaks in favour of the interpersonal interpretation that refers to women's lack of authority and power relative to men.

Moreover, there is a third difficulty concerning the explanatory power of the intrapersonal interpretation. Karbowski (2014, 443–444) has recently argued that Fortenbaugh's interpretation cannot explain why Aristotle attributes partial authority to women in the household but not in the state. Fortenbaugh presents his interpretation in a general way, suggesting that women's lack of authority over their emotions affects their ability to lead not only at the political level

---

[5] *EN* VII.6, 1148b31–33: "Where nature is responsible, then, no one would call these types un-self-controlled, any more than one would call women un-self-controlled because they have the passive rather than the active role in copulation." Translations from the *Nicomachean Ethics* follow Broadie and Rowe 2002, sometimes with slight modifications.

but also in the home. This conflicts, however, with Aristotle's conception of the domestic role of women. That Aristotle holds an asymmetric view with respect to the position of women at the political and the domestic level is shown in the following passage from Book VIII of the *Nicomachean Ethics:*[6]

> The community formed by man and wife is clearly of an aristocratic kind; for the man rules on the basis of worth, and in the spheres where a man should rule; those where it is fitting for a woman to rule he gives over to her. If the man lords it over everything, his rule changes into oligarchy; for the distribution in that case takes no account of worth, or of where his superiority lies. Sometimes women rule a household, because they have inherited property; their rule, then, is not based on excellence, but comes about because of wealth and power, as in oligarchies (*EN* VIII.10, 1160b32–1161a3).

Here, Aristotle explicitly admits that women are not completely subordinate to men at the domestic level. On the contrary, he attributes a limited authority to women within the household. Women's ruling over specific aspects of the household where men have no jurisdiction is appropriate at the domestic level in the case of specific decisions and actions that women are better than men at performing. Aristotle is not very explicit about these specific functions, but he indicates that the preservation of goods in the household is women's business, while providing the goods from outside the home is a man's job. Fortenbaugh's interpretation falls short when it comes to explaining why Aristotle attributes partial authority to women at the domestic but not at the political level.

Nevertheless, it is important to note that this criticism of the intrapersonal interpretation does not preclude Aristotle's viewing women generally as overly emotional compared to men. In fact, in the *Historia Animalium* IX.1 (608b6–18), Aristotle outlines typically female characteristics, describing women as more compassionate than men, more easily moved to tears, more jealous, more querulous, more apt to scold and strike, more prone to despondency, and less hopeful. Although this description suggests that Aristotle shares the view that women are in principle more emotional than men and, as a consequence, less able to control their emotions, he is not referring to this assumption when he claims that the deliberative part of a woman's soul lacks authority.

---

[6] *EN* VIII.10, 1160b32–1161a3: ἀνδρὸς δὲ καὶ γυναικὸς ἀριστοκρατικὴ φαίνεται· κατ' ἀξίαν γὰρ ὁ ἀνὴρ ἄρχει, καὶ περὶ ταῦτα ἃ δεῖ τὸν ἄνδρα· ὅσα δὲ γυναικὶ ἁρμόζει, ἐκείνῃ ἀποδίδωσιν. ἁπάντων δὲ κυριεύων ὁ ἀνὴρ εἰς ὀλιγαρχίαν μεθίστησιν· παρὰ τὴν ἀξίαν γὰρ αὐτὸ ποιεῖ, καὶ οὐχ ᾗ ἀμείνων. ἐνίοτε δὲ ἄρχουσιν αἱ γυναῖκες ἐπίκληροι οὖσαι· οὐ δὴ γίνονται κατ' ἀρετὴν αἱ ἀρχαί, ἀλλὰ διὰ πλοῦτον καὶ δύναμιν, καθάπερ ἐν ταῖς ὀλιγαρχίαις.

4.2 The interpersonal interpretation

The interpersonal interpretation comes in two versions: one *conventional* or *empirical*, the other *normative*. The conventional version construes the subordinate status of women as a social fact, a mere matter of convention. This version can be excluded immediately because it contradicts Aristotle's reference to moral psychology in *Pol.* I.13. Here, he uses psychological facts as a natural – not conventional – basis for his assumption of the subordinate status of women. The normative version, which is defended for instance by Deslauriers (2003, 229), views the claim that women's deliberative faculties are without authority as meaning that:

> [...] deliberations of women are subject to the authority of the deliberative faculty of men. That is because, on Aristotle's view, the deliberative faculty operates only in a particular domain, the household, which exists for the sake of another domain, the city. Because the household is for the city, the city is better than the household, and hence the rule of the former is without authority relative to the rule of the latter.

The normative interpersonal interpretation avoids the first and second difficulties because it interprets *akuron* according to its usual meaning, in the sense of powerlessness or lack of authority in a legal, political or socio-economic context, which appropriately describes the actual status of women relative to men. The interpersonal interpretation also meets the third objection because it explicitly refers to the different domains in which the deliberative faculties of women and men operate. It acknowledges the adequacy of female deliberative faculties in the domestic sphere, but at the same time it denies that women have the rational faculties required for political activity. An explanatory gap remains, however, for the interpretation does not explain *why* women's deliberative faculties are only suited to domestic affairs. To see why Aristotle considers women's deliberative faculties suitable only for domestic affairs, while they are insufficient for political activity, some scholars refer to the paragraph that immediately follows the description of the psychological differences in *Pol.* I.13. I will return to this passage below, since it helps to explain the limited accountability held by women for their actions. First, however, I will further explore Aristotle's attribution of certain parts of the soul to women and slaves. In order to analyse his distinction between different parts of the soul, it is illuminating to include slaves in addition to women and to compare the description in *Pol.* I.13 with Aristotle's outline of the human soul in *Nicomachean Ethics* I.13.

5 The rational and non-rational parts of the soul in the case of women and slaves

In *EN* I.13, Aristotle holds that the expert on ethical and political matters should have some knowledge of the soul to the extent that such knowledge illuminates the nature of virtue. This passage is the most detailed account of the nature of the human soul in Aristotle's extant writings. He starts his description by distinguishing between a non-rational and a rational part or aspect of the soul. The non-rational part comprises two aspects, the first of which is responsible for vegetative functions (such as nutrition and reproduction). This part is of no interest to the legislator because it does not share in human virtue and is not susceptible to reason. The second aspect of the non-rational part is rational in an extended sense, however, in that it is capable of obeying and being influenced by reason. This part of the soul is the "desiderative part in general" (*holōs orektikon*) which covers appetite and *thumos*, but presumably not wish.[7] This part, although it is non-rational, is at the same time rational insofar as it can listen to reason. With this said, it falls short of the rational part in the strict sense, which is capable of reasoning in its own right.

With this brief outline in hand, what parts of the soul does Aristotle attribute to slaves and women? I will start with the case of slaves. In *Pol.* I.13, Aristotle says that while these parts of the soul are present in all these people – namely men, women, slaves and children – they are present differently in each case. He continues with the remark that the deliberative part is missing in slaves. It seems natural to refer the phrase 'the parts' to the rational and non-rational parts of the soul mentioned previously. It then seems that Aristotle is attributing the rational part to slaves but denying them the deliberative part. This shows that we should not identify the rational part with the deliberative part and should instead conceive of the rational part as encompassing more than the deliberative part. This still leaves us with the question of which rational part, if not the deliberative part, belongs to slaves. The remark at *EN* I.13 helps to answer this: the non-rational part of the soul that is rational in the sense of being capable of obeying reason seems likely to be that part of the soul in which slaves also share. Looked at one way, it is rational because it can be influenced by reason, but without

---

[7] Cf. Lorenz 2006, 186; *pace* Price 1995, 110; for a longer discussion of this passage in *EN* I.13 see Lienemann 2018, 385–390.

sharing the same 'evaluative outlook' with reason.⁸ Looked at another way, it is non-rational because it is not capable of reasoning in its own right in the sense of not being able to deliberate and to reason (*hōsper sullogisamenos*), and presumably not even in the sense of forming beliefs on their own and being persuaded by reasons.⁹ The capacity for reasoning in its own right presupposes the deliberative part of the soul, which is rational in the strict sense.

At *EN* I.13, Aristotle explores how the non-rational part participates in reason in the case of the self-controlled person (encratic). The self-controlled person has strong and objectionable desires, which are in principle suitable for bringing her to act in pursuit of the objects of her non-rational desires. Yet in the case of the self-controlled person, the non-rational part, which is the source of her bad appetites, does not prevail but rather *obeys* reason. Aristotle compares the capacity of the non-rational part to listen to and obey reason with the way in which children listen to the advice of their fathers or friends. He adds that the non-rational part is in some sense persuaded by the rational part, which in some sense admonishes, warns, reprimands, and encourages. It is plausible to assume that Aristotle attributes to slaves this part of the soul, which can be classified as rational as much as non-rational depending on the perspective one holds. Nonetheless, what remains in dispute is how we ought to understand the capacity to be persuaded by reason. There are two possible interpretations on this front. The stronger version, defended by Cooper (1999b, 245), holds that persuasion presupposes being rational in the unqualified sense, such that the non-rational part is able to adopt the evaluative outlook of the rational part in the strict sense. Other scholars, including Lorenz (2006, 189) and Grönmoos (2007, 259), object (rightly, in my view)¹⁰ that Aristotle is not speaking about genuine persuasion in this passage, but rather uses the term in a looser sense (*pōs*). Encouragement and admonition do not necessarily involve reason; indeed, to encourage someone by invoking prospective pleasures or to warn someone by invoking prospective pains only re-

---

8 The designation 'evaluative outlook' is John Cooper's. Cooper holds the view that Aristotle argues that reason controls the non-reasoning desires "not just by getting them to 'follow' its directions (somehow or other), but by *persuading* them [...]" (Cooper 1999b, 245). In a remark on *EN* VII.6 and 7 Cooper maintains similarly: "Spirited desires, Aristotle points out, unlike appetites (however sophisticated), can or do directly incorporate some of the reasoned evaluative reflection that might lead (or might have led) to a decision to act as those desires themselves impel one to." (Cooper 1999a, 260–261).
9 Cf. *EN* VII.6, 1149a24–b3.
10 For an extended discussion of this point, see Chapter 10 in Lienemann 2018.

quires *phantasiai* on the part of the persuaded person, which Aristotle attributes to the perceptual faculty.[11]

If this interpretation of the cognitive capacities of slaves is correct, what then follows with respect to their accountability for their actions? According to my understanding of Aristotle's conception of accountability, to be accountable for one's actions in the fullest sense presupposes that a person shares in the rational part in the strict sense, because a genuine action is based on deliberation issuing in a decision about how to act (*prohairesis*). Slaves' actions cannot be based on a decision because they lack the deliberative part of the soul. Their actions are only praiseworthy or blameworthy to the extent that they are correct executions of their masters' orders. Slaves can be held responsible for adequately listening to the commands of their rulers, but they are not accountable for the quality of their actions, which they execute under the guidance of their masters without sharing their evaluative outlook.

I will now turn to the case of women. In *Pol.* I.13, Aristotle attributes all parts of the soul to women. This includes the deliberative part, but only in a qualified sense: in women, the *bouleutikon* is *akuron*, lacking authority. According to the distinction from *EN* I.13, this means that women have the non-rational part that is rational insofar as it is capable of obeying reason; beyond this, and unlike slaves, they share in the rational part in the strict sense – the part which is capable of reasoning in its own right. Obviously, the crucial question is how the restriction of women's deliberative capacities as *akuron* is to be understood. This can best be explained by reference to the architectonic relationship between husband and wife, as I will show in the next section. I will conclude this section with a brief preliminary remark on women's accountability for their actions. Since women have the capacity to deliberate, they are capable of reasoning in its own right. This means that women are in principle capable of deliberating about the best way to achieve a certain goal and to issue a decision to act. Thus technically, women do possess the capacities necessary for being held accountable for their actions in the full sense, namely the capacities of deliberation and decision-making. Nevertheless, Aristotle qualifies the deliberative ca-

---

11 Several remarks in the *Politics* also speak clearly in favor of the weaker interpretation, cf. *Pol.* I.5, 1254b20 – 24: "For he who can belong to someone else (and that is why he actually does belong to someone else), and he who shares in reason to the extent of understanding it but does not have it himself (for the other animals obey not reason but feelings), is a natural slave." and *Pol.* I.13, 1260b5 – 7: "Hence those who deny reason to slaves, but tell us to give them orders only, are mistaken; for slaves should be admonished more than children." [διὸ λέγουσιν οὐ καλῶς οἱ λόγου τοὺς δούλους ἀποστεροῦντες καὶ φάσκοντες ἐπιτάξει χρῆσθαι μόνον· νουθετητέον γὰρ μᾶλλον τοὺς δούλους ἢ τοὺς παῖδας].

pacities of women in a substantial sense. This suggests that women's accountability for their actions must also be qualified, as I will argue in the final section. First, however, it is useful to return to *Pol.* I.13, since it contains hints that will help us to understand the qualification placed on women's deliberative capacities. Moreover, it brings to light a crucial insight: these psychological differences are directly connected to different ways of participating in moral virtue. At the end, I will explore in detail the specific kind of moral and intellectual virtue that Aristotle attributes to women, which is also essential to determining their accountability for their actions.

6 The archetypal relation between the master craftsman and his assistant

Let us start by considering the following passage:[12]

> We must suppose, therefore, that the same necessarily holds of the virtues of character too: all must share in them, but not in the same way; rather, each must have a share sufficient to enable him to perform his own task. Hence a ruler must have virtue of character complete, since his task is unqualifiedly that of a master craftsman, and reason is a master craftsman, but each of the others must have as much as pertains to him. It is evident, then, that all those mentioned have virtue of character, and that temperance, courage, and justice of a man are not the same as those of a woman, as Socrates supposed: the one courage is that of a ruler, the other that of an assistant, and similarly in the case of the other virtues too (*Pol.* I.13, 1260a14–24).

After the description of the psychological differences at 1260a4–14, Aristotle continues at 1260a14–15 with an important consequence which is supposed to follow from the different deliberative faculties: the way in which subjects share in the rational part of the soul necessarily reflects the way in which they participate in moral virtues (or virtues of character). In other words: all subjects participate in moral virtues, but they do so differently, according to their deliberative faculties. In the next step, Aristotle refers to the relation between

---

[12] *Pol.* I.13, 1260a14–24: ὁμοίως τοίνυν ἀναγκαίως ἔχειν καὶ περὶ τὰς ἠθικὰς ἀρετὰς ὑποληπτέον, δεῖν μὲν μετέχειν πάντας, ἀλλ' οὐ τὸν αὐτὸν τρόπον, ἀλλ' ὅσον ἱκανὸν ἦ ἑκάστῳ πρὸς τὸ αὑτοῦ ἔργον· διὸ τὸν μὲν ἄρχοντα τελέαν ἔχειν δεῖ τὴν ἠθικὴν ἀρετήν (τὸ γὰρ ἔργον ἐστὶν ἁπλῶς τοῦ ἀρχιτέκτονος, ὁ δὲ λόγος ἀρχιτέκτων), τῶν δ' ἄλλων ἕκαστον ὅσον ἐπιβάλλει αὐτοῖς. ὥστε φανερὸν ὅτι ἔστιν ἠθικὴ ἀρετὴ τῶν εἰρημένων πάντων, καὶ οὐχ ἡ αὐτὴ σωφροσύνη γυναικὸς καὶ ἀνδρός, οὐδ' ἀνδρεία καὶ δικαιοσύνη, καθάπερ ᾤετο Σωκράτης, ἀλλ' ἡ μὲν ἀρχικὴ ἀνδρεία ἡ δ' ὑπηρετική, ὁμοίως δ' ἔχει καὶ περὶ τὰς ἄλλας.

ruler and ruled and connects this point to the different ways of participating in the moral virtues. He argues that the ruler must possess moral virtue perfectly or completely (*telean*) because he must fulfil the task of the master craftsman (*architektonos*). The ruler requires the deliberative faculties in the fullest sense because reason is a master craftsman. Aristotle calls reason (or the rational part of the soul) the master craftsman, because he views the rational part to be that part of the soul that rules by nature, whereas the non-rational part is naturally ruled. Although Aristotle is not explicit about the converse, we can assume that subjects only need limited deliberative faculties and that their moral virtues are imperfect. At the end of the passage, he describes the moral virtues of subordinates as assistant virtues (*hypêretikê*). Imperfect moral virtues seem to be appropriate for subordinates because the latter are ruled by nature and fulfil only subordinate tasks in the household.

Some scholars consider it important that Aristotle refers to the architectonic relation between master craftsman and assistant at this point.[13] He employs the architectonic relation in order to illuminate why only men's deliberative faculties are appropriate at the political level, while the female deliberative part of the soul's lacking authority is what makes women suited only to domestic roles. How can the architectonic relation be explored in more detail? At the beginning of the *Nicomachean Ethics*, Aristotle describes political science, the science of the legislator, as the 'most authoritative competence' (*kuriotatê*), which comprises the good of the whole state and which is "more beautiful and godlike" than the second essential competence, which is sufficient for making decisions concerning one's own life, i.e. the competence of the ordinary citizen (*EN* I.2, 1094a26–b11). Furthermore, he presents a hierarchical classification of the different disciplines performed in the state: political art is at the top of the hierarchy and is *kurios*, whereas other necessary disciplines such as rhetoric, strategy, and household management are subordinate to the art of politics because they fulfil subsidiary tasks which provide necessary assistance to the master discipline. It seems that Aristotle presupposes similar architectonic characteristics with respect to the marital relation. The master craftsman has authority over his subordinate assistants in the sense that he gives orders or commands to the latter, by which he controls and leads their actions. The master ought to have authority over his assistants because he alone has knowledge of the highest or best end. This epistemological point is very important. The ruler must have the ability to grasp the end or final good of a certain domain systematically. The subordinates, on the other hand, do not need to be able to grasp general ends. Because

---

13 See for example Karbowski 2014, 446–447.

they are guided by their masters, their actions are informed by the authoritative knowledge of their leaders. Subordinates need only the ability to understand the orders and to perform them adequately. Finally, Aristotle classifies the different disciplines, in line with the architectonic relation between master and assistant (cf. *EN* I.2). At the top is the master discipline of political science, which oversees the end of the whole state. In contrast, the other disciplines perform necessary subsidiary tasks that promote the ultimate end of the state. The activities of the assistant disciplines are subordinate to the master discipline because their contribution to the highest end is of a limited scope; they serve an inferior end that is part of the highest end but subsidiary to it, e.g. the provision of materials or tools. The assistants perform their tasks under the tutelage of their masters, who have the necessary general knowledge.

If we now return to the marital relation, it looks as if the characteristics of the architectonic relation between master craftsman and assistant also apply in a similar way to the relation between husband and wife.[14] The husband is by nature the ruler and has authority over his subordinates – his wife, his children, and his slaves. He is the natural ruler because of his superior deliberative abilities. Given that he alone possesses the rational part of the soul in the fullest sense, only he is able to grasp the ultimate end of the household systematically. By means of his authority with regard to the highest end, he is able to give orders to his wife in order to guide her in the fulfilment of her subsidiary household tasks. We have seen that Aristotle grants women some authority over specific domestic affairs where it is fitting for a woman to rule. With the exception of a few hints, he says very little about these specific domestic tasks, however. In Book III of the *Politics*, at 1277b24–27, he ascribes to women the task of preserving the property that the husband has acquired in the public sphere. This suggests that the role of women is clearly confined to the household. Although a woman has some authority in the management of the household, her domestic role is nevertheless subordinate to her husband's because her domestic activities are subsidiary to masculine activities. A woman is informed and guided in her actions by her husband, who exercises the relevant knowledge of the highest end of the household. Women only need the deliberative ability to understand and execute their husbands' orders in order to promote the highest end. With regard to specific matters, where women have authority to decide and act independently, the ability to grasp the ultimate end systematically with a view to freely deciding on a course of action is not necessary.

---

14 I here take up a suggestion made by Karbowski 2014, 446–448.

7 The moral and intellectual virtues of women

In the final section, I will focus on a point that I have only touched on so far, although it is crucial for determining the specific role and status of women at the domestic and the political level – namely the different kinds of virtues ascribed by Aristotle to men on the one hand and to women, slaves, and children on the other. In what follows, I will again focus on the case of women. At 1260a4–24, Aristotle argues that their different cognitive capacities explain how it is that men and women necessarily have different kinds of moral virtues. Since men's reason is more hegemonic (*hêgemonikōteron*, 1259b2) and is of the architectonic kind (*architektōn*, 1260a18–19), men necessarily have perfect or complete virtues of character. Women, by contrast, have only the assistant kind of reason, and thus partake only of imperfect moral virtues. This passage makes clear that Aristotle conceives of different kinds of virtues of character, relative to men and women. The different virtues of men and women reflect their different cognitive capacities and their correlate roles in the household and the state. The question I would like to address here is how we might specify the incompleteness of women's share in the virtues, both moral *and* intellectual. It is worth noting that, in the *Nicomachean Ethics*, Aristotle does not hint at such a distinction between different kinds of virtues of character. With this said, he assumes a distinction between different kinds or ranges of practical wisdom (*phronesis*) in Book VI of the *EN*:[15]

> Political expertise and [practical] wisdom are the same disposition, but their being is not the same. Of the disposition as it relates to the city, the architectonic form of [practical] wisdom is legislative expertise, while the form of [practical] wisdom at the level of particulars is given the generic name 'political expertise', and this is concerned with action and deliberation, since a decree is something to be acted upon, as what comes last in the process. This is why only people at this level are said to take part in politics, because only they *do* things, like various kinds of manual workers. With [practical] wisdom too, what is thought to be [practical] wisdom most of all is the sort that relates to oneself as an individual, and it is this that is given the generic name, i.e. '[practical] wisdom' (of those other forms of it,

---

15 *EN* VI.8, 1141b23–33: ἔστι δὲ καὶ ἡ πολιτικὴ καὶ ἡ φρόνησις ἡ αὐτὴ μὲν ἕξις, τὸ μέντοι εἶναι οὐ ταὐτὸν αὐταῖς. τῆς δὲ περὶ πόλιν ἡ μὲν ὡς ἀρχιτεκτονικὴ φρόνησις νομοθετική, ἡ δὲ ὡς τὰ καθ' ἕκαστα τὸ κοινὸν ἔχει ὄνομα, πολιτική· αὕτη δὲ πρακτικὴ καὶ βουλευτική· τὸ γὰρ ψήφισμα πρακτὸν ὡς τὸ ἔσχατον. διὸ πολιτεύεσθαι τούτοις μόνον λέγουσιν· μόνοι γὰρ πράττουσιν οὗτοι ὥσπερ οἱ χειροτέχναι. δοκεῖ δὲ καὶ φρόνησις μάλιστ' εἶναι ἡ περὶ αὐτὸν καὶ ἕνα· καὶ ἔχει αὕτη τὸ κοινὸν ὄνομα, φρόνησις· ἐκείνων δὲ ἡ μὲν οἰκονομία ἡ δὲ νομοθεσία ἡ δὲ πολιτική, καὶ ταύτης ἡ μὲν βουλευτικὴ ἡ δικαστική.

one is household management (*oikonomia*), another is legislation, another is political expertise, the last being split into deliberative and judicial) (*EN* VI.8, 1141b23–33).

At *EN* VI.8, 1141b23–33, Aristotle distinguishes between the architectonic form of practical wisdom of the legislator and the type of practical wisdom of the ordinary citizen, which is concerned with particulars. He adds that practical wisdom is primarily concerned with the individual, be it with respect to household management, legislation or political expertise. Without going into further detail, it suffices to note that Aristotle allows for a distinction between different kinds of *phronesis* in the *EN*.

In order to determine Aristotle's conception of different ranges of *phronesis*, another passage from Book III of the *Politics* is essential. In the context of this passage, at the end of Chapter 4, he discusses the ability and willingness of citizens in general to rule and be ruled in turn:[16]

> And whereas the virtues of these *are* different, a good citizen must have the knowledge and ability both to be ruled and to rule, and this is the virtue of a citizen, to know the rule of free people from both sides. In fact, a good man too possesses both [i.e. virtues of the ruler and of the ruled], even if a ruler does have a different kind of justice and temperance. For if a good person is ruled, but is a free citizen, his virtue (justice, for example) will clearly not be of one kind but includes one kind for ruling and another for being ruled, just as a man's and a woman's courage and temperance differ. For a man would seem a coward if he had the courage of a woman, and a woman would seem garrulous if she had the temperance of a good man, since even household management differs for the two of them (for his task is to acquire property and hers to preserve it). Practical virtue is the only virtue peculiar to a ruler; for the others, it would seem, must be common to both rulers and ruled. At any rate, practical virtue is not the virtue of one who is ruled, but true opinion is. For those ruled are like makers of flutes, whereas rulers are like the flute players who use them (*Pol.* III.4, 1277b13–30).

---

[16] *Pol.* III.4, 1277b1–30: τούτων δὲ ἀρετὴ μὲν ἑτέρα, δεῖ δὲ τὸν πολίτην τὸν ἀγαθὸν ἐπίστασθαι καὶ δύνασθαι καὶ ἄρχεσθαι καὶ ἄρχειν, καὶ αὕτη ἀρετὴ πολίτου, τὸ τὴν τῶν ἐλευθέρων ἀρχὴν ἐπίστασθαι ἐπ' ἀμφότερα. καὶ ἀνδρὸς δὴ ἀγαθοῦ ἄμφω, καὶ εἰ ἕτερον εἶδος σωφροσύνης καὶ δικαιοσύνης ἀρχικῆς. καὶ γὰρ ἀρχομένου μὲν ἐλευθέρου δὲ δῆλον ὅτι οὐ μία ἂν εἴη τοῦ ἀγαθοῦ ἀρετή, οἷον δικαιοσύνη, ἀλλ' εἴδη ἔχουσα καθ' ἃ ἄρξει καὶ ἄρξεται, ὥσπερ ἀνδρὸς καὶ γυναικὸς ἑτέρα σωφροσύνη καὶ ἀνδρεία (δόξαι γὰρ ἂν εἶναι δειλὸς ἀνήρ, εἰ οὕτως ἀνδρεῖος εἴη ὥσπερ γυνὴ ἀνδρεία, καὶ γυνὴ λάλος, εἰ οὕτω κοσμία εἴη ὥσπερ ὁ ἀνὴρ ὁ ἀγαθός· ἐπεὶ καὶ οἰκονομία ἑτέρα ἀνδρὸς καὶ γυναικός· τοῦ μὲν γὰρ κτᾶσθαι τῆς δὲ φυλάττειν ἔργον ἐστίν). ἡ δὲ φρόνησις ἄρχοντος ἴδιος ἀρετὴ μόνη. τὰς γὰρ ἄλλας ἔοικεν ἀναγκαῖον εἶναι κοινὰς καὶ τῶν ἀρχομένων καὶ τῶν ἀρχόντων, ἀρχομένου δέ γε οὐκ ἔστιν ἀρετὴ φρόνησις, ἀλλὰ δόξα ἀληθής· ὥσπερ αὐλοποιὸς γὰρ ὁ ἀρχόμενος, ὁ δ' ἄρχων αὐλητὴς ὁ χρώμενος.

According to Aristotle, the regular turn-taking between ruler and ruled requires the possession of two different sets of virtues on the part of citizens: one kind for the time spent ruling, another for the time during which they are ruled. Aristotle then applies this assumption explicitly to the marital relation between husband and wife. Insofar as the relation between husband and wife is a relation between a natural ruler and one who is naturally ruled, this presupposes different virtues on the part of the ruler and the person ruled. He therefore ascribes different sets of virtues of character, such as temperance and courage, to men and women. But this dichotomy does not merely concern the moral virtues. Aristotle applies the dichotomy to *phronesis* too, as the last part of the passage makes clear. He restricts practical reason to the male ruler and allows women only true opinion (*doxa alêthês*). This distinction is without parallel in Aristotle, and I am doubtful that it is sufficient evidence for denying any kind of *phronesis* to women.

In *Pol.* III.4, Aristotle's rationale for distinguishing between different kinds of practical wisdom is his concern for public order and peace. To this end, ruler and ruled need to have different kinds of practical wisdom because the willingness to be ruled presupposes on the part of the ruled a disposition to carry out orders and to act under the guidance of the ruler. Contesting the decisions of the rulers would undermine the hierarchical order of political rule and put the stability of the state at risk. Yet since political rule at the political level is not permanent, but rather shifts regularly between ruler and ruled, good citizens have to acquire both sets of character dispositions. Aristotle assumes that political rule is first learned by being ruled by others and by developing the obedient set of dispositions of character. As a male citizen advances to the position of ruler, he is capable of activating the disposition for leadership that he acquired while being ruled. In contrast, in the case of the marital relation between husband and wife, political rule is permanent, and a woman will not advance to the position of ruler. Therefore, Aristotle denies women practical wisdom, which belongs only to rulers.

The remark at *Pol.* III.4 suggests that women's cognitive deficiency essentially concerns their lack of practical wisdom. This lack is reflected in the fact that their deliberative capacity is without authority because practical wisdom is needed to grasp a general end and to deliberate about the means to that end. Furthermore, this lack of practical wisdom is reflected in the incompleteness of the moral virtues in which they share, which require practical wisdom to be perfectly developed. Karbowski offers an interpretation along these lines. He construes women's deliberative capacities as deficient (according to Aristotle) not only because they can never achieve a systematic grasp of general ethical value concepts, which are involved in practical wisdom and which inform the aim of human action, but also because their capacity to determine the means to an end is limited.

I would suggest, however, that this is too strong an interpretation, given that the denial of practical wisdom with respect to women in *Pol.* III.4 is unique. We have seen that Aristotle attributes some authority to women over specific domestic affairs. This suggests that he would also allow a limited kind of practical wisdom to women within the household. To be sure, this kind of practical wisdom is restricted, but it is a kind of practical wisdom nonetheless, one necessary for making decisions and giving orders on those domestic matters about which women decide and act independently of their husbands. This idea is given further support by the fact that, in *Pol.* III.4, the dichotomy between two kinds of practical wisdom is introduced in such a way that the ruler-*phronesis* does not categorically exclude the *phronesis* of the ruled. On the contrary, the idea is that, in the case of political rule, good citizens must acquire both kinds of practical wisdom, which they activate at different times and when appropriate. Aristotle's denial of unrestricted practical wisdom to women must be attributed to his assumption that female deliberative capacities lack authority. As long as he attributes some authority to women for specific matters within the household, however, this presupposes, in my eyes, that he is nonetheless prepared to ascribe to them a reduced form of practical wisdom.

Primary literature

Aristotle. 1998. *Aristotle. Politics*, by C. D. C. Reeve. Indianapolis: Hackett Publishing Company.
Aristotle. 2002. *Aristotle. Nicomachean Ethics. Translation, Introduction, and Commentary*, by Sarah Broadie and Christopher Rowe. Oxford: Oxford University Press.

Secondary literature

Baldry, Harold C. 1965. *The Unity of Mankind in Greek Thought*. Cambridge: Cambridge University Press.
Clark, Stephen R. L. 1975. *Aristotle's Man. Speculations upon Aristotelian Anthropology*. Oxford: Clarendon Press.
Cooper, John M. 1999a. "Reason, Moral Virtue, and Moral Virtue." In *Reason and Emotion: Essays on Ancient Moral Psychology and Ethical Theory*, edited by John M. Cooper, 253–280. Princeton: Princeton University Press.
Cooper, John M. 1999b. "Some Remarks on Aristotle's Psychology." In *Reason and Emotion: Essays on Ancient Moral Psychology and Ethical Theory*, edited by John. M. Cooper, 237–252. Princeton: Princeton University Press.

Deslauriers, Marguerite. 2003. "Aristotle on the Virtues of Slaves and Women." *Oxford Studies in Ancient Philosophy* 25:213–231.
Deslauriers, Marguerite. 2009. "Sexual Difference in Aristotle's Politics and his Biology." *Classical World* 102:215–230.
Föllinger, Sabine. 1996. *Differenz und Gleichheit. Das Geschlechterverhältnis in der Sicht griechischer Philosophen des 4. bis 1. Jahrhunderts v. Chr.* Stuttgart: Franz Steiner Verlag.
Fortenbaugh, William. 1977. "Aristotle on Slaves and Women." In *Articles on Aristotle – 2: Ethics and Politics* edited by Jonathan Barnes, Malcolm Schofield, and Richard Sorabji, 135–139. London: Duckworth.
Foxhall, Lin. 1989. "Household, Gender and Property in Classical Athens." *The Classical Quarterly* 39 (1):22–44.
Frede, Dorothea. Forthcoming. "Equal but Not Equal: Plato and Aristotle on Women as Citizens."
Frede, Dorothea. 2005. "Aristotle on Citizenship." In *Aristotle's Political Philosophy*, edited by Richard Kraut and Steven Skultety, 167–184. Lanham: MD.
Grönroos, Gösta. 2007. "Listing to Reason in Aristotle's Moral Psychology." *Oxford Studies in Ancient Philosophy* 32:251–271.
Heath, Malcom. 2008. "Aristotle on Natural Slavery." *Phronesis* 53/3:243–270.
Karbowski, Joseph. 2014. "Aristotle on the Deliberative Abilities of Women." *Apeiron* 47/4:435–460.
Karbowski, Joseph. 2012. "Slaves, Women, and Aristotle's Natural Teleology." *Ancient Philosophy* 32/2:323–350.
von Leyden, Wolfgang. 1985. *Aristotle on Equality and Justice. His Political Argument.* New York: St. Martin's Press.
Lienemann, Béatrice. 2018. *Aristoteles' Konzeption der Zurechnung.* Berlin/Boston: De Gruyter.
Lorenz, Hendrick. 2006. *The Brute Within.* Oxford: Oxford University Press.
Miller, Fred D. 1995. *Nature, Justice, and Rights in Aristotle's Politics.* Oxford: Clarendon Press.
Modrak, Deborah. 1994. "Aristotle: Women, Deliberation, and Nature." In *Engendering Origins*, edited by Bat-Ami Bar On, 207–222. Albany: SUNY University Press.
Morsink, Johannes. 1982. *Aristotle on the Generation of Animals. A Philosophical Study*, Lanham/New York/London: University Press of America.
Mulgan, Richard G. 1977. *Aristotle's Political Theory. An Introduction for Students of Political Theory,* Oxford: Clarendon Press.
Price, Anthony W. 1995. *Mental Conflict,* London/New York: Routledge.
Saxonhouse, Arlene. 1982. "Family, Polity, and Unity: Aristotle on Socrates' Community of Wives." *Polity* 15/2:202–219.
Schaps, David M. 1979. *Economic Rights of Women in Ancient Greece,* Edinburgh: University Press.
Scott, Dominic. 2010. "One Virtue or Many? Aristotle's *Politics* I 13 and the *Meno*." In *Aristotle and the Stoics Reading Plato* (BCIS Supplement 107), edited by Verity Harte, Mary M. McCabe, Robert W. Sharples and Anne Sheppard, 101–122. London: Institute of Classical Studies, School of Advanced Study, University of London.

Smith, Nicholas. 1983. "Plato and Aristotle on the Nature of Women." *Journal of the History of Philosophy* 21/4:467–478.

Part II: Hellenistic Philosophy

René Brouwer
Cynic Origins of the Stoic Doctrine of Natural Law?

Abstract: In this paper, I argue that the origins of the Stoic notion of natural law had an antecedent in Cynicism, which was closely linked to early Stoicism: the school founder Zeno of Citium wrote the work that made him famous in Cynic fashion, his immediate followers would also endorse Cynic doctrines. For the Stoics, humans can develop an awareness of the 'common law' as the rational force in nature that shapes everything in it; virtue consists in living in accordance with that law. In stark contrast to later 'Roman' Stoics, or thinkers influenced by them, like Cicero, who would use the notion of natural law to justify conventions, such as respect for private property, the early Stoics, following the Cynics, were willing to overturn conventional norms by appealing to nature. In addition to this anti-conventionalist strand, I suggest that the Cynics also advanced the doctrine further developed by the early Stoics that perfect humans would live in an ideal community governed by the common or natural law.

1 Introduction

The doctrine of natural law is often considered to have its origins with the Stoics (see e.g. Striker 1996). Here I would like to discuss the possible Cynic antecedents of this doctrine. As is well known, the Stoics shared the *negative* evaluation of law as convention with their Cynic teachers. Focusing on the negative elements Zeller (1922, 335) put it thus: "Die Wissenschaft hatte von dieser Bettlerphilosophie vorerst wenig zu erwarten; erst in der Stoa, als er durch anderweitige Elemente ergänzt, gemässigt und in den Zusammenhang einer umfassenden Weltsicht aufgenommen war, wurde der Cynismus in's grosse fruchtbar." The question that I will focus on here is whether there is more to Cynicism than anti-conventionalism, whether the Cynics also had a more constructive contribution to make, such that the early Stoics would have been able to develop their doctrine of law, starting out from these positive Cynic beginnings.

Before I start discussing this question it may be helpful to sketch briefly the Stoic doctrine of natural law, as it has been interpreted over the last decades,[1]

---

[1] Vander Waerdt 1989; Inwood 1999; Vogt 2008, 161–216; Brouwer 2011; Boeri 2013. For a different interpretation as a set of rules see Striker 1986; Mitsis 1999.

with the use of the bits and pieces that survived from or rather more often about the early Stoics in other authors.² The doctrine is this: the Stoics, from Zeno of Citium (334–262), the founder of their school, onwards, used 'law' (*nomos*) as one of the different names, including 'god', 'reason', 'fate' and 'Zeus' (see Diogenes Laertius 7.135, *SVF* 1.102, 2.580), they gave to the active principle within nature that shapes the world, each name bringing out a different aspect of this principle. For law see e.g. Aristocles of Messene (1st century CE?) *ap.* Eusebius of Caesarea (c. 260–339), *Preparation for the Gospel* 15.14.1–2 (*SVF* 1.98, LS 45G, 46G), but above all Cicero (104–43), *On the Nature of the Gods*, at 1.36 (*SVF* 1.162): "Zeno […] thinks that the law of nature is divine and that it has the power to order the right things and to forbid the opposite things" (*Zeno […] naturalem legem divinam esse censet, eamque vim obtinere recta imperantem prohibentemque contraria*). This interpretation of the law as a divine power can also be found in the *Hymn to Zeus* (*SVF* 1.537, LS 54I; for the most recent edition see Thom 2005), which was written by Cleanthes of Assos (c. 330–c. 232), Zeno's successor as head of the school. At l. 2, formulated in terms of traditional Greek religion, Cleanthes describes the law as the instrument of Zeus, "steering everything with his law" (νόμου μέτα πάντα κυβερνῶν). Pivotal in the Stoics' doctrine of law is the connection with 'reason' (*logos*), which they understood in a substantive, materialist sense as 'creative' fire, pervading everything and thus ordering the world (Sharples 1984; Brouwer 2014, 76 n. 90).

According to Stoic doctrine, human beings stand in a special relationship vis-à-vis this rational force in nature. Up till the age of seven or fourteen years onwards (the sources differ here), they naturally develop a faculty of reason.³ However, thereafter they themselves need to develop this reason further. According to the Stoics, then, the highest end in life is the perfection of human rationality such that the good human being acquires a completely rational or virtuous disposition, and thus becomes an active part of this rational force (Brouwer 2014, 91).

Furthermore, alongside the Stoic understanding of law as the rational force in nature, and the Stoic interpretation of the highest end as living in accordance with it, those human beings who have developed this perfectly rational disposition will form a community or city of sorts, consisting of all other perfect human

---

2 von Arnim 1903–1905 (= *SVF*) is still the standard collection of the extant evidence, Long and Sedley 1987 (= LS) offer a valuable selection, with commentary. In this chapter references will be made to both collections, wherever possible. For the extant evidence on the Cynics I will make reference to Giannantoni 1990 (= G.).

3 For a list of sources see further Brouwer 2014, 74 n. 75.

beings, governed by the 'common law', as reported by Plutarch, *On the Luck or Virtue of Alexander*, at 329 A-B (*SVF* 1.262, LS 67A):[4]

> The much admired *Politeia* of Zeno [...] is aimed at this one main point that we should not live together on the basis of cities or parishes, marked by their own interpretation of what is just, but we should regard all human beings as citizens and members of the parish, and there should be a single way of life and one order, like that of a herd grazing together and nurtured by a common law.

This passage can be read as a proposal for a universal community embracing all human beings that have brought their rational faculty to perfection.[5] That interpretation should at any rate be ascribed to Chrysippus, for which the evidence can be found in e.g. Cicero, *On the Nature of the Gods* 2.154, by Arius Didymus (presumably 1st century CE) *ap.* Eusebius of Caesarea, *Preparation to the Gospel* 15.15.4–5, and in the Plutarchean corpus, *On Homer* 119. I will return to these passages in Section 3.

This perfection is difficult to achieve, however: the Stoics maintained that the perfect human being had not yet come into existence (Brouwer 2014, 92–135), with the exception perhaps of Socrates at the end of his life, in prison (Brouwer 2014, 163–166). Rational human beings, who have not yet achieved that virtuous and perfectly rational disposition, can have a true insight into their place in the order of things, but lacking that solid disposition they will most of the time have to live according to the order of the whole, like dogs tied behind a cart – as in the famous Stoic image reported by Hippolytus of Rome (fl. 200 CE), *Refutation of All Heresies* 1.21.2 (*SVF* 2.975, LS 62A): ὥσπερ ὀχήματος ἐὰν ᾖ ἐξηρτημένος κύων – and suffer if they attempt to go against the course of the wagon. The Stoic theory of the emotions as incorrect judgments about one's place in the order of things finds its origins here (Graver 2007).

An implication of this demand for perfection is that the law as the one rational force in nature cannot be fully captured in terms of general prescriptions, since these do not take into account the specific circumstances. Zeno introduced new terminology for human beings who act in accordance with the law: only the sage performs 'right actions' (*katorthōmata*), in accordance with the specific circumstances, whereas imperfect human beings can at best perform 'proper func-

---

4 καὶ μὴν ἡ πολὺ θαυμαζομένη πολιτεία [...] Ζήνωνος εἰς ἓν τοῦτο συντείνει κεφάλαιον, ἵνα μὴ κατὰ πόλεις μηδὲ δήμους οἰκῶμεν ἰδίοις ἕκαστοι διωρισμένοι δικαίοις, ἀλλὰ πάντας ἀνθρώπους ἡγώμεθα δημότας καὶ πολίτας, εἷς δὲ βίος ᾖ καὶ κόσμος, ὥσπερ ἀγέλης συννόμου νόμῳ κοινῷ συντρεφομένης.
5 See e.g. Obbink and Vander Waerdt 1991; Schofield 1999, 64–92; Brouwer 2006, 2015a; Sellars 2007, 19; Vogt 2008, 161–216.

tions' (*kathēkonta*, also rendered as 'duties'), which have a reasonable justification only.[6] Laws as general prescriptions can at best offer an imperfect account of the actual course of this force in the world order.[7] The Stoics hence criticized *all* existing laws and constitutions in no uncertain terms. Zeno presumably did so in his *Politeia*, where we have to infer this from his prohibition of law courts, as reported in Diogenes Laertius 7.33 (*SVF* 1.267); Chrysippus did so, too, as can e. g. be inferred from the reproach that Diogenianus *ap.* Eusebius of Caesarea, *Preparation for the Gospel* 6.8.14 (*SVF* 3.324) directs at him: "How can you say that all positive laws and constitutions are wrong?" (πῶς δὲ τοὺς κειμένους νόμους ἡμαρτῆσθαι φῂς ἅπαντας καὶ τὰς πολιτείας;)

In their rejection of current laws and political arrangements, the early Stoics went so far as to state that perfect human beings could perform all kinds of 'embarrassing' or 'disturbing' actions, such as eating human flesh or having free sexual relationships, including incest. In later Stoicism these traits are often downplayed, especially among the 'Roman' Stoics, from Panaetius to Seneca, with the argument (among others) that these traits would merely represent an early phase in Zeno's thought.[8] According to these Stoics, whereas Zeno may have written the *Politeia*, his first work, 'on the dog's tail' (see Diogenes Laertius 7.4), a clear reference to his Cynic or doggish intellectual ancestry, later in his life Zeno would have abandoned his earlier, Cynic doctrines.

However, these attempts at downplaying were and must be in the end unsuccessful. The "disturbing theses" (Vogt 2008, 20) are an integral part, not only of Zeno's thought, but also of that of his successors, Cleanthes and Chrysippus. Evidence can be found in e. g. Diogenes Laertius, at 7.31–34 and 7.187–9, and in hostile sources, such as in *Against the Professors*, at 11.192–4, written by the Sceptic Sextus Empiricus (2nd century CE) and – perhaps most importantly – in *On the Stoics*, written by the Epicurean Philodemus of Gadara (1st century BCE), which survived in a mutilated papyrus from Herculaneum, brilliantly edited by Dorandi (1982). In this treatise, Philodemus attacks his philosophical adversaries by making clear that, first, other Stoics, such as Cleanthes, Chrysippus and Antipater, held the same opinions as Zeno in his *Politeia*, and that, second, they held these opinions in common with Diogenes of Sinope (mid 4th century), the founder of Cynicism. It is Diogenes' *Politeia* that Philodemus takes as a starting point. Since the authenticity of Diogenes' work was also subject to debate, Philodemus proceeds as follows: he first establishes the authenticity of Diogenes' *Politeia* by

---

6 See Diogenes Laertius 7.107 (*SVF* 1.230); Cicero, *Varro* 37 (*SVF* 1.231).
7 See Vogt 2008, Chapter 4; Brouwer 2011; Boeri 2013.
8 See Mansfeld 1986, 321, 347–349; Sellars 2007, 21–22; Brouwer 2008, 12–15.

means of quoting the Stoics quoting the *Politeia*, and then continues with the 'embarrassing' similarities in doctrine.

In Chapter 6 (of Dorandi's edition), Philodemus starts with Cleanthes' *On Dress*, in which Cleanthes mentioned and praised Diogenes' *Politeia*. He moves on to Chrysippus, presumably in order to make clear that the prolific Chrysippus referred to Diogenes' *Politeia* in several of his works. According to Philodemus, in his *On City and Law* Chrysippus makes mention of Diogenes' *Politeia*, where Chrysippus would have stated that weapons are useless (imagine the reactions of Philodemus' Roman readers!), for which Chrysippus in his *On Politeia* would have invoked Diogenes as an authority. Furthermore, in *On Things Not to Be Chosen for Their Own Sake* and in the first book of *To Those Who Think Differently about Practical Wisdom*, Chrysippus would have quoted Diogenes' doctrine on dice as currency. Perhaps with regard to these titles it could still be maintained that Chrysippus only recalls yet does not endorse these doctrines. But then Philodemus states that in his *On Life According to Nature* Chrysippus not only makes mention of Diogenes' *Politeia* but also agrees with it, even praising it in the fourth book of his *On the Virtuous and Pleasure*. The text becomes even more mutilated here, but the doctrine of man-eating is introduced from Chrysippus' *On Justice*. In Chapter 7 Philodemus then continues "to write about the good things of the men mentioned above" (τὰ καλὰ τῶν ἀνθρώπων ἤδη παραγράφωμεν, col. 18.1–2), i.e. Diogenes, Zeno and his followers. Sexual matters get most of the attention (masturbation in public; free sexual intercourse, with sisters, mothers and other members of the family, brothers as well as sons – sometimes even by force), but also their approval of killing fathers.

Cynicism is thus not just a phase in Zeno's thought, it is part and parcel of early Stoicism. About the role of the Cynic doctrines different interpretations are on offer, such as that the early Stoics would advocate outright anti-conventionalism (Goulet-Cazé 2003, 106–108) or that they would do so with regard to specific circumstances only (Goulet-Cazé 2017, 600). Even if the latter position may well be the correct one, the point, however, surely is that – just as for the Cynics themselves – the anticonventional doctrines allow for a radical rethinking of received opinions (the Stoics used the term 'paradox' here, in the literal sense of going 'against opinion'), even of what perhaps from a conventional point of view ought not be said or done, such that the perfect human being does the right thing in the given circumstances, for which the evidence can be found in Cicero, *Lucullus* 136 (*SVF* 3.599), Origen (c. 184–c. 253), *Commentary on the Gospel of John* 2.112 (*SVF* 3.544), and Diogenes Laertius 7.123 (*SVF* 3.642). The early Stoics thus followed the Cynics (or Socrates, for that matter) in advocating radically rethinking received opinions, and in specific circumstances also going against them.

The doctrine of law as developed by the early Stoics is thus more Cynic, more anticonventional than later versions or interpretations of this doctrine suggest. For students of the natural law tradition the anti-conventionalist aspect of the Stoic doctrine of law is often surprising and stands at any rate in stark contrast with the use of the Stoic doctrine by e.g. Cicero in the first century BCE or by Ulpian's pupil Marcian at the beginning of the third century CE, who both linked the notion of Stoic natural law with Roman law.

With regard to Cicero: in his *On the Laws*, Cicero made an attempt to connect the Stoic doctrine of law with Roman law.[9] In Book 1 Cicero makes the connection in a general sense; in Book 2 and 3 the connection is made with Roman law in the field of religion and magistrates respectively. Towards the end of his life, in his *On Proper Functions* Cicero offered a comparable connection between Stoicism and Roman law. A telling example is Cicero's presentation of justice as a Stoic virtue on the one hand and the protection of private property, one of the cornerstones of Roman law, on the other hand (Kaser 1971, 205; Capogrossi Colognesi 2016, 524). Whereas for the Stoics property is at best indifferent, in Cicero's presentation, the protection of private property would be one of the two main tasks derived from this virtue (see Pierson 2013, 45–52; Brouwer 2021, 103–125).

With regard to Marcian: in his *Teaching Manual*, Book 1, Marcian, a pupil of Ulpian, offers us the often-quoted passage from the beginning of Chrysippus' *On Law*, which is transmitted via Justinian's *Digest*, at 1.3.2 (*SVF* 3.314, LS 67R), and runs thus:[10]

> Law is king of all human and divine matters. Law must preside over things both fine and base as ruler and as guide, and thus be the standard of right and wrong, ordering animals that are political by nature to do as they should, and prohibiting them from what they should not do.

The definition is in fact a variant on the formulation that goes back to the 6th century BCE poet Pindar, which he (fr. 169 Mähler) introduced in the context of an account of Heracles' erratic behaviour. Chrysippus picked up on Pindar's

---

9 See Vander Waerdt 1989, 1994; Mitsis 1994; Asmis 2008; Schiavone 2017, 287.
10 ὁ νόμος πάντων ἐστὶ βασιλεὺς θείων τε καὶ ἀνθρωπίνων πραγμάτων· δεῖ δὲ αὐτὸν προστάτην τε εἶναι τῶν καλῶν καὶ τῶν αἰσχρῶν καὶ ἄρχοντα καὶ ἡγεμόνα, καὶ κατὰ τοῦτο κανόνα τε εἶναι δικαίων καὶ ἀδίκων καὶ τῶν φύσει πολιτικῶν ζῴων προστακτικὸν μὲν ὧν ποιητέον, ἀπαγορευτικὸν δὲ ὧν οὐ ποιητέον.

formulation and – following Zeno and Cleanthes – reinterpreted law in terms of the force in nature, as reason pervading the world. The Stoic understanding of law in which perfect human beings participate could hardly be more different from the Roman context of law as a systematic set of rules, in which the passage survived (Brouwer 2015b). In Lenel's reconstruction of the surviving passages from Marcian's *Teaching Manual* (numbers 42–183), it is placed among the first passages (number 44, Lenel 1889 1:652) and is followed – as usual in the tradition of the teaching manuals – by a systematic overview of the rules of law in sixteen books. Also in the *Digest*, in which these bits and pieces of Marcian's teaching manual can be found, Justinian – or rather Tribonian and his collaborators – place this quote from Chrysippus in the context of further general characterisations of the Roman legal sources, that is of statutes, *senatus consulta* and customary law.

Why the conservative Romans became so fond of such an unconventional school of thought remains an intriguing question, to which an answer may not so easily be given (Long 2018, 254). The softening up of Stoic doctrine by among others Panaetius and Cicero must have helped, such that at least some Romans might have lost sight of the controversial beginnings of Stoicism (Brouwer 2021, 35–36).

2 Positive doctrines in Cynicism

Whereas the influence of the Cynics in their radical anti-conventionalism on the early Stoics can thus not be denied, here I would like to deal with the question whether the Cynics also exercised a more constructive influence on Stoicism, notably in relation to the Stoic conception of law as the force of nature, with which perfect human beings live in accordance, and – if there are more than one of them – that these perfect human beings form a community. If so, the Stoics might have taken on board not only the Cynics' radical critique of existing arrangements, but also their alternative approach formulated in more positive terms, which they would then have developed further.

Before starting the discussion of the evidence regarding the constructive approach in Cynicism the problem of the sources cannot go unmentioned. Apart from the loss of most of the writings of the early Cynics, and apart from the fact that much of what survived is in the form of anecdotes, it is also important to be aware of the fact that the sources on Cynicism may have been misrepresented. Just as the Cynicizing traits of the early Stoics were played down by later generations, so Cynic doctrine was brushed up by later Stoics, who would thus have idealized Cynic doctrine, especially in the doxographies in Book 6 of Diogenes

Laertius, at 60–63, 70–73, and 103–105. In this idealising context Antisthenes (c. 445–c. 365) is often brought up, too, yet again as a moderating influence: with no extant direct references to this proto-Cynic by early Stoics, he is rather inserted in later doxographies, especially in the literature on successions (Brancacci 1992, 4072). In a recent overview article on the sources on Diogenes of Sinope (unfortunately somewhat perfunctory on the evidence in Diogenes Laertius, Book 6, and without reference to Philodemus), Overwien (2011, 120) may have stretched it a bit, where he answers the question as to "What Diogenes would have made of his Nachleben?" rhetorically, thus: "Diogenes würde vermutlich nur noch den Kopf schütteln und vor allen Dingen lachen." Shaking one's head is no option here, and we will have to deal with the tradition as best we can.

In discussing the positive doctrines in Cynicism, I will focus on the evidence of the two earliest generations of Cynics and pay particular attention to Diogenes of Sinope as the first Cynic and his pupil Crates of Thebes (c. 365–c. 285) as Zeno's first teacher. I will discuss the evidence under four headings: first, living according to nature, second, cosmopolitanism, third, interest in physics, and finally – more controversial – the evaluation of law as 'civilized' (*asteios*) in Diogenes Laertius 6.72–73.

2.1 Living according to nature

The first of these four headings, living according to nature, is reported in Diogenes Laertius, at 6.71 (fr. 271 G.). Diogenes not only characterises the good life as living according to nature, he also puts it into practice, valuing things according to nature:[11]

> In order to live the good life it is necessary to choose those efforts that are in accordance with nature rather than useless ones. Such things he said, and this is how he apparently lived, [...] by valuing things according to nature rather than those according to law.

The expression 'according to nature' of course raises the question what Diogenes meant by nature here. In his book on the Cynics, Desmond (2008, 132–159) offers a succinct overview of some different interpretations of nature among ancient thinkers. As for the Cynics, Desmond rightly focuses on the interpretation of simplicity, "stripping away unnecessary desires and customs" (Desmond 2008, 150,

---

[11] δέον οὖν ἀντὶ τῶν ἀχρήστων πόνων τοὺς κατὰ φύσιν ἑλομένους ζῆν εὐδαιμόνως. τοιαῦτα διελέγετο καὶ ποιῶν ἐφαίνετο, [...] μηδὲν οὕτω τοῖς κατὰ νόμον ὡς τοῖς κατὰ φύσιν διδούς.

cf. Helmer 2017, 52–54), which brings about freedom, independence and self-sufficiency (Desmond 2008, 150, cf. Rich 1956, 24).

It will suffice to mention just a couple of examples from the extant evidence on the Cynics' living the simple life, and hence of freedom, independence and self-sufficiency. A vivid account of Diogenes living the simple life is extant in Jerome (347–420), *Against Jovinian* 2.14 (fr. 175 G.). Jerome refers to Satyrus as his source, a 3rd century BCE Peripatetic author, one of the first to write biographies, with whose work he presumably was familiar via the lost end of Book 4 of Porphyry's *On Abstinence*.[12] This is the account:[13]

> He folded his cloak double to guard against the cold and had a backpack for a larder. [...] He was commonly known as someone who lived from day to day, begging for his needs from anyone whom he encountered, and thus acquiring his food.

As for Crates, typical for him are the accounts in which he renounces his property, thus 'setting himself free'. See Origen, *Commentary on the Gospel of Matthew* 15.15 (fr. 9 G.): "They say that he presented all his property to the people of Thebes, saying 'Crates on this day sets Crates free'" (φασὶν ἀποδόμενον πᾶσαν τὴν οὐσίαν τῷ Θηβαίων δήμῳ δεδωρῆσθαι, μετὰ τοῦ εἰρηκέναι ὅτι 'σήμερον ὁ Κράτης Κράτητα ἐλευθεροῖ') and Epiphanius, *Against All Heresies* 3.2.9 (fr. 16 G.): "Crates of Thebes (Boethia), who was a Cynic, too, said that poverty is the beginning of freedom" (Κράτης ἀπὸ Θηβῶν τῶν Βιωτικῶν καὶ αὐτὸς κυνικὸς ἔλεγεν ἐλευθερίας εἶναι τὴν ἀκτημοσύνην).

2.2 Cosmopolitanism

Another Cynic theme is cosmopolitanism. According to Diogenes Laertius 6.63 (fr. 355 G.), "When he [Diogenes the Cynic] was asked where he came from, he said: 'I am a citizen of the world'" (ἐρωτηθεὶς πόθεν εἴη, 'κοσμοπολίτης,' ἔφη). This report is echoed in later, 2nd century CE sources, such as Lucian and Maximus of Tyre. In *Ways of Life for Sale*, at 8 (fr. 80, ll. 27–9 G.), Lucian presents Diogenes in the setting of an auction, and makes Diogenes answer the buyer's questions in the following manner: "You are looking at a citizen of the world [...] striving to emulate Heracles" (Buyer: ποδαπὸς εἶ; [...] Diogenes:

---

[12] See Bernays 1866, 32, 159–163; Leo 1901, 118–124; Patillon, Segonds, and Brisson 1995, 40–41. Clark 2000, 194 is sceptical about Porphyry as Jerome's intermediate source here.

[13] *Diogenes palliolo duplici usus sit propter frigus: peram pro cellario habuerit:* [...] ἡμερόβιος *vulgo appellatus est, in praesentem horam poscens a quolibet, et accipiens cibum.*

τοῦ κόσμου πολίτην ὁρᾷς. Buyer: ζηλοῖς δὲ δὴ τίνα; Diogenes: τὸν Ἡρακλέα). Maximus of Tyre, *Oration* 32.9 (fr. 298 G.) presents Diogenes' cosmopolitanism in this manner: "Liberated from all distress, free, without a worry, without needs, without pain, he [Diogenes] inhabited the whole earth as if it were a single house" (ἄφετος παντὸς τοῦ δεινοῦ, ἐλεύθερος, ἄφροντις, ἀδεής, ἄλυπος ἐνέμετο τὴν πᾶσαν γῆν ὡς οἶκον ἕνα).

Cynic cosmopolitanism has been much discussed, and surprisingly enough, more often than not interpreted in a negative sense as an expression of the rejection of actual cities.[14] These interpretations are often based on the quote offered by Diogenes Laertius at 6.38 (fr. 263, 7 G.), which is introduced as follows:[15]

> He used to say that all curses of tragedy had happened to him. He was therefore:
> "Without a city, without a house, deprived of a country,
> a beggar, a wanderer, living from day to day."

The negative interpretation is obviously based on the first part of the quote, dominated by the adjectives with the negating alpha privative.

However, the statement of Diogenes is already coloured more positively, if we look at how Aristippus of Cyrene (c. 435–c. 356), one of Socrates' followers, and the founder of the Cyrenaic school, rejected traditional political communities. Since Aristippus was a contemporary of Diogenes, although from an older generation, some scholars even suggested a debate between Aristippus and Diogenes here. This is at any rate Aristippus' formulation of the rejection of particular communities, which can be found in Xenophon (c. 430–354), *Memorabilia* 2.1.13: "I do not shut up myself within a particular community but am a stranger everywhere" (οὐδ' εἰς πολιτείαν ἐμαυτὸν κατακλείω, ἀλλὰ ξένος πανταχοῦ εἰμι). In this context of Aristippus being a stranger everywhere, Diogenes' declaration that he is a citizen of the world already has a more positive connotation as an alternative to local citizenship. Rather than being a stranger, Diogenes the Cynic considers himself to be at home in the world, and that he as such is a citizen of the world (Moles 1996, 109–111; Sellars 2007).

In one of the doxographical sections of Book 6 of Diogenes Laertius at 72 (fr. 353 G.) this is expressed thus: "There is only one, real community, and that is the one in the world" (μόνην τε ὀρθὴν πολιτείαν εἶναι τὴν ἐν κόσμῳ). At Diogenes Laertius 6.105, in another doxographical passage, the end of living

---

14 Rudberg 1936, 1; Tarn 1939; Goulet-Cazé 1999, 733; Schofield 1999, 144; Overwien 2005, 333.
15 εἰώθει δὲ λέγειν τὰς τραγικὰς ἀρὰς αὐτῷ συνηντηκέναι· εἶναι γοῦν·
'ἄπολις, ἄοικος, πατρίδος ἐστερημένος,
πτωχός, πλανήτης, βίον ἔχων τοὔφ' ἡμέραν.'

in accordance with nature is given a social dimension. Those who live the simple life, at home in the world, live in friendship with others who live the simple life, too: "The sage is a friend to his kind" (καὶ φίλον τῷ ὁμοίῳ). Rather than a brotherhood of human beings, which is a theme among later thinkers, such as Panaetius and Cicero,[16] this passage speaks of a community of sages, of perfect human beings. Of course, these doxographical passages may have been stoicised; some scholars even outright attributed them to Chrysippus (Schofield 1999, 14; Pons Olivares 2009, 578). However, the positive account of cosmopolitanism can also be found in the extant evidence from Crates of Thebes (c. 365–c. 285), which is clearly reliable, and to which I will now turn.

For Crates' cosmopolitanism two short texts actually written by Crates himself can be taken into account: the so-called "Pera passage" and a fragment from a tragedy (see further Moles 1995, 143–144). This is the Pera fragment, preserved in Diogenes Laertius 6.85 (fr. 4 Diels 1901, fr. 80 G.):[17]

> There is a city, Pera, in the wine-dark sea of folly,
> beautiful and fat, though filthy, with nothing much inside.
> Never does there sail to it any foolish stranger,
> Or lewd fellow who takes delight in the rumps of whores,
> But it merely carries thyme and garlic, figs and loaves,
> Things over which people do not fight or go to war,
> Nor do they stand to weapons for copper coins or glory. (tr. Hard 2012, 229)

The Greek Pera is a variation upon Crete in the *Odyssey*, at 19.172–173, on which the first two lines are modelled. Pera, as retained or transliterated in the modern translations,[18] thus evokes a non-existent 'utopian' island, which is in the state of *tuphos* (l. 2). *Tuphos* can be understood both literally as 'mist' or 'smoke' as well as metaphorically as 'illusion' or 'folly'.[19] However, if Pera is taken literally, that is as 'backpack', the lines refer no longer to an ideal place somewhere else. The interpretation becomes thus, still in Hard's, but now adapted translation:

---

16 Giannantoni 1990, 4:545; Sellars 2007; Brouwer 2015a.
17 Πήρη τις πόλις ἐστὶ μέσῳ ἐνὶ οἴνοπι τύφῳ,
καλὴ καὶ πίειρα, περίρρυπος, οὐδὲν ἔχουσα,
εἰς ἣν οὔτε τις εἰσπλεῖ ἀνὴρ μωρὸς παράσιτος,
οὔτε λίχνος πόρνης ἐπαγαλλόμενος πυγῇσιν·
ἀλλὰ θύμον καὶ σκόρδα φέρει καὶ σῦκα καὶ ἄρτους,
ἐξ ὧν οὐ πολεμοῦσι πρὸς ἀλλήλους περὶ τούτων,
οὐχ ὅπλα κέκτηνται περὶ κέρματος, οὐ περὶ δόξης.
18 See e.g. Hicks 1925; Apelt 1967; Gigante 1998; Jürß 2010; Hard 2012, 94.
19 Decleva Caizzi 1980; Brouwer 2014, 153–157.

"The backpack as a refuge in the midst of a world of illusion that most people inhabit." With his backpack, then, fair and fat, the whole world has become Crates' city, with Crates being at home everywhere.

The second passage, from an unfortunately unnamed tragedy, yet again survived in Diogenes Laertius. According to Diogenes Laertius 6.98 (fr. 15 Diels 1901, fr. 80 G.), this passage offers "philosophy of a most elevated character" (ὑψηλότατον ἐχούσας φιλοσοφίας χαρακτῆρα), which is probably directed against those who maintain that Cynicism is not serious philosophy, but only a "way of life" (see Diogenes Laertius 6.103: αἵρεσιν καὶ ταύτην εἶναι ἐγκρίνοντες τὴν φιλοσοφίαν, οὐ, καθά φασί τινες, ἔνστασιν βίου). The following lines are presented as proof thereof: "My country is not one tower, one roof, / but the entire earth is my city [polisma] and my home, / readily at hand to serve as my dwelling" (οὐχ εἷς πάτρα μοι πύργος, οὐ μία στέγη, / πάσης δὲ χέρσου καὶ πόλισμα καὶ δόμος / ἕτοιμος ἡμῖν ἐνδιαιτᾶσθαι πάρα). Here again, Crates shows a positive allegiance to the earth that serves him as a city and home, 'readily at hand', and thus markedly not utopian.

It can thus be concluded that the Cynics present cosmopolitanism not just as a critique of existing communities, but also as an alternative. Cosmopolitanism in the Cynic fashion would thus consist in (and here I follow Moles 1996) having positive relations with 1) nature or the natural world (as opposed to the life in actual cities); 2) animals – after all Diogenes called himself a dog (see further Flores-Júnior 2005; Husson 2013); 3) other human beings, in so far as they are wise, such that they form a community, in which they have all things in common; 4) and finally, even the gods.

2.3 Interest in physics

The third theme is the Cynics' interest in physics. It is often maintained that the early Cynics were not interested in the study of nature (as e.g. by Husson 2011, 58, 161). The three following passages appear to confirm this lack of interest. Diogenes Laertius 6.103 (fr. 368 G.):[20]

> They choose to dispense with logic and physics, much like Ariston of Chios, to concentrate on ethics only.

---

20 ἀρέσκει οὖν αὐτοῖς τὸν λογικὸν καὶ τὸν φυσικὸν τόπον περιαιρεῖν, ἐμφερῶς Ἀρίστωνι τῷ Χίῳ, μόνῳ δὲ προσέχειν τῷ ἠθικῷ.

Diogenes Laertius 6.39 (fr. 371 G.):[21]

> To someone who was talking about astronomical matters, he [Diogenes the Cynic] said, "And how many days did it take you to get down from the sky?"

Stobaeus 2.1.23 (fr. 372 G.), in which Diogenes speaks to an astronomer, who is lecturing about the planets [lit. wandering stars]:[22]

> "It is not these that are wandering, but those over there," pointing to the people standing around.

Do these passages really imply that Diogenes had no interest in nature at all? Another, better interpretation is that Diogenes rather rejected the kind of knowledge of nature that cannot be put to moral use. A passage that survived in the Arabic tradition, fr. 374.1 Gutas,[23] in a set of sayings attributed to Diogenes of Sinope, conveys the point nicely: "He was asked: 'Which of the sciences is the most useful?' 'That which is practiced.'" A similar point is reported by Diogenes Laertius, at 6.27–28 (fr. 374 G.), where Diogenes criticizes students of literature, of music, the natural sciences and rhetoric. All their efforts are misguided:[24]

> The student of literature studies Odysseus' ills, rather than his own ills, the musician rather than tuning his lyre better tunes his soul, the natural scientist looking at the sun and the moon, overlooks things close by, and orators while talking about justice never practice it.

In a much-discussed passage, Diogenes Laertius 6.73 (fr. 132 G.), there is even evidence that Diogenes himself would have put a physical theory to use, explaining why eating flesh of animals or – indeed, here one of the disturbing theses pops up – why eating flesh of human beings is not 'strange' (*atopos*). It would stem from the Cynic's tragedy *Thyestes*, 'if really his', Diogenes Laertius adds, a remark which might be caused by the fact that the *Thyestes* could be an alternative title of the *Atreus*, mentioned by Philodemus, *On the Stoics*, col. 16.30 Dor-

---

21 πρὸς τὸν λέγοντα περὶ τῶν μετεώρων, 'ποσταῖος,' ἔφη, 'πάρει ἀπὸ τοῦ οὐρανοῦ;'
22 'οὐ γὰρ οὗτοί εἰσιν οἱ πλανώμενοι, ἀλλὰ οὗτοι', δείξας αὐτῷ τοὺς παρακαθεζομένους.
23 Gutas 1993, 503; Baldacchino 2014 offers only a translation in French of Gutas' English version.
24 τούς τε γραμματικοὺς ἐθαύμαζε τὰ μὲν τοῦ Ὀδυσσέως κακὰ ἀναζητοῦντας, τὰ δ' ἴδια ἀγνοοῦντας. καὶ μὴν καὶ τοὺς μουσικοὺς τὰς μὲν ἐν τῇ λύρᾳ χορδὰς ἁρμόττεσθαι, ἀνάρμοστα δ' ἔχειν τῆς ψυχῆς τὰ ἤθη· τοὺς μαθηματικοὺς ἀποβλέπειν μὲν πρὸς τὸν ἥλιον καὶ τὴν σελήνην, τὰ δ' ἐν ποσὶ πράγματα παρορᾶν· τοὺς ῥήτορας τὰ δίκαια μὲν ἐσπουδακέναι λέγειν, πράττειν δὲ μηδαμῶς.

andi, since Thyestes and Atreus are brothers, playing opposite roles in society (Dümmler 1901, 67–71):[25]

> He said that all things are in all things and go through all: for meat is not only in bread, bread is also in vegetables; and all other bodies also, by means of certain invisible passages mass particles find their way in and unite in the form of breath.

As commentators have remarked, this explanation may well rely on "a bit of popularized Anaxagorean physics" (Dudley 1937, 30), but is at any rate "scientific" (Höistad 1948, 144). We have thus reason to assume that Diogenes showed some interest in science, under the condition that it should have an ethical pay-off.

In this context of putting science to use, an intriguing poem on Diogenes' death cannot remain unmentioned. It is written by Cercidas of Megalopolis, usually considered a Cynic (Goulet-Cazé 1994), who is dated firmly in the 3rd century BCE (290–220), a couple of generations after Diogenes' death. The passage survived yet again in Diogenes Laertius, at 6.76–77 (fr. 54 Livrea, fr. 60 Lomiento), whereas bits of it apparently resurfaced in the Egyptian desert towards the end of the 19th century (*P. Oxy.* 1082, fr. 19 = fr. 14 Lomiento). This is the poem, with the introductory lines by Diogenes Laertius:[26]

> About his death the accounts differ: [...] One is that he controlled his breath, which is also the version of Cercidas of Megalopolis, who stated it in his *Meliambs* thus:
> The man from Sinope is no longer, who carried a staff,
> doubled his cloak, fed on aether, but he went up,
> after having closed his lips against his teeth and holding his breath.
> For Diogenes was truly a child of Zeus, a heavenly dog.

The starting point for Cercidas' poem appears to have been Diogenes' epitaph (preserved in the *Greek Anthology*, Book 7 no. 64 (fr. 110 G.); on the epitaph see further Häusle 1989): "Now that he [Diogenes] is dead, he has the stars as his home" (νῦν δὲ θανὼν ἀστέρας οἶκον ἔχει). Cercidas clearly plays on the

---

[25] καὶ τῷ ὀρθῷ λόγῳ πάντ' ἐν πᾶσι καὶ διὰ πάντων εἶναι λέγων. καὶ γὰρ ἐν τῷ ἄρτῳ κρέας εἶναι καὶ ἐν τῷ λαχάνῳ ἄρτον καὶ τῶν σωμάτων τῶν λοιπῶν ἐν πᾶσι διά τινων ἀδήλων πόρων [καὶ] ὄγκων εἰσκρινομένων καὶ συνατμιζομένων.

[26] περὶ δὲ τοῦ θανάτου διάφοροι λέγονται λόγοι· [...] οἱ δὲ τὸ πνεῦμα συγκρατήσαντα, ὧν ἐστι καὶ Κερκιδᾶς ὁ Μεγαλοπολίτης, λέγων ἐν τοῖς μελιάμβοις οὕτως·
οὐ μὰν ὁ πάρος γα Σινωπεὺς τῆνος ὁ βακτροφόρας,
διπλείματος, αἰθεριβόσκας ἀλλ' ἀνέβα
χεῖλος ποτ' ὀδόντας ἐρείσας καὶ τὸ πνεῦμα συνδακών.
ἧς γὰρ ἀλαθέως Διογένης Ζανὸς γόνος οὐράνιός τε κύων.

cause of Diogenes' death: breath recurs in *aitheriboskas* in line 2, which has been interpreted either as 'living in the open air' (Hicks 1925; Goulet-Cazé 1999) or as 'feeding on aether' (Livrea 1991, 236). The first interpretation would obviously allude to the fact that Diogenes preferred life in the open air. If so, why would Cercidas not have chosen to refer to plain air rather than aether? Aether is after all the divine element, which also rather nicely fits in both with the wordplay on Diogenes' name, which literally means 'child of Zeus', and the phrase 'heavenly dog'. Cercidas would thus have placed Diogenes' death, on an ethical level surely the ultimate expression of one's independence (see López Cruces 1995, 23–24), in a physico-theological context.

Of course, Cercidas' account is by no means evidence that Diogenes himself would have maintained such views (Goulet-Cazé 1992, 3914; Billerbeck 1996, 206). It has even been suggested that Cercidas would have presented us with a 'surrogate Stoicism' (Croiset 1911, 484). However, from the little that we know about Cercidas, he appears to have been rather critical of the Stoics, castigating a certain Kallimedon (in *Meliambs* 6a Lomiento), a pupil of Sphaerus, one of Zeno's favourite pupils (see further Knox 1929, xviii). It thus seems rather more plausible that Cercidas faithfully played on Diogenes' own interests in nature.

2.4 Law as *civilized*

The fourth and final theme is the characterisation of law as 'civilized' (*asteios*), at Diogenes Laertius 6.72–73 (fr. 353 G.):[27]

> Regarding the law he said that without it, it is impossible to live as a citizen; without a city there is no benefit in something civilized; and the city is civilized. Without law there is no benefit in a city; therefore law is something civilized.

At least three different interpretations of civilized have been proposed. First, 'civilized' expresses Diogenes' negative, 'pejorative', evaluation of actual cities and their laws (Schofield 1999, 132–134). The second interpretation takes it that 'civilized' should be taken to express the Cynic's positive evaluation of the city that is the world and the law that guides it (Moles 1995, 130 and 1996, 106 n. 4). This second interpretation resembles the later Stoic interpretation of law so much that – and this is the third interpretation – it has been maintained

---

27 περί τε τοῦ νόμου ὅτι χωρὶς αὐτοῦ οὐχ οἷόν τε πολιτεύεσθαι· οὐ γάρ φησιν ἄνευ πόλεως ὄφελός τι εἶναι ἀστείου· ἀστεῖον δὲ ἡ πόλις· νόμου δὲ ἄνευ πόλεως οὐδὲν ὄφελος· ἀστεῖον ἄρα ὁ νόμος.

that the argument is not Cynic at all, but rather a product of Stoics stoicising Cynicism (Goulet-Cazé 1982). Even if the passage is in itself ambiguous, in combination with the evidence under the other headings discussed here, a positive Cynic evaluation of 'civilized' – and hence of law – is at least likely.

It can thus be concluded that the extant evidence *does* allow for the conclusion that the early Cynics were not just radical anti-conventionalists. Cynic notions of simplicity, cosmopolitanism, and perhaps even law itself can be interpreted as a positive allegiance to a life that is simple, that is lived in the world and thus readily at hand, and perhaps even guided by the law of nature.

3 The constructive Cynic doctrines and early Stoicism

I will round off by discussing these positive Cynic doctrines as they reappear in Stoicism. As for the first theme, 'simplicity', the Stoic sage is characterised as simple. The evidence preserved by Stobaeus, at 2.108.11 (*SVF* 3.630), in which the sage is called – among other things – 'simple' (*haplous*), and capable of friendship, which well reflects the theme in Cynicism as discussed earlier. The sage lives the simple life, not needing anything but a virtuous disposition. It is in this context that his (or her) knowledge is also described as a 'simple good' (ἁπλοῦν δ' ἐστὶν ἀγαθὸν ἐπιστήμη, Diogenes Laertius 7.98 (*SVF* 3.102), see further Brouwer 2014, 158). All other things which are usually considered good are at best indifferent. As Tad Brennan (2004, 184) succinctly put it, in the phrase '*salva virtute*', indifferent things may allow for moral deliberation in relation to virtue, but in the end it is virtue only that counts.

As for the second theme, cosmopolitanism, as already noted in Section 1, the early Stoics developed this further, too. The sage's reason is fully in line with cosmic reason, and if possible contributes actively to it. If there is more than one sage, these sages will affect each other. The manner in which this happens is literally 'far-reaching'. This is how Plutarch, *On Common Conceptions* 1068F (*SVF* 3.627) states it:[28]

---

[28] ἄν εἷς σοφὸς ὁπουδήποτε προτείνῃ τὸν δάκτυλον φρονίμως, οἱ κατὰ τὴν οἰκουμένην σοφοὶ πάντες ὠφελοῦνται. τοῦτο τῆς φιλίας ἔργον αὐτῶν, εἰς τοῦτο τοῖς κοινοῖς ὠφελήμασι τῶν σοφῶν αἱ ἀρεταὶ τελευτῶσιν.

If a sage anywhere extends his finger using his practical wisdom, all the sages throughout the world will benefit. This is the work of their friendship, into which the virtues of the sages for their common benefit end.

Hermann Diels (1917, 6) rightly characterized this statement as 'etwas abenteuerlich', but the point is surely that sages related in this way are therefore also said to form a community, a Stoic doctrine preserved – via Eusebius of Caesarea, *Preparation for the Gospel* 15.15.5 (*SVF* 2.528, LS 67L) – by Arius Didymus, too: "A community exists amongst them, because they participate in reason, that is the law by nature" (κοινωνίαν δ' ὑπάρχειν πρὸς ἀλλήλους διὰ τὸ λόγου μετέχειν, ὅς ἐστι φύσει νόμος). A similar formulation can be found in Ps.-Plutarch, *On Homer* 119 (not in *SVF*): "This is the familiar doctrine of the Stoics, that there is one order, in which by nature gods and men rule together participating in justice" (ἐστὶ τὸ δόγμα ἐκεῖνο τῶν Στωικῶν, τὸ δὴ ἕνα μὲν εἶναι τὸν κόσμον, συμπολιτεύεσθαι δὲ ἐν αὐτῷ θεοὺς καὶ ἀνθρώπους δικαιοσύνης μετέχοντας φύσει). The Stoics' ideal community of sages thus does not refer to a political utopia in the sense of a group of sages that set up and form a local community together (see above n. 4). Rather, once a human being has perfected his or her own rational capacities, he or she will by virtue of having become perfect be a 'world citizen', participating on the highest level of being. If more human beings achieve perfection, they will be part of a community of sages, however far removed they may be from each other.

As for our third theme, interest in nature, this hardly needs further explanation: for the Stoics the study of nature is one of the three main areas of research (or parts of philosophy, as Zeno called it in his *On Reason* (see Diogenes Laertius 7.39, *SVF* 1.45, LS 26B, cf. Aëtius 1 Preface 2, *SVF* 2.35, LS 26A), alongside ethics and logic. Zeno and his followers would thus already have become interested in nature, due to the Cynics, an interest they would have developed further by their study of Heraclitus or Plato's *Timaeus*.[29] Fourth, and finally, the Stoic usage of 'civilized' (*asteios*) in connection with the city and law is developed in Stobaeus 2.103.12–17 (*SVF* 1.587, LS 67I):[30]

The law [...] is good, and likewise so is the city. With regard to the city being good, Cleanthes adequately put the following argument: "If a city is a habitable construction to which peo-

---

29 For Heraclitus see Long 1996; for the *Timaeus* see Betegh 2003.
30 τὸν γὰρ νόμον εἶναι [...] σπουδαῖον, ὁμοίως δὲ καὶ τὴν πόλιν. ἱκανῶς δὲ καὶ Κλεάνθης περὶ τὸ σπουδαῖον εἶναι τὴν πόλιν λόγον ἠρώτησε τοιοῦτον· 'πόλις μὲν <εἰ> ἔστιν οἰκητήριον κατασκεύασμα, εἰς ὃ καταφεύγοντας ἔστι δίκην δοῦναι καὶ λαβεῖν, οὐκ ἀστεῖον δὴ πόλις ἐστίν; ἀλλὰ μὴν τοιοῦτόν ἐστιν ἡ πόλις οἰκητήριον· ἀστεῖον ἄρ' ἔστιν ἡ πόλις.'

ple may have recourse for the dispensation of justice, then a city is surely civilized. A city is that sort of habitation. So a city is civilized."

Different from the *asteios*-passage brought up above, in Section 2.4, the meaning of *asteios* is here without a doubt a positive one, which is easily explained if we take both city and law to refer to the world. The theme was developed further with regard to the inferior person, who is inexperienced with the life in the city that is the world, and not familiar with the law pervading it. In the continuation of the Stobaeus-passage, at 103.24–104.5 (*SVF* 3.677), the non-sage or 'inferior person', who is the opposite of *asteios*, is introduced. This *agroikos* ('rustic') person lacks experience of the customs and laws of the city:[31]

> They also say that every inferior person is rustic. For rusticity is inexperience of the customs and laws in a city: of which every inferior person is guilty. He is also wild, being hostile to that lifestyle which is in accord with the law, bestial, and a harmful human being. And he is uncultivated and tyrannical, inclined to do despotic acts, and even to cruel, violent, and lawless acts when he is given the opportunities.

In the lines preceding Cleanthes' argument, at 2.103.9–12 (*SVF* 3.328), with which the theme is introduced, the Cynic undertones are even clearer: "Each inferior person is an exile, in as much as he is deprived of law and of a community in accordance with nature" (φυγάδα πάντα φαῦλον εἶναι, καθ' ὅσον στέρεται νόμου καὶ πολιτείας κατὰ φύσιν ἐπιβαλλούσης).

The extant sources on Cynicism thus provide substance to the characterisation of Cynicism as "the short cut to virtue" (σύντομον ἐπ' ἀρετὴν ὁδόν), as the expression goes in Diogenes Laertius 6.104 and 7.121, with the Stoics by implication following the longer road. Just as the early Stoics would do later on, the Cynics argued against law as convention. But as we have seen, they may also have contributed to a more positive conception of law as ordering reason. On the basis of their constructive doctrines on, first, the simple life, second, the world as a city, third, nature and, finally, law as civilized, the Cynics could thus have offered to the Stoics the starting point for more substantive theories about the nature of reality and the special place of human beings in it. If this is correct, the Stoics would thus have substantiated Cynic doctrine, developing it into the more theoretical interpretation of law as the rational force of nature, in which sages due to

---

31 φασὶ δὲ καὶ ἄγροικον εἶναι πάντα φαῦλον· τὴν γὰρ ἀγροικίαν ἀπειρίαν εἶναι τῶν κατὰ πόλιν ἐθῶν καὶ νόμων· ᾗ πάντα φαῦλον ἔνοχον ὑπάρχειν. εἶναι δὲ καὶ ἄγριον, ἐναντιωτικὸν ὄντα τῇ κατὰ νόμον διεξαγωγῇ καὶ θηριώδη καὶ βλαπτικὸν ἄνθρωπον. τὸν δ' αὐτὸν τοῦτον καὶ ἀνήμερον ὑπάρχειν καὶ τυραννικόν, οὕτως διακείμενον ὥστε δεσποτικὰ ποιεῖν, ἔτι δὲ ὠμὰ καὶ βίαια καὶ παράνομα καιρῶν ἐπιλαβόμενον.

their perfect reason participate. Cynic practical simplicity in the world at large would thus have developed into Stoic rational immanentism and thus have formed the basis for the Stoics' doctrine of natural law.

Abbreviations

G. = Giannantoni 1990.
LS = Long and Sedley 1987.
SVF = von Arnim 1903–1905.

Primary literature

Only editions, source collections, and translations explicitly mentioned in the text are listed here. Otherwise, the standard editions have been used, for which see e.g. the *Oxford Classical Dictionary*, edited by Simon Hornblower and Antony Spawforth, 4th edn (Oxford: Oxford University Press, 2012).

von Arnim, Hans. 1903–1905. *Stoicorum veterum fragmenta* 1–3. Leipzig: Teubner.
Cercidas. 1986. *Studi cercidei (P.Oxy. 1082)*, by Enrico Livrea. Bonn: Habelt.
Cercidas. 1993. *Cercidas. Testimonia et fragmenta*, by Liana Lomiento. Rome: Gruppo editoriale internazionale.
Cleanthes. 2005. *Cleanthes' Hymn to Zeus*, by Johan C. Thom. Tübingen: Mohr Siebeck.
Diels, Hermann. 1901. *Poetarum philosophorum fragmenta*. Berlin: Weidmann.
Diogenes the Cynic. 1993. "Sayings by Diogenes Preserved in Arabic", by Dimitri Gutas. In *Le cynisme ancien et ses prolongements*, edited by Marie-Odile Goulet-Cazé and Richard Goulet, 475–517. Paris: PUF.
Diogenes the Cynic. 2012. *Diogenes the Cynic. Sayings and Anecdotes. With Other Popular Moralists*, by Robin Hard. Oxford: Oxford University Press.
Diogenes the Cynic. 2014. *Diogène le Cynique. Fragments inédits*, by Adeline Baldacchino. Paris: Autrement.
Diogenes Laertius. 1925. *Diogenes Laertius. Lives of Eminent Philosophers*, by Robert Drew Hicks. Cambridge, MA: Loeb.
Diogenes Laertius. 1967. *Diogenes Laertius. Leben und Meinung berühmter Philosophen* by Otto Apelt, Hans Günther Zekl and Klaus Reich. Hamburg: Meiner.
Diogenes Laertius. 1998. *Diogene Laerzio. Vite dei filosofi*, 3rd edn. by Marcello Gigante. Rome: Laterza.
Diogenes Laertius. 1999. *Diogène Laërce. Vies et doctrines des philosophes illustres*, edited by Marie-Odile Goulet-Cazé. Paris: Le livre de poche.
Diogenes Laertius. 2010. *Diogenes Laertios. Leben und Lehre der Philosophen* by Fritz Jürß. Stuttgart: Reclam.
Giannantoni, Gabriele. 1990. *Socratis et socraticorum reliquiae*. Naples: Bibliopolis.
Knox, Alfred Dillwyn. 1929. *Herodes, Cercidas and the Greek Choliambic Poets*. Cambridge, MA: Loeb.

Lenel, Otto. 1889. *Palingenesia iuris civilis*. Leipzig: Tauchnitz.
Long, Anthony A., and Sedley, David N. 1987. *The Hellenistic Philosophers*. Cambridge: Cambridge University Press.
Philodemus of Gadara. 1982. *Filodemo. Gli Stoici* (PHerc. 155 e 339), by Tiziano Dorandi in *Cronache ercolanesi* 12:92–133.
Porphyry. 1995. *Porphyre. De l'abstinence Livre* 4, by Michel Patillon, Alain Ph. Segonds, and Luc Brisson. Paris: Les belles lettres.
Porphyry. 2000. *Porphyry. On Abstinence from Killing Animals*, by Gillian Clark. London: Duckworth.

Secondary literature

Asmis, Elisabeth. 2008. "Cicero on Natural Law and the Laws of the State." *Classical Antiquity* 27:1–33.
Bernays, Jacob. 1866. *Theophrastos' Schrift Über Frömmigkeit. Ein Beitrag zur Religionsgeschichte*. Berlin: Hertz.
Betegh, Gábor. 2003. "Cosmological Ethics in the *Timaeus* and Early Stoicism." *Oxford Studies in Ancient Philosophy* 24:273–302.
Billerbeck, Margarethe. 1996. "The Ideal Cynic from Epictetus to Julian." In *The Cynics. The Cynic Movement in Antiquity and its Legacy*, edited by R. Bracht Branham and Marie-Odile Goulet-Cazé, 203–220. Berkeley: University of California Press.
Boeri, Marcelo D. 2013. "Natural Law and World-Order in Stoicism." In *Nature and the Best Life*, edited by Gabriela Rossi, 183–223. Hildesheim: Olms.
Brancacci, Aldo. 1992. "I κοινῇ ἀρέσκοντα dei Cinici e la κοινωνία tra cinismo e stoicismo nel libro VI (103–105) delle 'Vite' di Diogene Laerzio." In *Aufstieg und Niedergang der römischen Welt* 2.36.6, edited by Wolfgang Haase, 4049–4075. Berlin: De Gruyter.
Brennan, Ted. 2005. *The Stoic Life. Emotions, Duties & Fate*. Oxford: Oxford University Press.
Brouwer, René. 2006. "Zeno's Political Philosophy: The City of Sages." To be consulted at http://www.archelogos.com/zeno/phessay.htm.
Brouwer, René. 2008. "On the Ancient Background of Grotius's Notion of Natural Law." *Grotiana* 29:1–24.
Brouwer, René. 2011. "On Law and Equity: The Stoic View." *Zeitschrift der Savigny-Stiftung für Rechtsgeschichte. Romanistische Abteilung* 128:17–38.
Brouwer, René. 2014. *The Stoic Sage. The Early Stoics on Wisdom, Sagehood and Socrates*. Cambridge: Cambridge University Press.
Brouwer, René. 2015a. "Stoic Sympathy." In *Sympathy*, edited by Eric Schliesser, 15–35. New York: Oxford University Press.
Brouwer, René. 2015b. "Ulpian's Appeal to Nature: Roman Law as Universal Law." *Legal History Review* 83:1–17.
Brouwer, René. 2021. *Law and Philosophy in the Late Roman Republic*. Cambridge: Cambridge University Press.
Capogrossi Colognesi, Luigi. 2016. "Ownership and Power in Roman Law." In *The Oxford Handbook of Roman Law and Society*, edited by Paul J. du Plessis, Clifford Ando, and Kaius Tuori, 524–536. Oxford: Oxford University Press.

Croiset, Maurice. 1911. "Kerkidas de Mégalopolis." *Journal des savants* 9:481–493.
Decleva Caizzi, Fernanda. 1980. "Τῦφος: contributo alla storia di un concetto." *Sandalion* 3:53–66.
Desmond, William. 2008. *Cynics*. Stocksfield: Acumen.
Diels, Hermann. 1917. *Philodemus. Über die Götter. Drittes Buch. Erläuterung des Textes.* Berlin: Verlag der Königlichen Akademie der Wissenschaften.
Dudley, Donald R. 1937. *A History of Cynicism*. London: Methuen.
Dümmler, Ferdinand. 1901. "Antisthenica." Diss. Bonn, 1882. Reprinted in his *Kleine Schriften* 1, 10–78. Leipzig: Hirzel.
Flores-Júnior, Olimar. 2005. "Cratès, la fourmi et l'escargot: les Cyniques et l'example animal." *Philosophie antique* 5:134–171.
Goulet-Cazé, Marie-Odile. 1982. "Un syllogisme stoïcien sur la loi dans la doxographie de Diogène le Cynique. À propos de Diogène Laërce VI 72." *Rheinisches Museum* 125:214–40.
Goulet-Cazé, Marie-Odile. 1992. "Le livre VI de Diogène Laërce: analyse de sa structure et réflexions méthodologiques." In *Aufstieg und Niedergang der römischen Welt* 2.36.6, edited by Wolfgang Haase, 3880–4048. Berlin: De Gruyter.
Goulet-Cazé, Marie-Odile. 1994. "Cercidas de Mégalopolis". In *Dictionnaire des philosophes antiques* 2, edited by Richard Goulet, 269–281. Paris: CNRS.
Goulet-Cazé, Marie-Odile. 2003. *Les Kynika du stoïcisme*. Wiesbaden: Steiner.
Goulet-Cazé, Marie-Odile. 2017. *Le cynisme, une philosophie antique*. Paris: Vrin.
Graver, Margaret. 2007. *Stoicism & Emotion*. Chicago: Chicago University Press.
Häusle, Helmut. 1989. *Sag mir, O Hund – wo der Hund begraben liegt*. Hildesheim: Olms.
Helmer, Étienne. 2017. *Diogène le Cynique*. Paris: Les belles lettres.
Höistad, Ragnar. 1948. *Cynic Hero and Cynic King*. Uppsala: Blom.
Husson, Suzanne. 2011. *La République de Diogène*. Paris: Vrin.
Husson, Suzanne. 2013. "'Revetir la vie des chiens', l'animal comme modele moral." *Archai* 11:69–78.
Inwood, Brad. 1999. "Rules and Reasoning in Stoic Ethics." In *Topics in Stoic Philosophy*, edited by Katerina Ierodiakonou, 95–126. Oxford: Oxford University Press.
Kaser, Max. 1971. *Das römische Privatrecht*. 2nd edn. Munich: Beck.
Leo, Friedrich. 1901. *Die griechisch-römische Biographie nach ihrer litterarischen Form*. Leipzig: Teubner.
Livrea, Enrico. 1991. "La morte di Diogene Cinico [1987]." Reprinted in his *Studia hellenistica*, 233–238. Florence: Gonnelli.
Long, Anthony A. 1996. "Heraclitus and Stoicism [1975–1976]." Reprinted in his *Stoic Studies*, 35–57. Cambridge: Cambridge University Press.
Long, Anthony A. 2018. "In and out of the Stoa: Diogenes Laertius on Zeno." In *Authors and Authorities in Ancient Philosophy*, edited by Jenny Bryan, Robert Wardy, and James Warren, 242–256. Cambridge: Cambridge University Press.
López Cruces, Juan Luis. 1995. Les Méliambes de Cercidas de Mégalopolis. Amsterdam: Hakkert.
Mansfeld, Jaap. 1986. "Diogenes Laertius on Stoic Philosophy." *Elenchos* 7:295–382.
Mitsis, Philip. 1994. "Natural Law and Natural Rights." In *Aufstieg und Niedergang der römischen Welt* 2.36.7, edited by Wolfgang Haase, 4812–4850. Berlin: De Gruyter.

Mitsis, Philip. 1999. "The Stoic Origin of Natural Rights." In *Topics in Stoic Philosophy*, edited by Katerina Ierodiakonou, 153–177. Oxford: Oxford University Press.

Moles, John. 1995. "The Cynics and Politics." In *Justice and Generosity*, edited by André Laks and Malcolm Schofield, 129–158. Cambridge: Cambridge University Press.

Moles, John. 1996. "Cynic Cosmopolitanism." In *The Cynics. The Cynic Movement in Antiquity and Its Legacy*, edited by R. Bracht Branham and Marie-Odile Goulet-Cazé, 105–120. Berkeley: University of California Press.

Obbink, Dirk. 1999. "The Stoic Sage in the Cosmic City". In *Topics in Stoic Philosophy*, edited by Katerina Ierodiakonou, 178–195. Oxford: Oxford University Press.

Obbink, Dirk, and Paul Vander Waerdt. 1991. "Diogenes of Babylon: The Stoic Sage in the City of Fools." *Greek, Roman, and Byzantine Studies* 32:355–396.

Overwien, Oliver. 2005. *Die Sprüche des Kynikers Diogenes in der griechischen und arabischen Überlieferung*. Stuttgart: Steiner.

Overwien, Oliver. 2011. "Das Bild des Kynikers Diogenes in griechischen, syrischen und arabischen Quellen." *Philologus* 155:92–124.

Pierson, Christopher. 2013. *Just Property. A History in the Latin West*. Oxford: Oxford University Press.

Pons Olivares, Daniel. 2009. "D.L. VI 93: Crates, 'ciudadano de Diógenes'. Una revisión del cosmopolitismo cínico." *Estudios clásicos* 12:575–582.

Rich, Audrey N.M. 1956. "The Cynic Conception of AYTARKEIA." *Mnemosyne* 4.9:23–29.

Rudberg, Gunnar. 1936. "Zum Diogenes-Typus." *Symbolae osloenses* 15–16:1–18.

Schiavone, Aldo. 2017. *Ius. L'invenzione del diritto in Occidente* [2005]. 2nd edn. Turin: Einaudi.

Schofield, Malcolm. 1999. *The Stoic Idea of the City* [1991]. 2nd edn. Chicago: University of Chicago Press.

Sellars, John. 2007. "Stoic Cosmopolitanism and Zeno's *Republic*." *History of Political Thought* 28:1–29.

Sharples, Robert W. 1984. "On Fire in Heraclitus and in Zeno of Citium." *Classical Quarterly* N.S. 34:231–233.

Striker, Gisela. 1996. "Origins of the Concept of Natural Law [1987]." In *Essays on Hellenistic Epistemology and Ethics*, edited by Gisela Striker, 209–220. Cambridge: Cambridge University Press.

Tarn, Willam W. 1939. "Alexander, Cynics and Stoics." *American Journal of Philology* 60:41–70.

Vander Waerdt, Paul A. 1989. "The Stoic Theory of Natural Law." Diss. Princeton.

Vander Waerdt, Paul A. 1994. "Philosophical Influence on Roman Jurisprudence?" In *Aufstieg und Niedergang der römischen Welt* 2.36.7, edited by Wolfgang Haase, 4851–4590. Berlin: De Gruyter.

Vogt, Katja. 2008. *Law, Reason, and the Cosmic City. Political Philosophy in the Early Stoa*. New York: Oxford University Press.

Zeller, Eduard. 1922. *Die Philosophie der Griechen in ihrer geschichtlichen Entwicklung* 2.1: *Sokrates und die Sokratiker. Plato und die alte Akademie. Im Anhang: Der gegenwärtige Stand der Platonforschung von E. Hoffmann*. 5th edn. Leipzig: Reisland.

Tim O'Keefe
The Normativity of Nature in Epicurean Ethics and Politics

Abstract: The Epicureans appeal prominently to nature in setting out their ethical theory. Four main such appeals are found in Epicurus and his followers: (1) the cradle argument and the appeal to our natural pursuit of pleasure as proof of pleasure's goodness; (2) the division between natural and non-natural desires; (3) the 'natural goods' of wealth, political power, etc.; and finally (4) the justice of nature being a pledge neither to harm nor be harmed. Despite this, merely being natural does not *per se* imply that something is choiceworthy or beneficial. For example, natural desires can be harmful in some cases, and some non-natural things, like money, are good. Human nature does determine what is good for humans, but only indirectly, insofar as it is natural for us to seek pleasure for its own sake. It is pleasure, not the natural as such, that is the criterion of choiceworthiness.

1 Introduction

Appeals to nature are ubiquitous in Epicurean ethics and politics. The foundation of Epicurean ethics is its claim that pleasure is the sole intrinsic good and pain the sole intrinsic evil, and this is supposedly shown by the behaviour of infants who have not yet been corrupted, "when nature's judgement is pure and whole." Central to their recommendations about how to attain pleasure is their division between types of desires, so that we know which desires we should seek to satisfy and which ones to reject: the natural and necessary ones, the natural but non-necessary ones, and the vain and empty ones. Elsewhere, the Epicureans talk about the 'natural goods' of political power and fame, and they contrast 'natural wealth' with wealth as "defined by empty opinion." Finally, in their politics, Epicurus claims that the "the justice of nature is a pledge of reciprocal usefulness, [i.e.] neither to harm one another nor to be harmed."

We may usefully raise two questions regarding these various appeals to nature. The first is: what is it for these things to be natural, i.e. what notion of 'natural' or 'nature' is at play here? (Furthermore, is there a *single* notion being used across these appeals, and if not, how are they related?) The second is: what normative work does a thing's being natural do? That is, what reason, if any, does a desire's being natural give me for pursuing the object of that desire and trying to fulfil that desire, as opposed to not doing so and trying to eliminate it, and similarly for the other appeals to nature?

This paper will have four main parts, each associated with one of the appeals to nature mentioned above: (1) the cradle argument and the appeal to our natural pursuit of pleasure as proof of pleasure's goodness; (2) the division between natural and non-natural desires; (3) the 'natural goods' of wealth, political power, etc.; and finally (4) the justice of nature being a pledge neither to harm nor be harmed.

2 The cradle argument and the goodness of pleasure

The Epicurean cradle argument is reported in several places. The fullest account comes at the start of Torquatus' account of Epicurean ethics in Cicero's *De Finibus* 1.30:

> Every animal as soon as it is born seeks pleasure and rejoices in it, while shunning pain and avoiding it as much as possible. This is behaviour that has not yet been corrupted, when nature's judgement is pure and whole. Hence [Epicurus] denies that there is any need for justification or debate as to why pleasure should be sought and pain shunned. He thinks that this truth is perceived by the senses, as fire is perceived to be hot, snow white, and honey sweet.[1]

At *PH* 3.194, Sextus Empiricus basically repeats Torquatus' observation that pleasure is naturally worth seeking because animals seek it out as soon as they are born and are not corrupted. Two other variations of the argument illuminate the contrast between uncorrupted infants and adult humans:

---

[1] Translations of *De Finibus* are from Annas and Woolf 2001. Translations of other texts are from Inwood and Gerson 1997. The following abbreviations will be used to refer to ancient texts: Aristotle, *Nicomachean Ethics* = *NE*; Cicero, *De Finibus* (On Ends) = *Fin.*; Cicero, *De Natura Deorum* (On the Nature of the Gods) = *Nat. D.*; Diogenes Laertius, *Lives of the Philosophers* = DL; Epicurus, *Kuriai Doxai* (Principle Doctrines) = *KD*; Epicurus, *Sententiae Vaticanae* (Vatican Sayings) = *SV*; Epicurus, *Letter to Herodotus* = *Ep. Hdt.*; Epicurus, *Letter to Menoeceus* = *Ep. Men.*; Lucretius, *De Rerum Natura* (On the Nature of Things) = *DRN*; Plato, *Republic* = *Rep.*; Sextus Empiricus, *Against the Learned* = *AM*; Sextus Empiricus, *Outlines of Pyrrhonism* = *PH*, Simplicius, *Commentary on Aristotle's* Physics = *in Phys*; Xenophon, *Oeconomicus* (Household Management) = *Oec.*

> [Epicurus] uses as a proof that the goal is pleasure the fact that animals, as soon as they are born are satisfied with it but are in conflict with suffering by nature and apart from reason [*logos*]. So it is by our experience all on its own that we avoid pain. (DL 10.137)

> Some of the Epicureans are accustomed to saying that an animal flees pain and pursues pleasure naturally and without instruction. For when it was just born and was not yet a slave to matters of opinion, just as soon as it was struck by the unfamiliar cold air, "it wept and wailed." And if it has a natural impulse to pleasure and a natural avoidance of painful exertion, then by nature painful exertion is something that is worth avoiding and pleasure is something naturally worth choosing. (Sextus Empiricus, *AM* 11.96)

Two themes are prominent in these passages. First, the fact that we 'naturally' pursue pleasure shows that it is good: and here it seems that this pursuit is 'natural' in the sense that we engage in it without tutoring or other learning. The second theme is that we should look to infant behaviour to discover what we naturally pursue because it shows what we pursue before we are 'corrupted'.

This usage of 'natural', where something is natural if it is congenital or built in to us, is not confined to our pursuit of pleasure. It is also the sense in which language and our preconception of the gods are 'natural'. For the Epicureans, all humans, without being taught, have a basic grasp of the gods, a conception which we get from 'nature herself' (*Nat. D.* 1.43). And language is not entirely a matter of human convention. Instead, the origin of language is 'natural' because early humans, like other animals, instinctively made different sorts of utterances in response to different sorts of stimuli, just as a stallion will make one kind of neigh when it is sexually aroused and a different sort of whinny when it is frightened (*DRN* V.1056–90). Epicurus says that these original 'lessons of nature' were added to by the discoveries of reason, when people decided to add words to their language that were not part of the original stock of natural names (*Ep. Hdt.* 75). But if this is the sense in which our pursuit of pleasure is natural, then the Epicurean appeal to the cradle seems deeply problematic, as it is unclear why what is natural (in this sense) should be normative. That is, how can we legitimately infer what we *should* pursue on the basis of we *do* pursue without tutoring or argument?

The problem here can be brought out by comparing Epicurus to Aristotle and the way in which he grounds his ethics in our nature, especially in his function argument at *EN* I.7. In it, Aristotle compares the human *ergon* (the human function or job) and the *erga* of artefacts. In the case of items that have functions, formal and final explanations – explanations which appeal to what something is and which appeal to goals or purposes – coincide. To be an eye is to be an organ which has the function of seeing. This function sets the *telos* of a functional item, and hence its good, because the good of something is its *telos*. Likewise, Aristotle believes that our theoretical reason has a function that it fulfils when it understands and contemplates the truths of cosmology and theology, and we can also perfect and express our rational nature in our practical and social lives. This functional understanding of nature is what allows Aristotle to appeal to our nature in order to discern what the human good is, an activity of the *psuchê* that expresses complete human excellence, i.e. excellence as a rational and social animal.

Whether Aristotle's appeals to human nature in his ethics presuppose his 'teleological biology', and if so in exactly what way, is controversial.[2] But for the purposes of illuminating what is going on with Epicurus, I do not need to stake out a definitive view on that question. Even Julia Annas, who thinks that Aristotle's ethics does not depend on his biology, attributes to Aristotle a strongly normative view of nature. She says that nature is "the goal or end of human development", which is not merely a description of how people *do* develop. Instead, it assumes that "we can distinguish between what forms an expression of a person's nature and forms a corruption of it – between a natural and an *unnatural* development." Annas notes that this notion of nature is 'strongly normative' (Annas 1993a, 137).[3]

The problem is that the Epicureans are at pains to deny *any* sort of normativity or teleology in their physics generally and in their biology specifically. According to Lucretius, organisms and their parts have no inherent purposes or functions, even though they are able to do various things (*DRN* 5 772–1090). Like Empedocles, the Epicureans think that just because the heart *does* pump blood, it does not follow that it is the *job* of the heart to do that. Instead, organisms that happened to have organs that allowed them to survive and reproduce, like a heart located in the chest rather than in the ankle, did survive and reproduce. That is why they are the ones around nowadays, whereas others died off. So how an appeal to nature is supposed to ground ethics is particularly enigmatic for the Epicureans.

The second theme of these passages, that we should rely on the judgment of infants about the goodness of pleasure because they naturally seek it "before they are corrupted", is also problematic. The obvious initial way to interpret these passages is that infants, who are not corrupted, seek what is actually good for us – pleasure – whereas people who are corrupted seek something other than what is good for us; i.e. something other than pleasure. One question immediately confronting such a view is why we should suppose that the untu-

---

[2] Defences of such a dependence include Irwin 1980; Leunissen 2015. Denials of it include Annas 1989, much of which is recapitulated in Chapter 4 of Annas 1993a, 142–158; Nussbaum 1995.

[3] See Annas 1993a, 138–141 for her fuller discussion of the role of nature in Aristotle's ethics.

tored behaviour of infants shows what is truly valuable for us to pursue. Aristotle, for instance, could plausibly complain that education and attending to arguments can give us better insight into what we should do. But let us leave this complaint aside for the moment.

The more central problem with this initial interpretation is that it does not square with the Epicureans' psychological hedonism, their view that *all* human behaviour is ultimately motivated by the desire for pleasure. Although the point has been disputed, I believe that several passages firmly establish that the Epicureans are psychological hedonists.[4] In *De Finibus* 1.23 the Epicurean spokesman Torquatus says that pleasure and pain "explain our every act of pursuit and avoidance." Likewise, Epicurus says that we "must practice the things which produce happiness, since if that is present we have everything, and if it is absent we do everything in order to have it" (*Ep. Men.* 122). Epicurus is here describing what we *do* strive for – happiness, i.e. pleasure – and from this observation derives the conclusion that we *ought* to do the things which allow us to obtain pleasure.

Finally, in *De Finibus* 1.42, Torquatus makes a quick argument that establishes normative hedonism, i.e. the intrinsic goodness of pleasure alone, on the basis of psychological hedonism, i.e. the thesis that pleasure is the only thing pursued for its own sake. This argument appeals to what motivates people generally, not infants in particular, and if people were not all motivated by the desire for pleasure, the argument would fall apart. I will look into this passage in more detail later, but for now, the relevant statement from it is: "the impulse to seek and to avoid and to act in general derives either from pleasure or pain."

So, given these apparent problems, how should we understand the Epicureans' appeal to the natural pursuit of pleasure by uncorrupted infants in the cradle argument?

2.1 The fact that we 'naturally' pursue pleasure shows that it is good

Epicurus appropriates the teleological framework of Aristotle's ethics. The highest good is that which we seek for its own sake and not for the sake of anything else, and everything else that we seek is sought for its sake. As I noted above,

---

[4] Most prominently, Cooper 1998 disputes that the Epicureans are psychological hedonists, but his arguments are given a detailed (and I believe convincing) rebuttal by Woolf 2004. For the sake of this paper, I will simply briefly give my own reasons for thinking Epicurus is a psychological hedonist.

when Epicurus appeals to nature to ground ethics, he should not be relying on an Aristotelian functional notion of nature, which allows us to distinguish between developments that fulfil our natural end as rational and social animals and those that are deviations from it. Absent such an appeal, we can still look to what we do, as a matter of fact, pursue for its own sake, and what we do approve of for its own sake. The Epicureans think that in order for something to exist for the sake of some goal, it must be the result of the intention of some agent (Simplicius *in Phys.* 198b29). Thus, value comes in at the level of intentional, goal-directed behaviour itself: the 'end' of some piece of behaviour is its good. And this behaviour, in turn, is motivated by our desires, which are also intentional and aim at some end. But then, to determine what actually is good requires us to engage in some empirical work: what *do* we seek for its own sake and approve of for its own sake? The Epicureans answer: pleasure. This sort of naturalistic metaethical theory, which posits that the good is what we seek for its own sake, need not be hedonistic: Ralph Barton Perry's (1924) naturalistic theory of the good is an excellent example of this. For Perry, goodness consists in being liked and sought for its own sake, and badness in being disliked and being avoided for its own sake. But he is not a hedonist because he thinks that hedonism's conception of what we seek for its own sake is much too narrow.

The argument for hedonism that the Epicurean spokesman Torquatus advances precisely fits with the naturalistic metaethics that I have outlined above: that we all *seek* pleasure for its own sake establishes that it is intrinsically *good* (*Fin.* 1.42):

> Furthermore, the impulse to seek and to avoid and to act in general derives either from pleasure or pain. This being so, it is evident that a thing is rendered right and praiseworthy just to the extent that it is conducive to a life of pleasure. Now since the highest or greatest or ultimate good – what the Greeks call the *telos* – is that which is a means to no other end, but is itself the end of all other things, then it must be admitted that the highest good is to live pleasantly.

It is not only our pursuit of pleasure that establishes its goodness, but also our delight in it. Epicurus' canon lists feelings of pleasure and pain as the criteria of choice and avoidance, with pleasure being familiar or congenial (*oikeion*) to us, whereas pain is alienating or foreign (*allotrion*) (DL 10.34). I have already mentioned *De Finibus* 1.30, where Torquatus says that every animal rejoices in pleasure, and goes to say that the truth that pleasure should be sought and pain avoided "is perceived by the senses, as fire is perceived to be hot, snow white, and honey sweet."

These behavioural and affective proofs of pleasure's goodness and pain's badness are not competing accounts. Instead, they work together: it is because we delight in pleasure for its own sake and abhor pain for its own sake that we seek pleasure for its own sake and flee pain. Epicurus' brief summary of why pleasure is the good appeals both to our instinctive pursuit of pleasure and our feelings toward pleasure (*Ep. Men.* 128–129):

> We do everything for the sake of being neither in pain nor in terror. As soon as we achieve this state every storm in the soul is dispelled, since the animal is not in a position to go after some need nor to seek something else to complete the good of the body and the soul. [...] And this is why we say that pleasure is the starting-point and goal of living blessedly. For we recognized that this [viz. pleasure] as our first innate good, and this is our starting point for every choice and avoidance and we come to this by judging every good by the criterion of feeling."

So the Epicureans ground our end, and hence our good, in our goal-directed behaviour and our pro-attitudes.

2.2 Infants and 'corruption'

Let us now turn to the issue of 'corruption' and what it means, and why we should look to the cradle in particular to establish what is good. Initially, the thesis that pleasure is good because we seek it for its own sake may not only appear hopelessly misguided, but also inconsistent with Epicurus' repeated insistence that we desire lots of things that we should not, that we make serious mistakes about what is good for us.

But in the *De Finibus* 1.55, Torquatus says, "There is no possibility of mistake as far the highest goods and evils themselves – namely pleasure and pain – are concerned. Rather error occurs when people are ignorant of the ways in which these are brought about." None of us are mistaken about what is good, but we make mistakes about what will bring us that good. Likewise, says Epicurus, all pleasures are good, but not all are choiceworthy, and all pains bad, but not all such as to be avoided. That is because some pleasures lead to more pain in the long run, and vice versa, so we have to think about the long-term consequences when choosing among pleasures and pains to make sure that we make our life overall as pleasant as we can (*Ep. Men.* 129–30).

This allows us to see how we can desire some things we should not, even if psychological hedonism is true: we have false beliefs about what we need to live pleasantly, for instance, believing that striving to accumulate as much wealth as possible is the way to make us secure and ensure we will be able to fulfil our desires. It also allows us to account for why infants are not corrupt, and the sense in which we often are. Animals and infants do not have empty and false judgments because they do not (robustly) have judgments at all. Some later Epicureans discuss how our reasoning abilities set us apart from other animals. We can calculate the outcomes of different possible courses of action, whereas animals have only 'irrational memory'. That is, they have repeated experiences that condition them to act in certain ways, and to find certain things attractive or repulsive, but they do not think through the outcomes of possible courses of action. That is because they do not understand concepts such as 'healthy' and 'expedient', and they cannot make causal inferences.[5]

Even though this development beyond the animal and infantile state is what allows us to be corrupted, this development is not as such a bad thing. We would not want to return to the cradle, even if it were possible. Infants obey the pleasure principle, going for whatever pleasure immediately beckons. Adults are still motivated by the desire for pleasure. But we need to move from the pleasure principle to the reality principle, delaying gratification when needed. Virtues such as courage do not come into being by nature, but by reasoning about what is advantageous (DL 10.120), and this is why Epicurus says practical wisdom (*phronesis*) is the source of all of the other virtues. Things like friendship and farming allow us to satisfy our needs better than we would be able to otherwise, and to face the future with serenity.

People who are 'corrupted' do not pursue something *other* than pleasure: instead, they pursue pleasure *badly* because of their false and harmful beliefs. And infants and non-human animals do not always pursue pleasure well. Instead, they pursue pleasure in a relatively simple and straightforward fashion, which precludes both the possibility of corruption but also of the sort of rational long-term planning that adults with practical wisdom engage in.

So, the cradle argument does not state that we ought to pursue pleasure because infants do, or that their behaviour is normative for us because they are uncorrupted. Instead, it starts from the observation that the good is what we pursue for its own sake and not for the sake of anything else, and we want to know what this is. Infant behaviour is (supposedly) a better and clearer guide to what we all pursue for its own sake. Discovering what we really desire is a problem because of self-deception and the opacity of our own motives. When discussing the fear of death, Lucretius furnishes some examples of how we can be blind to ourselves: a person restlessly moving from room to room, and from his city home to his country villa, not realizing that his ennui and misery is caused by his fear of death

---

[5] These Epicureans, Hermarchus and Polystratus, are discussed in Annas 1993b, 66–9. There is no reason to think that what they say regarding other animals departs substantially from what Epicurus would have said.

(*DRN* III.1053–75), and another who unconsciously believes that some part of him survives his death, and hence finds it horrifying to contemplate his body rotting, being incinerated, or being devoured, even though he denies believing that there is any sensation after death (*DRN* III.870–93). Torquatus acknowledges that many people *think* that the highest good is located in virtue alone. Such people are "beguiled by the splendour of a name" (*Fin.* 1.42) and we need to get them to see what they really value for its own sake. So, a study of what we *actually* desire for its own sake and approve of for its own sake is crucial for ethics.

3 Natural and non-natural desires

Now let us turn to the Epicurean division of desires. We will ask the same questions: what is it for a desire to be natural, and what normative work does a desire's being natural do? (That is, what reason, if any, does a desire's being natural give me for pursuing the object of that desire and trying to fulfil that desire, as opposed to not doing so and trying to eliminate it?)

Of course, the Epicureans do not make just a dichotomy between natural and non-natural desires, but a trichotomy, which is spelled out in a number of places. The overall trichotomy is reasonably clear, but there are still a few puzzles about how exactly it is supposed to work, because the reports are not entirely consistent. Let us start by looking through these reports.

Principal Doctrine 29 states the trichotomy this way: some desires are natural and necessary, some are natural but not necessary, and some are neither necessary nor necessary but are the result of a 'groundless opinion [*kenon doxan*]'. This is echoed in *Ep. Men.* 127, where the third class of desires is simply called *kenon*. A scholion to *Principal Doctrine* 29 fills out the trichotomy with examples, saying that the desire to drink when thirsty is natural and necessary, the desire for expensive food is natural but not necessary, while the desires for crowns and the erection of statues is neither natural nor necessary. It also reports that natural and necessary desires are ones whose fulfilment liberates us from pain. This echoes *Ep. Men.* 127, which however draws the distinction slightly differently. It says that necessary desires are necessary for at least one of three reasons: for happiness, or for freeing the body from troubles, or for life itself.

Finally, Epicurus characterizes the natural but not necessary desires as follows: "Among natural desires, those which do not lead to a feeling of pain if not fulfilled and about which there is an intense effort, these are produced by a groundless opinion and they fail to be dissolved not because of their own nature but because of the groundless opinions of mankind" (*KD* 30). This text is problematic, because elsewhere Epicurus seemed to identify the desires produced by groundless opinion with the desires that are neither natural nor necessary, whereas here he seems to classify at least some natural but unnecessary desires as based on groundless opinion.

Julia Annas has put forward the most detailed attempt to pull together these various reports. Natural and necessary desires, she says, are 'generic' desires for food, drink, clothes, etc. Such desires fit the criteria for being necessary for happiness, or for freeing the body from troubles, or for life itself. Natural but unnecessary desires are specific versions of these generic desires – for instance, the desire for lobster in particular, rather than food in general. It is natural to desire food but eating lobster in particular is not necessary to live happily, to free your body from troubles, or to continue to exist. And if it takes a lot of effort to get lobster, and you acquire the belief that you really do need lobster in particular so that you are put out when it is not available, then – because it is based on a groundless opinion that you learn – then the desire for lobster is no longer merely natural, but instead is neither natural nor necessary (Annas 1993a, 191–3).

I think that Annas' understanding of these passages is partially correct. But it does contradict another report, a scholion to Aristotle's *Nicomachean Ethics* (Usener 456). It says that the "desire for food and clothing" is a natural and necessary desire, "the desire for sex" is a natural but unnecessary desire, and "the desire for such-and-such (*toionde*) food and or such-and-such clothing or such-and-such sex" are examples of desires which are neither. Annas claims that "we have no reason to give this scholion authority, however, and it faces difficulties. (1) It cannot accommodate *KD* 30, which plainly implies that a desire can be either natural and non-necessary, or empty. (2) It makes the necessary distinction artificial; surely we have as much a need for sex as for clothing?" (Annas 1993a, 193 n. 29).

But I do not think Annas' reply quite works. The Epicureans plainly disagree with her thesis that we surely need sex as much as we need clothing. In his brief for vegetarianism, *On Abstinence from Killing Animals*, Porphyry reports that the Epicureans compare eating meat to having sex or drinking exotic wines. A desire for meat does not cause pain when it is not satisfied, and none of these three activities contribute to maintaining a person's life. Instead, they simply vary our pleasure, and our nature can continue on without fulfilling them (Porphyry, *On Abstinence* 1.51). And *Principal Doctrine* 26 states that the desires which do not bring a feeling of pain when not fulfilled are not necessary. So, by the Epicurean criteria, the desire for sex is not necessary. Similarly, DL 10.118 reports that having sex "never helped anyone, and one must be satisfied if it has not harmed." So, we have good reason to stick the desire for sex into the "natural but not necessary" bin, as reported in the scholion to Aristotle.

What about the report in the scholion that particular desires for such-and-so food, clothing and sex are examples of empty desires? I am not so sure this expresses a sharp disagreement with Annas' interpretation: the scholion could just be talking about those instances where the desire is informed by the false and groundless beliefs that I really do *need* a particular kind of food, clothing, or sex, where according to Annas those would be empty desires. In cases where I do not have those sorts of empty beliefs, when I am hungry I might not have a desire for generic 'food', like the cans of nourishment in the movie *Repo Man*. Instead, if I happen to see or remember a particular kind of food when I am hungry, then I might desire *that* food. As long I am not going to be put out if that sort of food is unavailable and can easily switch to something else, this sort of unnecessary desire would be acceptable. But the sort of attachment to eating lobster that Annas discusses, where I think that I need the lobster and will feel bad if I do not get it, is *not* natural but must be learned. This sort of harmful attachment is best avoided and must be extirpated if acquired. The above account is speculative, but it fits the texts and helps explain the scholion to the *Nicomachean Ethics*, showing how desires for a particular sort of food, drink or sex may fit into either category, depending on how it is held.

When it comes to the distinction between necessary versus unnecessary desires, we have both the examples of both kinds, and also – very helpfully – a set of criteria that allows us to see why some desires are in one category and some are in another. Unfortunately, with the distinction between natural and non-natural desires, all we get are the examples, on the basis of which we have to figure out ourselves what natural desires are supposed to have in common that makes them natural. But the basic use of 'natural' here seems to be the same as in our 'natural' pursuit of pleasure and also the ways in which our preconception of the gods and our use of language are 'natural'. They are congenital, not learned, and they are not based on *logos*.

What normative work is done by the appeal to nature in the case of desires? It is important but limited. The key text is *Vatican Saying* 21: "one must not compel nature but persuade her. And we will persuade her by fulfilling the necessary desires, and the [merely] natural ones too if they do not harm [us], but sharply rejecting the harmful ones." That some natural desires are harmful and must be rejected shows that the mere fact that a desire is natural does not imply that it is good or to be pursued. But natural desires are generally easy to get (*Fin.* 45), and so indulging in the fulfilment of natural but unnecessary desires, when they are not harmful, is usually prudent. More fundamentally, even when they are harmful, natural but unnecessary desires call for a different approach than vain and empty ones. Vain and empty desires, because they are based on false beliefs, can be subject to standard Epicurean cognitive therapy, exposing the basis for these desires and thereby helping to eradicate them. But natural desires, such as sexual desire, are not based on *logos* in this way, and so they can be managed but not eradicated. Another example is anger: Philodemus says that anger "is unavoidable, and is called natural for that reason." But anger can become empty (and unnatural) when excessive and towards the wrong objects.[6] Anger is disturbing, but the wise person is able to manage his natural anger in a way that does not interfere with his fundamental peace of mind.

4 Friendship, and the natural goods of wealth and political power

It is surprising that friendship is not mentioned anywhere in the Epicurean division of desires. It seems that the desire for friendship should be listed as a natural and necessary desire, because friendship fulfils one of the criteria for the object of such a desire: it is necessary for happiness (See *Fin.* 1.66–67). So it is tempting to include desires for social needs like friendship and a stable society among the natural desires, as does Annas (1993a, 196).

But the word translated as 'desire' in the Epicurean trichotomy is *epithumia* – which usually designates appetitive desires in particular, as it does in the *Republic*. The exact status of friendship can be illuminated by comparing friendship to the virtues – which the Epicureans themselves often do. The virtuous person will have the right desires and aversions (for instance, the courageous person will not fear death). Practical wisdom teaches us that the virtues are necessary and sufficient for attaining a pleasant life (*Ep. Men.* 132; *KD* 5). But even though the virtues are necessary for living pleasantly, we do not have an *epithumia* for virtue – that would be a category mistake. We reason out that the virtues are beneficial, and so we might acquire a *wish* to be virtuous, but that is not the same as an *appetite* for virtue. And the Epicureans put both courage and friendship into the category of such rational contrivances: "Courage does not come to be by nature, but by a reasoning out of what is advantageous. And friendship comes to be because of its utility" (DL 10.120 [B]). Friendship, say the Epicureans, is a means

---

[6] Philodemus *On Anger* XXXIX 29–31, as noted and discussed in Annas 1993a, 194–5. For more on Philodemus on anger, see Chapter 9 of Voula Tsouna 2007, 195–238. A controversial example of a natural emotion that can be managed but not eradicated is the fear of violent death at the hands of others, as argued for in Austin 2012. Although I do not agree with her specific proposal that the fear of violent death by others is natural, her discussion of managing but not eradicating disturbing natural desires is insightful.

to happiness devised by wisdom (*Fin.* 1.65, *KD* 27), and reason bids us to acquire friends when we realize that a solitary life is filled with fear and danger (*Fin.* 1.66).

The 'desire' for friendship here sounds less like an appetite, and more like what Aristotle calls *boulêsis*, or 'rational wish' – i.e. a desire for something based upon the belief that obtaining it is good for you (*EN* III.4, 1113a15 – 1113b2). And Epicurus uses a form of *boulêsis* in *Principal Doctrine* 7 in a way that comports with this Aristotelian sense:

> Some men want (*boulomai*) to become famous and respected, believing that this is the way to acquire security against [other] men. Thus, if the life of such men is secure, they acquire the natural good; but if it is not secure, they do not have that for the sake of which they strove from the beginning according to what is naturally congenial.

At the same time, for Epicurus, some things that we desire instrumentally because we believe that they will fulfil other desires of ours, like wealth, can still be the object of appetites, so *epithumia* for Epicurus is not restricted to bodily appetites. But that does not undercut the overall picture that Epicurus distinguishes between what we wish for and what we have an appetite for. Plato also says that money is desired by the appetitive part of the *psuchê*.

Here I should clarify that I am not trying to attribute to Epicurus Plato's tripartite theory of the *psuchê* from the *Republic*. Nor am I saying that he has a well-developed theory of rational and irrational elements in the *psuchê* like Aristotle does. But it is plausible that Epicurus is working with something like Plato's and Aristotle's distinctions between types of desires when he uses the term *epithumia*, and that this explains which items are included in his trichotomy of desires and which are excluded. More generally, for the Epicureans there are many affective states that are not desires: attitudes like gratitude, grief, resentment, and regret are pleasant or painful, but are not desires. We do not have an appetite or passion to recall delightful memories of past goods, but we can follow Torquatus' recommendation to do so in order to obtain joy (*Fin.* 1.56 – 7), and gratitude for past goods is central to the Epicurean ethical program.[7]

The 'natural good' of a contrivance, such as wealth, is the human need which it was originally devised to fulfil – such as reliably fulfilling our desire for food and other necessities in the case of wealth and gaining security from others in the case of fame.[8] Because of the Epicurean's psychology this is very closely linked to getting pleasure. But we can pursue these things in a way

---

[7] For more on grief, see Konstan 2013, and for more on gratitude, see Rider 2019.
[8] For more on the role of natural wealth in Epicurean ethics, see O'Keefe 2016, 39 – 41.

that actually is counterproductive to gaining this natural good and develop irrational appetites and passions for these things that lead to disturbance rather than peace of mind. When this happens, we need cognitive therapy to realize that our pursuit of these things is misguided.

Because he builds this purpose into his notion of wealth, Epicurus offers revisionist redefinitions of what truly counts as wealth and criticizes popular notions of wealth. We need little to fulfil our basic needs, and so, he says, "natural wealth is both limited and easy to acquire. But wealth [as defined by] groundless opinion extends without limit" (*KD* 15). In fact, if we measure it by "the goal of nature", poverty is great wealth and wealth without limits set on it is great poverty (*SV* 25), and in order to make a person wealthy, you should not give them money; instead, you should reduce their desires (Stobaeus *Anthology* 3.17.23).[9]

5 The justice of nature

Famously, Epicurus states in *KD* 31 that "the justice of nature is a pledge of reciprocal usefulness, [i.e.] neither to harm one another nor to be harmed", combining two conceptions of justice that were often thought to be opposed: conventional justice and natural justice. The sense in which justice is conventional for Epicurus is tolerably clear. At *KD* 33, Epicurus asserts that justice is not something that exists *per se*, but instead exists wherever there is a pact about not harming one another. Our agreements create justice, and Epicurus does not hesitate to draw out the implications of this theory: there is no justice (or injustice) with respect to animals that cannot make an agreement about not harming one another, nor between nations if they do not have a pact about not harming one another (*KD* 32). This comports with Aristotle's characterisation of conventional justice at *NE* V.7: certain things that were indifferent beforehand may be rendered just or unjust by our laws. We make driving on the left-hand side of the road unjust by declaring that people must drive on the right-hand side. But for Aristotle, unlike Epicurus, there exists natural justice in addition to conventional justice, which has the same force everywhere regardless of our decisions or opinions and which acts as a constraint on what may be conventionally just (*NE* V.7, 1134b18–1135a6).

But the sense in which justice is 'natural' is less clear. If my argument above has succeeded, justice obviously cannot be natural in the sense in which either the pursuit of pleasure or the desires for food and sex are natural. The pursuit of

---

9 Socrates offers redefinitions of wealth along similar lines in *Rep.* 521a and *Oec.* 2.2–10.

pleasure and the desires for food and sex are congenitally hard-wired into us, and into all other animals, apart from *logos*. As a human contrivance, justice is very much a product of *logos*. Human beings came together and formed societies in order to escape the threats posed by animal attacks and starvation which they faced in the wild, and they needed to devise laws and punishments in order to live together productively and peaceably in society.[10]

The Epicurean conception of the limits of our natural desires, however, can at least show that justice does not go *against* our nature in the way that it does in the social contract theory put forward by Glaucon in Book II of Plato's *Republic*. For both Glaucon and Epicurus, justice is an agreement we make in order to have a safe society, and we need society to escape the dangers of the wild. But for Glaucon, neither committing nor suffering injustice is a second best. It is a constraint we agree to because it is preferable to both committing and suffering injustice, but it is not as good as being able to commit injustice while not suffering it (*Rep.* 358e–359b). But Epicurus does not think that human beings are naturally aggressive and acquisitive. Instead, our natural desires are easy to fulfil. The fear of punishment is needed to keep fools in line, who otherwise would take others' goods, attack them, and otherwise harm them. The wise Epicurean does not desire great wealth, and he does not hate or envy others (DL 10.117). So, he does not have a motive to commit injustice. The laws exist for the sake of the wise, not so that they will not commit injustice, but so that they will not suffer it (Stobaeus, *Anthology* 4.143).

For a positive sense in which justice can be natural, we should look to other products of human reason, such as wealth, the virtues, and friendship: like them, justice is a human contrivance, and in that sense, it does not exist 'naturally'. But as an artefact, it has a 'natural good' insofar as it is devised for a purpose. Epicurus says that we have a *prolepsis*, or 'basic grasp', of justice as what is useful in mutual associations.[11] Epicurus' summary of justice as an agreement neither to harm not be harmed gives the basic content of what justice *is*, but we also have a basic grasp of what justice is *for*.

---

[10] For more on the origins of justice and how justice is not merely a non-aggression pact but allows people to coordinate their actions in order to fulfil their needs and escape danger, see O'Keefe 2001. For more on how the Epicureans' conception of justice fits with their conception of practical rationality, see Thrasher 2015.

[11] KD 37. We have a *prolepsis*, or 'basic grasp', of the meanings of some words, without need of additional proof. (*Ep. Hdt.* 37–8) *Prolepseis* are one part of Epicurus' canon of truth. For more on this topic and how *prolepseis* are supposed to solve Meno's paradox of inquiry, see Chapter 7 of Fine 2014, 226–256.

And just as in the case of wealth, where knowing the purpose of wealth allows us to re-evaluate popular notions concerning it, our grasp of the purpose of justice gives us a teleological standard, but one internal to our own practices, whereby we can evaluate the laws and conventions of our society. Laws that work, that actually help us live together peacefully and fruitfully, are just, while ones that do not are not. This allows for the requirements of justice to vary from place to place and time to time, and for a law that was previously just to cease being just, when it stops working. But generally speaking, what is just will be the same, insofar as what will be useful to help people live together will be the same (*KD* 37–8).

Finally, what normative work does the 'naturalness' of justice do? The main Epicurean justification for why a person should be just appeals directly to their hedonism, not to justice being natural in some way. Injustice, says Epicurus, is not bad in and of itself, but because of the fear of punishment (*KD* 34). By making injustice bad only because of its consequences, Epicurus allies himself with Glaucon's theory in the *Republic*, against Socrates' contention that justice is good not merely for the sake of its consequences, but for its own sake.

But we should not overstate the contrast with Socrates. Injustice is bad not only because it may bring punishment but because of the *fear* of punishment; this fear is (supposedly) inescapable (*KD* 35) and outweighs any benefits from acting unjustly. More crucially, the Epicurean defences of the virtues do not focus just on the ordinary bad consequences of vice. In his consequentialist defence of the virtues, Torquatus does mention how intemperance can lead to serious illness and a bad reputation. But Epicurus thinks that the vices are forms of psychic disease (Porphyry, *To Marcella* 31), and Torquatus stresses how the vices are disordered psychic states that inevitably cause distress simply because of what they are. The presence of dishonesty in the heart is disturbing, whereas justice "by its own power […] calms the spirits" and temperance "brings our hearts peace and soothes softens them with a kind of harmony" (*Fin.* 47–49). An unjust person who is held back from theft and assault by the threat of punishment may not fear being punished, but he is still in a bad way, because greed and wrath are in themselves disturbing states. This line of thinking is not terribly different from Socrates', although the Epicureans cash out the badness of vice in terms of the pain that the diseased psychic state itself causes, rather than the disordered state itself being bad.[12]

---

[12] How stark even this difference is depends on how we understand Socrates' task of praising justice in itself in the *Republic*. On most interpretations, this involves excluding any and all valuable consequences of being just, but on some less restrictive interpretations, Socrates may include certain types of consequences, e.g. those that justice brings about on its own or by its own

While the hedonic benefits of justice are what directly make it choice worthy, an appreciation of the natural good of justice, along with the natural goods of fame and wealth, plays an important role in living rightly. A person who knows what the point of justice is, what it is good for, can distinguish between just and unjust laws. He is able to see that justice benefits the members of a society in general, and that he has little or nothing to lose by adhering to its norms, unlike the fool who knuckles under only because he fears punishment. Likewise, the person who grasps what wealth is naturally good for can prudently gather together the limited resources he really needs to face the future with confidence, and he sees why popular notions of wealth are based on a misunderstanding of the role wealth should play in life.

6 Conclusion

Epicurus' ethics and politics are 'naturalistic' in some suitably broad sense, insofar as they are grounded on facts about what human beings are like naturally, what we desire and how we reason. And appeals to 'nature' are central to many areas of Epicurean ethics and politics. However, the relationship of nature to goodness is far from straightforward in Epicurus, and being 'natural' never *per se* makes something choice worthy or beneficial. Instead, in the case of pleasure, we are naturally 'hardwired' to seek pleasure for its own sake and delight in it for its own sake, and the good is what we seek and delight in for its own sake. So, our nature does determine what is good for us, but indirectly. Similarly, in the case of the desires, the fact that a desire is 'natural' to us does not make it good – some natural desires can be harmful. But whether a desire is congenital or learned will determine how to handle it, if it is harmful. Finally, human contrivances such as wealth and justice are not natural in the sense that the pursuit of pleasure and the desire for food are. But as contrivances, they have a 'natural good', a human need they were designed to satisfy, and knowing this natural good is crucial for using wealth properly, evaluating and perhaps improving the laws of my society, and conforming to just laws willingly and without resentment.

---

power, which would include some of the benefits the Epicureans mention. A recent example for this sort of permissive interpretation is Payne 2011.

Primary literature

Cicero. 2001. *Cicero: On Moral Ends*, edited and translated by Julia Annas and Raphael Woolf. Cambridge: Cambridge University Press.

Secondary literature

Annas, Julia. 1989. "Naturalism in Greek Ethics: Aristotle and After." *Proceedings of the Boston Area Colloquium in Ancient Philosophy* 4:149–171.
Annas, Julia. 1993a. *The Morality of Happiness*. Oxford: Oxford University Press.
Annas, Julia. 1993b. "Epicurus on Agency." In *Passions and Perceptions: Studies in Hellenistic Philosophy of Mind, Proceedings of the 5th Symposium Hellenisticum*, edited by Jacques Brunschwig and Martha Nussbaum, 53–71. Cambridge: Cambridge University Press.
Austin, Emily. 2012. "Epicurus and the Politics of Fearing Death." *Apeiron* 45 (2):109–129.
Cooper, John. 1998. "Pleasure and Desire in Epicurus." In *Reason and Emotion: Essays on Ancient Moral Psychology and Ethical Theory*, edited by John Cooper, 485–514. Princeton: Princeton University Press.
Fine, Gail. 2014. *The Possibility of Inquiry: Meno's Paradox from Socrates to Sextus*. Oxford: Oxford University Press.
Irwin, Terence. 1980. "The Metaphysical and Psychological Basis of Aristotle's Ethics." In *Essays on Aristotle's Ethics*, edited by Amélie Oksenberg Rorty, 35–54. Los Angeles: University of California Press.
Inwood, Brad, and Gerson, Lloyd P. [1988] 1997. *Hellenistic Philosophy Introductory Readings*. Indianapolis: Hackett Publishing Company.
Konstan, David. 2013. "Lucretius and the Epicurean Attitude toward Grief." In *Lucretius: Poetry, Philosophy, Science*, edited by Daryn Lehoux, Alistair D. Morrison and Alison Sharrock, 193–209. Oxford: Oxford University Press.
Leunissen, Mariska. 2015. "Aristotle on Knowing Natural Science for the Sake of Living Well." In *Bridging the Gap between Aristotle's Science and Ethics*, edited by Devin Henry and Karen Margrethe Nielsen, 214–231. Cambridge: Cambridge University Press.
Nussbaum, Martha. 1995. "Aristotle on Human Nature and the Foundations of Ethics." In *World, Mind, and Ethics: Essays on the Ethical Philosophy of Bernard Williams*, edited by James E. J. Altham and Ross Harrison, 86–131. Cambridge: Cambridge University Press.
O'Keefe, Tim. 2001. "Would a Community of Wise Epicureans Be Just?" *Ancient Philosophy* 21 (1):133–146.
O'Keefe, Tim. 2016. "The Epicureans on Happiness, Wealth, and the Deviant Craft of Property Management." In *Economics and the Virtues*, edited by Jennifer Baker and Mark White, 37–52. Oxford: Oxford University Press.
Payne, Andrew. 2011. "The Division of Goods and Praising Justice for Itself in *Republic* II." *Phronesis* 56 (1):58–78.
Perry, Ralph Barton. 1914. "The Definition of Value." *Journal of Philosophy, Psychology and Scientific Methods* 11 (6):141–162.

Rider, Benjamin. 2019. "The ethical significance of gratitude in Epicureanism." *British Journal for the History of Philosophy* 27 (6):1092–1112.

Thrasher, John. 2013. "Reconciling Justice and Pleasure in Epicurean Contractarianism." *Ethical Theory and Moral Practice* 16 (2):423–436.

Tsouna, Voula. 2007. *The Ethics of Philodemus*. Oxford: Oxford University Press.

Woolf, Raphael. 2004. "What Kind of Hedonist was Epicurus?" *Phronesis* 49 (4):303–322.

Philipp Brüllmann
Nature and Psychology in Cicero's *Republic*

Abstract: This paper defends two claims about Cicero's *Republic*. First, the argument of Books I and II calls for a discussion of psychological issues. If the ideas about the best constitution outlined in these two books are to make any sense, then certain assumptions about human psychology need to be true, or at least plausible. Second, in order to show that these assumptions are true or at least plausible, Cicero introduces, in *Rep.* III, a certain view of the cosmos. The dispute over naturalism vs. conventionalism about justice is used by Cicero as a vehicle for a discussion of psychological topics.

1 The naturalism of Cicero's *Republic*

It is not easy to say what role nature is supposed to play in Cicero's *Republic*. On the one hand, there are numerous references to nature in the extant remains of that work. Cicero does not hesitate to make use of arguments that are designed to provide politics with a natural basis, as for instance when he has Scipio, the host and major character of the dialogue, discuss the question why human beings live in states.[1] On the other hand, Cicero's attitude towards these arguments appears ambivalent. This is not just because many passages of his *Republic* reveal a sceptical attitude that seems to subvert the idea of seeking an objective and natural foundation for politics.[2] It is also because Cicero highlights more than once the

---

[1] As Scipio explains, the reason is not 'weakness' (*inbecillitas*) but 'natural herding' (*congregatio naturalis*). Human beings possess a natural impulse to form communities, so even if they could survive on their own, they would not want to do so (I.39–40). For the 'weakness' account, see III.23 and Plato, *Resp.* II 358e–359b (*adunamia tou adikein*). Notice that in IV.3a, Cicero locates the origin of political communties, along more Aristotelian lines, in the human wish for a happy life.

[2] A good example is the discussion of the simple constitutions in *Rep.* I, where we learn that each of them can draw for support on aspects of nature. Democracy can point out that "even for wild animals there is nothing sweeter than liberty" (I.55), so it would accord with nature to make liberty the most important good of the state. Aristocracy can observe that "nature has made sure not only that men outstanding for virtue and courage rule over weaker people, but that the weaker people willingly obey the best" (I.51), so it would accord with nature to establish a hierarchy within human society. Monarchy, finally, can refer to the fact that "through their investigation of the universe [men] have recognized that this entire world [is ruled] by [a single] mind" (I.56), so it would accord with nature that the state be ruled by one person as

importance of experience in political matters, of transmitted customs and of grown institutions, which counterbalances the naturalistic tendencies of his argument. A central illustration of this ambivalence is that the *Republic* offers two models for the ideal state: the cosmos, on the one hand, and the constitution of Rome, on the other.[3]

It seems safe to say, then, that the 'naturalism' of Cicero's *Republic* is neither simple nor straightforward (in contrast, e. g., to the naturalism of Callicles in Plato's *Gorgias*, which boils down to "look at nature and you'll see that I am right"). If we wish to understand the role of nature in Cicero's *Republic*, we must consider carefully how references to nature are put to work in particular contexts. This is the aim of the present chapter.

Book III of Cicero's *Republic* is famous for introducing the notion of a natural law. Scipio's friend Laelius refers to this notion in order to rebut the conventionalist account of justice propounded by Philus in the first half of that book. Apparently, Cicero here stages a familiar dispute over the question whether justice exists 'by nature' or merely 'by convention'. But this, I think, is only part of the story. For on closer inspection, we notice that there is a psychological background to this dispute.[4] Philus and Laelius proffer not only two different accounts of justice but also two different accounts of human psychology. This psychological background connects the argument of Book III with the argument of Books I and II. It treats a question provoked by Scipio's theory of the best constitution, or so I will argue. My claim is thus that Cicero uses the discussion of nature in Book III as a vehicle for the discussion of psychological topics. By spelling out this claim, I hope to contribute to our understanding of the role of nature in Cicero's *Republic*.

More specifically, I will defend two claims. First, the argument of *Rep.* I and II calls for a discussion of psychological issues. If Scipio's ideas about the best constitution, as outlined in these two books, are to make any sense, then certain

---

well. Unless otherwise noted, all translations from the *Republic* and the *Laws* draw upon Zetzel 1999.

[3] For the cosmos as a model, see *Rep.* I.14–34 (especially I.26–7) and, of course, the 'Dream of Scipio' (VI.9–28) (see Atkins 2013, 47–56; Miller 2014). For the idealized view of the Roman constitution, see *Rep.* II. The tension between these two models is a core topic of Atkins 2013. Though I do not agree with all of its far-reaching conclusions, I have profited a lot from this book.

[4] This connection has not been given the attention it deserves. Cf., however, the remarks in Woolf 2013 and Miller 2014.

assumptions about human psychology need to be true, or at least plausible.[5] Cicero is well aware of this. Second, in order to show that these assumptions are true (or to make them plausible), Cicero introduces, in *Rep.* III, a certain view of the cosmos.

Let us now look at these two claims in turn.

2 Politics and psychology: *Rep.* I and II

The first two books of Cicero's *Republic* develop an account of the best constitution of a state (I.33). The focus of this account is on the distribution of power (I.41–2), which is put in terms of the question who should possess the 'deliberative function' (*consilium*).[6] In reply to this question, Scipio first outlines the familiar scheme of six simple constitutions.[7] Three of them, monarchy, aristocracy, and democracy, seem acceptable to him. They have their flaws but also their virtues; and as long as "injustice and greed do not get in the way" (I.42), it seems to make no big difference whether the state is ruled by a single person, a group of chosen men, or the people (though Scipio shows a preference for the first option: I.60). Unfortunately, however, injustice and greed do usually get in the way. If that happens, the three acceptable constitutions change into their base counterparts: tyranny, oligarchy, and ochlocracy, respectively (I.44). The fundamental problem of the simple constitutions is hence their *instability*, which results in an endless 'cycle of constitutions' (I.45; 65).[8] The only way to escape that cycle, Scipio asserts, is to establish a 'mixed constitution', combining the virtues of the simple ones (I.45). This is the result of Book I. In Book II, Scipio tries to show that the Roman constitution represents the ideal form of such a mixed constitution. His argument is remarkable. Beginning *ab urbe condita*, Scipio sketches an idealized history of Rome that describes the elements of the Roman constitution as results of a huge learning process, spanning more than 500 years.[9] While some of these elements show the wisdom of those who introduced them (one of the good kings, e. g.), others react to situations of crisis, the deepest of which being the one that – due to the atrocities of the last king Tarquinius

---

[5] For the aims of the present paper, it is not necessary to decide the dispute over the role of scepticism in Cicero's *Republic* and *Laws*. On this question, see Atkins 2013, Chapter 1; Zarecki 2014, Chapter 1.
[6] On this notion, see Schofield 1995; Zetzel 1999, xxxviii.
[7] See Aristotle, *Pol.* III.7; Polybius, *Hist.* VI.
[8] On this concept and its background, especially in Polybius, see Atkins 2013, Chapter 3.
[9] On this strategy, see e.g. Asmis 2005.

Superbus – put an end to Roman monarchy (II.43–52). The best constitution, the best way to organize the distribution of power, is the constitution of Rome.

In the following, I will show that there is a psychological background to this argument. Scipio's statements about the best constitution rest on implicit assumptions concerning human psychology. To highlight these assumptions, I will focus on two core ideas in the argument of Books I and II: first, the idea of a ranking between the interests of the community and the benefit of the individual; second, the idea of a rule without sanctions. The first idea in particular is characteristic, not only for the *Republic* but also for Cicero's political outlook more generally. It deserves a closer look.

The contrast between common interest or benefit, on the one hand, and individual benefit, on the other, is not unfamiliar in ancient political philosophy. Aristotle, for instance, makes use of it in his own discussion of kinds of constitutions, claiming that good constitutions pursue the interests of the community, whereas bad constitutions serve the benefit of the ruler(s) (*Pol.* III.7). Also familiar is the idea that a political community could not survive if everyone pursued their own interests. Aristotle, again, refers to this idea in his discussion of consent (*homonoia*), the political kind of friendship. Consent exists, according to Aristotle, when the members of a community agree on what is beneficial (viz. for the community) and hence choose the same actions; when they do not, and compete about power and other goods, the community is in a state of faction (*stasis*) and hence decline (*EN* IX.6).

What seems different in Cicero is his inclination to talk about political matters quite generally in those terms. Cicero's perspective on politics is shaped by questions concerning common interest and individual benefit. One root of this tendency lies in his conception of the state. Consider the famous definition in *Rep.* I.39:[10] "The *res publica* is the property/concern of a people, but a people is not any gathering of men assembled in any way, but a gathering of some size associated in a partnership through agreement on law and community of interest."[11] According to this definition, we can talk about the state in terms of how the members of the political community relate to an entity that is called the 'public thing' (*res publica*). It has often been noted that Cicero's conception of that entity oscillates between the more literal understanding of '*res*' as 'property'

---

[10] On this definition, see the classic paper by Schofield 1995; cf. Atkins 2013, 128–38, who also offers some remarks on the comparison with Aristotle.
[11] *Est igitur [...] res publica res populi, populus autem non omnis hominum coetus quoquo modo congregatus, sed coetus multitudinis iuris consensu et utilitatis communione sociatus.* Translation modified.

and the metaphorical understanding as 'matter' or 'affair'.[12] But regardless of which understanding is at stake, the definition indicates what kind of questions will guide reflections on politics. Those questions will be about, e.g., whether or not the public thing belongs to (or is in control of) the people (III.43) and how well that thing is managed and taken care of. This kind of reification is completely unfamiliar from Aristotle.

Another important feature of the definition is its explicit reference to a community of interest. Scholars agree that Cicero's view of that community is inspired by the legal notion of a *societas*, a 'partnership' of shared profit and losses.[13] The relevant connection is concisely summarized by Jed Atkins (2013, 134):

> Scipio conceives of political society as a type of partnership, a cooperative enterprise undertaken for the common benefit of all its members. A people (*populus*) has partnered together (*sociatus*) in a common venture to manage a common property in which all members have an interest, the *res publica* or 'the property of the people.' This partnership is to be for the common advantage (*utilitatis communio*) and is governed by an agreement with respect to law/justice/rights (*iuris consensus*).

In a very specific way, the notion of common benefit is part of Cicero's definition of a state. Now common benefit is surely not a utilitarian aggregation or an average sum. It is the benefit of the community: what contributes to the persistence and flourishing of the 'cooperative enterprise'. And it is insofar as someone is a member of that community that his or her interests will somehow coincide with common benefit. Still, since being part of a community requires contributing something to it – to *share* benefits as well as losses – there might arise a conflict between what is to the benefit of the *res publica*, on the one hand, and what people perceive as their personal interests, on the other.

In the final analysis, such a conflict might turn out to be merely apparent, which means that under ideal circumstances, it would just not arise. There is good reason to assume that Cicero would agree with that.[14] But *Rep*. I and II

---

12 Cf. III.43–5, with Zetzel 1999, 76, n. 57. On *res* as property, see Atkins 2013, 131–2; Hammer 2014, 46–8. As Melissa Lane 2014, 245, points out, the same tendency applies to the term *publicum:* "In Roman thought, the common concern of the people included an emphasis on the concrete and material: what was *publicum* paradigmatically included collectively owned lands, revenues and provisions."
13 For a concise introduction, see the remarks in Hammer 2014, Chapter 1; Brouwer 2017; cf. Atkins 2013, 131–8.
14 What we know of Cicero's concept of the ideal statesman indicates that such a person would "scorn what is human" (VI.20) and understand that "the consciousness of noble deeds is itself the greatest reward for virtue" (VI.8; cf. the remains of Book V). This ideal also matches Cicero's concept of perfect virtue as referred to in *Off*. III.12–13.

are not about ideal circumstances. On the contrary, one crucial aspect of Scipio's strategy in those books is to identify causes of instability: factors that lead, or have led, to a crisis within the political community.[15] This helps him to bring out which conditions would serve the benefit and preservation of the state. It is in the context of this strategy that the abovementioned conflict between the interest of the state and the interest of an individual becomes salient.

According to Scipio, the major cause of instability is when people start to pursue their own profit while neglecting the benefit of the community. It is this kind of behaviour that was displayed by both Tarquinius Superbus (II.44–8) and the 'decemvirs', the commission of ten men, in the third year of their rule (II.62–3). By contrast, an important condition for the preservation of a state is that people are willing to do the opposite, i.e. to rank the interest of the community above their own benefit. Scipio refers approvingly to a number of figures in Roman history who are said to have done exactly this.[16]

This approach has two important implications. First, it establishes a fundamental contrast between the 'enemy' and the 'saviour' of the republic (which is highly characteristic for Cicero's political thought). Second, it introduces an ideal of self-sacrifice. In Books I and II, the saviour of the republic appears as someone who *renounces* her own well-being for the sake of the state. This again seems unfamiliar. We know of course the idea that the community is prior to the individual. Aristotle says so explicitly in *Pol.* I.2 (1253a18–29); and in *EN* I.2, he asserts that the good of the *polis* is greater and more complete than that of a single person (1094b7–9). But this is obviously a different kind of ranking. It does not rest on the concept of renouncement but on considerations of teleology or the whole-part-relation.[17]

---

15 Such factors can be features of the simple constitutions, like the fact that democracy does not recognize any degrees of status (I.43), or they can be events in the history of Rome, like the fact that in the third year of the rule of the decemvirs, all other institutions of the Roman constitution had been abrogated (II.62).

16 An important example is Lucius Iunius Brutus, who expelled the Tarquinians and "was the first in this state to show that in preserving the liberty of citizens no one is a private person" (II.46). Another is the father of Spurius Cassius, who put to death his own son when the latter was accused of the attempt to establish a monarchy (II.60). Note that in the preface to Book I, Cicero describes his own behaviour as consul and saviour of the republic in precisely those terms: "I did not hesitate to subject myself to the greatest tempests, even thunderbolts, of fate for the sake of saving my fellow citizens and for creating through my own individual dangers a peace shared by all" (I.7). Scipio's perspective is present right from the beginning.

17 Cf. also Aristotle's remarks on the claim that the virtuous person (*spoudaios*) would die if necessary for his friends and fatherland (*EN* IX. 8, 1169a18–b2). Even this kind of behaviour

In Cicero's *Rep.* I and II, by contrast, the concept of renouncement does not only play a prominent role, it is also backed by moral considerations. The behaviour of those who harm the community by pursuing their own profit is explicitly and repeatedly called 'unjust'.[18] This is not an *ad hoc* expression of disapproval but indicates a moral outlook according to which serving common advantage is a fundamental aspect of the virtue of justice. The fullest statement of this outlook can be found in *On Duties* (I.31; cf. I.29; III.24). In this work, Cicero offers an account of the virtues in which the relation between individual and society takes centre stage[19] and which focuses on the question of virtue and benefit. Since *On Duties* shows the same affinity for cases of conflict – like *Rep.* I and II, it deals with non-ideal circumstances[20] – we find the same tendency to describe as virtuous those who renounce personal advantage for the sake of the community (e.g. I.85–6).[21] What is more, Cicero here even outlines a hierarchy of communities, on top of which he puts the state. For "what good man would hesitate to face death on her behalf, if it would do her a service?" (*Off.* I.57). When it comes to a conflict of duties, it is hence the benefit of our country that we should serve first of all (*Off.* I.50–58), so that, e.g., "the good man will never, for the sake of a friend, act contrary to the republic" (*Off.* III.43).

We can now understand what makes the idea of a ranking of interests characteristic for the argument of *Rep.* I and II. And we can also understand, I think, why this idea rests on psychological assumptions. Scipio's use of it implies that human beings are able, in principle, to rank the benefit of their community above their own interests. This assumption is surely not trivial. On the face of it, it seems to require of someone to deliberately act *against* their self-interest.

---

is not explained by Aristotle as a form of renouncement but as way of "[assigning] himself more of what is fine" (a35–b1).

18 See I.64; II.43; II.50 (on the injustice of a king); II.51 (on Tarquinius Superbus' "unjust use of the power that he already had"); II.63 (on the injustice of the decemvirs and their unjust laws).
19 Note that this focus does not only concern justice. True courage, e.g., also does not fight for one's own advantage but for common safety or benefit (I.62–3; I.83; *Fin.* II.60). On this aspect, see Woolf 2015, 173–84. All translations from *On Duties* draw upon Griffin and Atkins 1991.
20 That means, it deals with the imperfect virtue of someone who is generally moved by what is honourable but sometimes finds himself confronted with cases in which the beneficial appears to conflict with it (*Off.* III.14–19).
21 One of Cicero's stock examples is the case of Marcus Atilius Regulus, which receives extensive treatment in *Off.* III (III.99–115; cf. I.39). As a consul, Marcus Atilius Regulus was captured by Carthaginian troops and sent to Rome to achieve the release of Carthaginian hostages. He swore an oath to return to Carthage if he should fail. Back in Rome, however, he advised the senate to *not* release the captives, since this would not be to the benefit of the *res publica*. Yet he kept his oath and returned to Carthage to be tortured and killed.

It is not at all clear whether such a behaviour is psychologically possible and, if so, whether it can be rational.

Let us now turn to the second core idea of the argument of *Rep.* I and II: the idea of a rule without sanctions. Here, we can be much briefer.

It has often been noted that unlike the Greeks, the Romans used to distinguish between two different kinds of power, which were named *potestas* and *auctoritas*.[22] The first, *potestas*, is the power of a king, a master, a father, or a military leader (then it is called *imperium*). This kind of power draws its force from the right to punish, the right over the life and death of those over whom the power is exterted, symbolized by the hatchet in the *fasces*. *Auctoritas*, by contrast, is a power based, not on the right to punish but on the leader's authority, which in turn is based on his or her qualities as a leader. The influence of someone who possesses authority is an influence of advice, and this advice is followed because of trust (*fides*) and respect, not because of fear. Traditionally, *auctoritas* was ascribed to the senate (II.57), which had a consulting function, whereas *potestas* was ascribed to the magistrates and, as *imperium*, to military leaders (cf. *Leg.* III.28).

In *Rep.* I and II, Cicero clearly holds *auctoritas* in high esteem. Not only does he more than once praise the advice of the expert.[23] But he also refers to a power without sanctions as part of his ideal. Scipio points out, for instance, that in the early days, people followed their kings deliberately and elected them on the basis of their virtue (II.24). It was a reputation for outstanding abilities that stood at the beginning of the rule of Romulus (I.64; II.4, 17, 20). And even Romulus, having acquired absolute rule, followed the authority and judgement of his council, the 'fathers' (*patres*) (II.14–15). After monarchy had been overturned, it was the authority of the senate that decided most things, while only some were done through the people (II.56). Conversely, it is a sign of decline when power is no longer grounded in authority but in fear. Tarquinius Superbus wanted to be feared, because he was afraid of being punished for his crimes (II.45). And as Cicero puts it in III.41, Roman power as well might be transformed from right (*ius*) to might (*vis*), "so that those who are now our willing subjects should be held by terror" (cf. *Off.* II.21–9).

That the ideal of a rule without sanctions is a characteristic feature of Cicero's approach is evident when we contrast Polybius. In Book VI of his *Histories*, Polybius offers an account of the Roman constitution as playing a decisive role in

---

[22] For a concise introduction, see Hammer 2014, 50–52, with literature. *Off.* II.21–2 offers an interesting sketch of different reasons why people submit to the command of another.
[23] See, e.g., I.12–13 on the authority of philosophers, the Seven Sages, and Cicero himself.

the city's marvelous story of success. Just like Scipio in *Rep.* II, he describes that constitution as 'mixed' and *therefore* stable. The cause of stability, however, is a different one in his book, namely, a balance of fear. The three elements of the Roman constitution (consuls, senate, people) depend on in each other in such a way that neither of them could accomplish anything without the help of the others and each of them can do serious harm to the other two.[24] In this way, the institutions are prevented from gaining too much power and forced, by fear, to cooperate. While for Polybius, this system of checks and balances is the basis of the Roman success, for Cicero, this success crucially depends on the personal qualities of the leaders (as emphasized in V.1–2a; cf. Powell 2012).

Again, it should be easy to see why this idea rests on psychological assumptions. If we take Scipio at his word, then a consideration of the expertise of a person can motivate someone to submit to that person's rule. It is sufficient to render that rule stable. But this is far from obvious. From the perspective of a thinker like Polybius, this idea of a deliberate obedience must appear rather naïve; it requires an argument.

So I hope to have established my first claim. Scipio's account of the best constitution rests on assumptions about human psychology. Since these assumptions are all but trivial – they invite some quite obvious objections – it seems natural to expect some remarks in their defence. The argument of Books I and II calls for a discussion of psychological issues. I think Cicero is well aware of that task and takes reflections on human psychology to be an integral part of his project.[25] In the following section, I will consider what Book III, and in particular the reference to nature, contributes in this respect. But before we turn to that book, some general remarks seem necessary.

The fundamental problem we are facing is that Books V and VI of Cicero's *Republic* are almost completely lost (with the exception of the Dream of Scipio), while of Book IV only snippets have survived. For Cicero's picture of human psychology, these books must have been relevant, for they treated questions of education, of the correct behaviour in social relationships, and of the emotional basis of that behaviour. We also know from Lactantius that Book IV contained remarks on the soul (IV.1). Any account of human psychology in Cicero's *Republic* will therefore be incomplete.

---

24 See *Hist.* VI.11–18; Hahm 1995. On the comparison between Cicero and Polybius, cf. Atkins 2013, Chapter 3, who also emphasizes the role of psychological background assumptions.

25 This of course is an important parallel between the *Republic* of Cicero and that of Plato. Note, however, that Cicero seems to reverse the order. Whereas Plato turns to the state in order to offer an account of the soul, Cicero turns to the soul (to human psychology), in order to support his account of the state.

This problem can be put more specifically. We know that in other contexts, Cicero draws a distinction between perfect and imperfect virtue and their respective psychologies (*Off.* III.11–18). This distinction is especially relevant for the cases we have been looking at, i.e. (apparent) conflicts between virtue and benefit; or in the terminology of *On Duties:* between the honourable (*honestum*) and the beneficial (*utile*). For Cicero, such conflicts belong to imperfect virtue alone, whereas in a perfectly virtuous person, they do not arise. It is beyond doubt, now, that Cicero's ideal state requires from its citizens a certain degree of virtuousness. But it is not at all clear *what* degree is required and *from whom*.[26] A full account of moral psychology in Cicero's *Republic* would have to answer these questions. But since we lack the relevant information (the ideal citizen is the topic of Books V and VI), our account will be incomplete in precisely this respect.

There is at least one thing we know, however. A key aspect in Cicero's picture of a good state of the soul is the rule of reason.[27] There is sufficient evidence in the extant text of the *Republic* for a view of the human soul which is based on a radical contrast between reason, on the one hand, and different kinds of irrational drives (e.g. desires or emotions), on the other.[28] The most famous expression of this view is the simile of the mahout and the elephant in *Rep.* II.67, which, following the lines of Plato's *Republic*, draws an analogy between state and soul:

> But in fact the man of foresight is one who, as we often saw in Africa, sits on a huge and destructive creature, keeps it in order, directs it wherever he wants, and by a gentle instruction or touch turns the animal in any direction. [...] So that Indian or Carthaginian keeps this one creature in order, one that is docile and used to human customs; but what hides in human spirits, the part of the spirit that is called the mind, has to rein in and control not just one creature or one easy to control, and it is not often that it accomplishes that task.[29]

---

26 There is some indication, e.g., that Cicero would draw a distinction between the ideal statesman, who takes virtue to offer its own reward (see above, n. 14), and the citizen of an ideal state, who is kept from crime by shame (though not by fear) (V.6).
27 See Miller 2014.
28 See, e.g., I.59–60 (anger should not rule our mind but vice versa); I.62 and 65 (what happens when the plebs are unrestrained in pleasure and desire); II.68 (fragments on the destructive power of the passions); III.37a (how the mind rules over the body [like a king] and over desires [like a master]); etc.
29 *Sed tamen est ille prudens, qui, ut saepe in Africa vidimus, immani et vastae insidens beluae coercet et regit beluam quocumque volt, et levi admonitu aut tactu inflecit illam feram [...] Ergo ille Indus aut Poenus unam coercet beluam, et eam docilem et humanis moribus adsuetam; at vero ea quae latet in animis hominum quaeque pars animi mens vocatur, non unam aut facilem ad subigendum frenat et domat, si quando id efficit, quod perraro potest.*

We find here the same tendency to think in terms of oppositions that we observed in the argument of Books I and II more generally. And although the ideal of a rule of reason is hardly unfamiliar in ancient philosophy, it seems fair to say that in Cicero the contrast is more radical than in Plato's picture of the tripartite soul or Aristotle's subtle account of the emotions.[30] On such a view of the soul, the basic problem in practical affairs is that people tend to give in to irrational drives of all kinds, while the solution is that these drives be controlled by reason. As Cicero puts it in *On Duties*, fear and desire are the primary causes of injustice (*Off.* I.24; cf. I.68). We should make sure that impulses obey reason (*Off.* I.102; cf. I.141) and be calm and free from every agitation (cf. I.132).[31]

This picture fits very well with our two core ideas. We have seen that Tarquinius Superbus aimed to establish a rule based on fear, while greed was the cause of his injustice. On the decemvirs in the third year of their rule, Scipio says: "In all their public actions they ruled the people greedily and violently and with an eye to their own passions" (II.63). Renouncement, on the other hand, seems to require that people master both fear and desire. And it seems quite plausible that a rule of *auctoritas* is a rule of reason.

With these observations in mind, we can now turn to Book III.

3 Psychology and nature: Book III

Book III comes at a point in the dialogue when the discussion of the best constitution is basically completed. As outlined above, Scipio has established two claims in Books I and II: first, an ideal constitution contains elements of monarchy, aristocracy, and democracy; second, the constitution of Rome shows how these elements are combined in the best possible way. Strictly speaking, the discussion could now turn to the next topics: by which customs and institutions the society should be formed (Book IV) and what the best citizen or statesman should be like (Books V/VI). The execution of that plan, however, is inter-

---

[30] This tendency to ground the argument on a stark psychological contrast can be observed in other works of Cicero, as well. See e.g. *Off.* I.101: "For the power of the spirit (*animus*), that is its nature, is twofold: one part of it consists of impulse (*appetitus*), called in Greek *horme*, which snatches a man this way and that; the other of reason (*ratio*), which teaches and explains what should be done and what avoided. Reason therefore commands, and impulse obeys" (Atkins' translation) (cf. also *ND* IV.10–11).

[31] *On Duties* abounds with examples for both the problem of disobedient passions or desires and the ideal of a rule of reason (e.g., I.66–9; I.80; I.122; I.136; II.18; II.37–8 etc.).

rupted by an objection: some people say that a state cannot be ruled without injustice (II.69), which means, apparently, that the gain and maintenance of power require some degree of ruthlessness in the pursuit of one's aims. Though this objection seems casual at first glance, it actually goes against the grain of Scipio's argument as developed so far. Scipio, as we have seen, treats injustice as the major threat, not as a precondition, for the persistence of a state. So it comes as little surprise, I think, that the objection is taken seriously. Its treatment is not only postponed to the next day but also integrated into a wider context. Taking one step back, the interlocutors engage in a general discussion about the value of justice. This discussion is the core of Book III.

Following the practice of the Sceptical Academy, the dispute about justice proceeds as an argument 'on both sides' (III.8). Book III first offers a speech 'against' justice, held by Philus, then one 'in favour of' justice, held by Laelius. After these speeches, Scipio offers his answer to the objection.[32] The gist of the speech of Philus (who emphasizes that he does not endorse the position he was told to defend: III.8) is that justice is a matter of convention: nothing is just by nature. His argument draws on at least two models. For one thing, it resembles in important respects Glaucon's challenge at the beginning of Book II of Plato's *Republic* (358b–362c, with Glaucon, too, acting as a devil's advocate).[33] For another, Philus claims to make use of the 'second speech' that was held by Carneades during his legendary visit to Rome in 155 B.C.[34] Of Laelius' speech only brief fragments have survived, but these fragments offer one of the most explicit state-

---

32 The answer is that without justice there is not even a state to be ruled (III.43). Note that this answer, as formulated in the surviving text, rests on the definition of the *res publica*, not on Laelius' defence (cf. Atkins 2013, 41).

33 In fact, some arguments in Philus' speech are clearly based on this passage in Plato. See in particular the distinction between the perfectly just and the perfectly unjust person (III.27; cf. Plato, *Resp.* II 361a–d) and the argument about the best and the second best option from the perspective of conventionalism (III.23; cf. Plato, *Resp.* II 358e–359b).

34 See III.8, 9, 21, and 29–30. Head of the Sceptical Academy, Carneades traveled to Rome as a member of an Athenian embassy of philosophers from three different schools. He caused sensation by offering one day a speech in favour of justice, the other day a speech against justice, thereby displaying the Sceptical method. Lactantius' summary of *Rep.* III takes Philus' speech to be a report of what Carneades actually said. But as Glucker 2001 convincingly argues, (i) there is no reason to assume that Lactantius had access to independent sources for Carneades' speech, and (ii) Philus' speech contains aspects that could not come from Carneades. A further point of reference for a conventionalist view of justice is of course Epicurus.

ments of the concept of a natural law, which is worked out more thoroughly in the first book of Cicero's *On the Laws*.[35]

The discussion about the *value* of justice turns out to be a discussion about its *basis:* is justice merely a matter of convention, or is it somehow grounded in nature? Familiar arguments are offered for both positions. Philus points out that the diversity of existing norms suggests a conventional basis of justice (III.14–17); Laelius refers to a certain view of the cosmos which indicates the existence of a natural law (III.33; cf. IV.1e–f).

In the following, I will show that there is a psychological side to this discussion, which connects the dispute between Philus and Laelius with the questions we raised at the end of the previous section.

Let us begin with the attack against justice. The first thing to notice is that conventionalist views of justice or the state are traditionally coupled with an egoist outlook entailing a descriptive and a normative aspect. In other words: those who proclaim, in ancient discussions, that neither the state nor justice are 'by nature' tend to share the assumption that human beings always pursue their own profit and are justified in doing so. (It is important to see that by rejecting the notion of a natural law, this outlook advocates a certain view of nature: a view according to which there is no natural 'order' that would provide our beliefs about justice with an objective point of reference. In this respect, the dispute about the *basis* of justice is a dispute about *nature*). As Plato's dialogues make clear, there are different options of spelling out the relation between conventionalism and egoism. But all of these options rest on the idea that if we wish to understand why such conventions exist, we need to understand who profits from them. This might be the rulers, who give laws that are to their own benefit; it might be the people, who profit from a mutual agreement not to harm each other; or it might be a weak majority, who use justice as a way of suppressing the stronger few.[36]

It is not easy to say whether this link between a conventionalist account of politics and a psychology of egoism is a necessary one.[37] But however that may be, Cicero for his part assumes that it is "the same people" who think that "jus-

---

[35] Again, this is a position that the speaker would perhaps not endorse, since in Book I, it was Laelius who raised doubts concerning the use of natural philosophy in practical matters (I.19) (cf. Atkins 2013, 53).
[36] The first is, of course, the position of Thrasymachus (*Rep.* I), the second of Glaucon (*Rep.* II), the third of Callicles (*Gorgias*).
[37] The *Crito* might be considered a counter-example, because Socrates here introduces the idea of a commitment to the laws of one's city, a promise that must be kept, for better or for worse (51c–52d).

tice is obedience to the written laws and institutions" and who measure "everything [...] by utility". He explicitly says so in *Leg.* I, explaining that if these people are right, then we have no reason to be just, unless it seems to our own profit; and "whoever thinks that it will be advantageous to him will neglect the laws and break them if he can" (*Leg.* I.42).

Now this is pretty much the view that Glaucon propounds in the opening passages of Plato's *Resp.* II; and it is also the view adopted by Philus. As Lactantius puts it in his summary of Cicero's *Rep.* III:

> The gist of his argument was as follows: that men ordain laws for themselves *in accordance with utility*, that is to say they vary in accordance with customs and have frequently been altered by the same people in accordance with the times.[38] (III.21a; my emphasis)

Since there are considerable gaps in the surviving text, the speech gives the impression of a rather loose collection of arguments. Even in this collection, however, the import of the egoist outlook is obvious. Philus' attack is fuelled by the conviction that human beings pursue their own profit and are right to do so.

In III.29 – 30, for instance, Philus argues that it is 'stupid' (*stultus*) to be just. To show that everyone would agree with that, he draws on a number of allegedly obvious examples. First, he refers to cases of buying and selling. Someone who is honest about the defects of what he sells, or the value of what he buys, is judged good but stupid, according to Philus, for he sells at a low and buys at a high price and thus suffers a financial loss (III.29). Then, he applies those criteria of profit and loss to 'larger issues', i.e. to matters of life and death, as illustrated by the famous example of the shipwrecked or that of the wounded soldier.[39] In such cases, it might well be 'good' (*bonus*) to rather die than commit the injustice of killing someone. But again, it is stupid, and as Philus insinuates, even the just man will not act as justice requires in that kind of situation. He will push off the plank the other shipwrecked and knock off the horse the wounded soldier (III.30). (We find here the combination of a descriptive and a normative aspect that was mentioned above.) In the political sphere, Philus maintains, we praise those who rule over as many people as possible. This is how Rome "grew

---

[38] *eius disputationis summa haec fuit: iura sibi homines pro utilitate sanxisse, scilicet varia pro moribus, et apud eosdem pro temporibus saepe mutata.*

[39] The shipwrecked: "So what will the just man do if he happens to be shipwrecked, and a weaker man has got hold of a plank? Won't he push him off and get on himself and use it to escape – especially since there are no witnesses in the middle of the ocean?" The wounded soldier: "Likewise, if in battle his own side is routed and the enemy is pursuing, and the just man gets hold of a wounded man on a horse, will he spare him at the cost of his own death, or will he knock him off the horse so that he can escape the enemy himself?" (III.30).

from a tiny nation to the [greatest] of all" (III.24b), and it explains why Rome does not allow its provinces to grow olives and vineyards (III.16).

In addition to confirming the psychological underpinnings of Philus' speech, these arguments reveal an interesting connection to the deliberations on the best constitution in Books I and II. Just like Scipio, Philus discusses cases of conflict between values. In line with his adopted egoism, however, he outright reverses the position of his host. When it comes to the test, as in the case of the shipwrecked or the wounded soldier, people would prefer their own benefit to the requirements of justice, and rightly so. This suggests, then, a reversal of attitude towards the concept of sacrifice (the idea of renouncing one's own benefit for the sake of the state) that we described as characteristic for Scipio's argument. If Philus is right, then people normally do not act like that; if they do, this is deeply irrational.[40] But Philus' argument also touches on the second core idea discussed above. If the psychology of egoism is correct, then the ideal of a deliberate submission to the laws of one's state or the rule of a competent leader is at best naïve. As Philus says in III.26, the 'least-dishonest' response to the question why people are just is that they fear punishment. This is the true reason why 'our', i.e. the Roman, laws are observed (III.18). In Philus' picture, there is only room for *potestas* but not for *auctoritas*.

So, it seems that in the speech of Philus the objections characterized as obvious in Section 2 come to the fore. Philus represents a view of human psychology according to which the story told by Scipio must seem highly implausible. Human beings are not made to put anything above their own profit; the request to do so has no rational basis. Neither are human beings made to follow someone without sanctions. The attention that is given to the speech of Philus – remember how the course of argument is interrupted – and the agitation it provokes (III.32) indicate that Cicero is not only aware of, but actually points out hat this story rests on assumptions that are all but uncontroversial. Philus' speech thus proves to be an attack against Scipio,[41] launched from the perspective of egoism and utility. Answering this attack gives Cicero the opportunity to put his account of the *res publica* on a securer basis. Let us now turn to the speech of Laelius and see what it offers on that score.

One strategy for answering the attack of Philus would be simply to reject his view of human psychology and offer an alternative. A number of passages in Ci-

---

[40] As an illustration, imagine how Philus would evaluate the case of Marcus Atilius Regulus mentioned above, n. 21.
[41] A direct reference to and rejection of Scipio's views is found in III.23: the mixed constitution is the result of a kind of bargain. Neither nature nor our wishes are the mother of justice, 'weakness is' (cf. above, n. 1).

cero's writings show how this might work. Drawing on the Stoic concept of social *oikeiōsis*, these passages claim that human beings are not at all bare egoists. Human beings possess a capacity for mutual affection and a corresponding impulse to take care of others. Though this impulse is most evident in the behaviour of parents towards their offspring, it can be directed towards other people as well, namely those we recognize as 'belonging to us' (*oikeion*). In fact, the other-regarding impulse can be directed towards all human beings indifferently, in which case it would provide a non-egoistic foundation of justice.[42]

It seems very likely that such a strategy was part of Laelius' defence. In the surviving fragments, however, there is no clear evidence for that, apart from a hint in a letter to Atticus (III.39a). What is clear enough, though, is that Laelius rebuts conventionalism by establishing a natural basis for justice and that he draws for this purpose upon Stoic views of the cosmos and universal law.[43]

It is my contention that there is a psychological side to this argument of Laelius, as well. The reference to the cosmos does not only offer a natural basis for justice, it also points to an alternative picture of human psychology. Cosmic nature helps to answer the egoistic challenge. (Notice that this contention is in line with Laelius' general outlook in Book III: his contempt for people who seem to always act for the sake of utility – wealth, in particular[44] – and his praise of those who explicitly reject that kind of reward: III.40.[45])

Consider the notorious paragraph III.33:

> True law is right reason, consonant with nature, spread through all people. It is constant and eternal; it summons to duty by its orders, it deters from crime by its prohibitions. Its orders and prohibitions to good people are never given in vain; but it does not move the wicked by these orders and prohibitions. It is wrong to pass laws obviating this law; it is not permitted to abrogate any of it; it cannot be totally repealed. We cannot be released from this law by the senate or the people, and it needs no exegete or interpreter like Sextus Aelius. There will not be one law at Rome and another at Athens, one now and another later; but all nations all times will be bound by this one eternal and unchangeable law, and the god will be the one common master and general (so to speak of) of all people. He is the author, expounder, and mover of this law; and the person who does not obey it will be in exile from himself. Insofar as he scorns his nature as a human being, by

---

[42] See *Fin.* III.62–9; *Off.* I.50–54. For further remarks on this strategy, see Brüllmann 2019.
[43] This model is introduced by Philus (!) already in I.19. Horn 2017 offers some arguments to the effect that Cicero draws upon a Platonic model. Since this question is not relevant for the present argument, however, we can safely put it aside.
[44] I refer here to Fragments 3 Inc. 4 on Sardanapalus and 3 Inc. 3 on the Phoenicians.
[45] Laelius thus returns to the kind of *exempla* that were used by Scipio.

this very fact he will pay the greatest penalty, even if he escapes all the other things that are generally recognized as punishments.[46]

This passage presents in a nutshell the characteristic features of the concept of a natural law, as it is developed more fully in *Leg.* I. Among these features are: (i) the claim that, unlike the changing conventions of different nations and states, this law is 'constant and eternal' and in some sense prior to those conventions; (ii) the claim that this law has a cosmological basis, i.e. it is a 'natural' law, ordained by the god, and concerns us insofar as we are parts of the natural order (cf. I.19); (iii) the claim that this law is identical with 'right reason'. Since the order of the cosmos is a perfectly rational order, the law of nature is an expression of perfect reason.

Most relevant in our context is the third claim, for it indicates how human beings get into contact with the natural law, which is by means of their capacity for reason. This capacity is not only something that human beings share with the cosmos, making them a privileged part of nature. It is also what enables them to understand the order of the universe, i.e. to grasp the natural law. In this sense the law needs no exegete or interpreter.

What is most interesting, now, is the idea that this 'grasp' has motivational implications. Here as in other contexts, understanding the natural law and obeying it are presented as two sides of the same coin (cf. *Fin.* III.20 – 22). Why so?

III.33 offers at least two hints concerning the answer to that question. First, we find at the end of the section a reference to undesirable consequences. Disobeying the natural law means acting against our true nature and thus paying 'the greatest penalty'. This is surely not in our interest. Second, there is the thought that 'good people', at least, grasp the natural law *as* something that binds them. In some way or other, these people take the contents of the natural law to be 'orders and prohibitions' that *apply* to them. The text does not explain how this is the case, and there might again be different options. But if we look at

---

46 *Est quidem vera lex recta ratio, naturae congruens, diffusa in omnis, constans, sempiterna, quae vocet ad officium iubendo, vetando a fraude deterreat, quae tamen neque probos frustra iubet aut vetat, nec improbos iubendo aut vetando movet. Huic legi nec obrogari fas est, neque derogari aliquid ex hac licet, neque tota abrogari potest, nec vero aut per senatum aut per populum solvi hac lege possumus, neque est quaerendus explanator aut interpres Sextus Aelius, nec erit alia lex Romae, alia Athenis, alia nunc, alia posthac, sed et omnes gentes et omni tempore una lex et sempiterna et inmutabilis continebit, unusque erit communis quasi magister et imperator omnium deus: ille legis huius inventor, disceptator, lator; cui qui non parebit, ipse se fugiet, ac naturam hominis aspernatus hoc ipso luet maximas poenas, etiamsi cetera supplicia quae putantur effugerit.*

other passages in the *Republic*, the most plausible answer seems to be that, by grasping the 'whole', i.e. the cosmos, we realize that it is more important than its 'parts', i.e. ourselves. As Scipio emphasizes at both I.26–27 and VI.20–25, taking the cosmic perspective leads to a reassessment of our values, in the sense that usual objects of our desires get outweighed by the requirements of the natural law.

Unfortunately, these two hints pull in different directions. Whereas the first seems in line with a psychology of egoism, adding to it the notion of what is *truly* in our interest, the second might be taken to mark a turn away from that kind of psychology. The concept of a natural law would then come with the proto-Kantian assertion that (some) people obey that law precisely without considering questions of utility.[47] Though the remaining fragments of the speech of Laelius do not allow to decide between these options, the following seems to be a plausible assumption.

On the one hand, the dialectical context of Book III does not require such a decision. On the contrary, it would perfectly suit the purpose of Laelius to be able to defend justice from different perspectives. On the other hand, there is some indication that the second option represents the true point of Laelius' reference to the cosmos. This is suggested by passages which refer to the argument on justice and nature as being concerned with the alternative between virtue and cleverness, between someone who does the right thing *because* it is naturally right (the *bonus*) and someone who does the right thing in order to avoid trouble (the *callidus*) (*Rep.* III.39a).[48] This characterization would be grossly misleading, I think, if the only point of Laelius were to identify what is truly in our interest (i.e. what trouble truly consists in). Furthermore, the second option fits much better with the ideal of a rule of reason that we identified as characteristic for Cicero's view of the human soul. The bulk of the relevant passages does not evoke a picture of reason as 'enlightening' our desires but a picture of reason as issuing commands to which desires obey. It is precisely this picture of command and obedience that III.33 endows with a natural basis.

Although the details might remain a matter of controversy, I take my second claim to be sufficiently established. In the speech of Laelius, Cicero introduces a view of nature which offers an alternative to the egoist outlook of Philus' attack

---

[47] It is this alternative that also troubles scholarship on the Stoic concept of natural law. For an excellent introduction, see Klein 2012.

[48] *Fin.* II.59 is explicit: "It is clear that if equity, faith, and justice do not derive from nature, and if all these things are measured by utility, then it is impossible to find any good man. Laelius said quite enough on this score in my work *De re publica*." The opposition of nature and utility, which seems puzzling at first blush, is in fact telling.

and in this way helps to defend Scipio's conception of the best constitution. It is in fact easy to see that Scipio's two core ideas make much more sense if Laelius is correct, since both the idea of our interests being outweighed and the idea of a deliberate obedience seem to be part of his picture.

4 Conclusion

In this chapter, I drew attention to the psychological background that links the argument about the value and the origin of justice in *Rep.* III with Scipio's account of the best state in *Rep.* I and II. I have shown that by adopting a conventionalist view about justice, Philus also adopts a psychology of conventionalism, which is a kind of egoism, based on the notion of utility. I have further argued that Laelius' rejection of conventionalism points to an alternative psychology. For his picture of the cosmos entails the idea that rational human beings will follow the law of nature deliberately. Cicero thus uses the (Stoic) cosmology of natural law to introduce the psychological backing required by his theory of the *res publica*.[49] To fully appreciate this strategy it helps to remember that, after the speech of Philus, Laelius finds himself in a similar situation as Socrates after Glaucon's challenge. But while Socrates replies to Glaucon with an account of the human soul, Laelius replies to Philus with an account of the cosmos. This seems to me a perfect example of the neither simple nor straightforward use of naturalist arguments in Cicero's *Republic*. It shows how Cicero adapts those arguments to the aims of his project, and it reveals, I think, that the references to nature are always worthy of a closer look.[50]

Primary literature

Cicero. 1991. *Cicero: On Duties*, edited by Miriam Griffin and Margaret Atkins. Cambridge: Cambridge University Press.

Cicero. 1999. *Cicero: On the Commonwealth and On the Laws*, edited by James E.G. Zetzel. Cambridge: Cambridge University Press.

---

[49] It should be noted that the psychological perspective seems to be a characteristic feature of Hellenistic references to nature, not present in the same way in Aristotle, for instance. Compare Aristotle's '*ergon* argument', which draws upon a function that is part of human nature, with the Epicurean/Stoic 'cradle argument', which is concerned with the object of our first impulse.

[50] I thank all participants of the workshop on nature and normativity, and in particular Peter Adamson, for their helpful comments.

Secondary literature

Asmis, Elizabeth. 2005. "A New Kind of Model: Cicero's Roman Constitution in 'De republica'." *The American Journal of Philology* 126:377–416.

Atkins, Jed W. 2013. *Cicero on Politics and the Limits of Reason: The* Republic *and* Laws. Cambridge: Cambridge University Press.

Brouwer, René. 2017. "'Richer than the Greeks': Cicero's Constitutional Thought." In *Ciceros Staatsphilosophie: Ein kooperativer Kommentar zu* De re publica *und* De legibus, edited by Otfried Höffe, 33–46. Berlin/Boston: De Gruyter.

Brüllmann, Philipp. 2019. "Elternliebe und Gerechtigkeit: Anmerkungen zur sozialen *oikeiôsis*." In *Philosophie für die Polis: Akten des 5. Internationalen Kongresses der Gesellschaft für Antike Philosophie in Zürich (6.–9.9.2016)*, edited by Christoph Riedweg et al., 357–79. Berlin/Boston: De Gruyter.

Glucker, John. 2001. "Carneades in Rome: Some unsolved problems." In *Cicero's Republic*, edited by Jonathan G. F. Powell and John A. North, 57–82. London: Bulletin of the Institute of Classical Studies.

Hahm, David E. 1995. "Polybius' applied political theory." In *Justice and Generosity: Studies in Hellenistic Social and Political Philosophy*, edited by André Laks and Malcolm Schofield, 7–47. Cambridge: Cambridge University Press.

Hammer, Dean. 2014. *Roman Political Thought: From Cicero to Augustine*. Cambridge: Cambridge University Press.

Horn, Christoph. 2017. "Die metaphysische Grundlegung des Rechts (*De legibus* I)." In *Ciceros Staatsphilosophie: Ein kooperativer Kommentar zu* De re publica *und* De legibus, edited by Otfried Höffe, 149–66. Berlin/Boston: De Gruyter.

Klein, Jacob. 2012. "Stoic Eudaimonism and the Natural Law Tradition." In *Reason, Religion, and Natural Law: From Plato to Spinoza*, edited by Jonathan A. Jacobs, 57–80. Oxford: Oxford University Press.

Lane, Melissa. 2014. *Greek and Roman Political Ideas*. London: Penguin.

Schofield, Malcolm. 1995. "Cicero's Definition of *Res Publica*." In *Cicero the Philosopher*, edited by Jonathan G. F. Powell, 63–83. Oxford: Clarendon.

Miller, Fred D. 2014. "The Rule of Reason in Cicero's Philosophy of Law." *University of Queensland Law Journal* 33:321–33.

Powell, Jonathan G. F. 2012. "Cicero's *De Re Publica* and the Virtues of the Statesman." In *Cicero's Practical Philosophy*, edited by Walter Nicgorski, 1–42. Notre Dame (IN): University of Notre Dame Press.

Woolf, Raphael. 2013. "Cicero and Gyges." *Classical Quarterly* 63:801–812.

Woolf, Raphael. 2015. *Cicero: The Philosophy of a Roman Sceptic*. London: Routledge.

Zarecki, Jonathan. 2014. *Cicero's Ideal Statesman in Theory and Practice*. London: Bloomsbury.

Raphael Woolf
Unnatural Law: A Ciceronian Perspective

Abstract: Cicero recognizes general moral principles independent of human convention, to which the actual laws and conventions that human societies devise must conform. Yet he believes that differences in local circumstances mean that the way in which conformity is realized may vary considerably across time and place. Conformity need not, and perhaps should not, imply uniformity. Furthermore, Cicero is attuned to the question of how societies develop towards a better realization of the natural law. Genuinely lasting improvement does not result from imposing wholesale change but by engaging reflectively and critically with tradition, custom and history. These points are established through a reading of three of Cicero's philosophical works: *De Re Publica*, *De Officiis*, and especially *De Legibus*.

1 Introduction

Is what is right and wrong merely a matter of convention, or are there moral principles that hold regardless of convention – principles that are, in the Hellenistic idiom, 'natural'? There exist, of course, human-made laws and conventions that set forth certain things as right and others as wrong. But one might ask where these laws and conventions derive their normative weight from. Is it the case that what makes something right or wrong is the fact of its having been laid down as such by some human process of, say, law-making? Or is a thing's rightness or wrongness grounded independently of its human prescription or proscription?

If one were inclined to answer the latter question in the affirmative, one might further say that our actual laws and conventions have normative force only if they are congruent with general moral principles that hold regardless of whether such principles are themselves enshrined in any human law or convention. Call this the normative priority of nature. Cicero, I believe, is committed to the priority thesis, but as often in his work, abstract philosophical positions receive a more complex colouring in virtue of his practical concerns.[1] He is anx-

---

[1] The commitment can be traced back to the early *De Inventione*, where Cicero asserts that law or right (*ius*) is originally derived from nature (*initium* [...] *eius ab natura ductum videtur*, II.65), the law of nature being given to us not by opinion but some "innate force" (*innata vis*). So too his concern for its practical import, as he grants the topic of natural rights some relevance to the

ious both to advocate and to set limits to the idea of there being moral principles that stand outside actual concrete laws and conventions, such as to serve as a test for the moral legitimacy of the latter.

I shall argue in particular that Cicero cautions against the idea that recognition of the existence of such principles means accepting that ideally there should exist everywhere a single set of laws and conventions applicable to all. This caution manifests itself in two main ways. Firstly, Cicero is keen to emphasise the importance of the local perspective. To the extent that he holds that there are universal principles, independent of human convention, to which the actual laws and conventions that human societies devise must conform, he believes that conformity is not to be achieved by disregarding the specific social and political circumstances that obtain at a given time and place. On the contrary, differences in local circumstances mean that the way in which conformity is realized may vary considerably across time and place. Conformity need not, and perhaps should not, imply uniformity.

Secondly, and relatedly, Cicero is suspicious of the idea that acknowledging the existence of universal principles mandates a headlong rush to implement them in full. Certainly, every society should strive to ensure that their concrete laws and conventions are not in breach of these principles. But achieving that may be, at best, a matter of slow and gradual progress; and given the complexity of human social organisation, even such progress cannot be expected to be smooth. One must, that is, recognize that genuinely lasting improvement is not a matter of wiping the slate clean and starting again, or imposing wholesale change regardless of what is already in place. It is, rather, in Cicero's view, by engaging reflectively but critically with tradition, custom and history that successful change is to be achieved.

I shall try to flesh out these points by considering how the notions of law, nature and country interact in three of Cicero's philosophical works: *De Re Publica*, *De Legibus* and *De Officiis*. Discussion of *De Legibus* will comprise the longest section, since it is in this work that the theory of natural law, construed as the idea that there exist moral principles of universal applicability, receives both its most extensive and, I shall suggest, most critical Ciceronian treatment.

---

orator's business while emphasising its remoteness from both Roman civil law and popular understanding (II.67).

2 De Re Publica

In the preface to *De Re Publica* Cicero claims that every correct moral precept enunciated by philosophers is derived from the work of those who actually established codes of law for their societies (I.2); and that the wider reach of the latter enterprise compared to that of the philosophers, who can barely get through to their own disciples, makes the lawmaker superior even to these theorists (*etiam eis* [...] *ipsis est praeferendus doctoribus*, I.3). Cicero says that such precepts are "brought into being and established" (*partum confirmatumque*) by the lawmakers (I.2). He does not mean, exactly, that the lawmakers invent them. Rather, they are said to be given shape through education and corroborated or enforced through custom and law respectively (I.2).

Those who operate in the practical realm thus seem to occupy an epistemically privileged position, with philosophers basing their own moral doctrines, to the extent that the latter are correct, on rules already formulated by those of a more practical bent. But this view in turn is more nuanced than one might suppose. Cicero speaks of the one who operates through formal civic authority as "compelling" (*cogit*) people to obey the law, whereas he cites the Platonist philosopher Xenocrates as remarking that his students are taught "to do of their own accord what they are compelled to do by law" (*ut id sua sponte facerent, quod cogerentur facere legibus*, I.3).

Overtly this contrast serves as part of Cicero's privileging of the lawmaker as a person of greater practical influence than the philosopher. But we are surely supposed to pause at this dictum of Xenocrates, whom Cicero has just described as being among the most distinguished of philosophers (I.3), a sentiment implying approval of the point that one should ultimately do what is right because it is right, not because the law commands one to do it. If so, then the philosopher has a crucial and distinct role to play in the moulding of good citizens, a role given important expression in the main body of *De Re Publica*, whose principal speaker Scipio Aemilianus (historically a distinguished politician and general who had led Rome to its final defeat of Carthage in 146 BCE) will speak of a "universal natural law" (*communis lex naturae*) which grants supreme authority based "not on the jurisdiction of the Roman people but on that of the wise" (*non Quiritium sed sapientium iure*, I.27).

I shall return to the connection outlined here between moral motivation and the concept of natural law in the discussion of *De Legibus* below. For now we may note that, while Scipio's formulation indicates a shift in emphasis, normatively speaking, from the practical political sphere to the theoretically ideal, progress towards the realisation of this ideal is pictured as incremental and uncertain. Cicero implicitly rejects, for example, the notion that it consists in recovering a social and political landscape whose features were fully displayed at some identifiable point in Rome's past. Movement towards conformity with the normatively natural comes, instead and inevitably, via the grind of the human political process and the development of institutions. In Scipio's narration of Rome's founding and early growth in the period of kingship, the military theme is pervasive – unsurprisingly given Rome's actual history – but for Scipio it is in the formation of the Roman constitution, as well as other civic reforms, that the kings' most valuable contributions lie.

Thus, Romulus' founding of the prototype senate and his deferring to its advice and authority is praised (II.14), while it is suggested that his military achievements were founded in part upon that relationship (II.15). Tullus Hostilius built meeting places from the spoils of war for the senate and the popular assembly, and also granted certain powers to the people (II.31). Ancus Marcius divided the spoils of his conquests among the citizenry, and built and settled a new city, the seaport of Ostia (II.33). Lucius Tarquinius doubled the size of the senate, and reorganized and expanded the equestrian order (II.35 – 6).

Scipio's catalogue of the royal reforms prompts Laelius to say that every king made good and useful additions (II.37). He recalls Cato the Elder's maxim, cited earlier by Scipio at II.2, that the constitution of Rome is superior to others, particularly those of Greece, because it is the work of many, not of a single individual. In the period after kingship Scipio recounts popular measures taken by the consul Publius Valerius and others (II.53 – 5). But Scipio is explicit that even with the new consular authority, which he describes as still "kingly in character" (*genere* [...] *regiam*), the combined power of that office and of the senate kept the aristocracy paramount (II.56); and this oppressiveness underlay the popular revolt against debt that established the Tribunate.

This view of the constitution as one that evolves without necessarily progressing in straightforward linear fashion illustrates the practical import of Cicero's engagement with the normative realm. If Cato is right that the superiority of the Roman constitution lies precisely in its developmental aspect, then there is no reason to think either that it ever reached, or should be expected to reach, a fixed and unchanging peak, exemplifying in full the moral principles that accord with nature.

In his preface to Book V, when speaking of his own time, Cicero does compare the work to be done to the restoration of a painting that has lost not only its original colours but its outlines as well, and firmly blames the political leadership (including, presumably, himself) for the corresponding state of the constitution, lamenting that ancient customs are "not just no longer practised but no longer known" (*non modo non colantur, sed iam ignorentur*, V.2). This paean to the old ways, however, hardly presents a straightforward path back: Cicero's analogy prompts us rather to ask how, if at all, customs no longer known are to be recovered. When Scipio turned at the close of Book II to consider the ideal political leader, the latter's virtually sole duty, which Scipio describes as comprising all the rest, was said to be that of "ceaselessly educating and examining himself" (*ut numquam a se ipso instituendo contemplandoque discedat*, II.69). This is not an attribute of one who thinks it is just a question of retrieving and reintroducing a previously perfected system. And it is, strikingly, not the attribute of a Platonic philosopher-ruler who has attained full knowledge already. New thinking will be required if the right principles, and the right methods of implementing them, are to be found.

Roman history itself receives an unsparing assessment when another of Cicero's speakers, Philus, undertakes to make the case for injustice at the start of Book III. Of course, as in Plato's *Republic*, the purpose of advocating injustice is to motivate counterarguments for justice.[2] But Cicero's practical orientation distances his treatment from Plato's. Firstly, in Cicero the topic of justice comes in the wake of his account of the state rather than as the occasion for it. Since, for him, any meaningful political proposals need a basis in reality, justice and injustice cannot be analysed before we have a concrete sense of the environments in which they occur. Secondly, and following from this, justice and injustice themselves need to be discussed by reference to actual historical circumstances, and Rome as principal representative of a highly developed society can hardly be excluded from this.

When Philus proclaims, in his role of injustice's advocate, that "the justice we are investigating is a thing of society not of nature" (*ius enim, de quo quaerimus, civile est aliquod, naturale nullum*, III.13), on the grounds that it would be the same everywhere if it were the latter, this does not seem wholly out of step with the material of the earlier books, with its emphasis on the foundational role of actual constitutions and codes of law. Philus goes on to cite various examples, including some pertaining to Rome, of how things considered morally right in one society are regarded as morally wrong in another, and how within the same society the same things may be regarded as right and wrong at different times.

Under the former category, Philus says that Romans themselves, "the most just of people" (*iustissimi homines*), are regarded as unjust – presumably, at

---

[2] To which one must add that Philus' speech is in a highly fragmentary condition. For a recent reconstruction see Zetzel 2017; and on the specifically Ciceronian character of the speech, Zetzel 1996, 302–4.

least, by those affected – for forbidding populations on the other side of the Alps from planting olive groves and vineyards, so that Rome's own would be more valuable (III.16). One doesn't need to be a vehement anti-Roman to think that the opposition might have a point here. And under the category of variation within a society, Philus points to the Volconian law passed at Rome in 169 BCE, which limited women's rights of inheritance and is described by Philus as "full of injustice to women" (*in mulieres plena est iniuriae*, III.17).[3]

Philus' testimony about variations in moral codes does not prove his point that there are no universal (in that sense 'natural') moral principles.[4] What it does suggest is that, if there are such principles, societies, even the best, move slowly and uncertainly towards them, and that the attainment and preservation of a more just order is likely to be a matter of constant revision and re-examination. It also hints that even if there are universal principles, their more detailed working out may require different sorts of realisation in different circumstances.

Now we know that Laelius, who responds with the case for justice, offers a defence of the justice of Roman rule, though unfortunately most of that portion of his response is lost. What we do have is a passionate and unequivocal assertion by him at III.33 of the notion of a perspective from which "there will not be one law at Athens and another at Rome, or one now and another in the future, but all peoples at all times will be bound by one eternal and unchanging law … founded and adjudged by god".[5]

This direction of travel, from the human realm towards that of the immortal and unchanging, had received an even more explicit evaluative colouring in Scipio's account of natural law back at I.27, in the transition to which he asked how anyone who has discerned the realms of the gods (*deorum regna*) can regard any-

---

3 Further discomfort for Rome is offered in Philus' assessment of the motives for imperial expansion. He suggests that the laudatory phrase "he expanded the boundaries of empire" that memorializes leading Roman generals implies that actually territory belonging to others was seized (III.24); and he wonders whether Rome's imperial conquests had anything to do with justice, however wise they may have been – Philus here establishing his contrast via a worldly sense of 'wisdom' that enjoins conquest and material gain (*sapientia iubet augere opes* […] *proferre fines*, III.24). Moreover, the unilateral repudiation by Quintus Pompeius of a treaty with Numantia may have been prudent but could not have been just (III.28).
4 As Peter Adamson suggests to me, citing for comparison Sextus' use of the mode of cultural differences, Philus' procedure may nonetheless be a sign of Cicero's own sceptical tendencies manifesting themselves.
5 *nec erit alia lex Romae, alia Athenis, alia nunc, alia posthac, sed et omnes gentes et omni tempore una lex et sempiterna et immutabilis continebit* […] *deus, ille legis huius inventor, disceptator, lator.*

thing in human affairs as noteworthy (I.26). We have, then, the presentation of a dual perspective. On the one hand the slow, concrete, imperfect journeys of individual societies towards a just order. On the other, the idea that what they are striving towards, and what has ultimate moral force, are universal principles applicable everywhere.

But 'everywhere' has itself, one might say, wide scope. It is not, as Scipio's account makes clear, confined to the earthly realm. It is natural law we are talking about, and the reach of nature is the totality of the universe. As Philus had asserted at I.19, the whole universe is a homeland given to us humans by the gods to share with them.[6] Philus' remark at the same time illustrates that there is complexity *within* the universal perspective as well.[7] Adoption of that perspective, as Scipio observed, makes us see how small the human realm is. But the human realm is also continuous with the divine, so that taking the divine perspective is not straightforwardly a rejection of the human one.

The main body of *De Re Publica* (as we have it) certainly speaks of our regarding the human realm too, even as against the divine, as important. After all, the opening conversation of Book I is represented as culminating in a turning away from reflection on the celestial realm to a focus on the earthly sphere (I.31–7). And despite the appeals to universalism, it is Rome that is held up both as the finest of nations and, I have suggested, a work in progress. The continuity of perspective between human and divine thus gives the sense that progress is possible, while the perspective from which the divine is presented as distinct and superior underwrites the idea that we have something to progress towards. The complexity of perspective manifested by *De Re Publica* evinces a recognition that the ideals we strive for must be fostered hopefully, but vigilantly and with a critical eye. In *De Legibus*, I shall now argue, this critical eye is turned towards the very notion of a universal perspective, on which the idea of natural law is founded.

3 *De Legibus*

Like *De Re Publica*, *De Legibus* looks to Rome as its model for the best society, while retaining the former work's sense that contemporary Rome, though failing

---

[6] *mundus hic totus, quod domicilium quamque patriam di nobis communem secum dederunt.*
[7] Though I cannot discuss it in detail here, this complexity is also, it seems to me, reflected in the work's famous closing Dream of Scipio, which emphasizes both the insignificance of the human realm in contrast with the divine (e. g. VI.20–23), and a continuity between the two realms (e. g. VI.26).

to live up to its past, is capable of improvement through evolutionary change. The laws that Cicero[8] actually proposes in *De Legibus* thus reflect in large measure the structure of the republican constitution that he takes to offer the most promising model of good government, but to have been undermined by the power struggles of his day. Innovation within this picture is therefore permissible, if modest, and not averse to borrowing from non-Roman (particularly Greek) traditions.

In *De Re Publica* V Scipio had affirmed that the political leader would be devoted to understanding justice and the laws, and will have examined their foundations, his principal interest in such study being its utility rather than the intrinsic pleasure of knowing (V.5). The discussion of law in *De Legibus* I offers an account of these foundations, Cicero using a similar phrase (*fons legum et iuris*, "source of justice and the laws", I.16) in previewing his account to the one used by Scipio in V.5. Thus, we are to see *De Legibus* as undertaking to supply this element of the ruler's outlook. The purpose of such an account is to set the parameters within which more concrete laws must fall and be judged. Law and justice are, in the first place, rooted in nature (I.18; I.20). Law is to be identified with the highest reason (I.18), with right reason (I.23), or more specifically with right reason in the realm of what is commanded or forbidden (I.33; I.42).

This, then, is evidently a normative account: it tells us what law, properly speaking, is; and that may be very different from the ordinary conception of law as written enactments that command or forbid in accordance with popular will (I.19). Unjust enactments are really anything but laws (II.11). What strays from the parameters of nature should not rightly be called laws at all; law is what is in conformity with "that most venerable origin of all things, nature" (II.13).[9] This framework allows, even encourages, critical comparison between actual laws, including as it may be those of Rome (I.42), and the standard of justice to which such laws ought to conform. More modestly, it licenses the legal theorist to consider revisions to legal codes in the light of considerations of justice. At the same time, Cicero is not building castles in the air. Rome, in his view, has produced the best concrete example of a good constitution. That means that the laws one proposes should be adjudged in terms of how well they fit the general character of that constitution (I.20; II.23; III.4), though that of course need

---

8 While I refer in this section to both author of *De Legibus* and main speaker within it as 'Cicero', tolerating some ambiguity of reference over what seems to me a certain artificiality in distinguishing the two by labelling the speaker as e. g. 'Marcus', the work's dialogue form is nonetheless integral to its construction; as we shall see, the relation between main speaker and interlocutors provides important material for interpreting the author's strategy.
9 *ergo est lex [...] ad illam antiquissimam et rerum omnium principem expressa naturam.*

not mean that they simply replicate the laws already in place. After all, earlier Roman legislators themselves will not necessarily have had that test in mind.

The relation between abstract principle and concrete realisation in the political sphere thus continues to be a theme that preoccupies Cicero. It is symbolized in the careful way he sets up, at the start of *De Legibus*, the idea of investigating the principles of law. The proposal arises in the wake of Cicero's rejection of the idea, at least for the time being, that he should turn his hand to writing Roman history, superficially because it would require too great a commitment of time (I.5–10). Why is that discussion there at all? History, one might suppose, has two features that distinguish it from a more philosophical approach to law. Firstly, it is descriptive rather than normative, attempting to show how things were, not prescribe how they should be. Secondly, and connectedly, it is essentially backward-looking, tasked with recovering and interpreting the past not laying down rules for the future.

Now one can evidently use the lessons of history to help make better provision for the future. And historical narrative is surely not alien to Cicero's scheme. In *De Re Publica*, after all, Scipio took pains to offer a broadly historical account of the development of the Roman constitution. Nonetheless, Cicero's refusal to take up the mantle of historian in *De Legibus* indicates that his aim is not to be bound by what is already in place, but to leave room for consideration of what ought to be. His discussion of natural law serves to manifest that aim, with his use of the concept of nature, or the natural, serving to highlight that he is conducting a normative enquiry. "We are", he says, "born for justice, and right is a matter not of opinion but of nature" (*nos ad iustitiam esse natos, neque opinione sed natura constitutum esse ius*, I.28).

But what is this nature that is thus contrasted with matters of opinion or convention? It is, in the first instance, human nature, as witnessed by Cicero's statement that 'we' are born for justice. We are all of the same species, and to that extent all alike (I.29–30), in particular in our possession of reason, which distinguishes us from other creatures (I.30). This explains the sense of mutual fellowship and union between human beings (I.28) and means that we are formed by nature to share justice and impart it to all (I.33). Not that we necessarily do this: nature is itself a normative concept – humans can fail to live up to their own nature, corrupted by the effects of bad habit and empty opinion (I.29; I.33). Nonetheless, Cicero argues, if one considers the endowments that humans share with each other, one will conclude that justice is the natural human condition.

But nature also refers, compatibly, to the nature of the universe as a whole, since the universe – "all of nature" (*naturam omnem*), as Cicero puts it – is governed by the gods (I.21). God in turn exercises governing power through the activity of right reason, which we humans, at least in our best condition, share with god (I.22–3). Reason is thus natural, in that it underlies the workings of the universe; and since we possess it too, as the divine element in us, in expressing our human nature it expresses our kinship with the gods as well. In sharing rationality with god, we are bound at the same time to the law that right reason expresses,[10] and since law in this sense implies justice (*ius*), Cicero can reiterate that gods and humans share citizenship of the whole universe, given that those who have law and justice in common have a common citizenship (*civitatis eiusdem*, I.23).

Cicero can thus claim to have shown that both law and justice are based in nature (I.33–4). Indeed he is anxious to show that if one does not conceive of justice as natural in this regard, then it is hard to make sense of the notions of justice and injustice at all. If we take the alternative as being to think of justice as simply consisting of human made commands and prohibitions, he argues that one should not even call a person unjust. One's responses to such commands and prohibitions will, rather, be a matter of calculation of utility. If one breaks a prohibition despite, say, the strong risk of punishment, then one might be considered incautious but not unjust (I.40).

Cicero's thinking is that to regard laws as no more than human artefacts – in that sense, as not based in nature – is to concede that reward and punishment are the only motives for obedience. But then it will be the rewards and punishments, not the justice or injustice of the act in question, that will be the measure of value or disvalue. But if that is so, then if one calculates correctly that, say, greater utility will arise from breaking a law than from obeying it, it seems that one has no reason to obey it. What is needed, rather, is a conception of justice as something sought, as Cicero puts it, "for its own sake" (*sua sponte*, I.48). That is, we must think of what is just as having an inherent normative force, in virtue of which it is to be pursued because it is just. And that means that justice must be more than simply a matter of human convention.

Whether or not we find Cicero's stance here convincing, it is important to note that there is a specific theory of justice that he appears to have in mind as the object of his critique – namely the Epicurean theory. Epicurus regarded

---

10 In Book II Cicero refers to the "true and original law" (*lex vera atque princeps*) as identified with the right reason of god (II.10). More precisely Cicero here labels god as "supreme Jupiter" (*summi Iovis*), a phrase that indicates at the same time a lofty remoteness from and a specific connection with Rome, an idea perhaps also indicated by Cicero's apparently interchangeable use of 'god' and 'gods' at I.21–3. For natural law as Jupiter's law see also *Philippic* XI.28, a context in which Cicero is nonetheless anxious that such law be ratified by the institutional authority of the senate (XI.29).

justice as precisely a matter of social agreements undertaken with the aim of maximising utility. Cicero refers to the Epicureans unmistakably, though not by name, at I.39 in terms of the theory that pleasure and pain are the measure of the respective goodness and badness of things, and of the denial that what is right should be pursued for its own sake rather than its consequences.[11]

One should further recall that Cicero's close friend Atticus features, along with Cicero's brother Quintus, as one of Cicero's two main interlocutors in the dialogue, and that Atticus is an adherent of the Epicurean school. So we might, given his presence, think all the more that there is an alternative point of view that is, in fact, not being given the opportunity to defend itself. Strikingly, Cicero does not even say that he thinks the Epicurean theory of pleasure is wrong; he says rather that he bids its proponents to abstain from all matters of government, which they neither know about nor have wished to know about (I.39).

It is true that the Epicureans, unlike the Stoics, generally maintained a quietist outlook and believed that by and large one should not be politically active. But they did have a specific theory of justice, as Cicero well knew, so he seems a little high-handed in excluding them from a conversation featuring that as one of its principal topics. What is more Cicero had adopted a similar attitude earlier in the book, when he asked Atticus at I.21 whether he would accept that the universe is governed by god. As Atticus' response makes clear, this is not what his school believes: Epicureans hold that though there are gods they play no governing role. Atticus nonetheless concedes Cicero's premise, so that he can see what will follow from it (I.22), and Cicero then proceeds to explain the theory of natural law that we have been discussing.

Epicureans are not the only ones whose views Cicero seems intent on marginalising in this context. Remarkably, at I.39 he asks the adherents of the New Academy to "be silent", since their habit of attacking any doctrinal view will cause "confusion" and result in the ruin of Cicero's "elegantly arranged edifice".[12] Now Cicero himself is a follower of the sceptical Academy, as we have just been reminded when Atticus comments ironically that Cicero of course is someone who does not follow his own judgement in debate but the authority

---

[11] There is here, as often, the question of how fair Cicero is to the Epicurean position. While the concept of nature evidently plays an important normative role in the Epicurean account of the good human life, Epicurus nonetheless seems to have held that the normativity of justice is, or can be, grounded on the content of specific local agreements. To this extent at least there is an important fault-line between him and a proponent of the concept of natural law.

[12] *perturbatricem [...] Academiam [...] exoremus ut sileat: nam si invaserit in haec quae satis scite nobis instructa et composita videntur, nimias edet ruinas.*

of others (I.36).¹³ Cicero replies that he indeed does not always accept the authority of others but that he is here trying to establish a foundation for states and cities (I.37).

Taken at face value this is surprising indeed. Although one can understand that having to deal with opposing views may make it harder to establish the kind of basis for systems of law and justice that Cicero has in mind, that could surely apply to any philosophical thesis and any sort of opposition. One might even suppose that attacking an edifice, however neatly constructed, might lead in the end to the construction of a stronger edifice.¹⁴ Cicero in fact says that he would like to appease the sceptics and dares not drive them off (I.39). So why just here does Cicero attempt to stifle debate? Why, in particular, does he draw attention to the fact that that is what he is doing? He need not have mentioned the sceptics, or for that matter the Epicureans, at all. He need not have chosen Atticus as a participant whom he could then ask not to dispute his basic premise.

Cicero clearly expects his readers to notice these moves. One might say that to announce loudly that one is closing down debate is itself to initiate a debate.¹⁵ Cicero, I suggest, uses the notion of uniformity of outlook to illustrate a crucial feature of the theory he is discussing. The idea of natural law is precisely the idea that there is a universal set of normative principles of equal applicability in all contexts. If this idea is correct, then there is indeed, in the end, no room for divergence of opinion about what justice is.¹⁶

At the same time Cicero's dismissal of the Epicurean and sceptical viewpoints reminds us that, in the real world as opposed to the ideal one of perfected reason, there are competing and critical opinions, and that the universalist theory itself is a product of a particular philosophical school.¹⁷ Just before Atticus' remark about Cicero's independence of thought, Cicero had drawn attention to the distinctive systematic methodology of the Stoics (I.36); and at I.38 he lists

---

13 For further defence of the view that Cicero retains allegiance to Academic scepticism in *De Legibus*, see Atkins 2013, 176–85; contra Glucker 1988, 48–50.
14 If Cicero's concern here is that "to unleash the full force of philosophical argumentation against the foundations of the city may do irreparable harm" – as suggested by Atkins 2013, 186 – one wonders how secure a foundation Cicero takes himself to be constructing in the first place.
15 For this reason I think there is more to Cicero's method here than "appeal to a consensus of philosophers" (Atkins 2013, 185).
16 This is not say that there could not, in fact, be conflicting ideas among advocates of natural law theory about what that set of principles was. But the theory itself mandates that one at most could be the right set.
17 Cf. *ND* I.36, where the thesis that natural law is divine is attributed specifically to Zeno.

the various adherents of the view that what is right should be sought for its own sake. And although he claims that Platonists, Aristotelians and Stoics have fundamentally the same idea here, even if Zeno the Stoic tried to claim originality by changing the terminology, it is still concrete individuals that are listed: Speusippus, Xenocrates and Polemo representing the Old Academy, Aristotle and Theophrastus the Peripatetic school, Aristo with his own distinctively austere viewpoint, and so on.

On the one hand, then, we have a vision of uniformity, representing a kind of ideal endpoint in which all is organized and measured in accordance with the same basic principles. On the other hand, we are asked to notice the messy, divergent voices (what else could justify their individual recognition?) that embody a range of perspectives and show where we are now and, perhaps, though the voices may change, where we will always be at any specific, historical moment – which is to say at some distance from an undisputed end-point. Cicero, as we saw, ostentatiously disclaimed the writing of history at the start of *De Legibus*, enabling him (so I argued) to leave room for the normative approach. But like his suppression of opposition to the universalist picture, the manner of his disclaimer serves to emphasize as much as diminish the importance of the historical perspective in a fully articulated political theory.

This is not to deny the weight that Cicero places on the idea that specific political systems are answerable to a set of unvarying basic principles. That remains the guiding theme of the opening book of *De Legibus* and is reasserted in Book II (8–14) before Cicero embarks on setting out his own legal proposals. But Cicero's careful construction also reminds us that a theory that denies variety of perspective is itself just one perspective, not immune from the critical claims of other perspectives, both theoretical and practical. Cicero is, after all, well aware that whatever basic principles he lays down "will not be accepted by all – that would be impossible" (*nec tamen ut omnibus probentur; nam id fieri non potest*, I.37). And this realism is not a grudging concession to others' obstinacy or his own inability to persuade, but a recognition, firstly, that in the human realm progress is made at the intersection of ideals and experience, and secondly, that each of those aspects may themselves have complex and competing elements.

Nature has stood importantly in Cicero's scheme for the continuity of the human and divine realms, and in that sense for the idea that there is one set of fundamental principles governing the whole universe. Although in *De Legibus* I nature has a privileged place, as against mere convention, we have also seen indications that Cicero does not regard the perspective of nature as the only one that ought to inform legal and political theory. Thus at I.17 he contrasted an enquiry into "the whole subject of universal justice and laws" (*tota causa*

[...] *universi iuris ac legum*), including explication of "the nature of justice" (*natura* [...] *iuris*) with the "small and narrow location" (*parvum quendam et angustum locum*) of Roman civil law. This contrast indicates the reach of the universal, while reserving a separately identifiable place for the local, which Cicero's choice of descriptive language seems targeted at capturing as such. If a set of immutable ideals is to function as the proper basis for testing and modifying actual legal and political structures, the realisation of such ideals in concrete form is a matter of meshing them with the particular complex and evolving societies whose well-being they are supposed to help optimize. It is no accident that Cicero speaks later of early Stoic political theory as "theoretically acute" (*verbo tenus acute*) but not addressed, as his is, to actual civic practice (*ad hunc usum popularem atque civilem*, III.14).

The inadequacy of the natural perspective on its own is reflected in a fascinating exchange at the start of *De Legibus* II about Cicero's homeland.[18] The work is set in Cicero's birthplace of Arpinum. Atticus, commenting on its natural beauty, remarks that just as Cicero traced everything back to nature in his preceding discussion of law and justice, so too nature is supreme (*natura dominatur*) in its ability to refresh the soul (II.2). It is already interesting that Atticus takes the notion of nature as it featured in the discussion of natural law, where it represented the whole universe, and applies it in a way that seems to contrast it with civilisation or the human made. He has just spoken of villas, marble walkways and panelled ceilings, as well as the landscaped water features that were a fashion for wealthy Romans, as comparing unfavourably with the natural features of Arpinum (II.2). Thus far nature trumps civilisation. But things get more complicated once Cicero acknowledges that Arpinum is indeed his homeland (*patria*), the place where he and his ancestors, who we are assured are "of very ancient stock", were born (II.3).

Cicero may be a son of the Arpinum soil. But as he says in response to Atticus' wonderment that he ever goes anywhere else when away from Rome, he rarely gets the chance to visit it. In fact Atticus expresses some surprise that Cicero should even call Arpinum, rather than Rome, his homeland, and asks if he has two homelands, Arpinum and Rome (II.5). Cicero after all is a Roman citizen and the people of Arpinum had been absorbed into Roman citizenship well before his birth. Cicero responds that while one can speak of people like him as having two homelands, one by nature the other by citizenship (*unam naturae, alteram civitatis*), or one by place the other by law (*alteram loci patriam, alteram iuris*), nonetheless one's first loyalty must be to the homeland of one's citizen-

---

18 For a concise discussion of the passage and its implications see Márquez 2012, 197–8.

ship, the all-embracing citizenship to which the name 'republic' attaches (*qua rei publicae nomen et universae civitatis est*) – that is, Rome (II.5).[19]

It is striking that law is placed here on the opposite side to nature, and privileged over nature.[20] Atticus' guileless favouring of nature over civilisation is implicitly rebuked by Cicero's recognition that it is civilisations, those most wondrous of human artefacts, that actually produce the institutions that enable human flourishing – including perhaps that ability peculiar to humans as a product of civilisation, the appreciation of nature as a thing of beauty. Instead of the whole universe being our homeland, and we its citizens (I.23; I.61), as the theory of natural law prescribed, it is now our concretely administrative city, seat of what is lawful by human construct, that is valorized as the location of our citizenship – and with it convention given primacy over nature.

What should we make of this? The opening of *De Legibus* II seeks to balance out the conception of law as natural that predominated in Book I with the reminder that it is the laws that humans actually devise that provide the context for any meaningful, let alone good, human life. Cicero goes out of his way at II.11 to contrast the expression of perfected reason with the laws that states make "variously and for particular circumstances" (*varie et ad tempus*), the latter being described as having the name of laws "by courtesy rather than fact" (*favore magis quam re*).

To be sure, then, such laws will be adjudged correct not by the simple fact that they have legal force – Cicero is after all even doubting whether in themselves they truly have such force – but by their congruence with basic principles of justice. In this regard Cicero sees "ancestral custom" (*mos maiorum*) as an important guide to the formulation of concrete laws, which seems to suggest some past time in which, thanks to the observation of such custom, things went well. Cicero somewhat encourages this view by telling Quintus, who observes in the wake of Cicero's listing of his religious laws at II.19–22 that they seem rather similar to "the laws of Numa and our own customs" (*legibus Numae nostrisque moribus*), that if he lays down any laws that did not previously exist as laws they would "pretty much" (*fere*) be based on ancestral custom, which had the force of law in those days (II.23). But mention of Numa also reminds us that the kings were neither individually nor collectively the last word in the evolution

---

[19] While the context makes clear that it is Rome to which Cicero refers, it may not be accidental that it is described now in language that seems to present it not in contrast with, but as rival for, the universal perspective.

[20] Cf. *Off.* I.21 where in the course of a defence of private property (including the right of Arpinates to the territory of Arpinum!) such property is said to be not anything natural but rather to fall under "the law of human society" (*ius humanae societatis*).

of the laws of Rome; and Quintus' comment invites us to reflect on whether Numa's laws and 'our own' customs refer to the same or different sets of prescriptions.

By a technique we have already seen deployed, Cicero uses an overt denial – in this case of genuine innovation – to cast a seed of doubt on the idea of there having been a fixed point in the past at which Rome's institutions were perfected such as to render genuine innovation unnecessary. The difficulty of such a view is brought into focus at II.40, where Cicero elaborates on his law that "the best of the ancestral rites be preserved." He quotes with approval the Delphic Oracle's response to a query from the Athenians, about which religious rites to uphold, that they should uphold their "ancestral customs" (*eas quae essent in more maiorum*). When the Athenians retort that such custom frequently varied (*saepe esse mutatum*), the Oracle advises to choose "the best", Cicero adding in his own name that "whatever is best is to be considered the most ancient and nearest to god" (*et profecto ita est, ut id habendum sit antiquissimum et deo proximum, quod sit optimum*).

The anecdote serves to draw our attention to the fact that nothing is fixed – not even the ancestral customs that Cicero had claimed he would resort to where new laws needed to be made. Cicero's respect for the most ancestral of the ancestral customs – whatever they turn out to be – need not be questioned. What his allusion to change encourages us to question is whether these are straightforwardly identifiable, and whether legal reforms can be based on winding back to what is both historically the hardest era to recover and by definition only the first stage in the development of the Roman tradition.

It also raises the unavoidable question: whose customs? Customs are in essence local, as the reference to the Athenians reminds us. But then there is a potentially awkward relationship between the ideal of universalism and the acknowledgement of custom. At II.35 Cicero discusses his proposal to outlaw the practice of nocturnal rites and asks what will become of the Greek mystery rites, such as those of Eleusis, into which many Romans themselves had been initiated. He adds that he is not making laws for the Roman people but for all "good and stable" (*bonis firmisque*) societies. Atticus replies that he assumed Cicero would exempt from his proposal those rites into which "we ourselves have been initiated" (*quibus ipsi initiati sumus*, II.36), and Cicero concurs, speaking in praise of the mysteries for their civilising effect. Atticus then bids him to apply his law by all means to Rome, but "not take away ours from us" (*nobis nostras ne ademeris*).

Atticus – original name Titus Pomponius – comes into his own here, his nickname bestowed for his love of Greek, and particularly Athenian, culture. As a partisan of that culture, he is allowed his plea for Romans to continue to immerse themselves in foreign rites, so long as the procedures inherent to those rites remain undertaken on foreign soil. Having 'lost' the right to assert his Epicureanism (Epicurus, let it be noted, was an Athenian), he 'wins' the right to carry on practising an aspect of Athenian culture that Cicero considers, in its own place, to be beneficial.

As in the case of Roman ancestral custom, so with Athenian cultural influence, one retains what is best. Athenian influence – Plato, Solon and others – on Cicero's proposals is often noted in *De Legibus* II (e. g. 38; 41; 45; 59; 64; 67), with Cicero referring to "your [Atticus'] Athenians" (*Athenienses tui*) at II.67. In so doing, Cicero again emphasizes the complex relation between universal and particular when it comes to the application of theory. Affirming that he is making laws for all decent societies, and hence that his prescriptions will not be limited to what originates at Rome, he at the same time presents this open-handedness as a response to the very particular enthusiasm of a Roman lover of Athenian practice. His inclusion of Greek ritualistic and legal aspects may coincide with what a pure reckoning of basic principles would deliver, but its motivation draws upon a rather richer brew of utility, custom and the admiration of a certain sort of Roman for all things Greek.

There is, moreover, an aspect of Cicero's pragmatism which leads to a dispute in which Quintus rather than Atticus is the protagonist. In *De Divinatione*, Quintus will play the role of defender of Stoic theology; and it is therefore no surprise that, unlike Atticus, Cicero does not need to ask Quintus to suspend any of *his* beliefs when he sets out the doctrine of natural law.[21] If anything, Quintus proves himself, by comparison with his brother, rather too hard-line a defender of uncompromising idealism. Cicero recognizes that some measures which might seem attractive and right on paper may not be wise to implement in the specific circumstances of particular societies. Thus, although commending Plato for the range of items that, in his own *Laws*, he forbade from being consecrated, Cicero confines himself simply to excluding land, bearing in mind he says, "human shortcomings and the resources of our times" (*vel hominum vitiis vel subsidiis temporum*, II.45). Plato's stringency about consecration may be admirable as an example of moral purity, but it would be impracticable to forbid, for example, flamboyant dedications of the spoils of war in a society of Rome's wealth and, implicitly, moral decadence. Cicero's realism on such matters perhaps sits ill with Quintus.

---

21 See e. g. *Leg.* I.21. Cicero nonetheless studiously avoids attributing natural law doctrine specifically to the Stoics, one reason for which, I take it, is that his own creative appropriation of it is paramount, as I shall argue further below in relation to *De Officiis*.

At any rate, when we come to *De Legibus* III, and its setting out of Cicero's laws governing the structure and exercise of Roman political offices, the brothers have a major dispute about the role of one significant element in that structure – the office of Tribune of the People. Now Cicero is hardly an uncritical admirer of the Tribunate; and he had earlier labelled three redistributive tribune laws as, from the normative point of view, not laws at all (II.14). Indeed, these serve as his chief legislative examples of what counts as unjust from the perspective of natural law. But Quintus picks up on the fact that Cicero, in the setting out of his proposals concerning public office, left the power of the tribunes intact, and in a passionate speech argues that the Tribunate tilts the balance of power in the state unfairly away from the aristocracy (III.19–22). Quintus praises the laws of Sulla, which forbade the tribunes from initiating legislation or holding any other political office after being tribune. Their powers were fully restored by Pompey, whom Quintus, despite the brothers' general favouring of Pompey, is unable to praise in that respect (III.22).

Cicero interestingly responds that Pompey had to have regard not just for what was best but for what was necessary (*non solum ei quid esset optimum videndum fuisse, sed etiam quid necessarium,* III.26) – that is, what was practicable given the constraints of the Roman political situation of the time. Pompey was "aware that this society could not be deprived of that power" (*sensit enim deberi non posse huic civitati illam potestatem,* III.26), the demonstratives making it clear that Pompey, as he had to, was taking account of the particular circumstances of time and place. The debate with Quintus is thus not only about ideals versus practice but about the idea of allowing the republican constitution to evolve – rather than see it as set in stone – precisely in order to preserve its essential character. Quintus is of the view that the Tribunate created an imbalance of power, yet he had earlier characterized Cicero's proposed laws about political office as almost the same as current arrangements, though with a few innovations. Cicero responds that his modesty in that regard is a recognition of the well-balanced state that Scipio had praised, based upon the wise provision of their ancestors (III.12).[22]

Ancestral wisdom (*sapientia maiorum*) is in turn praised by Cicero in defence of the establishment of the Tribunate, as the one measure which was able to stop the popular rebellion and, by at least giving the appearance of balancing the interests of ordinary people with those of the aristocracy, ensure the survival of the

---

[22] In *De Re Publica* itself a similar pragmatism is praised by Scipio at II.55 with regard to the granting to the Roman people during the early consulship of "a modest amount of liberty" (*modica libertate*) as a way of maintaining the authority of the leadership.

state (III.24). In expressing his conviction that evolution is the bulwark against revolution, Cicero reminds us that ancestral wisdom does not imply a fixed or monolithic outlook.[23] Incorporation of a role for popular leadership into the formal machinery of the state is likely to check rather than intensify the more savage expressions of popular will (III.23). The very modesty of his own innovations, then, acts as a practical demonstration of the evolutionary approach, against both the fixity of Quintus' stance and (what Cicero takes to be its probable consequence) the revolutionary transformation of the traditional order.

When Quintus suggests that Cicero's laws, insofar as they are based on the immutable natural law, will never be repealed, Cicero replies "certainly, just as long as the two of you [Quintus and Atticus] accept them" (*certe, si modo acceptae a duobus vobis erunt*, II.14). But Atticus is an Epicurean who doesn't, officially, even accept the principle of natural law; and Quintus' political stance sees every concession to popular power as misplaced.[24] Cicero knows, and via these personifications lets us know, that no law he proposes will be immutable.[25] Both history and theory, with their immutable tendencies to evolve, will see to that.[26] Far from this being an obstacle to Cicero's project, the notion that one comes closest to the ideals of nature only when one heeds the constraints of what is actual lies at its core. If we turn now to *De Officiis*, we shall see how this idea is pressed further in relation to the universalist aspirations of natural law.

---

[23] Compare Scipio's association, at *Rep.* II.30, of *sapientia maiorum* with ancestral willingness to incorporate and modify aspects of institutional arrangements from abroad; see here van der Blom 2010, 19.

[24] Annas 2013, 218 argues that Cicero presents his interlocutors as explicitly dissenting from his proposals at III.26 and III.37–8 "not to give the interlocutors any authority over the legislation" but to emphasize that persuasion rather than threat of force should be the basis of obedience to the law. Perhaps so; but Cicero's drawing of attention to his failure to persuade Atticus and Quintus seems more directly aimed at undermining the prospect of legislative permanence.

[25] See here Atkins 2013, 206–8; contra Inwood and Miller 2015, 145 who take the exchanges at II.13–4 to imply that Cicero holds anything not conforming to a criterion of immutability to be outside the scope of genuine law, and Straumann 2016, 45–6, who interprets II.14 as confirming that Cicero regards his proposed laws to be immutable.

[26] I am thus in broad sympathy with the view of Asmis 2008 that Cicero's own laws in *De Legibus* are intended to be congruent with, rather than having the status of, natural law. Ferrary 1995, 69, n. 52, who advocates a view of Cicero's proposed laws as being part of the law of nature (following Girardet 1983), speaks of *De Legibus* II.14 cited above as "go[ing] with the idea that the claim of Cicero's laws to form part of the *ius naturae* is confirmed by a *consensus prudentium*." Rather than establishing a consensus, that passage, it seems to me, is there to remind us of its elusiveness.

4 De Officiis

When Cicero sums up his position at the end of *De Officiis* I, he declares that in choosing what is appropriate, one must give priority to what upholds human social relations (*hominum societas*, I.160). An order of precedence is then spelled out: gods, country, parents, and then other relationships – the latter might include spouse, children, and other family members and friends (cf. I.54–8). Gods, scarcely mentioned before in the work, are present now less, it seems, because they are seen as providing the ultimate moral foundation than because of the contribution made by the commonalities of religion to social cohesion (cf. I.53; I.55; I.153).

Up to this point in the work it has been country that represents, for Cicero, the most important cradle of human flourishing. Family structures are the building-blocks of states (*quae propagatio et suboles origo est rerum publicarum*, I.54), but the nation encompasses everything that we hold dear (*omnes omnium caritates patria una complexa est*, I.57), and by implication is required for the maintenance of everything we hold dear, a thought reinforced by Cicero's immediate laceration of those who "are and have been hell-bent on utterly destroying their country" (I.57), a reference that presumably includes Mark Antony in the present tense and Caesar in the past.

This privileging of country, as that on which all other goods depend, is validated for Cicero by his witnessing of the turmoil created when its institutions are stretched to breaking point. It also stands as a practical delimiting of the scope of social relations, and correspondingly of the Stoic theory of human socialisation or 'appropriation' known (in Greek) as *oikeiōsis*, as expounded by Cato in *De Finibus*. Cicero clearly has that theory in mind when he discusses the character of human social bonds at *Off.* I.50–58, but the emphasis he places on it there is quite different. If anything, he adopts what might loosely be called a model of reverse *oikeiōsis*.

Cato had traced the concern that humans have for one another back to the bond between parent and child, the idea being that, as a normative ideal, the parenting impulse develops into a sense of kinship with all our fellow humans (*Fin.* III.62–3). Cicero, by contrast, *starts* in *De Officiis* with the universal sense of kinship (*est enim primum quod cernitur in universi generis humani societate*, I.50) and moves inwards, to the bond that exists between people of the same race and language, and then to people of the same country, emphasising the common political, legal, economic and religious framework that binds fellow-citizens together (I.53).[27] From there Cicero moves further inward to family relations, and then outward again, these relations being (as we noted above) the basis for civil society, the "nursery" (*seminarium*), as Cicero puts it, of the state (I.54). The metaphor reinforces the point that country is to be placed at the centre of the network of social relations that unite people, and paves the way for Cicero's declaration at I.57 that of all our ties there is none weightier or more dear than the one we have to our country (*omnium societatum nulla est gravior, nulla carior quam ea quae cum re publica est uni cuique nostrum*).

This, it seems to me, goes – deliberately so – right against the grain of Cato's account in *De Finibus*, and this in two main respects. Firstly, Cicero lays great emphasis here on the idea that human bonds come in varying degrees (*Off.* I.53; I.160) and that the concern owed to our fellow humans varies in proportion to the closeness of the relation we have to them (I.50). This admittedly provides a certain awkwardness given his objective of arguing that our most cherished status is that of citizen rather than family member, an awkwardness reflected in the two being treated as of equal rank at I.58, by contrast with how matters are put at both I.57 and I.160. Nonetheless this emphasis serves to play down the degree of concern we should reasonably hold for our fellow humans as such, in favour of the more concrete ties that arise from our identities as citizen and family member. Cato, whose main objective was to demonstrate the thesis that we do have rational concern for our fellow humans as such, makes no mention of degrees of closeness in his exposition.

Secondly, Cicero distances himself in this context from the Stoic idea, which flows from the thesis of a common humanity (or rather a common rationality), that the universe as a whole is a home shared by humans and gods. This emerges clearly when we see Cicero contrasting the "unlimited" (*infinita*) association of human with human, with the "more intimate" relation between citizens of a state (*interius etiam est eiusdem esse civitatis*, I.53). For Cato's Stoics the universe *is* a kind of state, of which all humans are citizens (*mundum autem censent* [...] *esse quasi communem urbem et civitatem hominum et deorum*, *Fin.* III.64; cf. *Leg.* I.61). That sentiment is, if one will pardon the pun, a world away from Cicero's declaration at *Off.* I.125 that what is appropriate for a foreigner or resident

---

[27] While parental love for children is said to be the origin of mutual human kinship in general at *Fin.* III.63 (*ex hoc nascitur ut etiam communis hominum inter homines naturalis sit commendatio*), at *Off.* I.53 Cicero traces more specific and local human attachments back to the phenomenon of general human sociability (*ab illa enim immensa societate humani generis in exiguum angustumque concluditur*).

alien is "to mind one's own business and not meddle in the affairs of a country that is not one's own".[28]

What lies behind this difference in outlook? The answer, it seems to me, is a theoretically grounded pragmatism that underlies much of Cicero's thinking on ethical and political matters and chimes particularly well with the objectives of *De Officiis*. His purpose is to give an account of human commitments that actually corresponds to the way human societies and value systems seem to be constructed. His adaptation of *oikeiōsis* signals his continuing debt to the resources of philosophical theory (Stoic in particular). But the way in which he utilizes that apparatus in support of a position in a radically different spirit from that of the original indicates the freedom Cicero takes himself to be permitted in pursuing the goal of practical progress. An unlimited commitment to our fellow humans is an abstraction too far for one who wishes to preserve and strengthen the ties that bind us in the real world; and so that commitment becomes not the climax but the starting point of his reflections on social cooperation and the human good.

Matters seem, on the face of it, somewhat different in Book III. Its principal thesis is that wrongdoing can never be of advantage to the wrongdoer and that acting honourably is always (also) the advantageous course. One fundamental prop of this thesis is the idea that to do harm to a fellow human being, or to profit at another's expense, is to undermine the bonds of human society on which we all ultimately depend (III.21–6). Cicero bases the prohibition of harm on the principle that we are by nature concerned with the interests of our fellow humans "just because they are human" (*ob eam ipsam causam, quod is homo sit*), so that all are bound in this regard by a "common law of nature" (*eadem lege naturae*, III.27).

Indeed, Cicero here rejects the view of those who say that we have obligations to our family, but not to our fellow-citizens, or alternatively that we have obligations to these but not to humanity more widely. Such views would dissolve the bonds that tie together, respectively, the state and the whole human race, in the latter case doing away with kindness, generosity and justice altogether (III.28). Yet while Cicero is rather keener to play up the universal human dimension here than he was in Book I, his outlook is, I think, in essence unchanged. He has no wish to deny that we have obligations to our fellow humans as such, on which the social virtues ultimately rest. But he continues to refrain from committing himself to the view that this makes us into citizens of the universe. As before, our fellow-citizens are treated as a separate category from humanity in

---

28 *peregrini autem atque incolae officium est nihil praeter suum negotium agere, nihil de alio anquirere minimeque esse in aliena re publica curiosum.*

general, Cicero affirming that while it is inhuman to prevent a foreigner from enjoying the amenities of the city, it is wrong to treat a non-citizen as a citizen (*nam esse pro cive qui civis non sit rectum est non licere*, III.47).

Cicero assures us that although the law of nature is indeed applicable to all, the laws of individual states are in basic accord with them, insofar as they forbid that harm be done to another for the agent's own profit (III.23). One's country, then, remains the fundamental reference-point for one's identity and interests as a social being. The ties of friendship, Cicero tells us, should be preferred to such things as wealth and pleasure, but one should in turn never do anything for a friend that is contrary to the interests of one's country (*contra rem publicam*, III.43), which "ought to be dearest of all" (*quae debet esse carissima*, III.95). And while there is a social bond that unites all humans, the one that unites fellow citizens is tighter (III.69).[29]

It is, surely, no accident that the authority of Rome's forefathers is correspondingly invoked here in favour of the view that the universal law of peoples is different from the civil law of a given state; the latter ought to include, but will not necessarily be identical with, the former (III.69).[30] The universal perspective is embedded in, and given substance by, the practical realities of human social organisation.[31] As we saw in the discussion of *De Legibus*, so too here ancestral ways are fashioned by Cicero into a thoroughly modern weapon, deployed not to represent a flawless past which it is our task to excavate and maintain unchanged, but to exemplify evolutionary flexibility and the sensitivity to time and place that is the defining feature of human convention and (one might add) the human condition.

The law of nature may, and should, regulate the laws of one's society; but Cicero's downplaying in *De Officiis* of the idea of a common universal home reminds us that progress occurs at a more local level. And this, I hope to have shown, is a preoccupation of Cicero's thought on these matters throughout. It is not, to reiterate, that Cicero rejects the universal perspective. What I have

---

29 *societas est enim [...] latissime quidem quae pateat omnium inter omnes, interior eorum qui eiusdem gentis sint, propior eorum qui eiusdem civitatis.*
30 *itaque maiores aliud ius gentium, aliud ius civile esse voluerunt; quod civile, non idem continuo gentium, quod autem gentium, idem civile esse debet.*
31 In III.69 Cicero contrasts both natural law and the law of peoples with civil law; I take the former pair to be extensionally equivalent in his usage (cf. *Tusc.* I.30 which identifies *lex naturae* with "the agreement of all peoples", *consensio omnium gentium*); but while the first member of the pair picks out the *source* of the authority of the law in question, the second adverts to its *application*, to any and all peoples, with the varying laws of particular states filling out its content in relation to their own conditions and circumstances.

tried to argue here is that his discussions of law, nature and country show an embrace of the idea, as paradoxical as it is necessary, that attention to the local perspective offers the best chance of bringing the universal perspective to the world.[32]

Primary literature

Cicero. De Finibus Bonorum et Malorum. L. D. Reynolds (ed.). Oxford: Oxford University Press 1998.
Cicero. De Officiis. M. Winterbottom (ed.). Oxford: Oxford University Press 1994.
Cicero. De Re Publica, De Legibus. J. G. F. Powell (ed.). Oxford: Oxford University Press 2006.
Cicero. Rhetorici Libri Duo Qui Vocantur De Inventione. Eduard Ströbel (ed.). Leipzig: Teubner 1915.
Cicero. Tusculanae Disputationes. M. Pohlenz (ed.). Leipzig: Teubner 1918.

Secondary literature

Annas, Julia. 2013. "Plato's *Laws* and Cicero's *de Legibus*." In *Aristotle, Plato and Pythagoreanism in the First Century BC*, edited by Malcolm Schofield, 206–24. Cambridge: Cambridge University Press.
Asmis, Elizabeth. 2008. "Cicero on Natural Law and the Laws of the State." *Classical Antiquity* 27:1–33.
Atkins, Jed W. 2013. *Cicero on Politics and the Limits of Reason: The* Republic *and* Laws. Cambridge: Cambridge University Press.
van der Blom, Henriette. 2010. *Cicero's Role Models: The Political Strategy of a Newcomer*. Oxford: Oxford University Press.
Ferrary, Jean-Louis. 1995. "The statesman and the law in the political philosophy of Cicero." In *Justice and Generosity*, edited by André Laks and Malcolm Schofield, 48–73. Cambridge: Cambridge University Press.
Girardet, Klaus. 1983. *Die Ordnung der Welt. Ein Beitrag zur philosophischen und politischen Interpretation von Ciceros Schrift* De Legibus. Wiesbaden: Franz Steiner.
Glucker, John. 1988. "Cicero's philosophical affiliations." In *The Question of "Eclecticism": Studies in Later Greek Philosophy*, edited by John M. Dillon and Anthony A. Long, 34–69. Berkeley: University of California Press.
Inwood, Brad and Fred D. Miller, Jr. 2015. "Law In Roman Philosophy." In *A History of the Philosophy of Law from the Ancient Greeks to the Scholastics*, edited by Fred D. Miller Jr. and Carrie-Ann Bondi, 133–65. Dordrecht: Springer.

---

[32] This paper modifies and expands on some themes from Woolf 2015. Earlier versions of the paper were read at Cornell University and LMU Munich. My thanks to the audiences on those occasions, and to Jim Zetzel for helpful written comments.

Márquez, Xavier. 2012. "Between *Urbis* and *Orbis:* Cicero's Conception of the Political Community." In *Cicero's Practical Philosophy,* edited by Walter Nicgorski, 181–211. Notre Dame: University of Note Dame Press.

Straumann, Benjamin. 2016. *Crisis and Constitutionalism: Roman Political Thought from the Fall of the Republic to the Age of Revolution.* New York: Oxford University Press.

Woolf, Raphael. 2015. *Cicero: The Philosophy of a Roman Sceptic.* Abingdon: Routledge.

Zetzel, James. 1996. "Natural Law and Poetic Justice: A Carneadean Debate in Cicero and Virgil." *Classical Philology* 91:297–319.

Zetzel, James. 2017. "The Attack On Justice: Cicero, Lactantius And Carneades." *Rheinisches Museum* 160:299–319.

Caroline Humfress
Natural Law and Casuistic Reasoning in Roman Jurisprudence

Abstract: "The Roman jurists, 'calculating with concepts,' did not need any natural law." (Christoph Kletzer). Focusing on classical juristic material, this essay argues that natural law was in fact one concept, amongst others, that Roman jurists calculated with. There is no evidence for Roman juristic treatises dedicated to natural law, yet as Levy noted in 1949: "Hundreds of texts are concerned with *ius naturale, naturalis ratio, rerum natura* and other phrases related to *natura* or *naturalis*. It is impossible to find a common denominator." The essay divides into two parts: first, it surveys a series of arguments drawn from those hundreds of juristic texts that relate to natural reason and natural law(s). Second, it analyses the Roman juristic method of "calculating with concepts." The argument throughout is that the common denominator which eluded Levy is the Roman jurists own, highly particular, type of case-methodology.

1 Introduction

"The Roman jurists, 'calculating with concepts', did not need any natural law."[1] Christoph Kletzer's statement neatly summarizes the celebrated nineteenth-century Prussian jurist Friedrich Carl von Savigny's understanding of the relationship between Roman and natural law. Natural law for Savigny "[...] was not a highly complex and eternally valid emanation of reason, but a mere abbreviation or simplification of positive law" (Kletzer 2007, 128). For Savigny (1814, 29), the fact that the Roman jurists "calculated with concepts" (*rechnen mit Begriffen*) which they had themselves developed, meant that they had no need for a systematizing natural law doctrine that stood 'behind', 'above' or 'beyond' their civil law. This basic understanding of the relationship between Roman and natural law can also be traced through the so-called school of the *usus modernus pandectarum* ("the modern use of the *Digest/Pandects*") that developed in the Netherlands and Germany from the sixteenth century onwards. Jurists associated with the *usus modernus pandectarum* attempted to resolve modern legal questions through the use of Roman civil law, more specifically through the use of the Roman emperor Justinian's *Digest* or *Pandects*, a text promulgated in

---

[1] Kletzer unpublished, 8; see also Kletzer 2007, 146.

533AD and mostly made up of heavily excerpted extracts from the writings of second- and third-century AD Roman jurists. As James Gordley (2013, 157) states:

> Unlike the late scholastics, the *iusnaturalists*, Pothier, Domat, and the later rationalists, they [sc. "the school of the *usus modernus pandectarum*"] did not try to resolve legal problems by means of higher principles [...] Typically, they did not dismiss the importance of the higher principles of natural law or of philosophy, although they did not apply them to legal problems. They began their treatises with accounts of law and justice that were squarely in the Aristotelian tradition, although these accounts became sketchier as time went on. Yet they rarely drew on these accounts to explain the Roman law.

Whereas seventeenth- and eighteenth-century jurists who worked within the tradition of the *usus modernus pandectarum* tended to neglect natural law, nineteenth-century German 'pandectists' such as Georg Friedrich Puchta and Bernhard Windscheid, who both worked within a Romanist tradition established by Savigny, framed their conceptual jurisprudence against contemporary natural law theorists (Haferkamp 2004). The nineteenth-century Pandectists may have been the "sworn enemies of natural law" (Grossi 2010, 106), but was Savigny right to claim that the Roman jurists themselves had no need for a natural law doctrine?

There is no evidence for any Classical Roman jurist (c.130BC–c.235AD), or indeed any 'epiclassical' (c.284–c.330AD), postclassical (c.330–527AD) or Justinianic (527–565AD) jurist, writing a treatise entitled *On Natural Law* or similar. According to William Warwick Buckland (1925, 29) the Roman jurists thought of *ius naturale* as: "[...] an ideal to which it is desirable that law should conform, but it was not really at any time, for them, a test of the validity of a rule of law." Jean Gaudemet (1952) concluded that natural law had a very limited place in Roman jurisprudence, as did Alberto Burdese (1954). Similarly, in his entry on 'Ius Naturale' Adolf Berger (1953a, 530) states that:

> Unknown to Republican jurists, the *ius naturale* is not considered by those of the Principate as a juristic conception denoting a special sphere of law, a particular category of law, or a system of legal norms. Nor do the occasional 'definitions' of the *ius naturale* found in the sources, give the picture of a certain uniformity of the conception, although the influence of Greek philosophy is evident.

The idea that *ius naturale* was not a juristic concept but rather a philosophical one is also found in Barry Nicholas' (2005) entry *Law of Nature* in the third edition of the *Oxford Classical Dictionary:* "For them [sc. the jurists] the philosophical natural law is no more than an ornament, carrying no suggestion that an inconsistent man-made law might be invalid."² In other words, Classical Roman jurists did not treat "the philosophical natural law" as a source of legal obligation above and beyond man-made ('human') law: the philosophical natural law was a mere 'ornament' to Roman jurisprudence.

In fact, much of the modern scholarship on natural law and Roman jurisprudence encompasses the broader question of the extent to which Classical Roman jurists borrowed abstract terminology from Greek philosophical sources (the classic argument in favour of juristic borrowing is Villey 1953; the classic argument against, Nocera 1962). More specifically, the question of philosophical influence on Roman jurisprudence also tends to include discussions on the extent to which Roman jurists borrowed or developed Ciceronian and/or Stoic concepts of natural law. In a subtle and persuasive article, Yan Thomas (1991, 204 and 209) concluded that: "On chercherait vainement dans le Digeste une formule équivalente au 'ius a natura' cicéronien. Pas davantage n'est admise la supériorité normative de la nature sur le droit [...] Aucune hiérarchie n'est suggérée entre droit naturel et droit civil, contrairement au modèle cicéronien." With respect to Stoic influence, on the other hand, Tony Honoré (2002, 80) has argued in a number of publications that Ulpian – a leading jurist and advisor to successive emperors of the Severan age (193–235 CE) – espoused "an outlook that is predominately Stoic." According to Honoré, Ulpian: "[...] shares with the Stoics the view that we are born free and equal and should live according to nature" (although note the qualification at Honoré 2010, 208: "It is a mistake to attribute to a lawyer a system of philosophy rather than a set of values. The nature of the discipline requires lawyers to be eclectic, to compromise between different aims"). As Schiller (1978, 560) wrote, perhaps with more than a hint of irony: "In spite of the fact that the attention paid by the Roman jurists to the concept *of ius naturale* may have been minimal, modern commentary on the subject is quite extensive."

In an important article published in 1949 and entitled *Natural Law in the Roman Period*, Ernst Levy accepts the premise that philosophical concepts of natural law played a very minor role in Classical Roman jurisprudence. Having explained that Cicero, schooled in Greek philosophy and rhetoric, developed a systematic idea of a law that is "above space and time", a law that has its "[...] very root and origin [...] in nature or, as [Cicero] also puts it, in God", Levy (1949, 45) turns to the Roman jurisprudence of the Classical era. As Levy (1949, 50) rightly argues, Roman juristic sources – in contrast with the writings of Cicero – do not offer an "unequivocal line of thought" on natural law. None-

---

2 See also Vander Waerdt 1994, 4887.

theless, continues Levy (1949, 50), the juristic sources are not barren: "Their wealth rather is disturbing. Hundreds of texts are concerned with *ius naturale*, *naturalis ratio*, *rerum natura* and other phrases related to *natura* or *naturalis*. It is impossible to find a common denominator." The lack of 'a common denominator', according to Levy, is due to the fact that the Roman jurists worked with multiple, different, meanings of 'nature':

> The outlook brightens, however, if different meanings are recognized and explained as such. Cicero, the philosopher, believes in a universal and eternal law. The jurists consider this type of natural law only in a minority of instances [...] As a rule, they refer to nature and preferably to the nature of things when they deal with factual situations of daily life. There the jurists feel at home. To master such problems they, and they alone, are called upon. They have to do with the law binding here on earth, and, if necessary, to be enforced by the courts.

For Levy, the hundreds of juristic texts referring to *ius naturale*, *naturalis ratio*, *rerum natura* etc. are all concerned with multiple, different, factual situations in daily life. Nature, for Levy, thus tended to be used by the Roman jurists as a 'yardstick' for measuring and determining the proper outcomes of the private law scenarios that dominated their collective thought. "For 'natural' was to them not only what followed from physical qualities of men or things, but also what, within the framework of that system, seemed to square with the normal and reasonable order of human interests and, for this reason need not be in need of any further evidence" (Levy, 1949, 51).[3]

Levy would thus agree with Savigny that the Roman jurists had no need for a *systematizing* natural law doctrine, but Levy also draws our attention to a fundamental aspect of Roman juristic thought: its method. If we return now to Christoph Kletzer and the argument that "The Roman jurists, 'calculating with concepts', did not need any natural law", I argue – to the contrary – that natural law was one concept, amongst others, that Classical Roman jurists calculated with.

In Section 2 below, I explore a number of specific examples of Roman Classical jurists using the concepts of natural reason and natural law in order to determine solutions to legal problems. Moreover, I will argue that on the few occasions where we do find what seem to be general philosophical or metaphysical statements about natural reason and natural law in Classical jurisprudential sources, those sources were most likely written with beginners in mind. In other words, what we tend to view as general definitions were originally intend-

---

[3] See also 54–55.

ed as initial 'footholds', which would enable those students who were (as yet) untrained in the highly specific kind of casuistic reasoning demanded by Roman jurisprudence to begin their steep ascent. In Section 3, we turn to Classical Roman juristic reasoning itself. As we shall see, the 'common denominator' which eluded Levy in his own analysis of those hundreds of Classical Roman juristic texts that contain phrases relating to *natura* or *naturalis* was the Roman jurists own, specific, type of casuistic method.

2 Roman law and natural law(s)

One of the most frequently quoted Roman juristic statements on the relationship between Roman law and natural law(s) was written by the second-century AD law teacher Gaius. Gaius' *Institutes*, based on an elementary set of lectures delivered to students in 160/1AD, was identified by Savigny in 1816 in a fifth-century palimpsest manuscript – one of only a handful of Classical Roman juristic texts to have survived independently from Justinian's sixth-century *Digest* compilation. We are not going to begin, however, with the famous reference to *naturalis ratio* that opens Gaius' *Institutes* (although we will return to this passage below). Rather, we start our exploration of how Roman Classical jurists worked out solutions to legal problems with an analysis of four highly specific examples, each of which highlights Gaius' casuistic use of the concepts *naturalis ratio* and *ius naturale*.

2.1 Calculating with concepts: *naturalis ratio* and the *ius naturale*

Our first example comes from Book 3 of a work by Gaius entitled *On Verbal Obligations*, excerpted by the Emperor Justinian's legal commissioners at *Digest* 3.5.38. The passage states that anyone paying a debt on behalf of someone else, even without his knowledge and agreement, frees him from liability, but a person cannot lawfully demand payment from another without his consent: "For both natural reason (*naturalis ratio*) and civil reason (*civilis ratio*) are in favour of our being able to improve another's position, even without his knowledge and agreement, but not of our being able to make it worse" (Mommsen, Krueger, Watson et al. 1985, Volume I, 108; translation modified). Gaius' statement that we are able to improve another's position without his knowledge and agreement is an example of a Roman juristic rule (*regula*): a general principle that serves as an interpretative elucidation of what the law is. According to the Severan jurist Paul: "A rule is something which briefly describes how a thing is. The law (*ius*) may not be derived from a rule (*regula*), but a rule must arise from the law (*ius*) as it is" (*Digest* 50.17.1 = Paul, *Plautius* Book 16; Mommsen, Krueger, Watson et al. 1985, Volume 4, 956). At *Digest* 3.5.38, Gaius first demonstrates the civil law 'as it is', then states the 'rule' that arises: both natural and civil reason agree that we can improve another's position, even without his knowledge and agreement, but we cannot make it worse.

Turning to our second example, this time from Gaius' *Provincial Edict* (Book 4) as excerpted at *Digest* 4.5.8 (Mommsen, Krueger, Watson et al. 1985, Volume I, 139; translation modified), we again see Gaius using civil reason and natural 'rights' to explain the law as it is:

> It is obvious that those obligations which are understood to have a natural warranty, do not perish with change of civil status, because civil reason (*civilis ratio*) cannot destroy natural rights (*naturalia iura*). Therefore, the action concerning the dowry, because it is framed with reference to what is right and just, continues to exist even after change of civil status.

As already noted, this passage comes from Gaius' commentary on the *Provincial Edict*, a formal legal source that belonged to a branch of Roman law referred to by scholars as the *ius honorarium* or *ius praetorium:* the law that was introduced by the 'praetors' (magistrates) at Rome, in the public interest, to aid, supplement and correct the *ius civile*. Gaius' specific question here concerns whether the praetors at Rome would grant an action for recovery of a dowry from someone who had lost their civil status. Gaius' answer is that the praetor would grant the action – and from the process of reasoning out that answer comes a rule that "civil reason cannot destroy natural rights." A similar process of reasoning can be seen in our third example, *Digest* 7.5.2, a passage again attributed to Gaius' *Provincial Edict* (Book 7). Here Gaius mentions a *senatusconsultum* – a decree issued by the Senate at Rome – that dealt with legacies which contain usufructs for goods that are consumed by the very fact of their use (for example wine, wheat, oil and, by analogy, coined money). The rule that Gaius states: "natural reason (*naturalis ratio*) cannot be altered by the authority of the senate" (Mommsen, Krueger, Watson et al. 1985, Volume I, 239; compare Gaius, *Institutes* I.83), is reasoned out from the Senate's specific decision to create a new class of 'quasi-usufructs' for this type of goods. Once again, Gaius' *regula* is reasoned out from the law as it is. The method of reasoning that underpins our fourth example, from Gaius' *Institutes* I.158, should be understood in the same way: "The agnatic tie is broken by status loss. Cognatic relationship, by contrast, is not affected by status loss. While the logic of state law can destroy rights founded on state law, it cannot affect rights founded on the law of nature" (Seckel, Kuebler,

Gordon and Robinson 1988, 103). Gaius first states the 'law as it is' and then identifies the *regula* that arises therefrom.

I have chosen to begin with these four, rather hard-core, examples of Gaius' casuistic problem-solving because it is precisely this kind of technical, specific, reasoning that lies behind what we today tend to read as general definitions of *naturalis ratio* and *ius naturale* in Roman juristic sources. Keeping in mind the fact that "a rule must arise from the law (*ius*) as it is", we can now turn to the celebrated passage that opens Book 1 of Gaius' *Institutes* (Seckel, Kuebler, Gordon and Robinson 1988, 19; translation modified), a text that probably originated as lectures to first year law students:[4]

> All peoples who are governed by laws and customs use law which is partly theirs alone and partly shared by all mankind. The law which each people makes for itself is special to itself. It is called city-state ['civil'] law, the law peculiar to that city-state. But the law which natural reason [*naturalis ratio*] makes for all mankind is applied in the same way everywhere. It is called the *ius gentium* because it is common to every nation. The law of the Roman people is also partly its own and partly common to mankind. Which parts are which we will explain below.

According to Gaius' *Institutes* 1.1.1 there is a law which natural reason makes for all mankind (*ius gentium*) and a law that each [civilized] people makes for itself (*ius civile*). As we saw in our first example above (*Digest* 3.5.38), these two *rationes*, the natural and the civil, can agree; but they can also differ, as in our second example above (*Digest* 4.5.8). Given that the civil law can destroy civil rights, but not natural ones – as we saw in our third and fourth examples above (*Digest* 7.5.2 and Gaius' *Institutes* I.158) – it must follow that the law of the Roman people is partly its own and partly common to all mankind. Gaius promises to explain to his students which parts of the *ius civile* are peculiar to the Romans and which parts are "common to all mankind", but he gives up on this explanation part way through Book 2 of the *Institutes*. In any case, by juxtaposing the opening statements of Gaius' *Institutes* 1.1.1 with the *regulae* stated in our four examples from Gaius' other writings, we can clearly see that his general definitions are not a priori statements, but rather arise out of his problem-solving casuistry. Gaius intended the general definitions given in Book 1 of his *Institutes* to function as provisional 'place-holders': he expected his students to move beyond them, once they had mastered the art of reasoning out from the civil law for themselves.

---

4 See also *Digest* 1.1.9.

The famous definition of the *ius civile* given at *Digest* 1.1.6 also originated in Book 1 of a pedagogic text: Ulpian's *Institutes*. The preamble to *Digest* 1.1.6 (Mommsen, Krueger, Watson et al. 1985, Volume I, 2) states: "The *ius civile* is that which neither wholly diverges from the natural [law] or the *ius gentium* nor follows the same in every particular. And so, whenever we add anything or take anything away from the common law, we make a law specific to ourselves, that is the civil [law]." If we leave to one side the complex and ultimately inconclusive debates concerning Justinianic interpolations to this passage, we can see that in broad outline it agrees with the text from Gaius' *Institutes* 1.1.1 quoted above. As *Digest* 1.1.1, 2 (Mommsen, Krueger, Watson et al. 1985, Volume I, 1), also attributed to Ulpian's *Institutes* Book 1, succinctly states: "Private law is tripartite, being collected out of natural, common or civil precepts." This idea of private law being collected out of natural, common (i.e. the *ius gentium*) or civil precepts is fundamental to the Roman juristic method. Roman jurists did not hypothesize an eternal or natural law from which human law ought to be derived, as the thirteenth-century Dominican Priest Thomas Aquinas did (see Figure 1). Rather, the Classical Roman jurists invariably began with the civil law of Rome and then worked outwards (see Figure 2), drawing upon 'natural' precepts in their problem-solving as and when the problem demanded.

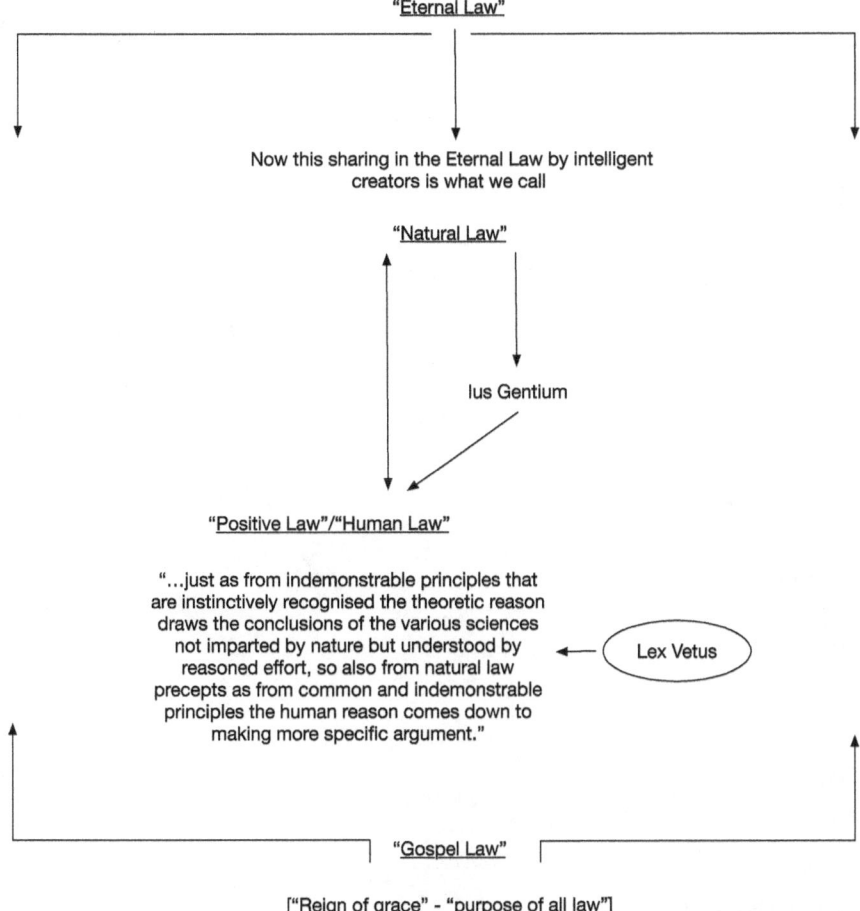

Figure 1: Representation of Aquinas' hierarchical scheme of law at Summa Theologiae Ia2 ae. 91

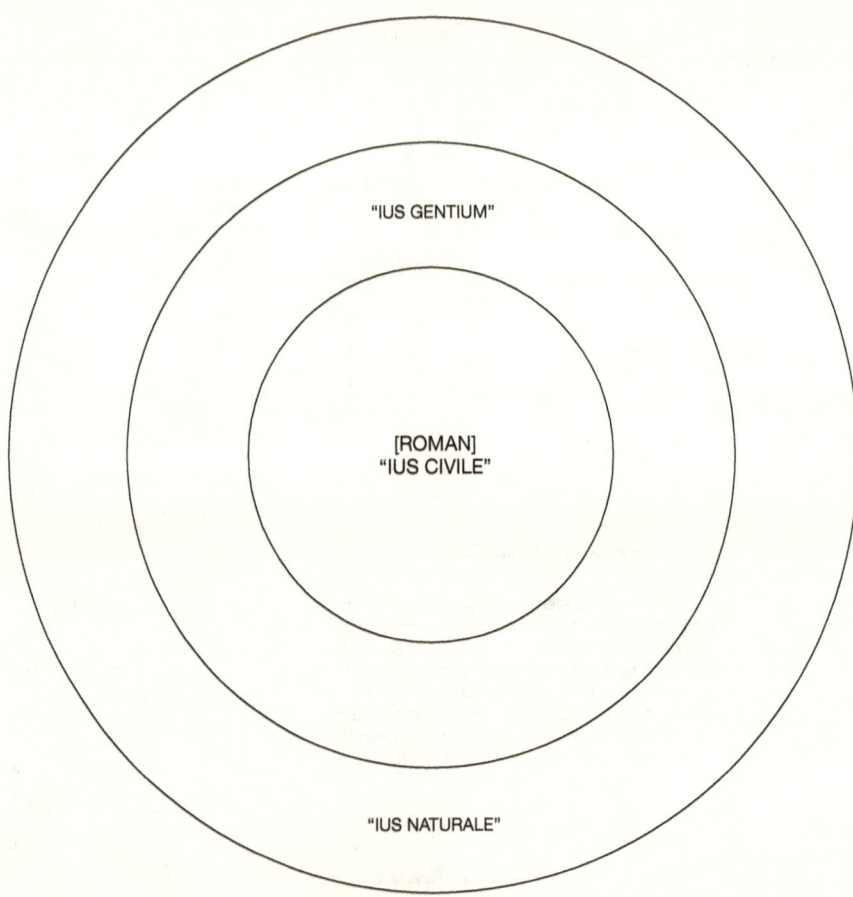

Figure 2: Classical Roman Juristic Framework

2.2 Does nature give rise to norms that are binding "in and of themselves"?

"Since ways of life are to be implanted, and not everything is to be sanctioned by written law, I will seek the root of justice (*ius*) in nature, which we are to take as our guide as we lay out the whole discussion" (Cicero, *On the Laws* 1.20).[5] Are there examples of Classical Roman jurists working with a philosophical concept of natural law or justice (*ius*), comparable to that of Cicero? *Digest* 1.1.1, attributed by Justinian's sixth-century compilers to Ulpian, *Institutes* Book 1, provides probably the most celebrated – and controversial – Classical juristic definition of natural law (*Digest* 1.1.1, 3; Mommsen, Krueger, Watson et al. 1985, Volume I, 1; translation modified):

> *Ius naturale* is that which nature taught all animals; for it is not a law specific to mankind but is common to all animals – land animals, sea animals, and the birds as well. Out of this comes the union of male and female which we call marriage, and the procreation of children, and their rearing. So we see that other animals, including wild animals, are taken to have experience of this law.

Berger (1953, 530) concluded that this Ulpianic definition of *ius naturale* is "striking by its peculiarity" and "has no juristic content at all." Roman legal scholars have long disagreed over the extent to which the text at *Digest* 1.1.1 may have been altered by its Justinianic editors in order to reflect a new and distinctive postclassical doctrine of natural law (see Justinian, *Institutes* 1.2.11). We should note here, however, that the text at *Digest* 1.1.1, 3 fits with the preceding statement at *Digest* 1.1.1, 2 that private law is collected out of natural, common and civil precepts. According to *Digest* 1.1.1, 3, the union of male and female which 'we' (sc. Romans) call marriage, together with the procreation of children and their rearing, are examples of natural precepts that are to be found within the Roman private law. *Digest* 1.1.1, 4 moves immediately onto the relationship between *ius gentium* and natural law: "*Ius gentium* is that which all human peoples observe. That it is not co-extensive with natural law can be grasped easily, since this latter is common to all animals, whereas the *ius gentium* is only common to human beings among themselves" (Mommsen, Krueger, Watson et al. 1985, Volume I, 1). As we have already seen, Gaius connected the *ius gentium* with *naturalis ratio* (Gaius, *Institutes* 1.1.1). Unlike Gaius, however, Ulpian specifies a difference between the *ius gentium* that all humans observe and the *ius naturale* that is common to all animals. Honoré (2002; 2010) suggests that this definition origi-

---

5 Quoted from Annas 2017, 173.

nated in Stoic philosophy, but ultimately there can be no definitive answer to the question of whether Ulpian (or any other Classical Roman jurist) systematically conceptualized *ius naturale* or *ius gentium* according to a particular philosophy or metaphysics. The crucial point is that Roman jurists were primarily interested in how – and to what extent – natural reason, natural law and the *ius gentium* interacted with the Roman civil law on a case-by-case basis.

The Roman concept of *ius gentium* also had a concrete, practical, context. From at least the late Republic, the court of the Peregrine Praetor at Rome heard cases involving foreigners (*peregrini*) who were freemen. Classical Roman jurists could thus be called upon by a Roman magistrate – as well as by private litigants – to advise on legal transactions with foreigners (i.e. freemen who were not citizens of Rome) or among foreigners.[6] The legal institutions which Roman jurists considered to be shared by all (free) men included the *ius commercii*, which covered basic commercial transactions such as informal sale, informal transfer of ownership, specific forms of promise, loan, partnership and other obligations; and the *ius connubii*, the 'right' or capacity to conclude a form of marriage, which would be recognized by Roman civil law, between a Roman and a non-Roman. In contrast with Early Modern 'philosophical' definitions,[7] the Classical Roman *ius gentium* should be understood as: "[...] those legal habits which were accepted by the Roman law as applying to, and being used by, all the people they met, whether Roman citizens or not" (Crook 1967, 29). The Classical *ius gentium*, like Ulpian's *ius naturale*, was a concept to work with.

The specific ways in which Classical Roman jurists used the concepts of natural law, natural reason and *ius gentium* in their casuistic reasoning can be seen in the following examples of juristic discussions relating to slavery, *patria potestas* and guardianship for minors. At *Institutes* 1.52 Gaius notes that, according to the Roman civil law, slaves are in the power of their owners; this power, however, must rest on the *ius gentium* "[...] for we can observe the same thing everywhere" (Seckel, Kuebler, Gordon and Robinson 1988, 45). Note that here Gaius makes good on his promise to specify which parts of the Roman civil law are "common to all mankind." Ulpian, in his *Institutes*, takes this reasoning a step further in order to explain the Roman practice of 'manumitting' (freeing) slaves: manumissions must also belong to the *ius gentium*, since all men are born free by natural law and where slavery is not known, manumission too must be unknown.[8]

---

6 See further Daube 1951.
7 Tuori 2012; Haakonssen 2017.
8 *Digest* 1.1.4pr, Ulpian *Institutes* Book 1.

Gaius' *Institutes* 1.55, on the other hand, go on to compare the power that masters have over slaves with the power that a Roman *paterfamilias* has over children born to a marriage concluded according to Roman civil law. *Patria potestas*, concludes Gaius, is a right which only Roman citizens have; it is an institution that belongs to the Roman *ius civile* alone. The fact that Roman citizens are unique in having their children "in power" (*in potestate*) is stated again by Gaius at *Institutes* I.189, but here he clarifies that the institution of guardianship for minors who have been released from *patria potestas* – for example by death of the *paterfamilias* – comes from the *ius gentium:* "The institution of guardianship for those who are still children is provided for by the *ius gentium*, because it is in accordance with natural reason for a young child to be ruled by a guardian" (Seckel, Kuebler, Gordon and Robinson 1988, 115). Again, we see here how definitions that we tend to assume are 'general' and 'a priori' were in fact arrived at via a highly specific juristic process of reasoning.

If we move beyond the beginners' handbooks (ie. the *Institutes*), we can begin to appreciate the complexity and subtlety of Roman juristic casuistry involving the concept of nature. Ulpian's discussion of 'natural obligations', for example, suggests that there are cases where nature can give rise to norms that are binding in and of themselves. *Digest* 44.7.14 (Ulpian, *Disputations*, Book 7) states: "Slaves are bound by civil delicts and, if manumitted, they remain bound. They are not bound by contracts in a civil way (*civiliter*), but in a natural way (*naturaliter*) they bind and are bound. Furthermore, if I pay a manumitted slave who gave me money on loan, I am released" (Mommsen, Krueger, Watson et al. 1985, Volume IV, 643). The broader legal question here involves changes to legal status: If a slave commits a delict whilst a slave and is then manumitted, he still has to answer for the wrong. But what of contracts and obligations? A slave was incapable of being a debtor, as defined by the Roman civil law – which partly led to the development of the Roman institutions of the *peculium* and the *actio de peculio*.[9] Debts not enforceable according to Roman civil law, however, were still 'debts'. Hence, as Gaius put it, debts incurred by a slave should be classified as natural obligations (*obligationes naturalis*, Gaius, *Institutes* III.119). In our passage, Ulpian states that slaves are bound by contracts in a natural way, rather than a civil way; moreover, contracts with a slave bind and are bound 'naturally'. Thus, if a slave gives money on a loan to a freeman they are both obligated 'in a natural way'; if the slave is subsequently manumitted, however, and I pay back the loan owed 'in a natural way', does the fact that the slave is now a free man create a new civil obligation, which is in excess of the natural one? Ulpian's an-

---

9 On which see Johnston 1995.

swer here is no, but the fact that this discussion originated in a text entitled *Disputations* implies that the issue was controversial. This is further supported by an extract from a work by Tryphoninus, a contemporary of Ulpian, given at *Digest* 12.6.64 and also attributed to a work entitled *Disputations*. It is exactly this kind of technical problem solving and juristic 'disputation' that provides the context for what otherwise might appear to us to be broad and general statements of (philosophical) principle.

In some instances, the way in which the sixth-century compilers of Justinian's *Digest* cut Classical juristic passages from their original context and pasted them as stand-alone statements creates a heightened sense of general, timeless, principles. For example, *Digest* 50.17.32 (Ulpian, *Ad Sabinum* Book 43) states: "As far as the *ius civile* is concerned, slaves are not regarded as persons. This, however, is not true under natural law, because, so far as natural law is concerned, all men are equal" (Mommsen, Krueger, Watson et al. 1985, Volume IV, 959; translation modified). According to Otto Lenel's reconstruction of Ulpian's *Ad Sabinum* (1960, 1173), the passage excerpted at *Digest* 50.17.32 was originally part of a detailed discussion under the title *On the Condition of Debtors*. Hence what appears in the *Digest* as a universal principle, namely that according to natural law all men are equal, in fact originated as a *regula* in the sense defined by the Severan jurist Paul. As the Italian scholar Carlo Alberto Maschi concluded in his 1937 study *La Concezione Naturalistica del Diritto e Degli Istituti Giuridici Romani*: "Far from being a supra-legal norm, the basis upon which the civil law in force is to be criticized or altered, 'nature' is an intra-legal principle, a corollary of the civil law as it is currently defined" (Colish 1990, 365).

2.3 Juristic arguments from the 'nature of things'

Maschi's argument that Classical – and Postclassical – Roman jurists invariably understood nature as an "intra-legal principle" rather than as "a supra-legal norm" has not been without its critics.[10] Maschi (1937, 2) was right, however, to stress that there are numerous instances in classical Roman juristic sources where the concept of 'nature' simply equates to 'that which is'. Air, running water, the sea and the seashore are not amenable to private ownership, thus they belong in common to all men 'by natural *ius*' (*Digest* 1.8.2; Marcian, *Institutes* Book 3; Mommsen, Krueger, Watson et al. 1985, Volume I, 24). Wild animals are free by nature and can be acquired by 'first taking', which is "a matter of nat-

---

10 For example, Jolowicz 1938.

ural reason" (Gaius, *Institutes* II.65 – 68; see also *Digest* 41.1.1; Ps.-Gaius' *Common Matters or Golden Things*, Book 2). Hence, as Ulpian argues, if a bear – 'wild by nature' – breaks loose and causes harm, its former owner cannot be sued for liability because he ceased to be the owner the moment that the bear escaped (*Digest* 9.1.1.10; Ulpian, *Edict* Book 18; Mommsen, Krueger, Watson et al. 1985, Volume I, 276). Ulpian uses the fact of the bear's wild nature to reason out a problem relating to liability for damages under Roman private law.[11]

Classical jurists also developed arguments from the 'nature of things' using analogical reasoning. For example, *Digest* 44.7.1, 12 (Ps.-Gaius, *Golden Words* Book 2) states: "It is clear in the nature of things that a lunatic, whether he makes a stipulation or a promise, performs no valid act."[12] *Digest* 44.7.1, 13 goes on to draw an analogy between the legal capacity of a lunatic and a minor: "Very near to him [sc. the lunatic] in position is a person who is of an age that he does not yet understand what is being done; but in respect of him a more benevolent view has been accepted; for one who can speak is regarded as being able lawfully to stipulate as well as to promise."[13] Having distinguished the lunatic from the minor, *Digest* 44.7.1, 14 reasons from the 'nature of things' as they pertain to a dumb person: "It is clear in the nature of things that a dumb person has no part in a verbal obligation" (Mommsen, Krueger, Watson et al. 1985, Volume IV, 640). *Digest* 44.7.1, 15 states that this is also the case for a [completely] deaf person, on the grounds that someone who promises must be able to hear the words of the stipulator and vice-versa. The *regula* that emerges across these discussions is that 'speaking' is a pre-requisite for the legal capacity to stipulate or to promise, but it is not the only pre-requisite (as is clear from the 'the nature of things' that pertain to the lunatic and the deaf).

Finally, with respect to Classical Roman juristic arguments from 'the nature of things', we should note a further, related category: appeals to normative principles that are said to exist according to 'natural reason' (*naturalis ratio*). For example, natural reason permits us to defend ourselves against attack (*Digest* 9.2.4pr, Gaius, *Provincial Edict* Book 7; also *Digest* 43.16.1.27, Ulpian, *Edict*, Book 69). It also invalidates a contract where "[…] the thing which we stipulated to be given is of such a nature that it cannot be given" (*Digest* 44.7.1.9, Ps.-Gaius, *Golden Words* Book 2; Mommsen, Krueger, Watson et al. 1985, Volume IV, 640). According to Peter Stein (1974), these kinds of Roman juristic arguments from natural reason underwent an important development between the Late Republic

---

11 See further Ashton-Cross 1953, 395 – 6.
12 Mommsen, Krueger, Watson et al. 1985, Volume IV, 640. On 'stipulation' see Berger 1953b.
13 Mommsen, Krueger, Watson et al. 1985, Volume IV, 640.

and early Empire, with a shift from "what is self-evident" to "what is universally valid." Tony Honoré detects a similar change in the concept of natural equity (*naturalis aequitas*). In the writings of Ulpian, 'natural equity' does not simply refer to what is self-evidently equitable: "The special feature of natural equity is that it operates even when the civil law does not cater for the problem [...] Natural equity is not fundamentally different from civil equity, but the equitable solution to a problem may or may not already have been embodied in the civil law" (Honoré 2002, 93). Again, we should note here that natural equity, like natural reason and natural law, was a concept used by classical jurists in order to solve problem cases within the Roman civil law – moving outwards to consider natural equity as and when the specific case demanded.

3 Casuistic reasoning in Roman jurisprudence

Classical Roman jurists used a particular kind of casuistic 'problem-thinking' and, in the process, developed and clarified a distinctive set of legal concepts and principles. Their objective, however, was not to arrive at a set of 'higher-level', governing legal principles or concepts, but rather to define the Roman *ius civile* case by case. As James Gordley (2013, 948) notes: "Their method did not require them to define their concepts or explain the relationship between one concept and some higher-level concept." The concepts that we find in classical Roman juristic sources: ownership (*dominium*), possession (*possessio*), contract (*contractus*) etc. – and, as I argue above, 'natural law' (*ius naturale*) and 'natural reason' (*naturalis ratio*) – are effectively 'working' concepts.

Classical juristic discourse reveals the concept of natural law 'at work' (in the Wittgensteinian sense referred to by Hart 1983, 277). We should not, however, assume from this fact that Roman classical jurists were only interested in "the factual situations of everyday life" (contra Levy 1949, 50). Their casuistic problem-case method was related – in various ways – to concrete, factual, situations. Nonetheless, in classical jurisprudential writing it was the "hypothetical case" that dominated (Frier 1985, 164):

> The hypothetical case is so characteristic of later Roman [classical] juristic casuistry that its unusual form and its importance are not always realized; in particular, it has little or nothing to do with Anglo-American 'case law'. Above all, cases in Roman juristic writings normally omit most references to contingent circumstances, even when it can be presumed that an actual case underlies the jurist's decision [...] the hypothetical cases in juristic writings serve a large number of purposes; they range from entirely plausible and everyday situations to which rules can be straightforwardly applied, to farfetched 'limiting cases' through which highly theoretical propositions can be elucidated.

As Fritz Schulz put it (1936, 51), Classical Roman juristic sources are casuistic in a peculiar way. They are not intended to showcase abstract principles by means of concrete or fictitious cases. Instead, they develop a series of predominately 'hypothetical' cases in which legal concepts and rules are identified, but are not abstracted from the cases themselves, in order to determine Roman legal solutions to Roman legal problems. *Definitio* (definition), for a Classical Roman jurist, was not a tool for generalisation or for the formation of abstract rules.[14] In sum, Classical Roman juristic sources show us the concepts of natural reason, natural equity and natural law 'at work', as part of the jurists' hypothetical case-method. As I argued in Section 2 above, where we (seem to) find general definitions of natural law in Classical Roman juristic sources this should be attributed either to the pedagogic nature of the text or to the editorial practices of the sixth-century compilers of Justinian's *Digest*.

According to Yan Thomas (1991, 227) the 'few' generalized reflections on nature that we find in Roman jurisprudence are solely a function of the jurists' casuistic reasoning: "Ces quelques réflexions ont été conduites à partir des seules opérations de la casuistique: Ce sont évidemment des opérations de la pensée. On y découvre, me semble-t-il, qu'il n'est d'autre nature, pour les juristes, que créé par eux. La cohérence du discours institutionnel vaut à la nature son statut – fort original – d'institution." 'Nature' was created by jurists, for jurists and it is the 'coherence' of the jurists' 'institutional discourse' that gives the jurisprudential concept its reality. Whether Thomas is right to dismiss philosophy as a source for jurisprudential thought remains an open question. What is more important, as I have argued above, is the recognition that Classical Roman jurists were not interested in defining concepts of nature, natural law, or natural reason, for their own sake. Nature, natural law, and natural reason were concepts to be calculated with – as such they played an important role in the search for Roman legal solutions to Roman legal problems.

4 Conclusion

The Roman jurists' method of calculating with natural law – and related concepts – is sharply different from medieval and modern uses of natural law. The difference does not lie, necessarily, within a casuistic approach. Casuistic argument was a feature of both medieval scholasticism and early modern humanism. Thomas Aquinas (1224/5–1274 AD), Hugo Grotius (1583–1645) and John Fin-

---

[14] See further Carcaterra 1966; Martini 1966.

nis (born 1940) all used casuistic reasoning, to varying degrees and extents, but their aim was to investigate how an abstract law of nature could be applied to concrete cases. Between the sixteenth and eighteenth centuries natural law arguments were made and developed in English, European and American courtrooms (Helmholz 2015). According to Helmholz, the nature, if not the detail, of these arguments exhibit a "remarkable consistency": "The law of nature was an abstract law. It stated some general principles, but most of them required refinement and specificity before they could be put into practice" (Helmholz 2015, 35). As I have argued above, the Roman hypothetical case method was strikingly different.

Classical Roman jurists did not begin with an abstract law of nature which was to be applied (or not) in practice. Instead, nature, natural law, and natural reason were working concepts, applied in the search for Roman legal solutions to Roman legal problems. This 'peculiar' kind of Roman juristic casuistry may, in fact, have left more than a trace in modern natural law discourse. As Knud Haakonssen (personal communication) has suggested, some early modern lawyers, in particular Samuel Pufendorf, understood the distinctiveness of Roman jurisprudential discourse and used it as a resource to challenge both Catholic and Protestant natural law theorists. Similarly, Ian Hunter (2010) has also identified "[...] a casuistical discourse where inconsistent principles are deployed strategically" in Emer de Vattel's *Le droit des gens*, a foundational text for modern histories of international law. As Savigny rightly understood, the Roman jurists had no need for a philosophical doctrine of natural law. But the fact that natural law was one concept – amongst others – which Roman jurists calculated with, left a distinctive legacy for some modern natural law 'theorists' to rediscover.

Primary literature

Gaius. 1988. *The Institutes of Gaius*, edited by Emil Seckel and Bernhard Kuebler; translated by William M. Gordon and Olivia F. Robinson. London: Duckworth.

Justinian. 1985. *The Digest of Justinian*, edited by Theodor Mommsen and Paul Krueger; translated by Alan Watson et al. 4 Volumes. Philadelphia: University of Pennsylvania Press.

Lenel, Otto [1889] 1960. *Palingenesia iuris civilis*, reprinted with supplement. 2 Volumes. Graz: Akademische Druck – U. Verlagsanstalt.

Secondary literature

Annas, Julia. 2017. *Virtue and Law in Plato and Beyond*. Oxford: Oxford University Press.
Ashton-Cross, D.I.C. 1953. "Liability in Roman Law for Damage Caused by Animals." *The Cambridge Law Journal* 11.3, 395–403.
Berger, Adolf. 1953a. Art. "Ius Naturale." In *Encyclopedic Dictionary of Roman Law*, by Adolf Berger, 530–1. Philadelphia: University of Pennsylvania Press.
Berger, Adolf. 1953b. Art. "Stipulatio." In *Encyclopedic Dictionary of Roman Law*, by Adolf Berger, 716–7. Philadelphia: University of Pennsylvania Press.
Buckland, William W. 1925. *A Manual of Roman Private law*. Cambridge: Cambridge University Press.
Burdese, Alberto. 1954. "Il concetto di "ius naturale" nel pensiero della giurisprudenza classica." *Rivista italiana per la scienze giuridiche* 8:407–421.
Carcaterra, Antonio. 1966. *Le definizioni dei giuristi romani. Metodo mezzi e fini*. Naples: Jovene.
Crook, John A. 1967. *Law and Life of Rome 90 B.C.–A.D. 212*. Ithaca, New York: Cornell University Press.
Daube, David. 1951. "The Peregrine Praetor." *The Journal of Roman Studies* 41.1–2:66–70.
Colish, Marcia L. [1985] 1990. *The Stoic Tradition from Antiquity to the Early Middle Ages. Volume I. Stoicism in Classical Latin Literature*. Leiden, New York, Copenhagen and Cologne: E.J. Brill.
Frier, Bruce. [1985] 2014. *The Rise of the Roman Jurists*. Princeton NJ: Princeton University Press.
Gaudemet, Jean. 1952. "Quelques remarques sur le droit naturel à Rome." *Revue internationale des droits de l'antiquité* 2:445–67.
Gordley, James. 2013. *The Jurists: A Critical History*. Oxford: Oxford University Press.
Grossi, Paolo. 2010. *A History of European Law*. Chichester West Sussex: Wiley-Blackwell.
Haakonssen, Knud. 2017. "Early-modern Natural Law". In *Cambridge Companion to Natural Law Jurisprudence*, edited by George Duke and Robert P. George, 76–102. Cambridge: Cambridge University Press.
Haferkamp, Hans-Peter. 2004. *Georg Friedrich Puchta und die 'Begriffsjurisprudenz'*. Vittorio Klostermann Press: Frankfurt and Mainz.
Hart, Herbert L.A. 1983. "Jhering's Heaven of Concepts and Modern Analytical Jurisprudence." In *Essays in Jurisprudence and Philosophy*, by Herbert L.A. Hart, 265–277. Oxford: Oxford University Press.
Helmholz, Richard. 2015. *Natural Law in Court. A History of Legal Theory in Practice*. Cambridge MA: Harvard University Press.
Honoré, Tony. 2010. "Ulpian, Natural law and Stoic influence." *The Legal History Review* 78.1–2:199–208.
Honoré, Tony. 2002. *Ulpian: Pioneer of Human Rights*. Oxford: Oxford University Press.
Johnston, David. 1995. "Limiting Liability: Roman Law and the Civil Law Tradition." *Chicago-Kent Law Review* 70.4:1515–1538.
Jolowicz, Herbert F. 1938. "Review of Carlo Alberto Maschi, *La concezione naturalistica del diritto e degli istituti giuridici romani*. Milan: Università del Sacro Cuore, 1937." *The Journal of Roman Studies*, 28:83–85.

Kletzer, Christoph. 2007. "Custom and positivity: an examination of the philosophic ground of the Hegel-Savigny controversy." In *The Nature of Customary Law: Philosophical, Historical and Legal Perspectives*, edited by Amanda Perreau-Saussine and James Murphy, 125–148. Cambridge: Cambridge University Press.

Kletzer, Christoph. Unpublished draft. "Hegel and Savigny on Customary Law."

Levy, Ernst. 1949. "Natural Law in the Roman Period." In *University of Notre Dame Natural Law Institute Proceedings*, edited by Alfred L. Scanlan, Vol. II, 43–72. Indiana: College of Law, University of Notre Dame.

Martini, Remi. 1966. *Le definizioni dei giuristi romani*. Milan: Giuffrè.

Maschi, Carlo Alberto. 1937. *La concezione naturalistica del diritto e degli istituti giuridici romani*. Milan: Università del Sacro Cuore.

Nicholas, Barry. [1996] 2005. Art. "Law of Nature." In *The Oxford Classical Dictionary* edited by Simon Hornblower and Antony Spawforth. Oxford: Oxford University Press.

Nocera, Guglielmo. 1962. *Ius naturale nella esperienza giuridica romana*. Milan: Giuffré.

von Savigny, Friedrich Carl. 1814. *Vom Beruf unsrer Zeit für Gesetzgebung und Rechtswissenschaft*. Heidelberg: Mohr und Zimmer.

Schiller, Arthur A. 1978. *Roman Law: Mechanisms of Development*. The Hague, Paris and New York: Mouton Publishers.

Schulz, Fritz. 1936. *Principles of Roman Law*. Oxford: Clarendon Press.

Stein, Peter. 1974. "The development of the notion of *naturalis ratio*." In *Daube Noster: Essays in Legal History for David Daube*, edited by Alan Watson, 305–316. Edinburgh: Edinburgh University Press.

Thomas, Yan. 1991. "*Imago naturae*. Note sur l'institutionnalité de la nature à Rome." In *Théologie et droit dans la science politique de l'État modern. Actes de la table ronde de Rome (12–14 novembre 1987)*, 201–227. Rome: École française de Rome.

Tuori, Kaius. 2012. "The Reception of Ancient Legal Thought in Early Modern International Law." In *The Oxford Handbook of the History of International Law*, edited by Bardo Fassbender and Anne Peters, 1012–1032. Oxford: Oxford University Press.

Vander Waerdt, Paul A. 1994. "Philosophical Influence on Roman Jurisprudence?" In *Philosophie, Wissenschaften, Technik. Philosophie*, edited by Wolfgang Haase, 4851–4901. Berlin: De Gruyter.

Villey Michel. 1951. "Logique d'Aristote et droit romain." *Revue d'histoire du droit français et étranger* 38:309–28.

Part III: **Late Antiquity**

Christopher Isaac Noble
Human Nature and Normativity in Plotinus

Abstract: Plotinus, following certain Platonic cues, maintains that 'we' and 'the true human being' correspond to the rational part of the human soul. This view is counterintuitive because it is natural to see ourselves and our humanity as including parts of the human organism additional to reason. In this paper, by way of considering Plotinus' contrast between the sage and the politically virtuous man, I propose that Plotinus' view that we are our rational part is best understood as expressing a teleological claim. Since our proper end is an activity of the rational part of soul, it is appropriate to identify our nature with the rational part of the organism alone.

1 Introduction

At *Ennead* 1.1, *What is the Living Organism, and What is the Human Being?*, Chapter 7, lines 14–24, Plotinus claims that 'we' and 'the true human being' are the rational part of the embodied human soul.[1] By contrast, the non-rational parts of soul and the body are merely 'ours'. Since Plotinus' claims about the identity of ourselves and our humanity are standardly presented as claims about the 'self', I will refer to this position as 'the rational self view.' This narrow identification of ourselves and our humanity with the rational part of soul has antecedents in the *Alcibiades I*, the *Republic*, and the *Phaedo*, as well as in certain statements in the *Nicomachean Ethics*.[2] Yet the rational self view, as stated, is counterintuitive. For

---

Note: I am grateful to the audience at the conference Nature and Normativity in Ancient Philosophy at the LMU Munich for their helpful responses to an early version of this paper, and to Peter Adamson and Andreas Anagnostopoulos for their valuable written comments on subsequent drafts.

[1] The rational part of the embodied human soul is also identified in this way at 1.1.10.3–10; 1.4.14.1–19; 2.1.5.17–23; 2.3.9.10–34; 4.4.18.10–21; 6.4.14.16–31, 15.35–41; 6.7.4–5.

[2] *Alcibiades I* (128e–133b) indicates that 'we' and 'the human being' are the soul, and has often been taken to imply that we are, more precisely, soul's rational part. *Republic* IV (588c–590a) and the *Phaedrus* (246a–254e) both offer 'images' of soul, in which the rational part is represented as a human being and the non-rational parts are represented as non-human animals. In the *Phaedo*, where the soul's intrinsic functions are presented as purely rational, Socrates is identified with his soul (115c-d). Aristotle, in various passages in the *Nicomachean Ethics*, suggests that the human being is or seems to be – either without qualification or 'most of all' – his ra-

https://doi.org/10.1515/9783110730944-013

it is natural to think that 'we' are subjects of the various actions and experiences that belong to the human organism, including those that involve our non-rational parts of soul and our bodies, such as a courageous action or experiencing a sensory pleasure. And we ordinarily understand 'the human being' to refer to the whole human organism rather than to some one part of it. What then does Plotinus mean to assert when he says that 'we' and 'the human being' are the rational part of soul, and why might he think that this claim is justified?

According to the most prominent interpretations, Plotinus' identification of the self with the rational part of soul reflects its status as a subject of a consciousness. Some interpreters appear to take the rational part to be our self because it is a subject of consciousness and reflexive self-awareness.[3] Others, noting Plotinus' claims that we may 'become' either the human organism or a transcendent intellect, depending on the orientation of our rational consciousness, hold that the self is to be identified with the rational part because it is a plastic subject that can adopt different identities.[4] However, there are reasons to be sceptical about these consciousness-centred approaches to the rational self view. One reason for scepticism is provided by Plotinus' treatment of the sage. Plotinus indicates that the sage distinguishes himself from other human beings by identifying himself with his rational part exclusively, and that this identification of oneself with rational soul represents an ethical ideal. This normative dimension of the rational self view is not easily captured by views according to which our rational part is the self because it is a conscious subject that is self-aware or that has a plastic identity. Another reason for scepticism about these interpretations of the rational self view is that they are not easily reconciled with several Platonic texts that Plotinus adverts to in support of the rational

---

tional part or his understanding (*EN* IX.4, 1166a13–17; IX.8, 1168b28–1169a3; X.7; 1178a2–8; cf. *Protrepticus*, fr. 6 Ross). Gill 2006, 4–14 characterizes these texts as offering 'core-centred' or 'essence-centred' approaches to personality.

[3] Gerson 1993, 122 claims that "to be an endowed self is to be self-aware," and Emilsson 2017, 285 presents the operative senses of self in Plotinus as that of an entity that is "capable of reflection" and "unifies mental phenomena." Remes 2007, 126, who identifies several distinct senses of 'self' in Plotinus, suggests that "the self [...] is a unified centre of awareness."

[4] This conception of the Plotinian self is well put by Hutchinson 2018, 7: "the self is a seat of awareness that fluctuates along these levels [of reality], belonging to the level of reality on which it focuses its attention"; see also Dodds 1960, 5; O'Daly 1973, 49; and Banner 2017, 148. Remes 2007, 240 identifies this plastic subject as one among several Plotinian senses of 'self'. Aubry 2008, 120–1 suggests that this plastic self ("le moi sans identité") is strictly speaking not our rational part, but a power for directing our consciousness that belongs to it and has the capacity to acquire different identities; but for a criticism of this interpretation see Chiaradonna and Maraffa 2018, 45–47.

self view. In these texts, Plato suggests that human beings are to be identified primarily with the rational part of the human organism, not because of its capacity for self-awareness or for acquiring an identity, but because it is our best part and is best qualified to rule.

In this paper, I will instead propose that the rational part of soul represents our self because of its teleological priority over the other of the parts of the human organism. In several passages, Plotinus indicates that the self is to be identified with our 'authoritative part'. This suggests that the rational part counts as the self because it is in some sense our principle of action. But in what sense is the rational part our principle of action, and why should our principle of action count as the self? In answer to this question, I will argue that Plotinus takes the principle of action for an individual to be the nature according to which that individual lives. Some individuals, who take the activities of the whole human organism to be constitutive of their end, make the whole organism their principle of action by choosing to live according to its nature. Sages, by contrast, who take their end to consist in the activity of the rational part alone, make the rational part their principle of action by living according to its nature alone and treating the other parts of the organism as mere instruments for its activity. Since an individual's principle of action varies with his or her ethical state, the self in a descriptive sense will vary from individual to individual according to whether they make their principle of action reason alone or inclusive of their non-rational parts. But, in a normative sense, the self is for everyone the rational part of the human organism, since the rational part represents what is naturally in authority and the nature according to which we ought to live. Because other parts of the human organism are not constitutive of that nature, it is proper not to see them as parts of ourselves. This view that our true self is the rational part is based upon a teleological view of the structure of a human organism, according to which the activity of the rational part represents our proper final end.

My discussion falls into three main parts. In Part 1, I discuss some standard interpretations of the rational self view and introduce my alternative proposal that the Plotinian self should be understood as a principle of action. In Part 2, I argue, by way of a consideration of Plotinus' contrast between the sage and the politically virtuous man, that an agent's principle of action is the nature according to which an individual lives. Finally, in Part 3, I consider why the rational part of soul is by nature our proper principle of action in this sense, and propose that Plotinus takes this status to follow from its causal priority over the rest of the organism.

2 The criterion for the self

Before turning to the rational self view, it will be useful to begin by outlining Plotinus' account of the make-up of a human organism. This account is the result of Plotinus' attempt to synthesize various Platonic claims about the soul and body, and to integrate these claims with his theory that all other existents derive from a single first principle. Like Plato, Plotinus holds that the human soul is a non-bodily existent, and can be intellectually active in a disembodied state (*Phaed.* 66b–67b, 76c-e, 80d–81a; *Phaedr.* 247c–248e). In its embodied state, this soul consists of rational and non-rational parts (*Resp.* IV 435b–441c; 9, 580d–581a; *Timaeus* 41d–42b, 69c–70b). While other texts leave open whether both our rational and non-rational parts are part of the original constitution of soul, the *Timaeus* settles this question in favour of the view that the original and basic component of our psychic make-up is a purely rational soul that has a secondary, non-rational soul conjoined to it under conditions of embodiment in the sub-celestial region (*Timaeus* 41d–42b, 69c–70b; cf. *Phaedr.* 246a-b, 253c–254e; *Resp.* X 611a–612a).[5] This composite soul is suited by its nature to animate the body of a human organism, though ethical failings can lead to its transmigration into the bodies of non-human organisms.

Following the *Timaeus*, Plotinus takes both our rational soul and our non-rational soul to be generated by more divine causes. To explain how they are generated, Plotinus appeals to a causal theory that he uses to explain how all other existents derive from his first principle, the One (or the Good). According to this theory, the One stands at the head of a series of causes that each generate, as the by-product of their internal activity, a further entity that is a less perfect 'image' or 'likeness' of themselves.[6] This productive pattern is now known as 'emanation' or 'double activity'.[7] In this series, the One produces a self-thinking divine Intellect, whose substance and object of thought are the Platonic Forms, and this Intellect in turn produces a purely rational Soul, which includes individual rational souls as its parts. These purely rational souls then produce our non-rational soul-parts, which include our sense-perceptual and nutritive faculties.[8]

---

[5] On this point see Lorenz 2006, 37–38.
[6] For this productive series, see 5.1.5–7; 5.2.1–2; and 5.4.1–2. For the production of the physical cosmos in particular, see 3.4.1; 3.8.1–4; 3.9.3; and 4.3.4.
[7] For double activity in Plotinus see Emilsson 2007, 22–68.
[8] There is some unclarity about the provenance of the nutritive faculty, *phusis*, which imparts form to the bodies of rational organisms. Some passages suggest that this derives from the rational soul of the cosmos, but others that it may derive from other individual rational souls. For discussion of this issue see Wilberding 2008, 427 n. 67.

Finally, the nutritive faculty that belongs to one soul in particular, the World-Soul, is responsible for generating and imparting form to primary matter in order to produce the elemental bodies. The World-Soul constructs the body of the cosmos as a whole from these bodies and administers it, while our own souls, when in an embodied state, oversee an organic body that is a part of the cosmic body.

According to the resulting picture of the human organism, there is, on the soul side of the soul-body divide, (1) a primary, purely rational soul (henceforth, 'rational soul') that is both the conscious subject of reasoning and theoretical understanding and the primary bearer of the species-formula (*logos*) for life as a human being.[9] In addition, there is (2) a secondary, non-rational psychic entity (henceforth, 'lower soul') that is responsible for psychic functions that involve the body (1.1.7).[10] This lower soul is comprised of the faculty of sense-perception and a sub-conscious nutritive faculty, whose operations include the formation of spirited and appetitive desires. On the body side of the soul-body divide, there is (3) a suitable organic body that is constructed by the nutritive faculty and receives from it a qualification – the so-called 'soul-trace' – which is a formal cause of the body's vital attributes (4.4.18). This living body together with the lower soul that animates it are sometimes referred to as 'the composite' (*to sunamphoteron*). When our rational soul is in the sensible world and is conjoined with the composite, it no longer engages in the single-minded contemplation of the Forms that characterizes its disincarnate state. Nonetheless, Plotinus maintains that an aspect of this rational soul – which interpreters often call the 'undescended' or 'higher soul' – remains continuously active in the intelligible world, even though its activity is not ordinarily present to our empirical consciousness (2.9.2.4–10; 3.8.5.10–12; 4.8.8.1–3; 5.1.10.13–31).

In *Enn.* 1.1, *What is the Organism (to zōon), and What is the Human Being (ho anthrōpos)?*, Plotinus suggests that what 'we' and 'the human being' are in the strict sense is the rational part of soul (1), whereas our 'lower' non-rational parts (2) and (3) are merely 'ours'. This is the rational self view.

> (T1) From these [Platonic] Forms, from which the soul alone receives its lordship (*hêgemonian*) over the living being, come reasonings (*dianoiai*), and opinions (*doxai*) and acts of intuitive intelligence (*noêseis*); and this is precisely where 'we' are. That which comes be-

---

[9] Since Plotinus claims that it is possible for our souls to live, not just as a human being, but also as a non-rational animal or even as a plant, the soul acts in each of these cases according to a different species-formula (*logos*) (6.7.4–5); for the reincarnation of human beings as non-rational animals in Plato see *Phaedo* 81e–82b; *Republic* X 620a–d; *Timaeus* 91d–92c.
[10] For Plotinus' lower soul see Caluori 2015, 152–179.

fore this is 'ours' but 'we', in our presidency (*ephestêkotes*) over the living being, are what extends from this point upwards. But there will be no objection to calling this whole thing 'living being' (*zōon*); the lower parts of it are something mixed, the part which begins on the level of thought is (I suppose) *the true human being*: those lower parts are the 'lion-like' [i.e. the spirited part] and altogether the 'various beast' [i.e. the appetitive part] [Resp. IX 588b–589b]. Since the *human being* coincides with the rational soul, when we reason, it is really we who reason because rational processes are activities of soul. (1.1.7.14–24, emphases mine)[11]

In this passage, Plotinus refers the view that 'the true human being' is the rational part of the soul to Plato's image of the parts of soul in *Republic* IX 588c–590a, which presents the rational part as 'the man within', the spirited part as 'lion-like', and the appetitive part as a 'many-headed beast'. Plotinus' view here is also indebted to the *Alcibiades I*, in which Socrates asks what 'we' (128e, 129b) and the 'human being' (129e) are, and contends that we correspond to what rules or uses the body and is 'more authoritative' (*kuriōteron*) in the organism, i.e. the soul (130d), whereas the body merely belongs to us (131a). Later, Socrates appears to narrow this initial identification of ourselves from the soul to the soul's rational part in particular, on the grounds that this is the locus of its 'good activity' and 'wisdom' as well as its other virtues (133b-c).[12] In keeping with the *Alcibiades*' view, here in T1 Plotinus cites its affirmation of the rational soul's leadership role and its distinction between ourselves and our possessions. This debt to the *Alcibiades* is corroborated by other passages in which Plotinus identifies the self with soul or with rational soul because it is 'authoritative' (*kurion*) (4.4.18.10–21; 4.7.1.20–25; 5.3.3.35–40). This Platonic background offers some context for understanding Plotinus' identification of ourselves with the rational part of the embodied soul. In the *Republic* IX passage, Plato urges that the soul's rational part represents the best and the distinctively human part of our souls, and that we ought to cultivate it and establish its rule over our animal-like parts. Similarly, in the *Alcibiades I*, Socrates' larger purpose is to persuade Alcibiades to identify with and care for his rational part on the grounds that it is his best part and is best qualified to rule. Like his Platonic sources, Plotinus

---

11 All translations of Plotinus are from Armstrong 1966–1988 in the Loeb series, sometimes with modifications.
12 The view that Socrates narrows the identification of the human being to reason or intellect is defended by Denyer 2001, 218 and 234–5 and Joosse 2014, 10–16, but for a criticism of this interpretation see Wasmuth 2016, 64 and 84–91. Cf. also Aristotle's claims that every 'composite' (*sustêma*) is its "most authoritative part most of all" (*to kuriōtaton malist' einai*) (*EN* IX.8, 1168b28–34), and that "each person seems to be his understanding, if he is his authoritative and best element" (*EN* X.7, 1178a2–8; cf. *EN* IX.4, 1166a13–17; IX.8, 1169a1–3).

is encouraging us to shift our conception of who we are away from the human organism as a whole and to assign the rational part authority over our lives.

Plotinus, of course, recognizes that we typically speak of ourselves as the whole human organism. Though he does not repudiate this broader way of speaking about ourselves, he suggests that this ordinary way of speaking is associated with a mistaken conception of who we are.

> (T2) But we say that the composite entity [of non-rational soul and body] is part of ourselves, especially when we have not yet been separated from body: for we say that 'we' are affected by what affects our body. So 'we' is used in two senses, either as including 'the beast' or as referring to that which even in our present life transcends it. 'The beast' is the body which has been given life. But the true human being is different, and clear of these affections; he has the virtues which belong to the sphere of intellect and have their seat actually in the separate soul [i.e. rational soul], separate and separable even while it is still here below. (1.1.10.3–10)

Here Plotinus recognizes the ordinary way of identifying ourselves as the whole human organism, and notes that one basis for this standard sense of the 'self' is the familiar fact that we tend to describe ourselves "as being affected by what affects our body." Yet he also observes that this ordinary self-conception is particularly characteristic of non-sages, who have not yet 'separated' themselves from the body like the philosopher of the *Phaedo*, and he reaffirms his view that the 'the true human being' is to be identified with rational soul. So, while we may speak of ourselves as the whole human organism, in the strict and primary sense our selves correspond to rational soul.

Though Plotinus contends that 'we' and 'the true human being' are to be identified with rational soul, he also maintains that 'we' may become something divine or sub-human. An individual is, he claims, "that according to which he lives" (6.7.6.17–18; cf. 6.4.14.24–31, 15.18–40), and we determine what we are by directing our rational soul's activity 'upwards' to intellect or 'downwards' to the non-rational parts of the human organism (1.1.11.5–8). In the former case, an individual is said to "become the object of contemplation," i.e. an intellect (4.4.2.3–14). In the latter, an individual may become a compound of his rational part ('the good self') and the rest of the organism ('the evil other') (6.4.15.38–40), or the rest of the organism alone (6.4.14.29–31). This view that we can live either according to intellect or our non-rational parts is given a more expansive treatment in a discussion of the transmigration of souls in *Enn. 3.4, On Our Allotted Guardian Spirit*.

> (T3) Therefore one must 'escape' to the upper world, so that we do not sink to the level of sense-perception by pursuing the images of sense, or to the level of the growth-principle by following the urge for generation and the "gluttonous love of good eating," but may rise to

the intelligible and intellect and God. Those, then, who guarded the man in them, become men again. Those who lived by sense alone become animals [...] But if they did not even live by sense along with their desires but coupled them with dullness of perception, they even turn into plants; for it was this, the growth-principle which was active in them, alone or predominantly, and they were taking care to turn themselves into trees. [...] Who, then, becomes a spirit? He who was one here too. And who a god? Certainly he who was one here. For what was active in a man leads him [after death], since it was his ruler and guide here too. (3.4.2.12–17 [...] 3.1–3)

In this passage, Plotinus indicates that in our next embodiment 'we' will 'become' the sort of living thing whose form of life corresponds to the part or set of parts that is our 'ruler or guide' and 'active' in this life. But Plotinus suggests that a human being who makes his dominant principle one that is proper to some other living thing is already in this life effectively a living thing of that sort by having adopted its natural activity as its end. Since what we become in this life is said to be a function of the 'orientation' of our rational part, Plotinus' proposal that our perceptual or nutritive faculties may come to be in this dominant position is presumably to be understood as the view that in this life a rational soul may place these parts in authority by coming to endorse their ends as its own.[13]

A central challenge for interpreting the rational self view is to explain why the rational soul counts as the self. Interpreters have tended to respond to this challenge by connecting rational soul's status as the self with consciousness.[14] This approach provides a principled reason to identify the self with rational soul rather than some other psychic part or faculty, and appears to find support in Plotinus' claim that intellectual or sub-sensitive activities of soul only reach 'us' when they reach 'perception' or 'thought' (4.8.1.1–11; 8.3–13; 5.1.12.1–15).[15] Some interpreters take rational soul to be the self because it is a subject capable of consciousness and self-awareness. Other interpreters have proposed, alternatively or additionally, that rational soul is the self because it is a conscious subject that can acquire different identities through the activities it adopts. This latter interpretation offers an elegant way to account for the facts that Plotinus claims that 'we' are rational soul, and yet that individual human agents may 'become' something more or less than reason: 'we' refers rigidly to the rational soul

---

13 This proposal takes a stance on how parts of the soul other than reason may come to rule in the soul of a human organism, namely, in virtue of reason's judgments or attitudes concerning the desires of our non-rational parts, rather than simply by an increase in the 'strength' of the desires in our non-rational parts relative to those of reason; cf. *Republic* VIII and IX.
14 For references see n. 3 and n. 4.
15 For these passages and rational soul's role in integrating our conscious experiences see Magrin 2015, 12–19.

or one of its powers, and what 'we' become are the substantive identities that this conscious subject acquires. In addition, this approach can accommodate Plotinus' programmatic claims that the self is what is in authority, insofar as the rational soul is ultimately responsible for determining the identity that we adopt.

There are, however, some reasons to be sceptical of readings that take Plotinus to identify our self with rational soul because it is a conscious subject of a certain sort. To begin with, though Plotinus maintains in T3 that the self in a descriptive sense can differ for different individuals, Plotinus' identification of the rational soul as what 'we' *really* are and as the 'true human being' is clearly intended to imply that we ought to identify ourselves with our rational part. This idea is especially prominent in his contrast between the sage's self-identification with reason and the non-sage's self-identification with the whole human organism. And Plotinus' contrast between the rational soul as the 'good self' and our non-rational parts as 'the evil other' confirms that the notion of the rational self is normatively loaded, and that this self is something with which an agent can and should identify (6.4.15.38–40). Yet, if the notion of the self is that of a conscious subject without a determinate identity, it is difficult to see how this notion can have the normative implication that we ought to identify with the rational part of soul. Moreover, and relatedly, it is unclear how readings that tie the rational self view to consciousness could represent a Plotinian construal of his Platonic sources. As we have seen, in claiming that the rational soul is the self, Plotinus appeals to Plato's claims that our rational part best represents our human nature, and that we are to be identified with the part that is authoritative in the sense that it is best suited to rule. But neither the programmatic passages where Plotinus distinguishes the self from what is not part of our self but external to it, nor the Platonic sources he cites, suggest that our self is defined by consciousness or by the capacity of that conscious subject to determine our identity.

In addition, there is reason to doubt the proposal that 'we' rigidly designates our rational part, and that 'we' become different in virtue of its acquisition of a new identity. Since rational soul is by nature a potential intellect, Plotinus can indeed claim that rational soul can become an actual intellect. But in the case of our non-rational parts – i.e. the perceptual and nutritive faculties of soul – it is harder to see how rational soul might be said actually to become these parts or to come to perform their activities, even if we 'become' something different through the assimilation of reason's goals to those of these non-rational parts. Plotinus' account of transmigration also calls into question the idea that rational soul determines what we are by acquiring a new identity. In *Enn.* 3.4, Plotinus contends that an individual's *daimōn* is a principle that presides in an inactive state over the principle that is active in an organism, so that, if, for example, a soul's active principle is sense-perception, then its *daimōn* is reason (3.4.3.3–20).[16] This suggests that, when our souls transmigrate into the body of a non-human animal, the rational part becomes the inactive *daimōn* and the active and ruling principle becomes the faculty of sense-perception. In such cases, 'we' acquire a new identity in our next embodiment, and cease to be human beings, not by reason itself changing its identity, but rather by a part other than reason coming to occupy the functional role of the dominant or ruling part of the organism. So, though it is true that the orientation of our rational soul and the orientation of its thoughts determines what we are in this life, it is not true that 'we' rigidly designates rational soul. Rather, Plotinus' general view is that what we are in this embodied life and what we become in the next is a function of the part of soul that plays the role of directing our actions, and in the case of non-human animals, the part of soul that plays this functional role will necessarily be a part of soul below reason. In explaining changes in the identity of the self, Plotinus thus identifies the self with what occupies a functional role rather than with a determinate but plastic subject.

There is, I think, another, more attractive way to explain why Plotinus takes the rational soul to represent our self. In a number of passages in the *Enneads*, Plotinus suggests that the self is what functions as one's principle of action. The evidence that this is indeed Plotinus' criterion for selfhood arises in two contexts. First, Plotinus sometimes suggests that soul, and more specifically rational soul, represents the self because it is by nature in authority. At 4.7.1.20–25, he contends that, by contrast with an organism's body, the soul is 'most authoritative' (*kuriōtaton*) and that, because it has this status, it is the human being 'himself'. This initial identification of the self with the soul is later, at 4.4.18.10–21, refined to the claim that 'we' are specifically the soul's rational part, and Plotinus again rationalizes this claim by stating that 'we' refers to what is "in a position of authority" (*kata to kurion*). This view is reaffirmed at 5.3.3.35–40, which claims that "we are this, the authoritative part (*to kurion*) of soul."[17] In these pas-

---

[16] Plotinus interprets an individual's guardian spirit (*daimōn*), not as a fixed and determinate part of soul, but as whatever plays the functional role of presiding over the dominant or active part of soul; on which, see Adamson 2017. Likewise, in an individual soul, just as the part of soul that plays the role of the *daimōn*, the part of soul that is dominant or active may change over time. In a human organism this dominant part of the composite embodied soul is by nature rational soul, though Plotinus makes clear in *Enn.* 3.4 that rational soul can effectively cede some or all of its natural authority to our non-rational parts.

[17] See also Plotinus' claim that if 'we' were mere parts of the World-Soul, so that our actions were determined by it, then "we are not ourselves, nor is there any act which is our own" (3.1.4.12–24); this passage suggests that being able to be in charge of our own actions is a necessary condition for being a self.

sages, Plotinus is clearly relying upon the view of *Alcibiades I* that we are our authoritative part. Though it is true that this part of soul is conscious, and so, that states of soul reach 'us' by becoming conscious states of rational soul, Plotinus' programmatic statements strongly suggest that his criterion for being the self is to be in authority rather than to be a conscious subject. Secondly, in addition to claiming that the rational soul is the self, Plotinus suggests that in practice the self for an individual varies with the part that is in charge of his or her actions. He contends that an individual is "that according to which he lives" (6.7.6.17–18; cf. 6.4.14.24–31, 15.18–40), and in *Enn.* 3.4 proposes that in the case of some individuals the part of soul that plays this role may even be the sense-perceptual or nutritive faculties of soul, when these set the ends for an individual. The common denominator of these claims is that the self is identified with whatever part of soul occupies the role of our principle of action. On the basis of this view, there is a fairly straightforward way to reconcile Plotinus' claims *both* that the self is our rational part *and* that the self for an individual may be an intellect or a sub-rational part of soul. Namely, the part of soul that is by nature our principle of action is our rational part (the self in a normative sense), yet in individual cases some part of soul inferior to reason may in practice function as an agent's principle of action (the self in a descriptive sense).[18] These claims are not in conflict, and indeed the normative idea that our true self is rational soul is the natural complement of the descriptive claim that an individual may (mistakenly) make something other than reason his principle of action. In the next section, I will offer additional support for this proposal and discuss what it means to be a principle of action by focusing on Plotinus' contrast between the sage and the individual with political virtue.

3 What a principle of action is

In the preceding section, I have proposed that Plotinus' criterion for the self is our principle of action, and that this criterion for the self is employed both in a normative sense, to refer to our proper principle of action, and in a descriptive sense, to refer to what serves as the actual principle of action for an individual. My goal in this section will be to clarify what Plotinus means by a principle of action. I will suggest that, for Plotinus, something qualifies as part of our prin-

---

18 In treating rational soul as our principle of action, Plotinus cannot be expressing the intellectualist view, accepted by Socrates and the Stoics, that our actions are invariably determined by judgments of rational soul. For, in that case, contrary to Plotinus' claims, it would never be true that something other than rational soul serves as a human organism's principle of action.

ciple of action, not by being the ultimate arbiter of our actions, but by being the nature according to which an agent lives.[19] This conception of a principle of action helps to clarify why Plotinus thinks that it is reasonable to identify one's principle of action as one's nature. In what follows, I will attempt to defend this interpretation of Plotinus' conception of a principle of action by focusing on his contrast between the sage and the man of political virtue.

In *Enn.* 1.2, *On Virtues*, Plotinus distinguishes between two grades of virtue: (1) inferior, practically oriented 'political virtues', which correspond to the virtues of *Republic* IV, and (2) superior, theoretically oriented virtues, known as 'purifications', that are identified with the virtues of the philosopher in the *Phaedo* and enable us to achieve the goal of 'godlikeness' presented in the *Theaetetus*.[20]

> (T4) Plato, when he speaks of 'likeness' [to God] as a 'flight to God' [*Theaet.* 176a-b] from existence here below, and does not call the virtues which come into play in communal life just 'virtues', but adds the qualification 'political' [*Resp.* IV 430c], and elsewhere calls all the virtues 'purifications' [*Phaed.* 69b-c], makes clear that he postulates two kinds of virtue and does not regard the political ones as producing likeness. (1.2.3.5–10)

This distinction is derived from the *Phaedo*'s contrast between the true virtues of philosophers ('purifications') and 'popular or political' virtue (*Phaed.* 64b–69d; 82a-b). But Plotinus finds evidence for the same distinction internal to the *Republic*. The description of the courage of the military class at *Resp.* IV 403c, as 'political' courage, together with the characterization of the philosopher-ruler as a craftsman of 'popular' virtue in the city at *Resp.* VI 500d, suggests to him that the political virtues referred to in the *Phaedo* are those described in *Republic* IV. This last passage, with its implicit contrast between true and 'popular' virtue, together with the claim that the introduction of knowledge of Forms results in "a still finer city and human being" (*Resp.* VII 543c-d), may also have suggested to Plotinus that the account of the virtues earlier in the *Republic* has been superseded by those of the philosopher, viz. by the purely intellectual virtues of the *Phaedo*.[21] Accordingly, following the *Republic*'s definitions of the virtues, Plotinus

---

[19] As we will see below, the Platonic ideal – suggested by *Republic* IV – that reason rule over the non-rational parts by determining the action to be performed is not sufficient to make reason an agent's principle of action in Plotinus' sense. For, if in performing this role reason identifies our good with a state of the whole soul, and lives according to its nature, then our non-rational parts are part of our principle of action by co-determining our final end.

[20] On the distinction between these grades of virtue and on its Platonic sources, see Dillon 1983, 92–105; Brittain 2003, 227–247; O'Meara 2005, 40–49; and Cooper 2012, 341–363.

[21] The relevance of the *Republic* VII passage was suggested to me by Dominic Scott.

holds that the political virtues are defined as a set of virtues that involve both the rational and non-rational parts of soul.

> (T5) [...] Practical Wisdom [*phronêsis*] in the reasoning part, Courage in the spirited part, Moderation in a certain agreement and harmony of the appetitive part with reason, Justice which makes each of these parts agree in "minding their own business where ruling and being ruled are concerned." [*Resp.* IV 427e–434d] (1.2.1.16–21)

By contrast, he treats the 'purifications' as intellectual virtues that belong exclusively to the rational soul, and as characterizing different conditions of a rational soul that grasps the Platonic Forms.

> (T6) Theoretical and Practical Wisdom [*sophia kai phronêsis*] consists in the contemplation of that which intellect contains. [...] So the higher Justice in the soul is its activity towards intellect, its Moderation is its inward turning to intellect, its Courage is its freedom from affections, according to the likeness of that to which it looks, which is free from affections by nature. (1.2.6.12–13 [...] 22–27)[22]

Plotinus' decision to limit the wisdom of the politically virtuous man to 'practical wisdom' (*phronêsis*) indicates that this individual has a kind of practical expertise that is not based in a theoretical understanding of the Forms. By contrast, his description of the sage as possessing "theoretical and practical wisdom" (*sophia kai phronêsis*), together with the fact that all of the other virtues are described in terms of reason's relation to the Forms, suggests that his practical wisdom does consist in his understanding of the Forms. It is also significant that the sage's 'purificatory' virtue has his rational soul as its subject, whereas the politically virtuous man's 'political' virtue has both his rational and non-rational soul as its subject. As we will see presently, this difference in the psychic subject of these different types of virtue reflects the sage's and the politically virtuous man's differing conceptions of the human good. In particular, in keeping with the idea that our good consists in the activity according to virtue, the sage's virtue belongs to his rational part alone because he identifies his good with an activity of rational soul, whereas the politically virtuous man's virtue pertains to

---

[22] That 'purifications' of 'soul' are states of reason specifically is confirmed by the subsequent contrast between these and the secondary purification of our 'non-rational part': "The soul will be pure in all these ways and will want to make the non-rational part, too, pure, so that this part may not be disturbed" (1.2.5.21–23); cf. the *Phaedo* (79a–84b) and *Timaeus* (41d–42b; cf. 35a–37c) for a usage whereby 'the soul' of a human being appears to refer to a purely rational substance.

his whole embodied soul because he identifies his good with an activity that belongs to both rational and non-rational soul.

The idea that the sage lives according to his rational part alone can be explained by reference to his view that his good consists exclusively in theoretical activity.

> (T7) If then the good life belongs to what has a superabundance of life (this means what is in no way deficient in life), *eudaimonia* will belong only to the being which lives superabundantly: this will have the best, if the best among realities is being really alive, is perfect life. [...] We have often said that the perfect life, the true, real life, is in that transcendent intelligible reality, and that other lives are *incomplete, traces of life*, not perfect or pure and no more life than its opposite. (1.4.3.23–29 [...] 33–41, my emphasis)

In this passage, Plotinus claims that the activity of the divine Intellect is the only mode of life that represents *eudaimonia* since only this primary form of life meets Aristotle's formal requirement that *eudaimonia* be something perfect or complete (*teleion*; cf. *EN* I.7, 1097a24–b5).[23] By contrast, other forms of life-activity, as mere images (or 'traces') of this life-activity, are incomplete or deficient, and so do not represent forms or parts of *eudaimonia*. Certainly, these other life-activities involve some form of goodness, but Plotinus does not think that having these qualitatively inferior activities, in addition to having the best possible activity, makes for a better overall life. According to this view, if a human being is going to acquire *eudaimonia*, he must do so by somehow acquiring this same activity.

> (T8) It is obvious from what has been said elsewhere that man has perfect life by having not only sense-life, but reasoning and true intelligence. But is he different from this when he has it? No, he is not a human being at all unless he has this, either potentially or actually (and if he has it actually, we say he is in the state of *eudaimonia*). But shall we say that he has this perfect kind of life in him as a part of himself? Other men, we maintain, who have it potentially, have it as a part, but the man who was well-off, who actually is this and has passed over into identity with it, is it. (1.4.4.7–16)

Here Plotinus contends that our rational souls can come to acquire this divine activity, and indeed can come to be this activity. His claim that the souls of human beings all initially have this perfect activity both potentially and as a part appears to refer to his doctrine that rational soul is by nature a potential intellect, and that soul actualizes this potentiality by coming to apprehend the

---

[23] Plotinus also contends that this form of life fulfills Aristotle's formal requirement that our final end be 'self-sufficient' (*autarkês*) (1.4.4.23–25, 5.22–24; cf. *EN* I.7, 1097b6–21); on this point see Gerson 2012, 19–20.

intellectual activity of its undescended part. Since Plotinus has identified well-being (*eudaimonia*) with this intellectual activity, the well-being of the sage, who acquires this intellectual activity, just consists in that activity of his rational soul. As suggested above, this position accords well with the idea that the sage's virtues consist exclusively in theoretical knowledge. Since the human good is identified with the theoretical activity of thinking the Forms, the corresponding virtues are aspects of this theoretical understanding.

Of course, the sage will continue to engage in certain practical activities. Still, the sage does not regard these activities as parts of his good, but at best 'necessary' and for the sake of something else.

> (T9) [continues T8] Everything else [viz. other than rational soul] is just something he wears [cf. *Phaedo* 87b–88b]; you could not call it a part of him because he wears it without wanting to; it would be his if it were united to him by an act of will. What then is the good for him? He is what he has, his own good [...] What he seeks, he seeks as a necessity, not for himself but for something that belongs to him; that is, he seeks it for the body which is joined to him; and even granting that this is a living body, it lives its own life and not the life which is that of the good man. (1.4.4.15–19 [...] 25–29)

Since, for Plotinus, the sage's superior, purificatory kind of practical wisdom consists in his theoretical knowledge, this knowledge directs his actions in the practical sphere. And, presumably, if the sage sees these actions as 'necessary', it is because his knowledge implies a recognition that certain actions are obligatory for someone in his situation. But his view that these activities are merely necessary rather than good reflects the idea that these practical activities are not part of his final end, i.e. *eudaimonia*. In reserving the designation 'good' for the sage's theoretical activity, Plotinus follows an established practice of restricting the term 'good' to things that have the sort of value that makes them contribute positively to our final end.[24]

Unlike the sage, the politically virtuous man does take certain practical activities to be constitutive of his own good.

> (T10) [...] if one carries out the so-called 'fine' [practical] activities as 'necessary' ones, and grasps that what is really fine is something else, one has not been enchanted – for one knows the necessity, and does not look to this world, and one's life is not directed to other things – but one has been enchanted in this way by the force of human nature and by appropriating (*oikeiōsis*) the life of others and also of oneself [...] for to pursue

---

[24] The thesis that only what contributes to or detracts from our happiness counts as good or bad has a precedent in Plato at *Euthyd.* 278e–282d and *Meno* 87d–89a, and is accepted by Stoics and Aristotelians; on this see Cooper 1985, 190–192.

what is not good as if it were good, drawn by the appearance of good by non-rational impulses, belongs to one who is led ignorantly to where he does not want to go. (4.4.44.18–23 [...] 31–32)

This passage, which contrasts the practical outlook of the sage with that of the non-sage, sheds some light upon Plotinus' view that practically oriented virtue includes states of the non-rational parts of soul. In keeping with the definitions of the virtues in *Republic* IV, the politically virtuous man must have a rational part that plays a dominant role in guiding our actions, the non-rational parts of soul must play some role in generating virtuous actions. Here Plotinus gives some indication of how this might be the case. Unlike the sage, the politically virtuous man views practical activity as 'fine' and as constitutive of the good life, and it is suggested here that an individual comes to have this attitude because his non-rational parts are the source of the belief that these activities are good.

This contrast between the sage and the politically virtuous man helps to clarify what Plotinus means by a principle of action, and why one's principle of action counts as the self. Since the sage, who identifies his good with theoretical activity, lives by the theoretical virtues of his rational part, he lives according to the nature of rational soul. Accordingly, the sage regards the parts of the human organism other than reason not as part of himself, but just as "something that he wears" (from T9). By contrast, since the politically virtuous man, who identifies his good with practical activity, lives by practical virtues of both the rational and non-rational parts of soul, he lives according to the nature of both his rational and his non-rational parts. In keeping with that mode of life, this individual is, and regards himself as, the whole soul or as the human organism. So in both the case of the sage and that of the politically virtuous man, their principle of action is the nature according to which each lives, and in so doing, each treats (and regards) that part of the organism as what they are.

In the next section, I will consider why it is correct, as the sage does, to treat rational soul as our principle of action in this sense. But first I would like to touch upon a problem that might be thought to arise from Plotinus' claim that the rational soul represents our self. This idea might seem to be in tension with Plotinus' suggestions that we should become something divine by assimilating ourselves to an intellect that thinks the Platonic Forms.[25] If being an intellect is our 'ideal' self, then how can our rational part also be what we really are? T2 suggests a reply to this puzzle. There Plotinus moves seamlessly between an

---

[25] For intellect as the 'real' or 'ideal' self, see O'Daly 1973, 25–26 and Remes 2007, 126. For the claim that 'we' are intellect, see 1.4.9.28–30.

identification of ourselves with our rational part (what "transcends 'the beast'": 1.10.6–10) and with our rational part in its intellectualized state, when it has been assimilated to intellect ("the true human being is different, clear of these affections; he has the virtues which belong to the sphere of intellect": 1.1.10–14). So Plotinus does not appear to take being our rational part and being an intellect to represent competing ideals, and, indeed, this position is a natural one for him to adopt. Our rational soul is by nature a potential intellect, and becoming an intellect is just for our rational soul to fully realize its own intellectual nature. If, like the sage, we come to make rational soul our ruling principle by orienting its activity towards our intellect, then our identification with our rational part will coincide with this rational part becoming an actual intellect. For this reason, Plotinus need not see identifying ourselves with our rational part and identifying ourselves with an intellect as representing distinct and competing normative ideals.[26]

4 Why is rational soul our proper principle of action?

In Part 1, I proposed that Plotinus identifies an individual's self with the principle of action. In Part 2, I maintained that, for Plotinus, something counts as a principle of action for an individual just in case that individual lives according to its nature, and that this conception of a principle of action makes intelligible the view that our principle of action represents who we are. But why does Plotinus think that rational soul is our proper principle of action in this sense, i.e. why we ought to live according to the nature of reason exclusively? After all, a human organism is a single living thing unified by an account (*logos*) that derives from the Form of a human being, so it is plausible to think that the whole organism represents our nature. Even if rational soul is the original and fundamental part of the whole human organism, and is the best part of this whole, it is not obvious that this should imply that it is right for us to live according to the nature of the rational part exclusively.

---

[26] In T3, Plotinus suggests that rational soul's realization of its own rational nature by its orientation towards 'higher' causes can even lead it to transcend human nature and become a spirit or a god. Presumably, in such cases, rational soul counts as something more than human because its intellectual perfection suits it to live a life superior to that of overseeing a human organism.

In taking the view that it is proper to live according to the nature of rational soul, Plotinus may be relying on an assumption that the function or end of a complex whole belongs to its essential part. In *Enn*. 6.7, Plotinus identifies a human being with the essential part of a human organism. Plotinus contends that the essence for a human being (*to einai anthrōpōi*) is that "which has made this man here below [i.e. the lower soul-body 'composite'], which exists in him and is not separate," and then goes on to claim that what plays this role is a rational soul operating with the species-formula (*logos*) for a human being (6.7.4.1–5.11).[27] Significantly, in this discussion, Plotinus assumes that the form or essence for a human being (*to einai anthrōpōi*) is simply equivalent to the human being (*ho anthrōpos*). Though Plotinus does not explain here why the human being should be identified with this essence, a reason for this view may be suggested by an appeal to the *Alcibiades I* in the immediate context. Plotinus contends that his definition of the human being agrees with Plato's definition of the human being in the *Alcibiades I* as what "uses the body" on the grounds that rational soul is the ultimate user of the body:

> (T11) But the man over this one belongs to a soul [i.e. rational soul] already more divine which has a better man and clearer senses. And this would be the human being Plato was defining, and by adding "using a body" he indicated that it rides upon the one which primarily uses a body [i.e. lower-soul], and the one which does so secondarily is more divine. (6.7.5.21–25)

In the *Alcibiades I*, Plato offers two prime examples of the identification of the 'self' with the essential part of a complex whole: the identification of 'the human being' with the soul that uses the body as its instrument, and the identification of the eye itself, not with the whole structure, but with the pupil, in which its 'good activity' occurs. In both cases, Socrates identifies the end of the whole with an activity of the causally primary part, and takes the other parts to be ancillary or instrumental to its end (129b–133c). Plotinus similarly appears to take the ultimate function or end for a thing to correspond to the activity that belongs exclusively to its essential part, on the assumption that the other parts will stand to their cause as its instruments (1.1.4.18–20; 1.4.16.20–29; 6.7.5.24).[28] On this picture, then, there is an intimate connection between rational

---

[27] For this definition of the human being, see Hadot 1987, 216–222 and Aubry 2008b, 275–276. Since, as noted above, rational soul generates the lower soul by emanation, and this lower soul constructs the body, rational soul would appear to be both the formal cause of the human organism as a whole and the efficient cause of its other parts.

[28] For Plotinus, our non-rational parts may also exist for the sake of rational soul's purposes. But, presumably, they do not exist for the sake of the agent's own final end, theoretical activity,

soul's status as essence of the human organism, and the view that we should identify ourselves exclusively with this part. Because our final end is by nature the activity of the essential part of the human organism, and the other parts are merely instrumental to its activity, it is proper for us to live according to the nature of rational soul alone.

Plotinus may also take the causal priority of the essential part of the human organism to imply that its activity qualifies as our final end in another way. As we saw in T7, Plotinus thinks that the perfect or complete activity that qualifies as *eudaimonia* consists in the activity of intellect, and that this activity is available to us because our own souls can engage in the same sort of intellectual activity. By contrast, other vital activities of the organism do not qualify as parts of our *eudaimonia* because they represent deficient forms of the perfect vitality of rational soul's intellectual activity: "the perfect life, the true, real life, is in that transcendent intelligible reality, and [...] other lives are incomplete, traces of life, not perfect or pure and no more life than its opposite" (from T7). Since our non-rational parts possess a deficient or imperfect form of life, it is hard to see how their activities could add in any way to the completeness or perfection of the life that is *eudaimonia*. Given this conception of our end, *eudaimonia*, as rational life, it is proper for us to identify the nature according to which we live as our rational part. The following text supports this proposal that Plotinus' identification of our human nature with rational soul is based in the superior value of its activity:

> (T12) A human being, and especially a good human being, is not the composite of soul and body; separation from the body and despising of its so-called goods make this plain. It is absurd to maintain that well-being (eudaimonia) extends as far as the living body, since well-being is the good life, which is concerned with soul and is an activity of soul, and not of all of it – for it is not an activity of the growth-soul, which would bring it into connection with body. (1.4.14.1–8)

---

which is most readily achieved when rational soul is dissociated from these parts. Plotinus' claim that the sage's practical activities are performed as necessities rather than as good – i.e. as part of our end – suggests that the rational soul would prefer to engage in theoretical activity exclusively, if possible. So it seems that any other parts of the organism, if their capacities are teleologically oriented to the purposes of the rational part, must be for the sake of the practical purposes that are 'necessary' for soul to perform rather than as activities that are part of its final end proper. For the view that both soul's theoretical activity and its 'practical' activity of imparting rational order to the cosmos are both 'essential functions' of Plotinian souls, see Caluori 2005, 75–93.

In this passage, Plotinus denies that the human being could be the soul-body composite on the grounds that *eudaimonia* does not include the so-called goods of the body. And he also indicates that *eudaimonia* cannot include the activities of our nutritive faculty, given the inferiority of its activity, which is made evident by its orientation towards the body's welfare. Since Plotinus suggests here that certain parts of the organism cannot be part of the human being because their activities or states are not included in *eudaimonia*, he appears to hold that the identification of the human being with rational soul is an implication of its axiological priority. It is worth noting that this axiological priority of rational soul is a consequence of the way in which rational soul is causally prior to the rest of the organism. As Plotinus puts it in T7, the life of our non-rational parts does not qualify as part of *eudaimonia* because they are mere 'traces' of the life enjoyed by rational soul, and this status of our sub-rational soul-parts as mere 'traces' of life is a corollary of the fact that the rational soul produces them by emanation. For when a cause produces its product by emanation, that product is a mere image of its cause and its activity possesses the character and value of that cause in only an attenuated form. So the sort of axiological priority that makes the activity of rational soul alone our final end, and that grounds our identification of ourselves with this part, is a consequence of the special sort of causally priority that rational soul has to the rest of the organism.

5 Conclusion

This paper began with the question why Plotinus thinks that we are only the rational part of the organism. In response to this question, I have made several points. First, I proposed that, contrary to the prevailing view, the relevant notion of the self is not that of a conscious subject that is self-aware or that acquires our identity. In addition to a lack of clear evidence that consciousness serves as Plotinus' criterion for selfhood, this approach has difficulty capturing the normative force of the rational self view, or of explaining how Plotinus could have found this idea in the Platonic texts that he treats as lending authority to this view. Instead, our most explicit evidence indicates that Plotinus, following the *Alcibiades I*, takes being a principle of action to be his criterion for being a self. Second, by focusing on Plotinus' treatment of the sage and the politically virtuous person, I argued that for Plotinus an agent's principle of action is the nature according to which an agent lives, so that it is intelligible that an individual's principle of action should be identified as who they are. Finally, I proposed that rational soul is by nature the nature according to which we *ought to* live because it is teleologically prior to the other parts of the organism, and suggested that this teleological priority is a consequence of its causal priority, in two ways. First, Plotinus holds that the proper end of the human organism belongs to rational soul because it is the cause of the human organism by being its essence, with the result that its other parts are mere instruments whose activities are not part of our final end. Secondly, because rational soul acts as the efficient cause of the other psychic faculties of the organism by emanation, the forms of vitality that constitute these psychic faculties, as mere 'images' of the vitality that belongs to rational soul, are deficient in a way that disqualifies their activities from being constituents of our final end.

It is worth noting that this conception of our natures may differ in important ways from the Platonic and Aristotelian views with which it has affinities. As noted above, Plato in the *Republic* suggests that the rational part corresponds in some sense to our humanity, while the *Alcibiades I* claims that the human being himself is the whole soul, and might be taken to suggest that our humanity might be more narrowly identified with reason. Similarly, Aristotle proposes that 'we' are our rational part, either without qualification or most or all. But despite these points of similarity, Plato, in the *Republic*, and Aristotle, in the *Nicomachean Ethics*, are generally thought to treat our nature as including more than our reasoning part, and to take living according to our nature to include the activities of soul-parts that are non-rational or that share in rationality in only an extended sense. For Plotinus, as for Plato and Aristotle, it is accepted that our end is an activity according to our nature. But Plotinus' conception of our nature as reason proper is more restrictive than that suggested by some Platonic and Aristotelian passages, and reflects his view that only the life of reason qualifies as our end. This more restrictive conception of the self may be traced, I have suggested, to Plotinus' view that rational soul is causally prior to the rest of the human organism given that he takes this causal priority to have the implication that rational soul's activity alone is constitutive of our final end.

Primary literature

Plato. 2001. *Plato: Alcibiades*, translation by Nicholas Denyer. Cambridge: Cambridge University Press.
Plotinus. 1966–1988. *Plotinus: The Enneads*, 7 Vols. translated by Arthur H. Armstrong. Cambridge (MA): Loeb Classical Library.
Plotinus. 1987. *Plotin: Traité 38 (VI,7)*, by Pierre Hadot. Paris: Cerf.

Secondary literature

Adamson, Peter. 2017. "'Present without Being Present': Plotinus on Plato's *Daimon*." In *Rereading Ancient Philosophy: Old Chestnuts and Sacred Cows*, edited by Verity Harte and Raphael Woolf, 257–75. Cambridge: Cambridge University Press.
Aubry, Gwenaëlle. 2008a. "Un moi sans identité? Le *hêmeis* plotinien." In *Le moi et l'intériorité*, edited by Gwenaëlle Aubry and Frédérique Ildefonse, 107–127. Paris: Vrin.
Aubry, Gwenaëlle. 2008b. "Individuation, particularization et détermination." *Phronesis* 53:271–289.
Banner, Nicholas. 2017. "The Indeterminate Self and its Cultivation in Plotinus." In *Selfhood and the Soul: Essays on Ancient Thought and Literature in Honour of Christopher Gill*, edited by Richard Seaford, John Wilkins, and Matthew Wright, 139–160. Oxford: Oxford University Press.
Brittain, Charles. 2003. "Attention Deficit in Plotinus and Augustine: Psychological Problems in Christian and Platonist Theories of the Grades of Virtue." *Proceedings of the Boston Area Colloquium in Ancient Philosophy* 18:223–263.
Caluori, Damian. 2005. "The Essential Functions of a Plotinian Soul." *Rhizai* 2:75–93.
Caluori, Damian. 2015. *Plotinus on the Soul*. Cambridge: Cambridge University Press.
Chiaradonna, Riccardo and Massimo Marraffa. 2018. "Ontology and the Self: Ancient and Contemporary Perspectives." *Discipline Filosofiche* 28:33–64.
Cooper, John M. 1985. "Aristotle on the Goods of Fortune." *Philosophical Review* 94:173–196.
Cooper, John M. 2012. *Pursuits of Wisdom: Six Ways of Life in Ancient Philosophy from Socrates to Plotinus*. Princeton, NJ: Princeton University Press.
Dillon, John M. 1983. "Plotinus, Philo and Origen on the Grades of Virtue." In *Platonismus und Christentum: Festschrift für Heinrich Dörrie*, edited by Horst-Dieter Blume and Friedhelm Mann, 92–105. Münster: Westfalen.
Dodds, Eric R. 1960. "Tradition and Personal Achievement in the Philosophy of Plotinus." *The Journal of Roman Studies* 50:1–7.
Emilsson, Eyjólfur K. 2007. *Plotinus on Intellect*. Oxford: Oxford University Press.
Emilsson, Eyjólfur K. 2017. *Plotinus*. New York: Routledge.
Gerson, Lloyd P. 1994. *Plotinus*. New York: Routledge.
Gerson, Lloyd P. 2012. "Plotinus on Happiness." *Journal of Ancient Philosophy* 6:1–21.
Gill, Christopher. 2006. *The Structured Self in Hellenistic and Roman Thought*. Oxford: Oxford University Press.
Hutchinson, Daniel M. 2018. *Plotinus on Consciousness*. Cambridge: Cambridge University Press.
Joosse, Albert. 2014. "Dialectic and Who We Are in the *Alcibiades*." *Phronesis* 59:1–21.
Lorenz, Hendrik. 2006. *The Brute Within: Appetitive Desire in Plato and Aristotle*. Oxford: Oxford University Press.
Magrin, Sara. 2015. "Plotinus on the Inner Sense." *British Journal for the History of Philosophy* 23:1–24.
O'Daly, Gerald. 1973. *Plotinus' Philosophy of the Self*. Shannon: Irish University Press.
O'Meara, Dominic. 2005. *Platonopolis: Platonic Political Philosophy in Late Antiquity*. Oxford: Oxford University Press.

Remes, Pauliina. 2007. *Plotinus on Self: The Philosophy of the 'We'*. Cambridge: Cambridge University Press.
Wasmuth, Ellisif. 2016. *Self-knowledge in Alcibiades I*. Cambridge University Ph.D. dissertation.
Wilberding, James. 2008. "Plotinus and Porphyry on the Seed." *Phronesis* 53:406–432.

Miira Tuominen
On Justice in Porphyry's *On Abstinence*

Abstract: This essay explores the notion of justice that emerges from Porphyry's arguments for abstinence from harming living beings. It first contrasts a notion of justice that includes non-human animals in its scope with another tradition in ancient philosophy, in which justice is restricted not only to human beings but to the citizens (*politai*) who share a community. Against this background, it is then argued that, although in a sense Porphyry takes the essence of justice to consist in the inner organization of the human soul so that reason leads and the irrational follows, he also lays great weight on the manifestation of inner justice in external action as restraint from injuring harmless living beings. Restraint from causing harm to living beings is argued to be constitutive of the higher degrees of justice, while the inner harmony of the soul and moderation pertaining to the tripartite soul is sufficient for a lower degree of justice.

1 The topic and aim of this chapter

In this essay, I shall explore the notion of justice that emerges from Porphyry's arguments for abstinence from harming living beings. I shall do so by first briefly contrasting a notion that includes non-human animals in its scope with another important tradition in ancient philosophy in which justice is restricted not only to human beings but to the citizens (*politai*) of a structured community or to the community (*polis*) itself. Against this background, I shall then argue that although Porphyry takes the essence of justice to consist in the inner organization of the human soul so that reason leads and the irrational follows, he also lays great weight on the manifestation of inner justice in external action as restraint from injuring harmless living beings. He insists that such restraint from injustice, as he also calls it, must be extended beyond the human species if one wishes to attain assimilation to god. As the reference to assimilation to god indicates, Porphyry does not claim that all justice would require restraint from causing harm to others from all people. Rather, abstinence from injuring living creatures is only required from such philosophers who aim at assimilating themselves to god that is the highest goal for a human being. Justice in this sense also is only possible to such philosophers because it requires knowledge about the true nature of justice that is acquired by a steady devotion to theoretical work. Moreover, against the objection that such wide extension of justice weakens and even breaks it down, Porphyry rather asserts that extending justice to non-human animals and plants makes justice stronger. Such an external manifestation of inner justice in abstinence from harming others is not political in the sense of being related to joint deliberation and action of people in a structured community. Neither is it political in the sense of requiring a constitution of a city that reflects or is isomorphic to the inner justice in the soul.

2 Justice in a *polis*

There is an influential discussion in ancient philosophical schools that articulates a political notion of justice. By justice being 'political' I mean, in this context, that it is in an important way related to joint deliberation and action in a structured community of human beings, a *polis*. One clear formulation of such a claim is found in Aristotle who calls the highest form of justice 'political' ([*to*] *dikaion to politikon, to politikon dikaion* e.g. *EN* V.6, 1134b13 and 18). Plato is also known for the view that it is, in a sense, the *polis* that is just when all its parts concentrate on their own business and do not meddle with that of the others. A similar kind of justice as *oikeiopragia* of course also pertains to the soul (IV, 434c8–10), and it would be exaggerated to claim that such justice is political in any more substantial sense than being structurally isomorphic to the justice of the *polis*. Moreover, in certain parts of the work, Plato's reflections on justice in the *polis* can be read as analogies for how justice must be understood in the soul, while other readings, such as the one adopted by Aristotle, take the political conclusions more literally. It needs to be stressed that I am surely not trying to make a case for Plato and Aristotle proposing solely a political notion of justice. My claim is rather that Plato and Aristotle carve out a discussion of justice as that of a city (*polis*) or that of the citizens (*politai*). For such justice, it is vital that the individuals work together in a structured community where they have different roles with respect to ruling and being ruled as assigned by the constitution (*politeia*).

There are of course a number of disputes over how to spell out the details of the view of Plato and Aristotle, and my aim is not to offer a substantial or original view of either. What is relevant for the present purposes is that insofar as justice is a matter of a structured human community working for a common goal, non-human animals will be excluded from its scope. I do not mean this as a general claim in the sense that a notion of justice pertaining to citizens could not in any sense apply to animals. In today's world, laws about the treatment of non-human animals guide and restrict the actions of citizens, and to the extent that people are assumed to have duties to obey the laws, animal justice can be incorporated into a citizen's moral duties. This, however, is an entirely different discussion.

Considering Aristotle's formulation of political justice, for instance, he maintains that it pertains to creatures or beings whose relations are "by nature governed by law" (*EN* V.6, 1134b13–14) and who have an equal share in ruling and being ruled. Such justice differs from justice in a household or in a village with respect to the relation between ruler and ruled. Aristotle famously criticizes Plato's view of justice precisely for making such relations static, so that some people merely have a share in ruling but not being ruled and *vice versa*. Ruling and being ruled also are notions that apply to human relations of power, and at least the kind of reciprocity that Aristotle values in such relations would not easily translate into human-animal relations. Non-citizens are also notoriously left outside it.

With respect to the Stoics, the question of whether their notion of justice is political in the sense explained above is more complicated. One general difficulty is related to the fact that our testimonies of a central source, Zeno's *Republic*, are not only scattered but often of a critical or polemical nature. In addition, there seem to be two different ways in which one can address the question of whether the Stoic notion of justice is political. First, one can ask whether the early Stoics' revisionary discussion of justice in their cosmopolitan ideal city of sages is related to joint deliberation and action in a structured community with specific roles for citizens. This is because in the evidence of the Stoic ideal more weight seems to be given to the citizens being wise than to ordering their mutual relations of ruling and being ruled. There is also controversy regarding the concrete political implications of Stoic cosmopolitanianism.

While Malcolm Schofield (1991) takes the notion of Stoic cosmopolitanianism, especially with respect to Zeno's *Republic*,[1] to be political in the sense of proposing a model for a cosmic city, such a view has been challenged, for example, by Katja Vogt. Although Vogt herself states that her view of Stoic cosmopolitanianism has political implications (Vogt 2008, 6–7), they are not necessarily political in the sense of being related to joint deliberation in a structured human community. Vogt's claim that all human beings should be treated as fellow-citizens, despite being formulated in terms of a cosmic *polis* and its citizens (*politai*), depends upon the idea that the *cosmos* is a dwelling-place for all human beings, not necessarily a structured human community. The implications Vogt draws

---

[1] Schofield's argument for Zeno's *Republic* being political is indirect in the sense that he argues for this on the basis of the claim that it needs to be continuing the tradition of Plato's *Republic* in this sense.

from this are related to following the law in the sense of "understanding what is of value or disvalue for human beings" (2008, 16), and the laws here refer to natural laws, not laws of existing cities (2008, 3–4). Such a theory does not necessarily ascribe different roles to different people with respect to ruling and being ruled.

Another possible reason that the Stoic notion of justice could be taken to be political is that its scope of application is determined through a process of *oikeiōsis*, turning to what is one's own or making something one's kin, translated as 'appropriation', 'affiliation', or 'familiarization.'[2] Ultimately this process needs to be extended to the whole of humanity, and in Hierocles' articulation (4.27.23,5 ff. Wachsmuth and Hense),[3] its last step is exactly to treat all human beings as one's fellow-citizens. Whether this has explicitly political implications is controversial. As far as I can see, Vogt would argue that it has, in the sense she understands what it means to be political. However, I would rather see the implications she draws as ethical, i.e. as pertaining to how one should treat other human beings and setting moral requirements on the basis of what is valuable to human beings.

Independently of how we answer the question about whether we can derive political implications for the Stoic notion of justice on the basis of existing evidence, non-human animals are excluded from its scope of application. This is one core claim for which Porphyry criticizes the Stoics in *On Abstinence* and I shall return to this criticism in the following section.

3 On the topic and argument of *On Abstinence*

Porphyry's *On Abstinence* is, in accordance with its title, a sustained argument for abstinence (*apochê*) from living or ensouled beings (*tōn empsuchōn*). It typically gets discussed as a treatise on vegetarianism, while some attention has also been paid to the arguments against animal sacrifice. However, I do not think we should read it merely as a treatise on vegetarianism with some arguments about sacrifice. First, the restraint from injuring harmless creatures that is identified as an important mark of the just person does not only refer to eating meat but also

---

[2] 'Appropriation' is used in Long and Sedley 1987, explained in 351; 'affiliation' by Vogt 2008, 5; 'familiarization' by Annas 1993, introduced in 148.

[3] = IV 671,7–673,11 found in Long and Sedley 57G; in Meineke's Teubner edition III 134, 1–136,2 = 4.84.23. The information about the different page and section numbers in different editions is found in Ramelli and Konstan 2009, lxxxi n. 147. I use Wachsmuth and Hense's numbering in the body text because it is found in the TLG.

to other forms of injury inflicted on animals. Secondly, a just person not only needs to refrain from injuring harmless animals but also extend justice to plants. In fact, it is not even clear whether humans, animals, and plants exhaust the class of creatures that should, according to Porphyry, be included in the scope of justice. When he sums up his arguments in Book 3 in its two final sections (3.26–27),[4] he first suggests that justice must be extended to living beings (*ta empsucha*). The term, although sometimes only used of animals and not plants, covers plants as well in the relevant sections (see e.g. 2.13.1=143,4–8 Nauck; 3.26.12=224,17–20 Nauck).[5] However, almost immediately after making the restriction to living beings, Porphyry goes on to state that a just person who abstains from injuring harmless creatures necessarily abstains from harming anything whatsoever (*pros pan hoti oun*, 3.26.10=224,8–9).

Thirdly, although the arguments about animals and plants and why one should not injure them are central to the treatise, I argue (in a monograph about to be completed) that the whole is structured around the common Platonic claim that one should strive to assimilate oneself to god to the greatest extent possible in bodily life. For Porphyry's *On Abstinence*, such a goal is relevant for several reasons. Firstly, this goal gives the treatise its structure. As Plato's seminal formulation has it (*Theaetetus* 176b1–2), such assimilation means becoming just and pious with wisdom (*phronêsis*). Although Porphyry discusses the virtues in a different order from the one in which they are mentioned by Plato, it is precisely piety (Book 2) and justice (Book 3) that form the focus of Porphyry's polemics. Arguably Book 4 has a special relation to wisdom, although the term *phronêsis* is not central there. In Book 4 Porphyry focuses on one specific objection to abstinence from Book 1 (1.13.5–1.14.1=96,23–24; 4.1.2=228,13–15) according to which no peoples and no sages had practiced abstinence, Pythagoras being the only lonely exception. In accordance with this objective, Porphyry focuses there on listing cases – often on tendentiously interpreted evidence to say the least – of peoples or sages, often priests who are taken to be philosophers, that testify to the contrary. However, although the assimilation to god as including piety and justice broadly speaking gives Porphyry's treatise its structure, the point should not be overstated. The virtue of purity is also central especially in Book 2, and the opening statement of Book 3 refers

---

4 Penned by Porphyry and not quoted from other sources. For the sources of Book 3, see Bouffartigue and Patillon 1979, 138–151.
5 The section numbers are found in the translations, the latter reference is to Nauck's Teubner edition 1963[2]. Nauck's line numbering is unfortunately not found in Clark 2000 or the French edition and translation by Bouffartigue, Patillon and Segonds.

to other virtues such as temperance and simplicity (3.1.1=186,16–17) that are argued to be best supported by abstinence.

Another way in which assimilation to god is important for the treatise is related to the group of people who need to practice abstinence. As Porphyry notes, it might well be that athletes, soldiers, orators, and craftsmen need meat, but one should not conclude from this that philosophers, let alone philosophers striving for divine assimilation do (2.4.3=134,1–13; 1.27). Therefore, the treatise is not an argument for vegetarianism as a common requirement of justice. Porphyry seems to assume that extending justice to non-human animals and plants requires that one knows and understands what justice really is and how it plays out in one's action. Given that this is a demanding cognitive achievement and requires time, study, and active exercise of one's reasoning powers, such understanding is only possible for people who focus their lives on such pursuits.

One might suspect that the fact that Porphyry gives such weight to the assimilation to god shows that abstinence from injuring harmless living beings is required only from Platonic philosophers. However, although central in the Platonism and Neoplatonism of late antiquity, godlikeness as the model for the best human life is also in a sense found in Aristotle (theoretical virtue), the Stoics (wisdom and happiness), and even the Epicureans (blessedness without concern for human affairs). Especially with respect to his polemics against the Stoics, Porphyry also suggests that given their notion of god as providential, benevolent, caring and beneficent (e. g. Plutarch, *Comm. not.* 1075e), they should extend similar beneficence beyond the scope of the human species, rather than arguing for the use, killing, and consumption of harmless living beings.

Porphyry's arguments for extending justice to (at least) all living creatures differ in a striking respect from most arguments about animal justice today. Much of today's discussions focus on the question of where to draw the boundary of creatures that deserve moral treatment. This general supposition leads to arguments about whether it is a certain kind of rationality that is required. How much human language does a creature need to understand in order to deserve moral treatment? How sophisticated do creatures need to be in terms of their ability to solve puzzles? How much self-consciousness do they need to exhibit? And so on. Others, by contrast, focus on the capacity to feel pain, and that capacity is singled out as being crucial for assessing the moral status of a creature. In Porphyry's case, animal rationality is prominent in Book 3 and animal capacity to feel pain is mentioned there as well. However, the occurrence of these themes does not entail that either of them would be the relevant criterion on which the moral status of living creatures depends for Porphyry. Rather, the discussions must be read in the framework of the overall polemics of the treatise.

In Book 3, Porphyry argues against the Stoic claim that justice does not extend to non-human animals because they are not similar to us (3.1.4=187,11–13) in the sense that they lack rationality while human beings are rational (Diogenes Laertius, *Lives of Eminent Philosophers* 7.129,6–8). The great majority of scholars have taken the arguments in that context to show that Porphyry himself subscribes to the claim about animal rationality with the conclusion that, contrary to the Stoic claim, animals must be included in the scope of justice, not excluded from it.[6] As opposed to the tradition, Fay Edwards has argued (2014; 2016) that Porphyry does not claim that animals are rational but assumes that they do not have reason. As she grants, however, this cannot be shown on the basis of *On Abstinence*; one must turn to other works by Porphyry, especially the *Commentary on Ptolemy's Harmonics*.[7] According to Edwards, Porphyry's argument about animal rationality in Book 3 of *On Abstinence* is thus purely dialectical or *ad hominem* in the sense that the Stoics should *on their notion of reason* ascribe rationality to non-human animals, while Porphyry himself does not accept the claim. This, however, is not vital for Porphyry's argument for animal justice because he does not make that depend on rationality (Edwards 2016).[8]

I agree with Edwards that the argument of *On Abstinence* 3 is primarily *ad hominem* and Porphyry is concerned with undermining the Stoics' grounds for denying animal rationality. More importantly, I agree that one of Porphyry's striking moves in *On Abstinence* is that he detaches the claim of animal justice from that of rationality. In fact, as I have pointed out above, for Porphyry it is not vital to show what kinds of achievements, cognitive or sensitive, animals must be capable of in order to deserve their status in the scope of justice. As mentioned, and this goes beyond what Edwards claims, he is not mainly concerned with where to draw the boundary of justice at all.

My main disagreement with Edwards concerns the ethical aspect of Porphyry's discussion (section 5 below), while I only disagree with her on two minor points on animal rationality. First, contrary to what she claims, I do not think

---

[6] Sorabji 1993, 46 n. 98 and 182 also referred to by Edwards 2014, 23 n. 1, 2016, 265 who gives an extensive list of those who endorse the traditional interpretation (or 'the consensus interpretation' as she calls it). The traditional reading is also found in Brittain 2002, 255–256; Caluori 2015, 193.

[7] Edwards 2014 is concerned with Porphyry's logical works; for the commentary on the *Harmonics*, see Edwards 2016; Chase 2010.

[8] The claim of animal rationality is called **PT** in Edwards 2016, and the claim of animal justice is similar to her **ET**: "If and only if X is rational, it is unjust for other rational beings to kill X for food." Note that I take the claim about animal justice in a broader sense than animals being killed for food; see Section 5 below.

that the fact that Porphyry does not ascribe rationality to animals (not at least in the full Platonic sense explained soon below) means that he would be downgrading animal cognitive capacities very much. Edwards (2016) argues that Porphyry limits animal cognitive achievements to such capacities as shrieking in pain and vocally expressing pleasure, which are possible on the basis of sensation and memory alone. She even suggests how to explain away the reference to 'Chrysippus' dog' seemingly engaged in inference according to the fifth Stoic indemonstrable (2018, 38–41). On some readings of what Plotinus makes of it at least, the full Platonic notion of reason requires that one regains cognitive contact with the Forms in bodily life, and that is a rather high cognitive achievement that eludes many human beings as well. From this perspective, rather advanced cognitive and linguistic achievements are possible on the basis of the capacity for *phantasia*, and no regained contact with the Forms is required.[9]

However, as I have repeatedly stressed above, for Porphyry's own purposes it is not vital to establish advanced cognitive achievements for non-human animals because their moral status does not depend on them. This also perhaps explains the striking fact that Porphyry does not explain in *On Abstinence* what he himself means by rationality. He gives the impression of agreeing with Pythagoras, his ancient predecessor and ally, on the point that where there is sensation and memory, there is reason (3.1.4=187,14–17). While Edwards (2016; 2018) takes this in the sense that human beings and animals are similar with respect to perceptions and passions of the soul, i.e. that to the extent that the capacities of perception and memory with feeling allow us to talk about rationality, non-human animals have it – but that Porphyry assumes this is not real rationality. This reading is of course possible. My second slight disagreement with Edwards on animal rationality is that I would rather be inclined to connect the dictum to Porphyry's general argumentative strategy. In general, Porphyry is concerned with listing all kinds of evidence to argue for abstinence, and he is not primarily concerned with pointing to the ways in which he differs from allies. It would probably be especially unwise for him to express open disagreement with Pythagoras on this point because Pythagoras is a rare example of a Greek sage (perhaps with Empedocles) who practiced abstinence and Porphyry refers to them as great authorities. Therefore, if someone is convinced by an argument that animals are rational in that they have sensations and memory and that this entails abstinence, Porphyry is not going to have a quarrel with them. In general, he

---

9 Human children, for example, learn to speak without the higher soul that is required for that kind of a contact (*Enn.* 1.1.11, 1–4). For the view that Plotinus assumes animals have lower souls, see Caluori 2015, 194; for reflections of what cognitive functions this entails for animals, see Emilsson 2017, 284.

might also avoid bringing in his own notion of rationality in the anti-Stoic polemics in order to leave it open that someone might be persuaded to abstain on the basis of those polemics.

I shall return to the question of how to understand Porphyry's own discussion of justice in Section 5 below. Theophrastus' arguments against animal sacrifice are important for Porphyry's view, and I shall consider them first in Section 4. Before moving to Theophrastus, however, a brief comment is needed on animal capacity to feel pain and its role in Porphyry's argument. It is a central factor in today's discussions largely due to Peter Singer's influential contribution, to the point that if such a capacity occurs in arguments about the moral status of animals, it seems that this must be the relevant criterion. It has in fact been suggested that this is the case for Porphyry as well (Girgenti 2001).[10] However, as mentioned above, animal sensitivity is not the criterion for Porphyry. Most importantly, plants belong to the scope of justice and Porphyry grants that animals differ from plants exactly by being sentient while plants are not. The argument referring to the animal capacity to feel pain is perhaps quoted or adapted from a lost work of Plutarch.[11]

> (T0) It is the nature of animals to have perceptions, to feel distress, to be afraid, to be hurt, and therefore to be injured. Plants have no perceptions, so nothing is alien or bad to them, nothing is harm or injustice: for perception is the origin of all appropriation and aversion, and the followers of Zeno make appropriation the origin of justice. (3.19.2=208,24–209,6; Clark's translation slightly modified)

This passage points to the difference between plants and animals such that the former are not afraid or hurt, do not feel distress and cannot thus be injured. This point is also used to argue that nothing is unjust to plants because they cannot be harmed. However, it would still be overhasty to conclude that this is Porphyry's argument for animal justice. The passage itself already makes the qualification that it is the followers of Zeno, i.e. the Stoics that make appropriation and thus perception relevant for justice. It might also be derived from a critical discussion of the Stoics by Plutarch, and thus we should not make far-reaching conclusions on the basis of it.

---

10 Sorabji 1993, 99 and 184 also detects the argument in Porphyry but leaves it slightly open what he takes the role of the argument to be in the whole of the treatise.
11 Sandbach 1969, 119; see also Bouffartigue and Patillon 1979, 144–147; 244 n. 5. The difference between plants and animals is not discussed in the surviving parts of Plutarch's *De esu carnium*, and the topic only makes a very brief appearance in *De sollertia animalium* (962f–963a), while they are treated on a par with animals in Solon's talk in the *Septem sapientium convivium*.

However, independently of the value of the passage as evidence of the Stoic view and whether it is from Plutarch, it has a specific role in the overall argument of Porphyry's *On Abstinence*. In Book 1, Porphyry reports a number of objections to abstinence and answers most of them in the course of the treatise. Unfortunately, however, he does not follow their order or indicate which objection he is addressing later on. The following objection in the form of a slippery slope is reported in Book 1.

> (T1) And if, as they say, plants have a soul too, what would life be like if we did not cut up either animals or plants! But if one who cuts down plants does nothing impious, neither does the one who cuts down animals. (1.18.1=99,8–11; Clark's translation)[12]

The objection is that one is entitled to eat animals because one has to eat plants anyway, and because both have souls, there is no difference in taking their lives. Although Porphyry does not accept the point that plants could not be harmed because they do not feel pain, this objection can be met with the kind of response quoted in (T1). Even if we use plants (Porphyry adopts Theophrastus' instructions for how to do that), it is not the same thing to 'cut down' an animal because they feel pain. Therefore, from the use of plants for nourishment we cannot conclude that we are justified to use animals in a similar way. All in all, although the capacity to feel pain is not a criterion for Porphyry of whether a living being can be harmed or not, he grants that animals can be harmed in a further way than plants through pain. However, the point is not a proto-Singerian argument for animal justice but builds on the role of pain in the Platonic framework. As Plato notes in the *Phaedo* (83d4–6), pleasure and pain are like rivets that fix the soul ever more tightly to the body. Causing pain to an animal thus prevents the liberation of its soul (e.g. 2.47). In this respect, plants and animals can both be harmed when their lives are taken but animals can also be harmed through pain.

4 Theophrastus: it is wrong to steal lives

In Book 2, Porphyry argues, quoting large extracts from Theophrastus' treatise *On piety* (*Peri eusebeias*), that rather than requiring animal sacrifice, piety or ho-

---

[12] The argument is one of the 'common objections' Porphyry quotes and later (in 1.26) ascribes to Heraclides of Pontus and Clodius of Naples. Bouffartigue and Patillon 1977, 28 suggest that Section 1.18–20 is probably from Clodius of Naples, who cites Heraclides of Pontus, but I withhold judgment about their claim.

liness (*eusebeia, hosiotês*) precludes it.[13] As I have indicated above, the arguments are not merely concerned with animal sacrifice, although that is central in the discussion, but Porphyry also quotes Theophrastus on how to use plants without violating justice. One justification that people might have had for animal sacrifice in Theophrastus' time was that it is a traditional way of expressing piety. Theophrastus argues, however, that although human beings have been sacrificing animals for a long time, the earliest generations did not do so – animals did not even exist then – and later the practice did not emerge from piety but was rather a consequence of some disasters that made harvest scarce (2.9.1=139,20 – 23; 2.12.1=142,1 – 3). When people had hardly enough to eat, they first started to sacrifice amongst themselves (2.27.1=156,1 – 5). In a slightly odd section (2.26) Theophrastus ascribes the transition from human victims to other animals to Jews whom he treats as if they were a priest caste among the Syrians. However, to show that even they supposed the act of sacrifice to be terrible, he tells how they made their offerings in the night, so that the all-seeing deity would not witness their transgressions. These early animal offerings were not eaten but wholly burned. However, as time went on, people forgot all piety and became insatiable, starting to eat the meat of the sacrificed animals and leaving nothing untasted (2.27.3 – 4=156,19 – 22).

Theophrastus' account of the origin of early human generations, their diet, and sacrificial practices makes the following central claims. (i) The account according to which the earliest generations survived entirely without nourishment from animals shows that human beings as a natural species are perfectly capable of surviving without meat. (ii) The alleged long and honourable provenance of animal sacrifice is a misunderstanding, and animal sacrifice only occurred as a result of a serious food crisis. (iii) As people have rightly denounced human sacrifice as well as anthropophagy, they should do so with respect to animals because both have their origin in the same calamities and have no rightful justification (see also 2.53.3=179,3 – 7).

According to Theophrastus, despite its traditional role, animal sacrifice is not pious because it is unjust not only in its origin but also as an action. Depriving a living being of its life is unjust because it means inflicting harm on it.

> (T3) Moreover, we ought to make only those sacrifices by which we hurt no one, for sacrifice, more than anything else, must be harmless to everyone. If someone says that god gave us animals, no less than crops, for our use, the answer is that when animals are sacrificed some harm is done to them, in that they are deprived of soul. So they should not be sac-

---

[13] For the quotations, see Bouffartigue and Patillon 1977, 17 – 29; for the text as in the context of Theophrastus' works, see Fortenbaugh and Gutas 1992, 405 – 433 = FHS&G **584 A-D**.

rificed. For sacrifice, as its name suggests, is something holy,[14] but no one is holy if he returns favours out of other people's possessions without their consent, not even if he takes crops or plants. How could it be holy, when injustice is done to those who are robbed? (2.12.3–4=142,13–22; Clark's translation with a minor modification)

In this passage, the injustice of depriving a living creature of its life is argued to be analogous to taking other people's possessions from them without their consent. Theophrastus also makes clear that similar principles that apply to animals also do to plants. The crucial claim thus is that sacrificing animals or plants is analogous to stealing and hence unjust. However, according to Theophrastus depriving a living being of its life or soul is an even greater wrongdoing (*to* [...] *deinon*, 2.12.4=143,1) than stealing external possessions from others.[15] This is because the soul of the animal is a greater good than any external belongings anyone might possess (2.12.4=142,22–143,3). Although he does not quite put it that way, he seems to assume that stealing is something inherently wrong and people usually recognize it as such.

However, from Theophrastus' perspective it is not only unjust and thus not pious or holy but also imprudent to try to bring gods gifts that are stolen from them as well. As the previous passage makes clear, Theophrastus maintains that the lives of animals and plants rightfully belong to those plants and animals, and this is why it is unjust to take it from them. However, he also claims that those lives or souls belong to the gods too because everything that exists is in a sense the property of the gods (2.13.3=143,16–17). To Porphyry the claim that lives of living creatures belong to the gods probably seems plausible, since the view that human lives belong to them is discussed in the *Phaedo* (62b). Despite its Platonic resonance, the claim creates some tension in Theophrastus' account. If we take lives of animals and plants, are we stealing from them or are we stealing from the gods?

Although Theophrastus and Porphyry do not articulate the explanation, Theophrastus would probably respond that the core of the wrongdoing is taking the life of an animal or a plant. If we do so, we are stealing a great good from a living creature, which means harming it in a very serious way. With respect to gods, we steal from them (because everything in a sense is their property). However, we do not steal an equally great good because we do not take their lives but external

---

14 Theophrastus plays on a superficial similarity between the word for a burnt offering (*thusia*) and holy things (*ta hosia*).
15 Aristotle also singles stealing out as one of those actions in which there is no proper measure but that are wrong already by their name (*EN* II 6, 1107a9–12). This is worth noting because Theophrastus' discussion of justice as quoted by Porphyry is not very Aristotelian.

belongings. It is not even clear whether we harm the gods in any way; they presumably thrive all the same. Therefore, the claim about stealing from gods seems to be a further reason not to take the lives of living beings, since it adds the dimension of imprudence to the account. It can be illustrated with the following analogy. If I am going to my friend's birthday party and take the flowers for my bouquet to her from her garden, I am stealing the lives of those flowers, which is wrong, but I also steal from her. Analogously to how I stole the flowers from my friend, the offerings to gods would be stolen not only from the plants and/or animals themselves, which would constitute the injustice of harming them, but also from the recipient of the token of gratitude or expression of honour. The reason why this would be imprudent is that while my friend might not notice that I took the flowers from her garden, the gods always will (2.24.5=153,20 – 22).

By claiming that taking lives of living creatures is similar but even greater as a wrongdoing than stealing external belongings, Theophrastus switches the burden of proof to the opponent. How can it be that even a minor wrongdoing of stealing external belongings is recognised as being wrong, while the major injustice that consists in taking the life of a living being is not? The point according to which it is unjust to take other people's possessions without their consent seems fair. However, it is not immediately evident how this translates to the case of animals and plants, given that we have no obvious way of determining whether they give their consent or not. Theophrastus does not discuss the animal case, and he might simply assume that an animal's attempt to flee, for instance, is sufficient evidence of their non-consent. While there was an ancient tradition claiming that sacrificial animals willingly yield themselves to sacrifice, Theophrastus does not seem to find this plausible even to the extent that he would argue against it.[16] However, he does discuss the case of plants.

To argue about the plant case, Theophrastus considers a possible objection according to which taking (the lives) from plants is not a wrongdoing because "it is not from the unwilling" (2.13.1=143,5; Clark's translation). While one might suppose this is because plants do not have a will, Theophrastus' argument proceeds in a rather different direction. He points to cases in which plants do something that is analogous to giving something willingly. For instance, even if we do not touch the trunk, trees let their fruit fall, and this sort of nourishment we can get from

---

[16] One objection to abstinence is also quoted in Book 1 in the form of a myth in which a bird allegedly flew to the altar herself (1.25.7=103,7–10), but Theophrastus and Porphyry do not seem to address the argument about animals offering themselves willingly.

plants without stealing from them.[17] Other ways of using plants without injustice (2.13) include taking leaves of a plant while leaving the organism alive and using agricultural products. If we let the plant as a whole live and take only its parts, we avoid harming it because we do not take its life, while using agricultural products is not a form of stealing, since, Theophrastus argues (2.13.3=143,17–19), human beings have contributed to the coming to be and the well-being of the crops by taking care of the soil and possibly watering the growth.[18] While Theophrastus has a rather positive view of agriculture – he also identifies the phase in which human beings had invented the skill but had not started to eat animals yet as a peak of human development – Porphyry would clearly prefer it if we did not have to eat at all (4.20.13=265,18–22). However, because of our mortal nature we are tied to the necessity of using plants for nourishment, and philosophers aiming at the assimilation to god must abstain from all avoidable injustice while doing it.[19]

Although Porphyry makes no explicit remarks in which he would disagree with Theophrastus on sacrifice, he recommends more radical forms of abstinence in the practices of piety for philosophers who strive for divine assimilation. While Theophrastean modest, blood-free offerings can be addressed to beneficent *daimones* who work as agents of cosmic providence (2.58), to divinities proper material offerings are inappropriate. To the god above all (*theos epi pasi*) that sits atop Porphyry's hierarchy of divinity – the details of which are not entirely clear – only pure silence[20] and pure thoughts should be offered, even words and discursive reasoning would be impure (2.34.2=163,15–22). As I have also suggested elsewhere (Tuominen 2017), the pure thoughts probably refer to

---

17 Theophrastus argues (as quoted by Porphyry in *On Abstinence* 2.13) for a similar case for taking honey from bees and milk from goats, provided that we human beings work for those animals and take care of them. In that case, the honey and the milk are like a salary for the work we did, and not like stealing. He underlines that we must make sure that the honey is not necessary for the bees (and the milk for the goats) in order to do this. I shall not discuss these cases in the present essay.

18 I do not think Theophrastus assumes everyone has to grow their own grain but rather allows some fair trade in acquiring agricultural products from other people without stealing.

19 He also notes that starving oneself to death is not an option because it would be wrong to take one's own life (1.38; 2.47).

20 Porphyry himself ascribes the view that pure silence must be offered to the god above all to 'a wise man' (2.34.2=163,16) that has since antiquity (Eusebius' *Preparation of Gospel* 4.10,17–13,1) been identified with Apollonius of Tyana. However, his account also resonates with Plotinus' distinction between two kinds of prayer, the lower ones being those directed at influencing the cosmic energies of *sympatheia* (*Enn.* 4.4 [28]), while the higher prayer does not even include entertaining silent thoughts, at least not in the sense of discursive reasoning, but is preparation for unification with the One in silence (V.1 [10] 6, 11–16), see also Rist 1967, 199–212. For Porphyry on prayer, see also Timotin 2015.

the Intellect's attempts to grasp the One in Plotinus (*Enn.* 6.9 [9] 3, 33–39). While all of Intellect's thoughts are pure, some are purer than others, and the purest are those that are directed to that which is 'before the Intellect.'[21] Since that must be the One, the purest thoughts are those that are directed at the One, although the Intellect cannot properly grasp it since the One is without intelligible shape (*Enn.* 6.9 [9] 3, 39).

Porphyry's guidelines for the piety of philosophers who strive for divine assimilation do not directly articulate his notion of justice, but there is one point that must be mentioned here. This is the way in which the expressions of piety suggested for philosophers aiming at divine assimilation differ from traditional sacrifice. While traditional sacrifice can be seen as the action of destroying something in the pursuit of some higher good (Vernant 1991, 290–302), Porphyry seems to assume that an offering to a good divinity must be good as well. Therefore, the offering not only needs to be entirely harmless and avoid destruction, it must also be similar to the real good in another sense. As Plato points out (in *Republic* I, for instance), the good is not a scarce resource that is diminished when shared. Material offerings could not be good in this sense. By contrast, arguably the contemplation of god and perhaps even pure silence are such that when one practices them and 'sacrifices' – or perhaps rather devotes – them to god, they are increased. The more one contemplates god and practices silence, the more one is able to do so.

However, although Porphyry requires philosophers aiming at assimilating themselves to god to practice (almost) entirely immaterial forms of piety, he does not reject or abandon Theophrastus' instructions or arguments about injustice. Quite the contrary. The Theophrastean guidelines for sacrifice in accordance with justice apply to offerings made to the beneficent *daimones* and they also become Porphyry's dietary instructions.

5 Justice according to Porphyry

We have now seen that although Book 2 of *On Abstinence* is mainly about piety or holiness (*eusebeia*, *hosiotês*) and why neither justifies animal sacrifice, it also contains important claims about justice articulated by Theophrastus that Porphyry incorporates into his own discussion. Porphyry does not explain in so many words what he means by justice. What he does say, however, is worthy

---

[21] Porphyry emphasizes that it is the contemplation of god (*theou theōria*) that we must direct to god (2.34.3=164,4).

of attention. After criticizing the Stoics for confusing justice with another virtue, love for the human species (*philanthrōpia*), he points out that:

> (T4) Justice lies in restraint and abstinence from harming everything that does not do harm.[22] This is how the just person is conceived of,[23] not that other [i.e. the Stoic] way; so justice, since it lies in harmlessness, extends as far as animate beings. (3.26.9=224,2–6; Clark's translation modified)

Porphyry does not argue for this in the context but probably assumes that his arguments against the Stoics throughout Book 3 have been sufficient to cast doubt on the restriction of justice to human beings, if not strictly speaking refute it. He does not articulate what he takes the Stoics to mean by justice but indicates that they derive it from *oikeiōsis*. While it is not clear what this would mean for the content of justice (or whether the Stoics themselves would accept the claim), *oikeiōsis* does give Stoic justice its scope of application. However, it is noteworthy that, in Cicero's *De officiis* (1.31, 9), restraint from causing harm is also listed as the Panaetian first principle of justice.[24] Therefore, Porphyry perhaps suggests that the Stoics should stick to this condition for justice and since they do not have sufficient grounds for excluding non-human animals from the scope of justice, they should extend restraint from causing harm to them as well.

However, as has been noted above, although Porphyry takes justice to lie in abstinence from causing harm, he does not define it in those terms, at least insofar as a definition is an account of an essence. Rather, he goes on to state immediately after the lines quoted in (T4):

> (T5) That is why the essence (*ousia*) of justice is that the rational rules over the irrational, and the irrational follows. For when the rational rules and the irrational follows, it is absolutely necessary for a human being to abstain from harming anything whatever. When the passions have been abased and appetite and anger have withered, and the rational part exercises the rule which is appropriate for it, assimilation to the Greater follows at once. (3.26.10=224,6–13; Clark's translation)

---

[22] This means harmlessness to human beings, i.e. the condition makes room for self-defense that is a central point in many objections in Book 1. Therefore, the harm does not mean the harm animals cause to other animals when eating them.

[23] καὶ οὕτως γε νοεῖται ὁ δίκαιος, οὐκ ἐκείνως. There is an error in Clark's translation (2000, 98) on this point ("this is how the just man thinks"). The correct form is medio-passive (νοεῖται), and a translation reflecting it is found in Bouffartigue and Patillon 1979, 188: '*C'est comme ceci que se conçoit l'homme juste.*'

[24] *Primum ut ne cui noceatur*. See also Epicurus, *Kuriai doxai* 31 for the claim that the justice of nature is a *symbolon* of the advantageous so that people would not harm or be harmed by each other.

According to Porphyry, the essence of justice thus is the inner Platonic justice. However, when the soul is just in that sense, the person necessarily abstains from causing harm to all things. In this he probably follows another Platonic claim, to which he refers in Book 2, according to which the good is never harmful and the bad never beneficial (2.41.1=170,18–19).[25] Neither, says Porphyry, does what is just do any harm (2.41.2=170,21).[26] The slight difference between Porphyry's formulation and that of Plato is that while Porphyry also articulates the claim in terms of what is just (*to dikaion*) here, for Plato it is the good (*to agathon*) that does not do harm (*Resp.* I, 335d7–12).

Porphyry does not explain what he means when claiming that justice lies (*keitai*) in harmlessness. What he says is that it necessarily follows from the inner justice of the soul. The claim that the essence of justice is reason's rule over the irrational in the soul thus seems to entail that inner justice is both necessary and sufficient for the kind of justice that Porphyry recommends for philosophers. The claim in (T5) just quoted, that reason's rule and the extinction of passions lead immediately to the assimilation to what is greater in the universe, also seems to imply that reason's rule is sufficient for reaching the goal of a philosophical life, assimilation to god. Although not building on the latter observation concerning assimilation to god, Edwards (2018) has argued that Porphyry's argument for vegetarianism on the basis of justice claims that philosophers should be vegetarian for the sake of inner justice, for the sake of moderation, and in order to be able to live a philosophical life. I shall not be concerned with the last claim about the philosophical life but will argue next that while reason's rule over the irrational is necessary and sufficient for the virtue of justice on the lowest level, there are higher degrees of justice on which it is necessary but not sufficient. Since it is for the higher degrees of assimilation to god that philosophers must strive, and since abstinence is necessary for them but not for everyone, philosophers also must act in accordance with the higher forms of justice that are productive of such greater assimilation.

Distinguishing different levels of justice is important for Porphyry's account of various degrees of godlikeness. When introducing such degrees, he first notes that people who only refrain from causing harm to their nearest and dearest will be contemptuous and greedy towards others because of being led by irrational impulses (3.27.2=225,7–11). Since they are not virtuous, he seems to assume, they are not godlike either. By contrast, a person who is led by reason and abstains from causing harm to fellow-citizens, strangers, and ultimately the

---

25 Cf. *Republic* 335d3: "the hot does not make cold."
26 οὐδὲ τοῦ δικαίου τὸ βλάπτειν.

whole human race is already virtuous. Such a person has inner justice and is more godlike (*theioteros* 3.27.2=225,15–16) than the first kind of person who lacks virtue. However,

> (T6) ... someone who does not restrict abstinence from causing harm to human beings but extends it also to other animals is more like god (*mallon homoios theō*); and if the extension to plants is possible, [the person] preserves the likeness (*eikōn*) even more (3.27.2=225,16–19; Clark's translation slightly modified).

Therefore, Porphyry grants that we can be just in the sense of having our reason rule over the irrational while only abstaining from harming human beings. This seems to exclude the possibility that abstinence is practiced for the sake of inner justice alone, since the latter is possible without the former. However, there is a higher degree of justice that does not consist of the inner organization of the embodied three-partite soul but also requires abstinence from harming non-human animals and even plants. Since abstinence is only required of philosophers aiming at assimilation to god, it seems that while non-philosophers can reach justice through reason's rule over the irrational alone, for philosophers it requires restraint from causing harm to others beyond the human kind.

Another work by Porphyry, his *Launching Points towards the Intelligibles* (also known as the *Sentences*), contains rather dogmatic pieces of Plotinian philosophy. In *Sentence* 32, Porphyry construes a rigid hierarchy of virtue building on Plotinus' more flexible reflections in *Enn.* 1.2. Porphyry's hierarchy is four-fold and contains political or civic virtues (*politikai aretai*), virtues of purification, theoretical virtues, and paradigmatic virtues. It seems that inner justice without abstinence from harming non-human animals and plants results in something like a civic virtue of justice. With respect to moderation, it is noteworthy that Porphyry takes it to belong to the level of civic virtue at which the goal is to act in accordance with human nature (*Sentence* 32, 30–31). Theoretical virtue, by contrast, requires freedom from passions (*apatheia*), and its goal is assimilation to god. Therefore, reason's rule over the irrational, which is also the description of moderation in Plato's *Republic* IV, seems characteristic of the lowest level of virtue pertaining to embodied three-partite souls, while philosophers aiming at assimilation to god need to free themselves from the passions altogether and aim higher than the mere full realization of human nature. This, together with the hierarchy of assimilation to god, speaks against inner justice and moderation being the goals for abstinence for philosophers according to Porphyry.

It is worth noting that the hierarchy of godlikeness including the assimilation to god as its highest stage does not refer to abstinence from causing harm to inanimate things. This might be taken to show that the remark according to which a just person abstains from harming anything whatever is not meant seriously in the sense that one could be just or unjust towards inanimate beings. However, the way in which the hierarchy is articulated does not necessarily mean that. Another possible reading is that while a just person abstains from harming all things, animate or inanimate, the injury one causes to living beings when taking their lives is so much greater than the harm caused to inanimate things when breaking them without good reason, for example, that the degree of one's assimilation to god does not depend on how one treats inanimate things. It might still be that Porphyry allows that a just person's inner justice also manifests in restraint from damaging inanimate things. This is not a crucial issue, but the fact that Porphyry leaves the matter slightly unclear is an indication that he is not concerned with drawing a strict limit for the application scope of justice as abstinence from causing harm to others.

The question of where to draw the boundary of the scope of justice is related to different intuitions concerning how the extension of justice affects it. On the one hand, one can take justice to be, as it were, a scarce resource that becomes weaker when extended wider. In Book 1 Porphyry reports an objection of this sort in a section confined to the Stoics (1.4).

> (T7) Someone who deals with such creatures [i.e. non-human animals] as he would with human beings, sparing them and not harming them, imposes on justice a burden it cannot bear, ruins what justice can do, and makes that which is alien destroy that which is appropriate. (1.4.3=87,23–88,4; Clark's translation)

The immediately following lines specify the objection by saying that if we do not spare non-human animals, we are unjust (and justice supposedly breaks down in this sense) or we do, and life becomes impossible and lacking in resources (1.4.3=88,4–7). This specification is quoted from Plutarch (*De sollertia* 964a1–3) but Porphyry does not mention his source. Porphyry's solution to the alleged dilemma is simply to reject its latter horn. Sparing (harmless) animals does not make life impossible or lacking in resources but is precisely the kind of life philosophers aiming at the assimilation to god should adopt. In a sense, Porphyry makes a concession to the general sentiment behind the objection just quoted (which resembles modern day objections to Peter Singer, according to which his theory of animal justice is too demanding). Porphyry grants that abstinence from harming animals is not required from everyone but is necessary for a higher degree of virtue of philosophers who aim at assimilating themselves to god to the greatest possible degree.

In Book 3, on the other hand, Porphyry's responds to the objection (which he briefly recapitulates in 3.26.5=222,25–26) by claiming its opposite. Contrary to what the objection maintains, justice does not become weaker or burdened when it is extended to non-human animals. Rather, extending it in that way makes one even more capable of being just to human beings (3.26.6=223,3–7). Moreover, while the objection claims that extending justice to non-human animals makes the alien (*allotrion*) destroy that which is appropriate (*oikeion*) (in T7 just quoted), Porphyry asserts that:

> (T8) [...] one who restricts justice to human beings is ready, like someone in a tight place, to jettison abstinence from injustice (3.26.7=223,12–14).

Porphyry thus argues that it is the restriction of justice to the human species that makes it weaker, not its extension to animals. In fact, he contends that such restriction makes it so much weaker that one is, in a difficult situation, likely to discard justice altogether. As opposed to the assumption that justice is a scarce resource weakened by extension, Porphyry rather assumes that it gets stronger the wider it is applied. The more we practice justice, the more we can be just, and thus justice to animals increases our justice to human beings.[27]

Porphyry also argues, as mentioned, that because of being restricted to human beings, the Stoic notion of justice collapses into another virtue, love or care for human beings (*philanthrōpia*, 3.26.9=224,1–2). Although love of humans is indeed a virtue, often connected to gods and perhaps Heracles as a somewhat puzzling Stoic sage, it is not the same as justice. However, Porphyry also criticizes the Stoics more severely for not seeing the cognitive capacities they take as rational in other animals because of self-love (*philautia*, 3.2.4=188,9). Porphyry seems to be referring to the kind of self-love Plato talks about in *Laws* V (731d6–732b4), although in the case of the Stoics the self-love is collective. In Plato, the self-lover only sees good in him or herself ignoring it in others, as "love is blind with respect to its object" (731e5–6). Analogously, the Stoics are eager to see goodness in human beings to such an extent that they fail to see it in non-human animals in this case, and they make species membership a condition of their love. Therefore, Porphyry implies that the Stoics should conduct independent enquiries into the respective cognitive capacities of human beings and non-human animals, when in reality they have a tendency of ascribing such capacities to human beings and denying them from non-human animals merely on the basis of species membership. In a word, from Porphyry's perspective, one

---

[27] This seems to be the converse of the modern-day 'dehumanization' argument for animal justice, according to which cruelty to animals brings about cruelty in human beings. The argument has traditionally been ascribed to Kant, although this has recently been challenged by Kain 2018.

should not decide the question of a creature's moral status merely by considering its species.

We are now in a position to return to the question of how justice as lying in restraint from injuring harmless creatures is related to inner justice. I have suggested that although the essence of justice for Porphyry is the inner one (reason leads and unreason follows), it is quite clear that it makes no sense to say that justice in this sense is extended merely to human beings or beyond the scope of our species. Therefore, it must be that the discussion of the scope of application for justice concerns its external manifestation in restraint from injuring harmless creatures (as in 3.26.9=224,2–6) or restraint from injustice (*ephexis tês adikias* 3.26.7=223,14 in T8).

Porphyry also refers to injuring harmless creatures as simply an injustice (in 3.26.7=223,14 quoted in T8) which entails that he also conceives of it as such. This in turn suggests that he endorses Theophrastus' claim that it is a wrongdoing (*to deinon*) and unjust to take lives of living creatures. Restraint from this kind of injustice must be extended to non-human animals and plants, and for the necessary use of plants as nourishment Porphyry follows Theophrastus' instructions.

Finally, the manifestation of the inner justice in action as restraint from causing harm to others does not make such justice political. It is a form of justice that human beings, when they come to know and profoundly understand the nature of justice, exert on animals and plants as well. Porphyry himself notes, when he makes his proper entrance in Book 2 after long quotations from Theophrastus, that it is not his task to discuss about political matters or the constitution in the treatise (*peri politeias* [...] *legein* in 2.33.1=162,20–21). He claims that he himself does not aim at abolishing any existing laws, although later on he points out that philosophers should not let themselves be changed by bad customs or practices (2.61.6=185,19–21). Therefore, while he does not make it entirely clear whether he would like to change existing laws, he insists that philosophers aiming at the assimilation to god should not, for instance, take part in animal sacrifice. However, the reform of sacrificial practices he suggests includes those proposed by Theophrastus. Perhaps Porphyry's claim that he is not aiming at changing the laws is related to the fact that such revision is derived from Theophrastus. One might also suggest that the dictum of not talking about politics or the constitution (*politeia*) refers to the fact that Porphyry leaves aside the kind of discussion that Plato devotes to the *politeia* in the *Republic*.[28]

---

[28] Yet another possibility is that Porphyry refers to Plato's denial in the *Laws* of renewing religious customs and practices. I am grateful to Julia Annas for a discussion on this point.

In addition to the claim that it is unjust to inflict injury on harmless creatures, another important assumption also made by Plato can be found in how the good is manifested both in piety and justice in action. We saw that Porphyry recommends for philosophers aiming at the assimilation to god such expressions of piety that do not require the destruction of anything. Rather, they are similar to the real Platonic good in the sense that the more one practices piety, theoretical contemplation of god, and silence, the more one is capable of doing so. In the case of justice, Porphyry argues against the Stoics that justice is not weakened or diminished when extended to non-human animals but its restriction to the human species does so. Extending justice to non-human animals and plants, by contrast, makes one even more capable of just action also with respect to human beings. Finally, it is justice and piety, together with wisdom, that constitute the assimilation to god, and justice to non-human animals and plants is required for such assimilation. Wisdom or knowledge is also required so that we can know and understand the world and the true natures of the virtues. This is one reason why the kind of justice that includes abstinence from injuring all living beings is not for everyone. It is for philosophers who can devote their lives to theoretical inquiry and acquire the knowledge that results from it, and that is needed in order to act in accordance with the highest forms of justice.

By way of conclusion, I have argued that Porphyry's notion of justice *On Abstinence* 3 is remarkable for several reasons. First, it is not based on the assumption that rational or sentient creatures alone deserve moral treatment from human beings. Porphyry even seems prepared to accept that an ideally just person abstains from harming all things, inanimate ones included, while the justice that partly consists in abstaining from depriving living creatures of their life is only possible towards animate creatures. Secondly, a central feature in Porphyry's discussion is the Platonic assumption that what is good cannot do harm. Analogously, Porphyry concludes that the more just – and consequently the more good – someone is, the more one is capable of abstaining from causing harm. It is remarkable, however, that in his hierarchy of godlikeness, he assumes the converse claim as well: the more just we are striving to become, the wider we must extend justice in the sense of harmlessness. Since philosophers who aim at assimilation to god to the greatest possible degree are striving to be as good as they possibly can, they must abstain from causing harm to others as much as is possible for a mortal creature. As I have argued, this entails that abstinence from harming living creatures cannot be for the sake of inner justice and moderation alone but that restraint from harming living creatures is a constitutive condition of philosophical justice.

Primary literature

Hierocles the Stoic. 2009. *Hierocles the Stoic: Elements of Ethics, Fragments and Excerpts*, by Ilaria Ramelli and David Konstan. Atlanta: Society of Biblical Literature.
Long, Anthony A. and Sedley, David N. 1987. *The Hellenistic Philosophers*, 2 vols. Cambridge: Cambridge University Press.
Porphyry. [1886] 1963. *Porphyrii philosophi Platonici opuscula selecta*, by August Nauck. Leipzig: Teubner.
Porphyry. 1977 and 1979. *Porphyre. De l'abstinence*, by Jean Bouffartigue and Michel Patillon. Collection des universités de France 1–2. Paris: Les belles lettres.
Porphyry. 2000. *Porphyry: On Abstinence from Killing Animals*, by Gillian Clark. London: Duckworth.
Porphyry. 2003. *Porphyre: De l'abstinence*, by Michel Patillon and Alain-Philippe Segonds, with Luc Brisson. Collection des universités de France 3. Paris: Les belles lettres.
Plutarch. 1969. *Plutarch, Moralia Volume XV: Fragments*, by Francis H. Sandbach. Cambridge MA: Harvard University Press.
Theophrastus. 1992. *Theophrastus: His Psychological, Doxographical, and Scientific Writings*, by William W. Fortenbaugh and Dimitri Gutas. New Brunswick/London: Transaction.

Secondary literature

Alesse, Francesca. 1994. *Panezio di Rodi e la tradizione stoica* (Elenchos). Napoli: Bibliopolis.
Annas, Julia. 1993. *The Morality of Happiness*. Oxford: Oxford University Press.
Brittain, Charles. 2002. "Non-Rational Perception in the Stoics and Augustine." *Oxford Studies in Ancient Philosophy* 22:253–308.
Caluori, Damian. 2015. *Plotinus on Soul*. Cambridge: Cambridge University Press.
Chase, Michael. 2010. "Porphyry on the Cognitive Process." *Ancient Philosophy* 30:383–405.
Edwards, Gemma Fay. 2014. "Irrational Animals in Porphyry's Logical Works: A Problem for the Consensus Interpretation of *On Abstinence*." *Phronesis* 59/1:22–43.
Edwards, Gemma Fay. 2016. "The Purpose of Porphyry's Rational Animals: A Dialectical Attack on the Stoics in *On Abstinence from Animal Food*." In *Aristotle Re-Interpreted: New Findings on Seven Hundred Years of Ancient Commentators*, edited by Richard Sorabji, 263–290. London/New York: Bloomsbury.
Edwards, Gemma Fay. 2018. "Reincarnation, Rationality and Temperance: Platonists on Not Eating Animals." In *Animals*, edited by Peter Adamson and Gemma Fay Edwards, 27–55. Oxford: Oxford University Press.
Emilsson, Eyjólfur K. 2017. *Plotinus*. London/New York: Routledge.
Girgenti, Giuseppe. 2001. "Porfirio nel vegetarianesimo antico." *Bollettino Filosofico: Dipartimento di Filosofia dell'Università della Calabria* 17:75–84.
Kain, Patrick. 2018. "Kant on Animals." In *Animals*, edited by Peter Adamson and Gemma Fay Edwards, 211–232. Oxford: Oxford University Press.
Rist, John M. 1967. *Plotinus: The Road to Reality*. Cambridge: Cambridge University Press.

Schofield, Malcom. [1991] 1999. *The Stoic Idea of the City*. Chicago: University of Chicago Press.
Sorabji, Richard. 1993. *Animal Minds and Human Morals*. Ithaca: Cornell University Press.
Timotin, Andrei. 2015. "Porphyry on Prayer: Platonic Tradition and Religious Trends in the Third Century." In *Platonic Theories of Prayer*, edited by John Dillon and Andrei Timotin, 88–107. Leiden: Brill.
Tuominen, Miira. 2017. "On Porphyry's Ethics of Piety in Book 2 of *On Abstinence*." In *On the Origins of Religion: Perspectives from Philosophy, Theology, and Religious Studies*, edited by Hanne Appelqvist and Dan-Johan Eklund, 77–95. Helsinki: Luther-Agricola Society.
Vernant, Jean-Pierre. 1991. "A General Theory of Sacrifice and the Slaying of the Victim in the Greek Thusia." In *Mortals and Immortals: Collected Essays* by Jean-Pierre Vernant, edited by Froma I. Zeitlin, 290–302. Princeton: Princeton University Press.
Vogt, Katja. 2008. *Law, Reason, and the Cosmic City. Political Philosophy in the Early Stoa*. Oxford: Oxford University Press.

George Karamanolis
Early Christian Philosophers on Society and Political Norms

Abstract: Writing, as they were, in a majority pagan society, some Christian Church Fathers were ready to critique political institutions and assert an exceptional status for the Christian community. This paper distinguishes two stages in the development of these 'antinomian' tendencies in early Christianity. In the first, Christian thinkers such as Justin Martyr, Tertullian, Eusebius, and Lactantius, seem to be disagree whether Christians make up a special part of the society they live in. Some accept pagan *political* norms while promoting specifically Christian *ethical* norms; others urge the replacement of both kinds of norms with Christian ones. This debate centers on the source of normativity: is it God, the emperor, nature, or, finally, reason? In a second stage, Augustine's *City of God*, inspired by the Stoic idea of the city of sages, envisions a distinct 'city' that unites Christians living under different earthly political regimes. Unlike earlier Christians, Augustine does not just distinguish but also connects ethical and political norms.

1 Introduction

Christianity was born in a non-Christian society. This is not a mere historical fact, as is the case with the other cults and religions that emerged in the Roman empire and coexisted with pre-existing religions and with indigenous Roman cultural and political norms. It was rather a cause of long-lasting frictions, debates, and often fierce polemics between Christians and non-Christians. From early on Christians considered non-Christian society and culture, Jewish and pagan alike, as erring and in need of conversion to Christianity. This is linked with the nature of Christianity, which was not just one more religion but an ambitious, holistic movement that aspired to transform almost every aspect of Graeco-Roman society, culture, religion, art, literature, language, and everyday concepts, as well as philosophy. Christians worked hard to establish a new identity within the pagan societies in which they lived. On the one hand, they argued that Christianity was nothing new but rather the fulfilment of the *Logos* operating within the history of humankind; on the other hand, they systematically criticized pagans and Jews for their beliefs, which they considered as an aberration of the *Logos*, as misguided and false. The Christian critique of pagan society, beliefs, and culture became a flourishing literary genre in the hands of early Christian intellectuals.[1] Writings against the pagans proliferated in the period from the second to the fifth century.[2] One standard topic was the Christian criticism of pagan norms and morals.

One might argue that this Christian critique should not be taken at face value, because it was politically motivated: the Christians aimed to justify their identity and win new members from the pagan camp. This is true to some extent. It is no accident, for instance, that the two *Apologies* of Justin Martyr (*ca.* 153–160) were addressed to the emperors Antoninus Pius and Marcus Aurelius, or that Athenagoras' *Plea for Christians* (*ca.* 177) was addressed to Marcus Aurelius and Commodus, as was also the case with Theophilus' *To Autolycus* some years later (181).[3] It is also true, however, that Christians had a serious problem from the outset, namely how they should fit into non-Christian society. Which norms of that society should they adopt? Did they have to abide by the laws of the society in which they lived, and if so, how should they assess the laws of non-Christians, which included for example laws ordaining the worship of the Roman emperor? Were some pagan laws just and others unjust, and what should be the criterion for that distinction? Should the criterion be a specifically Christian one? More generally, Christians had to decide whether to accept the existing pagan political order of the Roman empire, or instead aspire to create a new Christian one.

This cluster of problems is already addressed in the earliest Christian documents, such as Paul's letters and the *Letter to Diognetus*. In these writings we find claims to the effect that Christians are ordinary members of their contemporary non-Christian society, but Christians are also portrayed a special group, who follow norms based on a divinely ordained morality or a morality of revelation. Paul acknowledges the political authority of the state and encourages Christians to respect it on the grounds that the civic authorities are subordinate to God

---

[1] Criticism of Judaism is also strong in early Christianity, but this does not concern me here. Justin's *Dialogue with Trypho the Jew* became the model for later anti-Jewish literature.
[2] For instance, the works of Tatian and Ps.-Justin with the title *Against the Greeks*, Tertullian's *Ad Nationes*, Athanasius' *Against the Pagans*. The Christians described themselves as a separate race, *ethnos*, and indeed as a third race alongside Jews and pagans (see e.g. Clement, *Strom.* VI.5.41.6). On the building of Christian identity, see Lieu 2004, especially 238–268. On the intellectual debate between Christian and pagan thinkers see Karamanolis 2013, especially 31–48. Striking evidence for the Christian response to pagan society is to be found in the study of the Christian desecration of pagan artifacts; see Kristensen 2013.
[3] It is possible that Athenagoras delivered his apologetic work to the emperors when they were in Athens. His plea for the Christians has a political motivation, given the outbreak of persecution against the Christians by Marcus Aurelius, and the martyrdoms of Lyons in 177 (Eusebius, *Eccl. Hist.* V.1.1–4.3). See further Barnes 1975. On Athenagoras' *Plea* see further below.

(Rom. 13:1–4), but in the same context he goes on to specify the duties of Christians to one another (Rom. 13:8–15).[4] In the *Letter to Diognetus*, we hear that Christians are no different from other citizens in terms of conduct and customs, yet their manner of life is different: "they dwell in their own countries, but simply as sojourners. As citizens, they share in all things with others, and yet endure all things as if they were foreigners [...] They obey the prescribed laws and at the same time surpass the laws by their lives" (*Letter to Diognetus* Chapter 5). These two elements of Christian life, obedience to pagan laws and the wish to transcend them, point again to the difficulty faced by Christians, who saw themselves as adhering to divinely inspired norms yet also claimed to follow the norms of a non-Christian society, such as the laws of the Roman empire. It was a challenge for Christian believers in general, and Christian philosophers in particular. While the former dealt with the issue practically, the latter engaged with it theoretically. There was also a second-order challenge, addressed exclusively by Christian intellectuals, as to whether the ethical and political norms of non-Christian society should be replaced by Christian ones, and if so how this might practically be accomplished.[5]

In the following I will distinguish two stages in the way that Christian philosophers dealt with these challenges. In the first, Christian thinkers such as Justin Martyr, Tertullian, Eusebius, and Lactantius, seem to be divided on whether Christians make up a special part of the society they live in. Their diverging views on this issue bear on their assessments of contemporary political norms, and their answer to the question whether non-Christian norms should be respected or replaced with Christian ones. We will find two main models in the work of these Christian thinkers: one that distinguishes between political and ethical norms, accepting the pagan *political* norms while promoting specifically Christian *ethical* norms; and one that conflates political and ethical norms and urges their replacement with Christian ones. The debate centers on the source of normativity: is it God, the emperor, nature, or, finally, reason? We reach a new stage with Augustine, who in his *City of God* clearly distinguishes two cities or societies: the heavenly one, which is purely Christian, and the earthly one, which is only partially Christian. Augustine, I suggest, inherits the problems discussed by earlier Christians and suggests a complex solution, which is not only theoretical but also has, as I will try to show, a practical dimension that becomes apparent in certain passages in the *City of God* where Augustine speaks about

---

[4] Paul, for instance, takes Scripture and especially the life of Christ as a source of norms and a model of life; see Gal. 4:30, 1 Cor. 9:10, Rom. 15.1–3, Phil. 2:1–13. It has been argued that Paul accepted some pagan virtues. See Furnish 1996, 44–51; Rosner 2003, 212–226.

[5] For discussion see Fox 1986, 14–47.

state laws and society's norms more generally. I will argue that Augustine's vision is largely inspired by the Stoic idea of the city of sages, according to which virtuous sages make up a distinct group of citizens and, at least on one interpretation, a distinct 'city', despite inhabiting diverse earthly cities and being guided by diverse political orders. What is distinctive in Augustine's proposal is that, unlike earlier Christians, he does not just distinguish but also connects ethical and political norms. I will try to assess the relative advantages of this model over its predecessors.

2 Early Christians on society and human laws. Two levels of norms.

One of the earliest Christian philosophers to engage with the issue of non-Christian norms is Justin Martyr.[6] In his first *Apology*, Justin argues that both subjects and rulers are equally responsible for the prosperity of the state. He is critical of the ancient view, found in Plato's *Republic*, that rulers are given a privileged position (1 *Apol.* 3.2–4). Justin is not so much interested here in criticising Plato. He rather focuses on rejecting a view that might have been attractive for the two emperors he addresses, who are systematically presented in the *Apology* as examples of piety and devoted philosophers, namely that cities will attain happiness if rulers become philosophers.[7] Justin argues instead that the tasks of rulers and subjects are both divided and also common; the task of the subjects, especially Christian ones, is to make their lives and opinions transparent, while the task of the ruler is to judge well. Both, however, should lead a virtuous life and both are equally important for the happiness of the state:[8]

---

[6] On Justin Martyr, see Osborne 1973; more recently Minns 2010, 258–269.

[7] Τοὺς κατὰ ἀλήθειαν εὐσεβεῖς καὶ φιλοσόφους (1 *Apol.* 2.1), ὑμεῖς μὲν [...] εὐσεβεῖς καὶ φιλόσοφοι (1 *Apol.* 6–7), τοὺς ἄρχοντας [...] εὐσεβείᾳ καὶ φιλοσοφίᾳ ἀκολοθοῦντας (1 *Apol.* 3.9), ὑμᾶς, οἵ γε εὐσεβείας καὶ φιλοσοφίας ὀρέγεσθε (1 *Apol.* 12.19–20).

[8] I follow Marcovich's 1994 edition. 1 *Apol.* 3.2–5: Καλὴν δὲ καὶ μόνην δικαίαν πρό<σ>κλησιν ταύτην πᾶς ὁ σωφρονῶν ἀποφανεῖται, τὸ τοὺς ἀρχομένους τὴν εὐθύνην τοῦ ἑαυτῶν βίου καὶ λόγου ἄληπτον παρέχειν, ὁμοίως δ' αὖ καὶ τοὺς ἄρχοντας μὴ βίᾳ μηδὲ τυραννίδι, ἀλλ' εὐσεβείᾳ καὶ φιλοσοφίᾳ ἀκολουθοῦντας τὴν ψῆφον τίθεσθαι. οὕτως γὰρ ἂν καὶ οἱ ἄρχοντες καὶ οἱ ἀρχόμενοι ἀπολαύοιεν τοῦ ἀγαθοῦ. 3. Ἔφη γάρ που καὶ τις τῶν παλαιῶν. "Ἂν μὴ οἱ ἄρχοντες φιλοσοφήσωσι [καὶ οἱ ἀρχόμενοι], οὐκ ἂν εἴη τὰς πόλεις εὐδαιμονῆσαι." 4. Ἡμέτερον οὖν ἔργον καὶ βίου καὶ μαθημάτων τὴν ἐπίσκεψιν πᾶσι παρέχειν, ὅπως <μὴ> ὑπὲρ τῶν ἀγνοεῖν τὰ ἡμέτερα νομιζόντων τὴν τιμωρίαν ὧν ἂν πλημμελῶσι τυφλώττοντες αὐτοὶ <ἑ>αυτοῖς ὀφλήσωμεν. ὑμέτερον δέ, ὡς αἱρεῖ λόγος, ἀκούσαντας ἀγαθοὺς εὑρίσκεσθαι κριτάς. 5. Ἀναπολόγητον γὰρ λοιπὸν μαθοῦσιν

2. Every reasonable person would find good and fair the entreaty that subjects should give a blameless account of their life and thought and that rulers should similarly carry out their decisions, not with violence and tyranny, but as followers of piety and philosophy. In this way both rulers and subjects would fare well. 3. For one of the ancients said, "unless the rulers become philosophers, the cities cannot attain happiness." 4. It is our task then to offer to all the opportunity of surveying our life and teachings, so that we ourselves should not bear the blame for what those who do not really know about us do in their ignorance. But it falls to you, as reason demands, to give us a hearing and show yourself to be a good judge. For you will have no defense before God if you know the truth but fail to do what is right.

Justin clearly admits here that rulers, especially educated rulers like Antoninus and Marcus Aurelius, should be able to judge well, despite the fact that they are not Christians. Justin does single out Christians as a special, divinely favoured, class in his second Apology (2 *Apol.* 7.1), but he does not expect the emperors to appreciate that; he only expects the rulers to be inspired by piety and philosophy. If they do that, they will judge well and do what is just (*ta dikaia poiein*). This crucially involves tolerating the Christians and not charging them with imaginary crimes, as others do. Piety and justice are not specifically Christian characteristics for Justin; not only can they be found among pagans, but Justin clearly implies that they are valued in pagan society. This is why, a page earlier, Justin has referred to Plato's *Apology* 30c while arguing that the rulers who condemn the innocent harm themselves. For, according to Plato, doing injustice harms the unjust agent. Apparently Justin takes the view that there are several important values or norms, such as piety and justice, shared by all reasonable and educated people, Christians and non-Christians alike. In this regard Christianity continues to uphold values found in pagan culture.

Notably, Justin does not dispute the status of the Roman emperor or his claim to power. He rather grants this and takes it as a starting point for his reflections. The question is how the emperors should make good use of this right. As we have seen, he urges them to follow reason and stay true to their characteristic virtues, to piety and philosophy. Justin's emphasis on the virtuous character of the emperors is not just rhetoric, but functions as justification of their imperial authority. Justin must have said more on this topic in his *On God's Only Rule* or *On God's Monarchy* (Περὶ θεοῦ μοναρχίας), which is now lost; we know of its existence through the testimony of Eusebius (*H.E.* IV.18.4). Athenagoras' *Plea for Christians*, written around 177, may give us a hint that

---

<ὑμῖν>, ἢν μὴ τὰ δίκαια ποιήσετε, ὑπάρξει πρὸς θεόν. (3. καὶ οἱ ἀρχόμενοι: mss; del. Thalemann, Schmid, Marcovich. The deletion is justified by the distinction that Justin makes in what follows in his text).

would help us to reconstruct Justin's position. Athenagoras draws a parallel between the joint rulership of Marcus Aurelius and his son Commodus and that of God the Father and God the Son.[9]

> I wish that you, by yourselves, should discover the heavenly kingdom also! For as all things are subservient to you, father and son, who have received the kingdom from above (for the king's soul is in the hand of God, says the prophetic Spirit [Proverbs 21:1]), so to the one God and the *Logos* proceeding from Him, the Son, conceived as inseparable from Him, all things are similarly subjected.

This is a striking passage. Athenagoras not only compares the rulership of the Roman emperors with that of God, but further states that the Roman emperors have been granted their political authority from the Christian God. While imperial authority consists in being served and respected by all, God's power consists in having everything subjected to him. Justin Martyr may well have made a similar comparison in his lost *On God's Monarchy*.

Tertullian displays a similar attitude to the Roman emperor, whom he considers as part of the order of creation that ultimately depends on God's power.[10] More specifically, Tertullian suggests that on earth the emperor is what God is in heaven; he also claims that it is God who appointed the emperor to his position and granted him political power. The emperor's power, says Tertullian, comes from the same source that is responsible for our soul, namely God. Therefore, he continues, the Christians pray for the emperor's health because he serves God.[11]

> The emperor is great because he is inferior to heaven. He himself belongs to God, who owns heaven and all creation. This is whence the emperor comes, from Him who made man before making him emperor. The emperor's power has the same source as his spirit.

Tertullian's position resembles that of Athenagoras in deriving the political power of the Roman emperor from God and in claiming that the emperor is appointed by God, and that the emperor operates like God on earth. Yet in the same context, Tertullian goes further than Athenagoras by encouraging Christians to

---

9 *Plea for Christians* 18.2: Ἔχοιτε <δ' ἂν αὐτοὶ> ἀφ' ἑαυτῶν καὶ τὴν ἐπουράνιον βασιλείαν ἐξετάζειν. ὡς γὰρ ὑμῖν πατρὶ καὶ υἱῷ πάντα κεχείρωται, ἄνωθεν τὴν βασιλείαν εἰληφόσιν ('βασιλέως γὰρ ψυχὴν ἐν χειρὶ θεοῦ', φησὶ τὸ προφητικὸν πνεῦμα), οὕτως ἑνὶ τῷ θεῷ καὶ τῷ παρ' αὐτοῦ λόγῳ, υἱῷ νοουμένῳ ἀμερίστῳ, πάντα ὑποτέτακται.
10 On Tertullian's political views, see Barnes 1971.
11 *Apol.* 30.3: Ideo magnus est, quia caelo minor est; illius enim est ipse, cuius et caelum est et ommis creatura. Inde est imperator, unde et homo antequam imperator; inde potestas illi, unde et spiritus.

respect the emperor's rule,[12] a point also made implicitly by Justin. Elsewhere Tertullian explicitly denies the divinity of the Roman emperor, but this is because, he suggests, emperors are subordinate to God, and not gods themselves. Still he agrees with the Roman custom of granting the emperor divine honours after death (*Apol.* 13.8). We should not be surprised, then, to find Tertullian arguing that Christians should be loyal to the Roman emperor and that they should respect the laws and the customs of the society in which they live (*Ad Nationes* 1.17.4). Tertullian makes this point by way of responding to a common charge against Christians, according to which Christians do not abide by the laws of the cities where they live. In this context Tertullian makes an interesting comment about the nature of law.[13]

> The laws punish Christians. If the Christians did something wrong, this must become public. There is no law to prevent an investigation. In fact, an investigation functions in the interest of the law. How will you enforce the law if you pass over the very offense that the law forbids, failing to take account of the available evidence? No law can rely on its own account of its righteousness, but it owes such an account to those from whom it demands obedience. Moreover, a law becomes suspect if it shows no tendency to prove itself. Thus the laws against the Christians are rightly held to be worthy of respect and compliance, but only as long as no one knows what they punish. Once the truth is known, however, namely that these laws enforced their code with swords, crosses, and lions, they are vehemently rejected as supremely unjust [...] And an unjust law has no value.

Tertullian's aim here is to criticize the laws that punish Christians. Historians of this period tell us that there was no such specific law (Sherwin-White 1963; Barnes 1968). This, however, is not so important for us here, since there certainly were imperial decrees against the Christians or similar imperial decisions ordering the severe punishment and even execution of Christians.[14] The important point is Tertullian's way of arguing against the persecution of Christians; he condemns the absence of any investigation into the actual deeds of Christians. The existing evidence shows that this is true. Christians were arrested and punished

---

12 For a commentary on this chapter, see Waltzing 1931, 211–215. Sider 2001, 1–70 has (partly) translated and commented the *Apologeticum*.
13 *Ad Nationes* 1.6.4–7: *Christianum puniunt leges. Si quad est factum Christiani, erui debet. Nulla lex prohibit inquirere, atquin pro legibus facit inquisitio: quomodo enim legem observabis cavendo quod lege prohibetur, adempta diligentia cavendi per defectionem agnoscendi quid observes? Nulla sibi lex debet conscientiam iustitiae suae, sed eis a quibus captat obsequium. Ceterum suspecta lex est, si probare se non vult. Merito igitur tamdiu iustae in Christianos et reverendae et observandae censentur, quamdiu ignoratur quod presequuntur* [...] *Legis iniustae honor nullus est.*
14 Barnes 1971, 143–163, with reference to the relevant evidence.

for their identity and were proved innocent by denying their faith and by sacrificing to pagan Gods.[15] Tertullian asks what exactly the crime of Christians might be, and what exactly the legislation against them punishes. In this regard Tertullian continues along the line of reasoning established by Justin Martyr and Athenagoras, who appeal to the sound reason and the virtues of Roman emperors, who were apparently misled by widespread prejudices against the Christians. Unlike Justin and Athenagoras, though, Tertullian makes an important point about the nature of law. A law, he says, is not legitimate because of its status as law but because of its justification, an account of which should be available to all who are subject to the law. It is this account or justification that makes every law what it must be: an instantiation of justice. Tertullian makes no reference to Christian values or norms here. He implies that a law neither has to be inspired by Christian doctrine nor be issued by a Christian ruler; what is essential to the law is simply that it be just. Nor does Tertullian mention specifically Christian criteria according to which laws are just. A given law might be just or unjust regardless of the legislator's religious convictions. The upshot is that Tertullian declares loyalty to the current political order and to the imperial laws, insofar as they are indeed just. He has no expectations that Christians should be treated differently. Like Justin Martyr, Tertullian's only plea is for justice.

Tertullian differs from Justin Martyr, however, in claiming that the Christians do not make a special class, as Justin suggested. For him Christians are instead members of the same community to which everyone else belongs, namely the world (*Apol.* 38.3). The Christians, argues Tertullian, are not motivated by earthly or political concerns; they do not rule the world but only worship God and understand the Scriptures well (*Apol.* 39.3). Such motivations, though, do not set them apart from the rest of their fellow citizens. Rather, Christians are united with them in respecting the law and the emperor (*Ad Nationes* 1.17.3). There is an interesting passage in his *Apologeticum* (39.1–2, 8–9), where Tertullian claims that Christians are not only brothers to each other, as was commonly thought, but also to their pagan fellow citizens. Just like them, Christians also pray for their emperors, ministers, officers; for what binds all of them together is, Tertullian says, the law of nature, our common mother, as he calls it:[16]

---

15 See de Ste Croix 1963; Barnes 1971, 146.
16 *Apol.* 39.1–2, 8–9: *1. Edam iam nunc ego ipse negotia Christianae factionis, ut, qui mala refutaverim, bona ostendam, si etiam veritatem revelaverim. Corpus sumus de conscientia religionis et disciplinae unitate et spei foedere. 2. Coimus in coetum et congregationem, ut ad Deum quasi manu facta precationibus ambiamus. Haec vis Deo grata est. Oramus etiam pro imperatoribus, pro ministeriis eorum et potestatibus, pro statu saeculi, prerum quiete, pro mora finis […] 8. Sed et quod fratrum appellatione censemur, non alias, opinor, insaniunt, quam quod apud ipsos*

> 1. Now I myself will explain the practices of the Christian society; that is, after having refuted the charges that they are evil, I myself will also point out that they are good. We constitute a body as a result of our common religious convictions, the unity of our life, and the bond of our hope. 2. We form a group and a congregation aiming to besiege God with our prayers. This violence pleases God. We also pray for our emperors, their ministers and their powers, for the present state, or the peace in the world, for the delay of the end [...] 8. People fall into a rage over the fact that we call ourselves brothers. We are your brothers too, however, according to the law of nature, our common mother. And yet with how much more right are they called brothers and considered such those who have acknowledged one father, God, and who have drunk one spirit of holiness, who in fear and wonder have come forth from the one womb of their common ignorance to the one light of the truth? (Translation by Sider)

Tertullian does not deny that Christians make up a community and indeed a fraternity (*Apol.* 39.1–4), but he denies that this sets them apart from their fellow citizens. Rather, he says, they also count as brothers, since they have a common mother, nature.[17] Tertullian clearly refers to human nature here. All humans, he suggests, are brothers to each other by virtue of sharing both a mother and a father, human nature and God. Those who acknowledge God have more right to be called brothers, and such are the Christians. Tertullian does not specify here the sense in which humans have God as father, but he does so in *De anima*.[18] God, he says, breathed life into the first human and through him to all humans. It is God's spirit that makes up the human soul and is propagated from parents to children, from one generation to the next. The soul stems from God, the father, but its propagation is the work of nature, the mother.[19] It is in this sense, I take it, that all humans are brothers. Crucial for us here is that in Tertullian's view all humans share the same nature, and therefore we must be subject to the same law, the law of nature, although Tertullian does not specify here or elsewhere, as far as I know, how this law of nature relates to the specific laws of the state. The important point remains that, according to Tertullian, Christians do not make up a separate class of citizens but rather are connected to all others by virtue of sharing a common nature and belonging to the same society. They do what all others do: they work as sailors, farmers and traders, share the market

---

omne sanguinis nomen de affectione simulatum est. Fratres autem etiam vestri sumus iure naturae matris unius, etsi vos parum homines, quia mali fratres. 9. Quanto nunc dignius fratres et dicuntur et habentur, qui unum patrem Deum agnoverunt, qui unum spiritum biberunt sanctitatis, qui de uno utero ingorantiae eiusdem ad unam lucem expaverung veritatis?
17 See Waltzing 1931, 246–254.
18 See Karamanolis 2013, 193–198 with reference to further literature.
19 See Tertullian, *De anima* 11.1–3, 22.2 and the discussion in Karamanolis 2013, 193–198.

places, places of manufacture, inns, and baths (*Apol.* 42.1), and are subject to the same laws.

Yet while Tertullian emphasizes the common nature of all humans and the fact that all are subjects to the same law of nature, he also stresses the moral superiority of Christians. Tertullian argues that Christians abide by the law and it is the pagans who bring destruction to the state (*Apol.* 39.19–21), and he contrasts Christians with the moral flaws of pagans, including individual pagan philosophers (*Apol.* 46.8–47.10). Several other Christian contemporaries express similar views. Clement of Alexandria, for instance, speaks at great length about the aim of the Christian wise man to achieve perfection, which requires a specific sort of knowledge, central to which is knowledge of the Christian God and of Christian doctrine. The perfection sought by the Christian sage consists in becoming similar to God (*Strom.* VI.7.60.1–3), and this ideal involves, as in the case of the Stoics, the extirpation of all passions.[20] The critical point here is the distinction between two hierarchical levels of norms, the political and the ethical. Tertullian accepts the normative character of public laws, to which everyone including the Christians are subjected, yet he stresses the superiority of Christians at the level of morality.

This appears to be a widespread tendency among early Christians. We have already encountered it already in the writings of Paul and in the *Letter to Diognetus* (Chapter 5). We also find it in a pronounced form in Athenagoras' *Plea for Christians*. Athenagoras claims that the task of Christians is not merely to be just, but rather to be good and forbearing,[21] and he goes on to speak of Christian duties to themselves and to others with reference to Christ's resurrection (*Plea for Christians* 35–36). These are specific Christian values which are thought to be on a higher level than justice, and which could also be achieved by non-Christians. This dualism of norms, political on the one hand and moral on the other, is also implied in a passage of Theophilus' *To Autolucus*:[22]

---

[20] See further Bradley 1974; Karamanolis 2013, 226–228.

[21] οὐ γὰρ ἀπαρκεῖ δίκαιον εἶναι (ἔστι δὲ δικαιοσύνη ἴσα ἴσοις ἀμείβειν), ἀλλ' ἀγαθοῖς καὶ ἀνεξικάκοις εἶναι πρόκειται. "For it is not enough to be just (justice is to return measure for measure); but it is required of us to be good and forbearing" (*Plea for Christians* 34.3).

[22] I follow the text of Marcovich's edition 1995. *To Autolycus* I.11: Τοιγαροῦν μᾶλλον τιμήσω τὸν βασιλέα, οὐ προσκυνῶν αὐτῷ, ἀλλὰ εὐχόμενος ὑπὲρ αὐτοῦ. θεῷ δὲ τῷ ὄντως θεῷ καὶ ἀληθεῖ προσκυνῶ, εἰδὼς ὅτι ὁ βασιλεὺς ὑπ' αὐτοῦ γέγονεν. Ἐρεῖς οὖν μοι. "Διὰ τί οὐ προσκυνεῖς τὸν βασιλέα;" Ὅτι οὐκ εἰς τὸ προσκυνεῖσθαι γέγονεν, ἀλλὰ εἰς τὸ τιμᾶσθαι τῇ νομίμῳ τιμῇ. Θεὸς γὰρ οὐκ ἔστιν, ἀλλὰ ἄνθρωπος, ὑπὸ θεοῦ τεταγμένος, οὐκ εἰς τὸ προσκυνεῖσθαι, ἀλλὰ εἰς τὸ δικαίως κρίνειν. τρόπῳ γάρ τινι παρὰ θεοῦ οἰκονομίαν πεπίστευται. Καὶ γὰρ αὐτὸς οὓς ἔχει ὑφ' ἑαυτὸν τεταγμένους οὐ βούλεται βασιλεῖς καλεῖσθαι. τὸ γὰρ βασιλεὺς αὐτοῦ ἐστιν ὄνομα, καὶ οὐκ ἄλλῳ ἐξόν ἐστιν τοῦτο καλεῖσθαι. Οὕτως οὐδέ<νι> προσκυνεῖσθαι, ἀλλ' ἢ μόνῳ θεῷ.

Accordingly, I will pay honor to the emperor not by worshipping him but by praying for him. I worship the God who is the real and true God, since I know that the emperor was made by him. You will say to me, "Why do you not worship the emperor?" Because he was made not to be worshipped but to be honored with legitimate honor. He is not God but a man appointed by God [Rom. 13.1], not to be worshipped but to judge justly. For in a certain way he has been entrusted with a stewardship [1 Cor. 9:17] from God. He himself has subordinates whom he does not permit to be called emperors, for 'emperor' is his name and it is not right for another to be given this title. Similarly, worship must be given to no other person but to God alone. (Grant's translation modified)

Theophilus, along with Athenagoras and Tertullian, takes a similar position in presenting the emperor as God's appointed ruler, but he puts more emphasis on the difference between the emperor and God. The emperor, he argues, is not divine and accordingly does not merit worship, as God does, but only honour. The emperor deserves honour because he is appointed by God and his job is to judge justly. Theophilus claims, then, that Christians accept a hierarchy of authorities – God, the emperor and his officers – and also a hierarchy of the sources of norms. The emperor is responsible for justice in the state, while God is the ultimate source of norms. There is no conflict between the two, at least in principle, because the emperor has been appointed by God in order to bring justice to human society. Obedience to the law is a duty for Christians, since the emperor is appointed by God, but clearly Christians should acknowledge God as the sovereign source of all norms and obey God's commands.

One of the most interesting texts of this period for this question of the relationship between God and the Roman emperor is Eusebius' *Panegyric for Constantine (De laudibus Constantini)*. Eusebius presents Constantine as the model of a divinely elected Roman emperor, and goes as far as to compare him with God's *Logos*, who plays the role of a mediator between God and the world.[23] Eusebius tells us that through the *Logos* the emperor partakes of divine authority: "The emperor, receiving from the *Logos* of God a likeness (*eikôn*) of the Divine Sovereignty, in imitation of God himself, directs the administration of the world's affairs" (*LC* 1.6). The emperor's authority results from his imitation of the *Logos*. This becomes manifest in the emperor's behaviour: someone who declares allegiance to God is shaped not by passions, as previous Roman emperors had been, but by virtues, conforming with the divine model (*LC* 5.2–3). Constantine is thus depicted as the ideal emperor, the measure for past and future ones.

---

[23] Eusebius makes such claims also in the *Life of Constantine* I.4–6, probably written a couple of years after the Panegyric, i.e. in 337. Eusebius' *Panegyric* has been translated and discussed by Maraval 2001. There is an extensive literature on Eusebius' perception and presentation of Constantine; for a succinct account see Cameron and Hall 1999, 34–48.

Eusebius' project is innovative, but we should not forget that Athenagoras had already compared Marcus Aurelius and Commodus to God the Father and his Son. Eusebius is much more outspoken, of course, since Constantine is the first Christian emperor. Yet Eusebius too conforms to the tendency of a dualism of norms discussed above. In Eusebius' worldview, the emperor is responsible for the unity and stability of society, while God is for the entire world. We have, again, two causes of stability, order, and values: the emperor on this earth and God in heaven, with the former's authority derivative from the latter's.

So far we have seen variations of one Christian model, according to which Christian intellectuals accept and largely approve of the current political establishment and the political norms of their society, despite their pagan character. Although Christians disagree with each other as to whether they constitute a distinct group and how they are connected to non-Christians who share the bonds of common human nature, they are nonetheless unanimous in their political integration in pagan society and in their acceptance of the authority of the Roman emperor and of the political norms of pagan society, mainly the laws. They justify that approval by claiming that the Roman emperor is appointed by God. By making this claim the Christians distinguish two sources of normativity, political (the emperor) and moral (the Christian God).

3 Early Christians on society and human laws. One normative level

An alternative model to the one just presented would make Christianity the decisive criterion for political order and justice in society. This is what Lactantius does in his *De Ira Dei*.[24] The main aim of this work is to argue against the idea, widespread among pagan philosophers, that anger is incompatible with divinity. Lactantius argues that God can indeed exhibit anger when confronted with evil and that this is indeed the appropriate divine response to evil. He further argues that religion is crucial for the existence of society, since society is primarily characterized by order and justice. Religion, he argues, is crucial for avoiding the selfish actions that lead to crimes. It instils a fear of God in people (*De Ira Dei* 8.5–8). Without God and religion, he claims, there is no fear of the consequences of unjust actions, and without fear there can be no virtue or honesty. For Lactantius, the Epicureans for instance destroy society when they argue

---

[24] Lactantius' place in the climate of a changing empire is discussed by Digeser 2000.

against fearing the gods. The following passage captures Lactantius' main point well:[25]

> 5. And if God has nothing to do with the world nor shows any concern, why then should we not commit crimes whenever it is in our power to escape the notice of men and to cheat the public laws? Wherever we shall obtain an opportunity of escaping notice, let us take advantage of the occasion: let us take away the property of others, either without bloodshed or even with blood, if there is nothing else besides the laws to be reverenced. 6. While Epicurus entertains these sentiments, he altogether destroys religion; and when this is taken away, confusion and disorder of life follow. 7. But if religion cannot be taken away without destroying our hold of wisdom, by which we are separated from the brutes, and of justice, by which public life may be more secure, how can religion itself be maintained or guarded without fear? For that which is not feared, is despised, and that which is despised, is plainly not venerated. Thus it comes to pass that religion and majesty and honor exist together with fear; but there is no fear where no one is angry. 8. Whether, therefore, you take away from God kindness, or anger, or both, religion must be taken away, without which the life of men is full of folly, of wickedness, and enormity.

In this passage Lactantius, unlike earlier Christian thinkers, closely connects political and ethical norms in such a way that both have the same source. Public laws specify moral duties for citizens, but these derive from God. Without God and religion there would be confusion and disorder in public life, he suggests. On Lactantius' model we can, strictly speaking, have no society unless there exists a correct form of religion in that society, namely the Christian one. This is because religion is not only a personal matter, a personal conviction. It has an important social and political role, and functions as a political institution: religion sets public life in order.

Lactantius' emphasis on the political role of religion comes as no surprise, given that Roman religion once had that kind of role in Roman society. Indeed, one of the charges brought by Romans against the Christians was that the latter did not appreciate the political character of Roman religion when they rejected it

---

25 *De Ira Dei* 8.5–8: *5. Quod si negotium deus nec habet nec exhibet, cur ergo non delinquamus, quotiens hominum conscientiam fallere licebit ac leges publicas circumscribere? Ubicumque nobis latendi occasio adriserit, consulamus rei, auferamus aliena vel sine cruore vel etiam cum sanguine, si praeter leges nihil est amplius quod verendum sit! 6. Haec dum sentit Epicurus, religionem funditus delet; qua sublata, confusio ac perturbatio vitae sequetur. 7. Quod si religio tolli non potest ut et sapientiam, qua dictamus a belvis, et iustitiam retineamus, qua communis vita sit tutior, quomodo religio ipsa sine metu teneri aut custodiri potest? Quod enim non metuitur, contemnitur, quod contemnitur, utique non colitur. Ita fit ut religio et maiestas et honor metu constet; metus autem non est ubi nullus irascitur. 8. Sive igitur gratiam deo sive iram sive utrumque detraxeris, religionem tolli necesse est, sine qua vita hominum stultitia scelere immanitate conpletur.*

altogether as incompatible with Christianity. For Lactantius religion is primarily the acknowledgment of the Christian God, who is the cause of order in the world but also the source of ethical and political norms. The denial of religion in this sense leads to anarchy, injustice, and disorder. This becomes clear in passages where Lactantius argues that God is the source of justice: Christ, he says, is *doctor iustitiae* and *quasi viva lex* (*Div. Inst.* IV.23–24, IV.29). Accordingly, Lactantius speaks of a divine law that brings about justice, as other early Christian thinkers do (for instance Theophilus, *To Autolycus* 35.1). Quite telling is the following passage from *De Ira Dei*.[26]

> 5. Since, therefore, God has laid down a most holy law and wishes all men to be innocent and beneficent, is it possible that he should not be angry when he sees that his law is despised, that virtue is rejected and pleasure is made the object of pursuit? 6. But if God is the governor of the world, as he must be, he surely does not despise that which is even of the greatest importance in the whole world.

The passage makes clear that Lactantius does not distinguish two realms, a political and an ethical, an earthly and a heavenly one, as earlier Christian thinkers did, but rather conflates the two. He actually suggests that the kingdom of God reaches down to earth and should shape our social and political norms and values. God is not only the principle of cosmic order but also the principle of social and political order, that is, the source of justice in human society.

Apparently for Lactantius justice cannot be achieved in a society simply by abiding by the laws of the state, for they can be unjust, as Tertullian had already pointed out. Suppose someone takes the property of his neighbour without violating any law. No crime has been committed in a legal sense, but an unjust deed has been done. Both Plato and Cicero are sensitive to this problem and discuss such actions in order to show what justice really is.[27] For them justice is clearly not a matter of abiding by the laws but of doing what reason commands as just; and this requires the right psychological constitution, which includes right motivation and right views. Lactantius invokes Cicero's argument in *De Republica* to the effect that the law is one and immutable, arising from right reason and con-

---

[26] *De Ira Dei* 19.5–6: 5. *Cum igitur sanctissimam legem posuerit velitque universos innocentis ac beneficos esse, potestne non irasci, cum videt contemni legem suam, abici virtutem, appeti voluptatem? 6. Quod si est mundi administrator, sicut esse debet, non utique contemnit id quod est in omni mundo vel maximum.*

[27] See *Republic* I–II, *De finibus* II.58–60.

forming with nature, and the inventor of that law is God.²⁸ For Lactantius civic laws as such do not bring about justice, rather the right principles do; it is the conformity with these principles that confers authority to a law, a view reminiscent of Tertullian's relevant position discussed earlier.

For Lactantius the principles of just action crucially involve piety (*pietas*). This is nothing more than man's acknowledgement of the Christian God as the father of humans, of the *genus humanum*.²⁹ Unlike Tertullian, who makes God our father and nature our mother, Lactantius insists that God is both our father and mother (*Div. Inst.* IV.4.6). Man's acknowledgement of God as his only parent involves accepting God as source of order and justice. Here one may wonder how exactly God is such a source of justice. Lactantius, as far as I can see, does not answer this question directly. Yet he suggests that God is the source of right reason (*Div. Inst.* VI.8.6) and also of our social instinct (*Div. Inst.* VI.10.10). Lactantius appears to suggest that God is the creator of our nature and all its features. These are not neutral features of humankind but bearers of norms and values. They make us social animals and incline us to justice. In short, they make us what we are: humans. Lactantius then castigates the denial of religion, that is, the rejection of the Christian God, as the source of injustice, confusion, ethical and political disorder, exactly because such a denial makes us blind to the normative features of our nature crafted by God.

So far we have seen two early Christian models. In the first, Christians approve of the existing, non-Christian, political norms and institutions which account for order and justice in the state and accept the Roman emperor as the source of political norms. In the second model, which we have found in the work of Lactantius, political order and justice cannot be achieved merely by respecting the existing laws of the state but requires being motivated by the right kind of religion, namely Christianity, that is, by accepting the Christian God. On this view the existing human political norms must be replaced by Christian ones. Yet there is another possibility, namely that norms are derived from nature, more specifically, from human nature. Of course, God is the creator of human nature, as Lactantius claims, but this does not mean that He is specifically the creator of the norms pertaining to it. This is what Gregory of Nyssa will claim.

---

28 *Suspicienda igitur de ilex est, quae nos ad hoc iter dirigat illa sancta, illa caelestis, quam Marcus Tullius in libro de re public tertio paene divina voce depinxit* (*Div. Inst.* VI.8.6–9; citing Cicero, *De Republica* III.22.33). For a discussion of this passage, see Colot 2016, 145–147.
29 *Pietas* [...] *nihil aliud quam parentis agnitio* (*Div. Inst.* III.9.19). For a discussion, see Colot 2016, 150–152.

4 Human and divine laws: the question of slavery

Both Basil of Caesarea and Gregory of Nyssa take up the idea, already advanced by Tertullian, that all humans share a common nature, no matter their religious convictions or cultural backgrounds. Basil and Gregory strongly emphasize shared human nature, as opposed to the properties that distinguish individual humans. This emphasis is the result of their theological argument that the Persons of the divine Trinity share a common nature, namely the divine one, while also having distinct individual features. Gregory speaks at length about universal human nature in a section of his work *De hominis opificio* (l78D–185D). There Gregory argues that all humans share in God's image, which means that we all have an equal share in intellect, which crucially involves a capacity for self-mastery and free choice (τὸ αὐτοκρατὲς καὶ αὐτεξούσιον, 185AC).

This view is the basis on which Gregory argues quite strongly against slavery, maintaining that no man is a slave by nature, as already argued by the Stoics (DL VII.121–2). Early Christians take a somewhat ambiguous position on the question of slavery.[30] Justin, for instance, maintained that all humans whether free or slave are equally sons of God and have the same value, a view that we find repeated in several passages of Clement (*Paed.* 1.6.31, *Strom.* V.5.30.4). This view is in line with Paul's statement that there is neither slave nor free, neither woman nor man in Christ (Gal. 3:28). Such statements, however, do not explicitly condemn the idea of slavery. Indeed some Christians, like Gregory of Nazianzus, claim that slavery and freedom are the result of human deeds, of sinful or praiseworthy deeds (*De pauperum amore*, PG 35, 892AB).

The first Christian condemnation of the notion that slavery is natural is found in the work of Basil, who explicitly denies that slavery is a natural state for humans (*De spirito sancto* PG 32, 160D–161D). Basil stresses that there are no distinct natures for masters and servants, that all humans share the common human nature. Yet he admits that some people have a less developed capacity to deliberate (*bouleutikon*) and suggests that it is to their advantage to be guided by others (161 A).[31] Basil's brother Gregory of Nyssa takes a much more outspoken position on the issue of slavery.[32] He argues that there is only one human nature

---

[30] On the attitude of Christians towards slavery, see Ramelli 2016.
[31] One can reasonably speculate that Basil is guided here by Aristotle's ideas in the *Politics*, especially 1254a20–24.
[32] On Gregory's attitude to slavery, see Karamanolis 2013, 234–236; and in more detail Ramelli 2016, Chapter 5.

in which all humans share, namely the likeness of God's nature. Freedom, he says, is an essential feature both of divine and human nature, and if freedom is an essential feature of humans it cannot be taken away. Those who divide humans into masters and slaves introduce a division that is not intended by God and thus go against God's law (*antinomothetein*, Homily on Eccl. 335.5–7).[33]

> I owned slaves, males and females. What do you say? Do you sentence man, whose nature is free and with the power to decide, and to legislate against God, overriding his law, which is imposed in nature? [...] So then, tell me, who will sell and who will buy him who is made in the likeness of God and lord of all the earth, and who has inherited from God authority over all that exists on earth? Only God can do so, or better, not even God himself. For it is written that his gifts are irrevocable. God would not enslave human nature, he who by his own choice brought us back to freedom from the slavery of sin. If God does not enslave free nature, who should put his power over that of God?

Striking here is the use of the verb *antinomothetein*, which might be taken to suggest the existence of divine legislation. This is not a specific, codified legislation, of course; rather, God's laws are implied in the way human nature is made. This means that human nature carries with it certain norms. As already implied by Lactantius, it is not a neutral fact that humans are made in a specific way; instead human nature, being God's creation, has a normative character, that is, it dictates how we should treat ourselves and our fellow humans, and what behaviour towards others and ourselves cannot be tolerated. The careful study of human nature can show us what our duties towards ourselves and others are.

We find the same point of view in Nemesius' *De natura hominis*, which is dated to around the same time as Gregory's *De homimis opificio*. It is notable that Nemesius also criticizes those who legislate against God (*antinomothetein*, De nat. hom. 354 Matthaei) and follow human laws instead.[34] In his treatise Nemesius focuses on human nature and he, like Gregory, underlines its normative

---

[33] Gregory of Nyssa, *Homily on Ecclesiastes* IV, GNO Volume V, 335.5–7, 336.10–20: Ἐκτησάμην δούλους καὶ παιδίσκας. τί λέγεις; δουλεία καταδικάζεις τὸν ἄνθρωπον, οὐ ἐλευθέρα ἡ φύσις καὶ αὐτεξούσιος, καὶ ἀντινομοθετεῖς τῷ θεῷ, ἀνατρέπων αὐτοῦ τὸν ἐπὶ τῇ φύσει νόμον [...] τὸν καθ' ὁμοιότητα τοῦ θεοῦ ὄντα καὶ πάσης ἄρχοντα τῆς γῆς καὶ πάντων τῶν ἐπὶ τῆς γῆς τὴν ἐξουσίαν παρὰ τοῦ θεοῦ κληρωσάμενον τίς ὁ ἀπεμπολῶν, εἰπέ, τίς ὁ ὠνούμενος; μόνον θεοῦ τὸ δυνηθῆναι τοῦτο, μᾶλλον δὲ οὐδὲ αὐτοῦ τοῦ θεοῦ. Ἀμεταμέλητα γὰρ αὐτόν, φησί, τὰ χαρίσματα. οὐκοῦν ὁ θεὸς οὐ δουλοῖ τὸ ἐλεύθερον, τίς ὁ ὑπερτιθεὶς τὸν θεὸν τὴν ἑαυτοῦ δυναστείαν.

[34] "For how is a man not to be shunned when he makes laws contrary to God and instructs against the works of providence but does not even dare to speak against human law-making?" (translation by Sharples and Van der Eijk). Πῶς γὰρ οὐ φευκτός ἐστιν ἄνθρωπος ἀντινομοθετῶν τῷ θεῷ καὶ ἀντιπαρακελευόμενος τοῖς τῆς προνοίας ἔργοις, ὁ μηδὲ ταῖς ἀνθρωπίναις νομοθεσίαις ἀντιλέγειν τολμῶν;

character, which mainly consists in man's freedom to choose. Human law, he suggests, should not conflict with a law of nature, which has God as its author. Though Gregory and Nemesius make clear that the ultimate source of norms is God, these norms are still grounded specifically in human nature, which is created by God. Civic laws carry a normative force when they respect human nature; when they conflict with it, they conflict with divine legislation as well. To the extent that divine laws are made transparent in human nature, there is nothing abstract or mysterious about them. They are universal, yet also specific and concrete.

5 Two societies, heavenly and earthly

If we now move to Augustine, his sharp distinction between divine and human law represents a natural step forward. The former, he says, is immutable, universal, and eternal, whereas the latter is at best modelled on the former but remains an image of its model, therefore having the opposite features: it is mutable, fallible, temporal. The eternal law is not meant only for heaven, for an otherworldly society, but is the law of God, the supreme reason, which also orders human life, and is in this sense a law of nature, the law engraved in our hearts (*De lib. arb.* 1.6.15), by means of which we judge the actions of the others. The eternal law is the norm or the principle of justice, which makes the temporal law just and valid. In the following passage from a dialogue on free will, Augustine is in conversation with Evodius (*De lib. arb.* 1.6.15):

> *Aug.* Will not any intelligent man regard that law as unchangeable and eternal, which is termed the law of reason? We must always obey it; it is the law through which wicked men deserve an unhappy, and good men a happy life, and through which the law we have said should be called temporal is rightly decreed and rightly changed. Can it ever be unjust that the wicked should be unhappy and the good happy, or that a well-disciplined people should be self-governing, while an ill-disciplined people should be deprived of this privilege?
>
> *Ev.* I see that this law is eternal and unchangeable.
>
> *Aug.* I think you also see that men derive all that is just and lawful in temporal law from eternal law. For if a nation is justly self-governing at one time, and justly not self-governing at another time, the justice of this temporal change is derived from that eternal principle by which it is always right for a disciplined people to be self-governing, but not a people that is undisciplined. Do you agree?
>
> *Ev.* I agree. (Trans. Thomas Williams)

The distinction between divine, eternal law, and human, temporal law suggested here is also made evident in another passage from the same context in *De libero arbitrio* (1.3.6). Augustine asks Evodius whether adultery is unjust because the law forbids it, or whether the law forbids it because it is unjust. Evodius favours the latter option. An action should be judged as just or unjust according to a principle of justice, and the eternal law counts as such. It is infallible, universal, and immutable, whereas the human law is fallible and subject to change. Augustine summons us to abide by the eternal law if we want to be just. When there is a clash between eternal and temporal law, we should follow the former. For only eternal law qualifies as a law strictly speaking, because it is always just, and also because the authority of the law of the state comes only from the eternal law. Like earlier Christian thinkers, Augustine draws a contrast between the norms specified in Scripture, which bind the Christians, and the absence of such a normative framework in Roman society (*De civ. Dei* II.19). This is the reason, Augustine claims, for the decline of the Roman society, in which, as he says, injustice reigns (*De civ. Dei* II.19).

The question I would like to consider now is how this distinction between eternal and divine law on the one hand, and temporal and civic law on the other hand, is connected with the distinction between the heavenly and earthly cities central to *De civitate Dei*.[35] There must be some connection between the two, because in this work Augustine seeks to distinguish the norms which pertain to the city of God, the heavenly city, and those relevant to the earthly one. Let us first see what the defining characteristics of the two cities are. Near the end of Book 14, Augustine summarizes his argument so far as follows:[36]

> Two cities, then, have been created by two loves: that is, the earthly by love of self extending even to contempt of God, and the heavenly by love of God, extending to contempt of self. The one, therefore, glories in itself, the other glories in the Lord; the one seeks glory from men, the other finds its highest glory in God, the witness of our conscience. The one lifts up its head in its own glory; the other says to its God, "Thou art my glory, and the lifter up of mine head" [Psalm 3:4]. In the earthly city princes are as much mastered by the lust for mastery as the nations which they subdue are by them; in the heavenly city all serve one another in charity, rulers by their counsel and subjects by their obedience.

---

[35] For an introduction to Augustine's *De civitate Dei*, see O'Daly 1999; Weithman 2001, 235–237; Wetzel 2012.

[36] *De civ. Dei* 14.28: *Fecerunt itaque ciuitates duas amores duo, terrenam scilicet amor sui usque ad contemptum Dei, caelestem uero amor Dei usque ad contemptum sui. Denique illa in se ipsa, haec in Domino gloriatur. Illa enim quaerit ab hominibus gloriam; huic autem Deus conscientiae testis maxima est gloria. Illa in gloria sua exaltat caput suum; haec dicit Deo suo: Gloria mea et exaltans caput meum. Illi in principibus eius uel in eis quas subiugat nationibus dominandi libido dominatur; in hac seruiunt inuicem in caritate et praepositi consulendo et subditi obtemperando.*

In a nutshell, the difference between the two cities is that in the earthly city humans seek glory for themselves: they seek domination, they want to be like God, and as a result injustice and violence reign. In the heavenly city, by contrast, citizens love one another and God, seeking subordination and obedience to Him, acknowledging His dominion and supremacy. As a result, this is a city of peace and justice. The city of God includes the saints, the angels (*De civ. Dei* 19.7) but also some citizens dispersed in earthly societies (15.7). It is obedience to eternal law that brings peace to the heavenly city and it is the common love of God that unties its citizens (15.3). This is a perfectly ordered society, as opposed to an earthly city, which can be ordered only through the agreement of its citizens.[37]

> Peace between man and God is the well-ordered obedience of faith to eternal law. Peace between man and man is well-ordered concord. Domestic peace is the well-ordered concord between those of the family who rule and those who obey. Civil peace is a similar concord among the citizens. The peace of the celestial city is the perfectly ordered and harmonious enjoyment of God and of one another in God. The peace of all things is the tranquillity of order.

But what does this concord of citizens actually involve? Of course, the law is necessary in order to set limits to human selfishness, and as I have said, it must be framed in accordance with the eternal law (see also *De vera rel.* 58). The law, however, is the minimum required for the order of the earthly city; Augustine stresses that the city is also ordered by love, the love of its citizens for each other (15.3). We need to remember here that for Augustine love is essential for virtue. He actually defines virtue as a form of love (*De mor. eccl.* 1.25, 46), primarily of God and then of his creatures, other humans. Justice, for instance, amounts to loving one's neighbours (*De civ. Dei* 19.21), not merely giving them their due. It is love, rather than only law, that ties together the people of a city. In the case of the heavenly city, the city of God, its citizens are motivated by a particular kind of love, the love of the good, that is, Christ. This is the supremely just city. In it justice is nothing other but love for the good, for Christ. Augustine presents Christ as the ruler of the city of God (*De civ. Dei* 2.21), and Christ is completely just (*solus iustus*), indeed both just and justifying (*iustus et iustificans, De civ. Dei* 17.4). The heavenly city is just to the extent that its members connect them-

---

37 *De civitate Dei* 19.13: *Pax hominis mortalis et Dei ordinata in fide sub aeterna lege oboedientia, pax hominum ordinata concordia, pax domus ordinata imperandi atque oboedienti concordia cohabitantium, pax civitatis ordinata imperandi atque oboedienti concordia civum, pax caelestis civitatis ordinantissima et concordissima societas fruendi Deo et invicem in Deo, pax omnium rerum tranquillitas ordinis.*

selves to Christ through love. Some of the citizens of this supremely just city also live in earthly cities, but through their wisdom and relation to the good they rather belong to the heavenly city and are destined for eternal life with God.

One can see here the similarities with the Stoic idea of the city of sages already presented by Zeno. The heavenly city resembles the Stoic city of sages, a cosmic city (Schofield 1991). Both cities are ordered not because of laws but because of the supreme virtue and love of their citizens – their love for each other in the Stoic city, and their love of God and for each other in Augustine's heavenly city.[38] There has been some doubt recently as to whether the Stoics in fact held that there is a special community of sages, or that only the sages count as real citizens (Vogt 2008, especially 65–110). Even if the latter is the case, and only the fully virtuous sages count as citizens,[39] this could still have inspired Augustine, who would have known the Stoic thesis from Cicero.[40] For even in that case the Stoic city and Augustine's heavenly city are both unified by the virtue and mutual love of its citizens, not by civic laws. In both cases it is important to notice the relation between the city of the virtuous and the earthly city of the nonvirtuous (as it were). Augustine and the Stoics distinguish the ethical and political realms, while also connecting the two: the heavenly city of the just or wise citizens is the source of norms, yet the truly political state of affairs occurs only in the earthly city.

One can object here that the heavenly city is also a city, that is, a community. This is indeed an important feature of Augustine's conception. But the question is to what extent it really is a *political* community. In the earthly city people have property, jobs, interests, courts, enemies of the state; all these secular features are missing from the heavenly city. The latter is still a city but not in the same political sense that the earthly one is. Thus Augustine, following the Stoics, distinguishes a specifically political realm but also connects it with an ethical realm from which the norms come, and which is political in a real but rather extended sense.

Augustine thus avoids two dangers, which earlier Christians did not. If one separates the political realm, the realm of city life and law, from the moral one, then one may wonder why the civic law is normative and not an arbitrary set of rules. To answer this question, one must connect legislation and political order with moral order, that is, with some principle of normativity. Tertullian and also Lactantius seek to do this by making the civic laws derivative of God's and af-

---

38 For the role of love in the Stoic city of sages, see Schofield 1991, 25–56, and for the role of love in Augustine's heavenly city, see von Heyking 2001.
39 See Diogenes Laertius VII.32–33 and the discussion in Vogt 2008, 76–78.
40 See e.g. Cicero, *Academica* II.136.

firming that civic laws would otherwise be unjust. Yet they do not clearly address the question of how God's laws can be of a specifically political character, and thus adequate for shaping the laws of human society. How are God's rules applicable in human society, which is so different from heaven? One possible answer is that these norms are not God's, but natural laws, or laws pertaining to human nature, which was in turn created by God. This answer, which we find implied in Lactantius and Gregory, may explain the integration of some norms in human societies, such as the acceptance of human freedom. But it cannot account for all political norms observed in human societies.

Augustine avoids both dangers by distinguishing two realms, an ethical and a political one, an earthly and a heavenly city, while also closely connecting the two. By distinguishing them, he avoids the danger of underspecifying the character of the human political realm. Augustine acknowledges the specific political nature of human city life, where people work, have families, go to the baths and to market places. By connecting the two cities, though, he avoids the danger of the arbitrariness of norms operating in a human society, since the heavenly kingdom is also a city, a political society as it were, which means that its laws have a certain political character and as such can function as models for those of the earthly city.

6 Conclusion

I have argued that early Christians were seriously concerned with the political norms of their non-Christian societies and that they developed three main models for assessing them. In the first, Christians distinguished two sources of normativity, the earthly and political emperor, as opposed to the heavenly and moral Christian God. However, they also connected the two by claiming that the former derives authority from the latter, since the Roman emperor is appointed by God. The second model conflates political and ethical norms and argues for the replacement of non-Christian political norms. The Christian God is the only source of norms, and no human society can flourish unless men endorse Christianity, acknowledging the Christian God as the only source of normativity. We find this model especially in the work of Lactantius. Finally, the third model, put forth by Augustine, both distinguishes and connects the political and ethical realm. By doing so it avoids the danger of the arbitrariness of political norms as well as the danger of not appreciating the particular nature of the human political realm. The source of political norms is not God but a special kind of city, a city of perfectly virtuous citizens, the heavenly city of God.

Primary literature

Athenagoras of Athens. 1990. *Athenagoras Legatio pro Christianis*, edited by Miroslav Marcovich. Berlin and New York: De Gruyter.
Augustine 1957–1972. *Augustine City of God. Against the Pagans*, by E. McCracken et al., Cambridge Mass. (Loeb).
Eusebius of Caesarea. 1999. *Eusebius' Life of Constantine*, translated with introduction and commentary by Averil Cameron and Stuart G. Hall. Oxford: Oxford Clarendon Press.
Gregory of Nyssa. 1986. *Gregorii Nysseni in Ecclesiasten Homiliae*, by James McDonough and Paul Alexander, Gregorii Nysseni Opera vol. 5. Leiden: Brill.
Justin Martyr. 1994. *Iustini Martyris Apologiae pro Christianis*, by Miroslav Marcovich. Berlin and New York: De Gruyter.
Lactantius. *Lactance De ira Dei*, by C. Ingemeau. Paris: Éditions du Cerf (SC 289).
Tatian the Syrian. 1995. *Tatiani Oratio Ad Graecos, Theophili Antiocheni Ad Autolycum*, by Miroslav Marcovich. Berlin and New York: De Gruyter.
Tertullian. 1931. *Tertullian: Apology, De Spectaculis* by T. R. Glover. Cambridge, MA: Harvard University Press (Loeb).
Theophilus of Antiocheia. 1995. *Theophili Antiocheni Ad Autolycum*, by Miroslav Marcovich. Berlin and New York: De Gruyter.

Secondary literature

Barnes, Timothy D. 1968. "Legislation against the Christians." *Journal of Roman Studies* 58:32–50.
Barnes, Timothy D. 1975. "The Embassy of Athenagoras." *Journal of Theological Studies* 26:111–114.
Bradley, Denis J. M. 1974. "The Transformation of the Stoic Ethics in Clement of Alexandria." *Augustinianum* 14:41–66.
Colot, Blandine. 2016. *Lactance. Penser la conversion de Rome au temps de Constantin*. Firenze: Leo S. Olschki Editore.
Dodaro, Robert J. 2004. *Christ and the Just Society in the Thought of Augustine*. Cambridge: Cambridge University Press.
Fox, Robin L. 1986. *Pagans and Christians*. New York: Penguin Books.
Furnish, Victor P. 1996. *Theology and Ethics in Paul*. Nashville Tennessee: Abingdon Press.
de Ste Croix, Geoffrey E. M. 1963. "Why were the Christians persecuted." *Past and Present* 26:6–38.
Karamanolis, George. 2013 (2nd revised ed. 2021). *The Philosophy of Early Christianity*. Durham and London: Routledge.
Kristensen, Troels M. 2013. *Making and Breaking the Gods. Christian Responses to Pagan Sculpture in Late Antiquity*. Aarhus: Aarhus University Press.
Lieu, Judith. 2004. *Christian Identity in the Jewish and Graeco-Roman World*. Oxford: Oxford University Press.

Minns, Denis. 2010. "Justin Martyr." In *The Cambridge History of Philosophy in Late Antiquity*, edited by Lloyd P. Gerson, Volume I, 258–269. Cambridge: Cambridge University Press.

Miraval, Pierre. 2001. *Eusèbe Césarée. La theologie politique de l'Empire chrétien*. Paris: Les Editions du Cerf.

O'Daly, Gerard J. P. 1999. *Augustine's City of God: A Reader's Guide*. Oxford: Oxford Clarendon Press.

Osborne, Eric F. 1973. *Justin Martyr*. Tübingen: Mohr Siebeck.

Ramelli, Ilaria. 2016. *Social Justice and the Legitimacy of Slavery*. Oxford: Oxford University Press.

Rosner, Brian. 2003. "Paul's Ethics." In *The Cambridge Companion to St. Paul*, edited by James D. G. Dunn, 212–226. Cambridge: Cambridge University Press.

Schofield, Malcolm. 1991. *The Stoic Idea of the City*. Cambridge: Cambridge University Press.

Sherwin-White, Adrian N. 1963. *Roman Society and Roman Law in the New Testament*. Oxford: Oxford Clarendon Press.

Sider, Robert D. 2001. *Christian and Pagan in the Roman Empire. The Witness of Tertullian*. Washington: Catholic University of America Press.

Vogt, Katja M. 2008. *Law, Reason and the Cosmic City. Political Philosophy in the Early Stoa*. Oxford: Oxford University Press.

von Heyking, John. 2001. *Augustine and Politics as Longing in the World*. Columbia and London: University of Missouri Press.

Weithman, Paul. 2001. "Augustine's Political Philosophy." In *The Cambridge Companion to Augustine*, edited by Eleonore Stump and Norman Kretzmann, 234–252. Cambridge: Cambridge University Press.

Wetzel, James (editor). 2012. *Augustine's City of God. A Critical Guide*, Cambridge: Cambridge University Press.

Part IV: Medieval Philosophy

Peter Adamson
Against Nature: Two Critics of Naturalism in the Islamic World

Abstract: Two philosophers from the Islamic world, one Muslim and one Jewish, are discussed in this essay: Abū Bakr al-Rāzī and Judah Hallevi. Both of them were familiar with the occasionalism of Islamic theology and with the philosophical tradition and its denial of non-natural causation. They offer strikingly similar critiques of naturalism, that is, explanation in terms of immanent natures, arguing that direct divine action within the world may be a better explanation of so-called 'natural' phenomena. They present us with a God who operates directly within the cosmos, acting like a ruler who intervenes directly in the affairs of his subjects rather than a legislator who sets down laws and observes with detachment as the laws are carried out. Yet both al-Rāzī and Hallevi do acknowledge the efficacy of causes other than God.

1 Introduction

Nowadays, the phrase 'law of nature' is to some extent a dead metaphor. At least, in using this phrase we do not necessarily imply that the natural world has a legislator. In antiquity, though, the metaphor was still a live one. Detailed evidence for this has been provided by Wolfgang Kullmann, whose 2010 survey of the concept of the 'law of nature' in ancient philosophy shows that it goes back all the way to the Pre-Socratics. Heraclitus already draws an explicit connection between the divine and human legislators, whose laws (*nomoi*) are, he says, 'nourished' by the single law of god (fr. B114). Particularly central in Kullmann's reconstruction are the Stoics, who make Zeus a 'founder of nature'.[1] The predictability and regularity of natural phenomena are an expression of divine rationality. As so often, this Stoic idea was taken up by the Church Fathers, with the result that an originally pagan conception of the relation between the divine and the natural was well-known to the Latin Christian medievals.

Yet the medievals eventually came to conceive of this relation in a profoundly non-Stoic way. For the determinist Stoics, the workings of god are necessary

---

[1] As Brouwer 2013 pointed out in a review of Kullmann's book, one could give Plato a more significant role insofar as the *Timaeus* and *Laws* envision a divine craftsman who orders the cosmos in a law-like way.

and the cosmos cannot be other than it is, perhaps not even in the smallest detail.² The medievals thought otherwise. Especially the voluntarists of the late thirteenth and fourteenth centuries emphasized that God retains the capacity to order the world very differently, since it lies within his 'absolute' power to do anything that can be done. If both moral and natural laws remain constant within the world as He is created it, this is because of a 'covenant' God has made with humankind, which has its continued force simply because of divine will.³ Medieval voluntarism posed a significant challenge to Aristotelian philosophy, because that philosophy was no less committed to the necessity of nature than Stoic theology had been. As sceptically-minded fourteenth century thinkers like Nicholas of Autrecourt pointed out, it lies within God's absolute power to break from natural regularities by performing a miracle, giving us an experience of a non-existent object as if it existed, and so on.⁴ This shows that the study of those regularities does not rise to the level of the necessary, scientific knowledge limned in Aristotle's *Posterior Analytics*.

Broadly speaking, the Aristotelian response in the fourteenth century was to lower expectations. Ockham, Buridan, and Peter of Ailly all in various ways admit that absolute certainty may be unavailable but insist that we have the requisite knowledge to continue doing science. As Dominik Perler (2010, 390) has written, "all we can say is that if the natural course determined by natural laws continues, our mental states are reliably caused by material things and present them as they are. All we can strive for is this kind of hypothetical certainty." To put it another way, the thinkers of Latin Christendom eventually concluded that the philosopher may have knowledge of natural laws even if those laws are occasionally broken.

The same tensions played out in the medieval Islamic world. Most famous is the clash between al-Ghazālī and Averroes in their candidly titled works, *The Incoherence of the Philosophers* and *The Incoherence of the Incoherence*. Al-Ghazālī is usually taken to represent the viewpoint of Islamic rationalist theology, or *kalām*, and in particular of the Ashʿarite school. This tradition is fully committed to voluntarism. As al-Ghazālī (1997, 174) memorably says in his *Incoherence*, a book left in my library may miraculously transform into a horse and urinate all over my books while I am away. Since it would be possible for God to work such transformations, the only way I can have knowledge that things will proceed as normal is for God Himself to bestow that knowledge on me di-

---

2 I say 'perhaps' to take account of the idea that there could be causally inefficacious variations that differentiate individuals in successive world-cycles. See Long and Sedley, 1987, 52F-G.
3 For this much discussed topic see e.g. Oakley 1984 and 2002; Courtenay 1984 and 1990.
4 See further Perler 2006; Lagerlund 2010.

rectly. In general, the regularity we see in nature is the result of God's 'custom' (*sunna*), not of any intrinsic necessity in nature itself. Averroes (1954, 331) meanwhile adheres unapologetically to the Aristotelian line, insisting that causal relationships are necessary precisely because they are grounded in natures of which we can have demonstrative knowledge. If causes fail to take effect, this is simply because of external hindrance, as when talc prevents fire from burning something. Earlier representatives of *falsafa*, the tradition of Hellenizing and in particular Aristotelianizing thought in the Islamic world, would have agreed. For al-Fārābī and Avicenna, to mention only the two most famous names among the *falāsifa*, certain knowledge of necessary truths is the epistemic gold standard and it can be achieved through the pursuit of natural philosophy.[5]

What seems to be missing here is a moderate view, like that which would be adopted among fourteenth century Aristotelians in Latin Christendom. Was intellectual discourse in the Islamic world really divided so neatly into two camps, with the voluntarist and occasionalist *mutakallimūn* pitted against the necessitarian *falāsifa*? Here we reach the less familiar story I want to tell in the present paper. In fact there were numerous thinkers in the Islamic world who did not fall neatly into either camp. They were familiar with the *kalām* and the *falsafa* positions and wanted to distance themselves from both. I will consider two such figures, one a Muslim, the other a Jew. The Muslim is Abū Bakr al-Rāzī, who died in 925 AD and was along with Avicenna the most important medical author of the classical Islamic period. His philosophical output is mostly lost and known only indirectly through reports by other authors. I will however be focusing on a work (or more likely, part of a larger, otherwise lost work) that is extant, which comes down to us with the title *On Metaphysics*.[6] The Jewish thinker I will discuss is Judah Hallevi, who lived in Islamic Spain for most of his life before traveling east to the Holy Land, dying there in 1141. He was also a doctor, and a poet to boot, but his place in the history of philosophy is secured by a lengthy treatise called the *Kuzari*, in which he depicts the king of the Khazar people being converted to Judaism by a scholar who persuades him that this religion is superior to the belief systems of Islam, Christianity, and *falsafa*.[7]

---

[5] On levels of certainty in al-Fārābī see Black 2006, 11–46.

[6] Cited in my own translations from al-Rāzī, *Rasā'il falsafiyya* 1939. For an Italian translation and commentary see Lucchetta 1987.

[7] I use the Arabic text in Bashir 2012 cited by section number in my own translations. For an older English translation originally published in 1905, see Hirschfeld 1964. It has the same section numbers as the Arabic edition.

I juxtapose these two men not because I want to assert a direct historical link between them, but because they offer strikingly similar critiques of naturalism, that is, explanation in terms of immanent natures.[8] Both al-Rāzī and Hallevi argue that the *falāsifa* are overconfident in their appeals to the natures of things, and that direct divine action within the world may be a better explanation of so-called 'natural' phenomena. They present us with a God who operates directly within the cosmos, acting like a ruler who intervenes directly in the affairs of his subjects rather than a legislator who sets down laws and observes with detachment as the laws are carried out. This may make them sound like straightforward adherents of *kalām* occasionalism. But in fact, both al-Rāzī and Hallevi acknowledge the efficacy of causes other than God. For al-Rāzī, the phenomena that philosophers explain with reference to immanent natures can be better explained by appealing to *two* causes that are not immanent: God and the soul. Judah Hallevi concedes more to the philosophers, allowing that natural causes do have modest explanatory force. Yet he insists that a more significant role is played by direct divine causation.

2 Al-Rāzī against nature

Our discussion of al-Rāzī will require a brief primer on his controversial theory of the 'five eternal principles', namely God, the soul, matter, time, and place. A range of other authors, mostly hostile to al-Rāzī, inform us that in now-lost works he explained the generation of the cosmos in light of the interaction between these five things. God and the soul are designated as 'active' principles, which produce the cosmos out of eternal matter, which is 'passive'.[9] Time and place (also known as 'eternity' and 'void') are neither active nor passive, but must already exist in order for the cosmos to begin, since it must start at some moment and occupy some region of empty space. Creation occurs when the soul conceives a foolish desire to involve itself with matter. Had it been up to God, there would be no physical universe at all, since bodily existence always involves suffering. God allows the soul to make its unwise choice in order to let it learn from the mistake, as a wise father might allow a child to travel to a dangerous country to make the child appreciate his homeland.[10] Balancing out this

---

8 Mostly I will be focusing on causal explanation, but as we will see Hallevi extends his critique to the question of ethical naturalism, that is, the explanation of why certain actions are good or bad.
9 al-Rāzī, *Rasā'il falsafiyya*, 197.
10 Reported by Fakhr al-Dīn al-Rāzī 1987, Volume 4, 416.

tough love, God mercifully intervenes to ensure that the universe is as well-designed as possible and has good features that compensate to some extent for the inevitable suffering. For al-Rāzī the purpose of philosophy is to help the soul to free itself from its attachment to matter, so that it can be 'liberated' and return to its former state, now having learned its lesson.

None of this is explicitly mentioned in the text that comes down to us as *On Metaphysics*. I believe though that it provides the context for understanding al-Rāzī's critique of Aristotelian naturalism. The title *On Metaphysics*, as well as the ascription of the work to al-Rāzī, derives from the unique manuscript containing the treatise, which also preserves a short text by al-Rāzī describing the signs by which one recognizes a political leader who is favoured by God.[11] Despite the title, *On Metaphysics* as we have it is really a critical discussion of issues in natural philosophy, with particular attention given to issues we know interested al-Rāzī, namely medicine and the eternity of the cosmos. These are indeed the focus of the latter two sections of the work, which deal with embryology and the eternity question. Here I will limit myself to the first section (116–24), which critically discusses philosophical ideas about nature.

Al-Rāzī immediately identifies as his target "Aristotle and those who comment on his books", which is not a bluff: he goes on to show knowledge of the late antique *Physics* commentaries by Philoponus and Porphyry.[12] The Aristotelians, he says, think that the existence of nature is too obvious to need proof (presumably he thinks here of *Physics* II.1, 193a3–4). A focus on the question of whether a given principle stands in need of argument is characteristic of al-Rāzī. He elsewhere insisted that two of his five principles, namely time and place, are in no need of demonstration because they are simply obvious.[13] Apparently he gave the example of someone sitting in a dark house holding their breath, so as to be completely unaware of any motion, while still being cognizant that time is passing. The problem for the Aristotelian is that unlike time and place, nature is not something of which we are immediately aware. As al-Rāzī puts it:

> *On Metaphysics* 116: One may dispense with proof only for things that have been directly experienced, and for the intellectual first principles of demonstrations. But nature is not available to sense-perception, nor is the knowledge of it a principle for the intellect.

---

[11] See Kraus' introductory remarks at al-Rāzī, *Rasā'il falsafiyya*, 113.
[12] For this work as evidence on the reception of Porphyry's commentary in Arabic, see Adamson 2007.
[13] This aspect of his cosmology was in turn taken up by the later Fakhr al-Dīn al-Rāzī, who treats the earlier al-Rāzī as a proponent of this kind of "epistemic immediacy." See Adamson 2018 (where I discuss the thought experiment of the dark house), and Adamson 2017.

In the absence of direct, sensory evidence, it is no better to insist without argument that nature exists than to insist without argument that nature does not exist, as an opponent of the Aristotelians could do with equal justice.

This point is especially telling given that, as al-Rāzī notes without naming names, "another group of ancient philosophers" denied the reality of nature. We might – again, without necessarily asserting any historical connection – compare what he does here to methods of the ancient sceptics, as epitomized in the 'five modes' of Agrippa, as recorded by Sextus Empiricus.[14] He invokes both what Sextus would call the 'mode of dispute', by alluding to thinkers who rejected nature, and also the 'mode of hypothesis', stating that "something is not true just because people grant it, just as something is not wrong just because people disagree with it" (*On Metaphysics* 116). All this shows simply that if we are to accept the reality of nature, we will need to be persuaded by a good argument.

An attempt at such an argument is, according to al-Rāzī, provided by a further group of thinkers:

> *On Metaphysics* 116: Some philosophers (*falāsifa*) have come to our attention, who claimed that the proof of its existence is its actions, and its powers spread throughout the world that necessitate its actions, for instance fire and air going away from the center [of the universe], and water and earth towards it.

Though the adherents of this view likewise go unidentified, the proposal looks broadly Neoplatonic. We may be reminded of Plotinus, according to whom nature is the lowest principle of the cosmic hierarchy, below soul and intellect. But the remark about 'diffusion' links the passage especially to Philoponus, who in an influential passage said that nature 'descends' or 'permeates' (*katadedukuia*) into bodies.[15] That this is al-Rāzī's source seems to be confirmed later in the section, when he explicitly credits Philoponus with the thesis that "nature is a power that penetrates (*tanfudhu*) through bodies and governs them" (118).

It is in response to this argument that al-Rāzī first invokes a rival explanation for natural phenomena, namely that they are brought about directly by God:

> *On Metaphysics* 116–17: On what basis do you deny that God, great and exalted, is all by Himself that which necessitates the powers of all other actions, and the natures of things?

And later, with more detail:

---

[14] On which see Annas and Barnes 1985.
[15] For the relevant passage (Philoponus *in Phys.* 197–8) and its influence, see Lammer 2015.

On Metaphysics 120: If they say, "we find that material objects and animals are beneficially constituted in a way could never be imagined or understood by us, which shows that nature does this," then one may say to them, "on what basis do you deny that it is the Creator who does this, given that you have described nature with most of the attributes of the Creator? For you claimed that nature is an eternal, incorporeal substance, that does not change or alter, is unaffected by generation or corruption, governs the universe, and carries out its actions wisely and rightly. The only difference you allow between nature and God is that you suppose nature to be among immanent (*maṭbū'a*) things, rather than being separate and self-subsisting."

According to these passages, God and nature are at least equally good candidates for explaining such phenomena as the motion of elemental bodies. Though he does not say much about the rival scenario he is envisioning, at this stage it would seem that al-Rāzī has in mind a cosmology like that presupposed in *kalām*. This would be an occasionalist picture, as suggested by the remark in the first of the two passages that God would bring about things 'all by Himself' (*bi-dhātihi*), which I take it means "without the involvement of secondary causes." In other words, we need not hypothesize an immanent nature in fire to explain its upward motion, since we can just suppose that fire is moved directly by divine fiat.

Though al-Rāzī does not invoke the possibility of miracles, like al-Ghazālī or the fourteenth century voluntarists mentioned earlier, he does stress that empirical phenomena are 'necessitated' by nature, on the philosophers' view, and by God, according to the rival view. This is part and parcel of a more general strategy, in which al-Rāzī observes that the philosophers tend to portray nature as a cause that is very much like God in the *kalām* theory. Not only does nature necessarily bring about its effects, but it is also capable of "aiming at an end, making one thing so that another may exist", as if nature were "choosing, knowing, and wise" (118). Hence his accusation that the philosophers "have described nature with most of the attributes of the Creator." To illustrate the teleology the philosophers see in nature, al-Rāzī gives examples from the domain of medicine: in the generation of an embryo, nature forms organs for certain purposes, the eye for vision, the hand for grasping, the teeth for chewing (the last example of course evokes *Physics* II.8). Nature also has the role of restoring the body to health, something for which he quotes a well-known saying ascribed to Hippocrates, "natures are the healers of disease" (118).

As I've suggested, part of the force of al-Rāzī's polemic here is that, once we portray nature as being like God, there is nothing to choose between the two rival accounts. If God and nature are both capable of wisely selecting certain ends and then arranging things so that these ends are achieved, then either would be equally plausible explanations for such phenomena as the motion of fire, the formation of embryos, or recovery from illness. Yet al-Rāzī also wants to suggest that nature is a *less* plausible explanation, because it is hard to believe that nature is really wise or capable of means-end reasoning. Indeed, he asserts that the philosophers themselves think of nature as 'lifeless' (*mawāt*). And "how can that which is lifeless be wise, yet not discerning, rational, or capable of sense-perception? How can order and intelligence (*naẓar*) come from what is bereft of discernment and life?" (118). Notice that al-Rāzī is not anticipating modern-day doubts about Aristotelian natural philosophy by questioning the presence of teleology in empirical phenomena. Rather, he accepts that supposedly 'natural' things show the traces of intelligent design, but doubts that lifeless nature could be the explanation for that design. He turns against Aristotle the familiar Aristotelian example of goal-directed activity, namely housebuilding, pointing out that if nature cannot produce a house (for that we need a capable, living being), it is surely incredible to suppose that nature could form a human body (119).

If al-Rāzī were simply out to defend the *kalām*, occasionalist cosmology – whether sincerely or for dialectical purposes – then we would expect him to say that the human body is instead formed by God. As we'll see, this is exactly what Judah Hallevi is going to argue. But this is not what we find in al-Rāzī. Instead, he says:

> *On Metaphysics* 119: On what basis do you deny that the composition of the man is due to the rational soul rather than nature, and that the powers of growth and nutrition are due to it rather than nature? We turn the tables on you, ascribing to the soul what is due to nature, just as you ascribe to nature what is due to the rational soul.

As with the question whether God or nature offers a better explanatory principle, al-Rāzī is implicitly making two moves here. First, the soul is at least as good an explanation as nature, hence the last sentence with its suggestion of dialectical stalemate. But second, the stalemate can be resolved in favour of the soul rather than nature, on the basis of the now familiar point that things like the human body exhibit signs of wisdom. He treats Galen as an ally of Aristotle, thinking of Galen's paean to nature and its teleological operation in *On the Usefulness of the Parts*. And against Galen, he writes:

> *On Metaphysics* 120: You have described nature in two contrary ways. For you have said that nature makes this – meaning the teeth and the mouth – intentionally. But then you said that voluntary motion is one of the things done by the soul, and that intention belongs to the soul alone, just as volition belongs to the soul alone.

Similarly, he criticizes Porphyry for suggesting that nature can "act for the sake of something" despite lacking the power for intellection and volition (121). In general, al-Rāzī condemns these ancient thinkers for "making nature the cause of actions that can arise only from that which lives and chooses" (119).

I propose that we should read this stretch of al-Rāzī's *On Metaphysics* as an explanation of why his own cosmological theory does not give nature a status equal to that of his five eternal principles. He seizes upon the extravagant claims made for nature by 'the philosophers', and uses those claims against them: the more they insist that the natural world exhibits goal-directed activities, the less credible it is that nature could really be the cause of those activities. Far more reasonable to appeal to God, whom we know to be intelligent and capable of arranging things so as to achieve a purpose, and also to the rational soul, which has these same traits. What the Aristotelians explain with their appeals to nature, al-Rāzī can explain more convincingly with reference to God and the soul, the first two, 'active' principles of his own cosmology, which was equally outrageous to both the *falāsifa* and the *mutakallimūn* and was strongly criticized by members of both traditions.

Since he is here operating in the mode of refutation and not expounding his own theory, it remains somewhat unclear which teleological features are due to God and which to the soul. But the examples he considers suggest that God at least has jurisdiction over non-living things like the elements, whereas soul is responsible for forming and steering individual organisms. Even animals, al-Rāzī writes, exhibit 'choice and discrimination', for example when birds build their nests in high, inaccessible places or choose certain foods over others (122).[16] Does this leave anything for 'nature' to explain? Apparently not. As we have seen, al-Rāzī seems unimpressed by the philosophers' attempts to establish that nature exists at all, and as I've just suggested it would be in keeping with his cosmology to explain all life, and all teleological phenomena, with reference to the soul and God. Here in *On Metaphysics* he does note that the natural realm also includes many *non*-teleological features, such as the unwieldy horns that cause stags to get caught in tree branches, and the presence of useless breasts in human men.[17] But rather than putting the blame for such things on a distinct principle called 'nature', it seems that in his system what we tend to call 'natural evils' are just an unintended result of soul's association with matter.

We can find confirmation that *On Metaphysics* expresses al-Rāzī's own views and not just a dialectical engagement with Aristotelianism, by turning to a testimony found in the later philosopher-theologian Fakhr al-Dīn al-Rāzī (they are

---

[16] For his views on non-human cognitive capacities, see Adamson 2012.
[17] As noted by Lucchetta 1987, this stretch of the text draws on Theophrastus' doubts concerning teleology. See Gutas 2010, §22.3.

both called al-Rāzī because both hailed from the Persian city of Rayy). Within a discussion of design arguments for the existence of God, Fakhr al-Dīn refers to a lost work by the earlier al-Rāzī which, he claims, explicitly denied that nature can produce the wondrously well-designed features we find in the human body.[18] Al-Rāzī offered as an analogy the way that a jug has a wide neck for pouring in water, a body with dimensions that are neither too narrow nor too wide, so that water can be poured out at the right speed, and a handle that fits perfectly in the hand. Likewise:

> He mentioned something of the wondrous compositions in it and the forms that correspond to wisdom and advantage, and then said: the sound mind is aware that these wonderous and astonishing things in the composition of the body can come into being only from a wise and powerful [agent] who created the structure [of the body] through His power, and its wisely-chosen features through His wisdom.

Notice how close is the language here to what we've seen in *On Metaphysics*: God, but not nature, can be credited with the design of supposedly 'natural' things because He has power and knowledge whereas nature does not.

3 Judah Hallevi against nature

Judah Hallevi presents us with a very different sort of figure. He was Jewish and from the western end of the Islamic world in Andalusia, whereas al-Rāzī was Muslim and from Persia. Hallevi was a pious defender of Rabbinical orthodoxy, whereas al-Rāzī's scandalous writings led to frequent accusations of heresy from other Muslims. The text we will now be dealing with is also rather different from *On Metaphysics*. It takes the form of a lengthy dialogue, in which the Khazar king briefly interviews representatives of *falsafa*, Islam and Christianity, dismisses their claims to truth, and then embarks on a wide-ranging conversation with his Jewish spiritual advisor. Yet Hallevi likewise criticizes Aristotelian naturalism, and on much the same grounds we have just seen:

> *Kuzari* 1.76–7: *King:* "I observe them just leading us astray with these expressions, and making us give God an associate by saying 'nature is wise and active'. We even sometimes say it is a Creator, according to the drift of their remarks." *Scholar:* "Yes, but the elements, the moon, the sun and the stars perform actions by means of heating and cooling, moistening and drying. This carries no implication that they are wise, but rather that they are sub-

---

[18] See Fakhr al-Dīn al-Rāzī 1987, Volume 1, 223–4. My thanks to Fedor Benevich for bringing this passage to my attention.

servient. Giving form, determining, bringing forth, and anything in which there is wisdom due to a purpose, must be related to someone wise, powerful and dominating. Someone does no harm if he calls this thing that applies heating and cooling 'nature,' so long as he denies wisdom to it."

Like al-Rāzī, Hallevi is anxious that nature not be set up as an active principle alongside God, which would bring about its effects in a goal-directed and intelligent way. Instead, nature mindlessly brings about relatively crude effects, which seem to be restricted to causing the four basic Aristotelian contrarieties of heat, cold, moisture and dryness.

Of course, Aristotelians liked to think that one can explain quite a lot by invoking the manipulation of the contrarieties. It was even supposed that the success of astrology can be traced ultimately to the effects of the stars on these fundamental properties. To mention a simple example, astrologers were supposedly able to predict rainfall because of the 'moistening' effects of certain planets (Bos and Burnett 2000). As it happens, a contemporary and debating partner of Judah Hallevi named Abraham Ibn Ezra ascribed to this sort of theory, combining astrological ideas with Aristotelian cosmology. As Y. Tzvi Langermann has written, "the approach that constituted for Yehudah ha-Levi *the* philosophical norm, that is to say, that set of beliefs and opinions that makes up the particular 'philosophy' that threatened Jewish singularity and, therefore, had to be combatted in the *Kuzari*, is the very tendency towards naturalistic explanation, by means of astrological theory, of the differences among the various faiths" (Langermann 1993).[19] To this I would add that Hallevi is disturbed by the pretensions of natural philosophy quite generally. The claims of astrologers are simply a paradigm example of a broader, and pernicious, phenomenon.

As we have just seen, though, Hallevi openly concedes that appeals to nature can have some explanatory force. He is not an outright sceptic regarding nature like al-Rāzī.[20] His goal is to restrict rather than eliminate nature's causal efficacy. In one example of this moderate approach, he says that the balance of qualities is too exact and delicate to succeed without being steered by divine providence:

> *Kuzari* 3.53: Natural, generated things are all determined, balanced and proportioned in their mixtures from the four natures, and by the slightest adjustment (*bi-aysar amr*) they become perfect and well-shaped, and take on the animal or plant form to which they lay claim. Yet the slightest thing can corrupt the mixture of the form that shapes it. Haven't you seen an egg being corrupted by the least accident of excessive heat, cold, or movement,

---

19 See also Langermann 1997.
20 For more on Hallevi's use of skeptical arguments see Malachi 2018.

so that it fails to receive the form of a chicken? [...] So to whom is it given to determine the actions as far as the divine produces them, other than God alone?

In a passage just cited above, Hallevi said that 'nature' is simply a word for crude physical forces. It is improper to use the word for more sophisticated causal processes, which are in fact brought about by God.[21] In particular, it is God and not nature who creates organisms and grants them the powers distinctive of their various species:

> *Kuzari* 3.23: I gave you the example of the creation of plant and animal, saying that the form by which one plant is a different substance than another and one animal different from another is not a nature, but an influence from God the exalted, which the learned (*'ulamā'*) [merely] *call* 'nature' (*ṭabʿīa*).
>
> *Kuzari* 5.10: Anything possessed of these powers for growth, reproduction and nutrition, but is incapable of locomotion, is governed by nature according to the philosophers. In fact, though, it is God who governs it in a certain degree and disposition, which if you want, you can call 'nature', 'soul', 'power', or 'angel'.

Again, this does not mean that the elements have no causal effects, merely that these effects would be insufficient to bring about such phenomena as viable organisms.

This leaves 'natural' or physical forces as mere instruments that God uses to accomplish His will. In fact Hallevi envisions a chain of causes here, which is much like the chain invoked by astrologically inclined philosophers. God's influence is first of all ('without an intermediary') exercised upon the heavenly spheres, and the spheres in turn affect the four elements in the realm below the moon. This is why Hallevi said, in the first passage we cited from the *Kuzari*, that the heavens are 'subservient' to God. Supposing that they, or any other natural things, are the ultimate explanation for the generation and corruption is like supposing that the brain is the intellect: it is to mistake the instrument for the cause (4.3). To substantiate this claim, Hallevi mounts a sustained attack on the idea of 'bottom up' causation, in which organic forms would emerge from the mixture or combination of material constituents without any external help.

Thus, when the king mentions the philosophers' claim that "all generated things arise from the mixture of the four elements", the religious scholar re-

---

21 Helen Hattab informs me that in his *Philosophiae Naturalis Adversus Aristotelem* (1621, 255), Sebastianus Basso argued in a very similar spirit against Jesuit claims that Nature is responsible for human anatomy. In the passage Basso argues that Nature cannot be responsible for the construction of the veins if it lacks cognition. Rather a wise designer who seeks to achieve some goal must be given the credit, and this is God.

sponds that some source of wisdom is needed to distinguish substances into their different kinds. Blind nature may be able to produce the necessary material basis, but intelligence is needed to bestow *form* on those materials:

> *Kuzari* 4.9: We affirm that the material constituents (*mawādd*) of generation and corruption are on account of the spheres, whereas the forms are on account of their governor, who disposes them and arranges them as instruments for the subsistence of everything he wants to come to be, without our understanding this in detail. The astrologer claims to have a detailed and full understanding, but we deny that to him, and insist that no human grasps this.

For Hallevi the Creator is thus a 'god of the gaps', who explains what natural forces cannot. But here the gaps are sizable, with all substantial forms deriving from God's providential oversight. Hallevi is particularly struck by the cunning design of animals, which he takes to be a clear sign of "a wisdom that [human] minds cannot grasp in detail (*tafṣīl*), but only in general (*jumla*)" (3.11), and certainly not the result of the mutual interaction between the elements.

Hallevi thinks that the philosophers themselves understood this, which is why they postulated their so-called 'giver of forms' (5.2–4). This is an allusion to a theory first mooted by al-Fārābī, and then developed by Avicenna, according to which the lowest of the intellects associated with the heavenly spheres emanates substantial forms into suitably prepared matter. Hallevi does not so much target this thesis for refutation as make it the occasion for paying the philosophers a back-handed compliment. Even if they may sometimes talk like 'bottom up' materialists, in the end they see that a supernatural, 'top down' cause is needed. Unfortunately they misidentify the cause, granting to a mere celestial intellect the providential, form-giving role that is rightly God's. Here, we might see an echo of the sort of argument used more than once by al-Rāzī. Once we have agreed to invoke an active, powerful, knowing causal principle to explain the appearance of substantial forms, why not just say that this principle is God?

Still, as I say, Hallevi disagrees with al-Rāzī in that he is willing to label certain, admittedly rather humble, effects as the work of nature. For a really informative passage on this score we need to wait for the fifth and final book of the *Kuzari*. Here, Hallevi draws a distinction between two ways that things can be produced by God: either "by primary intention or by way of a chain" (5.20). The former would include "the evident ordering and arrangement in animals, plants, and the spheres, which no reasonable, thoughtful person would ascribe to chance, but rather to the intention of a wise artisan." The latter meanwhile is exemplified by fire's burning wood, something he explains in terms of the interaction of basic elemental qualities. Again, the contrast is aligned with that between form and matter. Crude interactions involving heat, cold, moisture and dryness are the domain of 'intermediary' and 'instrumental' causes, but these are inadequate to explain higher, organic forms. The latter are instead bestowed directly by God. Among the advantages of this theory, from Hallevi's point of view, is that it can undergird a theodicy. In particular, when humans are disobedient to God, this results from intermediate causes, not occasionalist divine influence (5.20).

Like al-Rāzī, Hallevi occupies an intermediate position between *falsafa* and *kalām*. The *falāsifa* are right that God does not do everything directly, but the *mutakallimūn* are right that He does much of what is supposedly done by nature. Where al-Rāzī recognized the soul as a lower, independent cause, Hallevi grants a limited scope for causal efficacy to matter and its basic qualities, and stipulates that if we use the term 'nature' properly, we will use it for this low-level kind of causation. As he puts it at the very end of the *Cuzari*, "our utmost aim is to discern, among natural things, that in which there is a cause that is not among natures, which we shall ascribe to a power that is not corporeal, but divine" (5.21). However, Hallevi takes a further step in the direction of the *kalām* position by affirming repeatedly that nature in this sense is subject to revision by God, in the form of miracles. And this stands to reason, when we consider that 'nature' is also traced to God's influence by means of a 'chain'. The thought seems to be that if God initiates such a chain from its top, He can also intervene to break a link further down in the chain.

This is vitally important for Hallevi, because miracles constitute the prime demonstration of Judaism. It is by invoking miracles recorded in the Torah, which were witnessed by too many people to be fraudulent, that the Jewish scholar initially convinces the king of the Khazars to convert. Now, Hallevi does seem to admit that miraculous events can be consistent with natural laws. A plague might be validated as miraculous and not as an example of 'the natural' (*ṭabīʿiyya*) simply by being made known in advance (1.83). But typically, he refers to miracles as events that 'breach' or 'overturn' (*qalaba*) the usual course of nature. It would be no exaggeration to say that Judaism itself stands or falls on the possibility that nature be overturned in this fashion, since Judaism requires a special relationship between God and the Jewish community, and God "has no connection with humankind except through a miracle in which things are transformed (*yaqlibu fī-hā al-aʿyān*)" (1.8).[22] Hence God

---

[22] Cf. *Kuzari* 1.67: the religious law speaks of "miracles and violation (*kharq*) of custom through the origination of things (*ikhtirāʿ aʿyān*), or the transformation of one thing into another, thus offering proof of the Creator of the world and His power to do whatever He wills, when He wills it."

speaks of Himself in the Bible not as Creator of the world but as the God of the Jews, who performed miracles for the Patriarchs (1.25; see also 2.54).

I mentioned at the outset of this paper the antinomy between Aristotelian philosophy of nature and Abrahamic belief in miracles, and mentioned too that the Latin scholastics resolved the antinomy by assigning natural laws the status of 'hypothetical certainty'. As Buridan observed, natural philosophy satisfies the criteria of Aristotle's theory of science, because it studies causal relations that obtain without exception – so long, that is, as nothing supernatural is going on.[23] There is no reason to think that Hallevi would disagree. We've seen that he does affirm the natural capacity of fire to burn wood, and more generally he is no opponent of the natural sciences. To the contrary, he tries to score points in favour of Judaism by asserting that the religious law is more informative on some scientific questions than the philosophers are. Its prescriptions regarding animal sacrifice, for example, show a greater insight into anatomy than can be gleaned from Aristotle or Galen (1.99; 2.64; 4.31).

But of course Hallevi is far less concerned for the niceties of Aristotelian epistemology than a thinker like John Buridan. So when it comes to address the conflict between natural philosophy and miracles, all his stress is on the fact that the regularities of nature are the work of divine will, and can thus be revoked whenever God sees fit:

> 3.73: Nature speaks through custom, the law through the breach of custom. The two may be reconciled: those customs that are breached were only natural [in the first place] because they were within the eternal will (*fī l-irāda al-qadīma*), conditional (*mashrūṭa*) upon it, and instituted according to it, since the six days of creation.

While miracles are ruptures in the custom of nature, they are also an expression of God's power over all things, which is normally expressed precisely in the natural regularities that miracles disrupt. The difference is not just that between the customary and the exceptional, but that between the direct and the mediated. Usually God does allow secondary causes to operate in the world, taking direct responsibility only for governance of the heavens and the granting of substantial forms. In a miracle, He cuts out the middleman, producing an event like the parting of the Red Sea 'without natural conditions' (*sharā'iṭ ṭabī'iyya*), acting "voluntarily, with intention, and immediately (*ikhtirā'an maqṣūdan awwaliyyan*)" (2.2). The initial creation of the universe was an event of this type, since of course no natural intermediaries could have been involved. Hallevi duly compares the working of miracles to the creative act in several passages. At one point, he

---

[23] See King 1987; Zupko 1993.

says that because miracles are "comparable to the first origination (*ikhtirā'*)", their occurrence "frees the soul of the faithful from the doubts advanced by the philosophers and materialists" (*al-falāsifa wa-l-dahriyya*) (1.91).

Let's round off this discussion of Judah Hallevi by bringing things full circle, and returning to the question of law. He does not quite compare the regularities of nature to a 'law' that can be broken, but he does use political metaphors to describe God's relationship to the world. The so-called 'naturalists' (*ṭabī'iyyūn*), he says, try to explain all things in terms of the natures of things that they can observe with their senses. Hallevi instead acknowledges that things are subject to God's *ḥukm*, a legal term that might be translated 'jurisdiction' or 'decree'. God's status as a 'king and lawgiver' is shown by the record of miracles in the Bible, such as His raising the dead back to life (3.17). If God is a king, He is a very involved one, not a detached monarch who delegates power to subordinates. Where the philosophers questioned whether God knows particulars, Hallevi's God knows every detail of His creation.

This point is made eloquently in a remarkable passage where Hallevi associates the philosophers with pagans, fire-worshippers, and atheists, all of whom deny the possibility of miracles:

> *Kuzari* 2.54: They agreed that no thing or action that shows itself in this world departs from the custom of nature. To the point that would-be philosophers, whose reflection is so subtle and belief so pure, determined that there is a first cause that does not resemble things and has no like, yet argued that He has no influence (*athar*) on the world, especially on particulars, deeming that He is above and transcends awareness of them, never mind creating something among them. But finally the purity of [the Jewish] community merited the descent of [God's] light upon them, and the working of miracles for them and breaching of the customs [of nature], that they might witness there to be a King who watches over and rules the mundane realm, who knows each thing whether slight or great, who requites the good and the evil, who bestows guidance upon hearts.

As the end of this quotation suggests, Hallevi sees a parallel between God's governance of nature and His governance over the norms of human behaviour. Just as the study of nature – in the properly narrow sense of material causation – is inadequate to account for the generation of plants, animals and humans, so natural reason is inadequate to determine right and wrong in the sphere of practical action.

At numerous places in the *Kuzari*, we can observe this parallel between the inadequate explanatory power of natural philosophy and the limited scope of merely human reasoning about norms. At one point, Hallevi draws that parallel explicitly:

> *Kuzari* 3.23: The determination of the relations that are required for human form are due only to the one who created them. Likewise God alone determines [which] living religious community (*milla*) deserves to have the divine command descend upon them.

The community in question being, of course, the Jews. They have been selected by God to receive the light of prophecy and a set of commandments that transcend what Hallevi calls 'rational (*'aqlī*) law' (1.81).[24] Such a law is knowable for anyone, whereas the 'divine law' is ordained by God (3.7). The reason we need the divine law is just like the reason we need God to bestow substantial forms when plants and animals are generated. As in the natural world, the demands of teleology in human practical affairs are too rigorous to be achieved without God's help, for "it is not within the scope of humankind to apportion the benefits of the faculties of souls and bodies" (2.50). We might, for instance, work out for ourselves that we occasionally need to rest from our normal activities, but God has ensured that we get just the right amount of respite by forbidding labour on the Sabbath (3.10).[25]

Here Hallevi anticipates an understanding of the religious law found in his more famous successor among Jewish Andalusian scholars, Maimonides. Generally speaking, Maimonides is much more open to the ideas of *falsafa* than Hallevi had been. Yet he too thinks that natural regularities can be overturned in a miracle (Langermann 2004, 147–72), and seems to have believed that those regularities are contingent upon God's determining activity.[26] In the religious law, too, we see that divine decrees have contingently determined and specified the norms that human reason can grasp in only a general fashion. The philosophers tell us to strive for virtue and that virtue lies in a mean between the extremes of vice, but so-called 'rational' laws are no substitute for the revealed law, which can be known only through a communication from God, since He has determined them contingently.[27] It may be that in developing such ideas, medieval Jewish thinkers were influenced by a voluntarist strand in Islamic legal theory. There too, we see that human reason is credited with the ability to discern what is 'beneficial' to the community, and some legal thinkers believed that this sort of insight can fill gaps left where the revelation fails to offer guidance.

---

[24] Cf. *Kuzari* 2.50: God's light cannot come from humans, "just as we say regarding the creation of an animal, for instance, that it did not create itself, but rather God formed it and brought it to perfection, since He saw which matter was apt for that form."

[25] For a similar position earlier in the Jewish tradition, including the example of rest on the Sabbath, see Rosenblatt 1948, 143–4.

[26] On the consequences of this see Seeskin 2005.

[27] Weiss and Butterworth 1975, 79. See further Weiss 1991, 76–7 for the contingency of religious legal injunctions.

But, with the exception of some rationalist jurists (especially among the Muʿtazilites), Muslim legal theorists usually refused to grant human reason the fully adequate scope that belongs to divinely decreed law. Humans simply do not have the epistemological resources to determine right and wrong in full detail, so we must depend on the religious law to learn how we should behave at the individual level and as a community.[28]

4 Conclusion

As I suggested towards the beginning of this paper, Abū Bakr al-Rāzī and Judah Hallevi occupy what may seem a rather anomalous position. They were neither *falāsifa* nor *mutakallimūn*, yet knew something about and drew on both *falsafa* and *kalām*. Actually though, this may not be so anomalous. A guiding principle of intellectual endeavour in the Islamic world was to avoid engaging in the uncritical acceptance of authoritative views known as *taqlīd*. A wide range of authors accordingly styled themselves as unbound and independent-minded critics, selectively adopting and rejecting theses from both Hellenizing philosophy and traditional Islamic religious science. One example would be the scientist al-Bīrūnī, an admirer of al-Rāzī who had sufficient knowledge of and critical distance from philosophy to send Avicenna a set of probing questions about Aristotelianism. We can also find certain mystics occupying the middle ground. Consider a sufi from Andalusia named Ibn Barrajān, who as it happens questioned naturalistic explanation in terms reminiscent of what we have seen in al-Rāzī and Hallevi:

> [The philosophers] said that nature is a subtle substance governing the creation of things. Now, if they mean by "substance governing the creation of things" that it is God, then it is true, and their mistake is simply in their using the names "nature" and "substance." Otherwise, they are far from correct, as nature is not what they claim to prove and define it to be, that is, something characterized with life, knowledge, agency, and desire, characterized therefore with wisdom and the ability to create.[29]

And we should notice that major figures who are standardly labelled as 'theologians' also made a show of occupying the no man's land between philosophy and theology – a no man's land that turns out to have been surprisingly well

---

[28] For voluntarism in the Islamic legal tradition, see Emon 2010. The position I am identifying as the dominant view, and comparing to what we find in Hallevi and Maimonides, is what he calls "soft natural law theory."

[29] Quoted from Akhtar 2017, 165.

populated. Though I mentioned al-Ghazālī above as a proponent of *kalām* occasionalism, in fact his stance on the topic miracles has been endlessly disputed by scholars. The difficulty of interpreting him has much to do with his ambition to draw selectively from the various intellectual currents of his day.[30] The same applies to Fakhr al-Dīn al-Rāzī, another 'theologian' whose breathtakingly original works are animated by the concerns of Avicennan *falsafa*.

Guided by individual judgment rather than rigid allegiance to any particular tradition, these figures made a habit of accepting some philosophical theses while rejecting others as excessive. Familiar examples would include belief in an eternal universe (rejected by both Abū Bakr al-Rāzī and Hallevi, and more famously by al-Ghazālī)[31] and Avicenna's notorious claim that God knows particulars only universally, which we've just seen Hallevi complaining about. As this paper has shown, the excessive philosophical views also included naturalism, the invocation of natures as fundamental explanatory principles. When Judah Hallevi points out that human understanding is not even up to the task of knowing when a given egg will successfully produce a chicken, he is showing that Aristotelian science promises more than it can hope to deliver. It pretends to study necessary relationships, then retreats to vague excuses like 'recalcitrant matter' to explain why some causes fail to produce their normal effects. To this we may add the looming threat that any natural process might be cancelled by a miracle at any time. It became increasingly clear in both the Islamic world and Latin Christendom that one faced a stark choice: either demote the causes of natural philosophy to the status of the 'hypothetically certain', or hold out for a cause that is linked to its effect by genuine necessity, and identify this cause as God.

---

30 The best evidence of this stance is his intellectual autobiography, the *Deliverer from Error*. For the much debated question of al-Ghazālī's true view on miracles in particular see Griffel 2009, which reaches a conclusion consonant with what I have just proposed here, namely that in the *Incoherence* al-Ghazālī wants to show that either occasionalism or a belief in non-necessary secondary causation would secure divine omnipotence.

31 For an overview see Adamson 2016. For the topic in Hallevi see 1.67: like fellow Andalusians Ibn Ṭufayl and Maimonides, he adopts the view that eternity can be neither confirmed nor disconfirmed by decisive proof (*burhān*).

Primary literature

Averroes. 1954. *Averroes' Tahāfut al-Tahāfut*, translated by Simon Van Den Burgh. Oxford and London: Oxford University Press and Luzac & Co.
Basso, Sebastianus. 1621. *Philosophiae Naturalis adversus Aristotelem libri XII In quibus abstrusa Veterum Physiologia restauratur et Aristotelis errores solidis rationibus refelluntur*. Geneve: Pierre de La Rovière.
al-Ghazālī. 1997. *The Incoherence of the Philosophers*, edited and translated by Michael E. Marmura. Provo, Utah: Brigham Young University Press.
Hallevi, Judah. [1905] 1964. *The Kuzari: An Argument for the Faith of Israel*, translated by Hartwig Hirschfeld. New York: Schocken Books.
Hallevi, Judah. 2012. *Al-Kitāb al-Khazarī, kitāb al-radd wa-l-dalīl fī dīn al-dhalīl*, edited by Nabin Bashir Freiberg: Al-Kamel Verlag.
al-Kindī. 2000. *Scientific Weather Forecasting in the Middle Ages: The Writings of al-Kindī*, edited and translated by Gerrit Bos and Charles Burnett. London and New York: Kegan Paul International.
Long, Anthony A. and David N. Sedley. 1987. *The Hellenistic Philosophers*. Cambridge: Cambridge University Press.
Maimonides. 1975. *Ethical Writings of Maimonides*, translated by Charles E. Butterworth and Raymond L. Weiss. New York: New York University Press.
al-Rāzī, Abū Bakr. 1939. *Rasāʾil falsafiyya*, edited by Paul Kraus. Cairo: Barbey.
al-Rāzī, Abū Bakr. 1987. *La natura e la sfera: la scienza antica e le sue metafore nella critica di Rāzī*, by Giulio A. Lucchetta. Bari: Milella.
al-Rāzī, Fakhr al-Dīn. 1987. *Al-Maṭālib al-ʿāliyya*, 9 Volumes, edited by Aḥmad Ḥijāzī al-Saqqā, Beirut: Dar al-Kitāb al-ʿArabī.
Saadia Gaon. 1948. *Saadia Gaon: The Book of Beliefs and Opinions*, translated by Samuel Rosenblatt. New Haven: Yale University Press.
Theophrastus. 2010. *Theophrastus, On First Principles*, by Dimitri Gutas. Leiden: Brill.

Secondary literature

Adamson, Peter. 2007. "*Porphyrius Arabus* on Nature and Art: 463F Smith in Context." In *Studies on Porphyry*, edited by George Karamanolis and Anne Sheppard, 141–63. London: Institute of Classical Studies, University of London.
Adamson, Peter. 2012. "Abū Bakr al-Rāzī on Animals." *Archiv für Geschichte der Philosophie* 94:249–73.
Adamson, Peter. 2016. "Eternity in Medieval Philosophy." In *Eternity: A History*, edited by Yitzhak Y. Melamed, 75–116. Oxford: Oxford University Press.
Adamson, Peter. 2017. "Fakhr al-Dīn al-Rāzī on Place." *Arabic Sciences and Philosophy* 27:205–36.
Adamson, Peter. 2018. "The Existence of Time in Fakhr al-Dīn al-Rāzī's *Maṭālib al-ʿāliya*." In *The Arabic, Hebrew, and Latin Reception of Avicenna's Physics and Cosmology*, edited by D.N. Hasse and A. Bertolacci, 65–99. Berlin: Walter de Gruyter.

Akhtar, Ali Humayun. 2017. *Philosophers, Sufis and Caliphs: Politics and Authority from Cordoba to Cairo and Baghdad.* Cambridge: Cambridge University Press.

Annas, Julia and Barnes, Jonathan. 1985. *The Modes of Scepticism: Ancient Texts and Modern Interpretations.* Cambridge: Cambridge University Press.

Black, Deborah L. 2006. "Knowledge (*'ilm*) and Certitude (*yaqīn*) in al-Fārābī's Epistemology." *Arabic Sciences and Philosophy* 16:11–46.

Brouwer, René. 2013. Review of Kullmann 2010. In *Zeitschrift der Savigny-Stiftung für Rechtsgeschichte, romanistische Abteilung*, 130:745–8.

Courtenay, William J. 1984. *Covenant and Causality in Medieval Thought.* London: Variorum Reprints.

Courtenay, William J. 1990. *Capacity and Volition: A History of the Distinction of Absolute and Ordained Power.* Bergamo: Pierluigi Lubrina Editore.

Emon, Anver M. 2010. *Islamic Natural Law Theories.* Oxford: Oxford University Press.

Griffel, Frank. 2009. *Al-Ghazālī's Philosophical Theology.* New York: Oxford University Press.

King, Peter. 1987. "Jean Buridan's Philosophy of Science." *Studies in History and Philosophy of Science* 18:109–32.

Kullmann, Wolfgang. 2010. *Naturgesetz in der Vorstellung der Antike, besonders der Stoa.* Stuttgart: Franz Steiner Verlag.

Lagerlund, Henrik (editor). 2010. *Rethinking the History of Skepticism: The Missing Medieval Background.* Leiden: Brill.

Lammer, Andreas. 2015. "Defining Nature: From Aristotle to Philoponus to Avicenna." In *Aristotle and the Arabic Tradition*, edited by Ahmed Alwishah, 121–42. Cambridge: Cambridge University Press.

Langermann, Y. Tzvi. 1993. "Some Astrological Themes in the Thought of Abraham ibn Ezra." In *Rabbi Abraham ibn Ezra: Studies in the Writings of a Twelfth-Century Jewish Polymath*, edited by Isadore Twersky and Jay M. Harris, 28–85. Cambridge MA: Harvard University, Center for Jewish Studies.

Langermann, Y. Tzvi. 1997. "Science and the *Kuzari.*" *Science in Context* 10:495–522.

Langermann, Y. Tzvi. 2004. "Maimonides and Miracles: The Growth of a (Dis)belief." *Jewish History* 18:147–72.

Malachai, Ariel. 2018. "Scepticism at the Service of Revelation? Preliminary Observations on Logic and Epistemology in Judah Halevi's *Kuzari*." In *Scepticism and Anti-Scepticism in Medieval Jewish Philosophy and Thought*, edited by Racheli Halevi. Berlin: de Gruyter.

Oakley, Francis C. 1984. *Omnipotence, Covenant, and Order: An Excursion in the History of Ideas from Abelard to Leibniz.* Ithaca: Cornell University Press.

Oakley, Francis C. 2002. *Omnipotence and Promise: The Legacy of the Scholastic Distinction of Powers.* Toronto: Pontifical Institute of Mediaeval Studies.

Perler, Dominik. 2006. *Zweifel und Gewissheit: skeptische Debatten im Mittelalter.* Frankfurt a. M.: Klostermann.

Perler, Dominik. 2010. "Skepticism." In *The Cambridge History of Medieval Philosophy, 2 Volumes*, edited by Christina van Dyke and Robert Pasnau, 384–96. Cambridge: Cambridge University Press.

Seeskin, Kenneth. 2005. *Maimonides on the Origin of the World.* Cambridge: Cambridge University Press.

Weiss, Raymond L. 1991. *Maimonides' Ethics.* Chicago: University of Chicago Press.

Zupko, Jack. 1993. "Buridan and Skepticism." *Journal of the History of Philosophy* 31:191–221.

Juhana Toivanen
"Like Ants in a Colony We Do Our Share": Political Animals in Medieval Philosophy

Abstract: This chapter discusses the reception of the Aristotelian concept of 'political animal' in thirteenth and fourteenth century Latin philosophy. Aristotle thought that there are other political animals besides human beings, and his idea of what it means to be a political animal was partially based on biological needs and desires that lead animals to live together. By analysing what medieval philosophers thought of other political animals – such as ants, bees, and cranes – and of the biological basis of the political nature of humans, the chapter elaborates on the precise meaning of the concept of political animal. It is argued that biological aspects play a significant role in medieval views, but at the same time medieval authors tend to distance human beings from other political animals by emphasising rationality, choice, and language as central factors for the social and political life.

1 Introduction

We know nowadays that social behaviour and even cultural learning are common in the animal kingdom (Laland and Galef 2009). Attributing culture to animals may be a more recent trend, but the idea that human beings are in a fundamental way similar to other social animals is an old one. As is well known, Aristotle claims that not only humans but also many other animal species – such as ants, bees, and cranes – can be considered as 'political animals' by nature (see, e.g., Aristotle 1984, 487b33–488a14), and medieval philosophers follow suit. According to them, human beings have a lot in common with other animals (De Leemans and Klemm 2007, 153–77), and one of the most salient similarities is the tendency to form organized communities, live in close association with other members of their species, collaborate and, if all goes well, contribute to the common good of the whole.[1]

---

[1] This similarity is acknowledged also in the main title of the present chapter, which is a quotation from the influential American punk band Bad Religion. Unsurprisingly, the original song has a strong political message: we should *not* be like ants but change the system that prey on the weak and poor.

Yet Aristotle also suggests that humans are political animals in a stricter sense. Rationality, language, and the ability to consider the normative dimension of justice transform the communities of human beings into something quite unlike beehives and ant colonies (see, e.g., Aristotle 1998, 1253a7–18; 1242a22–27; 1280a31–34). Understood in this way, human beings are the only political animals there are, since no other animal forms organized communities that aim for *eudaimonia* and involve considerations of justice. Modern scholars have adopted different strategies to resolve this apparent tension in Aristotle's view.[2] Some have argued that the concept of political animal does not have a fixed meaning: in a strict sense it excludes non-human animals, and when Aristotle applies it to them, he uses the term metaphorically (Mulgan 1974, 438–45; Cooper 1990, 222–25). Others have emphasized that Aristotle uses the concept in a biological sense and refers to activity and a way of life. According to them, the political life of humans is not different in kind but only an intensification and modification of the political life of ants, bees, and cranes. Understood in this way, being a political animal in the human way does not exclude all those traits that we find in other political animals, but only brings in an additional dimension of rationality. Political life admits of degrees, and therefore humans are political in the same way but to a higher degree than other animals (Depew 1995, 156–81; Labarrière 2004, 61–127).

Whatever Aristotle meant, his view is open to two radically different interpretations of the concept of political animal. It can be taken to mean either (1) an animal that is a part of a *polis*, a special kind of community that aims for a good life and is necessarily based on rational considerations of justice; or (2) an animal that collaborates with other members of its species in order to achieve a common goal. These two notions contributed to medieval discussions, but medieval authors usually did not explicitly address the tension between them. They were mixed together in complex ways, and it is not always clear how (and indeed, whether) they were supposed to form a unified conception of what it means to be a political animal.

The present chapter aims to shed light on medieval discussions that operate with this concept. The focus is on the period between 1260s and 1370s,[3] and the

---

[2] Instead of trying to resolve the tension, one may of course follow David Keyt 1987, 54 who claims that: "there is a blunder at the very root of Aristotle's political philosophy."

[3] The most important authors, in the order of appearance, are Albert the Great (c. 1200–1280), Peter of Spain (the Portuguese, who became the Pope John XXI and died in 1277), Peter of Auvergne (died 1304), and Nicholas of Vaudémont (flourished 1370s). The Peter of Spain that figures in the present chapter is not the same as the author of the influential logical work *Summulae logicales* (Pasnau and van Dyke 2010, Volume 2, 945–46).

chapter consists of three sections. Section 2 concentrates on political animals other than humans especially in the context of commentaries on Aristotle's zoological works. Section 3 examines commentaries on the *Politics* from the point of view of those psychological and biological traits that humans have in common with other animals, and the final section shows how certain medieval authors explicitly reject the idea that non-human animals are political. It is hoped that by analysing medieval discussions of political *animals*, and those aspects of the political nature of humans that are related to their animality, we will be in a better position to understand what exactly makes humans similar to other political animals on the one hand, and special in relation to them on the other.

2 Ants, bees, and cranes as political animals

The idea that there is no radical difference between the political life of humans and certain other animal species is most clearly presented in Aristotle's *Historia animalium*, which circulated together with his other zoological works under the common title *De animalibus*. This collection was translated into Latin twice, and although it was not among the most popular Aristotelian treatises, it received some attention from medieval scholastic philosophers (Asúa 1991, 5–189; van den Abeele 1999, 287–318). One of the most ambitious adaptations of this work is Albert the Great's (c. 1200–1280) massive *De animalibus libri XXVI*, which is only partially a commentary on Aristotle, as it contains material from many other sources, as well as Albert's own explanations and original views.[4]

In the course of his discussion, Albert mentions the political nature of animals several times. One of the first observations that he makes is related to the ways of life that different species follow: "the manners of birds and other animals are differentiated in another way, according to their behaviour (*operationes*) and ordering of their life. For one genus is that, which is always political and gregarious with many companions."[5] This is an important passage because it tells

---

[4] Albert left behind also a question-commentary *Quaestiones De animalibus*, which differs in certain respects from the more comprehensive *De animalibus*. Since the former is extant only as a *reportatio* made by Albert's student, it is bound to be less reliable. The relation between these two works is discussed in Asúa 1991, 180–87; Resnick and Kitchell 2008, 3–7.

[5] *Adhuc autem modi avium et aliorum animalium diversificantur aliter secundum operationes et regimen vitae. Quoddam enim genus est quod est civile et gregale semper cum multis sociorum* (Albert the Great 1916, 15 [58]). The translations of Albert's *De animalibus* are mine unless otherwise stated, but I have consulted Kenneth Kitchell's and Irven Resnick's translation in Albert the

us that the epithets 'political' and 'gregarious' refer to activities and ways of life rather than to any essential feature. Albert maintains that some animals are always political, and he continues by explaining that there are also animals that never live with other members of their kind. In between are those species that are political only occasionally, which means that they sometimes engage in activities that are counted as political, but not always. On this basis we may make a systematic division into three different ways of life that animals may lead:
1. Some animals live always together in groups (e.g. starlings).
2. Some animals live always alone, only meeting each other in order to mate (eagles, hawks).
3. Some animals 'dualize': they live sometimes alone and sometimes together with others (geese and cranes).[6]

The birds that Albert mentions are just illustrative examples. In principle, every animal species can be placed into one of these three categories, even though individual differences may be found within each species. Humans belong to the third group, because they sometimes withdraw from their communities in order to contemplate divine matters although they are gregarious and political animals by nature (Albert the Great 1916, 16 [59]; see Aristotle 1984, 488a7). The difference between humans and other dualizing animals is that humans usually live together and retreat only occasionally, whereas for geese and cranes it is the other way around. The differences between animal species are a matter of degree and not of kind.

Another important idea that becomes clear from Albert's analysis is that 'political' and 'gregarious' are not mutually exclusive terms. Political animals form a subcategory of gregarious animals, which means that all political animals are gregarious, but not the other way around:[7]

Great 1999. The references are to the Latin edition, but I give the page numbers of the translation in parenthesis.

6 Albert does not use the term 'dualize', but it is clear that he is alluding to a passage in Aristotle (1984, 488a2–7), where a similar division is made. For discussion, see Depew 1995, 157–59.

7 *Civitatense autem animal vocatur, quod ad imitationem civitatum omnia sua opera refert ad unum et agit unam actionem ad commune bonum pertinentem: nec tamen omne animal gregale cum sociis manens talem facit operationem in unum collatam. De hiis autem quae in unum conferunt operationes, est homo et vespa et apis et formica et grus. Sed in gruibus minus est manifestum quam in aliis, quia grues non conferunt in unum aliquam operationem, nisi curam vigiliae et ordinem volatus: alia autem animalia inducta conferunt multa in unum communitate negotiorum et ciborum, ex quibus communi consulitur utilitati. Horum autem quae sic communicant, quaedam regit rex, cui obediunt, sicut grues et apes et homines. Ista enim habent regem et principem solli-*

An animal is said to be political (*civitatense*),⁸ if it (imitating cities) directs all its operations to one [aim] and performs an action that pertains to the common good. Not all gregarious animals, which stay with their companions, perform such a joint operation. Among those animals that collaborate (*in unum conferunt operationes*), are the human, the wasp, the bee, the ant, and the crane. But in cranes this is less obvious than in the others, because cranes do not collaborate in any other action, except in taking care of guarding and setting order to their flight. The other mentioned animals collaborate in many things in a community of affairs and sustenance, which serve the common utility. Moreover, some of those who are united in this way are governed by a king, which they obey. Such are the crane, the bee and the human being. For they have a king and a leader, who takes care of the common utility. Some of the gregarious animals do not have a king. Such are ants and locusts, which wander about harmoniously in herds, as if the common care and city life (*urbanitas*) were entrusted to each of them.

The crucial factor that distinguishes political from gregarious animals is the ability to act together in order to promote the common good or to achieve a common goal (these two are not necessarily different things). Gregarious animals live together but unlike political ones, they do not aim at common good and they do not collaborate.⁹

The list of political animals includes at least ants, bees, cranes, wasps, locusts, and human beings. In addition to Aristotle's *Historia animalium*, medieval authors found information concerning the behaviour of these animals in Pliny the Elder's *Historia naturalis*, Isidore of Seville's *Etymologies* and various bestiaries. However, the idea that their behaviour makes them political is markedly an Aristotelian one, and in this respect, cranes are an illustrative borderline case. Most of the time they do not collaborate and they do not even live always together, but Albert counts them among political animals because they have two activities that require collaboration: when they gather somewhere to eat and sleep, one of them stands on guard for possible enemies; and they migrate in a V-formation where one of them acts as a leader, looking out for dangers and thus protecting the group (Albert the Great 1916, 7.1.6, 525 [616]). Albert says in another context that cranes *appoint* the guard and the leader (Albert the Great 1955, 1.8, 86; Albert the Great 2008, 28–29). Given that he demarcates between political and non-political animals by appealing to the way of life, cranes can be said

---

citum circa se de utilitate communi. Quaedam autem gregalium non habent regem, sicut formicae et locustae, quae per turmas egrediuntur concorditer, sicut unicuique eorum per se commissa sit cura communis et urbanitas (Albert the Great 1916, 16 [59]).

8 This rare term is sometimes translated as 'citizen' (*Dictionary of Medieval Latin from British Sources*, s.v. civitatensis), or 'urban' (Albert the Great 1999, Volume 1, 59).

9 From an Aristotelian perspective, the only new element here is the hierarchical classification. Other aspects come directly from him.

to dualize. In other words, even though it may be correct to classify cranes among political animals, they do not always act accordingly – they are political animals only occasionally.

On the basis of the foregoing, we may enumerate three interconnected criteria, which can be applied to non-human animals and which distinguish political animals from non-political ones:
1. Political animals collaborate in order to reach a common aim. This can be divided into:
    a. Acquiring material necessities for living (food, shelter, etc.).
    b. Achieving an end that is not related to daily needs (e.g. migration of cranes).
2. Political animals have a leader that promotes the common good.
3. Political animals have a division of labour.

Criteria (2) and (3) are not necessary for all political animals, but because they are often mentioned in discussions, and because they can be considered as indications of the political nature of a given species – having a leader or division of labour entails a common aim and shared action – let us consider them briefly before turning to the first criterion.

Many political animals were thought to have a leader or a king. A case in point is the bee. Medieval authors were commonly mistaken concerning the sex of the bee leader, but that does not alter the general philosophical point: having a leader marks certain species off from others.[10] Albert the Great draws the parallel between humans and bees to the extent that he mentions two types of problematic situations, which bees may face due to having a leader. The king of bees may turn out to be a tyrant, and there may be two or more leaders in one hive. The former case usually leads to a revolution, and the competition between several kings is resolved in a civil war (Albert the Great 1916, 8.4.3, 637 [736]).[11] Whether or not these scenarios can be attested empirically, the fact that Albert elaborates on them shows how far he is willing to take the similarity between the political life of humans and bees.

Non-human animals were thought to be organized in many different ways, and not all of them have kings. An illustrative example can be found in Guy of Rimini's (died after 1344) commentary on the *Politics*. He claims that conjugal

---

[10] *Etiam grues et apes eligunt sibi regem* (Radulphus Brito (?), *Quaest. Pol.*, fol. 1vb).
[11] The possibility of having several leaders is mentioned in Albert the Great 1916, 638 (737), 642 (742), and 652 (751). The last of these passages tells us that the community of bees resembles more an aristocracy than monarchy.

and political types of rule can be distinguished on the basis of having a permanent or a changing ruler, respectively:[12]

> 'Conjugal' and 'political' differ absolutely, because in a political rule the ruling persons and their subjects often change places. The reason for this is that this kind of rule belongs to equal persons, who are not different by nature from each other with respect to their freedom. One of them has been elected to rule the others for a certain predetermined time, and afterwards he becomes a subject, when another takes his place. And thus they alternate by succession after the manner of flying cranes, when one replaces another, who preceded him as a leader for a determinate time – this is said to be observed also in their night watch.

Guy uses cranes in order to illustrate his understanding of the key element that distinguishes political from conjugal type of rule. Presumably political rule can also be distinguished from monarchical and aristocratic governments, in which the leaders remain the same (see, e.g., Aristotle 1998, 1259b5–8; Thomas Aquinas 1971, 1.10, 113b; Thomas Aquinas 2007, 69–70). Cranes change their leader every now and then, and this trait marks a difference between conjugal and political ways of life, which are actualized in households and political communities. The fact that cranes have a leader indicates that they are political animals, or at least (to use the Aristotelian expression) that they dualize between solitary and political life.

Already these examples show that medieval authors did not hesitate to apply Criterion (2) and the concept of political rule to non-human animals. However, according to Albert the Great (1916, 627 [726–27]), there are animals that do not have a leader although they count as political. His examples of these include ants and locusts, which lead a political life although no-one among them holds any leading position. This means that this criterion is not necessary for being a political animal, even though it figures amply in medieval discussions.

What about Criterion (3)? Some political animals have quite sophisticated division of labour, while others have none. Bees are the prime example of the former:[13]

---

12 *Differt tamen coniugalis a politico simpliciter, quia in politicis principatibus transmutantur frequenter homines principantes et subiecti. Cuius ratio est, quia talis principatus est personarum equalium et quantum ad libertatem nil differentium per naturam. Per electionem autem unus certo et determinato tempore principatur aliis et postea fit subiectus sibi alio succedente. Et sic successione ad modum gruarum volantium alternantur, cum una qui dux determinato tempore antecessit, succedit alia loco eius, quod etiam dicuntur in nocturnis excubiis observare* (Guy of Rimini, *Super Politicam*, fol. 67rb).
13 *Quod autem omnibus quae inducta sunt mirabilius esse videtur, est quod quasdam habent operationes inter se appropriatas quasi quibusdam artificibus earum, sine quibus non potest subsis-*

> There is something which seems to be even more marvellous than all the things introduced so far. This is that bees have certain tasks that are assigned as if each went to certain of their craftsmen. Without these their society could not exist. It is just this way among people, where some are millers, some are cobblers or architects, and others are practitioners of various other crafts. The society of bees is based on the sharing of these tasks and thus some tasks are found to have been assigned to particular bees and others to others. Thus, the swarm is built up and held together by means of a sort of sharing among them.

Division of labour is essential for the survival of the beehive. By contrast, ants and locusts (which do not have a leader) represent species of political animals that do not seem to have a division of labour either. They have shared activities that aim at the common good, but they do not specialize in different tasks as the bees do. Instead, each of them has exactly the same function in the community. The connection between having a leader and division of labour is understandable, because one of the most fundamental types of division of labour holds between the ruler and the subjects. This is why the two last criteria can be considered to be the same.

Unlike Criteria (2) and (3) which are indicative but not necessary, the first criterion (collaborating in order to reach a common aim) is critical for distinguishing political from gregarious animals. Fulfilling it can be considered a necessary condition for being a political animal. It is not surprising that medieval authors emphasize it, given that it has a pivotal place in Aristotle's explanation for the difference between political and gregarious animals. The former have a *koinon ergon*, a common work, while the latter only live together without any kind of collaboration (Aristotle 1984, 488a7–488a10). They behave in the flock just like they would do alone, and while they may benefit from living together, their way of life does not count as political in the proper sense of the word. There are radical differences in the way the communities of different political animals are organized, but ants, bees, and cranes all fulfil Criterion (1). Human beings are similar to them in this respect. Yet, Albert also mentions one central difference between humans and other political animals: he writes that animals *imitate* the political life of humans. I shall return to this below, but it is good to keep in mind that although he considers many non-human animals as political animals, he does not mean that their way of life is completely similar to that of humans. It is

---

tere civitas earum. Sicut enim in hominibus quidam sunt pistores et quidam cerdones, quidam autem architecti et alii aliarum artium operatores, quorum communicatione subsistit civitas, ita inveniuntur quaedam operata appropriata quibusdam apibus et aliis alia quarum communicatione quadam construitur et continetur examen (Albert the Great 1916, 646 [745]). Albert writes about bees that: *Sed non solum artificiose operantur, sed etiam distribuunt opera inter se, ut una faciat unum opus et alia aliud* (Albert the Great 1916, 639 [739]).

an approximation and falls short in certain relevant respects, as we shall soon see.

Medieval philosophers tended to read Aristotle's zoological works in light of Avicennian psychology (Harvey 1975, 31–60; di Martino 2008; Toivanen 2013, 225–45). They used the machinery of the internal senses to elaborate on Aristotelian views, and they accounted for the social behaviour of non-human animals by appealing to the estimative power of the soul. Animals are capable of recognizing their own kin, apprehending the friendliness of other members of their species, and judging that life in a community is useful for them. All these abilities were usually attributed to the estimative power, as can be seen from the following passage by an anonymous[14] author:[15]

> Why a king is chosen only in the case of flying [animals], as is clear in the case of cranes? I answer that according to Avicenna, the estimative power is the highest power in animals, like the intellect in human beings. [...] For cranes make a leader and a ruler of the one who knows the routes better. And because they trust more those who are like them, they choose among [the members of] their own species. Or it can be said in another way, that animals choose a king on the basis of their aim: either against things that corrupt them from outside, like heat and cold (and in this way it is in the case of cranes, who migrate to warm regions in the beginning of the winter, and return in the beginning of the summer); or against things that corrupt them from within, like lack of food, and thus [they choose a leader who takes them] to eat leaves and herbs (and in this way cows and sheep choose their leaders); or [they choose a leader who guides them] in their proper actions (and in this way, bees choose a leader for themselves in order to construct a workshop, because one single bee does not know how to make honey).

The estimative power has an important role in accounting for the social behaviour of animals; a better estimative power means more complex social/political organisation (Toivanen, 2020). The author enumerates three functions that a leader may have in animal communities: warding off external threats, maintain-

---

14 The author may have been Peter of Spain or one of his students; at any rate, the work is based on Peter's *De animalibus* (Asúa 1991, 87–95).

15 *Quare solum in volatilibus rex eligitur, ut in gruibus patet? Respondeo quod secundum Avicennam virtus estimativa in animalibus est suprema sicut in hominibus intellectus.* [...] *Illum autem ducem faciunt et rectorem qui melius vias novit. Et quia de suo simili magis confidunt, ideo de sua specie eligunt. Vel potest dici aliter ut a parte finis rex ab animalibus eligatur: aut contra corrumpens extra ut est calor et frigidus, et sic est in gruibus qui in principio yemis pergunt ad calidas regiones, in principio estatis redeunt; aut contra corrumpens intus ut est defectus nutrimenti, et sic ad comestionem foliorum et herbarum, et sic vacce et oves eligunt sibi ducem; aut ad actum proprium, et sic apes ad construendum fabricam eligunt sibi ducem, nam una sola apis mellificare nequit* (Anonymous [Peter of Spain?] 1991, 361–62; I have slightly amended the punctuation). The same point is made in Albert the Great 1916, 496 [586].

ing material self-sufficiency of the community, and enabling the proper activity of the species in question. The same functions were attributed to political communities of human beings – the community provides clothing, housing, and military power against external threats; various material goods that lead to internal self-sufficiency; and the opportunity to live in accordance with reason, which is the proper activity of human beings (see, e. g., Thomas Aquinas 1979, 449; Thomas Aquinas 1971, 77b–78a; Giles of Rome 1607, 226–28 and 541–43). Just like humans need the political community in order to live according to reason and thus become humans in the full sense, bees cannot actualize their own function of honey-making without other bees. Collaboration is the only way to secure these goods, and this applies to humans as well as to other social animals.

Overall, Albert and many other medieval authors embrace the idea that humans are in relevant ways similar to other animals. The criteria that they use to distinguish political from non-political animals can be applied equally to humans as they are applied to bees and the like.

3 Human beings as political *animals*

As one might expect, the idea that human beings are political in a similar way as certain other animals entails that animality figures in the explanations for human social life. Medieval philosophers accepted the other side of Aristotle's theory, which emphasizes human rationality and the ability to use language (see the next section), but they also thought that humans are animals and have various biological needs and desires, which are relevant for sociability. Thus, it is no wonder that commentaries on the *Politics* often elaborate on the idea that human beings are political animals in the biological sense.

The biological basis of our political life is especially prominent when medieval authors discuss the idea that human beings live together in political communities in order to satisfy their material needs by collaboration (Criterion 1a above). It has been pointed out that Avicenna's influence on this matter is significant (Avicenna 1980, 531–32; Avicenna 1968, 69–70; Rosier-Catach 2015, 232–36; Fioravanti 1999, 19; Lambertini 1990, 277–325; Toste 2014, 149), but we should not overlook the fact that Aristotle himself claims that the political community was originally established for the sake of the preservation of life (Aristotle 1998, 1252b29–30). For instance, an anonymous commentator of Aristotle's *Politics* (the so-called Anonymous of Vatican) writes that:[16]

---

16 *Dicendum primo quod homo naturaliter est animal civile et politicum. Et hoc patet duobus vel*

It must be said first that a human being is a political animal (*animal civile et politicum*) by nature. [...] Because that is natural, which enables human beings to have sufficiency for their existence and their nature; but human beings receive sufficiency for their existence by being political; therefore etc. The major premise is apparent, because every human being naturally desires his existence and desires to be conserved in his existence, and [they do] this in order to participate in divine being. The minor premise is apparent, because by being political, a human being acquires things that are sufficient for his life and existence: one human being is not sufficient for himself but acquires his sufficiency through communication with others, because one skill prevails in one household and another skill in another household, and so forth, and by fitting these together they are rendered sufficient in their lives.

Human beings would not survive alone, and since a single household cannot meet all material needs, a political community is necessary. The argument appeals also to the division of labour (Criterion 3 above). Each separate household specializes in one product, and together they supply everything that is required for human life. From this perspective humans are political in the same way as ants and bees are: they collaborate in order to survive.

Human sociability is based also on another principle that we share with other animals: the desire to leave behind something similar to oneself. This desire or inclination aims at the preservation of the species, but it stems from the more basic desire for self-preservation. Animals do not live forever. They cannot continue their existence remaining numerically the same, and therefore their desire for self-preservation can be satisfied only in the formal sense by leaving behind an offspring. As Peter of Auvergne puts it:[17]

> The continuation of the species takes place only through reproduction [...] And therefore they [who cannot continue existing numerically the same] necessarily have a most natural desire, which is related to existence, which everybody naturally desires: they have this desire to reproduce, without which existence cannot be continued. [...] And therefore, such

---

tribus, quia id est a natura, per quod homo habet sufficientiam sui esse et sue nature; sed per esse civile vel politicum habet sufficientiam sui esse; ideo etc. Maior patet, quia homo quilibet appetit suum esse et conservari in esse suo naturaliter, et hoc ut participent esse divinum. Minor patet quia per esse politicum homo acquirit sufficientiam sue vite et sui esse, quia unus homo non est sibi sufficiens, sed per communicationem cum aliis acquirit suam sufficientiam, quia in una domo una ars regnat et in alia domo alia, et sic deinceps. Et per congruitatem illorum ad invicem redduntur sufficientes in vite eorum (Anonymous of Vatican, *Quaest. Pol.*, fol. 15vb).

17 *Hec autem continuatio in specie non fit nisi per generationem [...] Et ideo illa necessario habent naturalissimum appetitum, qui scilicet est in ordine ad ipsum esse, quod naturalissime omnia appetunt. Hunc inquam habent ad generationem sine qua illud continuari non potest. [...] Et ideo talia animalia [...] necessario appetunt combinationem maris et femine, sine qua non fieret generatio* (Peter of Auvergne, *Quaest. Pol.*, fol. 276rb).

animals [...] necessarily desire the combination of male and female, without which reproduction would not take place.

A couple of lines further down the text, Peter refers to Aristotle's *De anima* and states that animals desire to generate so that "they might participate in divine and immortal existence as much as they can."[18] As the only way in which mortal animals can partake in what is eternal and divine is by leaving behind a similar to themselves, the desire to leave behind something similar to oneself turns out to be a desire for a qualified immortality – insofar as such can be achieved by mortal animals.

All living beings, including humans, have this natural desire. Since most animals breed by copulation, the union between the biological sexes is a necessary means for satisfying it, and the union is natural for them. Like all forms of self-preservation, the desire to leave behind something similar to oneself manifests itself in the form of emotions.[19] Given that medieval authors thought that human beings can partake in the eternal and divine as individuals – due to the immortality of the soul and the resurrection of the body – their emphasis on this *animal*-desire as the basis of the union between man and woman is significant. Unlike other animals, humans could continue their individual existence without other people; but they could not continue their lives as human beings because their bodies are mortal like those of other animals. It is precisely due to this similarity that human sociability is accounted for by appealing to functions that we have due to our animality.

Also those animals that were considered unsocial and solitary (e. g. birds of prey) occasionally come together to mate, and thus having the desire to leave behind something similar to oneself does not alone make animals political or social. It does not even make them conjugal. Conjugal animals form more stable relationships and share their lives more than just to procreate – they feel companionship and raise and educate their offspring together. The development of a nestling into a bird is a natural process, but the nestling dies if it is left

---

[18] *ipso divino esse et immortali participent quantum possunt* (Peter of Auvergne, *Quaest. Pol.*, fol. 276rb). See Aristotle 1984, 415b3–8; Lennox 2001, 131–59.

[19] *Et ideo natura appetit semper esse. Hoc autem in rebus corruptilibus in uno individuo consequi non potest propter longe distantie a primo principio et ideo ne omnino naturale desiderium esset frustra reliquo modo complevit Deus continuam faciens generationem ut sic esse quod non potest conservari semper in uno individuo perpetuetur in suo simili. Et ideo omne generans naturale generat suum simile. Sic igitur in hominibus sicut in aliis animalibus et plantis inest naturalis appetitus relinquendi sibi similem in natura. Unde prima communicatio naturalis et principalis est communicatio viri et mulieris* (Guy of Rimini, *Super Politicam*, fol. 57vb–58ra).

alone before it is capable of taking care of itself. Many young animals must be fed and kept warm and safe before they can survive on their own. Although there are species in which the mother can do all this alone, Peter points out that in many cases both parents are needed to raise the progeny:[20]

> Further, it must be noted that one who acts according to this natural desire, does not intend only to leave behind similar to itself, but also to leave it behind in a perfect state. This is because it is natural for everyone to leave behind something that is not only similar in species and substance, but also in an equally perfect state, as far as possible. [...] In certain other animals, nutrition is not covered by the female alone but requires also the male, as is evident. Therefore it is necessary that both live together until the offspring has been raised perfect, as is clear in the case of many birds. Human beings are similarly in this condition.

Leaving behind something similar to oneself may require more than ensuring that one's child does not die. Peter claims that children need to be educated because otherwise they do not become rational animals in the full sense (Toste 2014, 129–33), and medieval authors hold that instruction plays a similar role in the development of other animals as well. For instance, Radulphus Brito (*Quaest. Pol.*, fol. 1b) claims that just as the development of rationality requires human contact, certain birds must teach singing to their nestlings.[21]

The desires for self-preservation and reproduction have an important role in medieval explanations for the sociability of humans and other animals. They are not social inclinations as such – they are ubiquitous in the animal kingdom, but they entail social life only when they cannot be fulfilled without collaboration and sharing. Yet, without these desires social forms of behaviour would not emerge. In this way, sociability is not a distinct psychological or biological trait but a feature that builds on such traits.

These traits are crucial for the emergence of conjugal life, but they are relevant also for political life. According to Aristotle's so-called genetic argument, the political community is the final outcome of a natural process that begins with the association of man and woman. Since this association has a biological

---

20 *Sed ulterius advertendum est quod agens secundum talem naturalem appetitum non solum intendit aliud derelinquere simile sibi, sed etiam derelinquere illud perfectum, quia naturale est unicuique non solum derelinquere simile specie et substantia, sed etiam aequale in statu perfectionis quantum potest.* [...] *In aliis autem animalibus nutritio non complectitur a femella sola, sed exi<gi>tur ulterius masculus, ut patebit. Et ideo necesse est ut commaneant ambo usque ad perfectionem [nutritionem] foetus* [MS: *fotus*], *sicut patet in pluribus avibus, et similiter homo est huius conditionis* (Peter of Auvergne, fol. 276va).
21 The idea that birds teach singing to their chicks is mentioned in Aristotle 1984, 536b17–19. See Fögen 2014, 225.

origin, the political community has biological roots as well. Moreover, human beings can satisfy their material needs only within a political community. Even though providing the material necessities for life, and thus enabling the full satisfaction of the desire for self-preservation, may not be the main function of the political community – good life, which can be acquired only through moral education and good laws, has a claim to that – it is clear that political life is at least indirectly a result of desires and inclinations that have biological origins. Although they do not constitute the whole explanation that medieval authors gave for the political nature of humans, they are a part of that explanation. Humans are political *animals*, and their political life stems partially from their biological needs.

Perhaps the most striking example of the role that animality plays in medieval conceptions of sociability comes from Peter of Auvergne's analysis of the Aristotelian dictum that human beings are political animals by nature. His argument leans heavily on the fact that humans are animals. As Marco Toste (2014, 125–43; 2012, 401–2) has shown, Peter qualifies his claim about the political nature of humans by making a distinction between two senses of nature:[22]

> But what is this nature? It must be said that a human being can be considered in two ways: either according to the nature of the species, or according to the nature of the individual, which is a certain material disposition—for we say that both of these are the nature of man. But a human being is not naturally political according to the first nature, I mean, primarily, in itself and absolutely, because a human being, according to what he is and insofar as he is a human being, is an animal and a body, and so forth, and rational. But he is imperfect or insufficient, not insofar as he is a human being or because of the nature of the species absolutely and in itself, but because that nature is considered according to its being in relation to matter. The reason for this is that a form is always continuous and perpetual by itself […] But in relation to matter, with which it constitutes one being, it cannot continue in its being remaining numerically the same […] Therefore, as all things desire naturally to exist (at least insofar as they can) and they desire also their continuation […] they neces-

---

[22] *Sed que est ista natura? Dicendum quod homo potest considerari dupliciter: vel secundum speciei naturam vel secundum naturam individui, que est aliqua dispositio materialis. Utrumque enim dicimus esse naturam hominis. Sed secundum primam naturam homo non est civilis a natura, dico primo et secundum se et absolute, quia homo, secundum id quod est et inquantum homo, habet quod sit animal et corpus et cetera, et quod sit rationalis. Quod autem sit imperfectus vel insufficiens, hoc non habet inquantum est homo et ex natura speciei absolute et secundum se, sed habet hoc ex natura illa considerata secundum esse suum respectu materie. Cuius ratio est quia forma de se est continuabilis semper et perpetua* […] *Sed in respectu ad materiam, cum qua consituit unum esse, non potest continuari in esse suo idem manens in numero* […] *Ergo cum omnia esse appetant naturaliter, saltim eo modo quo possunt, et etiam continuationem* […]*, necessario et naturaliter appetent id, per quod magis salvari et continuari possunt in illo esse. Hoc autem est civitas* (Peter of Auvergne, *Quaest. Pol.*, fol. 277ra–b, edition Toste, in Toste 2014, 134, n. 52).

sarily and naturally desire that by which they can better maintain and continue in that being. But this is a political community (*civitas*).

The argument is rather complicated, and we cannot go to the details here, but the main idea is to distinguish the nature of the species and the nature of an individual. The former refers to the common and essential features that are shared by all human beings, while the latter refers to individual properties that stem from different bodily complexions. Note that the individual bodily disposition does not figure in the quoted passage, which deals only with various aspects of the nature of the species. Peter argues that human beings are *not* political according to the nature of the species in itself, because the rational soul is immortal and does not need anything to remain in existence. By contrast, when the common human nature is considered in relation to matter, humans are political beings. The combination of the immortal soul and the mortal body needs material goods in order to remain in existence, and therefore it also needs other people.

The quality of the body becomes central when Peter turns to the individual nature, the bodily complexion that each individual human being has. He argues that only certain kind of body inclines to a social life. Some individuals have such deficient body that they are incapable of living with others, while others have such well-disposed bodies that they can live virtuously even in poor conditions of a solitary life. Most people fall in between these two extremes (Peter of Auvergne, 1.9, *Quaest. Pol.*, fol. 277rb). Peter obviously has in mind Aristotle's division between beasts, human beings, and gods (Toste 2014, 135–36), but he also reveals his Neoplatonic tendencies when he argues that the virtuous solitary person despises his body: "He would be disposed towards the body as towards an enemy, like Eustratius says, and he would have a heroic virtue, and he would choose a solitary life in order to speculate the highest things."[23] This heroic individual is able to concentrate on philosophical and religious speculation without other people, and although he is not self-sufficient in the material sense, he is able to distance himself psychologically from his body and cease caring for it. He overcomes his animality and ceases to be a political animal.

---

23 *Et ille tunc disponitur ad corpus sicut ad inimicum, ut dicit Eustratius, et habebit virtutem heroicam et eliget vitam solitariam ad speculandum altissima* (Peter of Auvergne, fol. 277rb, edition Toste, in Toste 2014, 139, n. 59). The connection to Book X of Aristotle's *Nicomachean Ethics* cannot be overlooked, but at the same time it should be remembered that Aristotle does not recommend a solitary life for theoretically happy persons. Instead, they live in a political community and spend their time with their friends. For a discussion on medieval conceptions of the relevance of friendship for a philosopher, see Toste 2008, 173–95.

Peter's position was not mainstream in all respects, but he establishes a strong connection between political nature and animality. Humans are social and political beings precisely because they are mortal *animals*. The animal body accounts for the inclination to lead a social life, and that kind of life is necessary for most of us, because otherwise we could not survive as bodily beings who have bodily needs – as biological beings, as animals.

4 More than the bee: language and rationality

All of the above goes nicely together with Aristotle's genetic argument for the naturalness of the political community: households, villages, and political communities appear in order to enable a self-sufficient life where no material needs go unfulfilled. But there is another side to Aristotle's theory. Especially his so-called linguistic argument suggests that the political nature of humans is not grounded solely on biological traits, but it involves rationality, language, justice, and moral virtue (1998, 1253a5 – 18). Aristotle begins his argument by arguing that human beings are *more political* than other animals. Although it is far from clear how the comparison should be understood, modern scholars have pointed out that it resonates with the discussion of political animals in the *Historia animalium* (Depew 1995, 162 – 70; Labarrière 2004, 99 – 127), and therefore Aristotle can be taken to suggest that the difference between humans and other political animals is a matter of degree. Our political life is not different in kind but only an intensification and modification of the way of life that we share with other political animals. Humans have a more complex but not essentially different organisation.[24]

However, Aristotle continues his linguistic argument by explaining *why* humans are more political than other animals: humans can use language and speak about what is just and what is unjust. Language, and by implication rationality, makes a difference. Due to this emphasis on rationality, the linguistic argument is easy to read in such a way that humans are the only political animals in the proper sense of the term, and that there is a qualitative difference or even a radical gap between the political life of humans and other animals. Depending on how the argument is interpreted, it entails either that non-human an-

---

[24] Depew 1995, 167 warns that Aristotle is not discussing desires or tendencies but about what animals in fact *do*. Yet, it is clear that their ways of life are based on their psychological capacities, which include habituation, desire, and cognition (see Aristotle 1984, 588a16–b3; Miller 1997, 30 – 32).

imals are political in a proper sense or that they are political only metaphorically.

These different viewpoints are reflected in medieval discussions. Albert the Great, who was one of the first Latin commentators on Aristotle's *Politics*, explains the linguistic argument without focusing on other animals. He only states tersely that the human being is a political animal: "more than the bee and any gregarious animal – that is, a kind of animal which sets up one ruler, like cranes follow one [leader] in a shape of a letter"[25] and clarifies that the difference is due to language, which enables humans to form real political communities. Only human communities are arranged according to justice and laws.

The same normative dimension is central also in Albert the Great's discussion of pygmies in his *De animalibus*. He notoriously argues that pygmies are not human beings, because they lack true rationality. They speak a language of a kind, but they are unable to talk about what is just and what unjust (Albert the Great 1916, 21.1.2, 1327–29 [1417]; Köhler 2008, 419–43; Resnick and Kitchell 1996, 41–61).[26] By consequence, they do not have real political community and laws but one that is based on instinct:[27]

> [...] the pygmy does not watch over a perfect political system (*civilitas*) or laws but rather follows the impulse of nature in such things, just as do other brute animals. [...] it has better apprehension than the other brute beasts, but it does not pay attention to the shame that results from disgraceful actions or the glory that results from that which is virtuous. And this is a sign that it has no judgment of reason, which is why it uses neither rhetorical nor poetical devices when speaking, which, nevertheless, are the least perfect of all arguments. For this reason it always dwells in the forests, presiding over, actually, no political system.

Albert establishes a connection between rationality, speech, and political life also elsewhere in the *De animalibus*. For instance, he argues that human beings are conjugal and political all the time when they participate in reason perfectly,

---

[25] [...] *plus omni ape et omni animali gregali, id est, in cuius genere principans constituitur unum, sicut grues unam sequuntur ordine litterato* [...] (Albert the Great 1891, 1.1, 14a).

[26] In a medieval context, language was considered to have two functions: it enables collaboration and makes normative discussions possible (Rosier-Catach 2015, 225–43).

[27] [...] *pigmeus civilitatem perfectam et leges non custodit, sed potius in talibus sequitur naturae impetum sicut et alia bruta animalia.* [...] *et ideo melioris apprehensionis est inter cetera bruta sed verecundiam de turpi, et gloriam de honesto non attendit. Et hoc signum est quod nichil habet de iudicio rationis: propter quod etiam rethoricis persuasionibus in loquendo non utitur neque poeticis quae tamen imperfectiores sunt omnium rationum: et ideo semper silvestris manet nullam prorsus civilitatem custodiens* (Albert the Great 1916, 21.1.2, 1328–29 [1417], translation by Kitchell and Resnick, slightly emended).

but wild humans (*silvestres*) and pygmies lack rationality and therefore they are not humans (Albert the Great 1916, 1.1.3, 17–18 [61]). He also claims that humans are the only political animals without qualification (Albert the Great 1916, 22.1.5, 1354 [1446–47]). It seems therefore clear that when he claims that pygmies are wild and suggests that rationality, language, and laws are necessary for a perfect political community, he means to contrast pygmies (and consequently other political animals) with humans, who lead a political life in the strict sense – a *perfect* political life, which is based on laws and transformed by the ability to speak about justice (Albert the Great 1916, 8.6.1, 671 [771]).

These claims are difficult to harmonize with what Albert writes elsewhere about the political life of non-human animals, unless we suppose that he uses the concept of 'political' in two different senses in his works. Both humans and other animals (including pygmies) can be said to be political, but not in the same way, and human communities are different in kind in comparison to communities of animals. According to this interpretation, Albert's rejection of the political nature of pygmies and his recurrent claim that other political animals only *imitate* the political life of humans (see, e.g., Albert the Great 1916, 1.1.4, 21 [65]) could be taken to mean that they are political only in a metaphorical sense. When ants, bees, cranes, and the like are compared to gregarious animals, the ability to collaborate is a significant trait that allows classifying them as political animals, but in comparison to humans their lives lack the crucial normative dimension. Their behaviour is in many ways comparable to the political life of humans, but nonetheless their communities are but imitations of the real political community of humans. The central functions are there, but in a truncated way.

And yet, the central functions *are* there. Pygmies and non-human animals have political communities, albeit not perfect ones. Humans may be the only political animals in the strict sense, but their political life is at least partially based on collaboration and other functions that Albert attributes to animals (Criteria 1–3 in Section 2 above). Within each of these functions, the difference between humans and other political animals is a matter of degree. Bees collaborate more than cranes; pygmies surpass bees; and rationality and language give humans the ability to collaborate in ways that are too complex for irrational animals. The perfect political community requires laws and reason, but imperfect imitations are not *altogether* different.

Albert (1916, 7.1.1, 498 [588]) hints in this direction when he writes that plants imitate the perfect reproductive action of animals by begetting something similar to themselves without intercourse – they have exactly the same function, only in a different way. Likewise, other political animals can be considered to be different since they lack the means for establishing a perfect political community, and since their communities stem from a partially different set of psychological abilities. Yet it seems possible to hold that political life is a matter of degree, even though absolutely speaking only humans are political animals who have perfect political communities. After all, the existence of a *perfect* community entails the existence of less-than-perfect communities, which suggests that they form a scale and admits of degrees.

Albert's view is a combination of two different conceptions of what it means to be a political animal. Biological and rational functions intermingle in a complex way. If we focus on the biological functions, the social and political life of human beings appears as an intensification of the political life of bees and other such animals: bees work together towards a common aim, and humans simply have a more sophisticated ability to collaborate due to language and rationality. By contrast, if we lay emphasis on the rational functions and abilities, the behaviour of other animals appears so different in comparison to humans, that their political life must be deemed to be nothing but an imitation of humans. The exact relation between these perspectives remains somewhat unclear in the case of Albert.[28]

Traces of a more definite distinction between humans and other political animals can be found in another discussion in the context of the commentaries on the *Politics*. Especially in the fourteenth century, philosophers begin to question the idea that human communities are completely natural. Take, for example, Nicholas of Vaudémont (flourished 1370s),[29] a Parisian master of arts who distinguishes different kinds of things on the basis of the process that makes them come about (Nicholas of Vaudémont 1969, fol. 4ra; see table 1).

Table 1: Classification of natural and artificial things according to Nicholas of Vaudémont

	Completed by nature	**Completed by art**
Initiated by nature	Plants	Wine, bread
Initiated by art	Grain	–

Wild plants are completely natural, because they do not require any human intervention in order to grow from seed to full blossom. Grain, by contrast, is sown by farmers, but afterwards nature takes over the process. And finally, wine and

---

28 Also Rosier-Catach 2015, 233 points out that Albert speaks about the political nature of animals both as a matter of degree, and as qualitatively different from that of humans.
29 For biographical information, see Flüeler 1992, Volume 1, 132–68; Courtenay 2004, 163–68.

bread are made of natural ingredients, but they are artificial in the sense that the final product is made by humans.

Nicholas argues that the political community belongs to the same category as wine and bread. It is initiated by nature but established freely by human beings: "Although the political community is initially from nature, it nevertheless is completed by art and choice. The first part is proved, because human beings are inclined to live in a political community. And the second part is proved, because it is completed by art and choice. Therefore etc."[30]

The key idea in this somewhat deficient argument is that the political community is natural only in the sense that humans have an inclination for it.[31] It must be brought about by human action, and although this requirement does not make it unnatural, Nicholas argues that its naturalness must be understood in a special sense: it is natural in the same way as wine is – which means that it is also artificial in the same way as wine is. The idea that natural causes and human action jointly produce human communities was applied also to the association between man and woman, which forms the core of household.[32]

Nicholas' view entails, among other things, a radical difference between animal and human communities. Beehives, ant colonies, and the temporal associations of cranes are completely natural. None of these animals has the ability to establish a political community such as we find among humans, for the simple reason that they act instinctually and cannot make anything that involves art, skill, or conscious decision. Nicholas' analysis shows that medieval authors have moved away from the biological understanding of what political life means – or at least they have started to emphasize those aspects of Aristotle's view that differentiate us from other animals.

---

30 *Quinta conclusio: licet civitas sit a natura iniciative, tamen ab arte et electione est completive. Probatur prima pars, quia homines iniciative se habent ad civitatem. Et patet secunda pars, quia ab arte est completa et ab electione. Igitur etc.* (Nicholas of Vaudémont 1969, fol. 4rb). I have corrected the 1513 edition on the basis of two manuscripts (see bibliography), but I refer only to the edition, which is more readily available.

31 The idea that the political nature of humans is nothing but an inclination was the mainstream view already in the latter half of the thirteenth century, and also the discussion concerning different senses of 'natural' (*iniciative* and *completive*) goes back to thirteenth century commentaries (Blažek, 2007, 315–32; Toste 2014, 121–56).

32 *[…] communicatio maris et femellae non est naturalis primo modo, quia non fit a principiis intrinsecis naturalibus. Secunda conclusio: quod talis communicatio seu coniugatio maris et femellae est naturalis secundo modo. Patet conclusio, quia iniciative est a natura et completive a voluntate, quia ibi oportet esse consensum et assensum utriusque* (Nicholas of Vaudémont 1969, fol. 5ra; here the Vatican MS has a radically different text, although the philosophical point is the same).

The same development can be seen in the interpretations of Aristotle's linguistic argument. Several authors either simplify it by omitting the comparison to non-human animals altogether or make a terminological move and claim that humans are more *social* than other animals. Thus, Walter Burley declares that: "Not only does it follow that human beings are naturally political and social, but also that humans are more social than any other animal."[33] As a result, humans are not depicted as being more political in comparison to the bee, which tacitly suggests that non-human animals are not political at all.

This trend reaches one culmination point when certain late fourteenth century commentators explicitly reject the political nature of non-human animals. Nicholas of Vaudémont provides a hierarchical taxonomy of the terms that refer to various ways of being social:[34]

> These terms – social, gregarious, and political – are related to each other in such a way that 'social' is an umbrella term (*superius*) for the other two. Wherefore every gregarious or political animal is social but not vice versa, because it loves the company of its own species. This is clear also because there is a kind of natural friendship among those who belong to the same species. 'Gregarious' applies properly only to other animals which roam in groups, as is clear from cranes and other birds. 'Political' applies properly only to human beings because political life aims at some virtue.

The criteria that Nicholas uses to sort different animal species into these categories are not very clear, but by making 'gregarious' and 'political' two distinct species in the genus of 'social', he rules out the possibility that there could be a smooth transition from one to the other. Only human beings count as political animals because political life is necessarily related to practical and theoretical virtues. As we have seen, already Albert the Great had these ideas in embryo, but Nicholas articulates them more sharply and definitely.

---

33 *Non solum sequitur quod homo sit naturaliter civilis et socialis, sed quod homo* [om. V] *est magis socialis quam aliquod aliud animal* (Walter Burley, *Expositio in Pol.*, fol. 5rb (V), 2va–b (CG)). The comparison is omitted by Anonymous of Vatican, *Quaest. Pol.*, fol. 16ra (Toste 2014, 175); Radulphus Brito(?), *Quaest. Pol.*, fol. 1rb (Toste 2014, 178); Anonymous of Milan (Toste 2014, 182); Anonymous of Oxford, *Extractio*, fol. 181ra; and Raimundus Acgerii, *Sent. Pol.*, fol. 49rb.

34 *Ista nomina – sociale, gregale et civile – sic se habent, quod sociale est superius ad illa duo. Unde omne gregale aut civile est sociale sed non econtra, quia diligit societatem suae speciei. Etiam patet quia quaedam est amicitia naturalis inter illa, quae sunt eiusdem speciei. Sed gregale proprie convenit animalibus aliis incedentibus per turmas, ut patet de gruibus <et aliis> ovibus. Civile proprie solum convenit hominibus, quia civilitas ordinatur ad aliquam virtutem* (Nicholas of Vaudémont 1969, fol. 5rb).

A similar approach is adopted by an anonymous fourteenth century author, who begins his answer to the traditional question concerning the political nature of humans with a terminological clarification that resembles the one made by Nicholas. However, there are significant differences in detail:[35]

> Every perfect animal is social with someone from its own species, as a male with a female. However, 'social' implies friendship, and therefore it is said that everything naturally comes together with (*applaudit*) and loves that which is similar to it. Therefore, every animal is social. 'Gregarious' is said only of those animals, which move about in herds, such as bees, ants, birds, and so forth. [...] 'Political' is said only of human beings, because the political community arises from participation of those who discuss with each other and are just, which takes place only among human beings.

There are certain problems in the manuscript, and the taxonomy could be spelled out more systematically, but there remains little doubt that the author suggests the following: (1) all animals are social and have social emotions towards at least some members of their own species; (2) animals that live together in larger groups, including the traditionally political ones such as ants, bees, and cranes, are gregarious; and (3) only human beings are political animals. Further down the text, the author provides his interpretation of Aristotle's linguistic argument which is consistent with this taxonomy. He emphasizes once more that only humans can be considered political animals: "Because other animals are not political, they do not need language. Therefore, they have only voice by which they signal to each other what is pleasurable or sorrowful, and [they signal] nothing about political justice."[36]

---

[35] [...] *omne animal perfectum est sociale cum aliquo de sua specie, sicut masculus cum femella. Verumtamen sociale denotat amicitiam, igitur dicitur <quod> 'omne simile applaudit et diligit naturaliter sibi simile.' Igitur omne animal sociale <est>. Gregale dicitur solum de hiis, quae incedunt per turmas, ut apes, formicae, oves, et cetera.* [...] *Civile* [*non*] *solum dicitur de hominibus, quia civilis communicatio fit <per> participationem conferentis et iusti, quae* [MS: *quia*] *solum habet locum in hominibus* (Anonymous Brussels, *Quaest. Pol.*, fol. 406va). The manuscript states that: "Political is *not* said only of human beings", but this must be a scribal error, as the continuation of the argument shows. A further justification for the omission of *non* is provided later in the same question. *Omne simile etc.*: Ecclesiasticus 13:19; cf. Aristotle 1984, 1155b7; Thomas Aquinas 1969, 444a124–30.

[36] *Cetera enim animalia, quia non sunt civilia, non egent sermone. Ideo solum habent vocem qua invicem significant quid delectabile aut tristabile, et nihil de iusto civili* (Anonymous Brussels, *Quaest. Pol.*, fol. 407ra). Nicholas preserves the comparison to other animals but claims that cognizing the normative element of justice belongs only to political animals (Nicholas of Vaudémont, *Quaest. Pol.*, fol. 6rb).

Both Nicholas and the anonymous author explicitly reject the Aristotelian idea that there are many animal species that count as political. Moreover, the anonymous author turns the linguistic argument on its head. The version handed down by Albert the Great and other thirteenth century philosophers states that humans are more political than other animals due to the ability to speak about what is just and unjust; the anonymous author, by contrast, suggests that humans need language because they are political. At least on the surface, he seems to think that language is an instrument that is needed in order to live a properly political life; if one is not political, there is no need for language.

Finally, the author puts forth an argument that draws from Cassiodorus' *Variae* 9.2. The ancient senator had mentioned the abilities of cranes – living in harmonious groups, taking turns in guarding, and alternating as the leader of the wedge – and concluded that they have a political community without kings. On the basis of this remark, the anonymous author suggests, someone might think that animals are capable of a political life and justice. Indeed, Albert and many other medieval philosophers used these abilities as criteria for establishing that cranes are political animals by nature, as we have seen. But the anonymous author claims that they are wrong: "I answer that such animals do not have a proper political government (*non politizant*), and they do not deliberate mutually about justice and injustice, but only by solicitude and certain natural instinct."[37] The actions of animals may appear similar to the forms of political life that are proper to human beings, but in reality they are based on a different set of psychological abilities and therefore radically different.

The idea that the political life of non-human animals is based on a natural instinct was not original, to be sure, but the way Nicholas and the anonymous commentator use it to reject their political nature reveals an important trend of narrowing down the scope of the concept of political animal. Neither of these authors breaks ground with the traditional observations concerning the behaviour of animals. They just do not think that collaborating and living together with other members of the species in an organized group, which may even have a leader, suffices to make an animal a political one. Being political becomes a necessary concomitant of the specific difference that sets humans apart from other animals; it turns into a trait that is as unique as rationality is in the animal kingdom.

---

[37] *Etiam quedam videntur politicare et iustitiam exercere. […] dico quod talia animalia non politizant proprie nec invicem conferunt de iusto et iniusto, sed solum sol<lic>itudine et quodam naturali insti<nc>tu* (Anonymous Brussels, fol. 407ra–b).

Nevertheless, the emphasis that these authors place on rationality and language does not mean that they would lose sight of the more basic functions of the political community. They acknowledge that it exists partially because it provides the material necessities for life (Anonymous of Brussels, *Quaest. Pol.*, fol. 405vb; Nicholas of Vaudémont, *Quaest. Pol.*, fol. 4ra). In other words, they do not forget Aristotle's idea that political community comes to be for the sake of living, although it remains in existence for the sake of living well. Political life may require rationality, but it still serves the function of keeping us alive, much in the same way as the (non-political) communities of animals.

5 Conclusion

Medieval views concerning political animals are complex because they oscillate between the ideas that (1) there are many political animals that are not humans and (2) humans are the only political animals in the proper sense of the word. The concept 'political animal' refers sometimes to biological and psychological traits that humans share with other social animals. Collaboration in order to reach a common goal, hierarchical structure within the community, and the inclination for the biological survival of the individuals and the species – all these are counted as traits that distinguish political animals from those that lead a solitary or gregarious way of life. By contrast, in some cases the concept of political animal is used in a stricter sense to denote a complex social life that is regulated by laws and related to justice, rationality, language, and moral virtue. Non-human animals are political in the former but not in the latter sense.

Whether this division between different ways to understand the meaning of the concept of political animal entails that non-human animals are less political than humans, or that they are only metaphorically political, is likely to vary from author to author. However, even when medieval authors end up rejecting the political nature of non-human animals, they do not discard the biological aspect of the concept altogether. They accept the behavioural similarity between humans and other social animals but question whether social behaviour counts as political when it does not involve rationality. In effect, they radicalize the difference between humans and other political animals without discarding the idea that humans are political due to their animality. The biological needs and desires that explain the behaviour of ants, bees, and cranes remain central for the political life of human beings. Rationality enables more complex forms of collaboration and social organisation, and it brings in the normative dimension of justice, but the political nature of humans is partially explained by appealing to the same factors that figure in the social life of animals.

In this way, medieval philosophers preserve the biological conception of what it means to be a political animal, but they tend to think that it is transformed by human rationality. Already Albert the Great defends this view, but he does not hesitate to call many non-human animals political. By contrast, certain fourteenth century authors presuppose that collaboration for the sake of the common good does not count as political unless it is coupled with rationality – even when it is done under a leader and with a division of labour. These later thinkers remove the ambiguity within Aristotle's view by explicitly denying the existence of non-human political animals. We are not like ants in a colony even when we do our share.[38]

Primary literature

Albert the Great. 1891. *Commentarii in octo libros Politicorum Aristotelis*, edited by Auguste Borgnet, Alberti Magni Opera omnia 8. Paris: Vivès.
Albert the Great. 1916. *De animalibus libri XXVI*, edited by Hermann Stadler. Münster: Aschendorff. [= *De animalibus*]
Albert the Great. 1955. *Quaestiones Super De Animalibus*, edited by Ephrem Filthaut, Alberti Magni Opera Omnia, Volume 12. Münster: Aschendorff.
Albert the Great. 1999. *On Animals: A Medieval Summa Zoologica*, 2 Volumes, translated by Kenneth F. Kitchell Jr. and Irven M. Resnick. Baltimore: The Johns Hopkins University Press.
Albert the Great. 2008. *Questions Concerning Aristotle's On Animals*, translated by Irven M. Resnick and Kenneth F. Kitchell Jr. Washington: The Catholic University of America Press.
Anonymous of Brussels. *Quaestiones in librum Politicorum Aristotelis*, Brussels, Bibl. Royale 863–69 (2916), fol. 402ra–436ra.
Anonymous of Milan. *Quaestiones super I-VII libros Politicorum*, quaestio 1.6., edited by Marco Toste, in Toste 2014, 181–86.
Anonymous of Oxford. *Extractio compendiosa dictorum in Politica Aristotelis*, Oxford, Bodl. Library 292, fol. 180ra–219ra.
Anonymous of Vatican. *Quaestiones super I Librum Politicorum*, Vatican, BAV Pal. lat. 1030, fol. 14ra–19rb (Partially edited by Marco Toste, in Toste 2014, 174–76).
Anonymous (Peter of Spain?). 1991. *Problemata*, edited by Miguel de Asúa, in Asúa 1991, 359–403.
Aristotle. 1984. *The Complete Works of Aristotle: The Revised Oxford Translation*, 2 Volumes, edited by Jonathan Barnes. Princeton: Princeton University Press.
Aristotle. 1998. *Politics*, translated by C. D. C. Reeve. Indianapolis/Cambridge: Hackett Publishing Company. [= *Pol.*]

---

[38] This research has been funded by the Academy of Finland and Riksbankens Jubileumsfond. Some results of this chapter have been published in revised and extended form in Toivanen 2021.

Avicenna. 1968. *Liber de anima seu sextus de naturalibus*, Volumes IV–V, edited by Simone Van Riet, Louvain/Leiden: Éditions Orientalistes/E. J. Brill.

Avicenna. 1980. *Liber de philosophia prima sive scientia divina*, Volumes V–X, edited by Simone Van Riet. Louvain/Leiden: E. Peeters/E. J. Brill.

Giles of Rome. 1607. *De Regimine Principum*, edited by Hieronymus Samaritanus. Rome: B. Zanetto.

Guy of Rimini. *Super Politicam*. Venice, BMarc. Lat. VI 92 (2492), fol. 57rb–142vb.

Nicholas of Vaudémont (Ps.-John Buridan). [1513] 1969. *Quaestiones super octo libros Politicorum Aristotelis*. Frankfurt: Minerva.

Nicholas of Vaudémont. *Quaestiones super octo libros Politicorum Aristotelis*, Paris, BNF Nal. 1130, fol. 2r–219r.

Nicholas of Vaudémont. *Quaestiones super octo libros Politicorum Aristotelis*, Vatican, BAV Vat. lat. 2167, fol. 1ra–139vb.

Peter of Auvergne. *Quaestiones super I-VII libros Politicorum*, Paris, BNF Lat. 16089, fol. 274r–319r.

Radulphus Brito (Pseudo?). *Quaestiones super librum Politicorum*, Baltimore, Johns Hopkins University cod. 9, fol. 1ar–4rb (Partially edited by Marco Toste, in Toste 2014, 177–81).

Raimundus Acgerii. *Sententia libri Politicorum Aristotelis*, Florence, BLaur. S. Marco 452 (20), fol. 49ra–75vb.

Thomas Aquinas. 1969. *Sententia libri Ethicorum*, Sancti Thomae de Aquino Opera Omnia, Volume 47. Rome: Ad Sanctae Sabinae.

Thomas Aquinas. 1971. *Sententia libri Politicorum*, Sancti Thomae de Aquino Opera Omnia, Volume 48. Rome: Ad Sanctae Sabinae.

Thomas Aquinas. 1979. *De regno ad regem Cypri*, Sancti Thomae de Aquino Opera Omnia, Volume 42, 417–71. Rome: Editori di San Tommaso, 1979.

Thomas Aquinas. 2007. *Commentary on Aristotle's Politics*, translated by Richard J. Regan. Indianapolis/Cambridge: Hackett Publishing Company.

Walter Burley. *Expositio in Aristotelis Politicorum libros*. Vatican, MS Borgh. 129, fol. 1r–148v (= V); Cambridge, Gonville and Caius Coll. 490/486, fol. 1ra–74va (= GC).

Secondary literature

Asúa, Miguel. 1991. *The Organization of Discourse on Animals in the Thirteenth Century: Peter of Spain, Albert the Great, and the Commentaries on "De Animalibus."* PhD dissertation, University of Notre Dame. Ann Arbor: U.M.I.

Blažek, Pavel. 2007. *Die Mittelalterliche Rezeption der Aristotelischen Philosophie der Ehe von Robert Grosseteste bis Bartholomäus von Brügge (1246/1247–1309)*. Leiden/Boston: E. J. Brill.

Cooper, John. 1990. "Political Animals and Civic Friendship." In *Aristoteles' "Politik": Akten des XI. Symposium Aristotelicum*, edited by Günther Patzig, 220–48. Göttingen: Vandenhoeck and Ruprecht.

Courtenay, William. 2004. "A Note on Nicolaus Girardi de Waudemonte, Pseudo-Johannes Buridanus." *SIEPM Bulletin de Philosophie Médiévale* 46:163–68.

De Leemans, Pieter and Klemm, Matthew. 2007. "Animals and Anthropology in Medieval Philosophy." In *A Cultural History of Animals in the Medieval Age*, edited by Brigitte Resl, 153–77. Oxford/New York: Berg.

Depew, David. 1995. "Humans and Other Political Animals in Aristotle's History of Animals." *Phronesis* 40/1:156–81.

Di Martino, Carla. 2008. *Ratio Particularis. Doctrines des Senses Internes d'Avicenne à Thomas d'Aquin*. Études de Philosophie Médiévale 94. Paris: Vrin.

Fioravanti, Gianfranco. 1999. "La Réception de la Politique d'Aristote au Moyen Âge Tardif." In *Aspects de la Pensée Médiévale dans la Philosophie Politique Moderne*, edited by Yves-Charles Zarka, 7–24. Paris: Presses Universitaires de France.

Flüeler, Christoph. 1992. *Rezeption und Interpretation der Aristotelischen Politica im späten Mittelalter*, 2 Volumes. Amsterdam: B.R. Grüner.

Fögen, Thorsten. 2014. "Animal Communication." In *The Oxford Handbook of Animals in Classical Thought and Life*, edited by Gordon L. Campbell, 216–32. Oxford: Oxford University Press, 2014.

Harvey, Ruth. 1975. *The Inward Wits. Psychological Theory in the Middle Ages and the Renaissance*. London: The Warburg Institute.

Keyt, David. 1987. "Three Fundamental Theorems in Aristotle's *Politics*." *Phronesis* 32/1:54–79.

Köhler, Theodor W. 2008. *Homo animal nobilissimum. Konturen des spezifisch Menschlichen in der naturphilosophischen Aristoteleskommentierung des dreizehnten Jahrhunderts*, Volume 1. Leiden/Boston: Brill.

Labarrière, Jean-Louis. 2004. *Langage, vie politique et mouvement des animaux: Études aristotéliciennes*. Paris: Vrin.

Laland, Kevin N. and Galef, Bennet G. (editors). 2009. *The Question of Animal Culture*. Cambridge, MA/London: Harvard University Press.

Lambertini, Roberto. 1990. "*Philosophus Videtur Tangere Tres Rationes:* Edigio Romano Lettore ed Interprete della Politica nel Terzo Libro del De regimine Principum." *Documenti e studi sulla tradizione filosofica medievale* 1/1:277–325.

Lennox, James G. 2001. "Are Aristotelian Species Eternal?" In *Aristotle's Philosophy of Biology: Studies in the Origins of Life Science*, 131–59. Cambridge: Cambridge University Press.

Miller, Fred. 1997. *Justice, Nature, and Rights in Aristotle's Politics*. Oxford: Oxford University Press.

Mulgan, Richard G. 1974. "Aristotle's Doctrine that Man is a Political Animal." *Hermes* 102:438–45.

Pasnau, Robert and van Dyke, Christina (editors). 2010. *The Cambridge History of Medieval Philosophy*, 2 Volumes. Cambridge: Cambridge University Press.

Resnick, Irven M. and Kenneth F. Kitchell Jr. 2008. "Introduction." In *Albert the Great, Questions Concerning Aristotle's On Animals*, translated by Irven M. Resnick and Kenneth Kitchell, 3–9. Washington: The Catholic University of America Press.

Resnick, Irven M. and Kenneth F. Kitchell Jr. 1996. "Albert the Great on the 'Language' of Animals." *American Catholic Philosophical Quarterly* 70/1:41–61.

Rosier-Catach, Irène. 2015. "Communauté politique et communauté linguistique." In *La Légitimité Implicite*, Volume 1, edited by Jean-Philippe Genet, 225–43. Paris/Rome: Éditions de la Sorbonne/École Française de Rome.

Toivanen, Juhana. 2013. *Perception and the Internal Senses. Peter of John Olivi on the Cognitive Functions of the Sensitive Soul.* Leiden/Boston: E. J. Brill.

Toivanen, Juhana. 2020. "Estimative Power as a Social Sense." In *The Internal Senses in the Aristotelian Tradition*, edited by Seyed N. Mousavian and Jakob L. Fink, 115–36. Cham: Springer.

Toivanen, Juhana. 2021. *The Political Animal in Medieval Philosophy: A Philosophical Study of the Commentary Tradition c. 1260–1410.* Leiden/Boston: E. J. Brill.

Toste, Marco. 2008. "*Utrum felix indigeat amicis:* The Reception of the Aristotelian Theory of Friendship at the Arts Faculty in Paris." In *Virtue Ethics in the Middle Ages: Commentaries on Aristotle's Nicomachean Ethics, 1200–1500*, edited by István P. Bejczy, 173–95. Leiden/Boston: E. J. Brill.

Toste, Marco. 2012. "Pro Patria Mori. The Debate in the Medieval Aristotelian Commentary Tradition." In *Il Bene Comune: Forme di Governo e Gerarchie Sociali nel Basso Medioevo*. Spoleto: Fondazione CISAM.

Toste, Marco. 2014. "The Naturalness of Human Association in Medieval Political Thought Revisited." In *La Nature Comme Source de la Morale au Moyen Âge*, edited by Maaike van der Lugt, 113–88. Florence: SISMEL-Edizioni del Galluzzo.

Van den Abeele, Baudouin. 1999. "Le 'De Animalibus' d'Aristote Dans Le Monde Latin: Modalités de Sa Réception Médiévale." *Frühmittelalterliche Studien* 33:287–318.

Jenny Pelletier
Ockham on Human Freedom and the Nature and Origin of Lordship

Abstract: This study explores the role of the will and the human capacity to act for the sake of ends in William of Ockham's account of the origin of political and social institutions. For him lordship (*dominium*), which the members of a human community possess over goods or over one another, is produced through human intelligent voluntary agency. In both his academic and political writings, he holds that intellect and will are needed to introduce the phenomena of ownership, property, and political rulership. Thus, only intelligent voluntary agents can institute social and political institutions, a use of powers given to us by God but exercised by humans in response to practical circumstances and for the sake of an end.

1 Introduction

William Ockham (*ca.* 1285–1347), controversial Franciscan philosopher-theologian and later rebellious political activist, excommunicated and convinced that the pope was a heretic, held the view that social and political institutions[1] come about by means of the human intellect and will working together.[2] A consequence of this view, for Ockham, is that social and political institutions are in a sense not natural. For, he famously also held that while the intellect is a natural power, the will is a free or voluntary power. By this he means that the will is not determined to perform one act over another but retains the power to act or to not act and to will or to not will. In drawing the distinction between voluntary and natural powers (and thus agency) Ockham opposes the realm of the natural and the voluntary. If social and political institutions come about through the cooperation of the intellect and the will, then they are not produced by means of a purely natural process but through "intelligent voluntary agency" (this term is

---

[1] I am using the term 'institutions' in an entirely non-technical way.
[2] To forstall any misunderstanding, it is important to note at the outset that for Ockham, the will and the intellect are not really distinct faculties or powers of the soul even though it is commonplace in the literature to refer to 'the intellect' and 'the will', a practice that I shall follow here. I will use 'intellection' and 'volition' to refer to the two kinds of really distinct acts that one and the same soul can perform.

used by Adams 1998 amongst others). To be sure, we can say that social and political institutions are natural in the sense that they arise by virtue of various acts of the rational human soul, which comprises the powers of intellect and will both of which are essential properties of being human. To have a will is part of human nature, even when that will is free and its acts are typically characterized as voluntary, and not natural.[3]

I intend to show that the human intellect and will lie at the origin of the emergence of at least one crucial social and political institution, namely lordship (*dominium*), which the members of a human community possess over goods (ownership or proprietary lordship) or over one another (political rulership or governance). Lordship, Ockham thinks, is produced through human intelligent voluntary agency and he holds this over his academic and political writings.[4] Given Ockham's distinction between natural and voluntary agency, there is a salient sense, therefore, in which lordship is not natural. Moreover, it is because human beings are intelligent voluntary agents that they are able to institute lordship, chosen in light of a perceived and desired end, as a viable and rationally satisfying means to achieve that end. Lordship has a purpose and a teleological explanation.

I will proceed first by analysing Ockham's account of lordship, both in the academic writings, where lordship is conceived of as a mental relation and

---

[3] It is not my intention to rehearse the tired discussion of Ockham's voluntarism, a debate that I will leave aside. I take it as obvious that Ockham provides a nuanced account of the relationship between the intellect (right reason, prudence, or practical intellect) and the will in his discussions of human action, ethics, and various themes in political philosophy. For an analysis of Ockham's purported voluntarism or naturalism, see Adams 1987b. She rightly concludes, to my mind, that Ockham is better thought of as a Franciscan Aristotelian who believes in natures and who privileges the will in the realm of the ethical, social, and political. For two interesting discussions connected to the debate in the realm of Ockham's political philosophy, namely divine command (God's will), human will, and natural law, see Kilcullen [1993] 1995; McGrade 1999.

[4] For a recent overview of Ockham's biography, see Spade and Panaccio 2016. Ockham's intellectual life abruptly changed course when, in 1324, he was summoned to Avignon on suspicion of heresy. He left behind a promising career in theology, having studied at Oxford and then the Franciscan convent in London. Once in Avignon, he became embroiled in the controversy over apostolic poverty against the pope on behalf of the Franciscan order. In 1328, he fled, finding refuge and protection for the rest of his life at the court of Louis of Bavaria, the Holy Roman Emperor. The poverty debate is widely considered to have been his introduction to political thought and, after the late 1320s, he never returned to his earlier speculative philosophical and theological interests. His *corpus* is thus divided into academic and political writings that abruptly cleave his career in two. In drawing on texts from both sets of writings, I am not making the strong claim that his speculative or 'academic' views inexorably entailed his political views.

more particularly as the mental relative term 'lordship' (Section 2), and in the political writings where Ockham describes lordship as a God-given power that human beings first exercised on their own initiative, thereby introducing ownership, property and political rulership into the social world (Section 3). On both accounts, the role of the intellect and the will are decisive (Section 4). I then turn to Ockham's view of the freedom of the will and its connection to his discussion of final causality, which we find in the academic writings (Section 4.1). Here, I discuss the distinction between natural and voluntary agency, and show that only intelligent voluntary agents can act for the sake of ends (in doing so, I admit that I am side-stepping a controversial issue in the literature on final causality in Ockham). I then return to lordship (Section 4.2), providing a reconstruction of the origin of ownership, its being brought about through the co-operation between the intellect and the will of its original 'institutors' as a means to end.

All of this is latent in the political writings. Ockham viewed social and political institutions largely as the result of human convention, agreement, and arrangement (e.g. Canning 2011, Chapter 4; Lambertini 2005) and the importance of human freedom in this has been the subject of some interest (Miethke 1991). An advantage of reading Ockham's academic writings alongside the political writings is that the former provide us with a very fine-grained analysis of the metaphysics and psychology of the human soul: its capacity for performing intellective and volitional acts, the freedom of the will, and its connection to final causality. The academic writings bring to bear an exceptional and characteristic degree of precision on these issues that is less forthcoming in the political writings.

2 Lordship as a mental relation

We first encounter lordship in Ockham's extended treatment on relations in the *Ordinatio*.[5] In d. 35, q. 4, Ockham discusses 'relations of reason'.[6] He lists lordship (*dominium*) along with money (*pecunia*) or value (*pretium*), conventional linguistic signification (*signum*), and slavery (*servitus*) as examples. Some of

---

[5] All translations are my own unless otherwise stated. Where I use a translation that has been published as part of a complete work, I cite the translation in the main text, providing the Latin text from Ockham's critical edition in the notes.
[6] I discuss the same passages in more detail in Pelletier 2020 with some differences in language. There, however, I am primarily concerned to determine the ontological status of lordship and ownership in particular.

these resurface in *Quodlibet* 6, q. 29, and q. 30. Since relations of reason will crucially depend on mental acts, I will call them 'mental relations', understood to mean mind-dependent relations. Real relations, as we shall see, are mind-independent. These texts have been extensively discussed in the literature, often as an appendix to Ockham's treatment of relations in general, where the overwhelming focus falls on real relations (Adams 1987a, 261–265; Henninger 1989, 136–140; Brower 2015). The main interest has been to determine whether he adopts a uniform approach to relations across the real and mental divide, and it seems that he does.

Despite casting some suspicion on the philosophical pedigree of the notion of mental relations, which he notes is absent from Aristotle, Ockham discusses mental relations to some extent, maintaining the consensus opinion that real and mental relations are distinct from one another (Ockham 1980, 699). Across the *Ordinatio* and the *Quodlibeta* his principal interest is twofold. On the one hand, he wants to get clear how mental and real relations differ from one another. On the other hand, he wants to show, in keeping with his general account of relations, that mental relations are not really distinct from their *relata*, namely, the very entities that are related. Relations, for Ockham, do not exist independently of what is related and with a handful of theological exceptions there are no relational entities in his ontology.

He typically conceives of relations in two ways, and this distinction is raised with respect to mental relations in *Ordinatio* d. 35, q. 4, where Ockham writes, "Concerning the first [question, namely what is a mental relation], I say that a mental relation can be understood in two ways: in one way as an utterance or concept conveying something or some things; another way as the signified [things] themselves" (Ockham 1979, 470).[7] In the first way, and this tends to be his preference for relations generally, relations are a class of term – an utterance or concept – that signify and connote entities conjointly (*in coniunctim*).

A side-note on the semantic terminology is necessary here, which has been much discussed in the literature (e.g. Panaccio 1999). Ockham exhaustively divides up simple terms that have signification into absolute and connotative terms. An absolute term like 'rose' signifies what it signifies (its *significata*) equally primarily, that is to say each and every rose in exactly the same way and without signifying anything else. Connotative terms signify what they signify unequally, that is to say some things primarily (their *significata*) and others things secondarily (their *connotata*). The connotative term 'red' primarily signi-

---

[7] *Circa primum dico quod relatio rationis dupliciter accipi potest: uno modo pro ista voce vel conceptu importante aliquid vel aliqua; alio modo pro ipsis significatis.*

fies things that are red, like paintings and roses, while secondarily signifying or connoting the patches of redness that inhere in those paintings and roses. On this first conception, relations are just relative terms, like 'similarity', 'causality', 'equality' that form a class of connotative terms. They have primary *significata* and secondary *connotata* that they conjointly convey.

In a second and admittedly non-Aristotelian way, Ockham thinks that we can conceive of relations as the related entities themselves, which can be conveyed by first-order relative terms. We can say that all patches of redness, for instance, are a similarity and they can be conveyed by the term 'similarity'. Either way the point is that relations are not relative entities existing in addition to the entities that are related whether we insist that a relation is best construed as a relative term or as the *relata* of the relative term.

Ockham describes a mental relation as "[...] when a thing cannot be such as it is expressed to be by that term without a concurrent act of the intellect or will" (Ockham 1979, 472).[8] On the first conception of a relation, a mental relation is a term, a concept or an utterance in a conventional language like Latin or English, that signifies things to be the sort of things that they are only by virtue of a concurrent intellection or volition – both of which are mental acts that connect those things to one another. Here, the terms 'lordship', 'slavery', etc. are mental relations. On the second conception of a relation, a mental relation is the set of things that are conjointly conveyed, signified and connoted, by a mental relative term, whatever those turn out to be. The idea is that the entities conveyed by the mental relative term are only related to one another in that respect (they might be related to one another in some other respect) because some intellection or volition has been performed at some point that links the one with the other. As I explain below, it is in this regard – the crucial performance of a mental act – that a mental relation differs from a real relation. A mental relative term like 'lordship', therefore, signifies what it signifies, its *significata*, while connoting the intellection or volition that connects its *significata* and whatever other *connotata* it may have to one another.

That the mental act in question is an intellection *or* volition is perhaps misleading. Ockham immediately goes on to give an example suggesting that a mental relation rests on at least one intellection followed by a volition. In this case, a mental relation seems to be a relation instituted by the will working with the intellect and not only the one or the other operating independently of one another.

---

8 *Alio modo potest dici 'relativum rationis' quando res non est talis qualis exprimitur esse per tale nomen, nisi concurrente vel actu intellectus vel voluntatis.* Ockham first discusses mental relations understood in a broad sense but this sense is not relevant for the case of lordship.

Pieces of metal can only be called 'money' once we have decided and thus willed to use those pieces of metal in exchange for goods, i.e. as having the function of exchange value. But, willing to use bits of metal in this way presupposes a prior intellection. Ockham 1979, 472 states:[9]

> For a spoken utterance is a sign and a coin is money or value only because, with a previous intellection, we wish to use the spoken utterance or coin in this way. And given that there is such a volition in us – or there was and there was no contrary volition – immediately, without anything else added, the spoken utterance is a sign and the coin money.

The term 'money' arises when we cognize an appropriate medium to which exchange value could be ascribed, i.e. these particular pieces of metal, then will to ascribe exchange value to those pieces of metal, and then coin the term 'money' or its equivalent in another conventional language.[10] I assume that we have to include an intellection that is our cognition or understanding of what exchange value is. Indeed, it seems likely that a reasonably complicated process would have to be carried out involving right reason prior to the performance of the volition by which it is decided that pieces of metal are 'money'. In the passage cited above, Ockham specifies that this volition could have taken place in the past and, unless it has been subsequently revoked, continues to hold in the present. This suggests that a mental relation can obtain over time even when the original institutor(s) of that mental relation is long gone. Presumably, however, present users of money, i.e. of coin used in exchange for goods, as well as the term 'money', must accept its original institution and this in turn entails that they perform intellections and volitions in the present.[11]

The example of 'money' or 'value' is used again in *Quodlibet* 6, q. 29, where Ockham writes (Freddoso and Kelley 1991, 586).[12]

> [...] a denarius is not said to have value except by virtue of the voluntary institution of the one who instituted it. And so ['value'] connotes an act of will and an act of understanding

---

9 *Quia vox non est signum, nec nummus est pretium nec pecunia, nisi quia praevio actu intellectus volumus sic uti voce et nummo. Et ex hoc ipso quod ponitur talis volitio in nobis – vel aliquando fuit et non fuit volitio contraria – statim sine omni alio additio, vox est signum et nummus pretium.* Translation with modification by Henninger 1989, 138.
10 I provide a more detailed analysis of this process in Pelletier 2020, 263–264.
11 Again, for a more detailed discussion on the relevant past and present volitions, see Pelletier 2020, 264–266.
12 [...] *denarius non dicitur pretium nisi per voluntariam institutionem alicuius institutentis, et ita connotat actum voluntatis et actum intellectus ipsius instituentis, sine quo actu nullo modo dicitur pretium. Et ideo potest dici relatio rationis* (Ockham 1980, 698).

on the part of the one who instituted it, without which acts [the denarius] would in no way be said to have value. And for this reason ['value'] can be called a relation of reason.

In this passage, Ockham explicitly refers to the '*voluntary* institution' (my italics) – the requisite performance of an intellection and volition – to institute a mental relation, the latter of which warrants describing such an institution as 'voluntary'. Further, he alludes here to the semantics of mental relative terms when he notes that 'value' connotes an "act of *will* and an act of understanding" (my italics). Notice that the disjunction from the *Ordinatio* passage is absent; here we have a clear case of an intellection *and* a volition taken together as being necessary for a mental relation to obtain. In short, 'value' signifies (1) bits of metal, and connotes (2) the goods for which those bits of metal can be exchanged as well as (3) the intellection(s) and volition(s) by which it was understood and then decided that those bits of metal would be so used.

That a mental relation implies an intellection and volition without which there can be no talk of a relation at all is of course how mental relations differ from real relations. In *Quodlibet* 6, q. 30 Ockham makes this quite obvious when he describes a mental relation as a relation that obtains by virtue of an "operation of the intellect" whereas a real relation obtains in the absence of any operation of the intellect. The similarity between Socrates and Plato in respect of their whiteness holds regardless of whether one connects the two men to one another by comparing the colour of their skin. The same cannot be said for money or slavery. Coins have no value and no one can be a slave unless it has been decided that coins can be exchanged for goods and that some human beings can own others. The terms 'money', 'lordship', and 'slavery' are relations that fundamentally rest on the voluntary institution of a past or present person or communities of persons connecting persons to persons (slavery), persons to things (lordship), or things to things (money). These terms convey certain members of the human community, the things that they use, consume, own, exchange, and so on, and the mental operations by virtue of which they have been connected to one another.

3 Lordship as a power

Ockham discusses lordship in two of his political works, where lordship is characterized as a power (*potestas*). The first text, *The Work of Ninety Days*, was Ockham's first political tract, composed between 1332 and 1334 as the immediate consequence of his involvement in the Franciscan poverty controversy in the 1320s. His involvement in that controversy, which took up questions about property, ownership, rights, and poverty, instigated his engagement with political philosophy.[13] The second text, written sometime between 1338 and 1342 is a treatise on papal and imperial power entitled, *A Short Discourse on the Tyrannical Government Over Things Divine and Human, but Especially Over the Empire and Those Subject to the Empire, Usurped by Some Who are Called Highest Pontiffs*. As part of a larger polemic against the claim that all temporal power finds its origin and legitimacy in the papacy, Ockham argues that unbelievers like the pre-Christian Romans can exercise true lordship over people and goods. This is because, he makes clear, lordship emerged in the human community in accordance with human law, not divine law. To press his case, Ockham gives a historical analysis of lordship.

Leaving aside divine lordship to focus on the human case, Ockham draws a preliminary distinction between common and exclusive lordship.[14] Common lordship was common to the entire human race, which, he writes: "God gave Adam and his wife for themselves and all their posterity" (McGrade and Kilcullen 1992, 88).[15] Common lordship was the power to manage and use temporal things for one's own benefit but precluded the possibility of dividing up goods in such a way that one made them one's own exclusively, that is by appropriating them to oneself so that no one else could control them. Exclusive lordship (*dominium proprium* or *proprietas*) is precisely the "[...] power of managing temporal things, appropriated to one person or to certain persons or to some particular collectivity" (McGrade and Kilcullen 1992, 88).[16] Exclusive lordship is ownership. An individual person or persons or a collective of persons (henceforth I will just refer to a person) can have ownership over, that is can own, things (goods, objects, etc.). Ownership is exclusive or private *per definition* and never common. A collectivity like a university does not have common lordship over, say, land, buildings, food, or clothing but owns those goods.

---

13 The topic of poverty, property, and power in Ockham and the broader Franciscan struggle against John XXII is vast. For a small selection of recent work, see Kilcullen 1999; Mäkinen 2001, especially Chapter 4 (though, she does not discuss Ockham at much length); Lambertini 2005; Shogimen 2007, Chapter 1; Canning 2011, Chapter 4; Robinson 2013, especially Chapters 1 and 2. For lordship in Ockham's political writings, see (amongst many others) Miethke 1969, 467–477 and more cursorily in Miethke 1991; Robinson 2013, Chapter 4.
14 I discuss the same passages with minor differences in language in Pelletier 2020, 254–255.
15 *Dominium commune toti generi humano est illud, quod Deus dedit Adae et uxori suae pro se et omnibus posteris suis: quod fuit potestas disponendi et utendi temporalibus rebus ad utilitatem suam* (Ockham 1997, 178).
16 *Aliud est dominium proprium [...] quod dominium est potestas principalis disponendi de rebus temporalibus appropriata uni personae vel certis personis aut alicui collegio speciali* (Ockham 1997, 178).

The entire human race would have continued to enjoy common lordship were it not for the fall (McGrade and Kilcullen 1992, 88–89):[17]

> [...] lordship common to the whole human race, existed in the state of innocence, and would have continued if man had not sinned, but without the power to appropriate anything to anyone except by use, as has been said. For since there would have been among them no avarice or desire to possess or use any temporal thing against right reason, there would then have been no necessity or advantage in having ownership of any temporal thing.

Under pre-lapsarian conditions, there was no ownership and therefore no property. Adam and Eve did not own the food they ate and the clothing with which they clothed themselves because of the love and concord that subsisted between them (Ockham 1997, 182).[18] They were able to manage and use the temporal goods that they needed without having to own them. This changes with the fall, which introduces greed, the desire to appropriate goods to oneself and a propensity to abuse temporal goods, which can be mitigated and controlled by the introduction and regulation of exclusive lordship.[19] After the fall, God gives human beings the power to establish ownership as a means to help human beings cope with the disastrous moral and psychological damage caused by their own sin and wreaked upon the human community at large.

Following the fall, both God-given powers, common and exclusive lordship, co-existed in the human community for a while.[20] Ownership and property did not yet actually exist but could, since God had only made it possible to divide up and appropriate goods between persons for their exclusive control (it is not clear in what sense lordship, a power, can exist given Ockham's ontological commitments but I will set this concern aside for now; this is the central question in Pelletier 2020). For Ockham, this entails that God did not ordain exclusive lord-

---

17 *Primum dominium, scilicet commune toti generi humano, fuit et permansisset in statu innocentiae, si homo non peccasset; sed absque potestate appropriandi rem aliquam alicui personae aliter quam per usam, sicut dictum est. Propter hoc enim, quod in eis nulla fuisset avaritia vel contra rationem rectam cupiditas possidendi vel utendi quacumque re temporali, nulla fuisset tunc necessitas vel utilitas habendi proprietatem cuiuscumque rei temporalis* (Ockham 1997, 179).
18 *Verisimile autem est quod inter Adam et uxorem suam tantus fuerit amor et concordia quod neuter voluit dominium proprium etiam pelliceae, qua utebatur, habere* [...].
19 In associating ownership and property with the fall, i.e. sin, Ockham endorses an Augustinian view that had inspired Franciscan thinking on this subject, see Brett 1997, 29–31; Mäkinen 2001, 84 (for Bonaventure); Canning 2011, 119 and 122.
20 *Et ideo post lapsum cum dominio, quod fuit in statu innocentiae, fuit potestas taliter appropriandi temporalia; sed proprietas non statim fuit post peccatum.*

ship even though it finds its source in God.[21] God permitted the members of the human community to act on that power if they chose to do so. The actual exercise of exclusive lordship, and therefore the inauguration of the phenomenon of ownership and property, did not take place until Cain and Abel first exercised that power (Ockham 1997, 179). Ockham declares, "For the first division of things, which would seem to have established exclusive lordship, seems to have been made between Cain and Abel" (McGrade and Kilcullen 1992, 92).[22] Abel was "compelled to make some such division of things by the malice of Cain, who wanted to oppress him violently and to appropriate everything to himself unjustly" (McGrade and Kilcullen 1992, 92).[23] Cain and Abel thus introduced ownership and property into human history for the first time. Exclusive lordship arises through human action performed in accordance with human law and not by divine law. In fact, in *The Work of Ninety Days*, Ockham (1963, 656) states that exclusive lordship over temporal goods was established by human ordinance or will.[24]

In *The Work of Ninety Days*, Ockham emphasizes the decisive role of human beings even more, specifically human-devised legal structures like courts. In *The Work of Ninety Days*, Chapter 2, where Ockham (1940, 308 and 310) defines his key terminology, he describes exclusive lordship as a human power of laying claim to a temporal thing in a human court, adding that on a narrower understanding of exclusive lordship one who exercises such lordship – the lord or owner – can treat that temporal thing in any way he or she likes as long as it is not forbidden by natural law. Ownership is not simply the division of goods between persons; it entails the right to defend one's ownership. Moreover, ownership includes the right to transfer one's ownership to another by means of human agreement, i.e. a contract (Ockham 1963, 487).

Ockham also conceives of lordship as political, and in this case too he characterizes it as power: "[...] God gave, without human ministry or cooperation, power to establish rulers with temporal jurisdiction, because temporal jurisdic-

---

[21] *Potestas ergo appropriandi res temporales personae et personis aut collegio data est a Deo humano generi* (Ockham 1997, 180).

[22] *Prima enim divisio rerum, quae constituisse dominium proprium videatur, videtur fuisse inter Cain et Abel* [...] (Ockham 1997, 182).

[23] *Hic autem non legitur [in Genesis] quod Deus dedit aliqua specialiter Cain et alia specialiter Abel; sed cum Cain malus fuerit et avarus, magis verisimile est quod Abel ex malitia Cain volentis violenter opprimere eum et appropriare sibi cuncta indebite, compulsus fuerit quodam modo divisionem rerum huiusmodi procurare* (Ockham 1997, 182).

[24] *Secunda conclusio, quam probant, est quod primum dominium temporalium proprium post lapsum fuit iure humano seu ordinatione aut voluntate humana introductum* [...].

tion is one of the things necessary and useful for living well and living politically" (McGrade and Kilcullen 1992, 90).[25] The implication is that, like ownership, the power to institute political lordship was granted by God but first exercised by human beings acting in accordance with human law. In the end, both exclusive lordship over property and political lordship over people(s) are ultimately human socio-political constructs. They emerge in human history due to the intellectual and voluntary actions of the members of human communities exercising certain powers that they have received from God in accordance with human law.

It follows from Ockham's analysis that despite the violence and conflict that becomes pervasive under post-lapsarian conditions, before actually instituting exclusive and political lordship, the first members of the human community were free to have acted otherwise. They could have chosen not to act on the power that God granted them or could have acted differently. Once they did, however, ownership, property, and political rule became entrenched within and across human communities of believers and unbelievers as morally-binding precepts. Ockham writes (McGrade and Kilcullen 1992, 91):[26]

> And therefore, just as unbelievers are bound by God's precepts and by natural law to honour father and mother and to do other things necessary to their neighbours, so, on occasion, they are bound to make such appropriation and to set up secular powers over themselves.

Though this might be taken to imply that exclusive and political lordship are absolutely and universally binding once instituted, persons or communities of persons under certain conditions can renounce, say, the right to own property (it is important for Ockham's position in the poverty controversy that the Franciscan order could renounce the right to own property but nonetheless use property owned by others).[27] Similarly, in times of necessity and in the interests of sustaining life, a person can licitly disregard someone else's claim to ownership and steal their property, e.g. food (this is because one cannot renounce one's natural right to use what is necessary for life) (Ockham 1997, 181).[28] In *The*

---

[25] [...] *data est a Deo, absque ministerio et cooperatione humana, potestas instituendi rectores habentes iurisdictionem temporalem; quia iurisdictio temporalis est de numero illorum, quae sunt necessaria et utilia ad bene et politice vivere* [...] (Ockham 1997, 180).
[26] *Et ideo, sicut infideles praecepto Dei et iuris naturalis tenentur honorare patrem et matrem et alia exercere, quae necessaria sunt proximis, ita tenentur in casu talem appropriationem facere et praeficere super se in saecularibus potestates* (Ockham 1997, 181).
[27] On the distinction between ownership and use and the poverty controversy, see n. 13 above.
[28] As pointed out by McGrade and Kilcullen 1992, 101, n. 56, ownership and property fall under Ockham's third kind of natural law, which is that law that holds by the dictate of reason 'on the

Work of Ninety Days, Chapter 11, Ockham explicitly argues that ownership (*proprietatis*) is superfluous because it is not necessary for the licit sustenance of human life (he uses the term 'human nature') (Ockham 1963, 411).

4 Human intelligent voluntary agency: the origins of lordship

We have seen that Ockham identifies 'lordship' as a mental relation in the academic writings, and this amounted to an analysis that emphasized the semantics of mental relative terms. The semantic focus is understandably absent from the political writings, where lordship as a social and political phenomenon takes center-stage and is construed as the power to appropriate goods, to defend one's claim to those goods in a human court, or to institute political rulers. What I would like to turn to now is the role of the human rational soul, the intellect and the will working together, that lies at the origin of lordship in both sets of writings, the academic and the political.[29] Lordship is produced through human agency, specifically intelligent voluntary agency. This entails that lordship is the sort of 'object' for which we can give a teleological explanation since we can explain why members of the human community would decide to institute it. Lordship is instituted for a reason, and in this regard it has a final cause of which we can be evidently certain.

4.1 Acting for the sake of ends: the will and final causality

Ockham's account of final causality is complicated. Marilyn McCord Adam's important article on the subject bears the subtitle *Muddying the Waters* (Adams, 1998; also see Brown 1987). One difficulty stems from reading his extensive discussion of final causality in the *Quaestiones variae*, q. 4 and his Expositio in libros Physicorum Aristotelis in conjunction with what we find in *Quodlibet* 4,

---

supposition' that a certain human or positive legislation has been set in place and agreed upon. They explain "Thus reason directs that once men exercise a power of appropriation granted by God (the grant and the exercise being acts done by God and man) to establish particular properties, then property that has been loaned must be returned [...] Natural law now requires respect for ownership rights."

29 Miethke 1991 discusses Ockham's conception of freedom and the will in the academic and political writings as well but without taking into consideration some of the detail that I will now discuss here.

qq. 1–2 especially. The problem is whether we can think of natural agents as acting for the sake of ends. It is abundantly clear that Ockham always holds that voluntary agents act for the sake of ends. But while it seems that some texts allow for the possibility of natural agents acting for the sake of ends in some sense, that is as having final causes, the *Quodlibeta* unequivocally reject this view, restricting final causality to the realm of rational, and especially human, agency.

I am going to set this discussion aside, focusing on the *Quodlibeta* where Ockham unambiguously draws a distinction between natural and voluntary agents, arguing that only the acts of the latter, agents possessing a rational soul capable of performing intellections and volitions, can act for the sake of ends at least so far as we can evidently know. On this view, to ask for what reason or to what end a natural agent performs an act, such as a fire burning or a stone falling, amounts to a category mistake (Ockham 1980, 299; Adams 1998 uses "category mistake").[30] What is distinctive about voluntary agency is the will, which is a free power that can act contingently and indifferently.

Ockham's treatment of the freedom of the will has been a subject of extensive commentary in the literature (see, amongst others, Adams 1986; Adams 1999; Normore 1998; Panaccio 2012; Schierbaum 2017, upon which my brief account and its references rely). There is no need to belabour the details here except to recall that the will is free because it wills contingently and indifferently (*contingenter et libere*) (e.g. Ockham 1967, 503; 1984a, 350–351). It has the power to produce an act or not, and furthermore this act can be a willing or nilling. Ockham holds, then, that the will has three possibilities open to it when the intellect presents it with an apprehended object: it can produce a willing, a nilling, or simply remain inert without producing an act, and this is irrespective of whatever the intellect (right reason, prudence, or practical intellect) might dictate it to do (Adams 1986, 13). The point is that the will is not naturally inclined to produce one act over another (e.g. Ockham 1980, 88; 1981, 351), or indeed to produce any act at all, at least not naturally in a strict sense. This is even when the intellect is telling the will that the apprehended object is good and should be willed, or bad and should be nilled (e.g. Ockham 1984b, 443; Adams 1986, 14). The will, furthermore, is a partial efficient cause of its own acts (Normore 1998, 35). This is what it means for its acts to be 'within' its power, allowing the will to be a self-mover that can bring about an act, its effect, without any external force acting upon it

---

30 [...] *diceret sequens praecise rationem quod quaestio 'propter quid' non habet locum in actionibus naturalibus, quia diceret quod nulla est quaestio quaerere propter quid ignis generatur; sed solum habet locum in actionibus voluntariis.*

(Ockham 1980, 89). Ockham grants that the will is not the total efficient cause of its acts; God and the apprehension of an object that the intellect provides are the two other partial efficient causes of the will's acts (Ockham 1984a, 359; 1984b, 393; Adams 1986, 11).

As a free power whose acts are within its own power, the will choses to set up its own ends and the means by which it aims to attain those ends (Normore 1998, 34). An end exercises a kind of causality that is known as final causality. In *Quodlibet* 4, q. 1, Ockham defines a final cause as that which is "[...] loved and desired efficaciously by an agent, so that the effect is brought about because of the thing that is loved" (Freddoso and Kelley 1991, 245).[31] Ockham does not specify what sort of effect is at issue here. A common-sense assumption is that he is talking about, say, walking or eating, which are physical acts the performance of which the agent has reason to think will allow her to attain the object – her end – that she loves and desires. They are external to the will and, therefore, only indirectly within the control of the will. Recent work, however, shows that this story is not quite so simple. Rather, the effect in question is a second 'complex' volition that is the agent's choice or decision proper to perform the requisite physical acts – the course of action – that presupposes a first 'simple' volition of loving some apprehended object.[32]

For example, I love my baby daughter and, assuming that my intellect informs me that she needs to be fed in order to preserve her well-being and given that in loving her I am invested in preserving her well-being, I will to feed her. Having willed to feed her, I then go through the physical acts of providing her with sustenance. Loving my baby sets her up as the end that explains why I will to feed her and then why I feed her. The first two acts are both volitions, the one a simple volition: loving my baby, and the other a complex volition: willing to feed her or willing to bring it about that she is fed. It is this second volition that is my decision to feed her. The third act is the doing or feeding itself, which is external to my will. So, the effect that is 'efficaciously' caused by virtue of loving or desiring an end – at least the first and immediate effect – is in fact another mental act, to wit the decision to pursue some course of action.[33]

---

[31] [...] *definitio causae finalis est esse amatum et desideratum efficaciter ab agente, propter quod amatum fit effectus* (Ockham 1980, 294).
[32] I am indebted to Panaccio 2012 and Schierbaum 2017 for what follows on incomplex and complex volitions (which is their terminology). Panaccio does not discuss this distinction in light of final causality but Schierbaum does.
[33] Schierbaum 2017, 133 writes: "As I see it, Ockham thereby wants to say that if a thing is desired in this way [as an end], then *what is effected in the first place is a choice to do or not to do*

Ockham does not think that we can prove that natural agents act for the sake of ends, ends that have been fixed by *some* will beforehand. One might well believe that God has fixed their ends and Ockham presumably does, but we cannot prove this by natural reason (cf. Normore 1998, 36). Natural agents always act in the same way unless impeded by an external force. There is no variation in how they act. This is because a natural agent is "[...] by its nature inclined toward one determinate effect in such a way that it is not able to cause an opposite effect" (Freddoso and Kelley 1991, 249).[34] Natural agents act in accordance with 'natural necessity', as when a stone falls to the ground or a fire burns. A stone shall always fall to the ground unless impeded from doing so, like when I throw it up in the air. Throwing a stone upwards is contrary to the action that it is normally inclined to perform, i.e. falling downward, and so this contrary action is deemed 'violent'. The argument seems to be that because there is no variation in how natural agents act unless hindered by some external force, we cannot infer that they have anything like a will that freely envisions ends and chooses means, since this would have the effect of varying their course(s) of action.

The case is different for intelligent voluntary agents. The will has no natural inclination that could be acted against since the will is no more inclined towards one effect – producing one act – than another. And, intelligent voluntary agents can tell one another that they acted in such and such a way and for such and such a reason; we can evidently know that human beings act for the sake of ends by experience. So, it is easy to see why Ockham would be sceptical of giving teleological explanations for events in the natural universe. For, his conception of final causality crucially relies on the activity of the intellect and the will working together to produce not only the love and desire for an object but also the decision to go after it. Clearly this suggests that only intelligent voluntary agents can act for the sake of ends, and therefore only *their* actions are susceptible to a teleological explanation, again at least as far as we can know evidently. It does not seem that natural agents have wills that are capable of producing volitions. But the human world is another thing entirely. Asking about the final causes for *our* acts, our simple and complex volitions, is utterly apt.

---

something. And it is by pointing to the desired thing that the choice can be accounted for [...]" (my emphasis).

34 A free agent [...] *non plus inclinatur ex natura sua ad unum effectum quam ad alium; sed de agente naturali* [...] *tale agens ex natura sua sic inclinatur ad unum determinatum effectum quod non potest causare oppositum effectum* (Ockham 1980, 300).

4.2 Instituting lordship for the sake of an end

This brings us back to lordship. The institution of lordship was first performed by means of the intellection(s) and volition(s) of a human being(s), what I will call the 'institutor' and which should be understood to be an intelligent voluntary agent(s) (my focus here will fall on the original institution of lordship rather than its later acceptance by present and future members of the human community). This volition, just by virtue of being a volition, is the sort of thing about which it is appropriate to ask, why was this volition performed? For what reason, in the case of ownership, for example, did the original institutor decide to connect some human beings to certain goods in such and such a way? The reason, ultimately, is the end or final cause of the volition by means of which ownership was instituted. In *Quodlibet* 4, q. 2, Ockham defines an end as what "[...] is loved and fixed beforehand by a will [...]" (Freddoso and Kelley 1991, 251).[35] His example is the love one bears towards oneself or another, a friend (*amicum amatum*).

Let us apply the foregoing material on volitions and ends to a reconstruction of the case of ownership. Ownership is originally instituted in part by the complex volition that is the decision to bring it about that some human beings are connected to certain goods in such and such a way, i.e. that they can exercise exclusive control over those goods, lay claim to them in a court, transfer them to someone else. This complex volition is performed because the institutor has a prior incomplex volition, which is the love he bears for himself or another. I take it that love of self entails, for example, desire for one's self-preservation, well-being, etc. The intellect sets forth how to achieve this end by performing various intellections, including the apprehension of the loved object, namely the agent himself, an understanding of the conceptual content of what shall be ownership, viz. that some human beings could be connected to certain goods in such and such a way, and the belief that if some human beings were so-connected to certain goods, this would be conducive to the agent's self-preservation or well-being. The agent's will finally performs the complex volition, the decision proper, and thereby (partially) institutes ownership. As such, we can say that the volition in question had an end and, moreover, that all the external acts necessary for the enforcement and regulation of ownership (e.g. the issuing of laws and punishment of theft, the writing up of deeds and contracts for property transference, etc.) that eventually develop within different human communities over time are also decided upon and performed for the same end.

---

35 [...] *finis est duplex: scilicet finis praeamatus et praestitutus a voluntate, puta cum aliquis operatur propter se amatum vel propter amicum amatum* [...] (Ockham 1980, 301).

We can see how this plays out in the story of Cain and Abel. Abel, confronted with Cain's avaricious and abusive appropriation of goods, understands that it is in his best interests and in the interests of the community, to institute and then regulate the ownership of property. They each decide to exercise the power that God granted them after the fall, bringing it about that they appropriate goods by exclusively controlling them. Both Cain and Abel make this decision in light of the love they bear themselves, for their own sakes. Abel also acts out of love for another if he is motivated to divide up goods with a view to the preservation and well-being of the human community.

There is a question as to whether the complex volition by which ownership is instituted is in fact as free as one might think. Ockham does not think that every volition is non-necessitated (see discussion in Panaccio 2012, 86–88; Adams 1986, 11). He argues that some volitions follow naturally from a prior and immediate volition (e. g. self-love) and an intellectual conviction (i. e. beliefs about how to preserve oneself and improve one's lot). The example he uses is an invalid who wills to be cured and understands that in order to be cured, she has to drink bitter medicine. In this case, her desire to be healthy and her understanding that she must drink the medicine in order to be cured cause what the literature calls a 'derivative volition', which is her volition to drink the medicine. This derivative volition is causally necessitated, following naturally upon a prior intellectual and volitional process (Ockham 1984b, 302).

What does this mean for ownership? Does the volition by which Abel decides to institute ownership follow naturally and thus necessarily from Abel's desire for self-preservation and his belief that, given the situation in which he found himself, to do so is the only (or best) means to achieve his end? If so, this might suggest that the institution of ownership is not achieved by means of a free and voluntary act but arises naturally and inevitably from the determinate psychological states of the members of the human community in response to their environment. Ockham indeed describes Abel as having been compelled (*compulsus*) to appropriate certain goods for himself in the face of Cain's oppressive violence and greed.

As commentators are quick to point out, derivative volitions are indirectly under the control of the will anyway, since the will can freely change, e. g. give up, the prior and immediate volition, like wanting to be healthy or loving my baby daughter (see Adams 1986, 11–12). The invalid could decide not to drink the medicine because she no longer desires to be healthy. So even if the complex volition by which ownership is instituted were necessitated in this sense, the institutor was free to choose the end in light of which he decided to institute ownership.

Moreover, the ownership case is far more complex than the invalid case. We do not easily agree about the means to the ends we seek to satisfy, having various potentially conflicting beliefs about what the best means would be to accomplish them, and we do not even necessarily agree about ends. This requires at the very least a minimal degree of reflection and deliberation even if acrimonious and ultimately oppressive, which is surely in part why people are led to articulate reasons for why a phenomenon like ownership and property ought to obtain. Despite Abel's precarious and threatening situation, he decided to institute ownership but he could have dealt with Cain in some other way or not dealt with him at all.

5 Conclusion

If lordship can be taken as representative of social and political institutions in general, then it would seem that only intelligent voluntary agents can institute social and political institutions. For, as we have seen, Ockham holds that lordship is established by virtue of the intellect and will working together, more precisely by the performance of individual intellection(s) and volition(s) of the members of the human community. He holds this across the academic and political writings with expected divergences. In the academic writings, after noting that lordship is a mental relation, his interest falls on the semantic features of mental relations as relative terms, i.e. of 'lordship'. In the political writings, Ockham wants to give an account of the origin of exclusive and political lordship, conceived of as powers. This origin is complex: the power to own property and the power to establish political rulership are given by God but instituted by human beings. We chose to act on these powers that God had merely made possible in the wake of the fall. Whatever social and political institutions human communities establish come about because of the intricate co-operation between the human intellect and will in response to the concrete and contingent challenges that human beings face together and often because of one another. The ubiquitous significance of the will in Ockham's account of lordship, which is a free power, is what justifies the claim that lordship is not instituted by a purely natural process. There is a sense, perhaps a very peculiar sense to be sure, in which lordship is not a natural social and political institution, indeed that no social and political institution could be wholly natural for Ockham.[36]

---

[36] This paper was written and finalized with the financial support of *Research Foundation – Flanders* (FWO) and *Riksbankens Jubileumsfond* (Sweden). I would like to thank Claude Panaccio

Primary literature

William of Ockham. 1940. *Opus Nonaginta Dierum. Capitula 1–6*. Opera Politica I, edited by Jeffrey G. Sikes. Manchester: University of Manchester Press.
William of Ockham. 1963. *Opus Nonaginta Dierum. Capitula 7–124*. Opera Politica II, edited by Jeffrey G. Sikes and Hilary S. Offler. Manchester: University of Manchester Press.
William of Ockham. 1967. *Ordinatio. Prologus et distinctio I*. Opera Theologica I, edited by Gedeon Gál and Stephen F. Brown. St. Bonaventure, NY: The Franciscan Institute.
William of Ockham. 1979. *Ordinatio. Distinctiones XIX–XLVIII*. Opera Theologica IV, edited by Girard I. Etzkorn and Francis E. Kelley. St. Bonaventure, NY: The Franciscan Institute.
William of Ockham. 1980. *Quodlibeta Septem*. Opera Theologica IX, edited by Joseph C. Wey. St. Bonaventure, NY: The Franciscan Institute.
William of Ockham. 1981. *Quaestiones in librum II Sententiarum*. Opera Theologica V, edited by Gedeon Gál and Rega Wood. St. Bonaventure, NY: The Franciscan Institute.
William Ockham. 1984a. *Quaestiones in librum IV Sententiarum*. Opera Theologica VII, edited by Gedeon Gál, Rega Wood and Romuald Green. St. Bonaventure, NY: The Franciscan Institute.
William of Ockham. 1984b. *Quaestiones variae*. Opera Theologica VIII, edited by Girard I. Etzkorn, Francis E. Kelley, and Joseph C. Wey. St. Bonaventure, NY: The Franciscan Institute.
William of Ockham. 1991. *Quodlibetal Questions*, translated by Alfred J. Freddoso and Francis E. Kelley. New Haven & London: Yale University Press.
William of Ockham. 1992. *A Short Discourse on Tyrannical Government*, edited and translated by Arthur S. McGrade, and John Kilcullen. Cambridge: Cambridge University Press.
William of Ockham. 1995. *A Letter to the Friars Minor and Other Writings*, edited and translated by Arthur S. McGrade, and John Kilcullen. Cambridge: Cambridge University Press.
William of Ockham. 1997. *Breviloquium de principatu tryannico*. Opera Politica IV, edited by Hilary S. Offler. Oxford: The British Academy.

Secondary literature

Adams, Marilyn McCord. 1986. "The Structure of Ockham's Moral Theory." *Franciscan Studies* 46:1–35.
Adams, Marilyn McCord. 1987a. *William Ockham*. Notre Dame: Notre Dame University Press.
Adams, Marilyn McCord. 1987b. "William Ockham: Voluntarist or Naturalist?" In *Studies in Medieval Philosophy*, edited by John Wippel, 219–247. Washington, D.C.: The Catholic University of America Press.

---

and Peter Adamson for their valuable comments on an earlier draft of this paper. I am also very grateful to Calvin Normore and Peter King for stimulating discussions on the concept of lordship in Ockham's thought.

Adams, Marilyn McCord. 1998. "Ockham on Final Causality: Muddying the Waters." *Franciscan Studies* 56:1–46.

Adams, Marilyn McCord. 1999. "Ockham on Will, Nature, and Morality." In *The Cambridge Companion to Ockham*, edited by Paul Vincent Spade, 245–272. Cambridge: Cambridge University Press.

Brett, Annabel. 1997. *Liberty, Right and Nature: Individual Rights in Later Scholastic Thought*. Cambridge: Cambridge University Press.

Brower, Jeffrey. 2015. "Medieval Theories of Relations." *Stanford Encyclopedia of Philosophy* (Winter 2015 edition), edited by Edward N. Zalta, https://plato.stanford.edu/archives/win2015/entries/relations-medieval. Accessed 24 June 2018.

Brown, Stephen. 1987. "Ockham on Final Causality." In *Studies in Medieval Philosophy*, edited by John Wippel, 249–272. Washington, D.C.: The Catholic University of America Press.

Canning, Joseph. 2011. *Ideas of Power in the Late Middle Ages, 1296–1417*. Cambridge: Cambridge University Press.

Coleman, Janet. 1988. "Property and Poverty." In *The Cambridge History of Medieval Political Thought, c. 350–c. 1450*, edited by James H. Burns, 605–648. Cambridge: Cambridge University Press.

Henninger, Mark G. 1989. *Relations: Medieval Theories 1250–1325*. Oxford: Clarendon Press.

Kilcullen, John 1995 [1993]. "Natural Law and Will in Ockham." *History of Philosophy Yearbook* (The Australasian Society for the History of Philosophy) Volume 1, 1–25. Accessed online 18 June 2018.

Kilcullen, John. 1999. "The Political Writings." In *The Cambridge Companion to Ockham*, edited by Paul Vincent Spade, 302–325. Cambridge: Cambridge University Press.

Lambertini, Roberto. 2005. "Poverty and Power: Franciscans in Later Medieval Political Thought." In *Moral Philosophy on the Threshold of Modernity*, edited by Jill Kraye and Risto Saarinen, 141–163. Dordrecht: Springer.

Mäkinen, Virpi. 2001. *Property Rights in the Late Medieval Discussion on Franciscan Poverty*. Leuven: Peeters.

McGrade, Arthur Stephen. 1999. "Natural Law and Moral Omnipotence." In *Cambridge Companion to Ockham*, edited by Paul Vincent Spade, 273–301. Cambridge: Cambridge University Press.

Miethke, Jürgen. 1969. *Ockhams Weg zur Sozialphilosophie*. Berlin: Walter de Gruyter & Co.

Miethke, Jürgen. 1991. "The Concept of Liberty in William of Ockham." In *Théologie et droit dans la science politique de l'État modern. Actes de la table ronde de Rome (12–14 novembre 1987)*, 89–100. Rome: École Française de Rome.

Normore, Calvin. 1998. "Picking and Choosing: Anselm and Ockham on Choice." *Vivarium* 36.1:23–39.

Panaccio, Claude. 1999. "Semantics and Mental Language." In *The Cambridge Companion to Ockham*, edited by Paul Vincent Spade, 53–73. Cambridge: Cambridge University Press.

Panaccio, Claude. 2012. "Intellections and Volitions." In *Emotion and Cognitive Life in Medieval and Early Modern Philosophy*, edited by Martin Pickavé and Lisa Shapiro, 75–93. Oxford: Oxford University Press.

Pelletier, Jenny. 2020. "Social Powers and Mental Relations. William Ockham on the Semantics and Ontology of Lordship and Ownership." *Oxford Studies in Medieval Philosophy* 8:248–276.

Robinson, Jonathan. 2013. *William of Ockham's Early Theory of Property Rights in Context.* Studies in Medieval and Reformation Traditions, 166. Leiden: Brill.

Schierbaum, Sonja. 2017. "Intellections and Volitions: Ockham's Voluntarism Reconsidered." In *The Language of Thought in Late Medieval Philosophy*, edited by Jenny Pelletier and Magali Roques, 125–136. Dordrecht: Springer.

Shogimen, Takashi. 2007. *Ockham and Political Discourse in the Late Middle Ages.* Cambridge: Cambridge University Press.

Spade, Paul Vincent and Claude Panaccio. 2016. "William of Ockham." *Stanford Encyclopedia of Philosophy* (Winter 2016 edition), edited by Edward N. Zalta, https://plato.stanford.edu/archives/win2016/entries/ockham. Accessed 18 July 2018.

Tierney, Brian. 1997. *The Idea of Natural Rights. Studies on Natural Rights, Natural Law and Church Law, 1150–1625.* Atlanta: Scholars Press.

Index of Names

Abraham Ibn Ezra   353
Adam and Eve   400–401
Adeimantus   3, 7n, 35–36, 43–44, 49
Aelius, Sextus   216
Aëtius   175
Agrippa   348
Albert the Great   366n, 367–372, 373n, 374, 381–383, 385–388
Alcibiades   42–43, 48, 51–53, 56, 274
Anaxagoras   70n, 71n, 172
Ancus Marcius   224
Antipater of Tarsus   162
Antiphon of Athens   vii, 5n, 6–8, 19–21, 24–25, 29–31
Antiphon of Rhamnus   7n, 21
Antisthenes   165
Antoninus Pius   318, 321
Apollonius of Tyana   306n
Aristippus of Cyrene   168
Aristo   233
Aristocles of Messene   160
Aristotle   viii, 44n, 46–47, 48n, 56, 59–70, 71n, 72–79, 81–90, 92–94, 96, 98–103, 105–109, 111–116, 119–127, 129–133, 135–136, 138–154, 182n, 183–186, 190–191, 193–194, 201n, 203n, 204–206, 207n, 211, 219n, 233, 269n, 282, 284n, 289–290, 294–295, 298, 304n, 332n, 344, 347, 350, 357, 365–369, 371–374, 376–381, 384–387, 389, 396
– *De Anima*   65, 67, 376
– *De Caelo*   78
– *De Motu Animalium*   124, 132
– *De Partibus Animalium*   69n
– *Historia Animalium*   116n, 143, 365, 367–369, 372, 380
– *Metaphysics*   46, 71n, 78–79, 132
– *Nicomachean Ethics*   47, 60n, 68, 76, 104, 109, 116, 120–121, 124, 126, 130, 132–133, 135–136, 141, 142n, 143–147, 149–152, 182n, 183, 190–191, 193–195, 204, 206, 269, 282, 289, 294–295, 304n, 379n
– *Physics*   69, 71n, 74, 78, 82, 123
– *Poetics*   84
– *Politics*   59–78, 81–90, 92–97, 99–105, 107n, 108, 110–116, 122–127, 129–132, 135–136, 138–140, 142, 144–145, 147–148, 150, 151–154, 203n, 204, 206, 332n, 366–367, 370–371, 374, 377n, 380–381, 383, 386n
– *Posterior Analytics*   123n, 344
– *Rhetoric*   121n, 122, 127
– *Topics*   106
Arius Didymus   161, 175
Athanasius   318n
Athenagoras of Athens   318, 321–322, 324, 326–328
Atreus   172
Atticus, Titus Pomponius   216, 231–232, 234, 236–237, 239
Augustine of Hippo   317, 319–320, 334–338, 401n
Averroes   344–345
Avicenna   345, 355, 360–361, 373–374

Basil of Caesarea   332
Basso, Sebastianus   354n
al-Bīrūnī   360
Bonaventure   401n
Brutus, Lucius Iunius   206n
Buridan, John   344, 357
Burley, Walter   385

Caesar, Gaius Iulius   240
Cain and Abel   402, 409–410
Callicles   5n, 29, 202, 213n
Carneades   212
Cassiodorus   387
Cato the Elder   224
Cato the Younger   240–241
Cercidas of Megalopolis   172–173
Chrysippus   162–165, 169, 300
Cicero, Marcus Tullius   viii, 159–161, 163, 165, 169, 182, 185–187, 191, 193, 201–211, 213–219, 221–243, 249–250, 257, 308, 330–331, 337

Cicero, Quintus Tullius   231, 235–239
Cleanthes of Assos   160, 162–164, 175–176
Clement of Alexandria   318n, 326, 332
Clodius of Naples   302n
Commodus   318, 322, 328
Constantine   327–328
Crates of Thebes   166–167, 169–170

Descartes, René   45–46
Diogenes Laertius   160, 162–163, 165–170, 172–176, 182n, 188, 191, 193, 298, 332, 337n
Diogenes of Sinope   162–163, 166–168, 170–173
Diogenianus   162

Empedocles   184, 300
Epicurus   vii, 181–187, 188n, 189–197, 212n, 230, 231n, 237, 308n, 329
Epiphanius   167
Eusebius of Caesarea   160–162, 175, 306n, 317, 319, 321, 327–328
Eustratius   381
Euthydemus   128
Evodius   334–335

al-Fārābī   345, 355

Gaius   viii, 252–254, 257–259, 261
Galen   350, 357
al-Ghazālī   344, 349, 361
Giles of Rome   374
Glaucon   3, 5–6, 7n, 8–11, 14–15, 25, 35, 195–196, 212, 213n, 214, 219
Gorgias   5n
Gregory of Nyssa   331–333, 338
Grotius, Hugo   263
Guy of Rimini   370–371
Gyges   3, 5–7, 9, 15

Heracles   164, 167, 312
Heraclides of Pontus   302n
Heraclitus   175, 343
Hermarchus   188n
Herodotus   22
Hippias   5n, 29
Hippocrates   349

Hippolytus of Rome   161
Hobbes, Thomas   vii, 60–61

Ibn Barrajān   360
Ibn Rushd *see* Averroes
Ibn Sīnā *see* Avicenna
Ibn Ṭufayl   361n
Isidore of Seville   369

Jerome   167
Judah Hallevi   343, 345, 350, 352–361
Justin Martyr   317–324, 332
Justinian   164–165, 247, 251, 257, 260, 263

Kallimedon   173
Kant, Immanuel   218, 312n
Kritias   5n

Lactantius   209, 212n, 214, 317, 319, 328–331, 333, 337–338
Laelius   202, 212–213, 215–216, 218–219, 224, 226
Leibniz, Gottfried Wilhelm   45–46
Locke, John   46
Lucian   167
Lucretius   182n, 183–184, 189
Lykophron   60

Maimonides   359, 360n, 361n
Marcian   164–165, 260
Marcus Aurelius   318, 321–322, 328
Mark Antony   240
Maximus of Tyre   167

Nemesius of Emesa   333
Nicholas of Autrecourt   344
Nicholas of Vaudémont   366n, 383–387
Numa Pompilius   235–236

Origen   163, 167

Panaetius   162, 165, 169, 208
Paul, the apostle   318–319, 326, 332
Paul, the jurist   252, 260
Peter of Ailly   344
Peter of Auvergne   366n, 375–380
Peter of Spain   366n, 373n

Philodemus of Gadara 162–163, 166, 171, 192
Philoponus 347–348
Philus 202, 212–215, 216n, 218–219, 225–227
Pindar 164
Plato vii, ix, 3, 5, 6n, 7n, 8, 21n, 25, 29–30, 35, 39n, 43–47, 51–53, 55n, 56, 70, 71n, 76, 98, 120, 126n, 128–130, 135, 137, 175, 182n, 193, 195, 201n, 202, 209n, 210–214, 216n, 225, 237, 269–272, 273n, 274–275, 277, 280, 284n, 286–287, 289–290, 294–295, 297, 302, 307–310, 312–314, 320–321, 330, 343n, 399
– *Alcibiades I* 269, 274, 279, 286–287, 289
– *Apology* 321
– *Crito* 14n, 213n
– *Euthydemus* 284n
– *Gorgias* 14n, 30, 202, 213n
– *Laws* 7n, 14n, 129n, 137, 237, 312, 313n, 343n
– *Lysis* 120
– *Menexenus* 7n
– *Meno* 284n
– *Phaedo* 70, 269, 272, 273n, 275, 280–281, 283, 302, 304
– *Phaedrus* 128, 272
– *Protagoras* 7n, 29
– *Republic* 3–19, 25–26, 29–30, 35–41, 43, 48–49, 51–56, 76, 98n, 126n, 128–129, 137, 182n, 192–193, 194n, 195–196, 197n, 201n, 209n, 210, 212, 213n, 214, 225, 269, 272, 273n, 274, 280–281, 284, 289, 295n, 307, 309–310, 313, 320, 330
– *Statesman* 85, 130
– *Symposium* 39n, 42–43, 48, 51, 53–54
– *Theaetetus* 52–53, 280, 297
– *Timaeus* 70, 137, 175, 272, 273n, 281n, 343n
Pliny the Elder 369
Plotinus ix, 269–290, 300, 306–307, 310, 348
Plutarch 161, 174, 298, 301, 311
Polemo 233
Polybius 203n, 208–209
Polystratus 188n
Pompeius, Quintus 226n

Pompey (Pompeius, Gnaeus) 238
Porphyry ix, 167, 190, 196, 293, 296–311, 312–314, 347, 350
Prodicus 5n
Protagoras 5n
Ps.-Gaius 261
Ps.-Justin 318n
Ps.-Plutarch 175
Pufendorf, Samuel 264
Pythagoras 297, 300

Radulphus Brito 377, 385n
al-Rāzī, Abū Bakr 343, 345–353, 356, 360–361
al-Rāzī, Fakhr al-Dīn 346n, 347n, 351–352, 361
Regulus, Marcus Atilius 207n, 215n
Romulus 208, 224

Sardanapalus 216n
Satyrus 167
Scipio Aemilianus 201–209, 211–212, 215, 218–219, 223–229, 238, 239n
Seneca, Lucius Annaeus 162
Sextus Empiricus 162, 182–183, 226n, 348
Simplicius 182n, 186
Socrates 3–6, 8–11, 14–15, 18–20, 29–31, 35–44, 48–51, 53–57, 70n, 71n, 120, 128–129, 148, 161, 163, 168, 194, 196–197, 213n, 219, 269n, 274, 279n, 287, 399
Solon 237, 301n
Speusippus 233
Sphaerus 173
Spurius Cassius 206n
Stobaeus 171, 174–175, 194–195
Sulla, Lucius Cornelius 238

Tarquinius, Lucius 224
Tarquinius Superbus 203–204, 206, 207n, 208, 211
Tatian the Syrian 318n
Tertullian 317, 318n, 319, 322–327, 330–332, 337
Theaetetus 52–53, 56
Theophilus 318, 326–327, 330
Theophrastus 233, 300–307, 313, 351n

Thomas Aquinas   122, 254, 263, 371, 374, 386n
Thrasymachus   5, 29–30, 213n
Thucydides   21
Thyestes   172
Torquatus   182, 185–187, 189, 193, 196
Tribonian   165
Tryphononius   260
Tullus Hostilius   224

Ulpian   164, 249, 254, 257–262

Valerius, Publius   224

William of Ockham   vii, 344, 393–411

Xenocrates   223, 233
Xenophon   20–21, 29n, 128–129, 168, 182n

Zeno of Citium   159–162, 164, 166, 173, 175, 232n, 233, 295, 301, 337

Index of Subjects

Accountability 135, 144, 147
Akrasia 141–142
Animal 63, 65, 71–75, 77, 79, 82, 84, 97, 123–124, 132, 170–171, 182–184, 186–188, 194–195, 257, 276, 278, 293–294, 296–308, 310–314, 351, 353–355, 357–359, 365–378, 380–382, 383n, 384–388
– political 59, 69, 71, 86–90, 92, 96, 105, 110–114, 164, 331, 365–372, 374–376, 378, 380–383, 385–389
Anti-conventionalism viii, 159, 163–165, 174
Aristocracy 131, 143, 201n, 203, 211, 224, 238, 371
Aristotelianism ix, 233, 248, 284n, 304n, 344–345, 347–348, 350–353, 357, 360–361, 365, 367, 369, 373, 394n
Auctoritas 208, 211, 215
Autarkeia 59–61, 67–68, 78, 87, 282n
Authority 25, 28, 122, 126, 135, 140–144, 147, 149–150, 153–154, 208, 223–224, 230n, 231–232, 238n, 243, 252, 271, 274–279, 318, 321–322, 327–328, 331, 333, 338

Body 15, 19, 39, 55, 64, 72, 97–98, 128–130, 187, 189–190, 210n, 269, 272–275, 278, 283, 286–288, 296n, 302, 325, 349–350, 352, 376, 378–390

Christianity ix, 82, 317–332, 335, 338, 343–345, 361
City 59, 63–64, 66–70, 71n, 72–78, 124, 137, 144, 151, 160–161, 168–170, 173, 175–176, 213n, 232, 243, 281, 294, 317, 319–321, 323, 335–338, 369
– city-state viii, 3–4, 101, 105, 142, 253
– ideal vii, 4, 295
Class 3–5, 137, 280, 321, 324–325
Community viii–ix, 60, 63–64, 67–68, 70, 72, 76–78, 81–82, 84n, 85, 87, 89–91, 94–116, 123, 127, 131, 133, 160, 165, 168–170, 175–176, 201n, 204–207, 293–295, 317, 324–325, 337, 356, 358–360, 365–366, 368–369, 371–375, 377–384, 386–388, 393–394, 399–404, 408–410
– ideal 159, 175
– universal 161
Constitution viii, 66, 76–77, 81, 84n, 114–115, 119, 121–122, 124–127, 130–133, 137, 142, 162, 201n, 203–204, 206n, 209, 224–225, 228, 238, 313
– best 201–204, 209, 211, 215, 219
– Roman 202–204, 206n, 208–209, 211, 224, 229
Conventionalism 201–202, 212n, 213, 216, 219
Convention 60–61, 120, 122–123, 133, 159, 176, 183, 196, 202, 212–213, 217, 221–222, 229–231, 233, 235, 243, 395
Cosmopolitanism 166–170, 174, 295
Cosmos 201–203, 213, 216–219, 273, 295, 343–344, 346–347
Courage 36–38, 40–43, 45, 47–50, 52, 54–56, 138, 148, 152–153, 188, 192–193, 201n, 207n, 270, 280–281
Cradle argument 181–183, 185, 187–188, 219n
Custom viii–ix, 22, 24, 122, 165–166, 176, 202, 210–211, 214, 221–225, 235–237, 253, 313, 319, 323, 345, 356n, 257, 358
Cynicism viii, 159, 160n, 162–168, 170, 174, 176–177

Deliberation 74–75, 83, 97, 109, 113, 135, 144, 146–147, 151, 174, 203, 295, 332, 387, 410
Democracy 50, 76, 114, 119, 125–127, 131, 201n, 203, 206n, 211
Desire vii–viii, 6n, 15, 27, 29, 37–39, 43–48, 50–55, 57, 64–65, 81, 90–91, 95, 97–99, 107n, 108–113, 116, 119, 128–129, 132, 146, 166, 181–182, 185–195, 197, 210–211, 218, 276, 346, 360, 365, 374–379, 380n, 394, 401, 406, 407n, 410

Education 4, 41, 124, 126, 132, 137, 142, 185, 209, 223, 225, 377–378
Eleutheria 119–120, 125, 130, 167
Emotion 141–143, 161, 192n, 209, 211, 376, 386
Emperor 317–325, 327–328, 331, 338
Epicureanism 181–197, 219n, 230–232, 237, 239, 298, 329
Equality 120, 126–127, 131, 138, 249, 260
Ergon 68, 183, 219n, 372
Essence viii, 83–84, 86, 100–102, 107–109, 114, 116, 286–287, 289, 293, 308–309, 313, 333, 336, 368, 394
Eudaimonia 62, 68, 75, 113, 282–283, 288, 366
Eudaimonism 60, 68, 70, 73, 78

Flourishing 62, 74, 87, 240
Freedom vii–viii, 28, 119–120, 125–129, 131–133, 136, 138, 152, 166–168, 201n, 206n, 238n, 242, 249, 258, 332–334, 338, 371
– aristocratic 119–120, 127–128, 130–133
– civic 120, 126, 130–131, 133
– democratic 120, 126–127, 130–131, 133
– personal 120, 126–130, 133
Friendship 12–13, 17, 57, 122, 125, 129, 146, 168–169, 174–175, 188, 192–193, 195, 204, 207, 243, 379n, 385–386, 408

God ix, 45–46, 72, 82, 87, 115, 121, 160, 170, 175, 183, 216–217, 226–227, 229–231, 236, 240–241, 249, 276, 285, 293, 297–298, 303–307, 309–314, 317–319, 321–338, 343–361, 379, 393, 395, 400–403, 404n, 406–407, 410
Good life 64, 68–69, 87, 101, 103, 108–109, 113–115, 116n, 132, 166, 187, 197, 231n, 235, 288, 298, 366, 378, 403
Gyges-thesis 5–9, 11–14, 19, 25, 29–31

Happiness 8, 69, 73, 78, 112–113, 115–117, 132, 185, 189–190, 192–193, 201n, 298, 320–321, 334, 379n
Hedonism 186, 196
– normative 185
– psychological 185, 188

Individual, human 28, 62–63, 72–73, 75, 77, 87–88, 91, 94, 117, 124, 129n, 204, 206–207, 271, 275, 277–280, 284–286, 332, 360, 376, 378–379, 400
– living being 65–66, 351
Injustice 6, 8–9, 11–17, 27, 29–31, 71–73, 86, 119, 125–126, 194–197, 203, 207, 211–212, 225–226, 228, 230, 293, 301, 303–307, 311–313, 318, 321, 323–324, 328, 330–331, 334–336, 380, 387, 402
Innatism 45–46, 48, 57
Intellect 132, 272, 274n, 275–277, 279, 281, 283, 285, 287, 332, 347–348, 354–355, 373, 393–395, 397–399, 404–410
– divine 272, 282, 306–307
Islam ix, 343–345, 352, 359–360
Ius 204n, 205, 208, 214n, 221n, 223, 225, 228–230, 234–235, 239, 243n, 247–254, 257–260, 325n, 403n

Judaism ix, 343, 345, 352–353, 356–359
Justice vii, ix, 6–9, 11–17, 24–28, 29n, 30, 36–38, 40–41, 45, 47–48, 50, 54, 71–73, 76, 84n, 86, 88, 119–123, 125–126, 132, 137–138, 148, 152, 161, 164, 171, 175–176, 194–197, 202, 205, 207, 212–216, 218–219, 225–235, 242, 248, 252, 257, 281, 293–303, 304n, 307–314, 318, 321, 324, 326–331, 334, 336, 366, 380–382, 386–388
– conventional 6n, 7, 121–122, 125, 133, 194–195
– inner 293–294, 309–314
– natural 6n, 7, 121–122, 123n, 125, 133, 181–182, 194–196, 230, 257, 308n
– political 295, 313

Kalām 344–346, 349–350, 356, 360–361
King vii, ix, 76, 126, 138, 164, 207n, 208, 224, 235, 358, 369–370, 373, 387
Knowledge ix, 35–38, 40, 43n, 46, 54–55, 57, 145, 149–150, 152, 171, 174, 225, 228, 281, 283, 293, 314, 326, 344–345, 347, 352, 360–361

Language 71–72, 86, 90, 112n, 116, 183, 191, 240, 298, 300, 365–366, 374, 380–383, 385–388, 395, 397
Law viii, 3–5, 22–30, 73, 88, 119–121, 123–127, 132–133, 142, 159–162, 164, 166, 173–176, 194, 196–198, 204–205, 207n, 213–216, 221–223, 225, 228–230, 232–239, 244, 248–249, 251–252, 257, 294–295, 313, 318–319, 323–324, 326–331, 336–338, 343, 346, 358, 378, 381–382, 388
– civil 222n, 234, 243, 247, 252–254, 258–260, 262
– common 159, 161, 242, 253–254, 257–259
– conventional 119, 122
– divine 333–336, 338, 359–360, 400, 402
– human 333–335, 338, 400, 402–403
– natural vii–viii, 62, 74–75, 79, 84, 121n, 122–123, 159–160, 164–165, 174–175, 177, 201–202, 213, 217–219, 221–223, 226–227, 229, 230n, 231–232, 234–235, 237–239, 242–243, 247–254, 257–258, 260, 262–264, 296, 324–326, 334, 338, 343, 344, 357, 394n, 402–403, 404n
– of states 243, 252, 296, 325, 331
– rational 359
– religious 356n, 357, 359
– Roman viii, 164–165, 222n, 234, 236, 247–249, 251–254, 257–259, 261
– universal ix, 216, 223, 243, 250
Lawmaker. *see* Legislator
Leader, political. *see* Ruler
Legislator 3, 66, 123–124, 145, 149, 152, 223, 229, 324, 343, 346, 358
Liberty. *see* Freedom
Logos 71, 74, 112n, 160, 183, 191–192, 195, 286, 317, 322, 327
Lordship vii, 273, 393–395, 397, 399–404, 408, 410–411

Moderation. *see* Temperance
Monarchy 66n, 124, 131–132, 201n, 203–204, 206n, 208, 211, 371

Naturalism viii–ix, 78, 84, 115, 116n, 186, 197, 202, 219, 343, 346–347, 352–353, 358, 360–361, 394n
– ethical 346n
– normative 59–62, 75–78, 79, 116n
Natural good 181–182, 193–195, 197
Natural quality 36, 45, 47, 49, 53–55, 57, 121
Nature vii–ix, 5, 59–70, 72–78, 81–86, 88–111, 113–116, 119–121, 123–126, 129, 132–133, 138–142, 144, 149–150, 153, 159–161, 165–166, 168, 170–171, 173, 175–176, 181–184, 186, 188–195, 197, 201–202, 209, 212–213, 215n, 216, 218–219, 221–222, 224–225, 227–230, 231n, 233–234, 242, 244, 249–250, 257, 259–261, 263–264, 271, 277–278, 281, 283, 285, 287, 289, 295, 303, 317, 319, 331, 345, 347–361, 368, 370–371, 376–378, 381, 383–384, 386–387, 393–394, 407, 409–411
– according to which someone lives ix, 271, 280, 285, 288–289
– cosmic 216
– divine 332–333
– human viii–ix, 5, 8, 14, 20, 22–31, 60, 63–64, 67–70, 72–73, 75, 81, 90–92, 95–97, 110–117, 122, 181, 184, 190, 197, 216–217, 219n, 229–230, 269, 277, 284, 285n, 286, 289–290, 306, 310, 325–326, 328, 331–334, 338, 365, 375, 378–380, 384n, 385–386, 388, 394, 404
– immanent 343, 345–346, 349
– in opposition to law vii, 5–6, 8, 20, 24, 26–31, 235, 239
– in relation to reason 74
– of children 122
– of communities 100–103, 109
– of leaders 35–36
– of living beings 95, 97, 110, 112, 114
– of persons 3–6, 8, 17, 52, 184, 280
– of philosophers 35–41, 44, 49–50, 54–55
– of states 74–75, 77, 81, 98n, 106, 114–115
– of the soul 3, 13, 15–19, 29, 31, 98, 272

– of things 54, 62, 67–68, 74, 79, 83, 105–110, 116n, 250, 261, 346, 358
– with a capital N 61, 66, 68, 70–71, 75, 78–79, 116n
Nomimon 3, 6, 8, 14–15, 17–18, 20, 24, 26, 29–31, 122
Nomos vii, 3n, 5, 7n, 24, 29–30, 120, 160, 164n, 175, 343
Norm viii, 59–62, 75, 81, 114–115, 197, 201, 213, 259–260, 318–321, 324, 327–328, 331, 333, 335, 337–338, 353, 358
– conventional 159
– ethical 317, 319–320, 326, 329–330, 338
– legal 3, 6, 8, 14, 17–18, 20, 24–26, 28–31, 248
– political vii–viii, 317, 319–320, 326, 328–331, 338
Normativity viii–ix, 62, 74, 81, 114–115, 181, 183–184, 188–189, 191, 196, 221, 223–224, 228–229, 231n, 232–233, 238, 240, 249, 261, 271, 277, 279–280, 285, 289, 317, 319, 326, 328, 331, 333–335, 337–338, 366, 381–382, 386n, 388

Occasionalism 343, 345–346, 349–350, 356, 361
Ochlocracy 203
Oikeiôsis 216, 240, 242, 284, 296, 308
Oligarchy 76, 114, 131, 143, 203
Order 54, 62, 79, 124, 129, 132, 153, 161, 175–176, 210, 213, 226–227, 239, 250, 324, 328, 330–331, 334, 336–337, 344, 350, 355
– cosmic 65, 71n, 78, 161–162, 330
– legal 60
– natural viii, 124, 217
– political 73
Organism 8, 10–11, 13, 16–17, 84, 114, 305, 351, 354
– human 24, 269–275, 276n, 277, 278n, 279n, 284–290
– the state as an organism 73, 81
Ousia 44, 72, 308
Ownership 258, 260–262, 393–395, 399–404, 408–410

Philosopher 35–40, 42–44, 52, 54–56, 208n, 223, 232n, 275, 280–281, 293, 297–298, 306–307, 309–311, 313–314, 320–321, 326, 344, 357–358, 379n
– corrupt 36, 42n, 49–51, 57
– natural 42–44, 47, 48n, 51–52, 56
– philosopher king ix, 3–4, 53, 225, 280
Phronêsis 151–154, 188, 281, 297
Phusis vii, 3–6, 8, 10–11, 13–14, 16–20, 23–31, 59–60, 67, 69, 71, 74–75, 85–86, 90, 99–101, 115, 166n, 175–176
Plant 5, 63, 65, 74–75, 77, 79, 84, 97, 293, 296–298, 301–302, 304–306, 310, 313–314, 353–355, 358–359, 382–383
Platonism viii–ix, 223, 233, 273, 281, 285, 297–300, 308, 314, 348, 379
Pleasure 13, 37, 39–40, 71, 112n, 128–129, 141, 146, 181–188, 191, 194–195, 197, 210, 231, 270, 299, 302, 330
Polis viii, 15, 24–25, 30, 59–62, 64, 67–69, 72–78, 81–83, 84n, 85–96, 99–113, 115–117, 121, 124, 127, 129n, 130–133, 138, 206, 293–295, 366
Politeia 76, 294, 313
Potestas 208, 215, 238, 258–259, 399, 402n
Principle of Action 271, 278–280, 284–286, 289
Prohairesis 63, 97, 109, 141, 147
Property, of the gods 304
– of the people 204–205
– private viii, 132, 137, 143, 150, 152, 159, 164, 167, 235, 329–330, 337, 393, 395, 400n, 401–403, 404n, 409–410

Rationality 138, 144, 159–160, 184, 186, 193, 230, 241, 289, 298–300, 312, 314, 350, 365–366, 374, 377–378, 380–383, 387–389, 405
– divine 343
– practical 195n
Reason 6n, 27, 71, 98, 109n, 112, 119, 123–124, 128–130, 132, 138, 145–149, 151, 153, 160–161, 165, 174–177, 183–184, 188, 195, 197, 210–211, 217–218, 228–230, 232, 235, 269, 271, 273–274, 276n, 277–279, 280n, 281–282, 286, 289–290, 293,

299–300, 309–310, 313, 317, 319, 321, 324, 330, 334, 359–360, 374, 381–382, 395, 398, 404n
– civil   251–253
– cosmic   174
– natural   247, 250–253, 257–259, 261–264, 358, 407
– practical   viii, 47, 116
– right   216–217, 228, 230, 330–331, 394n, 398, 401, 405
Res publica   204–205, 212n, 215, 219, 235, 241
Ruler   vii, 4, 35–36, 63–66, 70, 76, 85, 91, 97–98, 126–132, 135, 138–141, 143, 147–150, 152–154, 164, 204, 208–209, 211, 213–215, 224–225, 228, 238n, 239, 259, 274–276, 278, 281, 285, 294–296, 308–310, 320–324, 327, 335–336, 343, 346–347, 358, 370–373, 381, 387, 389, 393–395, 403–404, 410

Safety   vii, 127, 137, 193, 195, 207n
Sage   269–271, 277, 279, 280–285, 287n, 289, 295, 297, 300
– Christian   326
– Stoic   174–176, 312, 317, 320, 337
Scepticism   162, 203n, 212, 226n, 231–232, 348, 353
Security. *see* Safety
Self-sufficiency   59, 67, 72, 77, 85, 99–101, 103–104, 106, 109, 113–115, 117, 120, 166–167, 282n, 374, 379–380
Slave   vii–viii, 66, 77, 79, 81, 84n, 85, 90–91, 99, 101, 104, 119, 125–132, 135–136, 138–141, 144–147, 150–151, 258–260, 332, 395, 397, 399
– legal   125
– natural   63–64, 97–98, 125–126, 130–131, 332
Society   9, 20, 49, 57, 61, 64, 72–73, 90, 172, 192, 195–198, 201n, 205, 207, 211, 221–223, 225–227, 234, 236–238, 240, 242, 317–321, 323, 325, 327–330, 334–335, 338, 372
Sophist   vii, ix, 5–6, 20–21, 29–30, 50n, 60
Sôtêria   63, 91, 97, 127

Soul   ix, 3, 6, 8–11, 14–19, 29–30, 39–41, 49, 54–55, 68, 83, 109, 122, 124, 128–130, 132, 135, 140, 144–147, 171, 187, 209–211, 218–219, 234, 269, 272–274, 276, 278–279, 280n, 281n, 283, 285, 287–289, 293–294, 300, 302–304, 308–310, 322, 325, 346, 350–351, 354, 356, 358–359, 376, 393n, 395
– appetitive part of   15–16, 145, 193, 274, 281
– deliberative part of   135–136, 140–141, 143–150, 153–154
– estimative power of   373
– non-rational part of   98, 109, 124–125, 132, 140, 145–147, 193, 269–273, 276n, 278–279, 280n, 281, 284, 287n, 288, 293, 310
– nutritive faculty of   145, 277, 279
– perceptual faculty of   277, 279, 300
– rational   ix, 270, 272–279, 281–290, 350–351, 379, 394, 404–405
– rational part of   15, 17, 98, 109, 125, 129, 140–141, 145, 147–150, 193, 269–271, 273–279, 281–282, 284–286, 287n, 288–289, 308
– spirited part of   15, 50, 128–129, 145, 274, 281
Stoicism   viii, 159–166, 173–177, 216, 218n, 219, 231–232, 234, 237, 240–242, 249, 258, 279n, 284n, 295–296, 298–299, 301, 307–308, 311–312, 314, 317, 320, 326, 332, 337, 343–344
State   vii, 6, 20, 31, 81–85, 89, 93, 106, 107n, 113n, 115–116, 137–138, 142, 149–150, 153, 201, 203–207, 209n, 210, 212–213, 215, 217, 225, 232, 238–240, 318, 320, 325–327, 330–331, 337
– ideal   ix, 35, 38, 137, 202, 210, 219
Substance   72, 86, 272, 281n, 349, 354–355, 360, 377
– natural   69, 77, 83–84, 87

Temperance   36–39, 41–42, 45, 47–50, 52–56, 129, 138, 141, 148, 152–153, 196, 281, 293, 297, 310, 314

Teleology ix, 59–62, 64–75, 78, 81, 83, 107n, 125, 184, 186, 196, 206, 269, 271, 287n, 289, 349–351, 359, 394, 404, 407
Telos 67–68, 83, 183–184, 186
Tyranny 76, 115, 126, 131, 138, 176, 203, 321, 370

Virtue viii–ix, 37, 41, 43n, 53–55, 62, 73, 116–117, 124, 128–133, 135–136, 139–142, 145, 151–153, 159–161, 164, 174–176, 188–189, 192–193, 195–196, 201n, 205n, 206n, 207–208, 210, 218, 242, 269, 271, 297, 307, 309–310, 312, 319n, 320–321, 324, 328, 330, 336–338, 359, 379, 381, 385
– intellectual 126, 148, 151, 274–275, 280–285, 298, 310, 385
– moral 126, 129, 138–139, 148–149, 151, 153, 380, 385, 388
– natural 44, 47, 48n, 56
– political 279–282, 284, 289, 310

Voluntarism 344–345, 349, 359, 360n, 394n

Will 393–395, 397–399, 402, 404–410
– divine 344, 357, 394n
– freedom of 393–395, 403, 404n, 405–407, 409–410
Wisdom 38, 40, 203, 226n, 238–239, 274, 295, 297–298, 306n, 314, 329, 337, 349–350, 352–353, 355, 360
– practical 124, 135, 151–154, 175, 188, 192, 281, 283
Woman 36n, 70, 135–145, 147–154, 226
– difference between man and woman 139, 142, 151–153
– equality of man and woman 137
– relation between man and woman vii–viii, 63–64, 66, 83, 85, 90–91, 95, 97–99, 102, 104, 109n, 112, 140, 143, 147, 150, 153, 257, 376, 378, 384, 386